The Palgrave International
Handbook of Peace Studies

S0-BSU-494

JZ
5538
.P358
2011

690904750

Selection and editorial matter © Wolfgang Dietrich, Josefina Echavarría Alvarez, Gustavo Esteva, Daniela Ingruber and Norbert Koppensteiner 2011
Individual chapters © respective authors 2011

All rights reserved. No reproduction, copy or transmission of this publication may be made without written permission.

No portion of this publication may be reproduced, copied or transmitted save with written permission or in accordance with the provisions of the Copyright, Designs and Patents Act 1988, or under the terms of any licence permitting limited copying issued by the Copyright Licensing Agency, Saffron House, 6–10 Kirby Street, London EC1N 8TS.

Any person who does any unauthorized act in relation to this publication may be liable to criminal prosecution and civil claims for damages.

The authors have asserted their rights to be identified as the authors of this work in accordance with the Copyright, Designs and Patents Act 1988.

First published 2011 by
PALGRAVE MACMILLAN

Palgrave Macmillan in the UK is an imprint of Macmillan Publishers Limited, registered in England, company number 785998, of Houndmills, Basingstoke, Hampshire RG21 6XS.

Palgrave Macmillan in the US is a division of St Martin's Press LLC, 175 Fifth Avenue, New York, NY 10010.

Palgrave Macmillan is the global academic imprint of the above companies and has companies and representatives throughout the world.

Palgrave® and Macmillan® are registered trademarks in the United States, the United Kingdom, Europe and other countries

ISBN   978-0-230-23786-5   hardback

This book is printed on paper suitable for recycling and made from fully managed and sustained forest sources. Logging, pulping and manufacturing processes are expected to conform to the environmental regulations of the country of origin.

A catalogue record for this book is available from the British Library.

A catalog record for this book is available from the Library of Congress.

10 9 8 7 6 5 4 3 2 1
20 19 18 17 16 15 14 13 12 11

Printed and bound in Great Britain by
CPI Antony Rowe, Chippenham and Eastbourne

Contents

Section VI   Peace Thinkers

Tables and Illustrations

Preface

In fall 2005, Gustavo Esteva invited me to visit him at his house in San Pablo Etla, Oaxaca, Mexico. He introduced me to an idea, which he already carried in his mind for a time but considered too ambitious for realizing it alone. Gustavo and I have been friends for more than two decades now. I came across his writings when I was still a young academic at the University of Innsbruck, Austria. He was then already a well-known intellectual, publisher and activist in his country. He wrote his electrifying articles and essays against the hypocrisy of international help and development. His texts became enthusiastically discussed after the horrible earthquake that shattered Mexico in 1985, when the commons of the *barrios bajos* demonstrated their impressive capacity of taking the law into their own hands and, at the same time, illustrated the inability of the state's administration and the international organizations.

Gustavo was and is a fierce advocate of the commons, the vernacular cultures and their rights. As a young political scientist with special interest in Latin America, I was fascinated by his provoking ideas that seemed to provide a way out from the frustration of the so-called lost decade for development and the agonizing repetition of the failed development theories since the 1950s. I wanted to meet Gustavo and finally visited him on the occasion of a research project on Central American history. This first encounter resulted in the publication of the book *Fiesta* (1992), a title chosen to celebrate the self-healing potentials of the commons. My colleagues Markus Brunner and Martina Kaller, and myself, translated seven of Gustavo's most electrifying essays from Spanish or English into German and published them in one volume under the title *Fiesta*. Gustavo being the sole author of all these essays, the book was naturally issued under his name, but he never got tired of emphasizing that the book, which in this version has only been published in German, was our invention. The book was the first systematic and fundamental critique of developmental thought in the German-speaking world and it hit the scene. In spite of the immediate and excited rejection of the well-established circles of professional helpers, *Fiesta* was path breaking. Most of the by-then published concerns are nowadays mainstream and well accepted. This became especially true after the emergence of the Zapatista movement in Chiapas, which repeats and confirms many of Gustavo's considerations of earlier decades. Until today, Gustavo is closely related to this movement.

Before we met, both Gustavo and I were highly influenced by one of the most important lateral thinkers of the twentieth century, Ivan Illich. Born in Austria, Illich spent an important part of his life in Mexico and hence he connected our countries. More important than this biographical aspect is the fact that Illich combined two paramount philosophical streams of the twentieth century in his person. Above all, the *European* Illich was concerned with the renovation of the Catholic Church in the sense of the Second Vatican Council, whereas the *American* Illich was heavily inspired by the anarchistic ideas of Paul Goodman. This led to his famous critique on institutions such as schools and hospitals, technology and development, and combined his rather historical, sociological, theological or anthropological writings with the principles of Gestalt. This strange and hidden combination made him highly appealing. Gustavo became a prominent member of the inner circle around Illich in Mexico and the USA long before I met both of them. However, Gustavo and I shared the admiration of Illich's charismatic personality and this was the starting point for our cooperation and long decades of friendship.

All that happened long before Gustavo became founder and collaborator of the Universidad de la Tierra in Mexico and I UNESCO Chair holder for Peace Studies at the University of Innsbruck. Therefore, Gustavo's 2005 invitation seemed to be nothing but another episode in our common history. But what he proposed on this occasion was indeed a project of a lifetime and not to be mastered by one single person. He wanted to launch what he called an intercultural encyclopedia. Following Raimon Panikkar, Gustavo was thinking of looking for *homeomorphic equivalents* of some key concepts alluding to intercultural relations and basic social functions. The main idea was to find key words, such as *peace, development, democracy* and *land*, among many others, and invite outstanding thinkers from as many cultures as possible to discuss these key words from their point of view.

Gustavo wanted to avoid the usual attitude that experts write and speak about others as if they were objects of interest. He wanted everybody speaking about him, about her and their kind as being the key feature to identify the notions and messages of this project. The International Honors Program, which Gustavo used to collaborate with, was already interested and involved in the project. From the Garfield Foundation, Gustavo received funds to sponsor my visit to Mexico and finance some of the translations needed for the project, in the hope that any future proceedings could be used for grants for indigenous students.

I was very enthusiastic with this idea because I always advocated that *I* or *my opinion* do not express unscientific subjectivity, but that they are the precondition for inter-subjective communication in science. The image of having around thirty serious intellectuals of different cultural, religious and social backgrounds discussing these key concepts of intercultural communication respectfully among each other fascinated me from the very beginning. Gustavo wanted to start the series with the key word *peace*. As I had been coined a peace researcher over the intervening years, he asked me to coordinate the first volume.

We knew from the very beginning that this was an ambitious project but did not know how ambitious it would turn out to be. It is rather easy to find Western experts on everything, everybody and every place. However, even if one is rather well connected across many cultures, as Gustavo and I are, it is not easy at all to find people who are capable and willing to write about the most complex and intimate philosophical concepts of their own culture from a personal perspective. Such writing requires a high degree of self-manifestation on the side of the author and this is not only beyond the academic conventions of the West.

The fundamental practice of highly philosophical concepts, such as peace, and the academic writing style do not fit well together in many cases. People, who perceive peace as a harmonic flow of energy, rather meditate than write or speak about it. In these cases, the most valuable knowledge remains hardly accessible to an academic sphere. The wisest people may even be illiterate in these contexts. The moral interpretation of peace is very often related to a strict normative system, which does not allow philosophical doubts or discussions from a true believer's point of view. Therefore, even the best-educated and wisest people hesitate to publish profound analyses about their own belief and value system. In some other cases, when peace is rather perceived as a relational, societal concept, the contexts may not dispose about a proper vocabulary for translation into modern languages and normative systems. The word peace in modern English language could be a misconception of what they mean. Some of them, thus, refrain from trying to explain it at all. Finally, if taken seriously, peace is often a dangerous word for those who use it in totalitarian or authoritarian political contexts. Some invited intellectuals could not contribute because of that reason.

Furthermore, these distinguished people are very busy and will not accept short deadlines for the submission of the papers. We initially underestimated this fact. The question of speed versus quality arose, and we had to extend the deadline repeatedly for the sake of the quality of the entries. I could continue with this list of difficulties, but to cut a long story short, I say that gathering thirty authentic representative authors of different cultures in the world was a highly challenging endeavor that took us much more time than we had initially anticipated for this task. Therefore, at some point we decided to postpone the initially planned following volumes and concentrate on the realization of a single compilation on peace that we continuously called 'anthology.'

As time went by and the entries finally came in one by one, our own working conditions changed. The most significant alteration without any doubt was that the UNESCO Secretary General Koichiro Matsuura rewarded the MA Program for Peace Studies at the University of Innsbruck with the UNESCO Chair for Peace Studies in 2008. This charged the project with fresh energy and opened new options. As agreed in the contract between UNESCO and the hosting university, this project fitted perfectly into the tasks of the Chair. The anthology thus became a project of the newly established UNESCO Chair. This allowed us to integrate some of the very best alumni of our program or the corresponding Master of Peace Studies at Castellón in Spain into our list of authors. Elida Undrum Jacobson, Aurangzeb Haneef, Uzma Rehman, Alev Çakır, Samrat Schmiem Kumar and

Belachew Gebrewold are profound knowers of the peace cultures of their home and at the same time familiar with the philosophy of the trans-rational peaces as taught at the UNESCO Chair. This is a rare quality, which recommended them for our project.

The UNESCO Chair allowed also the sharing of immense publishing work among other authors. Josefina Echavarría, Daniela Ingruber and Norbert Koppensteiner, all of them distinguished core faculty members of the MA Program for Peace Studies at Innsbruck University, completed the editing team and supported us with highly valuable translations and editorial work, which finally guaranteed the quality of this volume.

All these developments required a new structure and finally we found our most valuable and preferred partner in the publisher Palgrave Macmillan. They integrated the project into their publishing concept and thus brought the anthology into its final shape as *The Palgrave International Handbook of Peace Studies: A Cultural Perspective*.

After all, we have to express our gratitude to Alexandra Webster from Palgrave Macmillan. Her advice to switch from the initial concept of an encyclopedia to a handbook is much more than a simple change of words. According to my experience, an encyclopedia of the cultures of peace will never be written. Too many are the diverging approaches, belief systems and contexts. Maybe someday we will dispose of a database, but this clearly exceeds the limits of a printed book.

Wolfgang Dietrich

Notes on Contributors

Astier M. Almedom, D. Phil., a native of Africa, is an Oxford-trained applied anthropologist with more than 25 years of experience in academic research and interdisciplinary scholarship in human behavioral and environmental sciences, including fieldwork in eastern Africa, Afghanistan and India. She is currently Director of the International Resilience Program at the Institute for Global Leadership, Tufts University. <www.bu.edu/pardee>

Ikuro Anzai was born in Tokyo. He is honorary director of the Kyoto Museum for World Peace at Ritsumeikan University, Japan, and specializes in radiological health science and peace studies. He also is an executive board member of the International Network of Museums for Peace and honorary director of the Nanjing International Peace Research Institute in China.

Alev Çakır was born in Vienna. She comes from an Alevi family originally from Anatolia. She studied Political Science at the University of Vienna and at the University of Warwick (UK). While studying an MA in Peace, Development, Security and International Conflict Transformation at the University of Innsbruck, she worked as a student's advisor. Her fields of interests include peace and conflict research, international development, migration and integration and Alevilik.

Wolfgang Dietrich was born in Austria. He is UNESCO Chair holder for Peace Studies and program director of the MA in Peace, Development, Security and International Conflict Transformation at the University of Innsbruck. He is faculty member at the Centre for Peace and Development Studies at the University Jaume I, in Castellón, Spain, and visiting faculty at the UN Peace University in Ciudad Colón, Costa Rica. He is currently completing the second volume of his trilogy *Variationen über die Vielen Frieden* (Wiesbaden: VS Verlag). The first volume, 'Deutungen,' was published in 2008 and will appear in English as *Variations on the Many Peaces: Concepts* in 2011.

Josefina Echavarría Alvarez was born in Medellín, Colombia. A BA in International Relations from the University Externado, she holds an MA in Peace Studies from the University of Innsbruck and a PhD in Peace, Conflict and Democracy from the University Jaume I, Spain. She lectures at the UNESCO Chair and MA Program for Peace Studies at the University of Innsbruck and at the MA in Latin American Studies, University of Vienna. Her latest book *In/security in Colombia* was published in 2010 by Manchester University Press. <www.echavarria.wissweb.at>

Marc H. Ellis is Professor of Jewish Studies and Director of the Center for Jewish Studies at Baylor University, where he is also Professor of History. He has lectured around the world on Jewish identity and the Middle Eastern crisis, including at the United Nations and the Carter Center. Over the years, he has written and edited more than twenty books, including *Toward a Jewish Theology of Liberation* (Waco: Baylor University Press, 2004 in its third edition), *Unholy Alliance: Religion and Atrocity in Our Time* (Minneapolis: Augsburg Fortress, 1997), and most recently *Judaism Does Not Equal Israel* (New York: The New Press, 2009).

Gustavo Esteva is a grassroots activist, a public intellectual and an independent writer. He was advisor of the Zapatistas in their negotiations with the government, in 1996. He participates in a number of organizations and networks at local, national and international level. He has published more than thirty books and hundreds of essays. He lives in a small Zapotec village in southern Mexico.

Munir Fasheh was born in Jerusalem in 1941. He was expelled from his home in 1948 and lived mostly in Ramallah, Palestine. He earned a Doctorate in Education at Harvard University in 1988 and has taught math and physics in Palestine and the US. He started a voluntary work movement in the West Bank region (Palestine) in 1971, where he also worked for five years as head supervisor of math instruction and dean of students at Birzeit University. He established the Tamer Institute for Community Education in 1989 in Palestine, which won the Astrid Lindgren Prize, and established and directed the Arab Education Forum from 1997 until 2007 at the Centre for Middle Eastern Studies at Harvard University. <www.almoultaqa.com>

Victoria Fontan is Associate Professor and Head of the Department of Peace and Conflict Studies at the University for Peace, Costa Rica. Her original specialization has been in insurgency studies, focusing on the role of humiliation in relation to the emergence of insurgencies, mostly in a Middle Eastern context. She has published on Lebanon and Iraq and has worked in both countries for the first ten years of her academic career. She is now shifting specializations towards the application of new sciences metaphors to Peace and Conflict Studies. She is currently finishing her second PhD thesis on the cybernetics of peace, greatly influenced by the work of Gregory Bateson and Evelin Lindner.

Johan Galtung is director of Transcend, founder of the Peace Research Institute, Oslo (PRIO), professor at the University of Hawaii and, among others, visiting professor at the Universities of Innsbruck, Granada, Ritsumeikan, Trömso and Witten, Herdecke. He is known worldwide as the 'father of Peace Studies' and has more than 1000 publications on peace and conflict transformation.

Arun Gandhi is founder and president of the Gandhi Worldwide Education Institute, USA. He is an eminent speaker and writer on the subject of nonviolence. <www.arungandhi.org> and <www.gandhiforchildren.org>

Belachew Gebrewold was born in Ethiopia. He is Lecturer of International Relations at Helmut-Schmidt University, University of the Federal Armed Forces in Hamburg, Germany, and teaches at the UNESCO Chair for Peace Studies, Innsbruck. His main research areas are conflicts in Africa and Africa in International Politics. His most recent publications include the edited volume *Africa and Fortress Europe* (Hampshire: Ashgate, 2007) and also *Anatomy of Violence: Understanding the Systems of Conflict and Violence in Africa* (Ashgate, 2009) and a co-edited work with Valeria Bello *A Global Security Triangle: European, African and Asian Interactions* (Routledge, 2009).

Arturo Guerrero is a social communicator and works as an activist, community radio producer and professor of communication and pedagogy. He was a book thief, DJ, phone operator for the police and a publishing advisor. He collaborated for seven years with Zapotec grassroots organizations and participates in the social movement of Oaxaca. He currently works with young Mazatecs and Mixtecs.

Aurangzeb Haneef was born in Pakistan. He studied Peace and Conflict at the Universities of Innsbruck, Austria, and Jaume I, Spain, with a specific focus in Islam and a general focus on religion, peace and conflict transformation. He recently graduated from Harvard Divinity School, United States, with a Master of Theological Studies degree, concentrating on Islam. He is involved with exploring the religion's capacity for peace building and conflict transformation through work and further research.

Peter Horsley taught Environmental Law at Massey University, New Zealand, and currently works with indigenous communities on sustainability projects in New Zealand and the South Pacific. He teaches in the Boston-based International Honors Program, with a focus on interculturality, sustainability frameworks, environmental law and policy, indigenous perspectives, knowledge systems, worldviews and ethics, and governance arrangements.

Daniela Ingruber works as editor-in-chief for the Austrian magazine *planet⁰*, based in Vienna. She is staff member of the UNESCO Chair for Peace Studies at the University of Innsbruck, where she lectures at the MA Program in Peace, Development, Security and International Conflict Transformation. She furthermore lectures at different universities in Europe and at the Institute of International Studies at Ramkhamhaeng University, Bangkok, Thailand. Since 2007, she also works for the *Diagonale* – Festival for Austrian Film. Among her latest publications is the book *bilder ohne wirklichkeit* (Vienna: Lit Verlag, 2009). <www.nomadin.at>

Elida Kristine Undrum Jacobsen is a researcher at the International Peace Research Institute, Oslo (PRIO). She is also program manager of the BA Course in Peace and Conflict Studies offered by Cultural Studies, University College Oslo in Pondicherry, India. She has an MA in Peace, Conflict and Development Studies from University Jaume I, in Castellón, Spain, and a BA in Journalism from Middlesex University, London, UK.

Hannes Kalisch was born in 1969. He is member of the Enlhet Community of the Chaco in Paraguay. Within the framework of the *Nengvaanemkeskama Nempayvaam Enlhet*, a working group composed of Enlhet and Toba-Enenlhet, he works for the recovery of the memory of the Enlhet-Enenlhet peoples and its subsequent dissemination in their respective tongues in the form of radio and TV programs, the production of videos and written texts. <www.enlhet.org>

Martina Kaller-Dietrich was born in Austria. She is Associate Professor at the University of Vienna, where her main teaching appointment is Global History with a regional focus on Latin America and as transversal thematic focus on the History of Nutrition. She is faculty member at the Centre for Peace and Development Studies at the University Jaume I, in Castellón, Spain, and at the Master of Arts Program in Peace, Development, Security and International Conflict Transformation at the University of Innsbruck, Austria. In 2008, she published the first comprehensive biography on Ivan Illich, entitled *Ivan Illich (1926–2002): Sein Leben, sein Denken* (Vienna: Bibliothek der Provinz).

Kam-Por Yu is a moral philosopher and senior lecturer in the Faculty of Humanities of the Hong Kong Polytechnic University. He has been Associate Professor in the Department of Public and Social Administration of City University of Hong Kong and research fellow in the Harvard School of Public Health. Among his latest publications is the book *Taking Confucian Ethics Seriously* (Albany: State University of New York Press, 2009).

Karlheinz Koppe was born in Germany. He is former chair of the German Society for Peace Studies, former secretary of the European Peace Research Association, former secretary general of the International Peace Research Association and Visiting Professor at the University of Münster, Germany. His special interest includes the peace movement and security policy.

Norbert Koppensteiner was born in Austria. He is a peace researcher, program coordinator of the MA in Peace, Development, Security and International Conflict

Transformation, and research and publications coordinator of the UNESCO Chair for Peace Studies at the University of Innsbruck. He is the author of *The Art of the Transpersonal Self* (New York/Dresden: Atropos Press, 2009). <www.koppensteiner. wissweb.at>

Samrat Schmiem Kumar was born in India. He holds an MA in Political Science, Contemporary History and Philosophy (University of Innsbruck, Austria) and an MA in Peace, Development, Security and International Conflict Transformation (UNESCO Chair for Peace Studies at the University of Innsbruck and UNESCO Chair for Philosophy for Peace, University Jaumé I, Castelló). He works as academic project coordinator and lecturer at the international undergraduate course in Peace and Conflict Studies hosted by Culture Studies/Oslo University College, in Pondicherry, India. Kumar is currently co-editing a volume on peace work in South Asia, and his most recent book is called *Bhakti – The Yoga of Love: Trans-rational Approaches to Peace Studies* (Vienna: Lit Verlag/Transaction Publishers, 2010).

Pat Lauderdale is Professor in the School of Justice and Social Inquiry at Arizona State University. He was recently appointed visiting scholar at the Center for Comparative Studies in Race and Ethnicity at Stanford University. His teaching and research interests include indigenous jurisprudence, racialization, diversity, global indigenous struggles, law and the social science, and international terrorism. In the 1980s, he helped create the Herbert Blumer Institute in Costa Rica with the goal of discovering and describing alternatives to violence and criminal law. His seminal book *Law and Society* (with James Inverarity and Barry Feld, Boston: Little, Brown and Co., 1983) has been translated into Japanese with a forthcoming version in Italian.

Syed Sikander Mehdi is a leading peace scholar from Pakistan. He is Convenor of the Peace and Cultural Studies Project, in Karachi, former chair of the Department of International Relations and former registrar of Karachi University. In 2008, he availed a ten-month Japan Foundation Fellowship in Kyoto and prepared a study on 'Building Peace Museums in Pakistan: Relevance of Japanese Peace Museums.' His research and publications focus on peace and nonviolent movements, peace building, culture of peace and peace museums, with particular reference to Pakistan, South Asia, Muslim Societies and Islam and Peace. <sikander.mehdi@ ymail.com>

Beatriz Molina is Professor at the Department of Semitic Studies and Director of the Institute of Peace and Conflicts at the University of Granada, Spain. Her research focuses on Peace in Mediterranean Cultures, with emphasis on the

Arab–Islamic world. She has participated in numerous research projects and published many articles and books on the subject.

Francisco A. Muñoz is Professor of History, former Director and Researcher at the Institute of Peace and Conflicts at the University of Granada, Spain. He has been research fellow at several universities in Europe and Latin America, has directed research projects, and published numerous works on history and peace studies.

Kofi Asare Opoku was born in Ghana. He earned a Master of Sacred Theology from Yale University and is Visiting Professor of Religion and Co-Chair of Africana Studies. His special interests include traditional African religion and culture, religious movements in West Africa, and African religions in the Americas. He is author of *Western African Traditional Religion* (Singapore/Accra: Far Eastern Publishers, 1978) and *Hearing and Keeping Akan Proverbs* (Pretoria: UNISA Press, 1997).

Uzma Rehman was born in Pakistan. She completed her Ph.D. from the Department of Cross-Cultural and Regional Studies (History of Religions section) at the University of Copenhagen, Denmark, in 2008. Her Ph.D. thesis dealt with the shrines of two eighteenth century saints (in Punjab and Sindh, respectively) in Pakistan. Her thesis demonstrates how identities of pilgrims and devotees are expressed and accommodated through multiple forms of expression namely social, sacred, ritual and literary, at the shrines of Waris Shah and Shah Lateef. Earlier, she did her Masters in Peace and Development Studies at the University of Jaume I, Castellon, Spain. She has also published a number of articles about the Sufi tradition in Pakistan.

Grimaldo Rengifo V. was born in Peru. He studied Educational Sciences and in 1987 he founded the PRATEC (*Proyecto Andino de Tecnologías Campesinas*/Andean Project of Peasant Technologies). Since then, he has been learning from native peasants approaches to agri/culture and supporting the search for alternatives to modern Western notions of development in the Peruvian Andes. The PRATEC offers courses on Andean agri/culture to schoolteachers and technicians who work in development programs. He is the author of numerous books and articles on development, agriculture and indigenous knowledge.

Amadou Lamine Sarr was born in Senegal. He studied Political Science and History at the University of Vienna, Austria. He is Associate Professor of History at the same university. His research foci lie on racism, global history, nationalism (with emphasis on African nationalism), colonialism, decolonization, Islam in/and Africa and fundamentalism. He is the author of various books, among them *Lamine Ibrahima Arfan Senghor (1889–1927): Das Andere des senegalesischen Nationalismus* (Vienna: Lit Verlag, 2007).

Swami Veda Bharati was born in the Sanskrit-speaking Vedic tradition of India. He earned his MA in London and D.Litt. at Utrecht University. He has been a traveling lecturer and Spiritual Guide since 1947. He holds the title of High Monk in the Swami Order of Monks and has worked as international Meditation Guide with fifty meditation groups around the world. He runs two ashrams in India, including a sophisticated laboratory examining neuro-physiological effects of meditation as well as an Institute of Interfaith Studies. He is Chancellor of the Himalayan Institute Hospital Trust (HIHT) University, in Dehradun, India. He is a published poet and author of fifteen books translated into many languages. <www.swamiveda.org>

Karma Lekshe Tsomo is an Associate Professor of Theology and Religious Studies at the University of San Diego, where she teaches Buddhism, World Religions and Comparative Religious Ethics. She studied Buddhism in Dharamsala, India, for fifteen years and received a doctorate in Philosophy from the University of Hawaii at Manoa, with research on death and identity in China and Tibet. She helped found Sakyadhita International Association of Buddhist Women and is the director of Jamyang Foundation, an innovative education project for women in developing countries. She has edited numerous books on women and Buddhism and authored *Into the Jaws of Yama, Lord of Death: Buddhism, Bioethics, and Death* (Albany: State University of New York, 2006).

Robert Vachon is Franco-American. He was deeply inspired by Raimon Panikkar's writings and since 1967 has consecrated his life to interreligious and intercultural research action alternatives to Western/Modern Culture. He has done so at the Intercultural Institute of Montreal (IIM), as co-founder and lifetime director of its journal *InterCulture*, which is published in French, English and Italian. He has been particularly involved with the indigenous and Mohawk traditional revival in North America. Joseph J. Baker presents his work and philosophy in *Robert Vachon: An Intercultural Life. A Spiritual Journey Engaging Religions and Cultures* (Oxford University Press, X Libris, 2007).

Nigel Young is a British Professor Emeritus in the Sociology Department and former Director of the Peace Studies Program at Colgate University, USA. He has written many books and articles on war resistance and peace movements. His areas of expertise are peace education, Anglo-American and European movements and the role of non-governmental relationships in promoting peace and global society.

Notes on the Edition

Our edition of the contributions that compose *The Palgrave International Handbook of Peace Studies* has followed a commonly accepted editorial principle: be as faithful as possible to the authors' writings. The aim, henceforth, has been to edit these pieces keeping in mind the authors' meaning, tone, nuances, style and manner.

The richness of this collection greatly resides in the fact that the authors stem from diverse traditions around the globe, which necessarily imply that their ways of knowing, their epistemology, also differs greatly. Sometimes, such understanding of knowledge enters in clear contradiction with the commonly accepted concept of authorship of Western scholarly writing. Thus, while some authors refer to ancient and common wisdom sources without further details and several convey invaluable oral knowledge, instead of intervening directly in the text, we have applied our faithfulness principle as consistently as possible and scarcely included editorial notes to facilitate the reading. To keep the coherence of the authors' endnote numbering, editorial notes appear at the foot of the relevant page marked with the abbreviation 'Ed.'

In the same line of thinking, most of the authors themselves have translated their own sources and so share with an English-speaking audience works, ideas and knowledge that would otherwise remain unavailable. When the author so indicates, such own translations have been marked in the body of the text with a simple '[trans. by author]' embedded in the reference.

A further discussion matter has been the necessity of gender-sensitive language. Instead of overriding the authors' use of female and male language forms, we have left this aspect as it originally appeared in the text because of the faithfulness principle: the references to gender/sex are, in and of themselves, part and parcel of peace notions. The designation of gendered subjects produces specific forms – bodily, emotionally, intellectually – of specific peace(s).

We so hope that the edition of this rich collection contributes to open up a microcosm of peace concepts. In this world we find poems, songs, high politics discussions, history and stories, personal accounts and conversations, debates on global and local relationships, carefully constructed observations, linkages between ancient traditions and current issues, and a thoughtful variety of conversations on what peace might mean, how it has been thought, named, experienced and felt, and how it could be imagined otherwise. This abundant material then is not just one fraction of a system; it speaks to the whole in the one peace.

Editorial Team of the UNESCO Chair for Peace Studies
Innsbruck, June 2010

Introduction

Wolfgang Dietrich

> Without interculturality, peace is only a utopia.
> Raimon Panikkar

Once the final publishing concept of this compilation was found, after the long period of formation and orientation as stated in the Preface, the editorial team, composed of Josefina Echavarría, Gustavo Esteva, Daniela Ingruber, Norbert Koppensteiner and myself had to structure the entries accordingly. We decided to start with the European ones, which are popular among conventional peace studies, and turn from there to all other narratives that classical peace research tends to ignore or neglect. We open the discussion with my chapter 'Beyond the Gates of Eden: Trans-rational Peaces.' This paper illustrates the history, the spirit and the work of the UNESCO Chair, which finally appears as the sole editor of the book. The concept of trans-rationality is not only a newcomer in the field of peace studies, but also the main inspiration of this book. The call for diverse political, social, philosophical and spiritual interpretations of peace and personal academic writing style stems from this approach. Therefore, this first chapter serves as a prolonged methodological introduction to the book.

From there we turn to the context of what I call the greater Mediterranean. Karlheinz Koppe's entry *'Peace*: The European Narrative' is a fine and short condensation of the conventional narrative on peace in Europe from a German idealist point of view. It contrasts my trans-rational approach and serves as umbrella for the following papers of Francisco Muñoz and Beatriz Molina *'Pax*: A Mediterranean Perspective,' Nigel Young's *'Peace*: A Western European Perspective' and Elida Undrum Jacobsen's *'Friðr*: A Northern European Perspective.'

Being historians from Granada in Spain, Muñoz and Molina focus on the smaller Mediterranean region and contribute a deep insight into the historical debate on peace in Europe. In a broader sense, their entry may be taken as a Romanic contribution, whereas Nigel Young starts from an Anglo-Saxon perspective. To a certain extent, Young's British–American background illustrates what I mean by the greater Mediterranean because Young doubts that there is something like a specific Anglo-Saxon contribution to peace theory. On the one hand, he perceives the British debate inseparable from the continental one. On the other hand, he expands it across the Atlantic. According to Young, these boundaries are diffuse and, up to a high degree, all European concepts are interwoven. This also becomes visible in Undrum Jacobsen's highly inspiring chapter on the Norse concepts. Even the very old notions of peace in Scandinavia, which are often falsely considered having been isolated, separated and wild in their understanding of peace out of fertility and harmony, demonstrate remarkable coincidences with the energetic concepts of the smaller Mediterranean. Throughout history, the syncretism increased and etymological notions often have been lost.

Astonishing therefore is not so much Young's observation of the interrelatedness of peace concepts everywhere in modern Europe, but rather the total nemesis of energetic peace concepts in the European collective memory. It seems that the invasion of the moral peace concepts successfully suppressed those energetic understandings and thus prepared the ground for the shallow syncretism of modern peace concepts. On the other hand, post-modern and trans-rational peace concepts may doubt whether this suppression was that successful. The increasing run on spiritual explanations of existence rather indicate a revival of those energetic concepts, and trans-rational peaces will propose to twist them with rationality.

On the opposite shore of the Mediterranean Sea we find the concepts of Shalom and Salam. It is a specific concern of this book not to allow them to appear as monolithic or antagonistic blocks. Therefore, we invited Marc H. Ellis, the founder of Jewish Liberation Theology, to present his arguments for us in '*Shalom*: A Jewish Perspective.' This lateral thinker might probably be challenged by orthodox or conservative voices. In the same way, Munir Fasheh's very personal presentation of a Palestinian perspective in '*Shalom/Salaam*: A Personal Palestinian Perspective' challenges any mainstream reading of peace. We are grateful to both authors for accepting our invitation because this specific region may need nothing more than dissent to the official narratives, which continuously deal with violence, (in)security and irreconcilable and merciless phantasms of a victorious peace. May these chapters contribute to the transformation of consciousness into alternative options to the so-called *Real Politik*.

In '*Salaam*: A Muslim Perspective,' Aurangzeb Haneef from Pakistan turns to the classical Moslem understanding of peace and emphasizes the peaceful grounding of this religion. The dogmatic concept of Islam does not make it easy to do this from a mere academic standpoint. I think that Haneef perfectly combines regard of the dogmatic prescripts and dedication to academic rigor. His is a hotly debated topic and the findings he arrives at will be disputed, but this will be true for many chapters in this book.

Uzma Rehman and Alev Çakır present two clearly deviating interpretations of the Sunni Muslim's mainstream understanding of Salam. The Sufi concepts of peace are often romanticized or challenged for not being orthodox. Therefore, I am specifically grateful that '*Salaam*: A Sufi Perspective' by Rehman comes from a very well-trained peace researcher who approaches the topic systematically and combines profound knowledge and aesthetic orientation with enlightening academic discipline. The same is true for the chapter on Alevism,

'*Salaam*: An Alevilik Perspective.' The unorthodox and liberal *Alevilik* culture is neglected in Turkey and fairly unknown outside of this country, in spite of the fact that millions of Alevis live in exile around the world. Alev Çakır's entry gives enthusiastic insight into their understanding of peace. We do not believe that the *Alevilik* concept of peace is any better than the Sunni's or the one of secular Turkish Kemalists, because better and worse are not criterion for peace, as Sufi Rumi stated centuries ago. Nevertheless, I am convinced that after the cultural reductionism that we suffered through best sellers like Samuel Huntington's *Clash of Civilizations* (1996), a more differentiated perception of peace cultures is a highly needed step to mutual understanding. This entry on a culture that lives in diasporas all over the world and is mainly absorbed by stereotypes on Islam is a perfect contribution to such a differentiation.

The treasonous richness and diversity of Indian peace cultures are a conceptual challenge for a project like ours. One could write some volumes of this kind just on India without ever achieving full coverage of its most important contributions to world peace discussions. Therefore, we concluded that it might be better to ask one single author to cover the full rainbow from an eagle's eye perspective and leave special aspects for separate contributions. Of course, this demanding goal could only be achieved by an extraordinarily open, experienced and wise mind. We are happy that we found in Swami Veda Bharati such a wonderful personality, who made the effort to write this remarkable contribution entitled '*Shanti*: An Indian Perspective.' This special case required more space than we used to offer other authors, because reducing these considerations to fifteen pages only would have made the endeavor impossible. I think that the result confirms perfectly the meaningfulness of this exception.

Indian peace philosophy did not only flourish in many different shapes within the subcontinent. Moreover, Indian-rooted concepts spread all over the world, where they have been integrated into local cultures and hence have produced an additional multitude of new approaches. The impossibility to cover all these aspects is not only true for India as a geographic term, but also for the most famous of its philosophical traditions, Buddhism. This led us to the conclusion that we shall not attempt to collect all variations of Buddhist peace interpretations but rather present one (less popular) example. In '*Shi wa*: A Vajrayana Buddhist Perspective,' Karma Lekshe Tsomo introduces the basically Nepalese peace thought of Vajrayana Buddhism and gives us an idea of how it is embedded into and related to the bigger and better-known traditions. Yu Kam-Por's '*He Ping*: A Confucian Perspective' and Ikuro Anzai's '*Haiwa*: A Shinto Perspective' relate the Buddhist approaches to Chinese Confucianism and Japanese Shintoism. The syncretism becomes evident in both cases and illustrates the enormous tradition, value and impact of the South- and East-Asian peace philosophies if they are understood as a corresponding and interwoven system of knowledge and wisdom, rather than as competing or – worse – clashing cultural constructs.

The insight into the importance of this field led us to another methodological exception. We wanted to know how Johan Galtung, in Europe commonly called 'the father of peace studies' and in his private life closely related to Japan, evaluates the contribution of Buddhism to peace philosophy. Therefore, his atypical contribution 'Buddhism and the World Peace' concludes the section on South- and East-Asian peace concepts.

In the case of all the countries and continents, which have been not only dominated by the British or one of the Romanic colonial styles but almost or totally been absorbed by their cultural belief systems, we decided to focus on the still remaining or resisting minority notions. Naturally, this can only be realized in an exemplary manner. We begin with Peter Horsley's contribution '*He Taura Whiri*: A Maori Perspective' on the Maori's understanding of peace, jumping from there to the Americas where Robert Vachon's '*Kayanerekowa*: A Mohawk Perspective' and Pat Lauderdale's '*Skennen*: A North American Indian Perspective' give us two native examples from the North. The Zapotec concept of Gustavo Esteva and Arturo Guerrero in '*Guelaguetza and Tu Chha'ia*: A Zapotec Perspective of What Others Call Friendship' represents Mesoamerica. Grimaldo Rengifo's '*Thaq*: An Andean–Amazonian Perspective' on the Andean peace thought and Hannes Kalisch's chapter '*Nengelaasekhammalhkoo*: An Enlhet Perspective' on the so-far almost undocumented community of the Enlhet in Paraguay and their understanding of peace, stands for the South.

The above-mentioned contributions on peace refer to minorities, which are framed by the dominating concepts of what I call the bigger Mediterranean, imposed on them by colonialism and modernization. Therefore, they do not represent states or nations. They are situated in regions but do not dominate them. However, introducing them in the place of a rather abstract construct in the kind of an Australian, Anglo-American or the Latin-American peace thought, they perfectly speak for the type of diversity that is still shaping the social reality of the hemisphere. Of course, there are many more minorities, which would deserve to be mentioned but considering the excellence of the quoted authors, we inclined our decisions in favor of these thrilling examples.

The case of Africa is even more difficult because, on the one hand, one does not find there a homogeneous culture of domination and, on the other hand, the diversity and density of vernacular cultures is extremely high. To ask for the profound meaning of all their peaces would be a very inspiring endeavor. However, for our project we could not do anything more but to take some examples from different directions of the continent. A more convincing logical structure could not be found. Nevertheless, the result for our purpose is rather similar as in the American case. Both Kofi Asare Opoku's chapter '*Asomdwoe*: A West African Perspective' on the Akan in the West and Belachew Gebrewold's entry '*T'ùmmu*: An East African Perspective' in the East, present differentiated and sophisticated peace philosophies far beyond the modern Mediterranean mainstream. This is completed by Lamine Sarr's entry 'African *Salaam*', which – in spite of all dogmatic rules – is another strong argument against a monolithic understanding of peace in Islam.

Drafting this book we repeatedly discussed the necessity of an own section on great peace thinkers and peace activists such as Mahatma Ghandi, Martin Luther King, Nelson Mandela, Adolfo Pérez Esquivel, Jody Williams, Morihei Ueshiba, the Dalai Lama and many more. It is precisely this 'many more' that brought us to the insight that such a section would rapidly explode towards a separate book. Too many people on this planet definitely deserve to be mentioned in such a project. Peace is for heroes and the good news is that they are abundant. Some of them are well known all around the globe, others who might be of the same factual importance are only popular among local or regional circles.

We finally agreed that Mahatma Ghandi would be the ideal representative of all well-known peace thinkers and peace activists. With Arun Gandhi's 'Mahatma Ghandi's Concept of Peace: A Grandson's Perspective,' we found a perfect solution for this conundrum. Satisfied with this, we concluded that the further essays on peace thinkers should rather focus on maybe less popular but highly influential lateral thinkers of the peace movement, rather than on the well-known and well-documented biographies of the usually mentioned big names. We finally selected a small group of thinkers and activists who basically deconstructed the notion of peace in their respective contexts. Their postmodern attitude was path breaking for the emergence of the trans-rational peace philosophy that inspired this compilation from its beginning.

Considering the above, it became evident that the current state of global affairs calls for a convincing personality who stands for the deconstruction of the stereotypical Muslim notion of just peace. The tribute to the less-known Khan Abdul Ghaffar Khan is a highly illustrative example of an applied nonviolent understanding of Islam. In our current world full of labels, fears and prejudices about the unknown other, Ghaffar Khan's concept can teach us all, Muslims and non-Muslims, so very much. We think that Sikander Mehdi's empathic chapter 'Ghaffar Khan: Gautama Buddha of Hashtnagar,' which verses on this unknown brother in spirit of Gandhi, is a highly inspiring statement for this book.

Still in the Indian context, Sri Aurobindo Ghose and Jiddu Krishnamurti may be among the most influential philosophers of the twentieth century, but they are hardly mentioned by mainstream peace researchers and not often acknowledged as path breakers of a non-modern but highly intellectual peace philosophy. With Samrat Schmiem Kumar we found an author who academically and biographically follows these important Euro-Indian cross-border commuters. He is a perfect representative of the younger generation of this current and hence an ideal author of the respective chapter 'The Inward Revolution: Aurobindo Ghose and Jiddu Krishnamurti.'

In the European context, the choice of our lateral peace hero was pregiven. This place was clearly reserved for Ivan Illich, the recently deceased inspiration for all the complete board of editors. Martina Kaller-Dietrich, who had recently published a highly celebrated biography of Illich, was the logical author of this chapter and we were very happy that she accepted our invitation to contribute to this book.

However, it is not easy to categorize Illich and he always refused to be placed in the circle of post-modern authors. Though this may be disputed, we respect the self-manifestation of such an influential thinker and therefore added a separate chapter on European philosophers whose reputation as post-modern pioneers has never been doubted: Gilles Deleuze and Jean-François Lyotard. Both are well-known philosophers but hardly counted as peace thinkers. In their case, it is not a question of the name that counts but definitely the door-opening effect of their philosophy on the contemporary understanding of peace. Deleuze, once an icon of structuralism, contributed essentially to the development of the post-structural understanding of society and therefore of peace. If someone carried the flag into this direction, it was Deleuze. And Lyotard in his writings created an understanding of plurality that allows us to talk about peaces instead of peace. Without that insight, this book would have never been written this way and the shift from the post-modern condition to the trans-rational cognition would be unthinkable. As the Innsbruck School of Peace Studies took up this thread and developed the new approach of trans-rational peaces, it was clear that one of our core faculty members should describe the context of this shift. Norbert Koppensteiner accepted the responsibility and contributed with his enlightening entry 'Pagans and Nomads: The Postmodern Peaces of Jean-François Lyotard and Gilles Deleuze.'

Africa offers a multitude of quite different peace heroes who would deserve to be mentioned in this book. We finally opted for Kenia's famous novelist Ngũgĩ wa Thiong'o because, on the one hand, his biography is a dramatic example for a lateral thinker's political and intellectual struggle for peace and dignity in the post-colonial context. On the other hand, what he has sown in the 1960s has become a strong popular movement after the turn of the millennium and our author, Astier M. Almedom, is not only witness but also activist of the movement 'Against all Odds.' Thus, her entry 'Ngũgĩ wa Thiong'o: Listening for Peace and Resilience in Africa from Makerere 1962 to Asmara 2000' serves as an eye-opener for many readers who are not so familiar with grassroots movements in Africa.

Raimon Panikkar, as I said earlier, was and is another crucial inspiration of this book. He is one more Indo-European lateral thinker in our list. For decades, he has been a fierce advocate of intercultural and interreligious dialogue. Gustavo Esteva, though neither European nor Indian but Mexican, was personally highly influenced by Panikkar and his initial idea for this book was derived from Panikkar's thoughts. Therefore, it was only natural to integrate Panikkar as a sort of *spiritus rector* into our compilation. And Gustavo Esteva as initiator and member of the editorial board is the logical author of this chapter 'Intercultural Inspiration: The Life and Work of Raimon Panikkar.'*

Finally, we wanted to nominate also a North American peace hero who should not be one of the famous idealist group. The number of convincing names is extremely high and all the criteria we applied failed in one way or another. After a long discussion, we chose Gregory Bateson. Though born in England, most of his professional life is correctly connected to the Palo Alto School in California. Beyond any doubt, his approach to system theory influenced many of the further peace thinkers we discussed and it illuminated several neighboring disciplines like humanistic psychology, communication theory and sociology. Bateson's influence becomes even stronger when seen from the perspective of so-called feedback loops of the interdisciplinary approach we follow. Without Bateson, the systemic understanding of peace studies and humanistic psychology can hardly be imagined. Without him, the work of the best-known peace and conflict workers of our time – from Paulo Freire to Adam Curle and John Paul Lederach, to name but a few – would be totally different. Of course, Bateson is not the source but just one of them, yet a highly remarkable and not well enough known one.

Therefore, we invited our colleague Victoria Fontan, Head of the Department of Peace and Conflict Studies at the UN Peace University in Costa Rica, to contribute with the entry 'Gregory Bateson: A Practitioner's Perspective.' She is an extraordinary experienced field worker and personal witness of the most spectacular international peace operations of the last ten years. Therefore, her approach to Bateson does not focus too much on the philosophical aspects but she re-reads him from a practitioner's point of view. This reminds us of the necessity to combine peace philosophy, especially if it appears in such a complex and advanced shape as Bateson's writings, with our contemporary applied peace and conflict work. By doing so, Victoria Fontan's contribution is a perfect final point of this section and the whole book, because her essay does not only conclude, but also at the same time it opens the chapter about the application and integration of all the knowledge and wisdom presented in this book into practical work.

Following the thrust of peaces and conflict transformation that underlie this book, such a chapter has to be constantly in the making, because the application of academic knowledge and cultural wisdom in concrete conflict work is a matter of the art and the science of every individual practitioner. Convinced followers of John Paul Lederach's elicitive approach to conflict transformation, we firmly disapprove of the seductive demand for prescriptive receipts and remedies.

---

* Ed. On August 26, 2010, during the final stages of editing this book we received the sad news of the passing away of Raimon Panikkar.

In the same line of thinking, we discussed the question whether we should integrate one or more general chapters on common global peace values and cultures. For example, UNESCO, which has supported this book project, has been promoting global peace and peace-building policy for a number of years and there is quite some academic work that requests the insertion of cultural activity into peace-building programs. The empowering nature of peace culture became increasingly recognized during the 1990s. In 1997, the General Assembly of the United Nations, anticipating the new millennium, declared the year 2000 to be the International Year of the Culture of Peace, and followed this in 1998 by declaring a Manifesto for an International Decade for a Culture of Peace and Non-violence for the Children of the World. The main impact of the commitment to a global peace culture by UNESCO was twofold; first, to emphasize the value of peace as a positive experience and value in everyday life and, second, to accelerate and promote interest in the cultural dimensions of peace building generally.

Established in 2001, the MA Program in Peace Studies at the University of Innsbruck was strongly inspired by the UNESCO's Manifesto 2000, which proposed to turn the new millennium into a new beginning, an opportunity to change, all together, the culture of war and violence into a culture of peace and nonviolence. The six cornerstones of the Manifesto 2000 are: respect the life and dignity of each human being; practice active nonviolence; share time and material resources; defend freedom of expression and cultural diversity; responsible consumer behavior; and new forms of solidarity. The MA program took the Manifesto 2000 as an argument to gather faculty and students from all around the world to fill these points permanently with new life, to explore our planetary understanding of peace and conflict transformation. From there, we concluded that there are as many peaces in the world as there are human perceptions and that the challenge for an academic program is to analyze the relation between these myriads of interpretations, evaluate their predominantly harmonious flow and find ways of transforming the sometimes-competing interests. Thereof resulted a Call for Many Peaces, formulating the specific character of the MA program. Gradually we developed a systematic understanding of different forms of peace. According to our findings, the main 'families' of peace interpretations are energetic peaces, moral peaces, modern peaces, post-modern peaces and trans-rational peaces.

We developed textbooks on this topic and in the context of our MA program all these interpretations are discussed and respected. However, the spirit of the Manifesto 2000 demands to promote our common understanding of peaces and it does not allow just to repeat the traditional wisdom, be it religious dogma or the scientific state of the art of previous epochs. According to the four leading principles of the program, scientificity, inter-culturality, inter-disci-plinarity and orientation on practical experience, we try to transgress the limits of conventional modern and post-modern schools of peace studies, which are

abundant all around the world. These topics have already been r̶
but more conventional handbooks on peace building and conte
resolution. As a result, we decided to draw the line here and rese
of international organizations, institutions, states and similar ent
project and concentrate in this book exclusively on the non-insti
between post-modern and trans-rational peaces.

It is precisely the philosophy of the trans-rational peaces with its reintegration
of spirituality into rational, modern and post-modern interpretations of peace,
which indicates that peace is in a permanent flow, that it has to be reshaped every
moment in every context and can never be kept in the cage of a rigid rational
structure. Moreover, a handbook does not claim to cover it all, to catch all the
meanings, to give a complete overview. We have not done that. We compiled
some thirty relevant opinions out of the myriad of peace perceptions and used
them to discuss peace in all its diversity and beauty. We hope that many are
willing to share this beauty with us, feel inspired to follow us on our adventurous
path, listen to the chimes of peaces and, ultimately, take the chance of a conscious
view on the depth of their own peace.

The ideas of Raimon Panikkar were our inspiration and guidance from the conception of this book. They accompanied us as it evolved. While reflecting on the challenges of our times and creatively exploring new intercultural paths, he died peacefully on August 26, 2010 in the place where he hosted friends and colleagues for decades. It was thus impossible to offer him this book, which pays homage to his wisdom, in person. We can well imagine his reaction to our late delivery: he would gently smile and forgive us.

Section I
Peace Concepts in Europe

1
Beyond the Gates of Eden: Trans-rational Peaces

Wolfgang Dietrich

> Out beyond ideas of right and wrongdoing, there is a field. I will meet you there.
>
> Dschalal ad-Din Muhammad Rumi*

My back pages

I was born and socialized in the Upper Inn valley. At that time, this was the most remote, conservative and least industrialized part of Tyrol, a western state of Austria. Many of my compatriots call this region 'The Holy Land' because throughout history Tyroleans were fierce advocates of the Roman Church.

When the students revolted in Paris, Berlin, Berkeley and Mexico, when Soviet tanks finished the political spring in Prague, when the Woodstock festival took place and the second General Episcopal Conference of Latin America was held in Medellín, I was still a boy. However, I consider myself a 68er because the spirit of this year reached Tyrol with a significant delay. When I began my studies at the University of Innsbruck in the mid-1970s, the academic mainstream was dominated by rigid positivism. Karl Popper was the hero of almost every academic attempt and the students' movement was fragmented with sectarian disputes about the writings of Karl Marx.

As always, this is not absolutely true, because Innsbruck was at the same time a hot spot of intellectual liberation and spiritual renovation of the Catholic Church. Karl Rahner,[1] one of the most influential Roman Catholic theologians of the twentieth century, spent almost all his academic life at the Theology Department of Innsbruck University. His work was groundbreaking in the development of what is generally seen as the modern understanding of Catholicism (Rahner, 1995). Rahner, who had attended lectures by Heidegger when he was a student,

---

* Sufi poet Dschalal ad-Din Muhammad Rumi (*1207, †1273) (in Collopy, 2002, p. 109).

3

argued that the finite subject's experience of the limited nature of knowledge and freedom amounts to a latent awareness of God. Such transcendental experience, according to him, is the 'condition of possibility' for knowledge and freedom as such (Fischer, 2005). I certainly cannot call Rahner as a liberation theologian, but his attempt to liberate theology from the strong Neo-Scholastic system, in which he himself was educated, was without any doubt path-breaking in the development of the following years.

Rahner died in Innsbruck on the very day I was promoted to Doctor of Law. His name and his writings continued to be a symbol for the spirit of the department, not necessarily of the university and much less of the city or the state. It may be true that people like Ignacio Ellacuria[2] or Segundo Montes,[3] who later became tragic heroes of the Liberation Theology and its understanding of peace,* were students of the same department, and many Latin American bishops and priests were highly influenced by Rahner, but the local public noticed little of the profound and advanced debates of those theologians.

This is remarkable because Austria's dramatic involvement in the most horrible wars of the twentieth century, the holocaust and the respective official narrative that attempts to justify the nation's mere existence, created an impressive list of trans-disciplinary lateral thinkers who, from my perspective, may be taken as an 'Austrian School' of peace theory and peace studies. The abundance of such brains in Austria is striking. Only a few called themselves 'peace researchers,' but many contributed to the significant changes of peace theory throughout the twentieth and twenty-first centuries.

The times they are a-changin': the 'Austrian school' of peace theory

Bertha von Suttner,[4] 1905 winner of the Nobel Peace Prize, was a leading figure in the peace movement of her time. Her 1889 novel *Die Waffen Nieder*, translated into English as *Lay Down Your Arms* (von Suttner, 1892), had still followed the idealist understanding of peace, whereas Sigmund Freud's[5] work (Freud, 1949) – along with Albert Einstein's theory of relativity – marks the first revolution of thought in the twentieth century. Of course, more than anything Freud was a doctor and a psychoanalyst, but his structural hypothesis is a blueprint for Johan Galtung's writings and, hence, constitutes a milestone in the development of the continental approach to peace theory. Furthermore, structuralism and post-structuralism, as philosophical schools, start from Freud's hypothesis. Since all post-modern approaches to peace theory derive from these streams, Freud can be considered one of their most important ancestors.

* Ed. For further discussions on the Theology of Liberation and Peace, see Chapter 28 on Ivan Illich.

Humanistic psychology, which strongly influenced the systemic theories of peace and conflict transformation in the Americas, turned against Freud rather than followed him. This began as early as Jakob Levy Moreno's[6] rejection of Freudian theory while still being Freud's student in Vienna. Moreno became interested in the potential of group settings for therapeutic practice, and developed the theory of interpersonal relations and the famous Psychodrama, which was a specific result of his Austrian experiences. However, humanistic psychology's turn against psychoanalysis would be unthinkable without Freud's approach as a first point of reference. Again, exiled Austrian lateral thinkers, many of them of Jewish origin, were among the founding fathers of systemic peace theory in the USA after the First World War. The most important is probably Ludwig von Bertalanffy.[7] His general systems theory is recognized as one of the greatest achievements of the science in the twentieth century. Since the 1950s, he was one of the most influential voices of American peace studies. Before that, he had studied in Innsbruck and Vienna, where he became professor before leaving Austria in 1948.

More than anything, Gestalt and humanistic psychology follow the 'here and now' principle. The legendary Esalen Institute in Big Sur and the Mental Research Institute (MRI) in Palo Alto, both in California, became hot spots of the path-breaking work of this branch. Moreover, among many Americans, Austrian Paul Watzlawick[8] was a key figure of this movement. In 1966, Watzlawick followed Virginia Satir as leader of the Palo Alto group and his communication theory opened the door for innovative methods (Watzlawick et al., 1974). John Paul Lederach's elicitive approach to conflict transformation would be unthinkable without the work of Watzlawick and his colleagues in California.

Gestalt and humanistic principles further influenced Austrian lateral thinkers, such as Günther Anders[9] (Anders, 1961), Leopold Kohr,[10] Robert Jungk[11] and Ivan Illich[12] (Kaller-Dietrich, 2008).* Like many of their generation, they were deeply traumatized by Auschwitz and Hiroshima and motivated by the concern about the conditions that gave rise to these horrors. Anders, the oldest of them, published epochal critiques of technology, capitalism and economic growth. He co-founded the antinuclear movement in 1954. In 1967, he served as juror in the Russell tribunal publicizing atrocities in Vietnam. He was one of the most important philosophical pacifists of the twentieth century.

Robert Jungk was another co-founder of the antinuclear movement. His book *Brighter than a Thousand Suns* (Jungk, 1958) had high impact. Like Anders, he was of German Jewish origin, but lived in Austria from 1970 until his death in 1994. Jungk was among the early promoters of *Mankind 2000*, an initiative directed toward establishing means for supporting integrative personal, conceptual and

---

* Ed. For more on Leopold Kohr and Ivan Illich as peace thinkers, see Chapter 28 by Martina Kaller-Dietrich.

societal development (Jungk and Galtung, 1969). Inspired by Wilhelm Reich and his conversations with Anders, Jungk created the method of the future workshops in Salzburg. From 1980 onwards, he was among the pioneers of the Austrian peace movement.

Leopold Kohr reshaped the anarchistic approach of the 'here and now' in his philosophy of the small (Kohr, 1957). His repeated call for human scale, community life, plurality, slow motion and development without aid was the blueprint for *Small is Beautiful: (A Study of) Economics as if People Mattered*, which his German friend Ernst Friedrich Schumacher[13] wrote in his house.

All of these Austrian thinkers contributed immensely to post-modern peace theory, yet without explicitly calling themselves either post-modernists or peace researchers. The same is true for Ivan Illich (1981), who, inspired by the writings of the American anarchist, poet and peace activist Paul Goodman, himself a founding theorist of Gestalt-therapy, became a worldwide popular critic of institutions such as schools and hospitals. Along with Anders, Kohr and Jungk, since the late 1960s, Illich was one of the most prominent voices against unlimited economic growth, technological progress and the idea of development. Illich was a Catholic priest of Jewish origin and his early inspiration was the reform movement of the Roman Catholic Church in the context of the Second Vatican Council. He witnessed the preparations of the Council from within the core group of regenerative thinkers and became its enthusiastic promoter. Illich advocated the liberation of theology but he never became a Liberation Theologian, because the reformist approach to religion unites within Illich Goodman's anarchist 'here and now.' This is perfectly expressed in Illich's famous option for the vernacular, which does not allow the idealistic future orientation of Liberation Theology.

Finally, Innsbruck was also an important station in the life of the physicist Fritjof Capra, born in Vienna in 1939. His books, the *Tao of Physics* (Capra, 1975) and *The Turning Point* (Capra, 1982), are epistemological milestones for the philosophy and science of the twentirth century and opened the way to transrational peace theory, which integrates the reductionist approach of modern and rational peace into the broader understanding of humanistic psychology and its derivates.

New morning: towards the turning point

At some point in the late 1970s, when all these ideas were disseminated in the Tyrolean environment they met people in profound transformation. Tourism and industrialization had transformed this mountainous Austrian state, once poor and rural, into a prosperous and modern place. The *Wirtschaftswunder*, the economic miracle, provided a life in abundance. Poverty could hardly be found in Tyrol at that time. Therefore, the social impact of the new emerged rather in the form of solidarity work for others in what was called 'the third world' and had little effect on conscious activities of collective self-actualization in the country. The Liberation Theology's re-establishment of the relationship with God was a concern for certain circles, but not really a big issue for the masses. In addition, the liberation from selfishness and sin was definitely sacrificed for the most appealing message: the emancipation from those constraints that limit one's capacity to develop freely and in dignity. In this specific context, we perceived the prevailing dogma of the conservative church's hierarchy and the general political climate that was, in a way, still bound to the legacy of Austro-fascism as the constraints we longed to be emancipated from. Liberation Theology came along with many further modern, post-modern and sometimes even revolutionary tendencies such as sexual liberation, anti-authoritarian education, civil and human rights projects, third world solidarity, the second women's movement, as well as peace and environmentalist initiatives. All these were represented and communicated in pop music, experimental theater and expressive dance, avant-garde cinema and more.

Of course, many of those things created inherent contradictions. It was not unusual for someone to drive a big car, watch a violent movie in the cinema while being engaged in the green, solidarity or women's movement. We wanted to save the world, listen to Bob Dylan,[14] win the national soccer league and have good sex. We were enthusiastic about imagining a brotherhood of men. We dreamed, idealized and experimented, but eventually we did not get a concrete result. The imagined brotherhood was still in our hearts when we became increasingly frustrated about our inescapable captivity in the neo-liberal rules of the 1980s. The 'permanent cultural revolution' was somehow on its way, but the syncretism of modernity produced some rather queer results, probably not only in my home country, and the brotherhood of men in this world remains elusive.

I am starting with this story because it illustrates perfectly the post-modern condition in which Peace Studies was framed in the West from the very beginning. I say the 'post-modern condition' because, although European intellectuals may have struggled already with structuralism at that time and started to read the early leftist interpretations of Nietzsche and Heidegger, a post-modern philosophy or a post-modern wisdom was not yet available. We were still searching for a new interpretation of the great narratives, be it the Christian or the Marxist one, until Jean François Lyotard's short but highly influential book *La condition postmoderne* (1979) gave the initial hint for a more profound discussion of our own emotional and intellectual condition.* From my perspective, this was the switch from post-modernity to post-modernism or from the post-modern condition to the post-modern cognition.

*   Ed. For further discussions on Jean-François Lyotard as peace thinker, see Chapter 29 by Norbert Koppensteiner.

There are no truths outside the gates of Eden: the call for many peaces

Lyotard provided us probably with the quickest access to post-modern philosophy, because his book was all about social and communicative plurality and plurality is the keyword for understanding this philosophy. I cannot repeat here the comprehensive and exuberant discussion of almost three decades, but I want to stress two points that are crucial for the further discussion of our topic.

First, plurality is not synonymous with the arbitrariness of 'anything goes.' The plurality of social contexts asks for a precise definition of their inherent properties for the understanding of their very being and intercontextual communication. Although the total number of these contexts is high, too high for the capacity of human perception, it is not unlimited. It is confined by the totality of human relations and can never exceed them. It is permanently flowing as human relations emerge and vanish. Thus, a philosophy of plurality of social contexts reflects the amazing potential of concrete human relations. It asks for limits, for definition, not for arbitrariness.

Second, plurality in post-modern philosophy is not a value comparable to 'truth' or 'reason' in idealism. It is not good or bad, it is simply a matter of fact. Plurality therefore shall not be reached in post-modernism, as advocates of a multicultural modernity would suggest. It shall not, because 'shall' in the ears of post-modern philosophers is the most violent word.[15] 'Shall' refers to the gap between the existing and the desired; it sacrifices the present for the promises of an idealized future goal. That which exists in the present is never good enough for the 'shall' and, hence, it creates a linear chronosophy[16] that leads us from an imperfect here and now into the promise of a great future. Post-modernism refuses this idealist imposition. It cares about the relations between finite human beings and the methods to make the world appear a bit more beautiful to them, but it does not try to make the world *per se* a better place. It knows that peace is only real when it is imperfect, unfinished and plural.[17] This distinction is crucial and it will be at the core of further considerations.

The post-modern quest for plurality is not limited to superficial matters of appearance, language or cultural habit. It targets much more the fundamental structures of society and the power that is imposed on them by specific narratives. Friedrich Nietzsche, the most important reference for post-modern philosophy, began by deconstructing morality. In 1886, he shattered the conventional wisdom of his time, stating that many forms of morality always exist simultaneously and at the same place, and that these are contradictory. Accordingly, an individual can never live a moral life as long as there is the belief that we can only rely on One ultimate moral principle (Nietzsche, 1983, p. 205). He, who claims to know what the One principle of morality is, seeks to exercise power over others. More than 100 years later, Gianni Vattimo, one of the most noted post-modern philosophers and interpreters of Nietzsche, labeled this observation as 'weak thought' (Vattimo, 1984), meaning a thought that does not resort to an ultimate principle such as God, reason, law, human rights, development, justice, progress or the like. Weak thought, according to Vattimo, is relational, restricted to the involved actors, defined, interpreted and transformed exclusively among and by them. Lyotard would add that it is not translatable into different contexts.

All this could be put aside as a sophisticated intellectual joke if there was not the supposition that post-modernism is the philosophical reaction to post-modernity, and not vice versa. Or to express it in simple words: at some point during that strange epoch into which I was born, an increasing number of people started wondering why we were doing what we were doing, because the then still dominating narratives had lost their power of conviction and apparently failed to explain the world. Whether we like it or not, we probably have to accept that the post-modern condition of societies provoked the radical revision of their fundamental principles, rather than being an intellectual conspiracy of some unscrupulous clowns who came along to fool the audience.

Nevertheless, as many have pointed out, post-modernism is not an epoch that follows modernity.[18] More precisely, it is an aspect of the modern condition, because reasonable doubt about the values of modern principles was there from their very inception. In this sense, not even Nietzsche was the 'founder' of what we could call a post-modern philosophy. Long before him, philosophers like Rousseau and Hume thought in a 'post-modern' way, as did the skeptical empiricism of Hobbes. Only the political impact of post-modern thought became stronger when the emotional and intellectual condition of post modern life, that is the frustration about the failed promises of modernism, became increasingly evident to more and more people.

As a reaction to suffering the anomy of modernity with all its political, social and psychological consequences, the mainstream of social sciences argued that one would just have needed higher doses of the same remedy to reach paradise on earth.[19] These were the advocates of development theories, progress, justice, democracy, technology and generally of universal values and strategies. Inspired by a more or less hidden logic of natural law, they did not turn away from the belief in an ultimate 'good' that should be evident for everybody. They argued for the universalism of human rights, international law, structural adjustment, good governance and global ethics.

The structuralism of the 1960s fairly neglected the responsibility of the subject for its own destiny and stressed the impact of 'structure,' the order of things, and the domination of the impersonal power in the capitalist world. This way of thinking even influenced the Second Vatican Council and can be easily identified in Pope Paul's Encyclica *Populorum Progressio* of 1967, which went so far as to call development another word for peace.

For peace is not simply the absence of warfare, based on a precarious balance of power; it is fashioned by efforts directed day after day toward the establishment of the ordered universe willed by God, with a more perfect form of justice among men. (Paul VI, 1967, §76)

The mentor of Liberation Theology, Gustavo Gutiérrez, then asked how the Catholic Church could make poor people believe that God loves them. Therefore, he made the poor, the excluded, the center of his theology. His main concern became to overcome poverty, not just as an economic or social phenomenon, but also as a multidimensional structure. To be Christian, according to him, meant to be a partisan of the poor and to live in solidarity with them.

Post-modernism tries to turn away from this common and 'strong' way of thinking. It challenges our minds by denying the legitimacy or even the very existence of any ultimate principle and reduces us to a relational, but rational, small and 'weak' multitude of social interactions. I once called the art of mastering them, of transforming the omnipresent bigger and smaller conflicts of daily life in a constructive manner, the 'many peaces' (Dietrich, 2006). We, human beings, are not too bad in that art. Kenneth Boulding (1989), the system theorist and founder of American Peace Studies, once estimated that more than 85 percent of all human conflicts are solved in an unspectacular and nonviolent manner. Our fascination for violence, however, makes it a permanent headliner and lets us forget about our most existential virtue.

Here we are back at the question of plurality and we notice how incompatible these many peaces are if we relate them to the One peace based in the One God that the Pope called development. The fundamental, insolvable contradictions between the modernizing Liberation Theology and post-modern philosophy are rooted in this presumption.

It is self-evident that this refers to Plato and his concept of truth, which shaped not only the intellectual debate of 2500 years, but also the perception of reality in everyday life in European cultures. If an absolute good exists, it must be possible to differentiate it from bad. If it is possible to identify the truth, it follows that one can separate it from the untrue or false. If there is objective beauty, it must be the ugly or at least the less beautiful that is different. If a personal God represents these values, the believers will be obliged to comply with his commandments if they do not want to follow Satan. If a Pope, a king or a cast of high priests represents the One God on Earth and interprets his will, the subjects have to obey and follow, fulfill the law and respect the rules. We are so used to this narrative that we did not even consider to change it when we substituted God by reason. There was a substitution of God by the state, but both types of powers coexist in modernity. In this sense, in modernity there is no brake from religious to secular constructions of the nation, but a coexistence in which religious and secular traditions invoke a national community. The secular priests of reason empowered themselves quickly as interpreters of the holy book of modernity and designated the reasonable administrators of modernity (Callahan, 2006).

If modern thought does not diverge as much from medieval or Hellenist philosophy as it appears at first glance, it should surprise no one that we discover an inherent legacy of domination within it. Post-modern philosophy tried to deconstruct the seemingly untouchable logic of this legacy. Let us take the example of justice.

It is hard to challenge the concept of justice in a modern Western context. Though people usually disagree greatly on what justice in a concrete situation means, they tend to agree that justice is a good thing. As soon as we disembed this belief from its abstract height and root it in a concrete personal conflict of parties, we see that when someone talks about justice for herself, she begins with the injustice she actually suffers. That is, justice is obviously only there as long as nobody mentions it. We cannot talk about mere justice in a concrete context, because as soon as we talk about it we name injustice. And in so doing, we construct the linear chronosophy that leads us into violence. Because if we talk about our own justice in a notoriously unjust world, we deplore our unjust situation in the present, which results from the injustice that we or our ancestors suffered earlier and we long for justice in the future. If we perceive the world like that, if justice for ourselves, and therefore injustice, is a concern, we build a world of revenge, envy and greed. We seek revenge for the injustice that our ancestors or we suffered before; we feel jealousy and envy because our present is not perfect; and greed, or as some say competition, is the energy that drives us into the assumption of a better future to be. If one combines all that with a high degree of ignorance or unawareness about one's own biases, one will end up in a rather unmerciful culture that makes the world an uncomfortable place. Some people call this progress, or development, and they view those who have doubts as conservatives, because in their linear chronosophy someone who is not progressive can only be conservative, backward and ignorant. As seen from their perspective, there is no alternative.[20]

Buddhists describe envy, greed and ignorance as the three elementary defilements and recommend twisting them through serious work on one's awareness. One can argue now that justice is not necessarily something that one claims only for oneself. I agree and if one selflessly seeks justice for others in the sense of a Buddhist *boddhisattva*, we call that compassion – but only if we do not abuse the others unconsciously as vehicles for our inner concept of greed, envy and jealousy. Many among us with idealist leanings tend to suppress this energy, unwilling to accept it as their own. Therefore, they project these properties into their narrative of others. The others, for example the 'poor,' the 'illiterate,' the 'uncivilized,' the 'homeless,' the 'underdeveloped,' the 'handicapped,' the 'migrants' and the 'orphans' in this sophisticated manner, become vehicles for one's own greediness that shall be satisfied once they are doing better. Compassion is only there if we are able to find resonance with the other and not if we give them the tune. I fear that this abuse happens frequently and definitely so in the failed history of the international solidarity work for development. The modern Christian contribution to this long-lasting tragedy is probably the irritating perpetuation and dissemination of the belief in justice. Irritation continues.

What I mentioned above concerning justice could also be said about security. Where absolute security prevails, nobody mentions it; or rather, where nobody talks about it, security prevails. As soon as we raise the question of security, we think of insecurity and normally we mean our own insecurity. The consequence is that we take measures to prevent aggression from others and, by doing so, we communicate that we perceive them as potential threats and that we dispose over sufficient weapons for defending ourselves. They cannot but take our fear-driven attitude as an unfriendly sign. They will respond to our fear and do the same. Finally, the fear will make one of us strike first to prevent the other from doing so. In that manner, fear creates violence.[21] Compassion would indicate the opposite, because it means that the fewer signs of fear, strength and defense we send into the world, the less we threaten others and the lower is the probability of an attack. Of course, this is risky, but risk is a bad word only in the ears of fear-driven people. Peace is for heroes. The concepts of peace in many cultures of the world acknowledge that and take the risk.

The concepts of justice and security are two appropriate examples to illustrate Boulding's main arguments. Yet post-modernists would say that the reason for Boulding's findings on the mainly nonviolent transformation of conflicts is that there exist only very few, if any, substantial conflicts in the world. Most conflicts are constructed by perception, created by fear, frustrated hopes, opinions, expectations, prejudices and stereotypes. Therefore, conflicts can hardly be solved because there are no substantial or just solutions, but the conflictive energy can be liberated by the deconstruction of perceptions, fears and hopes and so open the door for a multitude of previously unperceived options of interaction. This is what the art of conflict transformation means in a post-modern understanding. Hence, post-modernism would argue against all modern approaches that peaces will never emerge out of justice, comfort, development, progress or security, and even worse, they would state that the quest for them excludes the possibility of peaces. These require a plurality that allows the societal energy to flourish and flow in many ways. In short, peaces happen, they cannot be made.

Post-modern authors do not want to save the world or rather, in a seeming contradiction, they want to do so by refraining from it. Their merit is that they contributed to dissolve the mechanistic ideologies of the social and political branches of modernity, after modern science found that the universe is definitely no mechanic clockwork fueled by an external Creator God. On the other hand, post-modernity left the people in a shocking condition of anomy and atomy and the post-modern attitude does not help. Thus, the twentieth century ended with the need for new interpretations beyond the deconstructive limits of post-modernism. It seems to be the task of the new millennium to find new interpretations from where we derive our orientation, ethics, values and rules. I call these trans-rational peaces.

The chimes of freedom flashing: ethics and aesthetics of trans-rational peaces

Along the post-modern way of learning, to think peaces without a strong grounding, without an ultimate principle or God, we discovered the need for weak thought, as Vattimo (1984) says, for peaces understood as a dynamic, relational network of interaction and communication. Thus, peaces here are understood as an aesthetic momentum of an intersubjective, compassionate and harmonious resonance. If one follows this understanding by applying radically what I called the Austrian school after Fritjof Capra's *Turning Point* (1982), one finds trans-rational approaches to peaces. Trans-rational peaces transgress the limits of modernity and post-modernity by recombining the rational and modern with energetic elements and recognizing the importance of energy flow for the perception of peace.

Trans-rationality hence recognizes all earlier achievements of pre-modern civilizations and its practices. Pre-modern here comes close to pre-rational, but these terms are not identical in spite of the claim of modernity to differ from earlier stages of evolution precisely by the principle of rationality. However, it can hardly be denied that a multitude of rational wisdom emerged from pre-modern civilizations such as Buddhism, Hinduism and Dao, including Christianity, Islam and many more. Trans-rationality *twists*[22] such wisdom and its practice without romanticizing a Golden Age in a conservative manner. That is, it recognizes and integrates the pre-rational consciously into its own stock of knowledge, embedding, differentiating and reinterpreting it according to its own practice. It neutralizes eventual universalistic claims and enhances them to the actual level of common awareness. Pre-rational wisdom hence is embedded in rational consciousness.

Rationality in this context is equally considered to be a specific wisdom and methodology related to a certain epoch. Therefore, rationality is no longer treated like another name for God, as was the case in modernity and post-modernity, but as a useful tool that could be twisted into a broader interpretation of the world. Trans-rational, thus, is more than rational; it approaches spirituality, but not the ancient magic or mystic spirituality, which could be twisted as well as rationality for the generation of a trans-rational reinterpretation of the world. In the frame of peace studies, this implies that the magic and mystic wisdom of pre-modern and pre-rational civilizations, in its still existing or as well as in its already disappeared forms, do not have to be overcome, forgotten or deleted from our memory, nor do we have to adore them in a romantic, conservative manner. In a twisted manner, they must be recognized as common heritage of and for *all* human beings expressing the complete potential of our feelings, thoughts, words, actions and reactions. The more we suppress it in the name of rationality, the higher is the risk that it returns in an uncontrolled, violent and destructive manner, because we are all carriers of the complete memory and everyone has the potential to trigger disaster.

As pre-modern and pre-rational societies were and are highly spiritual, twisting their wisdom includes the recognition of spirituality as a constitutive feature of human nature. Thus, a trans-rational approach inevitably has to acknowledge the spiritual character of humankind and fashion adequate tools to handle this aspect with all the achievements of rational thinking and the application of further human virtues, some of them forgotten, others suppressed in the name of rationality. Such a concept allows transcending the contradictions of the modern age, without turning away from its most important achievements. For example, human rights can be recognized as a general achievement without insisting on their normative universality as stated in the respective declarations and covenants that disregard the cultural habits of many societies and hence create a lot of disagreement and irritation.

$E = mc^2$ means that material, visible existence is just one of many possible conditions of energy. From there derive some key insights of the trans-rational peace concept, which are:

a. There are no things but only networks and interrelations. The universe is an interwoven net of connectivity.
b. The Cartesian distinction between mind and matter, observer and observed is no longer upheld. We can never speak about nature without speaking about ourselves.
c. In nature, no static structures exist. Peaces are a dynamic equilibrium.

Trans-rational peaces thus transgress the limits of rationality that still characterize post-modernism. Trans-rationality is not a step backwards into pre-modern beliefs, it does not advocate magic or myth, but it reassumes the thread of spirituality that modernity fairly lost and twists it with the amazing experience of rationality to a broader perception of our existence. In this line of argumentation, our existence unravels a combination of ethics and aesthetics principled on trans-rational peaces.

Within ethics of trans-rational peaces, human beings are physical objects inter-connected via their superego. The individual here does not refer to a person but to a structure, a network of relations, such as families, kinships, clans, communities, guilds, companies, unions, villages, states or even the global society. The structure is neither fixed nor divisible, because being relational implies that it vibrates permanently. Ethics of peaces acknowledges this and provides the condition for unimpeded transformation. Therefore, global ethics is only peaceful if unchained from ultimate norms If applied dualistically, with the absolute notion of good and bad, of right and wrong, it necessarily loses its peaceful character. Ethics of trans-rational peaces relates but it does not bind.

The aesthetic of trans-rational peaces concerns human relations as well, but here it deals with the energetic level. It derives peaces from harmony.* Harmony is when the energy of life can flow unhampered. Hence, aesthetic of peaces is defined by the relations of what we call soul, atman or Id to each other and to the total that can be called God, brahman or existence. It is about the Dionysian aspect of being. The aesthetic of peaces refers to a transcendental experience. To a certain extent, it is metaphysical and, by virtue of being energetic, it builds an individual system. Yet this does not imply esoteric speculation, because the aesthetic of trans-rational peaces can certainly be perceived in the physical world as a property of the above-mentioned structures.

Ethics and aesthetic of trans-rational peaces are not exclusive or separated things. Peaces are simultaneously both ethical and aesthetic, as the ego is always driven by the superego and the Id. Consequently, peaces are simultaneously the object and property of relations, but due to the limitation in knowledge of the finite subject, depending on the cognitive interest they appear as the one or the other.

The concept of the individual is therefore a fen fire if the term is applied as the basis for an autonomous subject. However, if we define the individual as a *holon*,[23] meaning as an integrated whole of smaller holons and a subordinated part of a bigger system at the same time, we can perceive the individual, as stated above, either as an object or a property according to our own position and cognitive interest. Thus, internal and external in this context are helpful constructs for analysis. So are object and property. But, these boundaries cease to be helpful if we confuse them with reality or take them as separated spheres.†
In the world of holons, there is no internal without external as there is no object without property and vice versa. If this is true for the fundamental character of the individual, it is necessarily also true for the self-consciously perceiving subject.

---

* Ed. Energetic interpretations of peace are a major topic in this book and they constantly reappear in almost all of the chapters. For specific elaborations in Europe see the chapters that complement this Section I and for energetic notions of peace in the Middle East see especially Chapter 10. In Sections III, IV and V each chapter takes up energetic notions in its own distinct way.
† Ed. Munir Fasheh relates the problematic notion of individual as implying realities of separate spheres and its introduction into Arabic in Chapter 7.

There are no kings inside the gates of Eden: trans-personality and peaces

Recent neuro-scientific research gives clear evidence that human beings are equipped with an empirically evident *social brain*, that is a set of neurons that basically makes us cooperative and only competitive in exceptional situations (Bauer, 2007). Therefore, neuroscience confirms what Boulding (1989) and Muñoz (2006) have stated many times with different words: humankind is made for trans-personal peaces. Compassion is not an ideal but a property of humankind and this insight, more than anything else, unchains us from the modern ideology of competition in a ubiquitous and omnipresent natural war. This transgresses rationality and opens the path to trans-rational peaces. It liberates the Self from the ties of mere rationality.

This Self necessitates being understood in a holistic manner. For such comprehension, I relate Freud's structure of the person to Galtung's prevailing notion of peace.[24] Furthermore, by altering Freud's famous metaphor of the iceberg with Galtung's image of the iceberg of violence,[25] it becomes evident that peaces can only flourish if all interpersonal relational aspects are respected. Let me explain this connection in detail.

For defining violence, I use the metaphor of frozen, blocked human relations. Violence is then the objective expression of an omnipresent human property that becomes manifest when social relations *cool down* to a critical point, like water shows ubiquitous potential to turn into ice under certain conditions and temperature. The visible part of the iceberg above the surface thus corresponds with the play of the egos, the masks in the human drama. The physical aspects of conflict call our attention the most, especially if this implies direct violence. However, indeed this is just the surface. If we only mediate on that level, with whatever means from good services to so-called peace enforcement, we end up like Sisyphus cutting peaks of perpetually growing icebergs. Like the iceberg, violence is fueled from the depths.

We have seen that the Id of holons, such as individuals or groups, tends to long for more than is needed for substantial survival. It is driven by greed and envy and asks for what it considers to be justice. Being only an Id, just individual, it lacks the consciousness to realize that this search for individual justice creates both internal conflict and conflict in the relations with further holons. This drives and fuels the drama of the masks on the surface. Furthermore, if the aesthetic balance of energy gets lost, it produces what Galtung called structural violence, which eventually leads to direct violence of the masks on the surface.

The superego, however, also affects the drama of the masks by nurturing them with morals. The norms that are derived from morals, as we have seen, can again be objects or properties of holons. The individual, being unconscious of the holistic nature, takes them to be binding and demands them for the sake of their own security. If this binding perception of an individual obstructs the relational character of the structure, it will provoke what Galtung called cultural violence and can be simply defined as any intellectual concept that justifies structural violence. Hence, the superego drives the masks on the surface through intellectual and ethical but unconscious concepts. If these get out of balance, they once more push the drama towards physical violence.

Cutting the peaks of an iceberg will not make it disappear, but increasing the temperature of its surroundings will. Equally, the heat generated simultaneously by ethics and aesthetic of peaces can transform a violent situation into normal conflict transformation. Under this presumption, the egoic masks on the visible surface, as well as their potential attitudes and action of physical violence, appear as puppets on strings, as functions driven by the deeper structures. However, they are not mere delusion or *Maya*, as the East would say, because the images they produce retroact on the superego and thus form a substantial part of the bigger reality.

Taken seriously these arguments imply that peaces are inseparably twisted in all aspects of an individual, subject or person. Therefore, they are trans-personal objects and properties of human life. Moreover, if we agree that a person is a holon, we understand that the trans-personal cannot only perambulate all levels of a presumptively autonomous individual, but it inevitably transgresses all the constructed natural and social limits of this holon, because it is simultaneously and always internal and external, object and property.

As a result, the trans-personal concept of peaces indicates that there is a relevant trans-rational property of peaces. It is trans-rational because it transgresses the limits of rationality without being irrational or anti-rational. It rather twists rationality by balancing it and thus avoids becoming a tool of physical, structural or cultural violence; it twists rationality by memorizing it and thus keeping it available as ubiquitous human potential for conflict transformation; it finally twists rationality by enhancing it into the sphere of spiritual peaces. It defines a holon that transgresses the limits of rationality and trans-personal peaces, explores and experiences the spiritual sphere and is able to communicate it.

Philosophies and religions of ages stated that rationality is not enough to completely understand the point of such a message. As rationality is twisted on the spiritual level, it is necessarily a property of trans-rational peaces. Therefore, even a spiritually very limited rational person is not just a helpless object of manipulation by spiritual claims, orders or statements. Where the rational aspect is totally lacking, the presence of trans-rationality is very unlikely. In such a case, we have to expect cultural violence rather than trans-rational peaces. To a high extent, the trans-personal character of any peaceful relation empowers us to feel trans-rational peaces even if we are not able to understand them. If there is something like a spiritual sphere of existence open to our kind at all, then it follows that we human beings carry the potential and the property to experience it. Whether we just feel, believe or know this sphere is subsequently only a matter of a corresponding exercise.

Bringing it all back home: elicitive conflict transformation

From the acknowledgment of the concept of trans-rational peaces, elicitive conflict transformation follows as its respective method. As defined by John Paul Lederach (1995, pp. 55–70), elicitive conflict transformation draws out, highlights and catalyzes existing or communally held knowledge related to transforming conflicts between individuals, groups and communities, while the prescriptive approaches of modern and post-modern schools propose pre-created models. Elicitive conflict transformation starts from the assumption that the mere appearance of a mediator in a conflicting system is in itself a significant change. It understands the mediator as a constituting element of the conflicting, dysfunctional system. As an important difference to prescriptive methods, in an elicitive approach the mediator is never neutral. This requires a high awareness of such a mediating role. Therefore, the mediator has to develop a mature self-actualization and high consciousness about their own potentials, limits and properties before action. This method requires more subtle skills than any prescriptive tool and implies a thorough training of people who aspire to work in this field.

Lederach's innovative approach[26] would have been unthinkable without the enormous effort of humanistic psychology since the mid-1960s. It is an illustrative parallel to the so-called Austrian school that the founders, stars and heroes of this therapeutic movement, from Abraham Maslow[27] and Carl Rogers[28] to Virginia Satir,[29] Frederick Perls[30] and Ruth Cohn,[31] did hardly or not at all understand themselves as peace researchers. They rather called themselves therapists and social workers. However, they developed their knowledge about social systems, group settings, client-centered, family-centered or theme-centered therapy in Esalen and Palo Alto,[32] geographically and historically very close to the cradle of the North American peace research at Stanford University. Trans-disciplinary-orientated scientists, like Gregory Bateson,[33]* Paul Goodman[34] and Ludwig von Bertalanffy, build the missing epistemological link between these closely related disciplines. Both experimental fields finally produced the elicitive method of conflict transformation with its strong focus on the mediator as system-changing actor. The group therapy approach, as a method of conflict transformation, has already been explored by Jakob Levy Moreno but basically stems from Perls (1969) and Rogers (1970), who developed very different styles of Encounter methods. Virginia Satir, inspired by Bateson, introduced system theory into therapy and conflict transformation (Satir et al., 1991). She stated that the alteration of any

---

*   Ed. Gregory Bateson as peace thinker is discussed extensively in Chapter 32 by Victoria Fontan.

element in a system affects all the others and this again takes effect on the same element. Conflict, she said further, stems from dysfunctional relations within a system and/or incongruent communication styles of one or more parties. Her definition of the word transformation states that the parties use the conflictive energy for exploring and obtaining more options than they seemed to have before. One option is no freedom at all, two options are a dilemma (either/or) and three consciously perceived options are the minimum for calling conflict transformation the change of a social relation.

This definition, from my point of view, is still very helpful and distinguishes elicitive conflict transformation in a trans-rational frame from the one-dimensional and prescriptive modern notion of conflict resolution as well as from the evolutionist approaches of Ken Wilber (1995), who is mostly considered the initiator of the trans-rational approaches in psychology. In this specific aspect, the peace studies' understanding of trans-rationality pursued here clearly differs from Wilber's perspective.

Grounded on previous works, Ruth Cohn (2004) finally developed useful postulates and tools regarding the communication styles of parties and mediators. Her famous model of theme-centered interaction is a strictly relational concept of human communication in groups and focuses on the balance between theme, group and individual in group settings. It draws a seemingly simple triangular relation of the *I*, the *we* and the *theme*, all of them embedded in the general environment that she calls *globe*. Her first postulate 'Be your own chairman' calls for self-responsibility and focuses on the awareness of every actor's[35] internal disposition (*I*) and the external conditions (*globe*) in a relational (*we*) or factual (*theme*) conflict. This awareness given, one can take every situation as an invitation to decide on one's own and act responsibly for oneself and for others. Her second postulate reads 'disturbances first,' and is derived from the observation that in a system there are no coincidences; there is no division between inside and outside. Therefore, disturbances, whether they come from the individual, the group, the theme or the globe, have to be dealt with as a priority. Without the previous transformation of the disturbing energy, the flow of the system as a whole will be blocked, distracted or irritated. From these two principal postulates, Cohn draws a multitude of tools for authentic self-representation, authentic questioning, selective authenticity and congruent communication.

The feedback of these primarily American findings of mostly European emigrants had an enormous impact on continental peace research in Europe. Among others, the application of Capra's approach in peace studies led to the concept of trans-rational peaces, the Innsbruck approach. Based on this epistemological assumption, Lederach's principle of elicitive conflict transformation gained enormous importance and dynamic enlargement. The Master Program for Peace Studies at the University of Innsbruck made both approaches the main tenet of its curriculum. By doing so, it achieved high attention and recognition.

In 2008, the UNESCO Secretary General Koichiro Matsuura awarded the MA Program with the UNESCO Chair for Peace Studies. This prize can also be taken as a tribute to all the above-mentioned ancestors of the Austrian school, from Freud and Moreno to Illich, Rahner and Capra, just as a tribute to the heroes of humanistic psychology who prepared the path for Lederach's elicitive method.

The explicit invitation of the UNESCO Secretary General to develop this approach further by discussing and testing it everywhere in the world is an enormous motivation for the current representatives of that school. Many of the long time diffuse and contradictory developments of the Tyrolean environment, as described in the introduction to this chapter, suddenly converge into a concrete avant-garde project of peace studies. This international program is not and never was meant as a conventional Master study. Besides the high academic quality and the selective admission process, the Master is the result of a common regional endeavor, an expression of specific conditions. From its very beginning, the university cooperated with different institutions such as the Austrian Army, the Fire Fighter's Academy, the Red Cross, the Native Spirit Wilderness School and many further local organizations for providing the frame to the worldwide student's body to engage in a highly practical, experimental and self-actualizing training in the spirit of elicitive conflict transformation. The teaching methods refer to the above-mentioned founders of humanistic psychology, but apply and present equally more recent techniques such as the Nonviolent Communication model of Marshall B. Rosenberg (2003), Augusto Boal's Theater of the Oppressed (Boal, 1976), Morihei Ueshiba's Aikido (Ueshiba, 1996), Tatsumi Hijikata and Kazuo Ohno's Butoh Dance (Horton Fraleigh, 1999) and many more. It might be a matter of taste whether one takes this challenging curriculum as the best in the world, but it is certainly among the toughest.

Since its establishment, the UNESCO Chair for Peace Studies at Innsbruck University promotes the idea of trans-rational peaces and elicitive conflict transformation. For this end, there is no missionary attitude appropriate but rather the opposite. As both approaches emphasize the self-regulating potential of social systems, they encourage it in all contexts and call for the self-responsibility of conflicting parties. They neither claim almightiness nor deplore powerlessness. They advocate for the creativity of conflicting systems and support the potential of the self-healing power. Therefore, they focus on the perceptions and interpretations of peace(s) in particular social contexts of the world. This handbook starts from this understanding, honestly respecting every presented concept, accepting happily the myriad of contradictions between these approaches and the trans-rational thought itself and gazing amazed at the numerous options for peaces that result from the findings of the distinguished colleagues who present their concepts in this book.

I encourage you to follow up these multi-voiced and self-reflective chapters so that you can form your own views and you might, very well, come to different conclusions than I have. As said at the beginning of this introductory chapter, the many peaces remain open and intractable, and the manifestations and insights this collective collection prompts are equally open for you to assess and reappropriate.

Notes

1. *1904 in Freiburg, †1984 in Innsbruck.
2. *1930 in Portugalete, Spain. He studied in Innsbruck and was rector of the Universidad Centroamericana José Simeon Canas, when he was murdered by the Salvadorian Army in 1989.
3. *1933 in Valladolid, Spain, murdered by the Salvadorian Army in 1989 along with Ellacuria and further priests. He studied in Innsbruck from 1960 to 1963.
4. *1843 in Prague, †1914 in Vienna.
5. *1856 in Freiburg, †1939a in London.
6. *1889 in Bucharest, †1974 in New York.
7. *1901 in Atzgerdorf, †1972 in Buffalo.
8. *1921 in Villach, †2007 in Palo Alto.
9. *1902 in Breslau, †1992 in Vienna.
10. *1909 in Oberndorf, †1994 in Gloucester.
11. *1913 in Berlin, †1994 in Salzburg.
12. *1926 in Vienna, †2002 in Bremen.
13. *1911 in Bonn, †1977 in Geneva.
14. ...whose songs inspired the headlines I chose for this essay.
15. I take this specific argument from Marshall Rosenberg (2003).
16. Chronosophy means here the perception of social time.
17. These are the main arguments of Francisco Muñoz (2006).
18. This argument has been extensively discussed in Wolfgang Welsch (1994).
19. The topic has been raised again recently in the book of Kevin Rushby (2007), but of course the metaphor is much older and has been used frequently by myself already in the 1990s.
20. For example, Jürgen Habermas (1994).
21. This was also an argument of Friederich Nietzsche's 'Human, all too human' (*Menschliches, Allzumenschliches*) (Nietzsche in Koppe, 2001, pp. 175–176).
22. *Twisting* refers to the Heideggerian term *Verwindung*, interpreted by Gianni Vattimo (1992) as a non-dialectical form of overcoming the characteristic of a post-modern, pluralist notion of history.
23. The term *holon* was originally coined by Arthur Köstler (1976). It became very popular through its extensive use by Ken Wilber (1995).
24. I did that the first time in Dietrich (1998, p. 169).
25. Probably the most comprehensive definition among the myriad of his publications can be found in Galtung (1996).
26. Probably best elaborated in Lederach (2005).
27. *1908 New York, †1970 Menlo Park (CA).
28. *1902 Chicago, †1987 La Jolla (CA).
29. *1916 Neillsville (WI), †1988 Palo Alto (CA).
30. *1893 Berlin, †1970 Chicago.
31. *1912 Berlin.

32. Enlightening in this regard is Jeffrey Kripal (2007).
33. *1904 Grantchester, England, †1980 San Francisco (CA).
34. *1911 New York, †1972 New York.
35. That is party, client, mediator or therapist.

Reference list

Anders, G. (1961) *Burning Conscience: The Case of the Hiroshima Pilot Claude Eatherly, Told in his Letters to Günther Anders* (New York: Weidenfeld and Nicolson).

Bauer, J. (2007) *Prinzip Menschlichkeit: Warum wir von Natur aus kooperieren* (Hamburg: Hoffmann und Campe).

Boal, A. (1976) *Teatro do Oprimido e outras poéticas polítics* (Rio de Janeiro: Civilização Brasileira).

Boulding, K. (1989) 'A Proposal for a Research Program in the History of Peace,' *Peace & Change: A Journal of Peace Research*, 14, 4.

Callahan, W. (2006) 'War, Shame, and Time: Governance and National England and America,' *International Studies Quarterly*, 50, 395–419.

Capra, F. (1975) *The Tao of Physics: An Exploration of the Parallels between Modern Physics and Eastern Mysticism* (Boston: Shambhala).

Capra, F. (1982) *The Turning Point: Science, Society, and the Rising Culture* (New York: Simon & Schuster).

Cohn, R. (2004) *Von der Psychoanalyse zur themenzentrierten Interaktion: Von der Behandlung einzelner zu einer Pädagogik für alle* (Stuttgart: Klett-Cotta).

Collopy, M. (2002) *Architects of Peace: Visions of Hope in Words and Images* (Novato: New World Library).

Dietrich, W. (1998) 'Kulturelle Gewalt als Mittel und Indikator von Herrschaft im Weltsystem' in P. Gruber, K. Zapotoczky (eds.) *Globalisierung versus Demokratie? Plädoyer für eine umwelt- und sozialverträgliche Weltordnung* (Frankfurt/Vienna: Brandes & Apsel).

Dietrich, W. (2006) [1997] 'A Call for Many Peaces' in W. Dietrich, J. Echavarría and N. Koppensteiner (eds.) *Schüsseltexte der Friedensforschung/Key Texts of Peace Studies/Textos Claves de la Investigación para la Paz* (Vienna/Münster: Lit), 282–305.

Fischer, M. (2005) *The Foundations of Karl Rahner. A Paraphrase of the Foundations of Christian Faith with Introduction and Indices*, http://users.adelphia.net/~markfischer/Rahner000.htm, date accessed May 20, 2007.

Freud, S. (1949) *The Ego and the Id* (London: The Hogarth Press).

Galtung, J. (1996) *Peace by Peaceful Means: Peace and Conflict, Development and Civilization* (London/Thousand Oaks/New Delhi: Sage).

Habermas, J. (1994) 'Die Moderne, ein unvollendetes Projekt' in W. Welsch (ed.) *Wege aus der Moderne: Schlüsseltexte der Postmoderne-Diskussion* (Berlin: Akademie Verlag), 177–192.

Horton Fraleigh, S. (1999) *Dancing into Darkness: Butoh, Zen, and Japan* (Pittsburgh: University of Pittsburgh Press).

Illich, I. (1981) 'Peace vs. Development,' *Democracy*, 1, 2.

Jungk, R. (1958) *Brighter than a Thousand Suns: A Personal History of the Atomic Scientists*, trans. by J. Cleugh, (New York: Harcourt, Brace and Company).

Jungk, R. and J. Galtung (eds.) (1969) *Mankind 2000: Future Research Monographs* (Oslo: Allen & Unwin).

Kaller-Dietrich, M. (2008) *Ivan Illich (1926–2002). Sein Leben, sein Denken* (Vienna: Bibliothek der Provinz).

Kohr, L. (1957) *The Breakdown of Nations* (London: Routledge & Kegan Paul).

Koppe, K. (2001) *Der vergessene Frieden: Friedensvorstellungen von der Antike bis zur Gegenwart* (Opladen: Leske + Budrich).

Köstler, A. (1976) *The Ghost in the Machine* (New York: Random House).

Kripal, J.J. (2007) *Esalen: America and the Religion of No Religion* (Chicago: University of Chicago Press).

Lederach, J.P. (1995) *Preparing for Peace: Conflict Transformation Across Cultures* (Syracuse: Syracuse University Press).

Lederach, J.P. (2005) *The Moral Imagination: The Art and Soul of Building Peace* (Oxford: Oxford University Press).

Lyotard, J. (1979) *La Condition Postmoderne: Rapport sur le Savoir* (Paris: Minuit).

Muñoz, F. (2006) [2001] 'Imperfect Peace' in W. Dietrich, J. Echavarría and N. Koppensteiner (eds.) *Schüsseltexte der Friedensforschung/Key Texts of Peace Studies/Textos claves de la Investigación para la Paz* (Vienna/Münster: Lit), 241–281.

Nietzsche, F. (1983) [1886] *Jenseits von Gut und Böse*, Werke in vier Bänden, 4 (Salzburg: Das Bergland-Buch).

Paul VI (1967) *Populorum Progressio*, Encyclica from March 26, 1967, http://www.vatican.va/holy_father/paul_vi/encyclicals/documents/hf_p-vi_enc_26031967_populorum_en.html, date accessed May 12, 2007.

Perls, F.S. (1969) *Gestalt Therapy Verbatim* (Moab: Real People Press).

Rahner, K. (1995) 'Selbstvollzug der Kirche: Ekklesiologische Grundlegung praktischer Theologie' in K. Rahner *Sämtlich Werke*, 19 (Freiburg im Breisgau: Herder).

Rogers, C. (1970) *On Encounter Groups* (New York: HarperCollins).

Rosenberg, M. (2003) *Nonviolent Communication: A Language of Life* (Chicago: Puddledancer Press).

Rushby, K. (2007) *Paradise: A History of the Idea that Rules the World* (New York: Basic Books).

Satir, V. et al. (1991) *The Satir Model: Family, Therapy and Beyond* (Palo Alto: Science and Behavior Books).

Ueshiba, M. (1996) *Budo Teachings of the Founder of Aikido Ueshiba* (Tokyo: Kodansha International).

Vattimo, G. (1984) 'Dialectics, Difference, and Weak Thought,' *Graduate Faculty Journal for Philosophy*, 10, 1, 151–164.

Vattimo, G. (1992) 'Optimistic Nihilism' in *Common Knowledge*, 1, 3, 37–44.

von Suttner, B. (1892) *Lay Down Your Arms: The Autobiography of Martha Von Tilling*, trans. by T. Holmes (London: Longmans).

Watzlawick, P., J. Weakland and R. Fisch (1974) *Change: Principles of Problem Formation and Problem Resolution* (New York: W. W. Norton & Co.).

Welsch, W. (1994) 'Einleitung' in W. Welsch (ed.) *Wege aus der Moderne: Schlüsseltexte der Postmoderne-Diskussion* (Berlin: Akademie Verlag), 1–46.

Wilber, K. (1995) *Sex, Ecology, Spirituality* (Boston: Shambhala).

2
Peace: The European Narrative

Karlheinz Koppe

The concept of peace is shaped by many vastly different understandings, the best known of which is reflected in the old Roman word *pax*, which means to 'contract'. And, indeed, the Romans always took care to secure peace with the peoples they had subjugated via contracts with the local princes. Even today, this conception of peace has remained current and is accepted worldwide: The United Nations and regional areas of peace all around the globe are based on contracts between the participating states. Other conceptions of peace may also be of relevance, but in practical terms their importance remains far behind the concept of *pax*: the Greek notion of *eirene*, for example, actually only signifies a 'ceasefire' between wars,* the Russian word *mir* signifies 'peace' and 'world' simultaneously, whereas the Polish word *pokoj* conversely encompasses 'peace' and 'room.' People thus live in peace if – in the Russian understanding – peace reigns worldwide and – in the Polish understanding – they can retreat to their room.

The system of contracts also played an important role in early Europe. The Celtic conquests, to which even nowadays regional names like *Gaul* (France), *Galicia* in the northwest of Spain, *Galata* in central Turkey and *Galicia* in southern Poland testify, were followed by Germanic movements instigated by pressure from eastern peoples (Huns, Mongols, Hungarians, Slavs), who were looking for better spaces to live (the taking of land by the Ostrogoths, Visigoths, Vandals, Franks and many more), and were very often combined with a quest for adventures and loot (Vikings/Normans). The aims of this hunt for prey were, for example, the British Isles, but most of all the Roman provinces in Greece, on the Iberian Peninsula, in northern Africa and particularly the Roman heartlands of Italy.

The Germanic invaders nevertheless proved willing and capable of integration and adaptation. At first, they regarded the law of peace – *pax* – uncomprehendingly. They did, however, respect the right to hospitality, which is considered holy by all people of all times, but barely the rules of an ordered martial law.

---

* Ed. In Chapter 3, Francisco Muñoz and Beatriz Molina further discuss the peace notion of *eirene*.

Like the linguistically related words *frei* (free) and *Freund* (friend), *Friede* (peace, in Old High German: *fridu*) is derived from the Indo-Germanic root *pri* – 'to love, to spare' – and thus originally implies a state of love and protection which stresses the active moment of mutual help and support. Traditionally, peace is a social concept, it denotes a certain form of human living together. But *Freya*, the divine wife whose linguistic root also is related to *Friede*, was at the same time the patron of fallen heroes.*

During the last phase of the Roman Empire, Germanic tribes had not just obtained contractually (*pax!*) arranged areas of settlement; they also rose to high positions within the Roman ruling hierarchy. From the fourth century onwards, Germanic generals had the power to institute and topple emperors and Caesars according to their own interests. However, they could not avert the symptoms of fatigue and loss of civilization, decay and breakdown of the Roman Empire. With the disposition of the last Roman Emperor (Romulus Augustus) in 476, the Roman Empire – and with it the area of peace of the *Pax Romana* – had ended. The centrifugal forces under the leadership of Germanic tribal kings prevailed and for centuries defined the events of peace and war in an emergent Europe. From the fifth century onwards until the seventh and eighth centuries, the principal Germanic rulers were the Merovingian kings of the Franks, who still largely adhered to Rome's political, administrative and cultural structures. Only the eastern Roman Empire, at the very end no more than the close vicinity of Byzantium/Constantinople, survived the fate of western Rome for about a thousand years, until it fell prey to the Turkish (Muslim) Ottomans in 1453.

During the changing tides of the dissolving Roman Empire, a new factor emerged: the monotheistic understanding of belief originating in the antique Middle Eastern cultures (and Egypt) put an abrupt end to the peaceful coexistence of the affected populations. While the Hebrew–Israelitic–Jewish understanding remained focused on itself ('God's chosen people'), the Christian–Pauline understanding laid claim to an exclusive and absolute truth and to the implementation of this claim to power through violence. The Pope became 'God's representative' on earth. Emperors and kings were meant to be his military–political wings.

Initially, and until the end of the second century, the Christians and their bishops had followed the principle of nonviolence of Jesus of Nazareth, but with their recognition by the state, they rapidly began not just to approve war as means of extermination for non-Christians and heretics, but to praise it to the highest. The Bishop of Hippo, Augustine (354–430), in allusion to the stoics and most of all to Cicero (106–43), became the protagonist of 'just war' (*bellum iustum*) if the cause was just (*causa iusta*), the intention appeared morally right (*intentio recta*) and the responsibility was with a legitimate prince (*legitima potestas*). Augustine

---

*   Ed. *Freya* is discussed in Chapter 5 by Elida K. Undrum Jacobsen.

was the first to realize, about nine hundred years after Heraclites, that peace really was the stable pattern of relation between peoples and states and that war was only a – even if frequent – disruption: 'Just as there can be life without pain, but not pain without life, there also exists a peace without all war, but never a war without all peace' (Augustinus, 1955, p. 55). In other words, a war could not be directed towards conquest, revenge or punishment, but only towards the establishment of peace. Thus, Augustine continued in the vein of similar considerations of Plato, Aristotle and Cicero. It was also Augustine who early on realized the inner connection between peace and justice: *pax iustitiae opera* – peace is a labor of justice.

Augustine himself raged against the Nestorians, Donatists, Arians, as well as against Jews and pagans, even more horribly than Nero had done against Christians. Augustine asked the emperor to punish those people through war (and that meant extermination) – with the argument of just war. Many theologians even nowadays defend the Church Father and explain his war-cultural behavior partly in the conviction that he had acted according to God's commandment (not Jesus'!), and partly through indicating that Augustine had been a child of his cruel time and had been thusly shaped.

In a further development within the *recta intentio*, the *debitus modus* is added to the body of just war theory. *Debitus modus* implies a narrowing of the activities of war into legitimate means of war; among which for a long time has been the most important distinctions between combatants and non-combatants. Thomas Aquinas (1255–1274) and Francisco di Vitoria (1483–1546) developed the 'just war' doctrine further. Thomas so declared the extermination of injustice to be the main defining characteristic of 'just war.' Part of such injustice could also be an obstacle put in the path of the 'true faith'. With this, he bolstered the commonly occurring wars of 'Christian believers' against the 'infidels' and opened up the 'just war' doctrine for providing a justification for the Crusades. He also added the principle of *auctoritas principis* to the *legitima potestas*. Initially, Augustine had declared the *legitima potestas* as the third condition for leading a just war, which he understood as the legitimate power of the emperor and thus at that time as the universal power. But Thomas Aquinas added the *auctoritas principis*, which signified a shift in the power structures occurring after the end of the Roman Empire: not only the emperor, but every (ruling) prince held the decision on peace and war in his hands. The road towards a new understanding of peace, as Niccolò Machiavelli, Thomas Hobbes and Hugo Grotius defined it, was thus marked out.

Consequently, the 'Catholic' (implying 'worldwide') claim to power of the Church soon became the destroyer of the Roman Empire, which the emperors from Nero to Diocletian obviously had correctly recognized and which had triggered the prosecution of Christians in the first four centuries. Later, it violently destroyed the first positive success in coexistence between Jews, Christians and

Muslims: the Golden Age in Andalusia, rudimentarily also in southern Italy. Another consequence is the temporary re-conquest of the so-called 'Holy Land' through the finally unsuccessful Crusades, the 're-conquest' (*reconquista*) of Spain in 1492, as well as the cruel prosecution of non-Christian segments of the populations as well as of those Christian groups which had split from the – by then consolidated – Catholic papacy in Rome (*Arians, Gnostics, Donatists, Cathars*). In this manner, Christianity became the main cause for the development of war in foundational Europe.

The background for all wars in the Europe of the early Middle Ages until modern times was so formed by several factors: on the one hand, the Catholic papacy and the secular emperor were united in their claim to truth and power but, on the other hand, they were in competition with each other and, furthermore, within the Church itself power struggles were taking place – often or most of the time by worldly rulers or even just families, for example the exertion of influence on the successions of the Holy Chair, the exile of the Pope in Avignon (1309–1377) and the Controversy of Investiture (1075–1125). Likewise, princes waged war against the emperor as well as against each other. Niccolò Machiavelli (1469–1527) finally justified evil deeds as a moral necessity, even if only in extreme situations and in line with the reason of state, when he advised his prince: 'Therefore he needs to have a disposition, according to which he is prepared to let himself be carried by the winds of fortune and the changing of conditions and [...] not to let go of good whenever possible, but to turn towards evil, whenever necessary' (Machiavelli, 1986, p. 139). Thomas Hobbes (1588–1679) finally became the philosopher of the absolute power of the state originating in the prince, a power which on the one hand kept the subjects from killing each other (*homo homini lupus*), but on the other hand also reserved the right to assert the interests of the state against other rulers with the force of violence. From now on, the prince decided not only in practice, but also completely legally about war and peace (Hobbes, 1966, pp. 155–156). The right to conduct wars, the right to war (*ius ad bellum*) had finally led the just war (*iustum bellum*) ad absurdum. On this basis the Dutch lawyer and statesman Huig de Groot (*Hugo Grotius*, 1583–1645) formulated his great work *De iure belli ac pacis* (*On the Laws of War and Peace*), with which war and peace should finally be conducted in an orderly manner and which has since served as a starting point for international law.

Grotius' new approach consisted in perceiving humanity as a legal community above the states. Because natural law is considered universal, there exists not only a law of states but also an international law connecting states. Grotius nevertheless did not regard the community between the peoples as a model for a world-state, but he understood this community as a union of free states, which subordinate themselves to elementary moral obligations. The vision of a lasting or even perpetual peace was rejected by Grotius as an unrealistic utopia. Instead, his interest was in containing war and most of all subjecting it to legal norms.

Also during war a person remains a social being bound to law. Even against the enemy, he is bound by good faith. Part of the consequences for the laws of war, which Grotius derives from this conviction, is the distinction between combatants and non-combatants, the ban on torture and cruel acts of war and the debarment of acts of war against disarmed enemies.

This codification of war subsequently became a motive for further perceptions of peace.* The idea of the Crusades was no longer necessary as a motive for the establishment of peace, all the more so because the 'Turkish onrush' was losing force. Gottfried Wilhelm Leibniz (1646–1715) drafted an exposé in 1670 under the title '*Bedenken, welchergestalt Securitas publica interna et externa et Status praesens im Reich jetzigen Umständen nach auf festen Fuß zu stellen*' ('Considerations to put the *Securitas publica interna et externa et Status praesens* in the Empire on Sound Footing according to Current Circumstances'), which can only conditionally be seen as a peace concept. According to Leibniz' views, an imperial German state should secure peace in Europe and guide the power interests of the single European nations, mainly France's, England's, Spain's and Portugal's, towards the conquest and subjugation of territories overseas. This is the emergence of Eurocentrism, which subsequently should prove to be disastrous rather than fostering peace. According to Leibniz, the main instrument of inner-European peacekeeping should be an international court, *arbitrarum rerum*.

At the beginning of the early Middle Ages, the structures of civilization of the Roman Empire broke down within the span of a couple of generations; the cities became desolate, the channels and public baths decayed, agricultural crops declined; the latter probably also was a consequence of the depletion of forests for the generation of energy, burning of bricks, shipbuilding and the expansion of agricultural lands in connection with climatic changes. There can be no more obvious proof that civilizations can only bloom in peace and do not need war as impetus. This is also confirmed through the de facto standstill of civilization (on a low level) during the course of the continuous fights between the princes and bishops throughout almost the entire Middle Ages. This crisis of civilization was deepened during the high Middle Ages with the onset of the 'Black Death,' the plague introduced from Asia via the Mediterranean, which in waves carried off altogether about a third of the population of Europe.

The order of peace or (more to the point) the 'order of strife' of the Middle Ages rested on the idea of the *Pax Romana* as it was further developed by Augustine in connection with the theorem of 'just war.' To lead a 'just war' was a right reserved not only for the emperor of eastern Rome (remaining in Byzantium) and the western Roman Empire, about which the Pope and the German kings often quarreled also using the force of weapons, but also for other kings, patriarchs,

* Ed. For further discussions on different perceptions of peace, see Chapter 1 by Wolfgang Dietrich.

bishops and princes. The introduction of the concept of *pax* into daily life and the communal organization of the young successor states only proved this point: *paix*, *pace*, *paz*, *peace*. The Roman concept of *pax* encountered the understanding of peace of the Germanic peoples and principalities, who understood under this term mainly the inner relation among their kinsmen, but not the relations between different peoples.

In 1356 Emperor Charles IV issued the 'Golden Bull;' an edict towards the reorganization of the elections of the German king – and thus simultaneously the emperor – through the electors who formed the Electoral College. This way, the power struggles between the German princes could be contained, but not eliminated altogether. Other interests, like those of the mainly northern German cities united in the Hanseatic League and dynastic disputes of succession/marital politics, continued preventing the implementation of a European peace order. With the call for the Crusades (1096–1275) – not just for the conquest of Palestine but also for the forceful proselytizing of the not-yet Christianized peoples in the Baltic area through the Teutonic Order – the Church tried to unify the Christian princes, but without success.

Additionally, there was the Crusade against the Albigensians (1226–1229), a radical counter-Church for which the world was ruled by the devil and which had a strong influence in the southwest of today's France and had founded several dioceses there. This Crusade showed the collaboration between Church and kingship at its clearest, because the French kings used the war, which turned into a veritable genocide, to enlarge the territory of their state by about a third. The Crusades against the Turks also ended in a fiasco. Although a 'Kingdom of Jerusalem' was formed for about two centuries (1096–1291), the by-products were little Christian: not only were the Muslims and the few Jews living in Palestine and mostly in Jerusalem killed, but on the way there Jews were murdered all over Europe and mostly in the Rhine lands. Simultaneously, the Christian-Orthodox Byzantium, which had derived from the old eastern Rome, was conquered and in its place the so-called 'Latin Empire' (1204–1261) was formed.

After the Crusades, the European system of states was more disjointed than ever. With the death of Emperor Frederick II (1194–1250), who for some decades had fostered the coexistence of Christians, Jews and Muslims in southern Italy and Sicily and was anathematized by the Pope, the medieval empire had passed its high point and the decay of the imperial power in Germany and Italy had commenced. In addition, the papacy had gone beyond the zenith of its political power. The ban on Frederick II no longer had any effect. Frederick II also was the originator of the most important work of peace of the time, the *Landfrieden* (Public Peace) announced in 1235, which declared the royal suzerainty also for the princes and free imperial cities and which was confirmed in 1495 at the *Reichstag* (diet) of Worms as *Ewiger Landfrieden* (Perpetual Public Peace). It so terminated the *Gottesfrieden* (Truce and Peace of God – *tregua dei*), which had been declared on order of the Church in 1027 and lifted the right of force (*Fehderecht* – Right of Feud) of the landed nobility (including bishops and abbots) for the weekdays of Thursday (last supper of the Lord), Friday (day of crucifixion), Saturday (abatement from the cross) and Sunday (day of resurrection). On the other days, it was again allowed to fight, plunder and murder. In distinction from *pax*, the *treuga dei* meant, like the Greek *eirene*, only a limited period of ceasefire. On the other hand, for the affected people, mainly the peasants, it meant an improvement since they could do their work more securely on the 'feudless' days.

It seemed always that somewhere in Europe a war was being fought or a peace treaty was being signed, which usually did not last very long. In connection with the wars of the fifteenth, sixteenth and seventeenth centuries the decline and loss of papal influence became obvious. Nevertheless, the question of religious freedom dominated the political events, even if more in the background as a pretext for political struggles between the emperor, on the one hand, and the princes and imperial cities turned Protestants, on the other. In this manner, there occurred several wars in the course of the sixteenth century, which at first were settled in the *Augsburger Religionsfrieden* (Peace at Augsburg) which established the principle that each prince and imperial city could decide the religious affiliation of its subjects: whose realm, his religion (*cuius regio, eius religio*). Just as the Papacy and the Catholic Church had proven inutile as peacemakers, now also the Protestant Churches failed in this task, mainly because they, just a few decades after Luther's reforms, took on the character of established churches under the *cuius region, eius religio* rule and started to support the politics of their respective kings and princes.

The seventeenth century brought the temporary peak in the occurrences of war: the Thirty Years War (1618–1648) and the Treaty of Westphalia which ended it. The enormous damage that was done through this war befell almost exclusively the German imperial lands. The reduction in population is estimated to have been about 50 percent in rural regions and about 30 percent in urban areas. Almost 2000 manors and castles (feudal seats), more than 1600 cities and 18,000 villages were devastated. A peace agreement offered itself as a consequence of the political, economic and military fatigue, but nevertheless it played a crucial role in the political organization at the beginning of modern times: the late medieval chaos gave way to a relative order which, despite many infringements, lasted until the Napoleonic wars. From the point of view of the politics of peace, the time of the lansquenets – who descended marauding upon cities and villages – was over as they were steadily replaced by disciplined standing armies.

In this manner, at least part of the calls for peace, which had been unmistakable during the times of emergency in the Middle Ages and during the Thirty Years War, was heard even if it was not heeded. The most convincing caller for peace probably was Francis of Assisi (1182–1226). Francis was the descendant of a wealthy house and one day found himself so shocked by the poverty of the population on the one hand and the luxury of the Popes and bishops on the other hand, that he decided henceforth to live in poverty together with a group of equal-minded people in order to preach love and nonviolence. He was lucky not to be burnt at the stake for heresy, because in the same year in which he founded the community of his order (1209) the Crusade against the Cathars started – who also preached poverty and denounced the luxury of the Church. In contrast to the Cathars, however, Francis never questioned the authority of either Church or Pope. The Pope, in turn, used the 'protest' of the young Francis as a welcome argument to prove that already within the Church there would be enough space for spirituality of poverty and peace.

While Thomas Aquinas and his later interpreters integrated their insights of natural law into the tenet of the Church, other scholastics took different routes and hence were always in danger of persecution as 'heretics.' This held especially for Marsilius of Padua (about 1275–1342/43), who portrayed the claim of the Popes to have the last word in worldly issues as detrimental to peace and argued this point in what is probably the first document explicitly dedicated to keeping the peace: the Defender of Peace (*Defensor pacis*). The final chapter reads:

> This work shall be known as 'Defender of Peace', because it deals extensively with the most important causes which keep and maintain peace or quiet within the state, just as well as with those which evoke, prevent or eliminate the contrary thereof, namely dispute. [...] Furthermore government and people, as the primary elements of the community, can extract thereof, what has to be taken into consideration to keep the peace and freedom in the own land. (Marsilius, 1971)

Pierre Dubois (about 1250–1322), French theologian, lawyer and diplomat, developed plans to reform the politics of France. The Christian states should keep peace among them, form a confederation and put their disputes before an international court of arbitration to decide. This treatise, like most 'peace concepts' at the time, was only directed towards the peace among the Christian states. The reasoning was to be aware of the influence of the Pope in his capacity as territorial lord and in defense against his claim to suzerainty, and also to better repel the onrush of the 'infidel' Muslim Turks. Typical of this line of thought was the peace concept of 1464 by the Bohemian King George Podiebrad (1420–1471). One has to consider the French adventurer and manufacturer Antonio Marini as the true author of this 'Treaty of Alliance and Confederation,' which was sent to the French king and the High Council of the city of Venice. Without doubt, an ulterior motive of the treaty was to keep the Pope and the German Emperor out of Bohemian matters (secession of the Hussites from the Roman Church), and also to create a bulwark against the onrushing Turks. Furthermore, the plan contained some modern-sounding ideas: abstention of the confederated states from independent warfare, a sort of federal council of the participating princes, a federal assembly of their representatives, a common cabinet and even a federal court.

In this time, ideas of peace always ran the risk of not being heard. This is what happened, for example, to the first peace researcher of the newer history, Desiderius Erasmus of Rotterdam (1466–1536). In 1516 he received the commission of the Duke of Burgundy (later Emperor Charles V) – who at that time was only fifteen years old – to produce a study on the keeping of the peace. According to tradition he clad his investigation in allegorical clothing by letting peace itself appear as a person and complaining about his fate: *Querela Pacis* (The Complaint of Peace). The work was finished in 1517. It says:

> Almost no peace is so unjust that it would not be preferable to the seemingly most just war. Consider at first the different circumstances which war necessitates or brings with it, and you will see, what gain you have accomplished. [...] You have seen so far, that nothing has been achieved with alliances, that neither marriage and relation by marriage, nor violence and lust for revenge have helped. Now, confronted with this danger, show what reconciliation and benefaction can achieve. One war sows the next, revenge begets revenge. May now one friendship give birth to the other and one benefaction attract the other. (Erasmus, 1917)

This study was intended as a preparation for the first international peace conference and signified the first important document in which peace was formulated for humanity's sake and every kind of war was clearly refused. Translated into the language of modern peace research, Erasmus argued that military violence would not be an appropriate means to regulate disputes between princes and states, because it would harm the welfare of the state and its citizens more than it would benefit them. When Erasmus handed his work over to the duke's chancellor however, the young duke had long changed his mind and did not want to know about peace any more. And yet this little treatise has since had a lasting influence on many.

In contrast was the *Kriegsbüchlin des Friedes* (Little War-Book of Peace) of Sebastian Franck (about 1500–1542), a reformatory humanist who – coming from humble origins himself, he was a soap boiler and compositor – saw most of all the misery of the poor and the weak who had to suffer under the scourge of war. 'War has many "mistakes" and many "conditions" until it could be called just – especially in "these last times", in which a Christian war is as rare as a stork in winter' (Franck, 1968). From this viewpoint, he derived the conclusion: 'Thus war is bestial, against nature and reason, a pure folly and not human. And just like the Satan not then with the power and word of God, also may war not then through peace but through its opposite be fought and aborted. Heat has to drive out the cold, light the darkness. Likewise do I want here, armed with the weapons of peace to fight against all follies, fight and do battle' (Franck, 1968).

In the line of last peace plans before the Thirty Years War was also the 'The New Kineas' (*Le Nouveau Cynée*) of Emeric Crucé (1590–1648) and 'The Great Plan' (*Le Grand Dessein*) of Maximilien de Béthune, Duke of Sully (1560–1641). Addressed to the monarchs of his time, the exposé 'The New Kineas or Treatise on the Opportunities and Means to Found a Common Peace as well as the Freedom of Trade on the Whole Circle of the Earth' was published by the otherwise unknown Parisian scholar Emeric Crucé in 1623. The title was a recourse to antiquity. Kineas was a confidant of King Pyrrhos who, as second Alexander, wanted to found a great empire in the west and defeated the Romans with such heavy losses that his name became immortalized in the term of 'Pyrrhic victory.' The reasoning that wars do not pay was fundamental to Crucé. Therefore, he called not so much upon the way of thinking of the princes, but upon their self-interest (Raumer, 1967, p. 144). What is important is that Crucé was the first no longer to distinguish between peoples and religions but to include all humans – without a preferential position even for the emperor: Crucé sketched a universal peace instead of limiting his peace frame to the Christian occident. He furthermore argued that peace was necessary 'to give the freedom of trade and traffic to the whole world' (Raumer, 1967) and thus formed an idea that was further elaborated about 150 years later by Adam Smith in his work on *The Wealth of Nations*.

The Duke of Sully for his part ascribed his essay to the French King Henri IV who had been murdered twenty years earlier. His motive may have been to gain more attention for his treatise; a plan with which he also succeeded, for until modern times international lawyers referred to this draft, which sketched nothing less than a European federation as guarantor of peace. In this manner, the Great Plan appears as a report about the conceptions of the French king. Sully was predominantly occupied with a solution doing justice to Catholics, the Reformed Tradition (Calvinists/Huguenots) and Protestants (Lutherans) alike. Besides that the text was, with the exception of the description of the political and territorial delimitations, held so broadly that every legal scholar could interpret it however he imagined. Perhaps it was just the basic thought of a European balance of powers that fascinated the international lawyers of centuries to come.

The question also needs to be asked whether the Great Plan can really be counted as a 'Peace Concept,' because the most curious element in it is Sully's consideration to lead the accomplished peace of the federation of monarchs and republics through a 'holy war [...] against the enemies of the Christian name.' The latter implied a 'crusade as permanent form to secure the European life.' In this formulation, the antique Greek thought of a 'natural permanent war' returned to the discussions on peace. Sully's plan, like all peace concepts before it, had no success. But it still has fostered the dialogue about creating and maintaining peace through political means, even if it took another 300 years until the first practical implementation of its basic thought came into being with the constitution of the League of Nations (1919).

Slowly the insight started to spread that peace cannot be limited to Europe, but needs a universal character and that it has to be linked to justice for all humans. These thoughts were taken up in the 'Plan of Perpetual Peace' by Charles-François Castel – also called Abbé de Saint-Pierre (1658–1743) – who composed a concretization of Sully's Great Plan in 1713. So it reads with Saint-Pierre:

'1. The undersigning rulers will form a perpetual and irrevocable union amongst themselves and will name plenipotentiaries, in order to hold a permanent federal assembly or congress at a chosen place, in which all disputes of the undersigning parties shall be ordered or reconciled through arbitration or verdict.' Saint-Pierre nevertheless did not believe that the princes would agree to this plan, because 'through the perpetual peace they would lose all those resources. [...] Thus, what will they do to prevent that? That which they always have done, they will ridicule it.' (Castel, 1963, p. 86)

Saint-Pierre's plan, however, only became well known through the annotation of Jean-Jacques Rousseau (1712–1778), which was published after the latter's death in 1778. For Rousseau, who obviously identified with the plan, there is a close connection between peace and the realization of the social contract (*contrat social*). War for him is not an evil as such, but just the symptom of bad forms of government.

The last of the great treatises on peace before the French Revolution stems from the pen of Immanuel Kant (1724–1804). It is interesting that he chose the same concept as a title, which had been used by Saint-Pierre: *Perpetual Peace* (1795). And just like Saint-Pierre, Kant was rather skeptical about the realization of perpetual peace. He otherwise might not have chosen such an unconventional beginning for his treatise, namely to derive the title 'On Perpetual Peace' from the – by Kant himself designated as 'satirical' – 'sign of a Dutch innkeeper, on which a churchyard had been painted' and then to connect this to the consideration in the very first sentence, whether this title 'had for its object mankind in general, or the rulers of states in particular who are insatiable of war, or merely the philosophers who dream this sweet dream, it is not for us to decide' (Kant, 1925).

In his treatise, Kant had at first taken over Heraclites' old hypothesis about war as a 'normal state.' Thus the beginning of the second section reads: 'The state of peace among men living side by side is not the natural state (*status naturalis*); the natural state is one of war. This does not always mean open hostilities, but at least an unceasing threat of war.' Kant concluded: 'A state of peace, therefore, must be established.' He nevertheless had a clear vision of an ultimately permanent peace under the condition that in all states 'republican' constitutions would be introduced. For him it was hardly conceivable that the citizens would have to decree 'for themselves the calamities of war' (Kant, 1925).

Finally, a little quoted postscript from the following year (1796) should be remembered. It bears the title 'Announcement of the near Completion of a Treatise on Perpetual Peace in Philosophy' and the last paragraph reads: 'The commandment: you shall (even if it would be with the most pious intentions) not lie, if taken as the foundational principle of philosophy as a teaching of wisdom, would by itself not just effect the perpetual peace, but also be able to secure it for all future' (Kant, 1925). And yet he developed in the treatise rational republican justifications and conditions according to international law for the creation of a state of peace, perhaps not least of all out of the pacifistic conviction that standing armies (*miles perpetuus*) would be of evil: 'men paid to kill or to be killed seems to entail using them as mere machines and tools in the hand of another (the state), and this is hardly compatible with the rights of mankind in our own person' (Kant, 1925).

Kant even more importantly might have been the first author to combine his proposal with a true world citizen's right, using the term 'Human Rights' and condemning the inhuman colonial politics of the great powers of the time. In distinction to his often-Eurocentric predecessors, he recognized that perpetual peace – if it is to come to pass at all – has to be universal.

At the end of the seventeenth century and in the eighteenth century, the territorial and hegemonic wars had continued unabatedly. Most of them ended with a re-establishment of the peace order of Westphalia. It was also a dispute of succession that served the Prussian King Frederick II (Frederick the Great, 1712–1786) as pretext to extend his dominion to the detriment of Austria without any regards for the Perpetual Public Peace (*Ewiger Landfrieden*) and the peace order of Westphalia. In three Silesian wars (1740–1742, 1744–1745 and the Seven Years War 1756–1763) he struggled against a coalition in which at times, besides Austria, Saxony, France, Bavaria and Russia were also involved. Thus, he managed to establish Prussia as a great power in the concert of European states. This concert and the peace order of Westphalia were irrevocably destroyed when Napoleon Bonaparte terminated the disorder of the French Revolution (1789), gained first military successes, crowned himself Emperor Napoleon I (1804) and started his politics of conquest against Austria and Prussia (1806). He was aided by the first organization of a mass army (*levée en masse*). In a mere few years, he had conquered all of Europe and only England still resisted; a resistance which he tried to break with the so-called 'Continental Blockade' against the import of British industrial goods. His war against Russia (1812), which he tried to force into the Continental System, was the beginning of his defeat.

Interestingly enough, many of the territorial changes which Napoleon had forcibly introduced were upheld during the Congress of Vienna (1814–1815): the realignment of the Empire through the 'Principal Conclusion of the Extraordinary

Imperial Delegation' (*Reichsdeputationshauptschluss*, 1803), which meant an end to many small countries and particularly the Imperial Estates (*Reichsstände*) of the Church, the abdication of the Habsburgs from the crown of the German Empire 1806 through which the 'Holy Roman Empire of German Nation' ceased to exist, the perpetuation of the French system of civil administration and, in some cases, the legal structure following the example of the *Code Civil*. The German Confederation headed by Austria now took the place of the empire. In this Confederation, only thirty-seven sovereign princes and four 'Free Imperial Cities' were represented (before it had been at times more than 400 principalities and Imperial Cities). A completely new peace order had replaced the peace order of Westphalia. Even if the old semi-feudal states were reconstituted in most of the German and non-German states participating in the Congress of Vienna, the hope for a permanent peace remained at first a reality, which also was not stifled by the failed bourgeois revolutions of 1830 and 1848. The separation of the southern Netherlands and the erection of the kingdom of Belgium occurred peacefully.

But the hope proved to be deceptive. The earlier territorial claims of the princes were soon replaced by national movements of unification. Under the lead of Prussia and mainly during the chancellorship of Bismarck (1862–1890), a union of the German princes under the exclusion of Austria was attempted. In 1866, this issue led to war. Due to superior military equipment, Prussia claimed victory five weeks later, mainly because Austria was simultaneously militarily engaged in Italy. Through skillful misinformation (the so-called *Ems dispatch*), in conjunction with the occupation of the vacant Spanish throne, Bismarck then could goad France into declaring war on Prussia. This had the consequence that the southern German states, which had not become part of the northern German Confederation founded in 1866, entered the war on the Prussian side (1870–1871). On January 18, 1871, the Prussian King Wilhelm I was declared German Emperor in the Hall of Mirrors in Versailles. The Second German Empire was founded and from then largely decided on war and peace in Europe.

The national unification, even if on *Kleindeutscher Basis* (little German solution), was accomplished. Since the national unification of Italy also happened at about the same time, there now were five relatively homogeneous European states (Austria, France, England, Italy and Russia) facing each other and sorting out alliances. England took special care that the balance between these powers would not be disturbed. War and peace had a chance, but the involved parties and – chief among them – Germany were gambling on the card of war. Efforts of the newly founded 'Peace Societies' (Belgium, England, Austria and Germany) found very little commitment from the public, except for the 1889 novel-style book *Lay Down Your Arms* (*Die Waffen nieder!*) by Bertha von Suttner (1892).*

* Ed. See Chapter 1 by Wolfgang Dietrich for more information on Bertha von Suttner.

Karl Marx (1818–1883) and Friedrich Engels (1820–1895) of course also raised their voices. For them the cause of warlike violence lay in the relations of exploitation between capital and wage labor. To this diagnosis, they also attached a hope for peace, which the Communist Manifesto from 1848 formulated in the following way: 'in proportion as the exploitation of one individual by another will also be put an end to, the exploitation of one nation by another will also be put an end to. In proportion as the antagonism between classes within the nation vanishes, the hostility of one nation to another will come to an end' (Marx and Engels, 1959). At the beginning of the socialist workers movement there was thus the conviction that by putting an end to class antagonism war could be abolished as well and perpetual peace installed. The struggle to overcome the class antagonism is therefore the crucial means towards the realization of a stable peace. Nevertheless, the conclusion was not too far fetched that wars, if they hasten the revolutionary process, could be interpreted also as advancements on the road to peace.

Friedrich Engels, however, came to the conclusion that the destructions, which would be caused by a European war condensing the destruction of the Thirty Years War into three or four years, would not in fact further the hoped for socialist revolution, but on the contrary would destroy any hope for its advance. This is why the Second Socialist International advocated a politics of maintaining peace, but it still continued to connect this interest to avert war with the hypothesis that a war potentially could also further the revolutionary process. For this reason the First World War encountered the socialist parties in a situation in which they did not possess a common strategy about maintaining or reinstalling peace (Huber and Reuter, 1990, pp. 108–109).

Typical of the Marxist–Socialist (and later communist) notions of peace were the writings of Rosa Luxemburg (1871–1919). On the one hand, she was an untiring proponent for peace, rejected the war loans in 1914 and demanded a general strike of the socialist party in all countries engaged in the war (and subsequently was deeply disappointed when this call was not heeded). On the other hand, Rosa Luxemburg understood the concept of a stable peace only in connection with an overcoming of class antagonism. For her, class struggle and peace struggle were inextricably interlinked.

Also Friedrich Nietzsche (1844–1900)* took part in the debate with a remarkable peace-cultural comment, whose actuality for the last decade of the twentieth century was unmistakable:

> No government admits now, that it maintains an army to satisfy the occasional lust for conquest; but it shall serve for defense [...]. But this supposition is inhuman, so wicked and wicked more than war: well, at bottom it is already the summons and cause for war, because it, as I said, insinuates the immorality of

* Ed. For more on Friedrich Nietzsche, compare with Chapter 1 by Wolfgang Dietrich.

the neighbor and thus seems to provoke a hostile disposition and deed. From the doctrine of the army as means of self defense one thus has to abstain just as thoroughly as from the lusts for conquest. (Nietzsche, 1999, pp. 678–679)

Also the international women's movement became involved: the German women's rights advocate Anita Augspurg (1857–1941) organized the First International Women's Peace Congress in the middle of the war, from April 28 to 30, 1915 in Den Haag, even if without any chance of ever being heard.

The great powers had taken a rather minor incident, the murder of Franz Ferdinand, the Austrian heir to the throne in Sarajevo, as the cause to measure their strength, and 'once-and-for-all' prove their supremacy as well as get rid of economically annoying competitors. After grueling trench warfare and eight million fallen soldiers, France and England defeated the German Empire and Austria. In the last two years of the war, the victors had also been supported by American troops. The peace treaties of Versailles (1919), a classical peace dictate, witnessed the break-up the Austro-Hungarian Dual Monarchy, and reduced Germany in military terms to the status of a smaller middle power and chained it economically through severe and ultimately unrealizable demands of reparations.*

Today, there is no more doubt that this 'peace politics' in conjunction with the Great Depression (1929–1933) favored the rise of the National Socialists and the dictatorship of Adolf Hitler (1933–1945), and led directly into the Second World War (1939–1945), which was triggered by Hitler's provocative expansionist politics (occupation of Austria, partition of Czechoslovakia, attack on Poland). After futile diplomatic initiatives through the governments of England and France, both states declared war on the German Empire, a war which ended with 55 million fallen soldiers; 15 million killed civilians, among them six million Jews; 15 million refugees and displaced persons; massive changes in borders and enormous destruction of industrial structures and housing units through aerial bombings and artillery; and, finally, the division of Germany.

The peace politics after 1945 took a completely different direction as feared initially. The founding of the United Nations Organization (UNO) made the ban on war a norm of international law, but proved to be too weak to effectively implement it. The beginning of tension between the United States and their allied Western powers on the one hand, and the Soviet Union and the states that had been drawn into its spell on the other, in connection with the development of nuclear weapons, whose destructive potential had already been tested twice to end the war against Japan, triggered the so-called 'Cold War.' The period of 'Cold War' – or equally 'Cold Peace' – lasted until 1989, when the communist system of states collapsed together with the Iron Curtain and the Berlin Wall. However, additionally one needs to recognize and understand a political and economic

---

*   Ed. In Chapter 32, Victoria Fontan makes the case for discussing humiliation and war jointly.

self-interest not to repeat the mistakes of Versailles. One abstained from formal peace treaties, which were replaced by more or less formless declarations on the end of the state of war and increasing economic and military cooperation. Finally, the Cold Peace proved to be lasting despite the formation of the military defense alliances, NATO on the Western side and the Warsaw Pact Organization on the Eastern side, and despite the enormous production of weapons on both sides and the occasional crises prone to violence.

The new peace movement, which had already started in the 1960s in England,* was able to successfully mobilize millions of people at the beginning of the 1980s almost throughout all of Europe. However, the treaties on disarmament between West and East were rather the consequence of existing nuclear and other overcapacities of armament, than peace-political insights. This can be shown, among others, by the fact that after the collapse of the Soviet Union (1989–1990), at first world expenditure on armaments was reduced, but soon thereafter reached its former level.

In the interest of a growing economic development, but also as economic support to NATO, a network of peace-political contracts was created in Western Europe, which culminated in the step-by-step realization of the European Union (EU), whose twenty-five members (twenty-seven since 2007) agreed to substantial reductions of their sovereignty until after the creation of a common currency (euro). This is a worldwide unique peace region, even if it is still open, in how far it can really contribute to coping with societal sources of danger like pollution and scarcity of resources, underdevelopment in other areas of the world and the defense from terrorist attacks. Even if the European Union has not yet proven itself to be a peace-formative force or been able to solve latent inner conflicts (Northern Ireland, the Basque country, Cyprus, Balkans), European unification still remains the most important achievement of peace and a decisive contribution to a comprehensive understanding of peace.

An evaluation of the history of peace and war in Europe, from the dissolution of the *Pax Romana* until the prevention of catastrophe during the Cold Peace, should, however, not lose sight of its mental, cultural, economic and generally societal development. Europe has gained its impulse from the periods of peace, from this *eirene* which in classical Greece meant the lull in between the fights. To see only wars is a deception. What is important in this assessment is to emphasize the significance of peace in general and the periods of peace in particular. If these periods of peace are overlooked or neglected, Europe's history and society will be misrepresented.

In historical times, wars played only an inferior role for the majority of the populations – with the exception of regional devastations like the German lands during the Thirty Years War or during the two world wars. More significant problems were the dues and war taxes demanded of the populations by their

---

* Ed. More on England's peace movements is to be found in Chapter 4 by Nigel Young.

rulers, as well as the famines. War itself was for the amusement and intrigue of the powerful!

Although it is correct to say that military violence since the end of the Second World War has taken on new forms, it should not be overlooked that there has also been a significant reduction of military action. The primitive rule of force (*Faustrecht*) was first replaced by the Truce and Peace of God (*Gottesfrieden*), then by the Public Peace (*Landfrieden*) and the international laws of war and, finally, by the international ban on war in the Charter of the United Nations. Also, the development of democratic societies during the past two decades is an indicator that notions of peace can slowly prevail, even if there are still many deficits in this respect, especially within the democratic societies themselves.

Finally, in spite all of this, it remains to be noted that the notion of peace in Europe was able to assert itself only partially and that even today the economic, mental and constitutional development of Europe is still met by restrictions that impair its contribution to the configuration of world peace, economic reason and ecological security.

Reference list and further reading

Aristoteles (1989) *Politik: Schriften zur Staatstheorie* in F. Schwarz (ed.) (Stuttgart: Reclam).

Augustinus, A. (1955) *Vom Gottesstaat (De civitate Dei)* in W. Thimme (ed.) (Zürich: Artemins Verlag).

Bacon, F. (1982) *Neu-Atlantis* (Stuttgart: Reclam).

Beestermöller, G. (1990) *Thomas von Aquin und der gerechte Krieg: Friedensethik im theologischen Kontext der Summa Theologiae* (Köln: Kohlhammer).

Castel, C.I. (1963) 'Plan des Ewigen Friedens' in R.H. Foerster (ed.) *Die Idee Europa 1300–1946: Quellen zur Geschichte der politischen Einigung Europas* (Munich: dtv), 86–101.

Erasmus De Rotterdam (1917) *Querela Pacis: The Complaint of Peace* (Chicago: Open Court).

Franck, S. (1968) 'Das Kriegsbüchlin des Friedes' in S. Wollgast (ed.) *Zur Friedensidee in der Reformationszeit* (Berlin: Akademie-Verlag).

Hartmann, W. (1992) *Der Frieden im frühen Mittelalter* (Barsbüttel: Institut für Theologie und Frieden).

Hobbes, T. (1966) *Leviathan* (Stuttgart: Reclam).

Huber, W. and H.R. Reuter (1990) *Friedensethik* (Stuttgart: Reclam).

Kant, I. (1925) 'Zum Ewigen Frieden' in A. Messer (ed.) *Kants Werke*, 3 (Berlin: Knaur).

Leibniz, G.W. (1963) 'Bedenken, welchergestalt *Securitas publica interna et externa et Status praesens* im Reich jetzigen Umständen nach auf festen Fuß zu stellen' in R.H. Foerster (ed.) *Die Idee Europa 1300–1946: Quellen zur Geschichte der politischen Einigung Europas* (Munich: dtv), 79–85.

Machiavelli, N. (1986) *Der Fürst, Il Principe* (Stuttgart: Reclam).

Marsilius von Padua (1971) *Der Verteidiger des Friedens* (Stuttgart: Reclam).

Marx, K. and F. Engels (1959) *Werke* (Berlin: Dietz Verlag).

Nietzsche, F. (1999) *Menschliches, Allzumenschliches* (München: KSA).

Raumer, K. (1967) 'Zur Beurteilung der preußischen Reform' in *GWU: Geschichte in Wissenschaft und Unterricht*, 18 (Seelze: Friedrich Verlag).

Suttner von, B. (1892) *Die Waffen Nieder! Eine Lebensgeschichte* (Dresden/Leipzig: E. Pierson's Verlag).

3
Pax: A Mediterranean Perspective

Francisco Muñoz and Beatriz Molina

> Homo sum, humani nihil a me alienum puto.
> I am a human being, so nothing human is strange to me.
> Terence (ca. 190–160 BC)

Since its origins, the Mediterranean has exhibited numerous occurrences of peace, indeed, as many as there are historical characters, regions and moments, as peace, the peaceful regulation of conflict, is a tool which guarantees the success and survival of society. These peaceful episodes are portrayed in written sources and the historical reconstructions which researchers are able to piece together thanks to numismatic, epigraphic and archaeological sources. Peace, in practice and in theory, must have been present in all societies, as has been proven upon the appearance of the written word.

We are mainly concerned with three hypotheses: first, a wide range of peaceful occurrences existed in all societies and these also became reflected in the concepts and terminology that these societies used to express their ideas; second, that there is evidence of feedback between these internal, as well as external, peaceful events among different societies; and third, public and political examples of peace gradually adapted more audacious and elaborate criteria and forms. Finally, upon verifying this information, a Mediterranean universality of peace can be spoken of, a peace which is felt, lived, thought, written, deified and carried out with the objective of harmonizing personal, group and exterior relations.[1]

The present chapter, whose main purpose is to acquire a true sense of the semantic fields of the word 'peace' as originally portrayed in different Mediterranean cultures, is based on written Greek, Hebrew, Latin and Arabic sources. By examining the terms *Eirene, Shalom, Pax* and *Salam*, as well as other complementary concepts, the ideas held by each of these cultures regarding peace may be discovered. As follows, and after an introduction on Mediterranean interdependence, a section will be dedicated to each of these cultures, as well as general conclusions regarding Mediterranean peace.

An interdependent Mediterranean culture

Societies along the Mediterranean project their conflicts, yearning, needs and domestic projects on their exterior relations, thus making for both a troubled and a pacific *Mare Nostrum*, in which the majority of the disputes are settled in such a way so as to find the best solution for all concerned. Peace favors interior well-being and foments a more fruitful interdependence between communities. Therefore, the 'peace' achieved within each individual society promotes feedback among others.

Peace in the Mediterranean has occurred, therefore, on numerous occasions and in numerous places. Furthermore, peace coexists with a physical, human, historical, cultural or religious complexity ranging from the most global or generic to the most particular, occurring at all levels, from the smallest to the greatest degree. This complexity can bring about conflict and turn the Mediterranean into a tangled web that separates at its borders or, on the contrary, it may become an area of communication, depending on our ability to appreciate its wealth. It is necessary, thus, to deal with the Mediterranean from the recognition of its communities' relations, of all of the liaisons and interactions which favor the creation of a unitary space, which may be referred to as a 'Mediterranean woven fabric' and which may be considered the final result of minute interactions which, with the passage of time, become monumental. The development of the Mediterranean would not have occurred without these relations between each of the human entities that populate the area and are intertwined in such a way as to overcome geographical and cultural obstacles, going beyond states as well as physical and political frontiers. In these endless contacts among cultures, each one offers its experiences and models, so that by belonging to this common fabric, these models are transmitted, shared, strengthened, discriminated against or syncreticized (Harris, 2005; Muñoz, 2006).

A situation arises in which communication is favored, and the experiences of others may be shared and learned from. Effectively, women, men, children, youth, elders, Greeks, Romans, Byzantines, Turks, Jews, Christians, Muslims have had to define their exterior, international relations and integrate them in their particular views of the world, in the search for well-being. Countless experiences, cultural norms and institutions constitute their conceptions and practices in this sense. Since the invention of writing and the appearance of the graphic representation of peace, it is interpreted as a semantic symbol which expresses such projects and practices, and which is enormously developed in terms of ideas, treatises and projects. Thus, *Eirene, Shalom, Pax, Salam, Pace, Paix, Paz, Peace* or *Mir* are words which represent and sustain these practices, as well as other public and civic virtues with which they are related, such as hospitality, harmony, diplomacy, health, justice, equality, solidarity or liberty.

We know that cultural norms and institutional initiatives such as kings, pharaohs, sultans, magistrates, diplomats, embassies, assemblies, bishops, councils, leagues, monarchies, democracies, republics, federations or confederations have dedicated much of their energies to the pacific management of conflict, to the search for the community's well-being, in order to avoid war and promote peace. Peace is portrayed in various forms as a desire, an ethical horizon, a goddess, the establishment of diplomatic relations, the signing of a treaty, the end of a war, a political slogan or a social project. All of this activity is reflected in diverse epigraphic, numismatic or archaeological written sources, from treaties, agreements, missives or prayers, to the documents left by thinkers, philosophers, religious authorities, scientists or politicians. It is exactly this polysemous and flexible nature of peace that makes it such a useful resource (Pérez and Muñoz, 2004).

Largely, our historical reconstruction of the Mediterranean depends not only on the sources that have been passed down to us, but also on how they have been interpreted by historiography. As a result, in many cases, certain options have been overvalued in detriment of others. Thus, often violence is presented as having a greater influence on reality than peace, which would account for the fact that violence, as the 'fundamental' tool of dominant groups, has occupied a pre-eminent role in the historical documents, which, in the end, represent the sources that are available to us. The statement which claims 'history is written by the victorious' – in other words, the detainers of violence – is a good example of this reality. For example, the majority of written documents coming from Greece and Rome corresponds to such dominant groups, and the strong influence of these two civilizations over subsequent societies has made this documentation paradigmatic of Western civilization when, in fact, it only represents a part of reality, basically – and occasionally almost exclusively – that of elite power (Galtung, 1985, pp. 73–105; Muñoz and López, 2000).

By studying the different sources of information that demonstrate the pacific management of any type of conflict, we are able to reconstruct the cultural and ideological models that are related to peace. A historiographical deficiency exists in this regard, which is conditioned not only by methods, but also, curiously enough, by the original anthropological and sociological models. These are, to a great extent, the reasons for which the policies having to do with peace appear to be inexistent or deformed (Muñoz and Molina, 1998).

The processes related to the creation and strengthening of what might be identified as a *Culture of Peace* are largely linked to the demands and actions of civil and religious social groups which, in this way, promote actions we wish to recognize as 'pacifist empowerment', demanding participation in decision-making and the distribution of power.

The origins of the idea of peace

Peace is likely to have been present in all Mediterranean societies as an idea that, in one way or another, permeated all social actions. Thus, any concept of peace, whether developed in a domestic or religious environment, must have helped to establish links with the public arena; for example, the redistribution of resources to develop the population's well-being would be an activity that would have been carried out in the private as well as in the public and political spheres. For these reasons, it may be supposed that the religious or philosophical pacific precepts, the bases for social thought, would play an important part in both public and political life, as has been supported by written works on different Mediterranean cultures, such as in Hesiod's *Theogony*, in Greek culture or *Genesis* in Jewish culture, in which we find the first written words dedicated to peace.

Ancient Greece: *Eirene*

In ancient Greece, *Eirene* (peace) is represented as a goddess. The myth of her birth, as narrated by Hesiod in 700 BC, is quite eloquent, as *Eirene* is fruit of the union between Temis, the goddess controlling eternal law, and Zeus, governor of Mount Olympus and god of the sky and thunder. Wherever *Eirene* reigns, well-being and prosperity flourish. She is represented as being united to *Dike*, Justice, and *Eunomy*, Fairness or Good Government. They are intimately related, as are sisters, so that there is no peace without justice or good government, no good government without peace and justice, and no justice without peace and good government. Neither this formula to peace nor its origins are by chance, as the organization of the gods' world leaves no room for improvisation. *Eirene* and her sisters *Dike* and *Eunomy* are divinities of order, they are born as regulators of the kinds of conflict that are readily found in a community whose institution-alization is just beginning and they complete the creation and organization of the world. Therefore, peace, as well as justice and fairness, appear as natural, unchangeable, eternal principles. In Hesiod, *Eirene* is the one who 'flourishes' and represents more a moral, rather than a political, value (Martínez, 2000, pp. 254–290).

Upon the appearance of *Eirene* in ancient Greece, for the first time it becomes apparent how peace has been represented as a woman throughout our Western history. Peace was born having a feminine body and attributes in ancient Greece, embodied as a goddess, and her figure, always related to the ideas of prosperity and well-being, has lived on under diverse forms and abstractions throughout the centuries.[2]

Eirene represents, in the writings of the historians Herodotus and Tucydides, a solemn pact between actors, whether inside the polis or with outside communities, who wish to avoid war (*polemos*). For example, in the war between the Lydios and the Medes, the warriors interpreted an eclipse of the sun as a sign to establish peace. Consequently, mediators were assigned and a matrimonial agreement was enough to secure the pact. *Nobody is so foolish so as to choose war over peace.* In this way, *Eirene* continues to be a central concept in Greek politics, as it is linked to justice, liberty and autonomy. Greek orators such as Isocrates, Demosthenes, Aeschines and Andocides, during times of crisis in 400 BC, refer to *Eirene* as an instrument of stability that is of interest to democracy and the city. Isocrates appeals to the Panhellenic ideal as an argument for overall peace, a condition that is essential to social and political reconstruction. *Eirene* is not only an abstraction, or a situation of civic inactivity, but also that which designates the end of the war through a legal act and, in this sense, is considered as a premise as well as a consequence to social potential, military action and diplomatic activity. According to Andocides, *peace is made amongst equals, by coming to an agreement in regards to their mutual differences* (Alganza, 1998, pp. 123–152).

The search for peace between all Greek cities is manifested in the appeal to the *Koine Eirene* – Common Peace – and in the agreements which establish: *that by making a treaty of friendship and common alliance, they shall be friends and allies... and existing in harmony, the agreement shall be secured in the Acropolis.* The *Koine Eirene* has the horizons of a Panhellenic universalism, in that all citizens in all of the poleis and all communities should have complete autonomy in which to develop their rights.

As occurs in all languages, many other concepts complete the semantic field of the Greek *Eirene*. The term *synthekai*, meaning treaty, formal and public agreement, is, in many contexts, synonymous with peace. In other cases, *symachia* (alliance) is intimately related to *Eirene*: *that there be reciprocal peace and friendship, forever being friends and allies.* Later, we find the terms *philanthropy* and *eunomy* (benevolence). A special case is *homonoia* (literally harmony, coincidence of or equal thought or the same way of thinking), which portrays identity of thought as a way of communion and unity in itself, since the diverse manifestations of *homonoia* at different levels of human society are nothing but developments of this essential unity which take place when man shares a common way of thinking with others. Its areas of influence are as ample as the ways man has of forming groups. There is a *homonoia* for the city and another for the family, for meetings and for races, and even for oneself. *Homonoia* presents an extensive chronological presence, from 600 BC to 400 AD, during which, preserving its central semantic nucleus, it has diverse acceptances that vary in different times and spaces. Through the reading, translation and interpretation of more than 1000 literary and epigraphic references and, although its main meaning refers to the understanding between citizens, it is also used on other levels: relations between people, in marriage, with other poleis, etc. (Lorente and Muñoz, 2005).

Homonoia exists on many different levels although, in general, it may be said to be essentially a social concept, as our contact with others provides the fertile soil for the budding of all sorts of conflict, as our coexistence with others is always, willingly or unwillingly, problematic. Especially problematic are civil and political life since, by definition, they require the existence of at least two terms or subjects. The majority of us are in harmony with ourselves, at least most of the time, except when we experience interior plight as men of contradiction who are often troubled individuals, without peace.

Homonoia, as peace, guarantees that the components of a human group, whether it be a nation, a couple, a family or any other form of association, are maintained through the same will, in the same direction and with the same way of thinking at all levels and in all matters. By this definition, it does not seem that *homonoia* allows much personal freedom; however, the way of mutual personal restriction is the most appropriate for facilitating happy coexistence and social harmony. Greece was lacking neither in places nor people in which and in whom *homonoia*, which we include in the same semantic field as peace and pacific relations, served, on certain occasions, as an element which unified the citizens' consciences in a sole way of thinking which admitted neither freedom of thought nor dissidence.[3]

Jewish culture: *Shalom*

More or less contemporary to the Greek term *Eirene* is the Jewish *Shalom*, from the Old Testament, and from then onwards it has been present in all eras and aspects of life in the Jewish community, from early times, in pre-patriarchal history, when the Bible story refers to a pre-agricultural society.[4]* Only at special times and during a certain action, an individual acts as the 'leader' or representative of the community. The word *Shalom* comes from the root *ShaLaM* and represents a model of peace based on the idea of demonstrating a complete and perfect fact. There are other such terms related to peace, such as *ShaQat*, which portrays peace as rest, tranquility or silence. Both roots generate different terms that express the idea of peace in the Hebrew language, the most common and universal of which is *Shalom*.[5]†

The word *Shalom* is found on numerous occasions in the Old Testament. On the one hand, it is used with the meaning of *peace* in legal as well as historical, poetic–philosophical and prophetic books. It has the double meaning of peace and prosperity, which evolved from a negative vision, such as the lack of war, much more frequent in the Pentateuch and in historical books, to an ethical value, so frequent in the prophets. An example is Isaiah who calls on peace and justice for the liberation and glory of Jerusalem. On the other hand, and contrary to what is customary in Greek culture, *Shalom* is always masculine, and is also

---

*   Ed. For further discussions on this topic, see Chapter 6 *Shalom* by Marc H. Ellis.
†   Ed. Chapters 6 and 7 further discuss the word *Shalom* and peace from a Jewish and a Palestinian perspective, respectively.

found as a component of what are almost always the names of men – King Salomon is the most well known – only three correspond to women's names.

A bit later, the alliance with Noah agrees with an ethical view of man and nature as a growing value within the context of an ecological–social society, which looks for new experiences in favor of a more plural, just and pacific world. The expressions used to describe the confirmation of an alliance or treaty are numerous and, indeed, significant. One of the most frequent is that in which the different verbal forms are derived from the root *QuM*, whose primary meaning is to rise, be stable, last or complete. Messianism implies a peaceful world, which is reigned by the Messiah, the Prince of Peace. In the Hebrew language we find other concepts related to the idea of peace such as solidarity, justice or equality, which in numerous biblical passages are used as simple synonyms of peace, especially in the prophetic books; but there are also plenty of terms related to peace which are linked to Hebrew culture (Cano, 1998).

During the Diaspora, members of the Hebrew community would have to contribute by preparing the world for the coming of the Messiah and peace. This attitude led them to adopt a position of non-participation in violent acts: *Then they will forge from their hoes and their pruning shears./Nation against nation shall not raise its swords, nor shall they train to make war.*[6] The continuity of these teachings is evident in the rabbinic texts, which to a certain extent are no more than an exegesis of the Bible, for eight centuries, from 100 to 800 AD during the Diaspora of Israel, when its existence was precarious. Man's deep-rooted feeling of peace obligates Israel to make it part of its universe, in all of its religious representations.[7]

Roman culture: *Pax*

The Roman Republic gradually built an empire that settled in the Italic peninsula and, after 300 BC, extended throughout the Mediterranean. It represented a great empire which promoted, recreated and was based on an ancient Mediterranean scheme which developed over the centuries, and which now is superimposed by a centralization, until then unknown. *Pax* was not an unfamiliar concept in those circumstances, having clear origins from the beginning of the republic and used to mediate in private and local relations. Gradually, it acquired a public role in the relations among groups in conflict, and finally became a guarantor of the end of warlike activity. Therefore, it was sought after in one form or another in Rome, as well as in all of the communities implicated in such disputes.[8]

Peace is portrayed as an individual and group quality that acts in domestic and public spheres, which eventually becomes a goddess. Allowed entrance to the pantheon of the gods, which is reserved for those gods whose virtues or characteristics have played an important part in Roman history, the popular and inter-classist nature of peace is confirmed, which is a quality that makes it contemporarily operative in the relation between different social groups and the regulation of conflicts among them, as long as they participated in the same degree. This could be appealed by any of the actors concerned, in order to avoid confrontation and favor dialogue and negotiation. Seneca, perhaps in recollection of a biblical text, states: *that communities with a deep-rooted peace may prosper, that all iron may be used in the innocent labor of the fields, and the swords may remain hidden.* For these reasons, their validity transcends time and space, being: *universa, longa, aeterna, diuturna, perpetua, constans, sempiterna* and *futura,* becoming a guarantee for the well-being of future generations.

Many of Rome's conflicts with other communities along the Mediterranean were resolved through treaties and pacts that were, on the one hand, an expression of victory and, on the other hand, negotiation. Therefore, they should not be understood solely as an imposition of the strongest, but the result of the desires and longings of different contending factions, which preferred the ceasing of military action as a possibility of returning to daily life and their interests, to the waste and suffering of war. Indeed, peasants, merchants, women and even soldiers would have approved the signing of a treaty to end war and thus prevent the occurrence of worse situations or seen it as the beginning of a time of new hope. Similarly, political decisions should be guided by *virtus*, tolerance, mutual aid and peace. It was defended in this way by the stoic philosophers who so influenced Rome.[9]

However, perhaps the best example of peace as a political guide was the coining of money. It is a manifestation of Roman power – particularly that of the emperor – who, in this way, wanted to convey a sense of tranquility within the empire. Nevertheless, this idea is used as it is understood by the population who employs the currency, which, thanks to the polysemous nature of words, is associated with other areas of their lives. When in 27 BC Octavius was invested by the Senate as *Augustus*, his almost supernatural *autorictas* as liberator of Rome was recognized. This liberation is undoubtedly related to the idea of peace in that it liberates the citizens from internal tensions and, as well, guarantees peaceful frontiers. Aware of the power of image, he transferred that idea to his iconographic program, which he had begun years earlier. In this way, Augustus becomes an important reference in the diffusion and meaning of *Pax*. On the one hand, he was considered a promoter of peace, such as in *Pax* among citizens, *Pax* of the *res publica*, and is also responsible for imperial *Pax*. On the other hand, he may also be considered a promoter of the 'ideology' which, directly or indirectly, was present throughout his political and artistic program (urbanism, architecture, images, literature, etc.), and which will live on in the *Ara Pacis*. The emissions showing the sign of peace survive up until the middle of 400 AD during Constantine the Great and his successors, in spite of the changes and convulsions that had occurred especially during the later years of the empire, at which time its unity was threatened. *Pax*, until that moment, was most likely a symbolic attribute of unity.[10]

The emperors' interest in *Pax* was also promoted by the expectations of other sectors and activities of society. The merchants, more than any other group, represented the advantages of pacific coexistence in the Mediterranean. It is possible to say that similar sentiments were displayed, depending on the circumstances, by sectors such as the agrarian aristocracy, peasants, artisans, women and those who were sought after by the army. *Pax* could be unified, coordinated, conciliated or negotiated. Perhaps this explains Cicero's statement: *Nihil tam populare quam pacem* ('nothing as popular as peace'); peace was a beloved and beneficial value for the community, as it guaranteed the unity of things, tranquility of the spirit and dignity of the people. Moreover, Seneca said: *to wish for the return of peace is good for the victorious and necessary for the vanquished.*[11]

It may be said that the idea of *Pax* outlived the Roman Empire itself in that its uses and contents lasted throughout the centuries, up until our times as portrayed in the nouns *Paz, Pace, Paix*, which are present in the Romance languages. We undoubtedly interpret it as such, as in the societies in which the word and concept dwelled it was useful in defining the dynamics of pacific regulations. A large part of the legacy of the Roman Empire in general, and of Latin in particular, was deposited in the Roman Church, which thus transmitted the message of peace among men, and peace and respect to be distributed among institutions and the state.

Muslim culture: *Salam*

Islam emerged after 700 AD, bringing with it an important message of *peace*, which is reflected in the Qur'an and in the term *Salam*, as well as in other words and expressions that complement and enrich the contents of peace. However, as is well known, Islam is not only a religion, it is also a social, cultural and political phenomenon that, through the teachings of Mohammed, was to extend beyond the Arabian borders throughout the Mediterranean.* The teachings of the Prophet – which transcend religious life, penetrating social and political realms – contributed to the management of conflict and to satisfy the social necessities of the times through a set of regulating norms regarding the relations among individuals and groups, on an internal as well as an external level. The process saw, undoubtedly, violent circumstances; however, we believe that dialogue and negotiation predominated in the majority of the situations, resulting in numerous pacts and agreements that have been documented in the history of Islam (Molina, 1998).

Among the main objectives of the new religion that arose with Islam were to ensure, by way of moral perfection, the cohesion of the community and foster virtues such as solidarity, generosity, harmony, concord, justice and goodness.

---

* Ed. This book contains many variations of peace in Islamic cultures and on the word *Saalam* from diverse perspectives. See Chapters 7, 8, 9, 10 and 24.

However, in addition to these religious principles and virtues promoted by the message of Islam, there was a clear social project: solidarity. Solidarity, which is considered one of the religion's basic principles, was linked to goodness and generosity in the moral as well as the material sense.* Interior harmony would bring about social and even political harmony; honesty, as a moral virtue implying honesty as well as integrity, meant fairness in commercial operations inherent in a mercantile society; generosity, referred to in the Islamic religious precept as giving alms, meant putting material goods to good use, which contributed to greater social justice.

Therefore, it may be said that one of the proposals of the new religion was to try to promote attitudes with the tendency of achieving harmony and concord, and regulate in a pacific, nonviolent and persuasive manner the relations between members of a community. This is so in spite of the fact that, ultimately, the objective was the legitimization of power as, from a sociological point of view, great religions may be understood as resources in which to legitimize social order as a product of man's historical actions.

The Qur'an, which speaks directly of peace and other related virtues such as solidarity, honesty, compassion, forgiveness or harmony, contains sufficient elements in which to recognize the idea of peace in the growing Islamic community and, consequently, in the new society of later development. The study of the terminology related to peace, which appears in the Qur'an and its contextual analysis, allows us to establish existing links between its different meanings (religious, ethical, social, legal and political). Careful analysis provides for the distinction between at least two conceptions of peace: *internal peace*, related mainly to individual and religious realities, but also having to do with worldly and human aspects; and the other that may be denominated *social* or *external peace*, whose function was to regulate human relations among members of a group or different communities.

The first of these concepts – expressed fundamentally through the terminology related to the root *slm* – refers to a state of well-being and security associated with situations of harmony and prosperity, in not only a spiritual but also a worldly sense, and which is developed through notions and practices of tranquility, well-being and harmony. In regards to the second notion – which is expressed through the terminology derived from the root *slh* – it is portrayed mainly through the establishment of agreements, pacts and alliances as a way of solving conflict, a worldly security that would guarantee a new social order. The contexts in which this type of peace is mentioned are almost always associated with the regulation of the relations with other groups, such as Jews, Christians or infidels, as well as other cases of intra-communitarian regulation.[12]

* Ed. For further discussions on the concept of solidarity in Islamic approaches to peace, see Chapter 8 on *Salaam* by Aurangzeb Haneef.

In spite of these differences, both concepts – internal and external peace – are continually portrayed as being interrelated. It is supposed that at the onset of Islam, the different social groups were aware of the idea of peace, first, as a desire and a value to be maintained and, second, as a way of regulating conflict. It was a peace that was conceived initially as a desire for tranquility and individual well-being and, finally, as the need for a state of collective harmony which was achieved, in practice, through different compromises and agreements.

The idea of peace is related to the contexts in which the word appears, allowing it to be applied to social and political situations. Thus, for example, the idea of God – which continually appears as being related to peace – corresponds to the conception of divinity as a god who protects the faithful, is good, generous and capable of administrating justice as the sole guardian of authority.* These three divine attributes (protection, goodness and fairness) ultimately respond to the main attitudes and strategies, which the power or organizing system of the times would employ in order to regulate the coexistence of individuals belonging to a community and satisfy their basic needs: protect and safeguard the interests of the community, establish harmonious relations between its members and regulate political and legal order. Another important example is the notion of 'reward,' expressed by terms such as *ayr* or *razq*, which are continually associated with the attainment of peace. Although, literally, the reference is almost always to a spiritual reward in paradise, a semantic and contextual analysis of the terminology indicates that these expressions regarding the idea of reward are almost always linked to that of material payment as a way of satisfying the human need for subsistence (Molina, 1998).

The concepts and ideas related to peace, which appear in the Qur'an, serve as the basis for the subsequent development, often on an institutional level, of peaceful actions that were linked not only to the religious but also to social and political realms. The historical path of events itself, after the beginning of Islam, would go on developing, extending and refining the idea and practice of peace in Islamic societies, by adapting to new situations and experiences.

Mediterranean peace

Eirene, Shalom, Pax, Salam, along with other terms and concepts from Greek, Jewish, Roman, Islamic and Christian as well as other ancient and medieval Mediterranean cultures, shared an ample worldview of peace that was present in personal, domestic and public life and in which there was an undoubted acceptance of this criteria in the political arena of the governments of different societies. Although it is true that this represented a plural view of the world, there were numerous interactions among them.

* Ed. The question of Divinity and God in Islam, specifically on Sufism, is discussed in detail in Uzma Rehman's Chapter 9.

In each community, the semantic range of 'peace' meant that the same word could be used to interpret and favor the pacific management of conflict on different levels. The term 'peace' is often used, for example, in relation to agriculture as the means of securing provisions; similarly, it can be used to describe spiritual tranquility, consonance in personal relationships, affection, love or harmony among a group of inhabitants or citizens or in the running of the state. The end of war is especially noteworthy, as peace marks the end of hostility and the beginning of minimal agreements in which all those concerned win because it means the end of death and destruction. It may be said that any conflict or threat of violence can be dealt with by employing methodologies of pacific conflict management, peace.

Similarly, the word 'peace' completes its mission as regards the realms of the individual, the group and society, as well as in international relations. Its strong explanatory capacity is reinforced when its meaning is used and learned by different people. Therefore, for example, the personal greeting of peace allows us to understand the term as used in exterior relations between states and vice versa. Peace is united with other virtues, especially that of justice. There is no peace without justice. The invocation of peace in any area of life carries over into the other areas, which may account for its popularity – 'nothing is as popular as peace.' As it is used in diplomatic relations, it fosters contacts among different communities and promotes travel, thus favoring migratory movements, mixed marriages or exchanges.

Peace acquires special fortitude as part of religious life, as its relation to the institutionalized supernatural affords it strength and stability. In the Greek and Roman polytheistic religions, peace is presented as a goddess, *Eirene* or *Pax*, and is provided with the characteristics that grant it autonomy. On the contrary, in the Jewish and Muslim monotheistic religions, peace is managed directly by a sole god, on which its strength and complexity depend.

Finally, the coincidences within the semantic fields of *Eirene, Shalom, Pax, Salam* favor relations among them as common practices of the pacific regulation of conflict are identified, along with the words they represent. Similarly, there is room for multicultural learning and mutual reinforcement, as is already well known between the Greek and Roman cultures. The simple act of offering peace would open doors and resources.

This outlook may be expanded with an analysis of all the virtues implied in the conceptual and semantic fields of peace.[13] Moreover, it would be necessary to add the contributions of other cultures that, historically, have formed part of the Mediterranean framework. The area's human resources and the exceptional role the Mediterranean has played in fostering continual contacts, relations and similar lifestyles have meant that throughout history more civilizations have settled along the banks of this sea than perhaps anywhere else in the world. The range is so wide that it would be beyond the scope of this work to go into further detail, for which we must limit ourselves to the examination of brief references on the concept of peace in some of these cultures.

It is apparent how the roots *ShaLaM*, in Hebrew, and *SLM*, in Arabic – whose content, with diverse nuances, revolves around the basic notion of peace – have their parallels in other ancient Semitic languages, with similar meanings. Thus, in Phoenician, which bears a great resemblance to Hebrew, this root is documented as meaning 'to be complete.' In Assyrian, belonging to the eastern Semitic group, *shalamu* means 'to be complete, paid,' and *shulmu* 'prosperity.' In Aramaic, it means 'to be complete, saved,' and as a noun 'security, prosperity' and has the same meaning in Syriac, which belongs to the Aramaic group. In Sabateo, it has the meaning of 'peace,' as in Ethiopian, where the meaning of 'peace' is presented as 'security.' The similitude in meaning in different Semitic languages, as well as the existence of a common root, indicates without a doubt the existence in all of them of similar conceptions marked by mutual influences (Muñoz and Molina, 1998).

Different cultural groups, such as the Visigoths, Franks and Germanic communities, participated in the dismemberment of the Roman Empire. These cultures were to leave their marks on the different regions and contribute to the emergence, in the seventh and eighth centuries, of the Romance languages (Portuguese, Spanish, Catalonian, Provençal, French, Rhaeto-Romanic, Italian, Dalmatian, Romanian and Sardinian) in which the uses and terminology relative to peace can be researched through written sources and in the different Mediterranean Romance languages.

Within the great Hamito-Semitic family, mention must be made of the Berber or *tamazight* language and its different varieties. In regards to lexicon, one of the words commonly used for *peace* is *Salam*, undoubtedly borrowed from Arabic. More may be said – although there is a need for more in-depth research that would shed more light on certain aspects – of Turkish, which uses the terms *sulh* and *selâmet*, which are clearly of Arabic origin. However, the terminology of peace in this language is broader, spanning other terms which cover diverse aspects of the conceptual field of peace; as, for example, *baris* means 'peace,' 'reconciliation' and *huzur* 'rest,' 'tranquility,' 'spiritual peace' (Muñoz and Molina, 1998).

In Serbo-Croatian exists the term *mir*, whose meaning covers different ways of understanding *peace*: pacific relations between states; a non-bellicose state; public state without disorder; order, discipline; state without noise; silence; psychological balance; rest after work; a quiet state; peace treaty; reconciliation, flour (dialectic); the world; etc. It is possible that this term, which is common in other Slavic languages, existed earlier along the Mediterranean banks of the Balkans.[14]

In the Europe of the Middle Ages (especially 800–1100) the idea of peace – the *Pax* which came from the Roman Empire and which was embedded in Christian thought – once again served in the search for political re-equilibrium and social harmony. This movement was far-reaching, from its opposition to pillage and violence to spiritual and cosmological rearmament. The Catholic Church, due to its establishment and capacity, was the institution that headed that movement and sought for its repercussion in all areas within its sphere: the body, soul and society. The *Peace of God* (*Pax Dei*) meant limiting violent actions against ecclesiastical components and their properties in order to later extend to other acts of war and sectors such as agriculture and the poverty-stricken. The *Truce of God* (*tregua Dei*) limited the performing of violent acts, preventing Christians from fighting at certain times.* This movement saw the participation of not only ecclesiastical authorities, but also certain social movements, political institutions and authorities. In this sense, we may also make mention of 'heretic' movements (Cathars, Hussites, Waldesians, etc.), whose interpretation of the Gospel was taken to such extremes so as to oppose war, or the killing of one's own kind. Although, in fact, all political law was based on natural law, whose aim was to ensure order and peace with the purpose of allowing humankind to fulfill its temporal and eternal purposes.

Notes

1. In this sense, very significant is Wolfgang Dietrich's work on 'energetic peace,' which relates the gods of fertility to the concept of peace (Dietrich, 2006).
2. She has been associated with virtues, powers and symbols considered essentially feminine since the ancient world, which have been maintained almost until our days with the adaptations and additions inherent to the evolution of the notion of peace and the changes regarding all that is related to femininity.
3. The 'oaths of concord' were the institutionalization of the willingness to live in peace and harmony of the citizens of all of the Greek poleis. They have been handed down through literary works, such as the speech that Xenophon attributes to Socrates, as well as several other examples that have been conserved in inscriptions.

   In Rome, we have the word 'concord.' It served as an element to guarantee unity and coherence of the different components of the community. This 'deified' quality was used in mediation to ensure that social harmony and coexistence would prevail and transcend throughout the years of the republic and the Roman Empire. Concord was deified in public recognition of its importance. In the monetary minting of the Roman Empire, concord appears in legends and is personified as a feminine figure in different positions and holding various combinations of attributes, which coincide with the most publicly and politically valued virtues (*Pax*, *salud*, *tranquilitas*, etc.).
4. The dating of the books of the Old Testament is not exact, but it may be estimated that they belong to a period ranging from the oral traditions in 900 BC to the bindings of some texts in 300 BC.
5. The meaning of the root *ShaLaM* is similar in all Semitic languages; in Assyrian, *shalamu* means 'to be complete,' 'to be paid,' and *shulmu* 'prosperity;' in Phoenician – in form of pi'el – it means 'to be complete;' the same as in Aramaic and Syriac. In Sabateo and Ethiopian it means 'peace,' 'security.' Another practically synonymous root of *ShaQaTr* is *shalah/shalew/shalaw*, and means 'to be quiet,' 'to be tranquil,' 'live

* Ed. Karlheinz Koppe also examines the notions of Truce and Peace of God in Chapter 2.

in peace,' 'appease.' It contains in itself a series of meanings that include the idea of prosperity and well-being, as reflected in the name derived from this root *shalwah*. Cf. Cano (1998, 2000).

6. *Is* 2, 4; *Miq* 4, 3.

7. Cf. Pérez (1998). R. son of R. Elazar ha-Qappar says: So great is peace that even in times of war it [peace] should be proposed, as in this statement: '*When you reach a city to combat it, you will offer it peace.*' (*Dt* 20, 10), 26. *Is* 2, 4; *Miq* 4, 3.

8. Etymologically, *Pax* is the name of an action of feminine gender of the root *pak* – 'to fix by convention, solve by an agreement between both parties,' also *pag* – which normally defines a physical act. From these roots are also derived other terms such as *pango, pacit, pacunt, pacere, paciscor, pactus, paco, pacalis,* etc.

   The noun *pax* is present practically throughout the history of the Latin language, the history of Rome and is thus found in the works of many Latin authors from Pauto to Justinian, to cite some of the more notable ones, to Cicero, Salustius, Varro, Virgil, Livy, Lucano, Ovid, Pliny, Seneca, Valerius Maximus, Suetonius, Tacitus, Servius, etc., who use the word *pax* to define different activities in Roman societies. *Pax* in Rome is a useful concept to manage the problems and conflicts that occur in group(s), acquiring an enormous discursive potential and regulations to define the horizon towards which society should be oriented (Muñoz, 1998).

9. This is apparent in the politics of Tiberius and Gracchus, at the end of 200 BC, by Nero, thanks to the influence of Seneca, and the emperor himself, Marcus Aurelius, at the end of 200 AD.

10. Cf. Muñoz and Díez (1999). The most frequent type is a woman, as the personification and the divinity of *Pax*, dressed in a traditional tunic. In this way, *pax* establishes conceptual and semiotic links with diverse spheres and institutions within the Roman Empire.

11. *HerF.* 368.

12. The root *slm*, from which *Islam* is derived, originally had meanings ranging from 'integrity, security, well-being,' 'devotion, or obedience' to 'peaceful surrender' or 'greeting of peace.' The meanings of *slh* evolve from 'remove one's self from imperfection or be whole' to 'impose order,' 'reconcile,' 'reach an agreement.' See Molina (1998) and Gómez et al. (1997).

13. Often present in Greco-Roman culture, a good example of which are the Stoics, it may be compared to the Hebrew and Arabic cultures, and has a clear continuity in Christianity and humanism. Indeed, Justice, Prudence, Temperance, Strength, Clemency, Fidelity (faith) and Hope, to name only a few, remain in the Mediterranean culture to the present day.

14. However, in ancient Slavic the term *Pokoh* is also used, as is apparent in the root *pak* from Latin. Cf. Muñoz and Molina (1998).

Reference list

Alganza, M. (1998) 'Eiréne y otras palabras griegas sobre la Paz' in F.A. Muñoz and B. Molina (eds.) *Cosmovisiones de Paz en el Mediterráneo* (Granada: Universidad de Granada), 123–152.

Cano, M.J. (1998) 'Paz en el Antiguo Testamento' in F.A. Muñoz and B. Molina (eds.) *Cosmovisiones de Paz en el Mediterráneo* (Granada: Universidad de Granada), 28–61.

Cano, M.J. (2000) 'El pueblo de la alianza' in F.A. Muñoz and M. López (eds.) *Historia de la Paz: Tiempos, Espacios y Actores* (Granada: Universidad de Granada), 83–126.

Dietrich, W. (2006) 'A Call for Trans-Rational Peaces,' *Virtual Peace Library of the UNESCO Chair for Peace Studies at the University of Innsbruck*, http://www.uibk.ac.at/peacestudies/downloads/peacelibrary/transrational.pdf, date accessed June 13, 2009.

Galtung, J. (1985) 'La cosmología social y el concepto de paz,' *Sobre la paz* (Barcelona: Fontamara), 73–105.

Gómez, C., C. Pérez, B. Molina and A.R. Vidal (1997) 'Una lectura del Corán desde la paz,' *Miscelánea de Estudios Árabes y Hebraicos*, 46, 113–148.

Harris, W.V. (2005) *Rethinking the Mediterranean* (Oxford: Oxford University Press).

Lorente, M. and F.A. Muñoz (2005) 'Concordia un recurso a lo largo del tiempo para la construcción de sociedades pacíficas' in C. Pérez and F.A. Muñoz (eds.) *Experiencias de Paz en el Mediterráneo* (Granada: Universidad de Granada), 201–243.

Martínez, C. (2000) 'Las mujeres y la Paz en la Historia: Aportaciones desde el mundo antiguo' in F.A. Muñoz and M. López (eds.) *Historia de la Paz: Tiempos, Espacios y Actores* (Granada: Universidad de Granada), 254–290.

Molina, B. (1998) 'Aproximación al concepto de paz en los inicios del Islam' in F.A. Muñoz and B. Molina (eds.) *Cosmovisiones de Paz en el Mediterráneo* (Granada: Universidad de Granada), 229–264.

Muñoz, F.A. (1998) 'Pax Romana' in F.A. Muñoz and B. Molina (eds.) *Cosmovisiones de Paz en el Mediterráneo* (Granada: Universidad de Granada), 191–228.

Muñoz, F.A. (2006) 'La trama Mediterránea: Sobre los orígenes históricos del Mediterráneo (y de Europa),' *Saitabi*, 55, 29–43.

Muñoz, F.A. and B. Molina (1998) (eds.) *Cosmovisiones de Paz en el Mediterráneo* (Granada: Universidad de Granada).

Muñoz, F.A. and E. Díez (1999) 'Pax Orbis Terrarum: La pax en la moneda romana,' *Florentia Iliberritana*, 10, 211–250.

Muñoz, F.A. and M. López (eds.) (2000) *Historia de la Paz: Tiempos, Espacios y Actores* (Granada: Universidad de Granada).

Pérez, C. and F.A. Muñoz (2004) (eds.) *Experiencias de Paz en el Mediterráneo* (Granada: Universidad de Granada).

Pérez, M. (1998) 'Shalom: El modelo rabínico de la Paz' in F.A. Muñoz and B. Molina (eds.) *Cosmovisiones de Paz en el Mediterráneo* (Granada: Universidad de Granada), 63–123.

4
Peace: A Western European Perspective
Nigel Young

Peace as a process, not as a steady or finite state, means that there are many approaches and meanings to peace – and that they are constantly contested and changing – at different times, in distinct ways, in various contexts or cultures. To fasten on any etymology of peace is to grasp a set of bemusing paradoxes and contradictions: ambivalence, ambiguities – and even 'doublespeak' – 'War is Peace' to use Orwell's slogan from 1984, or 'Peace is our profession' – the motto of the US nuclear armed Strategic Air Command (SAC). Here I have named peace in terms of positive, pragmatic action, rather than in terms of ethics, or end states; dialectic can more easily accommodate unresolved tensions, when they are linked to peace as 'social action.'

If one decides to use categories in approaching global concepts of peace, then language may be as appropriate as geographical region or religion or continent. 'English speaking' is arguably the least inappropriate of those terms used to describe cultures on and beyond the eastern Atlantic shelf. Like Winston Churchill's phrase, here it only strictly covers mother-tongue speakers – yet already this connotes some imperial, Anglo-North American overreach, beyond the Atlantic!

In dealing with this subject, we are confronted by two major contradictions. First, that the detachment of English, British or 'Anglo' traditions from others (e.g. 'European' is problematic) – the notion of an 'Anglo-Saxon' world – is part of the racist baggage of late nineteenth century parlance: England was only Anglo-Saxon for a brief period between the collapse of the Roman Empire and the Norman French dynasty. As a result Latin, French, Danish/Norse, Celtic (British) had as much linguistic importance in creating English as the peasant tongues of the Northern Germanic–Frisian tribes (e.g. Saxons) (Stenton, 2001). Second, in theoretical and conceptual terms, at least the English-speaking peace traditions have produced little of note, as we shall see.

Concepts of peace in the British and North American contexts have, from a religious and philosophical point of view, been both narrow and distinctly unoriginal. Indeed, with the exception of one or two figures, such as John Ruskin and Henry David Thoreau, they have been highly derivative also. William Penn took certain ideas from Quakerism and reactions to the Hobbesian England of the Civil War to his Pennsylvanian experiment. Payne created populist rhetoric that spanned the American and French revolutions with rights of free-born (English) men and Rousseauite optimism. Those who derived inspiration from the Church – from figures such as Augustine of Hippo, Thomas of Aquinas and Erasmus of Rotterdam,* did so from a cosmopolitan European Christianity, centered on Rome. So what is there to write about, when the native traditions of the English-speaking countries is so lacking in original concepts and ideas? What was special about the tradition was not a contribution in words but a focus on deeds: Practical peace-making, implementation of utopian schemes, peace plans and proposals, and the rationalization of capitalist contract or free trade imperialism as a formula for peace. But what also derived from mainland Europe in particular was a secular, radical tradition of thought; anarchist, socialist, communist, which informed a more measured and nonviolent approach to practical peace and radical change; civil disobedience, the evolution of the strike and other methods of the labor movement as a nonviolent methodology. This was the basis of the socialist internationalism of Keir Hardie and the Independent Labour Party (ILP) and it fed the tradition of war resistance and non-cooperation that spread worldwide.

In North America, these ideas were directly transplanted by immigrants like Goldmann and taken up in a pragmatist American variant by figures like Debs and Randolph Bourne. But again, even via the British Isles, the inspiration was often Continental Europe. John Dewey's instrumentalism was the liberal version of John Stuart Mill, as opposed to anarcho-socialist praxis.

These cross fertilizations with European ideas and practices underline the artificiality of separating out the mongrel traditions of Britain and North America from those of Continental Europe. And indeed, in the British Commonwealth, for example, Gandhian ideas† were imported to Britain after 1920 from India and to the US especially in the 1950s, where Mohandas Gandhi made an impact on the civil rights movement when his ideas of *Satyagraha* were taken up by pacifists. Moreover, even beyond Europe this conceptual hybrid drew inspiration from Japan, China, Vietnam and other Asian traditions. Westward migration of people and ideas fused with the instrumental, utilitarian, Deweyite pragmatism, not only with the US, but on both sides of the Atlantic. There were moments of true inspiration – Quakerism in the 1650s, for example. But the fundamental 'Anglo-American' bent was in concepts of diplomacy, law – especially between states, contractual obligations, mediation and arbitration – not in metaphysical deliberation, but in praxis. Moments of subsequent renewal like the 1920s and

* Ed. For further information on all three of them, see Chapter 2 by Karlheinz Koppe.
† Ed. More information on Gandhi's life and philosophy is provided in Chapter 25 by Arun Gandhi.

the 1950s brought low-level innovation, for example 'conscientious objection' and 'nuclear pacifism' in the UK, and then the conceptual apparatus of the New Left; but even here the inspiration was Albert Camus rather than Bertrand Russell!

Even the distinction of English as an emerging global language – or at least lingua franca – is purely instrumental. It has arguably been the major language since the nineteenth century in communications about peace, and even from the seventeenth century it was a key instrument rivaling Latin, Spanish and then French. It was practical and convenient, and had a well-developed vocabulary. In other words, utility, not theoretical sophistication, was the key: it makes it a relevant category, expanded by political, economic and military hegemony – and eventually cultural hegemony, of which language was part. But it was not the language of the 'philosophers' or Hegel, and even the usages of the term 'peace' betray these characteristics. At best it is (or appears) neutral – the language of mediation or pacification, not harmony or social advance.

Through the help of etymology, the English usage of the term 'peace' can be divided into negative and positive (but largely passive) categories.

The etymology of peace in English includes meanings of 'rest,' 'silence,' 'death,' 'passivity,' to be left alone (like the German *Friedhof*), in other words, it is, like Johan Galtung's terms, essentially 'negative' peace. In the negative category, one places absence of war and treaties to end war, as well as 'law and order' ('keeping the peace,' 'breach of the peace,' etc.). More positive are the usages of peace as harmony or friendship and individual peace, stillness, peace of mind, serenity, rest – but eventually returns to the (negative?) 'rest in peace,' or 'at peace' (dead!). These too are passive concepts. If one applies a fourfold analysis of these one is approaching the usage of peace as active – and as used by the peace movement; nonviolent social change, conflict transformation, resistance – to war and nuclear weapons and direct action or civil disobedience.

Table 4.1 Positive and negative peace

	Positive	*Negative*	
Active	Nonviolent action, social change	War resistance, nuclear disarmament	*Active*
Passive	Friendship Harmony Serenity	Stillness; rest Silence Pacification	*Passive*
	Positive	*Negative*	

The Romano-Christian traditions of *Pax*,* official peace stemming from a strong state or a strong church (or a strong state-church), passed on into concepts of peace through law and order, laws of war, and the 'just' war theory – an early

* Ed. Compare with the *Pax Romana* in Chapter 2 by Karlheinz Koppe.

form of 'arms control.' This was accomplished also by the concept of pre-emptive peace; armed strength as a peace-based deterrent: 'prepare for war to keep the peace' – including the pacification of conflict: 'defense, internal and external.' English magistrates were called JPs (justices of the peace); enforcing peace through the rule of law (nationally and locally), the deterrence of crime and affirming centralized sovereignty (Leviathan).

The evolution of contract (possessive, capitalist individualism) modified this; as Johan Galtung puts it, a major source for some Western traditions of international law is based on peace as a contractual, conscious and mutually agreed-on relationship (Galtung, 1996), meaning 'treaties must be observed.' Contract 'softened' the state in some ways, allowing more 'liberalized' claims against state power. But this same state-peace was based on strength; in most English-speaking societies legality gave legitimacy to the very monopoly of violence, to territoriality, perhaps leading to the use of the army as internal peacekeeper and the early acceptance of massive deterrence (battleships, nuclear weapons) by Western liberal democracies, but not standing armies.

One area where this tension is particularly fraught and interesting is civilian conscription for compulsory military service. Universal conscription developed for mass mobilized armies in Continental Europe after 1793, and then, except for the English-speaking countries, became an almost universal institution in the next 120 years. By 1970, it had spread worldwide, but not until 1915–1917 did Britain, Australia, New Zealand* and even the United States of America introduce mandatory armed service for males of so-called 'military age' – usually 17/18 to 35 years or older.

It is true that conscription had made an unpopular and brief appearance during the American Civil War (1860s), but equally important was the emergence in these same Western countries of ideas of conscientious objection to forcible military service, in peacetime – or wartime. The origins of this concept lie in the English Civil War of the 1640s–1650s and were institutionalized in Quakerism. There were strong movements both for and against conscription in the nineteenth century, but more specifically objection to several other state compulsions, such as vaccination in the late nineteenth century, crystallized the notion. It is true that such concepts spread to several other northern European states, including Norway and Tsarist Russia; but in the period after 1918 it was in the English-speaking states that legalized objection made its most rapid advances, i.e. in the next 50 years. Later in the twentieth century as draft resistance grew, mass civilian armies (and conscription) began to decline, and the right of 'objection' became accepted by almost all non-authoritarian states – and some authoritarian ones: rights are further strengthened and duties diminished. These 'terms of trade' are about power, organization and resistance, rather than 'peace concepts.'

* Ed. For more details on New Zealand and peace, see Chapter 16 by Peter Horsley.

Nevertheless, both were embodied in legal and cultural conceptualizations and became part of peace movements and peace culture.

What does war resistance have to do with peace? In the most primitive utopian-pacifist slogan, simply 'wars will cease when men refuse to fight.' The tiny numbers of such refusers had significance far beyond that of a 'prophetic minority:' unpopular wars and conscriptions did spark mass unrest, protests, strikes, resistance – even social revolution: certainly political repression – and change. There is seen to be a potential limit on states' power to make war; even totalistic nation-states needed to legitimize and popularize (e.g. make patriotic) their military ventures. War resistance, however futile and doomed in its immediate effect, sets in motion a process of questioning war-making states in general. The absence of such states is no guarantee of even a negative peace, but it is conceived of as a positive evolution.

The attempt to put conscientious objection into the US constitution and the later attempt to outlaw war were symbolic, utopian gestures, but they help define this English-speaking concern with legislating rights – expanding the liberal or libertarian space for individuals against the state that many socialists seeking social justice from above – by a socialized state – found difficult to accept. The relative weakness of Marxist socialisms is linked to this antipathy to top-down theories, in the English-speaking world – a preference for incremental, even experimental steps towards peace could lead to vacillation, compromise and considerable hypocrisy, but it also gave space for popular initiatives and social creativity from below, lacking in some authoritarian traditions such as those of the new communist parties.

As the first nation-states emerged, they often did so through a peace of pacification, internal colonialism. The 'exception,' the Dutch Republic, would have pacified the Walloons, had not the Spanish Empire turned back their war of national liberation between 1580 – and the treaty of Breda (1650). Both Great Britain (the United Kingdom) and the United States of America are clear models of this. The pacification of Wales, the west, the north, Scotland (as late as 1746) and Ireland maintained the hegemony of a London-centered English 'peace,' albeit with the loss of French-speaking dominions (Parisian domination of the provinces was equally part of French national expansion). Similarly in North America, the pacification of the west, the Indian wars, the defeat of Mexico and finally the defeat of a slave-owning south consolidated power in the industrial northeast. This exemplified a 'might-is-right' element in *Pax Americana*, which extended into the Monroe doctrine, 'manifest destiny' and the ideologies of Theodore (Teddy) Roosevelt. The US role of intervention in the Caribbean (Cuba, Central America and eventually most of Latin America) exemplified this dimension of US 'internationalism,' imperial rather than liberal, and an abiding tension in US foreign policy strategy.

At this point – to shift from 'peace' from above to peace from below – it is essential to note the popular bases of peace praxis emerging in social movements from Quakerism and other puritan groups onwards, and by 1815 it had become a genuine social movement in its own right. I will treat the modes of peace practice in the English-speaking world in eleven categories: they are not discrete but overlapping and they are not equivalent but vary in size, importance and longevity. For example, religious peace action continues vigorously, despite a change in character, over more than 350 years.

Religious peace praxis was often retreatist or quietist (as in Quakerism), but when confronted by repression or persecution by authorities, refusal or non-cooperation, or 'bearing witness,' it became a form of resistance to the state: the obeying of a high law (conscience, the inner light), rather than state law. In some cases, especially in North America, this produced martyrs. From this 'left wing Puritanism' based on small, democratic meetings – stressing justice, nonviolence and radical egalitarianism, many peace strands evolved, including conscientious objection and radical dissent of a secular kind.

The new social radicalism that emerged in the late eighteenth century had both political and religious roots. After the bloodletting of the period 1790–1815, especially in Europe, this movement was increasingly anti-militarist and utopian. The first peace societies emerged. This tendency criticized the use of armed force to repress internal rebellion and dissent and was deeply skeptical of conscription – and even more of standing armies.

At this stage a bifurcation begins between a radical, extra-parliamentary, Republican, even 'Jacobin' use of the peace movement, one which overlaps with the labor movement, and on the other more mainstream liberal, parliamentarist and middle class, focusing on utilitarian, pragmatic solutions. The first wing, stemming from sympathy with the American and French revolutions, prioritized social justice, egalitarian democracy and mass action. The second wanted to reform the state, liberalize democracy, create international institutions, but rejected both the creation of utopian alternatives and social revolution. The methods of the first were mass protest, strikes, non-cooperation, fraternization, direct action. The second chose lobbying, petitions, deputations, conferences, letter writing, pressure group activity of all sorts. Somewhat apart from both, were the utopian communities, especially in North America, founded on peace principles, often libertarian and experimental and including pacifist leaders in their ranks: sometimes religious and sometimes secular, they continued to overlap with wings of the peace movement.

Anti-conscriptionism was strong in many parts of Europe, but only in the English-speaking world did it survive until the First World War – it was both religious and secular, and worked both as a liberal pressure group and as radical resistance. Socialist anti-militarism was, however, somewhat divided on conscription as a peace issue – with some believing that the draft democratized (and thus might stop) the war and the army. Others believed that by arming workers, this might lead to insurrection, mutiny and desertion. It was also argued that mass (universal) conscription was fairer than selective systems. But overall the anarchist view – that this was 'involuntary servitude' and should be refused – held sway. In the case of the Vietnam War, the argument that the draft radicalized and deepened opposition in society – and the armed forces – was given some force.

Internationalism of two kinds became prevalent in the English-speaking world in the latter half of the nineteenth century. The first was the liberal internationalism of free trade, expansionist capitalism and the Atlantic democracies. In terms of praxis, this was focused on the international rule of law, treaties, the growth of inter-governmental and inter-parliamentary linkages, of international institutions, like the Red Cross, and global communications (the World Postal Union). It fostered peace conferences, courts of arbitration and international justice, and a more transparent diplomacy. The influence of British philosophy and political economy, Adam Smith, Jeremy Bentham, James and John Stuart Mill – and then Richard Cobden and John Bright – as well as constitutionalism (Walter Bagehot) and jurisprudence, was strong.

The second tradition, growing from the activism of the emerging mass working class movement in England, was the increasing internationalism of early socialism. It drew much from pre-Marxist, and non-Marxist (Proudhonian) socialism in Continental Europe; but Paine, Owen and some Chartist leaders emphasized links with movements abroad. The international conferences between 1815 and 1860 were harbingers of the internationalism culminating first in the Paris Commune and then in the Second International 1880–1914. Less ideological than its continental counterparts, this tradition was fiercely anti-militarist up to the First World War, when nationalism proved divisive in the event of mass mobilization. Nevertheless, strikes against war and resistance to military service did take place, especially in the United States in 1917–1918, which led to the crushing of both socialist parties and labor unions.

Out of the failed praxis of 1914–1918 emerged three kinds of action or tradition. In the first place, a new, secular and more radical pacifism emerged from groups like the ILP and the No Conscription Fellowship. This expanded into internationalism in the War Resisters' International in 1921. The First World War proved a watershed, dividing those who were against war, but unwilling to refuse and resist military service (or to oppose all wars), and those who not only totally opposed all war, but were ready to refuse to fight for the nation in arms, whatever the penalties, whatever the context.

The second tradition, again emerging out of a split women's movement in 1914–1917, was a feminist–pacifist internationalism, which helped in the formation of the Women's International League for Peace and Freedom in 1915. This tradition was revitalized in the new women's movement after 1980 with transnational protests and women-only actions against nuclear bases, in nonviolent blockades. In the interim, spokeswomen like Sylvia Pankhurst, Vera Brittain and Virginia Woolf maintained opposition especially to the targeting of civilians (e.g. aerial bombing).

The third tradition of communist internationalism after Vladimir Ilyich Lenin quickly became a counterpart of the state peace of Western governments. As the Soviet Union's notion of peace evolved and dominated the English-speaking communist parties and movements, the concept of peace evolved to suit the needs of Russian foreign policy. Soviet Marxism was deployed to determine the stance on each peace issue, and in each peace movement or campaign 'front organizations' were created to pursue efforts approved by Moscow (like the Stockholm Appeal in 1950).

The main conceptual innovations of the period 1918–1950 came not from socialism, but from Mohandas Gandhi,* whose ideas were taken up by radical pacifists in the 1920s, by parts of the labor movement in the 1930s, by the US civil rights movement in the 1950s and 1960s, and by the emerging nuclear disarmament (nuclear pacifist) movement, also in the 1950s and 1960s. Civil disobedience, nonviolent direct action, the boycott, the sit-in, the blockade, all used Gandhian campaigns as models. Many Second World War resisters adopted a utopian Gandhian philosophy to work not only in these campaigns, but in a wide range of peace, social change and social justice projects and utopian projects.

By the 1960s, alternative security concepts, civilian resistance and nonviolent defense became part of the remit of peace organizations. In the discussion of such themes, peace research began to flourish, especially in the English-speaking context. Despite the contributions of the Norwegians Johan Galtung and Arne Næss, and Austrian and German thinkers like Robert Jungk and Leopold Kohr,† the most extensive growth was in North America and the UK. This intellectual movement, sparked by Lewis Richardson in the UK in the 1930s and then spread from the 1950s, was developed in North America by Kenneth Boulding, Anatol Rapoport, Quincy Wright, Theodore F. Lentz and Thomas Schelling, and in Britain by John Burton, Michael Nicholson, Adam Curle and Paul Smoker, and contributed in the interchange with North American ideas and social theory (Sorokin, Coser, etc.). The evolution of the conceptual apparatus of peace studies deriving from such research-led discussion had a significant effect on the development of peace education, which was especially strong in England.

It also influenced the emergence of the second wave of the nuclear disarmament movement after 1979, which was considerably more sophisticated than the nuclear pacifist movement of 1957–1963. Like the former, it was led by intellectuals but was more committed to a trans-European strategy 'beyond the blocs.' Unilateralism (taking action whatever the action of other states) was

* Ed. Chapter 25 is exclusively dedicated to Gandhi as peace thinker.
† Ed. See also Chapter 1 by Wolfgang Dietrich.

diluted, but transnational linkages energized political dissent on both sides of the Atlantic: it remained fiercely non-aligned and made nonviolence a principle of action.

Both in the 1960s and in the 1980s, many of the traditions and concepts re-emerged – indeed the New Left (1956–1972) may be seen as an attempt to synthesize inherited ideas and forms of praxis, with new social methodologies created as 'experiments with truth.' Despite its militant rhetoric, this movement was overwhelmingly nonviolent and anti-war – and indeed decentralist. Media coverage and internal divisions tended to distort this perception, but its contribution to peace theory in the Western context was real enough; the new women's movement and the environmental security (Greenpeace) movement of the 1970s are its natural heirs. Indeed, from Gandhi's first actions in South Africa to contemporary ecological activism, there is a strong conceptual link.

Finally, we have to deal with state-sponsored peace in the English-speaking world. The state-sponsored peace of the Soviet Union was never translated into a party in power in these countries, but nevertheless an anti-communist, anti-appeasement (referring to appeasing Nazism) official concept of peace did hold sway in the West during the Cold War. Security, deterrence, balance of power, counter-insurgency, containment, this was the language that supported the Strategic Air Command ('Peace is our Profession'), the 'peacekeeper' missile, UN peacekeeping in Korea – as well as later the Peace Corps and the United States Institute of Peace, both offspring of the State Department and close to the CIA.*

At the non-official level, the Moral Re-armament movement, and other conservative, pro-free market organizations, as well as the anti-communist McCarthyite movement in the US, led to projects like HUAC (the House Un-American Activities Committee) which, with the FBI, pursued the non-communist peace movement as well as the 'peace-fronts.' For a long time the academic field of international relations was closely aligned with Western state policy; however, gradually peace research had the effect of widening the international relations paradigm and making it more 'liberal' and open to peace studies.

Clearly, 'aligned' movements, supporting the armed policy of a given state, fell outside the realm of peace concepts used by most of the peace traditions considered in this chapter.

Conclusion

Can one draw any conclusions from the previous discussion? One point clearly is that most of the praxis analyzed in the Atlantic world had little or no theoretical

---

* Ed. On the relationship between the Peace Corps and the CIA, see Chapter 28 by Martina Kaller-Dietrich.

basis – and that its concepts were generally poorly developed. The second is that peace practice in the English-speaking world was as divided over approach – goals, methods and tactics – as the theoretical traditions elsewhere were. The third is that conceptually this movement drew most of its ideas from other societies. The English-speaking world has some unique characteristics relating to peace work, but this is as much related to historical situation, political evolution and geo-social context as it is to the history of ideas and concepts.

Insofar as there was originality, it was in practical theories, evolved through action – trial and error – very much parallel to Gandhian methodology.

Reference list and further reading

Arendt, H. (1958) *Origins of Totalitarianism* (New York: Schocken Books).

Brock, P. and N. Young (1999) *Pacifism in the 20th Century* (Toronto: Syracuse University Press).

Galtung, J. (1996) *Peace by Peaceful Means: Peace and Conflict, Development and Civilization* (London: Sage).

Hinsley, F.H. (2008) *Power and the Pursuit of Peace: Theory and Practice in the History of Relations between States* (Cambridge: Cambridge University Press).

Howard, M. (2008) *War and the Liberal Conscience* (Irvington: Columbia University Press).

Krippendorff, E. (1971) 'The State as a Focus of Peace Research,' *Peace Research Society Papers*, 14, 47–60.

Moore, B. (1979) *The Social Origins of Dictatorship and Democracy: Lord and Peasant in the Making of Modern World* (Harmondsworth: Penguin).

Stenton, F. (ed.) (2001) *Oxford History of England*, 2 (Oxford: Oxford University Press).

Young, N. (1976) *War, Resistance and the Nation State* (Ann Arbor: University Microfilms International).

Young, N. and M. Shaw (1983) *War Resistance, State and Society* (London: Macmillan Press).

5
Friðr: A Northern European Perspective

Elida K. Undrum Jacobsen

Long the goddess sought her lover,
O'er parch'd sands and mountains cold;
From her eyes, all swoln with weeping,
Dropp'd round tears of purest gold.
All, who 'neath love's fever languish,
Hence derive their burning care;
Freya's anguish
Each true lover's breast must share.

Adam Oehlenschläger*

Introduction

When thinking about old Nordic history, who does not have the image of the rough and masculine warrior Viking? The climate of the north made Scandinavia a seemingly 'impenetrable' sphere, a millennia ago described by writers from the Mediterranean region as on the brink of a distant, cold and symbolically world's 'end' in the north, the border of the seventh sea, and close to an eternally ice-covered sphere.[1] From this distant north, where there were 'more wild animals than people,' came the brave, powerful Viking who traveled far, looted land without fear and stood with honor in battle against his enemies. The representation of the masculine conqueror is part of a historical narration that has overshadowed other conceptions of the Nordic past. However, it is not representative of the everyday life of the Norse, which was founded in a livelihood of agriculture and fishing, and where female powers were seen as essential for life. In this image, the masculine and the feminine unite in notions of fertility and harmony.

This chapter explores the etymological root of the Scandinavian meaning of peace, which dates back to the Viking age.[2] Rather than identifying peace

---

* Oehlenschläger in Pigott (1839, p. 213).

through modern parameters, such as justice, ethics and politics, the chapter explores the word as it is found meaningful in the context of Norse society. The etymological root of peace is thus presented through two principal features of the Norse milieu: the cosmology of the Viking age and the rites and rituals of the Norse. These two prisms enable an understanding of the societal function of peace in the Viking age. Peace as a concept is here found to be represented in notions of fertility and harmony; it is concerned with the growth of crops, fertility of the soil, reproduction of animals and good health of human beings. The chapter thus unveils a concept of peace that is situated in the feminine and energetic nature of its roots.*

The Viking age

The Viking age broadly speaking lasted from the late 700s to the late 1000s AD; however, to understand and appreciate the Norse worldview more comprehensively one will have to take into consideration archeological material dating from the whole period of the Iron Age from 500 to 1000 AD (Solli, 2002, p. 22). What follows focuses on the notion of peace in this period of the Scandinavian past, although the chapter will in addition conclude by taking into consideration the changing context and conception of peace from the Middle Ages until today. This chapter will only provide parts of an insight into the notion of peace in the old Scandinavian context, as it is not possible to discover a full picture, 'origin' or an 'accurate' description of the Norse *Weltanschauung*. The Norse worldview is not part of a doctrinaire system, nor is it a systemized set of beliefs. The old Scandinavian cosmology was for the most part conveyed orally from generation to generation through ritual performances, narrations of myths, scald songs and poetry. Runic letters were known and used by the Germanic world from about 200 or 300 AD; however, they are found mainly providing only shorter inscriptions on stone and wood, and as such are complementary sources to a larger insight into Norse society. One is thus bound to understand the Norse existence from an 'outsider's' perspective.

A contemporary understanding of Norse reality is as a result challenged by the barrier of written text. The mythology is not written down on Norse premises, as the Nordic culture was 'silent' until Christianity, Latin letters and scrolls to write on came to the Nordic sphere around the year 1000 AD. The predominantly Christian and male writers would not recount in detail the actuality of pagan worship. And as most of this literature is written some two centuries after the Nordic countries were Christianized, we are left with a 'patchy and often contradictory record' (O'Donoghue, 2007, p. 67). Despite this ambivalence, the

---

*   Ed. For a discussion on the energetic definition of peace interpretations, see Chapter 1 by Wolfgang Dietrich.

vast research done, based on archeological findings, place-names and scald poems, laws and other written sources from the Christian Middle Ages, demonstrates that these sources can tell us *something* about the Norse rites and cults.[3]

The etymology of peace in Scandinavia

The contemporary expression for peace in Scandinavian languages is *fred*.[4] Etymologically, this modern word for peace in Norway, Sweden, Denmark and Iceland stems from the same old Norse root *friðr*, which signifies *love*. The word can also be found interpreted as meaning 'friendly relations.'[5] The words *frilla* (lover) and *frjá* (lovemaking) both stem from the same root as the word *friðr*. All of these notions position the word as a binding and unifying force, a dynamic relationship. *Friðr*, *frilla* and *frjá* are also related to the word *fri*, which can mean both 'free' and 'proposal' (to marry).

In written sources from the pre-Christian era as well as the Middle Ages, the word *friðr* is especially found in the fertility cult formula *til árs ok friðar*. The first part of this aphorism, *til árs* (for good yearly harvest) included a wishing for the fertility of the earth and growth of crops. The term *ok friðar* (for peace) expressed a wish for societal togetherness and tranquility which was desirable for all forms of procreation. This peaceful condition concerned the harmony between people and gods, which ensured good and ripe crops, that the animals reproduced and that humans and animals enjoyed good health. The cult gathering brought about a state of *friðr*, peace (Steinsland, 2005, p. 279).

The Nordic cult formula *til árs ok friðar* – fertility and good year – contained conceptions of a harmony that was upheld when everything in the cosmos was in tune with god-given principles (Steinsland, 1997, p. 87). As we will explore below, these god-given principles were not bound by codes of ethical behavior, but through a performed dynamical relationship between gods, human beings and the cosmos. Peace as fertility and lovemaking is personified in fertility gods, who granted peace as love and fertility to the earth and human beings. The recipients of the offering *til árs ok friðar* were the gods *Frøy* (Frey, Freyr) and *Frøya* (Frejya, Freija) who were the guarantors of peace, prosperity and love.

From its etymological roots, we can thus establish that *friðr* signifies peace as 'love' and/or a 'friendly relation.' In the Norse cult, peace is found represented in fertility, harmony and lovemaking. In this conception, peace is a cosmic and societal harmony that concerns the richness of the earth and the health of the animals and people. Furthermore, *friðr* includes an ongoing communication between humans and gods through cult practices, which in turn nurture cosmological balance and is as such maintained through cyclical and collective offerings to the god and goddess Frøy and Frøya.[6] But what does peace as 'love' actually mean in the Norse context? This chapter explores the concept of *friðr* in the dynamic relationship between humans, gods and other powers in the

Norse worldview. Peace cannot be found here as an absolute truth, it is rather a collective harmony that is lived and performed by the Norse people.

Friðr: A cosmological peace

The meaning of peace is always situated in its context. In Norse society, the main components of this context are human beings and their relation to the gods and other cosmological forces. The cosmology is narrated though the myths, and in myths one finds answers to how the world was created, and how laws of nature, death and life came into being. Myths can be seen as a compass which people use to orient themselves in the reality of the world.[7] However, this mystical worldview should not be understood literally or as a geographical world-image, as the sea-going Vikings were skilled in geography. The cosmology is rather a symbolical world-model, which can be seen as an expression of a common world, in which people found their place and where questions about life could be overcome. Only through 'decoding' the mythical imagery-language can we begin to understand a Norse world-image (Steinsland, 1997, p. 24).

The old Scandinavian cosmology informs about the function, existence and order of the universe and humans and other beings' place in the cosmos. Here, the world is illustrated as a circular disk in which the one 'home' (circle) is placed outside another, with natural boundaries such as mountains and deep valleys separating them from one another.[8] In the middle of the world lies the center – the home of the *Æesir* (Ásir) gods, *Åsgård*. From this center radiates a tremendous energetic potential of divine will and creativity out into the cosmos (Steinsland, 2005, pp. 98–99). The Life Tree *Yiggdrasil* (meaning Yggr, *Oðin's*, horse) stands in the holy center of Åsgård. At the divine source of the Life Tree are the three female powers that spin the destiny of humans and gods, *nornene*. The tree has one root in the death realm, one in the realm of the *jotner* (giants) and one with the gods and humans (Mundal, 1990, p. 3; Holtsmark, 1989, p. 71). Outside Åsgard lies *Midtgård*, where human beings live, and outside Midtgård is *Utgård* (the farm outside), where the chaos forces prevail and where oppositional powers radiate towards the center. Humans thus live in the middle of chaos and divine – in a constant tension between different powers.

The Norse cosmos can be seen as a macro-reflection of the social system, which was primarily run by means of agriculture and fishing. The *gård* (farm) was the central social entity, where communal activity was organized. The Life Tree, or destiny-tree, is a holy symbol of the cosmic center, as well as a symbol of the kin and life on the farm. Every farm had a holy farmyard tree that should not be cut down or harmed.[9] The tree also symbolizes a threefold existence that binds the chaos forces, gods and humans, and death together in the cosmic space. Outside the farm was the cultivated land marked by the border of a fence, and outside the farmland, the wilderness. Similar to the untamed nature, at the same time unsafe and bursting with resources and knowledge vital for life, the forces in Utgård – giants, dwarfs and other powers – can be dangerous for human beings and for the gods. The outside forces are represented in the mythology as endangering the godly and human survival, and are to evoke the end of the world, *Ragnarok*.[10] The Norse world is fragile and dangerous. However, chaos forces are also the source of creativity and knowledge that are necessary for existence, and thus not to be closed out of the godly and the human.

The Norse worldview explicates a life-experience where the energies of existence are experienced as poles that both attract and divert from each other, and where the world is ceaselessly dynamical. The gathering, opposition and tension in the relationship between the male and the female is experienced as a basic force of life. The ambivalent relationship between giants (chaos) and gods (order) is in the same way reflected in the manly and womanly powers that in their meeting form the basis of creativity and new creations in the cosmos. It is the obligation of the gods and humans to constitute a functioning cosmos out of an energetic chaos (Steinsland, 1997, pp. 20–21, 73).

The unification of male and female, seed and soil is in the Norse myths a symbol for fertility and harmony. In this chapter peace out of love is explored in the interrelation between humans, gods and cosmos, which unveil the meaning of *friðr* to the context of Norse society.[11] *Friðr* is a central conserving element of Norse reality, animatedly performed in Norse rituals, and part of the Norse *ethos*.

Peace out of fertility and harmony

Below I will explore the concept of peace through the mythological narrative of the fertility gods. The concept of peace in Norse society is embodied in the gods Frøy (the Lord, the seed, the ruler) and Frøya (the Lady, the female ruler) who grant peace out of love, fertility and harmony in a highly erotic and energetic way. The Norse cosmovision appreciated a variety of goddesses and gods, mainly separated into two kith and kin – the Æsir and the Vanir.[12] The gods *Njord*, *Frøy* and *Frøya* are the only three Vanir gods that are part of the larger Norse mythology.[13] As opposed to the warrior and order function of Æsir gods such as Oðin and *Tor*, the Vanir gods are described as more concerned with lovemaking than war. The position of the Vanir gods as predominantly Nordic, as opposed to the Æsir gods which are common-Germanic, places them as powerful fertility gods in the Nordic context. In the Viking age, Frøy is the god of peace and prosperity, whereas Frøya is the goddess of love and lovemaking. The two gods are twins, and together they represent female and male love. Their father is the sea god Njord, and although their mother is unknown, she is known to be Njord's sister.

The different gods and goddesses of the Norse cosmology have been worshipped under diverse names in different regions and at different times (Näsström, 1998,

p. 18). Although this chapter's main focus is on the Viking age, it is significant to mention that research on the pre-Christian Scandinavian customs reveal the existence and continuation of a more ancient fertility cult of Mother Earth as the peace-giver in the Scandinavian region prior to the Viking age.[14] Mother Earth as a peace-giver is not solely an old Germanic heritage, but can be found in many Indo-European language cultures. Many of these share similarities to the gods and goddesses in Norse mythology.[15] Findings of goddess-statues, neck-rings, human bodies and a buried wagon can point to the existence of the cult in south Scandinavia.[16] This aspect would demand further research into the concept of peace in the pre-Viking era. In addition, cult-worship of the god Njord has been linked to the more than fifty-six sacral 'holy white stones' that witness an old phallus cult that took place in Scandinavia in about 400–600 AD. These stones have often been found in areas related to Njord names, a third of them near graves (Steinsland, 2005, pp. 144–150).[17] It is thus believed that in the Viking age Njord became a less present god, while Frøy replaced him as the principal deity of fertility and peace of the Vikings.

Frøy symbolizes peace as fertility as the highest vegetation god of the Norse. He rules over rain, sunshine and growth of the earth. He is mastering the natural forces that ensure that the harvest is good and that beings remain healthy. As the principal fertility god, he is invoked to bring about good crops. Embodying peace out of harmony, both Frøy and Frøya symbolize the highest form of lovemaking and lust, and their cult contained strong sexual elements. The activities of the fertility gods were strongly associated with sexuality. They were responsible for the union that made life continue: man and woman, seed and soil. Frøy is represented mainly through the symbol of the phallus, which stands for spontaneous life energy and becoming life. He is also represented with the symbols of the sword and ship, which are also phallus/fertility symbols.[18] As the god of love, Frøy will give everything, apples of gold, his precious sword or his horse, for the one he desires.[19]

Frøya's many characters make her the primary goddess of lovemaking in the Viking age. Similar to her brother, she promotes fertility in plants and the earth, but she is primarily known for her mastering of love between man and woman. In the myths, she is described as light and fair, and other chaos powers such as giants and dwarfs are constantly attracted to her. As the foremost fertility goddess, Frøya's most important function is to arouse the desire to make love. 'She is, as one might expect of a fertility goddess, constantly associated with sex: her legendary necklace, the Brisingamen, is paid for by sex with the dwarfs who made it' (O'Donoghue, 2007, p. 48). Frøya is also known for having sexual relations with all the elves and gods, including her own brother, and for being a *fordæða* (a witch).

The goddess does not hesitate to use her attractive powers to gain golden chains. She has plenty of gold and her daughters are called *Hnoss* (the jewel, the glittering) and *Gersimi* (gemstone). She is by other names and attributes called *Vanadis* (the Vanir's woman), *Menglad* (the one who loves necklaces), *Gullveig* (golden liquor), *Mardoll* (who shines above the ocean), *Syor* (sow or the protector), *Thrungva* (the longing one), *Skjalv* (the goddess of marriage) and *Gevjon* (the giver of good gifts), who is an agrarian goddess who masters sorcery, and has the qualities of virginity and erotic looseness. Under the name *Horn* (linen), *Frøya* is connected to the harvest of linen, which was celebrated with rites and belongs to fertility as female. The linen seeds were called the 'semen of the women' and were to be planted on Friday, Friggs-day. *Frigg* (the beloved), who is the wife of the most powerful Norse god, Oðin, is also impossible to tell apart from *Frøya*. Her name etymologically stems from *frjá*, to love. Both Frøya and Frigg have sexual relationships with their brother and father and are both trading sex for gold. According to Näsström (1998), Frøya has over time been separated into two goddesses, representing the 'weeping mother' and the 'lusty lover.'[20]

Peace and death

Frøy and Frøya thus represent peace out of fertility and harmony. However, as central fertility forces they are also in control of the underworld and the destructive, through death, power and sorcery. The Vanir gods as presented in the myths grant cosmic peace out of three aspects: life, regeneration and death. Eros and death are also strongly present in the Norse myths. Life and death are experienced as eros, and eros is energy.[21] Frøya is described as a *blotgydje*, which can mean both 'offering goddess' and 'offering priestess.' Frøya rightfully bears the role of the death goddess. She resides in *Folkvang* (people's battlefield, warlords' plain) and, similar to the Valkyries goddesses, she goes to the battlefields.[22] As the goddess of death, she chooses half of the fallen warriors killed in battle, in which the Æsir god Oðin takes the other part to Valhall. The god Frøy lives in *Alvheim* (the home of the elves), which connects him to the *alfár*, elves, who are also fertility forces in the Norse mythology connected to the death sphere.

Ideas like punishment or reward after death were not mentioned in the Norse myths; rather death was depicted as a lust-journey, or a meeting with the dead and eros (Steinsland, 1997, pp. 102–103). The Nordic religion revealed several different conceptions about the afterlife. One either went to Frøya in *Folkvang*, Odin in *Valhall* (the hall of the dead) or to the goddess *Hel* (for those who did not die in battle) and the goddess *Ran* (for those who drowned). The journeys to Frøya, Hel and Ran are depicted in Norse myths as love-meetings with the dead and the goddess, for the most part kings and heroes. Norwegian religion researcher Gro Steinsland (1997, p. 122) finds in her investigation on Norse myths death as a love-meeting, a Holy Wedding – a love alliance that binds life and death. In numerous archeological findings the love-couple are depicted together as lovers, the oldest one dating back to ca. 1000 BC showing a man and a woman stretching their arms out towards each other, the man with his phallus upright towards her. We thus have to conclude, she states, that literary and archeological sources give evidence that ideas about a wedding in death, and the connection between eros and death, are ancient beliefs in Nordic mentality.

The alliance between two oppositional forces is, as mentioned above, a central understanding of Norse cosmology. This mythological aspect also represents alliance and power. The Holy Wedding in its deeper symbolical meaning is the unification of the creator-force and the cosmological order (Nässtrōm, 1998, p. 88). Myths about the Holy Wedding would represent the erotic unification of two extreme opposites, such as giants and gods, which could again create something new and powerful. In Norse mythology the proposal of the god Frøy to the giant woman *Gjerd* witnesses symbolisms of a king-ideology.[23] Both the large Norse ruler dynasties, Ynglingætten of Uppsala in Sweden and Laderjalsætten of Hologaland in Norway, legitimized their position through the wedding-myth, by claiming to be descendants of Frøy (Steinsland, 2005, p. 406).[24]

The gods Frøy and Frøya are described in a plurality of functions that make them the gods of peace as love in the Norse context. These attributes are mythical representations that make them the Lord and the Lady of the Viking age. However, the gods would not be represented in myths were they not also a part of the daily existence of the people. The Norse worldview or mythology was an integral part of the culture and tradition.

Peace in public cult rituals

Rituals and cults were the 'tools' that enabled humans to come in contact with the mythical world, and through which human beings moved to both the otherness of time and of space of the mystical realm. People were born into the cult-community. It was thus not the *personal belief* that mattered, but the *siðr* (customs) centered on holy performance, rites and cult-practice. Here, people who did not participate in the offerings – rather than those who did not believe in the gods – were perceived as god-less (Solli, 2002, pp. 36, 80). Norse customs thus differ in many ways from 'universal' religions such as Christianity and Islam. The communication between humans and gods was of decisive relevance to the welfare of the society. In everyday life, it was important that the gods were well-willing, granted fertility for the earth or the animals and therefore one did offerings of many kinds (Schjødt, 1999, pp. 47–49).

Cult is thus a central conserving element of the Norse society. It was the cult that maintained *friðar*. For analytical purposes, we may separate the cult practice into two main categories, the public cult, which was primarily following cyclical times of the year and held by the authorities of the society, and the private or local cult-practices, which mainly concerned the household and were found in the everyday. The fertility gods were very important to both these cult-practices.

The most important public Norse cult-practice was *blót*. The noun *blót* can be connected to the verb *blóta*, offering, which also contains the meaning 'to strengthen:' one strengthened the gods with the offerings. Etymologically it could have meant to soak or splash (blood on the offering table) and offerings are often described with the word *rjóða* (red color). The offering sacrifices are generally interpreted as having the function of pleasing the gods, ensuring fertility, perpetuating the well-being of the community and/or forming a communion with the sacred. Sacrifices could be violent, bloody and frightening. They were symbolisms of a greater sacrifice that was needed in order to sustain societal harmony.[25] The offerings also served to transform social conflict: 'an act of violent and bloody sacrifice during these temporary gatherings may have served to draw attention away from interpersonal conflict and channel it in other ways' (Lucas and McGovern, 2007, p. 24). The yearly and cyclical offerings preserved the societal harmony that concerned the connection between humans and gods. However, there were also sacrifices in times of crisis, such as threats from disease, war or unfertile seasons. Offerings for crises could be both animal and human offerings (Näsström, 2001, p. 219).

Collective feasts bound humans and the gods in a fellowship, and communal offerings took place three times a year. In the Viking age, the main winter and autumn offerings were dedicated to the peace god Frøy. A large fertility *blót* also took place in the spring, to guarantee the summer's fertility and harvest, for 'good growth and peace.' The autumn feast celebrated the harvest and thanked the fertility gods for peace and prosperity: 'There is plenty of place-name evidence for a Frey cult throughout Iceland and Scandinavia, and it is especially significant, given Frey's role as a fertility deity, that fields were often named for Frey' (O'Donoghue, 2007, p. 62). At the autumn offering, the first drink would be dedicated to Frøy and Frøya *til árs ok friðr*.

The cult-formula *til ars ok friðr* expressed a wish that the farmland should be growing well and that there should be peace/love in a certain period, without interruption of any kind (war, sickness, death). In relation to the harvest, the god Frøy is depicted in myths as journeying through the land during autumn to bless the season and endorse all forms of peace as prosperity to the people, and the Norse would carry ships or wagons with a deity of Frøy over fields in order to bless them and ensure good growth. The ritual continued until far into the Middle Ages; however, at that time the Frøy deity was substituted with local saint-images (Steinsland, 2005, pp. 144–154; Näsström, 1998, p. 75). Sources regarding mid-summer celebrations are few and sporadic. However, there is a possibility that there were larger feasts also in the summer containing a strong presence of fertility rites (Näsström, 2001, pp. 225–227).

The winter feast for the god Frøy, *Jol*, in the month *jylir*, intended to assist humans and gods to overcome the darkness and the cold.[26] Greasy food, heavy drinks and the gathering of kith and kin made the feast a central aspect of the mid-winter offering. It represented the exuberance of the farm, lasted for several days and it was a bad sign if it ended too early. The gods were invited to taste the abundance of the household, in order to assist them in ensuring the prosperity of the living in the year to come (Näsström, 2001, p. 222). Frøy's holy animal, the pig, was the main offering, but there is also evidence of oxen and horsemeat as part of the celebration.[27] The holy gatherings were celebrated with the offering of food and drinks to the gods, which the people consumed in communion. *Alu or øl* (beer) was essential to these feasts, where ritual toasts for the gods Oðin, Tor, Frøy and Njord were a widespread practice. The Vikings also toasted the deceased forefathers, or they drunk a *bragefull*, which entailed making promises for heroic acts one would do in the future. This drink was believed to grant humans powers, lift people to another sphere, and was only drunk on bigger occasions. Important celebrations such as birth, marriage and death were also celebrated with the holy drink (Steinsland, 2005, p. 277).

The notion of peace is essential to pre-Christian fertility cult-practices, which were centered on *ár ok friðr*. The offerings brought people together in a holy congregation, and through the sacrifices people united with each other and with the fertility gods. Other words that were central to the cult-gatherings were *heilag*, holy, and *heill*, luck. These notions point to the centrality of the cult: the holy meeting recreated harmony and order and a sense of togetherness. The cult gatherings were also important to the society's economic system. At the larger communal offerings, everyone would partake with foods and goods, and the sharing and redistribution of commodities at these gatherings was essential to the overall function of the society. In some cases, such as with the king dynasty in Uppsala, Sweden, the king or ruler would be the central distributor of the goods and resources, and would thus be seen as the guarantor of the execution offering rituals *til ars ok friðr* (Steinsland, 2005, pp. 274–280).

The public cult-rituals maintained the societal and holy order, and conserved and justified the role of the societal authorities. The men were in charge of the larger and public offerings, as well as political and juridical discussions, but within the more local cult connected to the well-being of the farm and farmland, women were often the cult-leaders. In the local cult-practice, where the people of the house would sacrifice both animal and non-animal offerings to the relevant gods, collective powers, especially female, played an important role. Frøy and Frøya were called for also in the private cult, which mainly concerned the inner borderlines of the farm.

Peace in local cult rituals

It is believed that Frøya and Frøy were the recipients of local and esoteric offerings to the collective powers *diser* (female powers) and elves. It is believed that offerings to the elves were received by Frøy (Holtsmark, 1989, p. 93), whereas offerings to the female powers were received by Frøya. The purpose of these offerings was to retain health after death or an accident, or it was connected to the harvest and ripeness of the soil, and human and animal reproduction. However, due to the erotic and 'secret' character of some of these rituals, it is difficult to access their meaning in written sources (Näsström, 1998, p. 150; Steinsland, 2005, p. 345).

These private offerings could also be offerings to the forefathers. The Norse were preoccupied with death and both archeological and Norse literature shows that in the Viking age people had manifold conceptions and ideas connected to death, funerals and the afterlife; expressed through myths, symbolisms, rites and cult (Steinsland, 1997, pp. 97–98). The Vikings performed both burial and cremation rituals. There was no conception of *eternal* life after death; death was an invitation to a new dimension of existence where there were different possibilities than in life. Fundamental to this understanding was the belief that the deceased still protected kith and kin, and the kinship thus included both living and dead. As such, it was a dimension that could be crossed into also by the living. Graves from the Viking age reveal much about the rituals of the Norse.

Frøy was, together with his twin sister, associated with local *rites de passage* such as childbirth and marriage.[28] However, although one can affirm that both Frøy and Frøya have mythical symbolisms connected to these rituals, little is known of how the gods were actually invoked in the rites. Childbirth was an unsafe process both for the mother and the child, as such different forms of powers were often called to assist, and Frøya is known to have been called for at births. The child, when born, was attuned to his/her destiny from the female powers under the Life Tree (Steinsland, 2005, pp. 328, 336). Marriages served as important rituals not only for the two who married, but for the whole kin and society: through marriages, two kin became connected by law. Weddings were performed by the bride and the groom taking each other's hand. The last wedding drink would be proposed for Frøya (Näsström, 2001, p. 235; 1998, p. 185).

Peace in societal relations

One cannot speak of a 'universal' concept of peace in the context of Norse society, neither is the peace found in this chapter representing a moral or ethical position. There was no notion of morality *per se* in the Norse customs.[29] Societal borderlines were rather formed through patterns of honor and shame; manifold, composite and crossing beyond reason and needs (Steinsland, 1997, p. 35). The communal peace belonged to kith and kin and concerned the balance of forces in the cosmos of the Norse. The communal aspect of *friðr* is found in the demarcation of its etymology in granting human belonging to the kinship. *Ætt* is connected to the verb *eiga*, meaning 'that which belongs to one' or 'that one is related to' (Steinsland, 2005, p. 362). Children inherited from both the mother's and father's side of the family and thus the family relations were complex and important. The formation of the society and laws drew lines of hierarchical structures. Those on the top of the hierarchy, as expected, had more benefits than those at the bottom. At the very bottom was the *trell* (slave) who was owned by another person and thus was named *ufri* (not free). Life as a *trell* was a life without any basic rights and the social status was inherited. However, the farmer/owner could decide to release the slave from his/her status, *frjálsa* (liberate, set free), and lift her/him into the free constituency.

The clearest social borderline was thus marked within the very notion of peace, of which peace meant societal belonging. Around each individual, there was a circle of peace, *friðr*, out of holiness, stemming from the word *heill*, whole or undamaged (Steinsland, 2005, p. 367). No person was allowed to break this holiness, and any breach of this law onto an individual, such as shaming or sexual violations, was considered an infringement of the honor of the whole kin. Being part of the kinship is thus directly related to a notion of peace. The worst that could happen to a human being was to be excluded from the societal belonging and kinship, and to lose property and personal peace; to become *útlegd* or *friðlauss* (peaceless; meaning outlawed) (Steinsland, 1997, p. 36).

Central to the Norse *ethos* were traits such as loyalty, friendship and honor (Solli, 2002, pp. 35, 71). Honor served as a demarcation line that ensured that people followed the laws of the society. Although the Norse society did not have any juridical body, social conflict was solved in a highly organized way. The *ting* (assembly) was a gathering of free men within a geographically marked-off territory, which served the purpose of discussing laws and matters that concerned common interests. As soon as the area in which the *ting* would be held was settled, it was considered holy and one was not allowed to bring weapons there or disturb the *friðr*. The condition of *friðr* was endorsed by the god Frøy: '[i]n accordance with Freyr's peacekeeping role, he banned weapons from his temples. Bloodshed on his sacred land angers him' (Gimbutas, 1999, p. 195). A man who brought weapons, or broke the holy peace, would be called *varg i veum* (a wolf on the holy place) (Steinsland, 2005, pp. 371–372).

Knowledge and transcendence

Above, *friðr* is found to be a central signifier for the societal togetherness brought about by cult-gatherings, as well as a forming aspect of the *ethos* of the kinship. Rather than a moral code of right and wrong, honor and shame were markers of the Norse societal boundaries. Another demarcation line in the Norse society was gender, and the roles attributed to the two sexes. In Norse society, dress codes and codes for behavior constructed a clear line between what was considered manly and what was considered female. However, in some cult-practices the performances aimed at crossing beyond the general societal boundaries, and selected people performing the rites could transgress into behavior that would normally be met with despise. This contact with the godly world could only be achieved through the crossing of the regular societal boundaries (Solli, 2002, p. 235). Frøya, the goddess of lovemaking and death, was also the goddess of the most powerful and unbound practice in the Viking age: *seiðr* (sorcery, magic).

The practice of *seiðr* did not nurture fertility, reproduction and health as normally assigned to the Vanir-cult. It was primarily a practice performed by women and, in contrast to the public and private rituals, a practice that belonged to the margins of society. Its relevance to the concept of peace lies in the transcendental function of the practice, which is a necessary trait for gaining knowledge and power in order to keep the cosmos in balance. The Norse worldview included a vision of powerful forces both in the external world and in the internal depth of the human psyche that, through dangerous or unconventional excursions and practices, were to be used, fought and tamed in order to generate energy, gain powerful insights and keep a cosmological balance. In her role as the goddess of lovemaking and sorcery, Frøya represents the highest form of transcendence.

The Norse believed that humans had an outer soul, a *fylgje*, which had an animal skin and could leave the body. The *hugen*, thought, could also leave the body, especially in dreams; those who lost the thought went mad. The Norse word for soul was *ond*, which has the same etymological root as *ånde* (to breathe). *Seid* led to ecstasy, and in ecstasy the soul left the body and one could do soul-travel or get help from spirits to see into the future (Solli, 2002, pp. 129–130, 173). The Norse worldview was an open life view where the quest for knowledge was limitless (Steinsland, 1997, p. 127). It was in transcendence that the highest virtue and ultimate power resided: knowledge. The ritual access to the realm of the gods did not only aim to connect with the powers, it *was* power (Steinsland, 2005, p. 29). *Seid*-practice could reveal that which was hidden, in presence and future, and find that which had gone missing. The collective survival of the kin was thus dependent on finding a powerful sorcerer who could generate knowledge, do soul-traveling and connect to the forefathers and gods (Solli, 2002, p. 167).

The Viking society thus included complex societal agents that as mentioned above were dynamic and relational. Cult-rituals could be collective gatherings ensuring fertility and harmony. But they also functioned as energetic, cultural agents that could perform social critique and creative stimulation. Above all, the rituals created contact with the non-human powers of the cosmos.

Although the main focus of this chapter has been the old Norse understanding of peace, it cannot be representative for an old Scandinavian past without mentioning the Sami conception of the word. The similarities between the Norse customs and the pre-Christian Sami religion are many, including the ecstatic practices, such as *seid* and shamanism, and divinatory techniques to predict the future and past (Andersen, 2008). Contact and exchanges of goods between the Norse and the indigenous Sami population in Scandinavia were recurrent in the pre-Christian era, and they were considered equal 'partners' until the kingdom gradually changed the societal power structure during the Middle Ages (Solli, 2002, pp. 194–197). Thus, '[i]n spite of different cultures with different languages, different ways of living and different religions the contact between the Nordic people on the Scandinavian peninsula and their Sami neighbors must have been rather close' (Mundal, 2000, p. 346).[30] The Sami languages have no word for war. The word for peace, *rafí*, can mean to be in harmony, to have soul-peace. Furthermore, the expression can also be connected to the underworld, as in the expression *ráfen oadit*, which means to sleep in peace (not be bothered by the subterranean).

The moral peace

Christianity came late to the Scandinavian countries compared to the rest of Europe. The Norse had known about Christianity and been in contact with the religion through trading and looting, long before the Nordic countries were Christianized.[31] The concept of peace in the context of a Christian Scandinavia as unified under kingdoms requires a more comprehensive analysis than will be provided below. However, in order to place the etymological meaning of peace in a contemporary understanding, it is necessary to situate the old Norse concept in the larger societal and political changes that came about with the Christianizing of Scandinavia from about 1000 AD.* As described above, in the pre-Christian era, the concept of peace was rooted in the deep culture of Norse society. Peace belonged to kith and kin, and concerned an ongoing exchange with the Norse gods. With the new religion, the relationship between human beings, gods and the cosmos would be challenged with a new belief system and a new set of laws drawn along moral and ethical lines.

The Christianizing of Scandinavia can be seen in close relation to the power changes with the congregation of one kingdom from about 800 to 1000 AD. Norse customs did not disappear because they were a dying form of religion, but because they were not compatible with the new power-political circumstances (Solli, 2002, pp. 232–238). From around 1000 AD, the establishment of a new set of laws that followed the Christianizing of northern countries brought about a reinterpretation of the word peace as love: there was a banning of Norse god-worship; peace as harmony, fertility and lovemaking were no longer accepted in their erotic and female nature; the practice of *seid* was forbidden; and new laws changed the form of rituals.

---

* Ed. In the Introduction and Final Remarks, different 'peace families' – among them moral peaces – are explained in a more lengthy manner, referring precisely to what Jacobsen here mentions in regards to how the notion of peace changes and is changed by morality and religious norms.

The Christian law forbade the housing of pagan god images and punishments for not obeying this law were hard. The highlights of Christian missionary tales were the destruction and burning of pagan god-images; by destroying the image one destroyed the power of the god (Steinsland, 2005, p. 293). Where the Norse *siðr* had its main focus on kinship, Christianity focused on individual sin and destiny. In the new religion, Christianity, these concepts were to form the normative frames for human beings in life as well as death:

> It must have been difficult for people in Nordic countries – especially in inner parts where knowledge of the Christian faith was poor – to comprehend the essential contents of a human life bound to sin and need for liberation and blessing. That sin and liberation should be the basis of view of human life and ethics was something fundamentally new in relation to the moral playing rules of the pre-Christian society. There, moral demands were governed by a pattern of honor and shame. (Steinsland, 1997, p. 157 [trans. by author])

With Christianity came one God, omniscient and good. In this worldview, existence is experienced in dualisms, good and evil, not in a constant dynamism, which was the cosmovision of the Norse. Christian laws from the Middle Ages forbade strongly the practice of all forms of sorcery: *seid* was named as witchcraft and forbidden by the priesthood, and if caught and judged guilty one became outlawed from society. The fact that there was a stark attention drawn to this topic in the laws shows that sorcery and rituals must have been widely practiced throughout the Middle Ages: 'Out from written sources it is not an exaggeration to say that we *know* that there was an endeavor to combat Pagan phenomenon such as *seid* and sorcery throughout the Christian Middle Age. Especially women accused of sorcery got a misfortunate destiny' (Solli, 2002, p. 77 [trans. by author]). Sorcery had been an active and dynamic rite that could change and transform knowledge on the divine and this practice threatened the Christian priesthood and doctrine. With the establishment of a male priesthood, female participation in religious rites or customs faded away, and this changed the position and role model of women in Nordic countries. Women, who earlier had an equal status to men in the farmland, now became subjugated to men in both the public and private belief system.

However, researchers also point to the continuity of some of the rituals of the pagan traditions, even after Norway was officially Christianized. One example of this is how places still carried names of pagan gods, without having shown signs of changes throughout the Middle Ages (Rindal, 1996, p. 17). The autumn rites of peace as fertility and growth were not completely rejected with the change in religion. For example, in the older *Gulatingssloven* from the western part of Norway, it states that the farmers should brew beer before All Saints Day 'and all should bless this beer with thanks to Christ and The Holy Maria for good growth and peace (*til árs ok friðar*)' (Näsström, 1998, p. 151). The celebration of Virgin Maria became very popular in the Nordic countries, and many of the names and functions that had earlier been attributed to the goddess Frøya and the Vanir gods were now captured in the image of the Holy Mother. She would be called for at birth and weddings and at cyclical, yearly celebrations. Perception of death changed radically (Solli, 2002, pp. 73, 179, 233–239).

Most importantly to the notion of peace as fertility and harmony, however, is the changing view on sexuality that came about with the Christianizing of Scandinavian countries. Female powers that had been part of the Norse cosmology were not appropriate for the new religion where gender-moral and the moral of sin/salvation became coexistent and inseparable (Solli, 2002, p. 71). The goddess Frøya, representing lovemaking, eroticism and sorcery, would be deemed a witch and a prostitute, a work of the devil (Näsström, 1998, p. 188). The erotic and dynamic symbolisms that had formed the fertility cult and the concept of peace would change during the Christian Middle Ages. Although cult-practices are known to have continued, the concept of peace as love can be seen to have changed into a love out of morality, a peace to be found in the granted salvation of the Christian god.

The contemporary peace

As this chapter has demonstrated, the notion of peace in Scandinavian discourses and practices does not possess a 'fixed' meaning or values. Rather, it holds diverse meanings at different times and contexts which, as part of the belief system and internalized in the society, have become a rarely questioned, shared phenomena.[32] In the context of contemporary Scandinavian society, the word peace can be found somewhat detached from its etymological root. In its modern form *fred*, peace, predominantly signifies an 'absence of war.' It also means an absence of social conflict or disagreement of which comes the vernacular expression *leve i fred*, to live in peace (with one's neighbors). In addition, *fred* can be a condition of silence and harmony, from which comes the expression *sjelefred*, which can be translated as soul-peace or peace in death. Although these expressions for peace have dissimilar connotations in today's society than in the Viking age, they still carry remainders of an old Scandinavian past.

The concept of peace as found in an old Norse context speaks from a past that is relatively unknown to contemporary popular and academic discourses on peace. The old Scandinavian meaning of peace as *love* in harmony and fertility thus remains a concept to be explored further. From a peace research perspective, the legitimate question might arise: Where do we place the etymological meaning of peace as found in Norse mythology and cult-practices in contemporary peace science and which relevance do we appoint to it? As presented in this chapter, the etymological notion of peace is rooted in the language and context of Norse and thus can claim to have a cultural validity in the Viking era. A trans-disciplinary approach may be an insightful way of interpreting peace in Norse society in relation to contemporary peace research. European and Scandinavian peace research would be broadened with a deeper integration of etymological and mythological interpretations of peace.

Notes

1. Persian Ibn Horradadbeh (820–912 AD) is the first author mentioning the people *al-rus* and thus the Nordic region. He describes the region as the world's 'end.' For elaboration on other old sources describing old Norse Scandinavia see Solli (2002, pp. 24–25).
2. The 'Norse' language was formed in the syncope of the time period 500–700 AD.
3. See, for example, Steinsland (1997, 2005), Solli (2002), Mundal (1990, 2000), Gimbutas (1999), Onsell (1999) and Näsström (1996, 1998, 2001).
4. *Fred* means peace in today's Norwegian, Swedish and Danish. In Icelandic, peace is *friður*.
5. See Ordnett (2009) and Avdeling for Leksikografi (1986) for these two meanings of peace.
6. The time was perceived as cyclical, and there were as such no 'historic' events, rather an ongoing continuation following the rhythm of the agricultural work. See Steinsland (2005, p. 106).
7. See, for example, Solli (2002, p. 79), Steinsland (1997, p. 18).
8. According to Thorpe (2001, pp. 114–115) there are in total nine worlds in Norse mythology: *Muspellheim* (abode of Muspell's sons), *Åsgard* or *Godheim* (world of Æsir gods), *Vanaheim* (abode of the Vanir gods), *Midtgard* (the world of men), *Alfheim* (for the elves), *Svart-alfheim* (inhabited by swart-elves and dwarfs), *Utgard* (inhabited by *jotuns* or giants), *Helheim* (the death realm of Hel) and *Niflheim* (the farthest north, inhabited, older than heaven and earth).
9. See Steinsland (2005, pp. 107, 271) and Steinsland (1997, p. 35) for further elaboration on the symbolism of the Life Tree.
10. Ragnarok is the end of the world, of human beings and gods, which will begin by the death of the most beautiful of all gods, *Balder*, and end with a large, gruesome war in which the humans will assist the gods against the giants and other powerful chaos forces. The myth about Ragnarok also reveals that after the end of the world, a new world will arise. See Holtsmark (1989, p. 68).
11. This understanding of peace resonates with energetic peace cultures of the Great Mother (Dietrich, 2008). Peace in an energetic cosmovision is situated within the notion of fertility and harmony and sees a primordial cosmic energy as the source of all being. Human existence is perceived as the micro-cosmos which participates in harmony with the macro-cosmos. In an energetic concept of peace, there are only dynamical relationships. For further elaborations on energetic concepts of peace and the Great Mother, see Dietrich (2008, pp. 36, 94–98).
12. According to place-names *Tor*, *Frøya*, *Frøy*, *Njord* and *Oðin* appear to have been the most popularly worshipped gods in Scandinavia during the Viking age. See Näsström (1998, p. 13).
13. In Norse myths, the Vanir gods came to the Æsir after what is described as a 'first war,' which ended through an agreement sealed with each side spitting into a vessel and exchanging hostages, whereupon *Njord*, *Frøy* and *Frøya* are given to the Æsir. Even

though the Vanir gods stand equal to the Æsir in their new home, they never lose their particular attributes. For further elaboration on the myth about the 'first war' see Steinsland (2005, p. 136), Solli (2002, p. 38) and Edwardes and Spence (2003, p. 180).

14. Researchers agree that Njord is identical with the peace goddess Nerthus described in the Roman Publius Cornelius Tacitus' *Germania* during the first century AD and their etymological root is identical. According to Tacitus, the goddess Nerthus was worshipped by several Germanic tribes as Mother Earth. At certain seasons she would travel in her chariot, accompanied by festival rejoicings and she would spread peace and plenty over the length of all lands she passed (Edwardes and Spence, 2003, p. 124). The spring feast was joyful, and no war was fought and iron (weapons) was to be hidden away. All belonging to her was sacred, and could only be touched by the priest. The same aspects of the peace and fertility cult are in the Viking age found in the gods Frøy and Frøya. See Solli (2002, pp. 39, 115–116) and Näsström (1998, p. 54; 1997, p. 107) for further elaboration.

15. For example, the Roman goddess Kybele. See Näsström (1998, p. 57).

16. The discovery in Denmark in the 1800s of a buried wagon that was highly decorated points to the possibility that there was an old Norse cult similar to that of Nerthus in south Scandinavia. See Steinsland (2005, p. 147).

17. In Norway, there are about 30 place-names that can be connected to the Njord-cult (Solli, 2002, p. 39).

18. The ship is also a symbol for the death ship. See Näsström (1998, p. 44).

19. The 'apples of gold' represent in Norse myths youth that was granted to the gods (by having a bite of them). It is also a fertility symbol. The sword can be seen as representing the phallus. 'The one he loved' is here referring to the giant woman Gjerd and Frøy's proposal to her as told in Norse myths. See Steinsland (2005, p. 155).

20. It is considered that Frøya, as with many other great goddesses of Indo-European heritage, has been worshipped under many names in the course of time and through various interpretations has become separated into different goddesses. See Näsström (1998, pp. 56, 95–97, 116–122, 128–129) for further elaboration on the separation of one goddess Frøya into goddesses under various names and attributes of Frøya.

21. Näsström (1998) sees Frøya, as the Great Goddess of the Nordic region, as encompassing life, death and regeneration. I have in this chapter considered both Frøy and Frøya as important in representing the three aspects.

22. The Valkyries are goddesses that reside with the god Oðin in Valhall. They go to the battlefields where they choose warriors that will in death come to Valhall to join the gods in endless war mongering and feasts to prepare for the final battle, which will lead to Ragnarok, the end of the world.

23. For an elaboration on this myth and its relevance to the king dynasties (through the symbols of a ring, apples and a stick), see Steinsland (2005, pp. 393–420).

24. In Scandinavia the so-called *gullgubbene*, small golden plaques, which are reminiscences of cult rituals from 600 to 900 A.D. have been found. Many of these show men and women in a loving embrace, which might imply the Holy Wedding between god and goddess (Näsström, 1998, p. 40). The Holy Wedding as a ritual is connected to power, as described in relation to the fertility god Frøy. It is believed that these plaques can witness a cult practice in the pattern of the wedding of Gjerd and Frøy (Steinsland, 2005, p. 400).

25. Several of the Norse myths expressing offering ideals connect it to the acquiring of knowledge and power or to the god's wish to gain more resources to combat antagonists. It was not only the human beings who offered to the gods, to strengthen them or to receive their good will, but the gods would also offer themselves to gain

power or knowledge necessary to retain cosmological harmony. The greatest warrior god, Oðin, offered his own eye, and hung in the Life Tree for nine days and nights, in order to gain knowledge and the power of the Runes. See Solli (2002, p. 162).

26. The world *jol* has survived as a marker also for the Christian winter celebration of the birth of Jesus Christ. Christmas in Scandinavian languages is also today called *jul*.

27. See, for example, Steinsland (2005, p. 275; 1997, p. 88). Towards the summer – the time of the year when the Viking raids begun – the offering was dedicated to Oðin for victory and luck in war.

28. *Rites de passage* can be explained as transition rites and are important in cultures to move from one condition to another. They can be initiation rites. See Solli (2002, pp. 88–93).

29. See Solli (2002) and Steinsland (2006) for an elaboration on the Norse ethos.

30. The pre-Christian Sami conception of the world was three dimensional: an upper part for the heavens and heavenly gods (heaven), a middle part for humans (earth) and a lower up-side-down world, which is the land of the dead (underworld). The *noaid* is the most important communicator between these three worlds/dimensions, and had to go through hard tests and rites, such as meeting with his/her *gadzer*, help-spirits, to be chosen for this task. Central to the pre-Christian Sami conception of reality is that almost all beings, humans and animals, have two souls, one connected to the body and the other to a 'freesoul' attached to the inner being. The latter can leave the body and travel. See Solli (2002, pp. 172–173).

31. The Vikings settled in regions far from their homeland, including Iceland, the Faeroe Islands, Man, Hebridene, Ireland, Normandy, Greenland and Newfoundland. See Steinsland (2005, p. 97).

32. See Fry (2006, p. 83) and MacGinty (2006, p. 15) for an elaboration on the importance of historical and contextual interpretation of peace.

Reference list

Andersen, O. (2008) Personal Communication (November 13, 2008).

Avdeling for Leksikografi (1986) *Bokmålsordboka: Definisjons- og rettskrivingsordbok* (Oslo: Universitetet i Oslo & Universitetsforlaget).

Dietrich, W. (2008) *Variationen über die vielen Frieden*, Band 1: Deutungen (Wiesbaden: VS Verlag).

Edwardes, M. and L. Spence (2003) *Dictionary of Non-Classical Mythology* (Montana: Kessinger Publishing).

Fry, D.P. (2006) *The Human Potential for Peace: An Anthropological Challenge to Assumptions about War and Violence* (New York/Oxford: Oxford University Press).

Gimbutas, M. (1999) *The Living Goddesses*, edited and supplemented by M. Robbins Dexter (Berkley: University of California Press).

Holtsmark, A. (1989) *Norrøn Mytologi: Tru og Mytar i Vikingtida* (Oslo: Det Norske Samlaget).

Lucas, G. and T. McGovern (2007) 'Bloody Slaughter: Ritual Decaptivation and Display at the Viking Settlement of Hofstaðir, Iceland,' *European Journal of Archaeology*, 10, 1, 7–30.

MacGinty, R. (2006) *No War, No Peace: The Rejuvenation of Stalled Peace Processes and Peace Accords* (New York: Palgrave Macmillan).

Mundal, E. (1990) 'Forholdet mellom gudar og jotnar i norrøn mytologi i lys av det mytologiske navnematerialet,' *Tidskrift för nordisk personnamnsforskning*, 8 (Uppsala: Studia Anthroponymica Scandinavica).

Mundal, E. (2000) 'Coexistence of Sami and Norse Culture – Reflected in and Interpreted by Old Norse Myths,' paper presented at the 11th International Saga Conference, *Centre for Medieval Studies* (Sydney: University of Sydney), 346–355, http://www.arts.usyd. edu.au/departs/medieval/saga/pdf/346-mundal.pdf, date accessed December 10, 2008.

Näsström, B.M. (1996) 'Freyja and Frigg: Two Aspects of the Great Goddess,' in J. Pentikäinen (ed.) *Shamanism and Northern Ecology* (Berlin: Mouton de Gruyter), 81–97.

Näsström, B.M. (1998) *Frøya: Den store gudinnen i norden*, trans. by Kåre A. Lie (Oslo: Pax Forlag A/S).

Näsström, B.M. (2001) *Forn Scandinavisk Religion: En Grundbok* (Sweden: Studentlitteratur).

O'Donoghue, H. (2007) *From Asgard to Valhalla: The Remarkable History of the Norse Myths* (London: IB Tauris & Co. Ltd).

Onsell, B. (1999) *Jordens Moder i Norden* (Stockholm: Carlssons Bokförlag).

Ordnett (2009) *Kunnskapsforlagets blå språk og ordbokstjeneste*, http://www.ordnett.no, date accessed January 10, 2009.

Pigott, G. (1839) *A Manual of Scandinavian Mythology Containing a Popular Account of the Two Eddas and of the Religion of Odin*, illust. from Oehlenschlager's Danish Poem the Gods of the North (London: William Pickering).

Rindal, M. (ed.) (1996) *Fra Hedendom til Kristendom: Perspektiver på Religionsskiftet i Norge* (Norway: Ad Notam Gyldendal).

Schjødt, J.P. (1999) *Det Førkristine Norden: Religion og mytholgi* (Copenhagen: Spektrum/ Forum).

Solli, B. (2002) *Seid: Myter, Sjamanisme og Kjønn i Vikingenes Tid* (Oslo: Pax Forlag A/S).

Steinsland, G. (1997) *Eros og Død i Norrønne Myter* (Oslo: Universitetsforlaget AS).

Steinsland, G. (2005) *Norrøn Religion: Myter, Riter, Samfunn* (Oslo: Pax Forlag A/S).

Thorpe, B. (2001) *Northern Mythology: From Pagan Faith to Local Legends* (London: Wordsworth Editions Limited).

Section II
Peace Concepts in the Middle East

6
Shalom: A Jewish Perspective

Marc H. Ellis

> The world is a creation, not a reflection, not semblance, not play. The world is not something which must be overcome. The world is a created reality, a reality created to be hallowed.
>
> Martin Buber

Shalom is known throughout the world as the Hebrew word for peace. But it also is related to *shelemut*, meaning wholeness. Included here is a sense of harmony, of right living and relation.* In classical Hebrew, the opposite of *Shalom* is not war but *mahloket*, which means divisiveness or quarrel. The struggle to overcome this divisiveness is the task of *tikkun olam*, the mending of the world, traditionally with reference to the struggle to bring about God's rule on earth. As Arthur Green, the Lown Professor of Jewish Thought at Brandeis University, points out, in contemporary usage *tikkun olam* 'refers to the betterment of the world, including the relief of human suffering, the achievement of peace and mutual respect among the peoples, and the protection of the planet itself from destruction' (Green, 1999, p. 175). *Shalom* is the place from which the mending of the world goes forth; the mending of the world ushers in an era of *Shalom*, the messianic time when brokenness and divineness comes to an end.

In their journey through time, these ancient words have become conceptual frameworks and foundational images through which Jews live and see the world. Therefore, they are ancient and always conceptual; primal and renewed. For Jews, the question is always one of the now, infused with layerings from the past that reverse our modern understanding of history as a linear rendering of the human journey with progress at the center.† This history is, for the most part, without interruption; the only exception is the temporary break of retrogressive corruption or a barbarism defined as primitive. The forces of history will be

---

* Ed. In Chapter 3, Francisco Muñoz and Beatriz Molina discuss the word *Shalom* and peace within a Mediterranean framework.
† Ed. For more on linear chronosophy see Chapter 1 by Wolfgang Dietrich.

triumphant and, successfully combating regression, the linear march of history continues on without abeyance.

Inherent in this advance is a universalization of what once was particular, and at the same time a cleansing of the primal. Universal history is empire on the largest scale; to become a reality the intermediate empires must be combated and ultimately excised from history. The ancient that does survive is then pressed into the service of the universal.

Yet at times the ancient becomes contextualized in another, more subversive way. It becomes a challenge to empire and when defeated becomes an exile. Still this displacement continues on in a fragmented manner, awaiting another day and time. At some point, it becomes the fuel of a new consideration of the world and its possibilities; it may even become the foundation for the emergence of a new particularity.

Is this the trajectory of Jewish history, mirroring the complex interaction of ancient and contemporary, particular and universal, empire and the search for community? The Exodus narrative, then and now, carried by the Israelites and then the Jews, is now released into the world as the foundation for those who struggle for peace, justice and reconciliation in a world characterized by the cycle of violence and atrocity. The words themselves and the conceptual sensibility they invoke – *shalom, tikkun olam* – are needed now more than ever.

The drama unfolds. In this need, the Jewish people as a whole fail their own appointed destiny. The community, at least those who have adopted empire as their cause and security, employ the terminology in the service of a linear history that they themselves have been victims of. Thus, the very depth of peace and the mending of the world become forms of violence; as protection to the recently surviving community, the Jewish establishment substitutes empty gestures for the real engagement in an attempt to disguise culpability with the pretense of innocence. Is it any different with any other community or nation?

Here I write of the people Israel now emboldened with a state. Also of the Holocaust, the six million, who perished under the ideological banner of the Third Reich and the silent complicity of the religion of Europe, Christianity: Israel as an understandable response to the helplessness of the Jews of Europe; nationalism as the possible repair of the Jewish world *after*; misunderstanding, tragic yet understandable, that placing Jewish before state would change the nature of nationalism. After suffering so often under the various banners of collective undertakings, Jews should have known better. Paradoxically, Jews *were* the warning points, the trip wire, of collective insanity of the engaged collectivities but also of mobilized religiosity.

No more. Today the Jewish establishment in America and Israel has modified the Jewish tradition of ethics and morality almost out of existence; the words are mouthed, the meaning transformed. A marginalized people have come into power, as have alliances that once were arrayed against us. A Constantinian

Judaism has arisen that embodies the concord of synagogue and state much like the earlier pact of church and state in the era of Constantine and beyond. Religion in service to the state is the subservience of religion to power; all the political, economic, intellectual and spiritual resources of the community are then oriented to this service. Those values and abilities that once confronted unjust power are reoriented toward security and affluence of the community, even if both are purchased with injustice toward others.*

Yet the reality is complex. Emerging in the wake of the neo-conservative shift in the Jewish world are other Jewish individuals and groups, progressive and more, who stake a claim to the history of Jews and Judaism as a counterforce to empire. For them the journey of the people of Israel is found in a particularity that moves toward community within and peace with other communities, a communal enterprise characterized by a dual thrust of particularity and universality. Opposing Constantinian Judaism, these Jews are found in Israel, America and elsewhere; they are dissenters within, though they are often seen, at least by Constantinian Jews, as outsiders to the Jewish community. Though the issues are wide ranging and variegated, the central issue of dissent revolves around the use of new-found Jewish power in the world, especially against the Palestinians,† and the particular alliances made to project that power, especially alliance with white dominance and America in a global capitalist system.

Still more complexity. The civil war between Constantinian and progressive Jews, a war over the very meaning of Jewish existence in the world, is confronted by another, even smaller group of Jews, Jews of conscience. These Jews see that a further critique of Constantinian and progressive Jews is needed; indeed Jews of conscience see a fundamental alliance of the two in their inability to confront fully the assimilation of the Jewish community to the values of affluence and empire. The main issue here is, once again, Palestine and the refusal of progressive Jews to deepen their critique of Israel's historic and enduring policies toward the Palestinians.

For Jews of conscience the very enterprise of Israel is called into question. For example, while progressive Jews limit their critique to Israeli policies in the occupied Palestinian territories after Israel's victory in the 1967 war, Jews of conscience point to the very injustice of the creation of the state in 1948 and the massive Palestinian refugee crisis it engendered. As options for the future, progressive Jews have supported the Oslo Accords and the Geneva Accords as possible compromises that Jews and Palestinians should agree on; Jews of conscience have raised serious questions about the viability and the very justice of such accords that leave so little for Palestinians and do not raise the possibility of a healing of the land and both peoples in mutual equality and justice.

---

* Ed. In Chapter 1, Dietrich offers an in-depth discussion of the relationships between moral and modern understandings of peace and notions of security and justice.

† Ed. Munir Fasheh examines peace in Palestine through his personal lenses in Chapter 7.

So a civil war on a number of levels and a serious one at that. After the Holocaust, can Jews be criticized, from outside or within, for seeking a power that prohibits another event of mass death? In a world that stood by as the Jews were murdered *en masse* in the heart of civilized Europe, can we expect Jews to seek an arrangement with the world where they are dependent on the protection of others? Too, the question of God, an important consideration for a people whose existence is in its origins political and religious, is at stake. Jews could not depend on humanity *or* God for rescue. Thus the logical, compelling sensibility is the systematic pursuit of empowerment without regard for collateral damage, an understanding that both Constantinian and progressive Jews have of the Palestinians.

The emergence of Holocaust theology, 1966–1988

The need for empowerment is clearly political but the framework for that politics is also important. In the aftermath of the Holocaust, a series of intellectual and spiritual searches began that issued into books, lectures and conferences to form a coherent and recognizable body of work known as Holocaust theology. Broadly considered, this theology spoke to the Jewish people, to the heritage and contemporary journey of the Jews; it probed the Biblical and Talmudic narratives of God, the covenant and the prophetic as they applied to the situation of people after the Holocaust and with the emergence of the state of Israel. This Holocaust theology movement had two distinct phases, the first from 1966 to 1974, the second from 1974 to 1988.

The first phase particularly dealt with God and the covenant: What could Jews believe about a God who had chosen the Jews as a people and promised to be with them, but had been absent during the Holocaust? After the Holocaust, could Jews affirm their reality as a covenanted people, with or without God? None of the Holocaust theologians affirmed God as certainty after the Holocaust; all affirmed the need for Jews to continue on as a people after the Holocaust. There was also an agreement that only through empowerment could the continuity of the people be structured in a material way: Israel is that structure, embodying the millennial hopes of the return to Zion and the concrete need for a safe haven against the threat of another Holocaust.

Both God and the covenant – indeed the Holocaust itself – were articulated within the victory of Israel in the 1967 Arab–Israeli war. That victory allowed the questions of the Holocaust to surface in a public way for the first time. Israel, known and admired within the broader Jewish world, was also raised to a new level of public articulation. Thus, in a short period of time these two events, for the most part unnamed and marginal to Jewish identity, became central to Jewish discourse and identification. Moreover, from that moment on the two events were twinned not only chronologically, the Holocaust ending in 1945, Israel becoming a state in 1948, but also conceptually. In some ways the center of Jewish religiosity and affirmation shifted precipitously in the wake of the 1967 war; to this day normative Judaism sees a critical discussion of either – how the Holocaust is used as a place of unaccountability, Israeli policies toward the Palestinians – as an attack on Judaism and Jews. Indeed, they are seen unequivocally as anti-Semitic acts.

In the wake of the 1967 war and the consolidation of Holocaust theology as normative for Jews around the world, the discussion of anti-Semitism shifted from personal and collective prejudice against Judaism and Jews to personal and collective opposition to Israel (or Israel's policies) as the 'new anti-Semitism.' Here, Jewish authors were concerned with criticism of Israel as a desire to undermine Israel as a state; they saw it as a threat to Jewish empowerment. The threat, ostensibly one of a political nature and thus to be negotiated in a political framework, was more often seen as a threat to Jews everywhere, the ignition of a new round of anti-Semitism that would end in another Holocaust.

So criticism of Israel, especially Israel's policies, was not seen as a political debate in which people could take different sides. Rather it was seen as an assault on the very survival of Jews everywhere, an assault on the Judaic that Jews in their history were quite familiar with. The situation of Jews in the world had changed and at the same time had not changed. The world was and still is anti-Semitic. The only defense was a good offense.

Within the Jewish community, unity was essential. After the Holocaust and now with Israel under assault, Jews could not afford to split on the issue of empowerment. Coupled with the charges of anti-Semitism to those who criticized Israel from outside, the label of self-hate was often applied to even those Jews who supported the establishment of the state of Israel but vocally opposed the dispossession of the Palestinians in 1948 and the furthering of that displacement after the 1967 war and the conquest of Jerusalem, the West Bank and Gaza. Jews who criticized Israel were, consciously or not, aiding the enemy whose criticisms were not, by definition, political, but anti-Semitic.

The caution here within the Jewish community, one articulated by Holocaust theology, was that with the new questions about God and the covenant, as well as the need for Jewish empowerment, the prophetic voice in Jewish history and contemporary life had to be quieted. So often and correctly critiquing the unjust power of others when Jews were without power, the prophetic voice might, if focused on the Jewish world, endanger Jewish empowerment in Israel and elsewhere. Thus, the prophetic might help accomplish what anti-Semites (and Hitler and the Nazis) hoped for: the demise of the Jewish people. In short, the Jewish prophetic could help hasten another Holocaust.

The first phase of Holocaust theology began with the publication of Richard Rubenstein's *After Auschwitz* in 1966 (Rubenstein, 1992) and ended with the long essay 'Cloud of Smoke, Pillar of Fire,' by Irving Greenberg (1977). Greenberg's essay was delivered during an extended conference on the Holocaust held in St. John the Divine Cathedral in New York City in 1974. In that conference, two other major Holocaust theologians also spoke, Elie Wiesel, himself a Holocaust survivor and later to become a Nobel laureate, and Emil Fackenheim, an internee in Nazi Germany and later a philosopher at the University of Toronto.

Greenberg's essay, especially, ended the first phase of Holocaust theology because he summarized the main trends of Holocaust reflection, while at the same time adding distinctive understandings of Jewish reflection and action after the Holocaust. Greenberg's summary also signaled an end of the distinctive, powerful understandings of Holocaust theology in the theological realm. The second phase of Holocaust theology would concentrate much more on the political ramifications of Holocaust theology, especially with regard to Jewish empowerment and Israel.

From 1974 to1988, the consolidation of Holocaust theology continued apace but now in the context of an Israel increasingly removed from the heady days of the 1967 war. This period saw the beginning and consolidation of the Israeli occupation of the West Bank and Gaza, as well as the increasing settlement activities of religiously based, messianically oriented movements, political and religious sentiments quite foreign to Holocaust theology.

The second phase of Holocaust theology also witnessed the emergence of Palestinian opposition to the occupation and Israel's controversial invasion of Lebanon in the early 1980s. The Lebanon war, which featured among other events the bombing of Beirut and the first organized Israeli opposition to its own governmental policies, was followed by the first Palestinian uprising in 1987.* Like the war in Lebanon, the uprising and especially Israel's brutal response to it, highlighted increasing international criticism of Israel's foreign policy and, for the first time, Jewish opposition within Israel and the diaspora to these same policies.

The Lebanon war and the uprising occasioned the final creative essay of Holocaust theology, again penned by Irving Greenberg. Its title summed up the journey of the Jewish people in the last forty years: 'The Ethics of Jewish Empowerment' (Greenberg, 1995). Like his previous essay, though now recognizing that the position of Jews had changed radically since the Holocaust and the creation of Israel, Greenberg pleaded for Jews to maintain a sense of sobriety in the face of increasing external and internal pressures to adopt a politics either of repression or of pacifism. His emphasis, instead, was on a middle ground: after the Holocaust, it was a religious obligation for Jews to be empowered; Jews should judge their empowerment not by perfection but within the process of what Greenberg labels 'normalization.'

Normalization means that Jews, now empowered, are responsible for their own empowerment and the critique of policies promulgated by Israel and supported

---

*   Ed. On the various significances of the first *intifada*, see also Chapter 7.

by the Jewish establishment in America. Normalization also means that the external and internal calls for Jews to be better than other nations – to be held to a higher standard – could be heard only if that 'better' supported Jewish empowerment. Jewish power, again obligated, had rights and responsibilities that took precedence over ethics and morality. Within empowerment, ethics had to be discussed and parsed; ethics that called Israel to a too high standard had to be judged as inauthentic to the contemporary Jewish situation.

Hence, the prophetic call, so deep and resonant within the Jewish tradition, could, if not disciplined, also become a call for collective suicide. Empowerment and the prophetic could coalesce on the fringes of the Jewish world: the Jewish establishment has to choose power over the prophetic lest another Holocaust commence.

The meaning of the prophetic *after*

From the beginning of the Jewish journey, the question of peace has been shadowed by the need for repair of the world. A disordered world needs *shalom*; *shalom* comes within the process of *tikkun olam*. Yet the most distinctive aspect of the Jewish journey is neither peace nor the repair of the world; it is the prophetic that balances both peace and repair, or rather calls both to account. There can be no peace without justice, nor can the world be repaired if only that repair is felt by the powers that be.

The prophetic as it emerges in the Jewish journey is comprised of a series of judgments constrained by the treatment of the widow, orphan and stranger. In a strange and original reversal, those on the margins are the final arbiters of the justice or injustice of the powerful. In another reversal, the judgment is rendered within and upon the community; for the survival of the people Israel is dependent on that judgment. Indeed, injustice can bring the entire enterprise to a halt; Israel's destiny is chartered for liberation, a turn away from justice spells Israel's demise.

The Exodus and its yearly celebration in Passover portray this quite clearly. Israel, now a nation of slaves, is freed under the direction of a God of liberation, the true God with real power, demonstrated in this movement from slavery to freedom. The Egyptian gods are false precisely in their reliance on magic and foretelling; the God of Israel is real in the dynamic that breaks the power of empire. Empire is thus exposed as a form of magic structured to oppress; Israel as a community will be structured around justice for those on the margins so that in the end, at least within Israel, there will be no one on the margins.

The God of liberation works on the political level as part of a religious sensibility that has justice at its core. The God of Israel can be praised – indeed must be praised. Yet that praise can only be accepted within the context of a just social, economic and political order that is built into the dynamic of Israel's life, in turn rooted in the day of rest, the Sabbath, the seventh day of the week, and the Sabbatical year and Jubilee year, the seventh and fiftieth year, thus the Sabbath year and crowning year of the Sabbath of Sabbaths.

The day and years of rest are for all, even slaves and animals. Agricultural fields are to be left untended, debts are forgiven, land redistributed. The Sabbath, Sabbatical, Jubilee cycle is structured into the life of Israel and it complements, in a concrete political way, the words of the prophets, who begin to appear in Israel after its entry into the Promised Land. The prophets appear when this structure is violated, when the marginal begin to appear within Israelite society.

The analogy is clear and repeated often: the widow, orphan and stranger being mistreated in Israel is the same treatment as that meted out to Israel by the Egyptians. The corollary, that a society that mistreats its own citizens for power and gain is, no matter the language or claim, really worshipping a false God, is leveled at Israel. Israel cannot be in right relation with the God of Israel if Israel practices injustice. Moreover, Israel is not above suffering the fate of Egypt. Worship their gods and the true God will punish and banish you from the world stage. Again, the religious and political are intimately tied together. At least in the Bible, empowerment without justice is fated.

In some obvious way, the Holocaust is a direct confrontation with the Exodus story, the God of liberation challenged by an absent God. But another challenge is the traditional understanding of the reason God punishes a wayward Israel, for injustice, which also means straying from God's teaching. Embedded in this understanding of chastisement and punishment is the prophetic, indeed the entire structure of the Hebrew canon, for if Israel cannot be chastised and punished for transgressions, then the God of Israel has lost his power both to liberate and to admonish. The prophetic is the extension of the Exodus and the God of Israel, but to be both, God has to be present to the people and acknowledged by them.

In Holocaust theology, the Holocaust is presented as counter-testimony to the Exodus, a formative event in the history of the Jewish people that casts doubt on the very foundations of the Biblical God. This includes questioning the presence of God and the notion that Israel's suffering on account of its sins can be invoked in the case of the Holocaust. Whatever the sins of the Jewish people, no matter if God judged them for having strayed from God's teachings, the systematic murder of six million Jews cannot be justified. Almost a million and half children were murdered in the Holocaust. Could God have judged them guilty of sins warranting a death sentence?

The prophetic: Where does it come from? Another question posed by the Holocaust. In the history of Israel, the prophets are summoned by God to speak his word to the people. God instructs the prophets, places words in their mouths, challenges them to continue, inspires them through their travails and protects them. Their mission is God's; the distinguishing mark of the prophet is that the prophet carries God's revelation. In some ways, the prophet is God's revelation to Israel as Israel can understand. Of course, the choice is Israel's to follow God's word or warning as spoken by the prophet. If Israel turns its back on the prophet, the road to perdition is sealed. The language of God through the prophet is tough, emotional and condemnatory. And yet it is sealed within the Hebrew canon. Directed at Israel, it even sees the victory of other nations over Israel as part of God's plan for a sinful Israel. Sinful Israel experiences a defeat; the imagery of the suffering that follows is comparable to the sufferings of Jews in the Holocaust.

Holocaust literature needed a new language to describe the suffering of Jews in the death camps – how do you describe to those who have not experienced the death camps the inhumanity and brutality of it all – but that new language is really quite old. Adjusted for time and context, such language can be found in the Hebrew Bible itself. But in the Holocaust such imagery is not attributed to God, or to God's wrath or punishment. In the Holocaust, the prophet does not speak the language of death; to hold otherwise would be to make Hitler a prophet. The language of death thus has to proceed without God or the prophets. That is why, again unlike the Hebrew Bible, for Holocaust theologians there is no way back from the Holocaust. The return to God promised by God through the prophets – if only Israel will turn back to God – is nowhere to be found in Holocaust theology. Death of the innocent is therefore surrounded by a solitude and hopelessness that is not found in the Bible.

Is the state of Israel such a hope, a response to the Holocaust without God? Could the formation of Israel be a prophetic response to the Holocaust? Could the Holocaust be without God and Israel be with God?

Holocaust theology does not answer these complexities directly. On the one hand, exile and return, suffering and redemption, are deeply embedded in Jewish history; they comprise an important, perhaps defining, rhythm in the canonical text. On the other hand, Holocaust theologians reject this pattern with regard to the Holocaust as it would seem to justify, retrospectively, the Holocaust. Since their general sense is that the Holocaust is a *novum* in Jewish and world history placing it within the old dynamic would generalize the Holocaust. In their minds, this would then minimize the horrors of the Holocaust. Would this do the same to the state of Israel, and minimize the importance of the state? Holocaust theologians see the emergence of the state of Israel as another *novum* in history. Could they be worried that if the state of Israel is found within the general rhythm of Jewish history that it too might then be liable to the critique for injustice that comes within that dynamic?

Thus, the Holocaust and Israel exist, at least for Holocaust theologians, in a vast solitude, cut off from the dynamics of Jewish history yet issuing directly from it. What results is needed for the protection of both events from ordinary interventions. Holocaust theologians surround both events in an almost God-like protection – without God.

The argumentation is thus extreme; carrying forth events in history as sacred – without the sacred – is an arduous task. It has to be done, for without this protection the entire enterprise of Jewish history, already teetering on the edge of disaster, is at risk. What protects Jews from disaster is Jews themselves, but herein lies the difficulty. How can formative events in Jewish history be insulated from the patterns of Jewish life that Jews live within, even with the questions and doubts raised within those events?

The plight of Jews of conscience is therefore difficult, if not impossible. Jews of conscience argue from the depths of tradition without traditional language, a seemingly secular enterprise but in line with Holocaust theology's difficulty in speaking in overt religious terms *after*. They also probe more deeply than Holocaust theologians do because they refuse the sanctified aura of the Holocaust and Israel. In probing the lessons of the Holocaust, Jews of conscience speak prophetically with regard to Palestinians. They are therefore correctly singled out by normative Judaism as aligning themselves with the prophets of old. In an age where the prophets are seen as threatening the Jewish establishment and empowerment, they are consigned to the periphery more or less as enemies of the Jewish people.

Yet, minus religious language, was not that the plight of the prophets in the Hebrew Bible? Declared as enemies of the people and the state – in empowerment one and the same thing. Thus, what appears to be a *novum* in Jewish history may not, on closer examination, be that at all. That includes the separation of certain events as sacred, not to be disputed or discussed in certain ways. The tabernacle is declared off limits, as are certain areas of the temple. To intrude into these spaces is to face the wrath of God and the people. Do the Holocaust and Israel fulfill these sacred roles in contemporary Jewish life?

The prophets saw the declaration of sacredness in the face of injustice as idolatry. Do Jews of conscience simply carry this tradition forward, charging Constantinian Judaism as encouraging and practicing idolatry? Simply put, Jews of conscience are unable to say *shalom* without justice; they cannot practice *tikkun olam* in empire.

In the wake of the Lebanon war, one Jewish writer put the dilemma aptly when she wrote of contemporary Jewry as torn between Israeli power and Jewish ethics. Alas more than two decades later, the situation is even worse, so that the very words of peace and repair are suspect.

Has it always been so with or without God?

Reference list

Green, A. (1999) *These are the Words* (Woodstock, VT: Jewish Lights Publishing).

Greenberg, I. (1977) 'Cloud of Smoke, Pillar of Fire: Judaism, Christianity, and Modernity after the Holocaust' in E. Fleischner (ed.) *Auschwitz: Beginning of a New Era? Reflections on the Holocaust* (New York: Ktav).

Greenberg, I. (1995) *Yitzhak Rabin and the Ethic of Jewish Power* (New York: National Jewish Center for Learning and Leadership).

Rubenstein, R. (1992) *After Auschwitz: History, Theology and Contemporary Judaism*, 2nd edn (Baltimore: Johns Hopkins University Press).

7
Shalom/Salaam: A Personal Palestinian Perspective

Munir Fasheh

> There is no path to peace. Peace is the path.
> In matters of conscience, the law of majority has no place.
> The future depends on what we do in the present.
>
> Mahatma Gandhi

Two worlds

When Columbus and his sailors came ashore, carrying swords, speaking oddly, the Arawaks ran to greet them, brought them food, water and gifts. Columbus wrote:

> They brought us parrots and balls of cotton and spears and many other things, which they exchanged for the glass beads and hawks' bells. They willingly traded everything they owned [...]. They were well-built, with good bodies and handsome features. They do not bear arms, and do not know them, for I showed them a sword, they took it by the edge and cut themselves out of ignorance. They have no iron. Their spears are made of cane. They would make fine servants. With fifty men we could subjugate them all and make them do whatever we want.

The aim of converting people to Christianity (which Columbus claimed before he left) was quickly forgotten and greed became the main driving force.

The contrast between how Columbus saw and treated strangers and how the Arawaks did is very telling: while Columbus saw strangers as potential servants, slaves, resources and subjects to subdue and control, the Arawaks' behavior embodied hospitality, generosity, loving, giving and being good. It meant running towards strangers and greeting and saluting them. The Arabic word for

99

peace – *salaam* – has two meanings: one is close to the meaning in English and the other is 'greetings and salutations.'

Peace for the Europeans who first set foot on the Bahamas meant subduing others to silence and servitude. The subduing aspect seems to be a common thread in European thinking and practices including how they perceived science, knowledge and learning. Francis Bacon, 'father of modern science,' for example, defined science as 'subduing nature.' Whereas peace with strangers for the Arawaks embodied good relations, peace for Columbus embodied obedience. Columbus was on a mission from the royal court and acted accordingly; the Arawaks were acting out of their free spirit. One was the extension of institutions; the other was a manifestation of harmony in living.*

Peace is relational

The relation between Arawaks and Europeans is what I experienced as a Palestinian starting with the days when I first came in contact with missionaries, and with education (which was imposed by the British on the people of Palestine in the early 1920s). Since then, I have been living and experiencing two worlds: the world of my parents and our community, and the official world of institutions and professionals. That contrast was made more striking because as I lived a large part of my life under Israeli military occupation, I found that we were protected (until 1993) from organizations such as the World Bank, which needed some form of 'national authority' in order to enter our communities. That meant we had to depend on ourselves for almost everything. The 'backbone' of our lives was our relations with one another, and what the community, surroundings and culture had. In 1993, a drastic shift happened: we moved from people who lived with hope to people who live with expectations. I will come back to this idea – which was developed by Ivan Illich – later in the chapter.†

Over the years, I felt that what most characterized the relationship between the two worlds is the seeming inability of the Europeans to see, feel, understand and deal with people who lacked what they considered civilized and valuable. It was difficult – it seems – to see others who lacked the 'right' symbols as a source of understanding, knowledge and wisdom. Judging from the behavior of World Bank 'experts,' who came to Palestine after 1993, that attitude and perception seem to have never changed. The style, the words and the structures have changed but the logic, perceptions and conceptions have not. Even when a Westerner goes with an open mind and open heart to study a community, culture or people outside the European world, s/he usually goes armed with words and concepts

---

*   Ed. The differences in peace notions as born out of institutions and as born out of harmony are also discussed by Wolfgang Dietrich in Chapter 1.

†   Ed. Further Ivan Illich's contributions as peace thinker are traced in Chapter 28.

that determine to a large extent how s/he sees, perceives and understands the world. This is also true, in general, about educated people from the communities that are being studied. When an educated person, for example, goes to study Lebanon, armed with the idea of secularism, s/he has already lost the ability to see Lebanon in its uniqueness, richness and diversity. Similarly, when a person looks at Palestine through the concept of nation-state, s/he is already missing the ability to see the depth of the Palestinian experience. To be more personal, prior to 1976, the only way I could see my mother was through words I internalized, such as illiterate and uneducated. Using the measures of the institutional world, I could not see anything of value in her. I was 35 years old when I started to realize the treasure she had within her – which our educated minds and modern eyes cannot see or detect (Fasheh, 1990). An educated mind is one that usually sees the world through words, rather than seeing words through the world.

The most distinctive aspect of my life that I can recall is the fact that it was mainly 'made up' of relationships. Since I was seven years old, when we had to leave our home in Jerusalem in 1948, physical surroundings kept being shattered and destroyed. Every ten years or so, a war took place and occupation of new Arab land followed.* In between, destruction was continuously taking place: confiscation of land, uprooting trees and killing and jailing people. I lived more than half of my life in Ramallah under Israeli military occupation. There was hardly any peace at the political and physical levels. Yet, at the level of relations with people (within the family and community) I felt deep peace.[1] I am talking here about warm, nurturing and good relationships; about free, non-contractual, non-official and non-formal relationships that are full of aliveness and embody dignity, humility, generosity, hospitality and freedom. These nurturing relationships have been the main source of feeling peaceful, within me and with people around me. When I read the phrase 'aesthetics of harmonious relations' in Wolfgang Dietrich's Transrational contribution (2006) and his assertion at the end that 'more than anything the word peace describes the relations between human beings [...]. It is relative and relational,' I felt the meanings of these words in a very personal way. I felt they expressed what I have been experiencing since I was a little boy growing up in Ramallah. My contribution in this volume revolves around the aesthetics of harmonious relations that I experienced throughout my life in the community and culture in which I grew up. I will start with stories that manifested 'harmonious relations,' then mention relations that I experienced within institutional–official–formal settings (where people are treated as spare parts in a machine and, thus, could be changed at the boss's or owner's discretion). Then I will talk about the Palestinian experience as

---

* Ed. Chapter 6 offers diverse understandings of Jewish politics and religious views on this issue.

a magnifier of what is happening in the world at large and some principles that are basic to peace at the personal and interpersonal levels.

Stories that embodied harmonious relations in my experience

First story: Since 1948, I lived mainly in Ramallah. When we first moved there, we lived eight people[2] in one room for several years. That was what my family could afford. This room was where we slept, where my mother and aunts worked sewing clothes, where my sisters and I played, and where we ate. In spite of the fact that we just lost everything, and had hardly anything to live on other than what my mother and her sisters got from sewing clothes, and in spite of the extremely small space we lived in, I felt inner peace, and peace with people around me, that still nurtures me at levels that are very deep. I felt the interpersonal communal peace in Ramallah in spite of displacement, pain, deprivation and poverty that were produced as a result of the creation of Israel.

Second story: When I was in school in the 1950s, I had a very dear friend in the same class. Teachers kept telling my friend and me 'we wonder who is going to be first in the class this year.' We hated it and did not know how to stop them from poisoning our friendship. Finally, we thought of something. We agreed that I write his name on my exam papers and he writes mine on his. They soon discovered what we were doing, and we agreed to stop doing that if they stop playing their game. My friend and I felt that our relationship was much more important than playing the game of competing over symbols. That and similar experiences were the basis of the conviction that grew within me over the years, namely that the very idea of measuring people against each other, along a linear vertical measure that claims objectivity and universality, is a basic source of violence that comes covered with claims, such as 'living up to one's potential.' I became convinced that inner peace and peace in a family or community are shattered if the worth of people is controlled by institutions and professionals.

Third story: The first Palestinian who established schools along the modern path was Khalil Sakakini who built his first school in Jerusalem in 1908. Most schools then were missionary. The level of 'contamination' that characterized institutionalization of learning, however, was not yet very deep among people. Thus, for example, grades did not make sense to Sakakini. Aspects that were very dear to his heart, and which he practiced in his relationship with teachers and students, were dignity of students, honest and beautiful relationships among all, an inspiring relationship with the Arabic language and an intimate and friendly relationship with nature: an aesthetic combination of harmonious relations with people, culture and nature. He refused, for example, to 'teach' the geography of Palestine through textbooks and, instead, he encouraged his students to know Palestine by walking. Many of his students walked from Naqoora in the north to Rafah in the south and all around. The principal of the school in Ramallah where I studied was a student of Sakakini. Every Saturday he closed the school early and took all teachers and students for a hike in the valleys and hills around Ramallah – which he considered as part of the curriculum. That habit of walking in the countryside never left me. There are certain trees, caves, rocks, springs, hills and valleys that I still remember from those days. Intimate relations developed between them and me; in a sense, they became like friends. Every time I pass by something that became part of me, I feel I want to stop and say hello. This is what Palestine means to me: it is a web of relations; it is feeling the 'aesthetics of harmonious relations' with people, community, culture and nature. Palestine has never been an abstract official entity to me but relations that keep nurturing my life. They have been a basis of inner peace in my life.

Fourth story: In 1963, I hit a man with my car. He was walking along the roadside and it was dark and raining heavily. The way that accident was settled followed a path totally dependent on relations, which included my family and his family. It took several months and visits. In the last visit, where agreement had to be concluded, I went to his home. They put a rope around my neck – as part of tradition – indicating I was 'captive' to be freed only after arrangements are made. After that was done, the man whom I hit came into the room, pulled the rope off my neck, which meant I was free again, and we hugged. Then all those who were present from both sides hugged each other, and food was served and a big celebration took place. It was not a deal between two lawyers in a courtroom competing about who would win, but a way that I felt is not only more human but also more fair. That experience confirmed within me that the dwelling place of peace is in the hearts and relations among people, and not among professionals.

Fifth story: When the Greek Orthodox Church refused to marry my parents because they were first cousins, they got married in a Catholic church. Their relationship was more important to them than their relationship to an institution. It was possible for my parents to do that because they were still living the tradition where marriages were basically between persons and families; institutions and priests were formal and secondary. If their loyalties were to an institution, it would have produced anger rather than peace within them.

Another story, the sixth, which also involves my father, took place in the 1930s when he agreed with my uncle to open a grocery store in Jerusalem. My father told my uncle that he has only one condition: not to sell cigarettes or alcohol. He refused to sell them not because there was a law against selling them, not because selling them was against custom and not because of research then that proved they were harmful, but because he saw their effect on people, like coughing all the time because of smoking. He could not feel peace within him if his relation to people embodied harm. My uncle's argument was that they were not going to force or encourage people to smoke; people were free to choose whether to smoke or not. My father said that he was also free to choose to refuse to sell what he believed is harmful to people. Two diametrically different perceptions of freedom! In my father's perception, his relation to people, and not making profit, constituted his freedom to decide and act.

Seventh story: In 1978, my father came back after a demonstration in Ramallah where he saw two Israeli soldiers holding a little boy by his hair and smashing his face against the wall. He stopped the car and went down. One soldier pointed his gun at him and ordered him to get back in his car and leave. He came home very disturbed and his face was red. I will never forget his comment after he told us what he saw: 'these cannot be Jews.' In a sense, he was defending Judaism against the behavior of the Israeli soldiers!

The eighth story is about a practice that was common among Christian Palestinian women in Jerusalem who could not conceive, and so they would go to Hebron, an Islamic town, to pray under the tree of Abraham, a Jewish symbol, to Christ! Living the three religions in one practice is an aesthetic instance of harmonious relations. It is worth mentioning that the attitude of my parents in these stories embodied a way of living that is alien to believing in 'pure' identities. Each one of us is a unique combination of many 'worlds,' where a person can be 'home' for several worlds that live together in a harmonious way within the same person. It is also worth mentioning that such harmonious relations have gradually been disappearing by Palestinians who were educated and, thus, made to believe in a single undifferentiated path for progress.

Ninth story: Al-Khader is a village near Bethlehem.[3] Al-Khader is the name of a saint who is revered by both Muslims and Christians in Palestine. The village is inhabited by Muslims but has a church that carries the name of the saint. Both Muslims and Christians celebrate al-Khader's day inside the church. Some Muslims even baptized their children as a form of blessing and not as a sign of conversion. That practice, using Dietrich's words (2006), is a good example of respect and recognition towards others, rather than of tolerance and assimilation. People interacted with one another in a way that transcended the difference between them without dissolving them into one shapeless 'whole.' To me, that practice embodied peace within each person, and among persons, who participated in it. It is a beautiful example of harmonious relations. Every person kept his/her beliefs but when they met, there was a lot that they celebrated and shared together. The church did not belong to one group but was a space where relations among people were nurtured and deepened. Again, these relations were first questioned, and have been disappearing, by Palestinians – both Muslims and Christians – who were educated by the British system, which was introduced into Palestine in the early 1920s. They looked at such practices as a sign of ignorant illiterate people. They were prisoners to their textual minds that see the world through words, abstractions, definitions and identities – which made it difficult for them to see how such practice brought peace into people's hearts and into their relationships.

Tenth story: The voluntary work movement I was part of in the 1970s brought together people of all ages and backgrounds. Every Friday and Sunday we walked to a village, refugee camp or wherever work was needed and did what people wanted us to do.[4] It was free, inspiring, energizing, alive and brought a lot of happiness, joy and meaning into people's lives, creating peaceful feelings within each person and among people. It created a 'web' of beautiful relationships and friendships. When it became institutionalized, it lost a lot of its energy, spirit and beauty.

I felt that spirit of the 1970s again during the first *intifada* (1987–1991). Both periods were most inspiring in my life. They were wonderful manifestations of what people do and how they relate to one another when institutions and professionals are 'paralyzed.' Such spirit cannot be captured in words and concepts, and cannot be fully comprehended by the mind. The closest words I can use to describe both periods are inspirational and spiritual. People's actions were not a result of plans and organized ideas, but manifestations of what they internalized through living in a community and culture that embodied that spirit. They were examples of acts and abilities that have been vital in people's lives for thousands of years. What I started realizing, since the early 1970s, was how useful the mind and language are in organizing, planning, competing, controlling, winning and executing, but how limited they are in their ability to comprehend life in its fullness, richness, depth, beauty and diversity, and how limited they are in their ability to 'see' how things fit together, in a natural way, because minds usually look for mental connections only. That realization made me always ask what is ignored/belittled/disvalued/made invisible by talking only about what the mind can understand and language can express. This question is crucial in discussions concerning peace.

One similarity between the 1970s and the first *intifada* was the fact that there were no authoritarian leaders – there were inspiring leaders – and no funds, and no one appointed him/herself as a change agent or spokesperson of social change. The two periods consisted mainly of people and communities in relation with one another. Institutions and organized groups were either marginal, like in the 1970s, or closed down by Israelis, like in the first *intifada*. The absence of authoritarian leaders and the lack of intervention by institutions provided freedom and released energy within people to act autonomously, and use 'structures' that were part of the community and culture such as neighborhoods and mosques. People did what they thought they could do and what they thought was good to do – and were ready to face consequences and punishment by the occupying army. What took place during the two periods is close to what I believe Gandhi meant by self-rule. The two periods dismantled within me the modern myth that people cannot govern themselves, and cannot function and manage their lives without institutions, professionals and leaders directing them all the time. I cannot think of any time in my life other than these two periods where I felt people more energized and alive, and having beautiful relations. I already mentioned some examples from the 1970s above; I will tell here two stories from the first *intifada* to illustrate that spirit.

The first is a story about a common scene during the first *intifada*: a number of Israeli soldiers harshly beating a young man in his early twenties in the central district of Ramallah. Several women rushed toward the scene shouting and trying to pull the soldiers away from the young man. Suddenly, a woman carrying a baby ran up and started shouting at the young man, 'I told you not to leave the house today, that the situation is too dangerous. But you didn't listen; you never listen to me.' Then she turned to the soldiers and said, 'Beat him; he deserves this. He never listens. I am sick of my life with him.' Then back to the man she cried, 'I am sick of you and your baby; take him and leave me alone.' She then pushed the baby into his arms and ran away. The soldiers were confused. Finally, they left the man and went on. A few minutes later, the woman reappeared, took back her baby, told the young man to go to his home and wished him safety and a quick recovery. I then realized that they were total strangers to one another.

The woman was not acting or pretending; and she was not a superhuman or a hero, as many like to characterize Palestinians. Nor, on the other hand, was she a subhuman or a member of a non-people, as many Israeli and Western experts portrayed Palestinians for decades. She was simply acting humanly, in a spontaneous and compassionate way. What she did was the result of feeling a relation with a stranger that prompted her to do something. It is a manifestation of attentiveness, aliveness, spontaneity, love, freedom and taking risks. Her action brought out the hope in human beings: how incredible and how unpredictable human beings can be. Above all, she did what she felt was good – an attribute that is usually forgotten in a world dominated by rational explanations, such as power relations or oppressors vs. oppressed. She acted outside laws and customs, outside paradigms, outside the intention of producing social change, and without evaluating, figuring out or thinking of consequences. She even risked the possibility of getting her baby harmed. She did not ask where the young man was from, or to what political or religious group he belonged. She did what she felt was good and right. She brought peace to herself, to the young man, and probably to the heart of some soldiers.

The second story that embodied the spirit of the first *intifada* was communicated to me by Kamal Abdul Fattah, Professor of Geography at Birzeit University, and concerned a boy in Jenin who was running away from soldiers, and entered a house, where a woman was sitting on a chair, preparing food. When she saw the terror in the young boy's eyes, she told him to hide under her gown. For her, doing what was in her judgment good was more important than thinking whether it was appropriate or in accordance with custom. Her love for a 'stranger' and the impulse to do something to protect him were far more important than obeying a law or conforming to a custom or asking whether her action was appropriate or not. Her action was again a manifestation of love, doing good, being attentive and alive and spontaneous, acting in freedom and taking a risk – all at once.

It is exactly in the sense embedded in the actions of the two women that I use the word love here. Their actions manifested that love is stronger than rules, laws and customs, and that it is intimately connected to doing good.[5] Love and doing good are not possible without freedom, where people are driven from within to do what they feel is good.

The fact that both stories involved mothers is significant. What kept, and is still keeping, Palestinian communities functional, and kept peace in the hearts of children, have been such acts by people who did what they did as a matter of living, with a manifestation of love for others and for one's ways of living, and not as a result of planned and organized thinking. It is exactly in this sense that mothers in Gaza and in refugee camps in Lebanon, for example, have been indispensable in the survival and sanity of people there, in spite of the insanity of what Israel has been doing since the 1950s – almost non-stop. I believe one day the Gaza mothers will be looked at as an embodiment of the miracle of humanity. They cannot think of life separate from relationships. Their attitude and deeds are manifestations of peace, to the contrary of news reports.

As final examples, I would like to give two stories that reflect the centrality of relations among people in bringing peace into a community: one from Mexico, the other from India. During a visit to Oaxaca, Mexico, Gustavo Esteva* told me something that keeps inspiring me. He said that one issue the Zapatistas raised with the Mexican government was that they want to live according to their own ways and traditions, one of which is living without jails. They believe that a person who does harm to another or to a community points to something wrong in the relations among people and not in one individual. This means that the community has to make an effort to reflect on relations among people rather than put the blame and punish one person.[6] This is radically different from putting people in jail as a way of bringing peace into a community, as well as radically different from demanding the improvement of jails.†

The other example is from India. When the British put tax on salt, a law that Gandhi considered unjust, his action was not to beg the British to change it. He did not get into empty arguments with them about rights. He, instead, acted very strongly in a way that embodied dignity, love, freedom and doing good.

---

* Ed. Gustavo Esteva and Arturo Guerrero co-author Chapter 19. Their discussion on Zapotec notions of peace as friendship echoes the arguments developed here by Fasheh in terms of peace as relational and the obstacles that texts and institutions pose to peace as harmony.

† Ed. In a similar vein, in Chapter 17 Pat Lauderdale develops in depth the differences between punishment and retributive justice from healing and restorative community processes concerning North American Indian nations.

He walked 241 miles along with thousands of fellow Indians, until he reached the sea, where he dipped his hand into the salty water showing how ridiculous and stupid the British law was. It was a manifestation of self-rule, dignity, justice and freedom. Peace is void and meaningless without them.

Aspects related to peace within the culture in which I grew up

In all the above stories, peace embodied good relations among people and included living in a way that transcended personal interests and, instead, embraced some common good. Much of what I said above springs out of the culture in which I grew up, which may be similar to other cultures. They manifest the fact that peace is relational and, thus, cannot be separated from culture. That is why translations of foreign words have always been fascinating and revealing to me. They act as eye-openers to aspects in the culture I grew up in, to aspects of people whose minds become glued to texts or other official symbols such as TV images and to aspects of dominant ideology in general. It is significant to mention here that we do not have words in Arabic for 'individual,' 'privacy,' 'education,' 'nationalism' and 'nation-state.' I am mentioning these specific words because their meanings in English are contrary to what is embedded in the stories I mentioned above insofar as that 'peace is relational' and contrary to having harmonious relations. With time, I realized that the absence of words in Arabic that correspond to these words is not a manifestation of deficiency in the language and culture but of the fact that our world is different, i.e. the absence is a manifestation of pluralism in living. By forcing words in Arabic to mean what these words mean in English, we would bring into our thoughts, perceptions, actions and relations dimensions that – in my experience – proved to be violent and non-peaceful.

The word 'individual' in English, for example, refers to one who can live and be defined without any relation to anyone, anything or nature.[7]* Not having a word for 'individual' in Arabic is not a manifestation of lack in thinking or in the language but a fact that reflects how Arabs live and perceive people. Why should we – as Arabs – have a word for something that we do not experience in our lives? It makes perfect sense not to have a word for it. Unfortunately, instead of realizing that the absence was really an indication that our world is different, 'educated' Arabs struggled to find a word in Arabic that is equivalent to 'individual.' Finally, they chose a word and forced it to become part of the language people use, which ended up 'contaminating' our thinking and perceptions. The word they chose was *fard* – which means something totally different from 'individual.' It means 'a person out of many persons who belongs to a certain group.' For example,

---

*   Ed. Wolfgang Dietrich discusses the different connotations that 'individual' can have as autonomous subjects and as holons in Chapter 1.

fard min afrad al'aela/alqabeela/almajmoo'ah/almujtama' – an individual of many individuals who form some social entity: a family, tribe, group, community; i.e. a person who is always part of a whole, in relation to others – never separate and isolated.

In other words, the fact that we do not have a term in Arabic for words such as 'individual' tells us something about our worldview and should signal an alarm – that it has no roots in our lives and we have to be cautious in using it. It is an opportunity to tell our children/students about the many 'worlds' that exist, each of which reflects certain perceptions, values and realities. In other words, by forcing a word to mean 'individual' where in fact it does not, it does not only confuse and distort, but also loses an opportunity to explore a beautiful concrete example of what pluralism means. It is very hard for me to see how peace can be achieved as long as we go on believing in universal thinking, in the sense of a single undifferentiated path for progress.* Having a pluralistic attitude towards life, knowledge, meanings and ways of living is crucial in relaxing people's minds and bringing peaceful feelings into one's life. In other words, I do not feel that the concept of individual is in harmony with peace as I experienced it in my life, which always embodied relations with one's surroundings.

'Individual' is connected to 'privacy,' another word that has no synonym in Arabic – again for the same reason: why create a word for something that people do not experience? Again, the word used in Arabic for 'privacy' does not mean the same as in English. It was when I went to the US for the first time (1965) that I realized that the *living* meaning of 'privacy' has no translation in Arabic. It is the same with education, nationalism and nation-state: education is connected to institutions and professionals and did not spring out of living; Arabs could not find in their experience anything similar to this fabricated word. Nationalism and nation-state are connected to modes of thinking and living that are alien to Arab societies and cultures. The idea of having artificial arbitrary lines called international borders and official sense of belonging, and the idea of having a 'pure' nationality that defines a person's identity, is something that was forced on us in our region after the First World War by the British and French[8] to extend their control over the region – militarily, politically, culturally and economically. When I visit Jordan, Syria or Lebanon, for example, I do not feel I am in another country. Nationalism and nation-states are the source of a lot of violence against people, communities and cultures in all the cases I am familiar with.

It is interesting to point out that the word for peace in Arabic – *salaam* – refers to both peace (as in English) and to salutation.† It reflects what Arabs in ancient

---

*   Ed. Chapter 1 offers a succinct definition of linear chronosophy and the challenges it poses to peace. This is also discussed by Marc H. Ellis in Chapter 6.

†   Ed. This book offers manifold readings, contextualizations and interpretations of *Salaam* in the various chapters that make up Section II Peace Concepts in the Middle East as well as in Chapter 3 on Mediterranean perspectives.

times seem to have believed: to feel peaceful, one always has to recognize the existence of others in a way that embodies connectedness and warmth.

Another aspect of Arab culture that reflects a very special relationship between two people is the fact that a good segment of the Arabic language is devoted to the dual form – *al-muthanna*. It is different from 'couple,' it is not a legal relation and it does not dissolve the two into a new whole. It basically asserts that the relationship between the two is very special (almost like their baby), very important to both but separate from both – having its own existence and its own growth path. The absence of *al-muthanna* – from European languages – has been crucial in how Europeans perceived and related to others. The absence of the *dual*, the relation of 'I and you,' from their languages led – it seems – to its absence in their consciousness, perceptions and thinking.

Al-muthanna embodies a logic that is different from Aristotle's and Hegel's. In Aristotle's logic, another person is either identical to me or not-me, either I or not-I, with no third alternative. In Hegel's logic, it is possible for 'you and I' to form a new synthesis, one expression of which is referring to one's spouse as 'my other half.' In the logic embedded in *al-muthanna*, you remain you and I remain me, but there is a third 'creature' – which is the relationship – that is created between us and becomes very important for both of us. In other words, the two persons keep their separate selves but form a relation that keeps growing and it becomes impossible to live anymore without it being part of their lives.

The absence of *al-muthanna* is much more serious than what Europeans can comprehend and, unfortunately, more than what many Arabs realize. Those who believe that Aristotle and Hegel exhaust all kinds of logic are handicapped in their ability to see, let alone understand, the logic embedded in *al-muthanna*. It is not an intellectual concept that can be understood solely by the mind; it is very hard to comprehend if one never experienced such relationships. This explains at least partially why a person like Huntington cannot see civilizations in any way other than in conflict; he sees others at best through Aristotle's or Hegel's logic: either identical to me or a negation to me or, at best, can form a new synthesis with me. It also explains why missionaries could not see my parents' Christianity.[9] This handicap in Huntington and missionaries is due – at least partially – to the absence of *al-muthanna*. In this sense, *al-muthanna* is a cultural treasure that helps us have a different perception of the world.

The first *intifada* forms a special part of the Palestinian experience, a part that embodied cultural aspects, which were the 'essence' of that period. What inspired me most in this regard were *al-Jame'* and neighborhood committees, both of which carried within them relations among people. For me, the *intifada* is still a hidden treasure within Palestinian collective memory and consciousness, waiting to be expressed as an inspirational experience of a different world in living and relating. It was sort of a 'cultural revolution' but, unlike others that carry the same name, it was neither organized nor planned. It grew as a natural response to an oppressive situation – military occupation – driven mainly by what is available in people, in the community, in culture and in nature. In this sense, culture – like blood in the body or a river in the landscape – nurtures everything it touches; unless, of course, the culture, blood or river is polluted.

Part of the culture I grew up in is Eastern Christianity and Islam. Both were inspiring to me, and to what I am saying here in particular. Jesus, for example, said that if you say that you love God but you hate your neighbor, you are a liar. In other words, one's relations with others manifest one's love for God. In his life, Jesus replaced all commandments by one: love one another. Spontaneous good relations among people that stem from their hearts were for him the essence of life. In Islam, a story that I loved ever since I heard it is the one where a man from *al-badiyah*, the Arabic word for desert but with different connotations, went to Prophet Mohammad and asked him if he could tell him in one sentence the essence of the religion he was calling people to follow, and according to his answer, the man would decide whether to be a Muslim or not. The Prophet pondered on the question and then said: 'religion is how people treat one another' (*ad-din huwa al-mu'amalah*). The man said, 'then I am a Muslim.' The 'essence of religion' – in what Jesus and Mohammad said – dwells in one's relations with others, in how people treat one another.

A most inspiring example in Arab culture, which revolves around relations, is a statement by Imam Ali. It is connected to the worth of a person and to the source of that worth. According to it, the worth of a person does not come from symbols, institutions and measures that claim to be objective and universal but, rather, from the person's inner harmony and from one's relations to people, community, culture and nature.[10] The 1400-year-old statement is: قيمة كل امرئ ما يحسنه (*qeematu kullimri'en ma yuhsenoh*), which means that the worth of a person is what s/he *yuhsen*, which, in Arabic, has several meanings that together constitute the worth of a person:

- The first meaning refers to how well the person does what s/he does – which requires knowledge, skills and tremendous mental discipline (*itqaan*);
- The second refers to how beautiful and pleasing what one does is to the senses, the aesthetic dimension – which requires a high degree of sensitivity;
- The third meaning refers to goodness, in the sense of refusing to harm self, others, or nature – which requires tremendous self-discipline and high ethical standards;
- The fourth refers to what one gives of oneself, and not what one delivers as ready made from others, which requires valuing one's experience;
- The fifth meaning refers to how respectful of people and ideas the person is in discussions and interactions with others – which requires both humility and dignity.

What is significant is that the meanings are not given by authority of any sort but by people as they experience life and make sense of it in a particular place and time, by people in relation to one another and as co-authors of the various meanings of *yuhsen*.

Worthiness is not a purely intellectual concept but essentially an existential relational one; it stems from perception of self and from interactions with one's surroundings. In this sense, it is a beautiful way – regarding one's worth – of transcending both institutional violence, as practiced in schools, universities and institutions, in general, through evaluations and grades and cultural violence, as practiced by people who claim monopoly of the meaning of customs. The worth of the person is not determined by a committee or institution outside the person and community and not by culture as fixed rules and meanings, but by the person and the people one interacts with. This necessarily means that the meanings of the word *yuhsen* have to be 'created' anew in every case, place and time. This naturally can be influenced by culture and by various practices in other places, but with a dimension that is extremely crucial: the right of every person to independently investigate the meanings of *yuhsen* in a particular time and place.

The statement transcends what exists in a respectful way; for example, it has no specific content but, rather, meanings stem from living and interacting. In this sense, it reflects a pluralistic attitude. Progress – according to *yuhsen* – is not to improve along a path that is determined by an authority but in the sense of doing what one does in an increasingly better way, increasingly beautiful, good to the community and in a way that is more respectful and stems from within. The measure, thus, is not how one scores against others but a constant reflection on how well one's work is, how beautiful, good, respectful and whether it stems from within. In this sense, the statement is in harmony with Dietrich's stress that peace is relative and relational. Moreover, the statement transcends discussions concerning categories such as pre-modern, modern or post-modern.

Imam Ali's statement protects people – in relation to one's worth – from the tyranny and arbitrariness of institutions and professionals; and it protects people from structural and cultural violence. What is significant is that such protection is done through culture itself: the statement being part of the Arab–Islamic civilization. It is a beautiful example of 'changing traditions in traditional ways,' one of the inspiring principles of the Zapatistas.

One last aspect of the culture in which I grew up is that there is no peace as long as money is used to enslave people and rob their humanity. One aspect where I see Christianity and Islam converge very strongly is in relation to making money out of money, what is referred to as interest. In Islam, *riba*, the word for interest, is absolutely forbidden. In Christianity, the only time we read that Jesus was ready to be 'violent' was when he carried a whip and kicked the moneylenders out of the temple. Two thousand years later, a statement entitled 'Fifty Years are Enough' issued in 1995 by All Africa Conference of Churches, on the occasion of fifty years for the establishment of the World Bank and IMF, carried the same message: 'Every child in Africa is born with a financial burden which a lifetime's work cannot repay. The debt is a new form of slavery as vicious as the slave trade.'

Logic and relations within the institutional world

At the same time as I was experiencing the 'aesthetics of harmonious relations' within my family, community and culture, I was also experiencing another kind of relations within another world: the world of institutions and professionals. My first experiences of this other logic and relations were in education and religion, via schools and missionaries. In both, the stress was on symbols such as language as the measure. For example, according to both institutions – using their measures – my mother was ignorant. If you asked her, for example, about what Jesus said, she could not cite one sentence except maybe 'love one another.' Later, I realized that she was a person whose life embodied what I believe to be Jesus' spirit – naturally and beautifully. Similarly, if you asked her about any mathematical fact, she could not cite any; yet – as I wrote about her in several places – her knowledge of math still amazes me and I still cannot understand it!

The attitude and logic of the institutions of education and religion disturbed my inner peace vis-à-vis my relationship with my parents and, in particular, with my mother and people labeled as illiterate. I still remember vividly how I used to feel ashamed when missionaries preached to my parents because they made me feel that they were ignorant. I have not come across any missionary who was curious about how my parents embodied Christianity; all they seemed interested in was how to preach and convert them to their respective denominations.

One impact of education and institutional religion was dulling my senses to see what was there: the beauty, richness, knowledge, wisdom and abilities in my parents, and in my community and culture. I was conditioned to believe that they had nothing of value, simply because they did not measure up to what was considered valuable by institutions and professionals. The attitude and logic of both institutions made me realize that one of the most – though subtle – forms of psychological perceptual violence was the belief that there is nothing in a person, or a community or a culture, that one can learn from. This made me realize the power of words in dulling senses. Although I felt the warmth, beauty, love and freedom that characterized my parents' ways in living, and I was living and enjoying relations within the community that were nourishing, I internalized the institutional perspective that there was nothing in my parents' ways of living or in the community that was worth learning from. Put differently, I internalized the assumption that there are people who know and people who are ignorant in some absolute sense, and that the role of the first is to educate, preach, empower or conscientize the second. I feel very strongly now that this is a subtle form of violence.

What made the attitude of missionaries particularly disturbing to me was the fact that Palestinian Christians form the only indigenous Christian community in the world. They are the ones who carried the spirit from one generation to another starting when Jesus walked on the land of Palestine. What was significant about missionaries was not what they said as much as how absent my parents' Christianity was in their consciousness. The impact of foreign churches, which pulled many Palestinian Christians out of our traditions, and the establishment of Israel, which uprooted most Palestinian Christians from Jerusalem, led to the disappearance of this special and precious group from Jerusalem. It is a loss that cannot be recovered. In this sense, I belong to a dying 'species' that is extremely important.

I now believe that relations among people within institutions are void of life, honesty, dignity and humility, and that they are always connected to measuring, controlling and wanting to win 'converts.' There is right and wrong, not as opinions but as decisions by some authority. I mentioned earlier the difference between the worth of a person in educational settings and one's worth according to Imam Ali's statement.

Peace without dignity and respect is lifeless and shallow. Dignity and respect by necessity include humility and freedom. As I mentioned above, one of the deepest and most subtle forms of disrespect and lack of humility is when one believes that there is nothing one can learn from the other. This attitude has been a main justification of much of the evil done to others by Europeans: they are nothing, so we can do whatever we please with them. Institutionalizing what is natural in people, such as learning, healing, relating, marrying, caring, etc., has been an important basis of this attitude. I became very conscious of this attitude in its various manifestations: in education, it made me believe that the worth of a person can be measured by numbers; in politics, it made me believe that we cannot manage our daily affairs and govern ourselves without governments and institutions; in bringing up children, it made me believe that we need experts; in agriculture, it made me believe that a person who reads thirty books, but rarely touches plants and soil, is better than a farmer who feels plants and 'talks' with animals. What is alien, lifeless and rootless is considered real, while what has been part of people's lives for thousands of years became worthless!

Palestine as a magnifier: peace prior to 1993 and post 1993

The Palestinian situation and experience have been inspiring to me because they served as a magnifier, through which I could see and comprehend the world at large.[11] I use 'Palestinian' here not as a national or political identity but in an experiential existential sense. I already mentioned that I experienced both the lack of peace and deep sense of peace, both of which have been almost a daily part of life. Part of the reason for this magnifying aspect is that everything is in flux in Palestine, the pace at which things happen there, and aspects that became accepted in other societies are either still in the making or do not exist in Palestine.

The idea of nation-state is one example of this magnifying aspect of the Palestinian situation. If we look at what has been happening since the Palestinian Authority was created in 1993, we would see a very revealing case of the 'true nature' of the modern concept of nation-state.[12] It was immediately accompanied by words such as development, progress, rights, peace, democracy, governance and reform. All these words became part of the rhetoric, and always conveyed positive connotations.

In practice, however, I watched how they were distractions from what was happening on the ground: expectations replaced hope as a way of living; the language of rights overshadowed dignity; the pattern of consumption in living became much more prevalent as a lifestyle; individualistic gains and greed overcame feelings of community and solidarity; personal interests replaced communal good; and depending on authority gradually eliminated the sense of responsibility in managing daily affairs. In other words, people were robbed of abilities and became disabled – as persons and as communities.

Prior to 1993, relations 'defined' people; they formed the backbone of our lives. Post 1993, official and institutional relations took over. They became connected to rules, regulations, laws, and to consumption and its values – control, winning, greed, etc. In other words, there has been a gradual transformation of people from fully attentive and responsible people, able to do and manage a lot of daily and life necessities, to groups quarreling over artificial positions and privileges; from people who were able to take care of themselves into individuals who complain and demand authority to do what they could do before; from a people whose dignity shattered one of the most advanced control systems in the world to a society full of NGOs dumping all sorts of useless information and teaching all kinds of fast formulas – 'à la McDonald's' style in fast food. Worst of all, the inner peace that we enjoyed within each person and among us started disappearing and in its place an abstract peace became the topic. Peace that Israel is trying to impose is like peace in a zoo, where each species/group lives in a special cage, separated from one another. There are guards to keep every group in its place and separate from others. Naturally, some species have more privileges than others: more space, more freedom to move, the right to steal from others, etc.

What has been happening in Palestine since 1993 is a miniature of what happened in so many other places, where the 'national struggle' for liberation was reduced to a struggle for a nation-state, whose main function is to control people in the name of unity, progress and development, and in the service of big corporations and dominant powers.[13] As all other nation-states after World War II, the role that was assigned to the Palestinian Authority carried within it the virus of development, which was claimed to be the savior but which, in fact, was the virus that destroyed the internal immune system in us as persons and in our community – a kind of social AIDS virus. In Palestine, this virus came much later than in other places, because of Israeli military occupation. We were protected from development simply because we did not have a national authority, which meant that organizations such as the World Bank could not enter our communities. The Oslo deal, in practice, was a plan to create a make-believe authority, which has no authority at all except to do harm to people, and allow organizations such as the World Bank to take control of certain sectors such as economy and education. What we ended up with in reality were three kinds of occupation: the continuation of the Israeli military occupation, the World Bank economic occupation and occupation of the mind mainly through education and development projects. The one that is most dangerous in my opinion is the occupation of minds, because it is the subtlest, and it is the one that defeats us from within. One most effective tool in occupying minds, formulating perceptions, limiting imaginations and determining actions has been professional words and official meanings.*

I would like to elaborate a little more on transforming us from a people who had hope to people who live with expectations, an idea developed by Ivan Illich.† In spite of all the disasters that took place since the British occupied Palestine after the First World War, and especially after 1948 when Israel was created and the majority of Palestinians were expelled and more than 400 villages were completely destroyed, and also the new occupation that took place in 1967, along with its miseries – I say that in spite of all that, hope has always been the driving emotion and energy among Palestinians and the main thread in our social–spiritual–cultural fabric. After 1993, hope was radically transformed by reducing it to a hope of having a pseudo-nation-state, with all that this carries within itself in the form of expectations.

In other words, prior to the Oslo deal, we were living with hope, while after it, expectations dominated our outlook, our words, the boundaries of our thinking and the horizon of our imagination. Expectations determined our actions and relationships with one another. They created new values and new lifestyles. Distractions became more prevalent; the consumption pattern in living gained deep roots; material possessions became more desirable; and control, winning, competition, profit and greed became more dominant as values. Traits such as hospitality and mutual acts of solidarity started disappearing. Learning increasingly meant sitting in workshops for few days and getting certificates at

* Ed. Ngũgĩ wa Thiong'o coined the expression 'colonization of the minds,' which echoes Fasheh's critique of the occupation of the minds and the importance of language in this enterprise. For more on this peace thinker see Chapter 30.
† Ed. See Chapter 28 for an exploration of Ivan Illich.

the end, and often with a ceremony – usually filled with harmful drinks and food – as a way to give value to an empty, lifeless and meaningless process.

Peace that existed prior to 1993, as a manifestation of harmonious relations, was transformed into an empty slogan and a whip to beat anyone who got out of line with the official peace as dictated by Israeli terms and means. In a sense, it became a word that blocked real peace from gaining roots. Prior to 1993, the peace I felt was inner and communal peace. After 1993, it became a slogan associated with agreements that totally ignored people's lives and realities. It became an abstraction and part of an ugly political game. We did not gain peace outside us and, in addition, we lost it inside and among us. The situation among Palestinians has been a constant deterioration, all in the name of progress, development and building a nation-state.[14]

After the Second World War, development replaced direct military rule in stealing resources and controlling nations politically, economically and culturally. It accomplished this mainly via national banks, national governments, national curricula and national mass media. It did it in the name of help, assistance and spreading democracy. Again, the Palestinian situation serves as a magnifier through which we saw the hypocrisy of Western powers in their naked reality: not one of them honored the choice of people!

In spite of that, people who live in a way reflecting that the common good is higher in their lives than personal interests and symbolic gains, continue to be present working with hope, energy and aliveness – within Palestinian society and probably within others.

Moving into the future

A basic principle that I have been trying to live by for many years is that whatever we do we should try to make sure that what we gain does not rob us from what we have. Any peace that robs us from inner or interpersonal peace is not worth having. In other words, seeking peace through formal structures that ignore relations is doomed.

This means, first, that we cannot talk about peace as just a treaty or agreement and, second, we cannot think of peace separate from other aspects in life. We cannot go on talking about peace at an abstract level and ignore what is happening on the ground. Also, we cannot talk about peace while we continue encouraging the consumption pattern in all its aspects, including comparing people and nations along linear measures that claim to be objective and universal. We cannot afford to go on deceiving our minds via rootless disconnected words. Peace cannot be attained if we continue to believe in a single undifferentiated path for progress – one of its manifestations is monopoly of education over learning. Peace cannot be attained if we continue to let institutions monopolize abilities and functions that can be done by people, such as learning, healing, bringing up children, caring and entertaining.

One aspect that characterized the 1970s and the first *intifada* – when I felt peace in the community very deeply – was the transcendence of personal interests. People transcended their narrow interests and worked for a larger good, they were doing what is good for the larger community. The feeling that the interest of the larger community is at least as important as personal interest was a source of peace within and among people.

This is exactly where we as Palestinians fell into the trap of dominant words and perceptions, which made us lose sight of what we already had. Dominant perceptions and conceptions of peace blinded us to see the richness and diversity of what peace meant to us in our practices, communities, culture and relations. It is exactly at this level and in this sense where I feel the most meaningful and exciting challenge we face as Palestinians: articulating our own experience, perspective and practice of peace. This includes rethinking education and the nation-state in light of what happened in Palestine since the British occupied it after the First World War.

More than anything else, living in Palestine was what helped me heal from much of what I internalized while growing up. I taught Newtonian physics, Cartesian mathematics and Aristotelian logic for many years. It was my experience since the 1970s that shattered my blind acceptance of a universal path in knowing, learning, relating and living. That led me, in particular, to question what is dumped on us by authorities of all kinds – including scientific and mathematical authorities. In teaching the law of gravity, for example, I said:

> Whether you believe that there is a force of attraction between you and the chair or not, is not of any importance to your life. What is important is how you perceive that claim. If you accept it just because it comes from some authority, then it is much healthier to reject it, or at least, to put it on hold until you either drop it or find personal understanding of it. If accepting it deepens your unconditional unquestionable acceptance of authority and deepens your mistrust of your senses, then it is better not to accept the claim. It is important to trust senses more than authority.

Part of relational living is to trust one's senses in life more than official, professional or authority claims. That attitude brought peace to me and to many students. Being in harmony with one's senses and feelings is crucial to feeling inner peace.

This led to a conviction that has been a main part of my thinking and living for many years, namely the importance of co-authoring meanings of the words I use. One main area where I practiced this in my work is related to the worth of a person in the sense of what s/he *yuhsen*.[15] Co-authoring does not only refer to language but to any form of expression that one feels comfortable with, music, dancing, planting, child upbringing, style of living, treatment of others. It is worth mentioning that people – especially children and 'illiterates' – create meanings, rules and measures all the time, in harmony with their experiences and contexts. It is institutions that block this natural ability in people. The co-authoring I try to embody in my life builds on what is beautiful, inspiring, healthy and abundant in people, communities and cultures.

Notes

1. What is happening in Lebanon at the time of this writing (August 2006) seems to embody similar feelings. In spite of tremendous destruction at the physical level, yet – judging from emails of friends – harmonious relations have been developing among them.
2. The eight people were my parents, three aunts, my two sisters and myself.
3. See Lance Laird's dissertation at the Divinity School at Harvard (Laird, 1998).
4. That was the main topic of my doctorate dissertation at the School of Education at Harvard University.
5. It is interesting to mention that as I am typing 'doing good' the computer kept trying to change 'good' to 'well' – as if doing good is meaningless and, in some sense, wrong!
6. This is similar to dealing with a student by expelling him/her from school vs. dealing with the student in a way that sees the locus of any problem in relations among people. That is why Sakakini, whom I mentioned earlier, never believed in punishing students in his schools.
7. CV, for example, is a series of parallel pieces of information that says almost nothing about the person's convictions or about how s/he relates to the world around him/her: to people, community, culture and nature.
8. Through the Sikes-Pico agreement in 1916 in which they divided the region between them.
9. See, for example, the journal *Cornerstone* (2006).
10. Within the Arab Education Forum (2006) that I established and have been directing since 1998, Imam Ali's statement has been the guiding principle in the Forum's thinking and practice.
11. At least it sheds light on aspects in today's world as well as exposes dominant symbols, words, meanings and measures.
12. This is so even though what is taking place in Palestine is not a full state.
13. When I look around the world, I see nation-states that are characterized by peace in the sense of dead minds, dulled senses, high-speed tools and machines and consumption pattern in living. The so-called peace agreement in 1993 is an empty word because it ignored the realities in which people live. Peace was dictated by Israeli terms and means.
14. It is interesting that people in the Indian subcontinent early in the twentieth century – such as Gandhi, Tagore and Mohammad Iqbal – saw the poison and drug in the idea of nation-states outside colonizing nations, where the idea served such nations to control markets inside their states and outside.
15. All that became central in my work within the Arab Education Forum (2006) and the Qalb el-Omour project. For details, see the website of the Forum (2006), which although is mostly in Arabic, there is enough in English to give the reader a clear idea.

Reference list

Arab Education Forum (2006) http://www.almoultaqa.com/, date accessed June 13, 2009.
Cornerstone (2006) 'The Forgotten Faithful', 40, http://www.sabeel.org/pdfs/Cornerstone%20
    40final,%20Spring%202006.pdf, date accessed August 2006.
Dietrich, W. (2006) 'A Call for Trans-Rational Peaces', *Virtual Peace Library of the UNESCO
    Chair for Peace Studies at the University of Innsbruck*, http://www.uibk.ac.at/peacestudies/
    downloads/peacelibrary/transrational.pdf, date accessed June 13, 2009.
Fasheh, M. (1990) 'Community Education: To Reclaim and Transform what has been Made
    Invisible', *Harvard Educational Review*, 60, 1, 19–35.
Laird, L. (1998) *Martyrs, Heroes and Saints: Shared Symbols of Muslims and Christians in
    Contemporary Palestinian Society*, ThD in Comparative Religion (Cambridge: Harvard
    Divinity School).

8
Salaam: A Muslim Perspective
Aurangzeb Haneef

> Assalaam-o-Alaikum: May Peace be upon you!
> Arabic Islamic greeting

Introduction: culture, Muslim culture and Islam

By now, there is an increasing agreement among scholars and practitioners that culture is an important matter that should be given its due consideration in international peace and conflict resolution and negotiations. Scholars such as John Paul Lederach and Kevin Avruch have done seminal work in this area. The present effort of the editors to bring out an *International Handbook of Peace Studies: A Cultural Perspective* may also be seen as an acknowledgment of such an increasing consensus. Further, it is evidence of an ongoing commitment to understand peace and its different manifestations in various cultural settings in order to provide alternatives to dominant discourses of peace and conflict resolution.

But what is culture? There are about 160 existing definitions of culture (Avruch, 1998, p. 6). So, though it may be easy to acknowledge that culture plays an important role, it is surely more complex to agree on the nature and dynamics of such a role without an understanding of exactly what culture is. According to Edward Taylor in *Primitive Culture* (1870) and cited by Kevin Avruch (1998, p. 6), culture is 'that complex whole which includes knowledge, belief, art, morals, law, custom, and any other capabilities and habits acquired by man as a member of the society.' Thus, it is a mix of many elements and each has its own role in the dynamics of culture. It follows from this definition that a culture constitutes belief among other things. In turn, a belief also constitutes a whole culture of its own, which is 'capable of forming personal and social identity and influencing subsequent experience and behavior in profound ways' (Appleby, 2000, p. 9). A belief system, or simply a religion, thus not only forms part of a culture but also influences that culture with its own set of values, rituals and habits to the extent that often the line between culture and religion is blurred. Therefore, terms have been derived such as 'religious cultures,' to signify not only that a certain culture has a significant role of religion, but also that a certain religion is so pervasive in a society that it builds up the capacity to form its own culture. This explains the emergence of such terms as Muslim culture, Jewish culture, Hindu culture and so on.

Indeed, similar to any other group of people, Muslims are inspired by their religion, as well as influenced by their local cultures. Therefore, there can be no single and homogeneous 'Muslim culture.' This is also the reason why there can be no single manifestation of the religion 'Islam' since religion is imagined and expressed differently in its diverse followers. The original textual sources may be the same but their interpretations, visualizations and implementations differ with time and place, and so with culture.* Having said this, it cannot be ignored that there are still some commonalities attributed to the religion that transcend boundaries and cultural differences to form a distinct blend of local culture and religion. These are worthy of being called a Muslim culture since Islamic values and principles manifest themselves as influential determinants of values, rituals and social habits in a society. It is in this vein, and following from the point that often religion and culture are inseparable, that I explore the religious roots of a culture where Islam plays an influential role; 'a way of life' as commonly held among Muslims. The Muslim culture deeply embedded in Islamic values and principles experiences peace, conflict and violence in a particular manner. It is this particularity that I wish to bring out in this chapter.

Islam and peace?

The phenomenon of 'Islam as news' in the non-Muslim world has been around for some time, but mostly it made headlines after the Islamic Revolution of Iran in 1979. Edward Said (1997) analyzes in detail how the media and 'expert' coverage of this and other events in the Muslim world in the 1970s considerably enhanced an already existing problematic image of Islam and Muslims, which only gained strength with future events such as September 11, 2001. 'Islamic terrorism' has become a household term since then.

Though many Muslims challenge this construction and present Islam as a peaceful religion, most of them do not fully recognize the ambivalence in the textual resources (Qur'an and Hadith), which is then selectively used by some to justify acts of violence against fellow Muslims and non-Muslims. 'Peaceful Islam' remains largely rhetoric in the midst of violent conflicts involving Muslim communities around the world.

---

* Ed. This argument of religion as way of life and specifically in regards to Muslim culture can also be found in Chapter 3 on the Mediterranean.

Fortunately, one positive result of this onslaught on Islam is that some Muslim scholars have taken up the task of examining the problem. They have attempted to revisit the Islamic intellectual history and tried to explore classical Islamic doctrines, in the context of contemporary developments as regards prevailing discourses on international law, global politics, human rights, democracy, social justice, economic systems, war and peace and intercultural and interfaith relations. In doing so, many have attempted, on the one hand, to counter the negative image of Islam, and on the other hand, to present Islam as a dynamic system which promotes social justice, peace and an active and thriving community. They have done so by using the same ambivalence present in the textual sources, either by selective usage of the text or by attempting to reconcile the differences and presenting an overall view. As a result, what is now being recognized more widely is that there is a discourse in classical and contemporary Islam which actively promotes such concepts as human rights, democracy, pluralism, nonviolence and, hence, peace. These attempts have taken the form of debates that are most consequential for the future of the Islamic religious tradition itself.

These intellectual efforts have two foreseeable results. First, these efforts would help to overcome the negative image of Islam in the West. Second, these would also enable Muslims to make informed judgments about their own conduct towards fellow Muslims and non-Muslims in the light of new and renewed religious knowledge. Some of this knowledge was previously overshadowed due to the lack of sufficiently available and independent Muslim scholarship on contemporary issues, and overwhelmingly selective religious and political discourses that encouraged extremist ideologies to address conflicts.

Some of this knowledge will be presented in this chapter to show how peace is conceptualized in Islam, what the different approaches are through which peace is sought to be established, and what the underlying principles and values are that determine resolution of conflicts.

Islam: A System of *Salaam*

Before discussing various Islamic approaches to peace, it is important to see how peace is conceptualized in Islam.

From the Tables 8.1 and 8.2 it is interesting to note that *Salaam* has taken the meaning of 'peace,' whereas Islam has taken the meaning of 'submission' or 'surrender.' Both meanings – peace and submission – come from the same root and therefore it can be deduced that there is an inherent link between the two. Islam means submission in peace or one enters peace when one submits or surrenders to the system of God, which is revealed in the Qur'an. According to Said et al. (2001, p. 7), this etymological link between *Salaam* and Islam 'suggests a condition of peace, security, wholesomeness, and safety from harm that is attained through surrender (*taslim*) to the Divine.' Qureshi (1989, p. 134) also cites a verse from the Qur'an to explain this link: 'Only he who surrenders to God with all his heart and also does good, will find his reward with his Lord, and will have no fear or regret' (Qur'an: 2: 112). Here, 'no fear or regret' signifies a condition of peace and tranquility.

Table 8.1   *Salaam* and Islam

In Arabic, peace is translated as *Salaam*. The root word from which it is derived is *Salamah/Silm*, which means to admit, to consent, to submit, to reconcile, to keep safe, whole, peace, peaceful (Hava, 1970). The name of the religion *Islam* is also derived from the same root as *Salaam*. Literally, *Islam* means submission, obedience (Hava, 1970).

Table 8.2   Etymology of *Salaam**

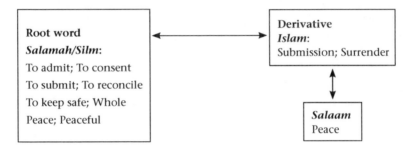

For many Western readers the meaning of Islam as submission or surrender to the Divine could be troublesome. Submitting one's ego to a belief or an unseen person called 'God' whose existence cannot be proven rationally or scientifically is probably unappealing if not abhorrent. This is especially true in the case of Western experience of religion, mainly Christianity, where Inquisitions, Crusades, Pogroms and wars conducted in the name of religion and Divine Will, have given religion and 'submission/surrender' a negative connotation. Therefore, the words 'submission' and 'surrender' should be seen in a slightly different light.

In Islam, these words carry a meaning that goes beyond simply following orders from the unknown. Harris (1998, p. 113) suggests that perhaps 'reconciliation with God' is a better term in order to convey the meaning of Islam by avoiding the 'semantically loaded' terms of submission and surrender. Reconciliation with God assumes good relations between people and deity. In times of desperation and hopelessness, people turn towards God and 'submit' to the Divine Will and pray for guidance. This act of submitting serves as an intangible support system, which produces positive psychological impulses that help people deal with their problems while believing that there is someone more powerful who loves them,

*   Ed. The etymology of *Salaam* is also explored in Chapters 3 and 7.

takes care of them, who is in control and to whom they 'submit.' According to Siddiqi (2001), the full meaning of Islam as submission is:

- To give oneself fully and completely to God;
- To enter into a covenant of peace with Him;
- To accept the path of wholesomeness and perfection which God made available for humanity through His prophets and messengers throughout history and finally through Prophet Muhammad.

Thus, apart from being in reconciliation with God, Islam also requires Muslims to submit to the system of Qur'an through which they can walk the path of wholesomeness and perfection. 'The keynote of the Qur'anic revelation could be characterized as integration and wholeness through surrender to God. This essential theme is expressed in a universalistic spirit, suggesting a world view premised on tolerance and inclusiveness' (Said et al., 2001, p. 7). Thus, peace with God is made by submitting oneself to Him through His message and peace with humankind is made by doing good.

Islam is the system of *Salaam*. Many scholars consider Islam to extend beyond submission to God's will, to define Islam as 'the making of peace' (Abu-Nimer, 2003, p. 45). 'The paths of righteousness and virtue that lead to God are also called *subul al-salam* or paths of peace (Qur'an, 5: 16). Hence, the Qur'an calls Heaven as *Dar al-Salam*, which is the home of peace and perfection (Qur'an, 10: 25)' (Siddiqi, 2001). Maulana Wahiduddin Khan (1999, p. 45) cites a verse from the Qur'an to deduce that attaining a state of peace in the soul is the spiritual goal of Islam: 'O tranquil soul, return to your Lord, well pleased and well-pleasing Him' (Qur'an, 89: 27–28). The daily greeting of Muslims is *Assalaam-o-alaikum* (may peace be upon you) that is also derived from the Qur'an (10: 10).

Siddiqi (2001) further explains: '*Salam* is an active and dynamic involvement to keep and to restore the right order. *Salam* is both an individual quest for peace and harmony for one's self and it includes the concern for the well-being of all people regardless of their races, colors or genders.' According to Siddiqi (2001), 'there are three major components in the concept of peace (*Salam*) in Islam.' These are:

- Inner peace and harmony in the life of every individual;
- Social cohesion in the community;
- Treatment of tensions and conflicts.

Thus, *Salaam* begins from the individual peace, expands to the harmony in the immediate community and encompasses conflict resolution at all levels. It aims for the peaceful whole.

Hashmi (1996, pp. 148–149) identifies several essential assumptions based on the Qur'an, the first two of which are summarized here: the first is that human fundamental nature is one of moral innocence and each individual is born with knowledge of righteous behavior. 'This moral awareness is eroded as each individual encounters the corrupting influences of human society (Qur'an, 30: 30).' The second is that it is the nature of humans to live in harmony and peace with other living beings on earth. This is a responsibility assigned by God to humans as His vicegerent on this planet (Qur'an, 2: 30). 'True peace (*Salam*) is not merely an absence of war; it is the elimination of the grounds for strife or conflict, and the resulting waste and corruption (*fasad*) they create. Peace, not war or violence, is God's true purpose for humanity (Qur'an, 2: 208).' Similarly, according to Kadayifçi-Orellana (2004, p. 43):

> Various uses of the term 'peace' in the Quran suggest that the Islamic concept of peace is wider than the absence of war. These uses recommend that peace is a positive state of safety or security, which includes being at peace with one-self, with fellow human beings, nature and God. Based on these verses, Islamic scholars associate peace with a wide range of concepts. These concepts include but are not limited to, justice and human development, wholeness, salvation, perfection and harmony.

These principles mentioned by Hashmi and elaborations given by Kadayifçi-Orellana, interestingly coincide with the explanation of the concept of peace from the perspective of peace and conflict research as 'reduction of direct, structural, and cultural violence' (Galtung, 1996, p. 223). A further distinction is between negative peace and positive peace. Galtung defines negative peace as the 'absence of violence of all kinds' (1996, p. 31) and positive peace as 'a cooperative system beyond "passive peaceful coexistence", one that can bring forth positively synergetic fruits of the harmony' (1996, p. 61). Each kind of peace can be further analyzed into its direct, structural and cultural aspects.

The Islamic equivalent of negative peace could be the Arabic concept of *Sulh*, 'which means only the end of hostilities or the implementation of truce,' while that of positive peace could be *Salaam*, 'which means an enduring peaceful relationship based on mutual respect' (Bangura, 2005, p. 6). *Sulh* is absence of war while *Salaam* insists on promotion of social justice. This positive conception of peace (*Salaam*) in Islam 'therefore suggests a condition of order – a proper equilibrium of parts – from which a pattern of harmony can emerge. This condition is both internal and external; upholding it is the responsibility of every Muslim' (Said et al., 2001, p. 7).*

---

*   Ed. For more on the concept of internal and external Islamic approaches to peace, see Chapter 3.

Since *Salaam* captures the equilibrium and wholeness, it is intricately linked with the idea of *Ummah*: the idea that all Muslims are one nation as a whole. On a communal level, each Muslim is linked with another through the concept of *Ummah*: 'The Nation where the boundaries are more spiritual and socio-cultural than geographical' (Elmandjra, 2005, p. 5), which fosters unity, peace and harmony among Muslims who are bound by one faith. Any other distinction becomes secondary. The concept of *Ummah* also coincides with the concept of *Tawhid* (unity or oneness of God) and that of *Wahdat-al-Wujud* (unity of existence). It follows from *Tawhid* that God is one and united. Since all beings are God's creation, each is linked to Him. Therefore, each creation is linked with each other through this special link with God. This is the transcendent unity of all creation. Such unity among Muslims is demonstrated through the concept of *Ummah* that supports peaceful relations between individuals and communities through equilibrium and wholeness that is envisioned in *Salaam*.

Islamic approaches to peace

The aforementioned conceptualization of *Salaam* in Islam can be concretely imagined and achieved through various approaches. These approaches are derived from a vast body of literature on Islam. According to Said et al. (2001) the main five Islamic approaches to peace are as follows:

- Power Politics: Peace through Coercive Power;
- World Order: Peace through the Power of Law;
- Conflict Resolution: Peace through the Power of Communication;
- Nonviolence: Peace through Will Power;
- Transformation: Peace through the Power of Love.

The authors acknowledge, '[w]hile there are some pundits who would question the Islamic authenticity of one approach or another, all five represent ongoing conversations as well as areas of experimentation. [...] Islam is one, but its manifestations and practices are multiple' (Said et al., 2001, pp. 16–17). These five Islamic approaches represent 'new ways of organizing knowledge about Islam, within the context of emerging global perspectives on the promotion of human solidarity and the full utilization of cultural and spiritual resources for the advancement of peace' (Said et al., 2001, p. 21). Such coverage of Islamic approaches cannot be conclusive as there could be other possible resources for inquiry into Islamic teachings and traditions.

The first approach of Power Politics presupposes a 'pessimistic reading of human nature.' It advocates the use of 'Islam as a language for legitimation of power and authority and for the preservation of social order' (Said et al., 2001,

p. 17). This approach supports state authority, strives to maintain negative peace and accepts political necessities created by internal and external threats.

The second approach of Islamic World Order takes an ethical approach and perceives Islam as a 'way of life.' It attempts to institutionalize principles and values that could create a 'humane and just order.' 'Peace is a condition of order defined by the presence of such core Islamic values as justice, equity, human dignity, cultural coexistence, and ecological stability, and not merely an absence of direct violence' (Said et al., 2001, p. 18). This and the remaining approaches in a way advocate positive peace.

The third approach of conflict resolution strays away from the state and institutional levels towards the societal and communal levels. It focuses on the Arab–Muslim traditional practices of reconciliation, mediation and arbitration. 'They affirm a restorative conception of peace and justice, encompassing notions of compensation for losses, attentiveness to issues of "face" or social esteem, renunciation of retribution for the sake of the whole, and forgiveness' (Said et al., 2001, p. 19).

The fourth approach of Nonviolence suggests peaceful strategies with a complete prohibition on the use of violence to fight against oppression and injustice. 'Adherence to Islam requires nonviolent solidarity* against oppression, the promotion of renewal through broad-based social movements, and training for programs of direct nonviolent action' (Said et al., 2001, p. 20). It follows the idea of 'Peace by Peaceful means' by Galtung (1996) that means should be according to the ends. It is based on the premise that true and lasting peace cannot be achieved through the use of violence. Only peaceful means can lead to peaceful ends.

The fifth approach of Transformation of Human Heart and Mind lays down love for divine and all creation as a precondition for harmony. 'This approach defines peace as a condition of all-embracing harmony perceived through the inward renewal and transformation of human consciousness' (Said et al., 2001, p. 21). Such 'renewal takes place within each person through inward cleansing and loving surrender to the divine' (2001, p. 21). Its principles were developed and spread by 'spiritual brotherhoods and fellowships' normally called Sufis and their practice is called Sufism (*Tasawwuf*), a loose understanding of which is Islamic Mysticism or Spiritualism.†

Each Islamic approach to peace described above functions on a distinct set of principles and values. Often, the same principles can be found under more than one approach. Thus, all these approaches, despite being diverse, have common elements that derive from some basic principles and values found in Islam. It is important to mention that Abu-Nimer (2003) has discussed seventeen such

---

* Ed. For further discussion on the concept of solidarity in Islam, see Chapter 3.
† Ed. See Chapter 9 by Uzma Rehman devoted to Islamic Sufism.

principles and values, which support Nonviolence and Peacebuilding in Islam. Similarly, other scholars, such as Qureshi (1989), Saiyidain (1997) and Khan (1999) have also discussed some of these principles under a different organization and approach. Out of these principles and values, some have been presented in this chapter which are common to most approaches and which constitute the system of *Salaam*.

The common Islamic principles and values that constitute *Salaam*

Some of the common Islamic principles and values that support the system of *Salaam* are discussed briefly as follows.

Universality

The Qur'an transcends the boundaries between race, religion, color and gender and reaches out to all humanity. It is not just limited to so-called Muslims. People from all faiths including Muslims are part of this system. The Qur'an calls to everyone: 'Easy have We made the Qur'an to understand: So, is there any one who will pay heed?' (54: 17). Further, we learn from the Qur'an that all people belong to a single community (2: 213). The Qur'an (35: 24) emphasizes that there was no part of humanity where messengers were not sent. Hence, the clear proofs, or scriptures or the Book, do not just belong to the people from Arabia, or Asia, or the present-day Muslim populations, but to the whole of humanity. It also shows that the same truth was sent to people who existed before. The Qur'an does not reject earlier revelations. In fact, it confirms them. It further claims that if God had wanted, He could have made all people into one nation (professing one faith) but this diversity in faith is by God's will (5: 48–49).

It is important to mention here, as also explored further in a later paragraph, that regarding sanctity of life, the Qur'an does not discriminate on the basis of race, religion, nationality or other distinguishing features of people. Killing one human being is like killing all humanity and saving one life is like saving the entire human race (Qur'an, 5: 32). It is applicable equally to all human beings. According to Wahiduddin Khan, the main goal of all religions is to create a 'spiritual unity' between all human beings, without which there is little hope of peace and harmony (Khan, 1999, pp. 41–42). Islam fulfills this condition through unity of God, unity of nature and unity of humanity.

Non-compulsion, plurality/diversity and tolerance

The Qur'an lays clear instructions that there must be no compulsion in the matter of faith (Qur'an, 2: 256). Even the Prophet has been warned that he is simply a messenger whose job is to remind people, but not to watch over them (Qur'an, 88: 21–22) and not to compel the people to believe (Qur'an, 10: 100). If there is disagreement, instead of resorting to violence, one should say, 'for me my actions, for you yours. You are not answerable for my deeds, or I for what you do' (Qur'an, 10: 41). These signs indicate that a person should just do his/her duty (if he/she thinks he/she has the truth) and share his/her ideas with other people. This is all one can do. Compulsion should be avoided.

At another place, in the matter of belief, it is said, 'To you your way, to me my way' (Qur'an, 109: 1–6). The diversity in faith and belief is by God's will (Qur'an, 5: 48, 10: 99, 11: 118). God has made humankind into diverse nations and tribes so that they may know each other (Qur'an, 49: 13). A Muslim must believe in all apostles and make no distinction between them (Qur'an, 4: 150–152). Thus, a Muslim can neither be disrespectful to any of the apostles nor can he disbelieve the truth of their message because he must believe in what was revealed to them before Prophet Muhammad.

As discussed in the above section on universality, the Qur'an (5: 48–49) not only 'recognizes the legitimate multiplicity of religious convictions and laws' (Abou El Fadl, 2002, p. 17) but also states that Christians, Jews or anyone who believes in God and the Last Day and does good deeds has nothing to fear or regret (Qur'an, 2: 62, 5: 69). It is interesting to see in the previous verses that the Qur'an, which is supposed to be the Holy Book of Muslims, is also talking about Jews and Christians, or anyone else for that matter, being rewarded. No single nation or people have a monopoly on salvation. It clarifies that in the eyes of God, those who believe in God and do good deeds are worthy and there are no other criteria for elevation. A Muslim or Jew or a Christian after reading this has no reason to consider himself/herself superior to others simply on the basis of religion, because there may be good people in all religions. Thus, a sense of universality and tolerance prevails. This is a strong reminder for Muslims not to develop a superiority complex and to judge others harshly.

Therefore, keeping in view this plurality, there remains no justification for compulsion. Instead, Islam cultivates tolerance and respect towards the 'other.' This may hold true for monotheist religions only, which preach one God. It is proper to say that Islam rejects polytheism. Therefore, it can be asserted that Islam is *intolerant* towards polytheism and idol worship. Islam does condemn the beliefs and practices of polytheists and idol worshippers but it does not permit a Muslim to deal with them in an arrogant and unjust manner. Polytheism is the very negation of the Qur'an, 'therefore, it was constitutionally impossible to share with the polytheists any respect for the alleged associates of God. But Islam has done what it could. If it could not enjoin respect, it has enjoined courtesy' (Qureshi, 1989, p. 16). This is also confirmed from the Qur'an (6: 107–108). Thus, a Muslim is not allowed to abuse people who follow polytheist ideologies. He/She may be unable to respect their ideologies as possible truths, since he/she disagrees with those ideas, but extends courtesy and shows tolerance towards them.

A look at the Islamic history also provides several examples of tolerance towards other religions and acceptance of this plurality on a state level. Prophet

Muhammad and some of his successors entered into several treaties and agreements with other states and with many Christian and Jewish tribes living around the city-state of Medina. Saiyidain (1997, p. 165) presents one such treaty between Prophet Muhammad and the Christians of Najran in 630 CE as an example of tolerance and respect towards people of other faiths. In another treaty of Jurjan entered into by the Prophet's successors, 'there is full protection for their life, property, religion and religious law and no changes will be made in them' (Saiyidain, 1997, p. 165). Denny (2004, p. 133) also cites the example of a governance document called the 'Constitution of Medina' concluded by Prophet Muhammad to regulate relations between Arab and Jewish factions, as a 'promising model for contemporary Islamic peacebuilding and international and interreligious relations, taking into account vastly different issues of "space and time" in a global context of international relations.'

According to Karen Armstrong, '[i]n the Islamic state [of Al-Andalus in Spain], the three religions of Judaism, Christianity, and Islam had been able to live together in relative harmony for over six hundred years' (Armstrong, 2001, p. 6). After the defeat of Muslims in Spain and as a consequence of Spanish Inquisitions that followed, many Jews who were expelled from Spain were given refuge in the Ottoman provinces of North Africa and Balkans (Armstrong, 2001, p. 8). We find another example where non-Muslims living under Muslim control were given complete freedom to practice their faith. This was the time of the Great Mughal ruler Akbar (1542–1605 CE) in India. 'He deliberately set about creating an empire in which the followers of various religions could coexist' (Eickelman, 2002, p. 120). While he supported Islamic institutions, he also encouraged the practice of reason and dialog between religions. He married non-Muslim women and appointed non-Muslims to his court on important positions. Under him, the empire expanded its boundaries to other states and communities and remained mostly peaceful.

Lamenting on the little attention given by classical Muslim scholars to the affirmation of diversity and tolerance towards others in the Qur'an, Abou El Fadl says: 'The classical commentators on the Qur'an did not fully explore the implications of this sanctioning of diversity, or the role of peaceful conflict resolution in perpetuating the type of social interaction that would result in people "knowing each other"' (Abou El Fadl, 2002, p. 16). It is interesting that in the modern Islamic discourse this is finally being rectified with several scholars[1] writing on diversity of faiths and their acceptance in the Qur'an and the importance of these principles in the context of peace.

Even though this aspect of Islamic theology has been underdeveloped, from the historical evidence 'it is fair to say that Islamic civilization was pluralistic and unusually tolerant of various social and religious denominations' (Abou El Fadl, 2002, p. 16). Hashmi (2002, pp. 32–33) agrees with this assertion as far as the pre-modern period is concerned, but grieves that the same is not true in the case of modern Islamic societies and states. Generally, scholars of the 'Qur'anic exegetical tradition tended toward conservatism and exclusivity when dealing with the Qur'anic views of the other' (Hashmi, 2002, pp. 35–36). He goes on to suggest, 'if modern Muslims are to build tolerant and pluralistic societies based on Qur'anic teachings, they must also be prepared to chart a new exegetical discourse' (Hashmi, 2002, p. 36), which I believe is in the making.

Dignity of life

After recognizing the universal outlook of the Qur'an and seeing that it affirms plurality and promotes tolerance, it is now useful to see how 'life' is perceived in the Holy Qur'an: 'that whosoever kills a human being, except (as punishment) for murder or for spreading corruption in the land, it shall be like killing all humanity; and whosoever saves a life, saves the entire human race' (Qur'an, 5: 32). Killing has thus been forbidden except for just cause (Qur'an, 17: 33).

The story of two sons of Adam, *Habil* (Abel) and *Qabil* (Caine), in the Qur'an (5: 27–30) is an illustration of the sanctity of life and of rejecting violence. In the story, *Qabil* is the aggressor and *Habil* is nonviolent. In the end, *Qabil* kills *Habil*. For Muslims, it is clear from this story that the one who chooses aggression and violence is damned, but the one who chooses nonviolence, endurance and suffering is dear to God. It is also worth noting that taking one's own life is also forbidden in the Qur'an (4: 29–30). Thus, it is clear that human life holds the highest value. It is a gift of God and must not be destroyed except in the pursuit of justice. This aspect will be discussed further in the next sections.

Patience

Patience is pointed out as one of the greatest Islamic virtues. The Qur'an has instructed humans to be patient in their dealings (Qur'an, 3: 134, 3: 186, 3: 200, 42: 43, 74: 7, 103: 1–3). God has promised to be kind to those who were victimized but endured patiently against all odds (Qur'an, 39: 10). People have been asked to be patient and not to hurry in punishing others for their deeds (Qur'an, 16: 126, 46: 35). There are many other verses in the Qur'an that deal with patience and its positive effects on human relations. While explaining patience (*Sabr*) in the Arabic language in Islam, Abu-Nimer cites Abdullah Yusuf Ali:

> *Sabr* implies many shades of meanings, which is impossible to express in one English word. It implies (1) patience in the sense of being thorough, not hasty; (2) patient perseverance, constancy, steadfastness, firmness of purpose; (3) systematic as opposed to spasmodic or chance action; (4) a cheerful attitude of resignation and understanding in sorrow, defeat, or suffering, as opposed to murmuring or rebellion, but saved from mere passivity or listlessness, by the element of constancy or steadfastness. (Yusuf Ali in Abu-Nimer, 2003, p. 71)

Thus, *Sabr* is more than just passivity and waiting. In many ways, it parallels the various shades of Gandhi's *Satyagraha*, which is also an active way of exercising perseverance and constant struggle in a peaceful way.* It is important to quote Khan (1999, p. 170) at length here as he clearly brings forth the distinction between violence and nonviolence with the help of the concept of *Sabr* in Islam:

Patience implies a peaceful response or reaction, whereas impatience implies a violent response. The word *sabr* exactly expresses the notion of nonviolence, as it is understood in modern times. That patient action is nonviolent action has been clearly expressed in the Qur'an. According to one tradition, the Prophet of Islam observed: God grants to *rifq* (gentleness) what he does not grant to *unf* (violence). The word *rifq* has been used in this hadith as an antithesis to *unf*. These terms convey exactly what is meant by violence and nonviolence in present times. This hadith clearly indicates the superiority of nonviolent method.

A non-passive, active and dynamic exercise of *Sabr* is in fact active nonviolence. Further, violence is not worthy of God's blessings. Its opposite, gentleness, is a preferred method of dealing with human relations. Logically, gentleness is a consequence of patience. Patience is enjoined on all peoples many times in the Qur'an and there are numerous traditions of the Prophet Muhammad emphasizing the need of patience in human relations. There is thus a clear indication of the divine inspiration and preference towards a culture of nonviolence through the practice of patience.

Forgiveness and reconciliation

The virtues of patience and forgiveness go together. This is the first in a series of steps leading towards reconciliation and long-lasting peace. From an Islamic point of view, one cannot practice patience and be revengeful at the same time. People are told to control rage and to forgive (Qur'an, 3: 134, 16: 110, 42: 37). They are instructed to respond peacefully (Qur'an, 25: 63, 16: 126). Choosing peace is more difficult than resorting to violence. But this choice can make the difference in conflict relations. The Qur'an goes further and proclaims that patience and forgiveness is a sign of strength and resolve (42: 43) and in a way supports the 'nonviolence of the strong,' which Gandhi so often proclaimed.

Forgiveness can have a transformative effect on human relations. This is the basic step towards reaching reconciliation. There is probably no better way to transform a conflict into friendship than as prescribed by the Qur'an: 'Good and evil are not alike. Repel evil with what is better. Then you will find your erstwhile enemy like a close, affectionate friend' (Qur'an, 41: 34). Evil may mean

---

* Ed. In Section VI on Peace Thinkers, see Chapter 25 on Ghandi.

violence/oppression and good may mean patience/no-nviolence. This injunction is similar to Christ's teaching of 'love your enemies.' In another instance, mutual consultation in settling affairs is also praised along with forgiveness (Qur'an, 16: 110). It shows that patience, forgiveness and mutual consultation go hand in hand and are the necessary vehicles for reconciliation and peaceful resolution of conflicts.

One of the most famous examples from the Islamic history concerning forgiveness is the bloodless victory of Mecca by Prophet Muhammad and his companions. In spite of the oppression and injustices perpetrated by the Meccans on Prophet Muhammad and his companions during the thirteen years of Meccan period, upon victory, Muhammad was magnanimous. He declared general amnesty for all.

In the Arab–Islamic context, the rituals of settlement (*Sulh*) and reconciliation (*Masalaha*) are important vehicles for peaceful conflict resolution, 'both of which are often referred to simply as *sulh*' (Irani and Funk, 2001, p. 182). 'The word [*Sulh*] itself has been used to refer both to a ritualized *process* of restorative justice and peacemaking and to the actual *outcome* or condition sealed by that process' (Irani and Funk, 2001, p. 183, emphasis in original). The purpose of *Sulh* is to end immediate hostilities. As mentioned earlier, it signifies negative peace. It encourages restorative justice and creates conditions to deter revenge against the perpetrator. The parties vow to forget the negative past and initiate new and friendly relations for a positive future. If successful, this process can lead to long-lasting peace, *Salaam*, or positive peace.[2]

Mediation and arbitration

In the Qur'an, promotion of peace between two parties is encouraged through diplomacy and mediation: 'If two groups of believers come to fight one another, promote peace between them [...], make peace among them equitably and be impartial' (49: 9). In another instance, those who promote reconciliation and peace are commended (Qur'an, 4: 114). This may include dialogue, negotiations, facilitation, mediation and arbitration.

An early example of mediation was the one between the Muslims of Medina and the Quraysh tribe of Mecca. A battle was averted through the offices of an Arab tribe that was friendly to both parties (Salmi et al., 1998, p. 131). While he was living in Medina, Prophet Muhammad had at least twice accepted arbitration. Perhaps the most famous case of arbitration in early Islamic history was of that between the fourth caliph Ali and Muawiya, the governor of Syria (Salmi et al., 1998, p. 132). There were two arbiters in this case, one nominated by each party.

Regarding arbitration on personal matters, the Qur'an says, '[i]f you fear a breach between them, appoint one arbiter from the people of the man and one from the people of the woman. If they wish to have a settlement then God will reconcile them, for God is all-knowing and cognizant' (4: 35). Thus, mediation and arbitration are important tools of peaceful conflict resolution and well embedded in Islamic traditions that help to achieve a settlement (*Sulh*) and ultimately restore the state of peace (*Salaam*).

Justice

Peace and justice are deeply connected. Peace is said to be a consequence of a state of social justice and order. This relationship is not only emphasized in Islam but also by several non-Muslim scholars. The conditions of social injustice, corruption and oppression equate to structural violence, which affects the society in a pervasive way. In many situations, it provokes a violent reaction from the oppressed. Therefore, it is necessary to address this cause to achieve a stable and long-lasting peace in the society.

The question arises: How does Islam establish its priority between peace and justice? Traditionally, according to Khadduri (1984, p. 162), justice 'had to prevail, if necessary, by the sword.' However, if justice can be achieved through peaceful means, without using the sword, then there is no risk of 'breaking the peace' and therefore, there is no need for setting the priority between peace and justice. Both hold the same position and importance. The establishment of justice or social order essentially follows the first approach of Power Politics and the second approach of Power of Law, as mentioned previously. The Islamic state uses law to establish a just social order for the sake of peace. The same can be achieved through nonviolent means within the fourth approach of Nonviolence.

In Islam, justice has many aspects for which many different words are used in Arabic. However, the most commonly used word is *Adl*. According to Khadduri (1984, p. 8), '[t]he literal meaning of "Adl" in classical Arabic is thus a combination of moral and social values denoting fairness, balance, temperance and straight-forwardness.' In the Qur'an, justice is one of the most emphasized principles. To achieve this end, everybody must be treated equal (Qur'an, 4: 58, 4: 135). True and honest testimony of the witness is encouraged and emphasized (Qur'an, 2: 283, 5: 8). Further, Khan (1999, p. 169) points out that God abhors corruption (*Fasad*) (Qur'an, 2: 205), and that God does not love those who create disorder and spread corruption in the land (Qur'an, 5: 64). This corruption and disorder is the antithesis of *Salaam*, which claims equilibrium and right order that leads to a state of safety, security, unity, wholeness and peace.

Therefore, in order to restore *Salaam*, the Qur'an urges Muslims to stand up firmly for justice (16: 90, 4: 135, 5: 8). It urges Muslims to fight for it and those who do not do so are considered accomplices of the oppressors (Qur'an, 4: 75–76). Demanding action against wrongdoing is permitted; however, patience and forgiveness are still preferred (Qur'an, 42: 39–43). This fighting against injustice and oppression, and demanding an action against certain wrongdoings, is sometimes interpreted as a divine injunction to wage a violent campaign. However, the same ends can also be achieved through peaceful means. The divine injunction for a violent response to injustice and oppression is mainly supported by an occasional allowance of force in the Qur'an and the often-misconstrued notion of *Jihad*. It is useful to consider each, one by one.

Jihad

The instrument with which Islam sought to achieve its objectives of establishing a just social order and peace was *Jihad* (Khadduri, 1984, p. 164). It is said to have both violent and nonviolent manifestations, which suggests, 'Islam's ultimate goals might be achieved by peaceful as well as violent means' (Khadduri, 1984, p. 164). It is in fact a perfect example of the *Ambivalence of the Sacred* (Appleby, 2000) where the original text has been interpreted in contrasting ways. Unfortunately, *Jihad's* violent manifestation is most acknowledged while the nonviolent one has been largely ignored.

Jihad in Arabic means striving, struggle, exertion, effort, attempt (Hava, 1970; Noorani, 2002, p. 45; Harris, 1998, p. 96; Küng, 2005, p. 259; Khadduri, 1984, p. 164; Abou El Fadl, 2002, p. 19), 'denoting that the individual is urged to use his utmost endeavors to fulfill a certain function or carry out a specific task' (Khadduri, 1984, p. 164). Various forms of *Jihad* or struggle are presented. These are *Jihad* by heart, *Jihad* by tongue, *Jihad* by hands and *Jihad* by sword (Khadduri, 1984, pp. 164–165). There is, however, a general consensus among scholars that *Jihad* by heart or spiritual *Jihad* is the best form of *Jihad*. This is commonly known as the Greater *Jihad*. *Jihad* by sword is its lowest form. It is commonly known as the Lesser *Jihad*.

The Greater *Jihad* is essentially self-struggle. It implies that each Muslim strives to become a better human being. In doing so, the follower of *Jihad* can also benefit his or her community. This inner struggle is one of the basic principles in Sufism.*

The Lesser *Jihad* is said to be the violent struggle. Islam prohibited war in all other forms except in the form of *Jihad* (Khadduri, 1966, p. 16). But, even in its most violent manifestations, *Jihad* is not a Muslim 'Holy War,' as rightly observed by Küng (2005, p. 259): 'The combination of the words "holy" and "war" does not appear in the Koran; according to Islamic understanding, a war can never be "holy".' Abou El Fadl (2002, p. 19) also confirms: 'Holy war (*al-harb al-muqaddasah*) is not an expression used by the Qur'anic text or Muslim theologians. In Islamic theology war is never holy; it is either justified or not, and if it is justified, those killed in battle are considered martyrs.' Perhaps, Lesser *Jihad* or violent struggle is equivalent to the concept of 'Just War' in Christianity. Khadduri (1984, p. 165) accepts this without qualifications, whereas Hashmi (1996, p. 164) agrees that there are similarities between the two concepts.

Khadduri (1984, pp. 164–173; 1966, pp. 57–60) also traces the evolution in the interpretation and manifestation of the concept of *Jihad* in classical

---

*   Ed. In Chapter 9, also a thorough discussion on inner *jihad* can be found.

Islamic discourses between the eighth and the fourteenth centuries from being a defensive war against anyone, to an offensive war against unbelievers, to a defensive war against unbelievers, and back and forth. This constant evolution in the meaning of *Jihad* was induced by changing circumstances of each era where Muslim scholars debated and interpreted *Jihad*, among other concepts, in the light of existing realities of their time. 'Many classical jurists adopted an imperialist orientation, which divided the world into the abode of Islam and the abode of war, and supported expansionist wars against unbelievers. But this view was not unanimous' (Abou El Fadl, 2002, p. 20). Thus *Jihad* was one of the doctrines that was used to regulate the relations between Muslims and non-Muslims in a political context that rendered the concept of *Jihad* susceptible to interpretations to suit the political needs of its time and place.

In contrast to the violent manifestations of the Lesser *Jihad*, a few other scholars such as Wahiduddin Khan limit the understanding of *Jihad* to the Greater *Jihad* only. Khan does not subscribe to the manifestation of *Jihad* as physical fighting. He explains *Jihad* and the difference between violent and nonviolent struggle as follows:

> Jihad means struggle, to struggle one's utmost. It must be appreciated at the outset that this word is used for nonviolent struggle as opposed to violent struggle. One clear proof of this is the verse of Qur'an (25: 52), which says: Perform Jihad with this (i.e. the word of Qur'an) most strenuously. (Khan, 1999, p. 171)

In this case, performing *Jihad* with the Qur'an would mean an ideological struggle, as it is a book of ideology rather than a sword or a gun. He explains it further, 'In the light of this [aforementioned] verse of the Qur'an, *Jihad* in actual fact is another name for peaceful activism or nonviolent activism. Where *Qital* is violent activism, *Jihad* is nonviolent activism' (Khan, 1999, p. 171). So, he puts all that is nonviolent activism under *Jihad*, purifying *Jihad* from all its violent manifestations. He further categorizes *Qital* as violent activism.

However, things are murkier than this. Interestingly, at most occasions *Qital* instead of *Jihad* is used in the Qur'an to express warfare. The doctrine of warfare can be extracted from the Qur'an on its own by exposing the various forms of the Arabic word *Qital* without leaning on the doctrine of *Jihad*. But traditionally, the doctrine of warfare in Islam has absorbed the doctrine of *Jihad*.

Various forms of the Arabic root *q-t-l* (*Qital* being one of those) are used forty-four times in relation to warfare. Similarly, various forms of the Arabic root *j-h-d* (*Jihad* being one of those) are used ten out of forty-one times in the Qur'an in relation to warfare (Landau-Tasseron, 2008). Although it is only a small number of times that *Jihad* has been used in connection with warfare, curiously it is sufficient enough to make the interpretation of *Jihad* as warfare the dominant one. Thus, *Jihad* has been largely used instead of *Qital* to denote the Islamic doctrine of warfare.

By making warfare the dominant interpretation of *Jihad* and *Jihad* the dominant representation of warfare, the warfare was given a moral and holy connotation that is normally ascribed to *Jihad*, thereby inflating the appeal for warfare. Since separating *Jihad* from warfare is not entirely possible, since at least on ten occasions *Jihad* is used in connection with warfare in the Qur'an, an effort should at least be made to highlight *Jihad's* essential meaning of nonviolent struggle, which is overshadowed. Distinguishing, and not necessarily separating, *Jihad* and *Qital* would also help to check unnecessary co-option of *Jihad* to legitimate or holify and even exaggerate the necessity of war.

The Qur'an allows the use of force in limited circumstances as described below. It should be noted that all verses selected in the following sections contain the word *Qital* or its derived form in Arabic, to expressly state the use of force. It will also be clear that the Qur'anic use of force is always in *reaction* to an act of war, injustice or oppression. It never allows the first use of force. In the end, an attempt will be made to reconcile the Qur'anic injunctions on nonviolence and peaceful conflict resolution, and the use of force within the context of *Salaam*.

Self-defense

While keeping a peaceful and nonviolent approach towards a conflict situation, the Qur'an realizes that there will be times when war is imposed upon people and in order to save themselves, people will need to respond with violence. Therefore, it allows the use of force, but only in case of self-defense. 'Fight those in the way of God who fight you, but do not be aggressive; God does not like aggressors' (2: 190). There are two very important laws or restrictions laid out in the above injunction. First, it allows people to use force in repelling attacks from other people. It allows so only in case of self-defense, as it is apparent: 'fight those who fight you.' The second restriction is that people should not exceed the limits of the necessity of war. It means that people who respond forcefully should be defensive and not aggressive. This rule is also repeated with a further clause for peace: 'But if they are inclined to peace, make peace with them, and have trust in God, for He hears all and knows everything' (8: 61). Further, '[i]f they keep aloof and do not fight, and offer peace, God has left you no reason to fight them' (4: 90). Thus, if the attackers rebound or stop their aggression and offer peace, then it is obligatory to choose peace over war.

In a few other places in the Qur'an, killing is allowed in a situation of war (2: 190–192, 4: 89–91). It should be remembered that in these verses and elsewhere, 'the Koran's calls to war reflect the specific situation of the Prophet in the Medina period and the particular nature of the Medina suras [chapters in the Qur'an]. Precisely those calls to fight against the polytheistic Meccans cannot be used today as a principle justifying the use of force' (Küng, 2005, p. 264). These calls to fight are limited according to the aforementioned principles of being defensive and preferring peace to violence.

There are many limitations placed on the use of warfare by several classical Muslim jurists (Salmi et al., 1998, pp. 119–130). These are at least equal to, and may exceed, the limits placed by the Geneva Conventions. The point of contextual interpretation as mentioned by Küng is further elaborated upon by Noorani (2002, pp. 52–56) by referring to several interpretations of the above verses from some Muslim and non-Muslim scholars of Islam. Unfortunately, some Muslims take these verses out of context and use these to justify violent actions against non-Muslims in general.

Oppression and injustice

The Qur'an gives permission for, and sometimes obligates people to fight against, oppression and tyranny, as shown in the following verse, but as other verses discussed above, this fight is in reaction to the act of oppression. 'So, fight them till all oppression ends and judgment is wholly God's. If they desist then verily God sees all they do' (Qur'an, 8: 39). At another place, '[w]hat has come upon you that you do not fight in the cause of God and for the oppressed, men, women and children...those who believe fight in the way of God; and those who do not, only fight for the powers of evil' (Qur'an, 4: 75–76).

So, the people are encouraged to stand with the oppressed and to fight for their rights. Those who do not are considered accomplices of the oppressors. It is interesting that some international law experts have also recognized justification for this kind of response against oppression. According to Ilesanmi (2000, p. 151), '[w]hen State managers substitute private gain for the common good and violate the inherent, although not absolute, rights of their fellow citizens, their actions constitute "systemic violence", which is no less aggressive and invasive than infliction of physical harm.' Under such oppressive systems, rebellion by people is a '*responsive* action...a necessary act of "self-defense" and "*counter* violence", taken as a last resort to protect the innocent' (Campbell in Ilesanmi, 2000, p. 155, emphasis in original). What Ilesanmi and Campbell are suggesting from the viewpoint of international law has been suggested by the Qur'an, in the aforementioned verses, which gives the right to fight against oppression. Permission to fight is also given at another place in the Qur'an (22: 39–40):

> Permission is granted those who fight because they were oppressed. God is certainly able to give help to those, who were driven away from their homes for no other reason than they said: 'Our Lord is God.' And if God had not restrained some men through some others, then monasteries, churches, synagogues and mosques would have been razed, where the name of God is honored most. God will surely help those who help Him; verily God is all-powerful and all mighty.

In the above verses, first, a clear permission is granted to fight against oppression. Second, the words 'if God had not *restrained* some men through some others' are of significant value. The word 'restrained' signifies use of force. It means that God let some men use force to stop other men (God allowed reaction or defense) so that the places of God's worship are not razed.

Two points are worth noting here. The first is the use of force for the sole purpose of defense or protection. The second is the inclusion of houses of worship of religions other than Islam. It does not mention only the Muslim house of worship, the mosque, but it acknowledges that in all houses of worship God's name is honored. This further confirms the earlier assertion that Islam is universal in its approach and includes all within its system. It enjoins people to use force to protect places of worship, not only mosques, but churches, monasteries and synagogues as well.

Commenting on the allowance of force in the Qur'an, Qureshi takes into account the political and social consequences of a complete prohibition of force. It is important to quote him at length:

> A total prohibition of force will naturally result in disobedience, because what can the oppressed do, if not fight, in the last resort? When a doctrine is found to [be in] conflict with the law of existence, it will not be obeyed. And what is more, it will result in a general disregard for moderation, and even law. Therefore, the right thing would be to preach that force is to be considered a divine gift, and as such, a sacred trust to be used only for the sake of justice. It should never be prostituted for aggression or injustice. It is a weapon for protection, not destruction. And more than this, it is too sacred a weapon to be used without thought. If used at all, it should be used only in the last resort. When all other attempts have failed and some great injustice is still crying for redress then, and then only, is it to be used. (Qureshi, 1989, p. 59)

This use of force as supported by Qureshi, falls under the general aim of Islam, which is restoration of order and social justice in a society, which is a prerequisite for long lasting peace.

Mediation

One more verse from the Qur'an on the use of force would have been especially appropriate to quote if a comparison with modern peace theories was being made. Nonetheless, it will be used here to show as much as possible the complete philosophy of the use of force in the Qur'an and how it professes to achieve peace in different situations.

> If two groups of believers come to fight one another, promote peace between them. Then if one of them turns aggressive against the other, fight against the

aggressive party till it returns to God's authority. If it does so, make peace among them equitably and be impartial. Verily God loves those who are just. (49: 9)

There are three important messages in this verse. The first is the promotion of peace between two warring factions. As mentioned in the previous section on mediation and arbitration, the promotion of peace may include dialogue, negotiations, facilitation, mediation and arbitration. The second is the use of force against a party, which, after rejecting peace initiatives, resorts to violence and aggression against the other party. The Qur'an allows using force against the aggressing party until it is ready to come back to the table. And then third, it instructs the peacemakers to be impartial and just in their dealings with both parties.

It may be recalled from the tables above that the meaning of *Salaam* includes 'to keep safe' – safety from harm as well. It is in this context that the principles of the use of force should be looked upon. Using force or violence for self-defense, fighting against oppression, and mediation are allowed for the sake of human safety and security. In modern peace discourse, these are loaded terms but let us just take these at their face value: safety and security of life from harm. To this end, sometimes force is necessary to repel force. This is of course a short-term objective to achieve negative peace.

Ambivalence of *Salaam*: nonviolence and/or use of force?

After analyzing Qur'anic injunctions on the use of force in the case of self-defense, oppression and injustice, and especially the one above concerning mediation, the question of 'peaceful conflict resolution' arises. On one side, the Qur'an encourages nonviolence and on the other, sanctions use of force and violence. These are two different approaches towards the same goal. An attempt is made to reconcile this ambivalence found in the concept of *Salaam* in this section.

Many writings are available in classical Islamic literature dealing with these issues. Some contemporary scholars have also attempted to address these topics. There are three main approaches towards war and peace in Islam, as briefly mentioned by Kadayifçi-Orellana (2004, pp. 40–42) and in relative detail by Abu-Nimer (2003, pp. 25–47). The first approach is the 'offensive' approach. The scholars in this category believe that Islam holds the exclusive truth, and believers must actively engage in fighting offensive wars to establish God's system, including attacks on civilians if necessary. The second approach is the 'defensive' approach. The scholars in this category recognize that Islam allows use of force in certain conditions, the most obvious of which is 'self-defense.' Accordingly, Muslims may use force in the face of oppression and persecution in order to defend themselves and to establish justice and restore harmony. The third approach is the 'nonviolent' approach. Scholars in this category believe that nonviolent resistance is the *preferred* method to fight against injustice and for resolving conflicts according to the Islamic principles.

Now, the question arises: Which approach or interpretation is correct? The answer to this question is not final and continues to be the subject of intense debate. Bassam Tibi (1996, p. 129) would suggest: 'Instead, there are a number of different traditions, each of which draws selectively on the Qur'an to establish legitimacy for its views of war and peace.' Tibi is talking about the *Ambivalence of the Sacred* and interestingly recognizes that under different circumstances, different verses of the Qur'an could be applicable. Through this ambivalence, it is also important to recognize that there are peaceful traditions available from the Qur'an in abundance, which foster nonviolence and peaceful conflict resolution, as has been shown in preceding sections. Therefore, a better question would be: How can these different approaches be reconciled in an attempt to keep an overall view of the Qur'anic message?

According to my present knowledge of the Qur'an and what I have been able to present, fighting (*Qital*) against injustice and oppression is allowed, and sometimes obligated, but how this fight is to be fought is not defined in the Qur'an. Maybe one verse can act as a guiding principle: that the recompense of a crime shall be its equivalent (Qur'an 42: 40). Here it does not explain 'equivalent' in quality (a direct or indirect response) or in 'quantity' (respond to what extent?). Therefore, it can be assumed that it means equivalent in both, quality and quantity. To express the point in contemporary peace research terminology, this approach would mean:

- First, the response to a situation of direct violence and aggression, such as war, could be self-defense, which is equivalent in quality (direct response against direct aggression) and quantity (not aggressive: limited to its necessity);
- Second, the response to a situation of indirect or structural violence (injustice and oppression) could be an indirect or structural response, which is using nonviolent struggle for change. So, the reaction would depend upon the action.

But, using another verse in the Qur'an creates a dilemma. It says: 'repel evil with what is better. Then you will find your erstwhile enemy like a close, affectionate friend' (Qur'an, 41: 34). Following this principle, how can one respond to violence with violence? There seems to be a contradiction between the two verses, which propose two entirely different approaches. However, quite interestingly, an amicable reconciliation between the seemingly two opposite commandments is provided by the second part of the first verse: 'but whoever forgives and makes right, then his reward is upon God' (42: 40).

In short, if one is left with no choice but to use force against a threat to one's survival, then it is allowed. However, forgiveness, patience and therefore nonviolence are the preferred choice. On the one hand, while acknowledging the political realities of a given situation, the Qur'an tries to achieve a higher moral approach towards addressing conflicts on the other hand. This is what could be called 'idealistic realism' (Hashmi, 1996, p. 151). The Qur'an realizes that some people might have to resort to the use of force in order to resist and repel direct violence. This is based on a practical and immediate solution for survival against a direct threat. Therefore, in this case, fighting or violent activism (*Qital*) is sanctioned in some places. However, acknowledging a higher moral ground and realizing the need for long-lasting peace, the Qur'an takes a nonviolent approach towards resolution of conflicts. Thus, there is a choice available to humans according to the given situation. It must be made clear that this choice is not between fighting and not fighting. As shown previously, one is not only allowed to fight, but is also obligated to fight under oppression and injustice. The choice is between two ways of fighting: violent and nonviolent according to the given situation, in order to restore order, harmony, safety and a sense of wholeness – peace – *Salaam*. In other words, both nonviolence and violence have their role in the system of *Salaam*.

Another way of looking at the two seemingly contrasting ways is to place them in sequence. First, force is allowed to repel aggression, achieving a ceasefire, a settlement: *Sulh* – a state of negative peace. Then, using forgiveness and reconciliation to move to a state of harmony, equilibrium and wholeness: a state of positive peace – *Salaam*.

Conclusion

The Qur'anic references can arguably be said to signify the 'Islamic' in the Islamic culture, while the various manifestations of these principles in a particular cultural setting can be called the 'cultural,' as in the case of the Arabic practice of *Sulh/ Masalaha*. The Islamic, in other words, signifies the commonalities, while cultural aspects and histories signify the particular manifestations of those commonalities resulting in a unique blend called the Muslim culture.

From a cultural perspective, in Muslim societies, contemporary models of peace and conflict resolution based on secular principles will neither have a large acceptance because of their Western orientation, nor will these be as effective as when these are based on religion, because Islam still has a profound influence in Muslim communities. It is also important to recognize that sources of nonviolent alternatives from either Hinduism/Jainism (Gandhi) or Christianity (Martin Luther King Jr.) will be rendered useless, unless those alternatives are shown to be deeply embedded in Islamic traditions. The notion of 'Cultural Triumphalism' has currency in the Western culture – the triumphant culture – but holds no ground in Islamic societies. Muslims are proud of their religious culture and would resist any imposition of principles and values that are seen to have roots outside their own tradition.

Therefore, it is important to reclaim and highlight the knowledge buried in the ashes of the Muslim history and reorient it according to the present times. The reasons for the success of early Islam lay in its societal project and governance – its stress on justice, social order and absence of violence. Therefore, it was more concerned with 'establishing' peace in an era of tribal warfare than exploring philosophical and theoretical shades of 'peace,' which was done later in a time of relative peace when Muslims established their own state and Islamic intellectual thought began to develop. This is perhaps also the reason why the Islamic approach towards establishing peace is that of 'idealistic realism.' While proposing a higher moral approach of nonviolence towards addressing conflicts, the Qur'an allows a violent approach in certain cases out of the necessity of survival. While accepting the ideal, it does not ignore the real. This is the reconciling point in the seemingly obvious ambivalence in the system of *Salaam*. It may be appreciated that the overall message of *Salaam* is mostly nonviolent and tends towards positive peace after a state of negative peace has been achieved.

It has been shown that having been a thriving civilization, Islamic traditions are rich in principles and values that support a just social system where every being is in harmony with each other, thus creating a sense of completeness and wholeness where one can live in peace – *Salaam*. If that harmony is disturbed, then there are alternatives available, both violent and nonviolent, to restore that system of peacefulness.

Notes

1. A few notable works are by Qureshi (1989), Hashmi (1996), Khan (1999), Sachedina (2001), Abou El Fadl (2002), Masud (2002) and Abu-Nimer (2003).
2. For a curious reader, a summary of the complete *Sulh* process is given by Mousalli (2001, p. 187) in an Arab–Islamic context.

Reference list

Abou El Fadl, K. (2002) 'The Place of Tolerance in Islam' in J. Cohen and I. Lague (eds.) *The Place of Tolerance in Islam: Khaled Abou El Fadl* (Boston: Beacon Press).

Abu-Nimer, M. (2003) *Nonviolence and Peacebuilding in Islam: Theory and Practice* (Gainesville: University Press of Florida).

Appleby, R.S. (2000) *The Ambivalence of the Sacred: Religion, Violence and Reconciliation* (Lanham/Boulder/New York/Oxford: Rowman & Littlefield).

Armstrong, K. (2001) *The Battle for God: A History of Fundamentalism* (New York: Random House).

Avruch, K. (1998) *Culture and Conflict Resolution* (Washington DC: United States Institute of Peace Press).

Bangura, A.K. (2005) (ed.) *Islamic Peace Paradigms* (Dubuque/Iowa/Kendall: Hunt).

Denny, F.M. (2004) 'Islam and Peacebuilding: Continuities and Transitions' in H. Coward and S.G. Smith (eds.) *Religion and Peacebuilding* (Albany: State University of New York Press).

Eickelman, D.F. (2002) 'Islam and Ethical Pluralism' in S.H. Hashmi (ed.) *Islamic Political Ethics: Civil Society, Pluralism, and Conflict* (Princeton/Oxford: Princeton University Press).

Elmandjra, M. (2005) 'What Future for Islam in Europe?' Paper presented for Club of Rome and Islamic Cultural Centre of Valencia, Valencia, September 15, 2005.

Galtung, J. (1996) *Peace by Peaceful Means: Peace and Conflict, Development and Civilization* (London/Thousand Oaks/New Delhi: Sage).

Harris, R.T. (1998) 'Nonviolence in Islam: The Alternative Community Tradition' in D.L. Smith-Christopher (ed.) *Subverting Hatred: The Challenge of Nonviolence in Religious Traditions* (Boston: Boston Research Center for the 21st Century).

Hashmi, S.H. (1996) 'Interpreting the Islamic Ethics of War and Peace' in T. Nardin (ed.) *The Ethics of War and Peace: Religious & Secular Perspectives* (Princeton/New Jersey: Princeton University Press).

Hashmi, S.H. (2002) 'A Conservative Legacy' in J. Cohen and I. Lague (eds.) *The Place of Tolerance in Islam: Khaled Abou El Fadl* (Boston: Beacon Press).

Hava, J.G. (1970) *Al-Faraid Arabic-English Dictionary* (Beirut: Catholic Press/Dar el-Mashreq).

Ilesanmi, S.O. (2000) 'Just War Theory in Comparative Perspective: A Review Essay,' *Journal of Religious Ethics*, 28, 1, 139–155.

Irani, G.E. and N.C. Funk (2001) 'Rituals of Reconciliation: Arab-Islamic Perspectives' in A.Z. Said, N.C. Funk and A.S. Kadayifçi (eds.) *Peace and Conflict Resolution in Islam: Precept and Practice* (Lanham/New York/Oxford: University Press of America).

Kadayifçi-Orellana, S.A. (2004) 'Religion, Violence and the Islamic Tradition of Nonviolence' in *The Turkish Yearbook of International Relations*, XXXIV (Ankara: Ankara Universitesi Basimevi).

Khadduri, M. (1966) *The Islamic Law of Nations: Shaybani's Siyar* (Baltimore: The Johns Hopkins University Press).

Khadduri, M. (1984) *The Islamic Conception of Justice* (Baltimore/London: The Johns Hopkins University Press).

Khan, M.W. (1999) *Islam and Peace* (New Delhi: Goodword Books/Al-Risala).

Küng, H. (2005) 'Religion, Violence and "Holy Wars",' *International Review of the Red Cross*, 87, 858, 253–268.

Landau-Tasseron, E. (2008) 'Jihād' in J.D. McAuliffe (ed.) *Encyclopaedia of the Qur'ān* (Washington DC: Brill).

Masud, M.K. (2002) 'The Scope of Pluralism in Islamic Moral Traditions' in S.H. Hashmi (ed.) *Islamic Political Ethics: Civil Society, Pluralism, and Conflict* (Princeton/Oxford: Princeton University Press).

Mousalli, A.S. (2001) 'An Islamic Model for Political Conflict Resolution: *Tahkim* (Arbitration)' in A.A. Said, N.C. Funk and A.S. Kadayifçi (eds.) *Peace and Conflict Resolution in Islam: Precept and Practice* (Lanham/New York/Oxford: University Press of America).

Noorani, A.G. (2002) *Islam and Jihad: Prejudice versus Reality* (London: Zed Books).

Qureshi, I.H. (1989) *The Religion of Peace* (Karachi: Royal Book Company).

Sachedina, A. (2001) *The Islamic Roots of Democratic Pluralism* (New York: Oxford University Press).

Said, A.A., N.C. Funk and A.S. Kadayifçi (2001) 'Islamic Approaches to Peace and Conflict Resolution' in A.A. Said, N.C. Funk and A.S. Kadayifçi (eds.) *Peace and Conflict Resolution in Islam: Precept and Practice* (Lanham/New York/Oxford: University Press of America).

Said, E.W. (1997) *Covering Islam: How the Media and the Experts Determine How We See the Rest of the World* (New York: Vintage Books).

Saiyidain, K.G. (1997) *Islam: The Religion of Peace* (New Delhi: Dr. Abid Husain Memorial Trust/Har-Anand Publications).

Salmi, R.H., C.A. Majul and G.K. Tanham (1998) *Islam and Conflict Resolution* (Lanham/New York/Oxford: University Press of America).

Siddiqi, M.H. (2001) 'Islam is Peace,' http://www.pakistanlink.com/religion/2001/1102.html, date accessed October 15, 2004.

Tibi, B. (1996) 'War and Peace in Islam' in T. Nardin (ed.) *The Ethics of War and Peace: Religious and Secular Perspectives* (Princeton/New Jersey: Princeton University Press).

9
Salaam: A Sufi Perspective

Uzma Rehman

> There is no peace at the lower level of living, i.e. the level of one's human ego. On the inner spiritual path, one becomes enlightened, rising above all common differences of the culture, language, creed and religion as the enlightened one is travelling towards the inner reality whose essence is eternal love.
>
> Baba Jaan Sarkaar Dr. Muhammad Youssuf Shaheen Shah

Introduction

Historically speaking, Sufism or the mystical dimension of Islam has been accommodated in a variety of cultural contexts. Sufism has especially been active in the form of Sufi orders and followers of Sufi way of life in societies such as the Indian subcontinent (Eaton, 1978, 1997), Indonesia (Geertz, 1968), Turkey (Hammarlund et al., 1999), Egypt (Hoffman, 1995), and parts of Morocco (Gellner, 1984), Sudan (Mahmoud, 1997) and Senegal (Samson, 2000).* An example of this is the active presence of the Sufi literary and institutional traditions in several Muslim-majority societies as well as its increasing popularity among Western societies, especially at transnational levels (Werbner, 2003; Malik and Hinnells, 2006). Popular Sufism – in both its institutional and literary forms – is not only practiced in several Middle Eastern, African and Asian societies, it has also been operating in Western societies such as Europe and America[1] since the 1960s and 1970s especially with immigration from Asia, the Middle East and Africa to these countries. The popularity of Sufism in the West has especially been on a rise in recent years (Hermansen, 2006, pp. 28–29). In the case of the Indian subcontinent,† the Sufi tradition is said to have flourished in the Indian society due to its 'multi-racial, multi-religious and multilingual pattern' (Nizami,

---

* Ed. Section V of this book focuses on peace concepts in Africa. On Islamic understandings as Rehman mentions, see especially Chapter 24 on African *Salaam*.
† Ed. In Chapter 11, Swami Bheda Vharati offers a rich overview of peace notions in India.

1999). It is therefore not surprising that Sufism is considered to have potential for peacemaking.

Scholars trace abundant material within historical Islamic sources – the Qur'an,[2] the *Hadith*[3] and the Prophet's *Sunnah*[4] – that sheds light on the techniques of peace and conflict resolution (Said et al., 2001; Abu-Nimr, 2000/01, 2003). The Islamic concept of peace is often linked with Sufism.[5] Scholars of conflict resolution and peace studies argue that shared aspirations exist for peace in religious traditions (Boulding, 1986, p. 501). It is this perspective that points to the role of the Sufi tradition.

Sufism is considered a form of spirituality that 'transcends socially defined boundaries of religion' and that defines culture 'as a resource whose function is to express our humanity in ways that make us more human' (Said and Funk, 2004). Scholars argue that Sufism is as relevant for the contemporary world as it has been for centuries (Ernst, 1997; Nasr, 2000). Others speak for its relevance for people's practical lives (Michel, 2005). Sufism is also said to contain solutions for the anxieties in individual and collective lives of people especially in a globalized world that poses unique challenges to societies (Said and Funk, 2004).

In this chapter, I use three dimensions of Sufism to explore its role in peacemaking:

1. The theosophic[6] dimension of Sufism constitutes the philosophy and tenets that are based on the Islamic belief of *Tawhid*[7] or the concept of *Wahdat al-Wujud*.[8] I explain the Sufi concept of peace through its notion of unity in diversity, and its spiritual interpretations of the Islamic concepts such as *jihad*, justice, and so on.
2. The institutional dimension of Sufism entails the popular tradition of Sufi *khanqahs* and *dargahs*[9] that is based on egalitarian principles and has inclusive structures and organization. The popular institutional dimension of Sufism combines beliefs and rituals related with saint-reverence that are shared by Muslim and non-Muslim populations living in certain societies. This has sometimes given rise to syncretistic traditions.
3. The popular literary dimension of Sufism is perceived to have an interreligious appeal. In most cases, the Sufi poetry relies not only on imagery and on concepts of Islamic background, it also borrows features from the literary genres and cultural traditions existing in the host societies where Sufism came to establish itself.

I use the case of Sufism in the Indian subcontinent because it illustrates how its theosophic, institutional and literary dimensions contribute to peacemaking. The Indian subcontinent is known to be a historically diverse society with multireligious, multicultural and multilinguistic traditions coexisting for centuries. Sufism also found a social environment in the Indian subcontinent that was suitable to its theosophic, institutional and literary dimensions. It is where Sufi institutions and literary traditions maintain their popular appeal to this day. In this regard, the Sufi concept of peace is related to cultural pluralism. In order to investigate this, I will first define the concepts of peace, culture and cultural pluralism.

Peace culture as cultural pluralism

The term 'peace' is defined both negatively and positively. In a negative connotation, it may mean 'freedom from war and unrest,' while a positive definition of peace is linked to 'well-being and fulfilment as goals of religious and social life' (Parrinder, 1987, p. 221). The term 'culture' used here may be understood broadly as 'the symbolic aspect of human existence,' to use Johan Galtung's words (2003). Based on this definition, a 'culture' contains religious, social, intellectual and linguistic elements within or even beyond a particular geographical context.

Elaborating on peace culture, Elise Boulding (1998) remarks that it is the 'creative management of differences [that] is at the core of peace culture.' To her, '[a] peace culture maintains creative balance among bonding, community closeness, and the need for separate spaces. It can be defined as a mosaic of identities, attitudes, values, beliefs and patterns that leads people to live nurturingly with one another and the earth itself without the aid of structured power differentials, to deal creatively with their differences, and to share their resources' (Boulding, 1998). Boulding considers Sufis and Anabaptists as nonviolent holy peace communities within Islam and Christianity, respectively.

Defining cultural pluralism

Drawing on Boulding's understanding of a 'peace culture,' I will define cultural pluralism as a term that not only means the presence of culturally diverse groups within a geographical, political or social context, but also an amiable interaction between them based on mutual recognition and friendly exchange of ideas, practices, genres of popular devotional, literary and musical traditions contributing to composite cultures, while at the same time maintaining their original character. In this perspective, it is imperative for a tradition to maintain its original character, since assimilation of any one culture by another – for example, assimilation of a minority culture by a majority culture – would not amount to cultural pluralism but rather to cultural imposition.

In this chapter, I use the cultural-pluralist approach to link the theosophic, institutional and literary dimensions of Sufism to the concept of peace. Cultural pluralism, openness to cultural diversity and adaptation to diverse social environments can serve as a barometer for assessing the role of a tradition in peacemaking. According to this approach, it is under the umbrella of Sufi principles contained in its theosophical tradition that cultural pluralism has been practiced in popular Sufi institutions – historical *khanqahs* and present *dargahs* or tombs of saints – as well as transmitted through the literary legacies of Sufi saint-poets.

Extending Boulding's (1998) analysis, we can then argue that a cultural-pluralist approach:

1. Acknowledges diversity and multiplicity of the divine creation and at the same time an essential unity among these.
2. Recognizes that structures, organization and functions of Sufi institutions are based on egalitarian principles whereby people's diverse social, religious and ethnic backgrounds are recognized, accommodated and creatively employed for attaining effective systems of transmission of broad-based values led by overarching universal principles.
3. Maintains that the literary and musical traditions provide a link between the Sufi traditions and the popular devotional practices such as saint-reverence through metaphors and symbols from the folk traditions; that the literary and musical tradition contained in Sufism refers to the local religious, cultural and social traditions and is not homogeneous in its contents and references.

Sufism and cultural pluralism

If one considers the concept of peace linked to cultural pluralism, as Boulding does, religious systems contribute to peace in societies by allowing diverse devotional and popular practices to coexist and flourish. This undermines sharp boundaries between diverse religious beliefs and devotional practices. In fact, diversity of faiths is considered a source of knowledge and insight. Sufism proves well to these requirements. The reason for using the three dimensions of Sufism is to explore close links between its theosophic, institutional and literary forms with the cultural-pluralism approach.

Background: definitions of sufism

There is a variety of views among Sufis about the definition of *Tasawwuf*[10] (Arabic term for Sufism). The word 'Sufi' is linked to the Arabic word *Suf* meaning 'wool,' thus the word '*Sufi*' meaning 'a wearer of a woollen garment' (Gilchrist, 1986, p. 346). The term can be historically traced back to the pre-Islamic mystics (Lings, 1975, p. 46) who wore woollen garbs as a sign of simple and ascetic lives they were prone to lead. The term '*Sufi*' is often linked to the Arabic word '*Safa*' meaning 'purity' (Lings, 1975, p. 46). Although the latter term is preferred by most Sufis since the Sufi discipline has inner purification at its heart, others may not approve of either of the definitions ascribed to Sufism. The eleventh century Sufi saint from Persia (who later came to settle in Lahore, Pakistan), Ali bin Uthman al-Jullabi al-Hujwiri, stated that Sufism is too exalted to be etymologically derived from a genus. According to him, the word 'Sufi' refers to a person on the mystic path who has abandoned all else but God (Al-Hujwiri, 1953, p. 34).

Carl Ernst (2005b) defines Sufism as a 'wide-ranging phenomenon.' According to this definition, Sufism refers to 'scriptural interpretation, meditative practices, master-disciple relationships, corporate institutions, aesthetic and ritual gestures, doctrines, and literary texts.' While referring to Sufism as a heterogeneous phenomenon, Carl Ernst rejects its generic character. He further contends that Sufism is 'firmly rooted in particular local contexts, often anchored to the very tangible tombs of deceased saints, and it is deployed in relation to lineages and personalities with a distinctively local sacrality' (Ernst, 2005b, p. 22).

Sufis trace their spiritual tradition back to the Islamic sources – the Qur'an, the *Hadith* and the *Sunnah* of the Prophet Muhammad. They claim their roots back to Prophet Muhammad who was himself 'a Sufi on his way to becoming a Prophet' (Rizvi, 1978, p. 20). Prophet Muhammad was born in Makkah in 571 AD. He often spent time in solitude inside a cave in Mount Hira near Makkah. At the age of forty, during one of his moments of solitude, he received divine revelation in the form of the Holy Qur'an. Sufis believe that Prophet Muhammad passed on secret spiritual knowledge and practices to his cousin and son-in-law, Ali Ibn Talib. It is from there that the Sufi tradition started. All Sufi orders trace their roots back to the Prophet and Ali Ibn Talib (Subhan, 1960, p. 7).

Islam is said to have spread in the world through a variety of processes. According to one view, Islam was spread in the Indian subcontinent through 'conquest, immigration and conversion' (Mujib, 1967, p. 20). Another view points to the peaceful role of missionaries and Sufi saints as main sources of the spread of Islam (Arnold, 1896). With the processes linked to the spread of Islam, the accompanied Sufi tradition also spread in different parts of the world. From the twelfth century onwards, Sufism became institutionalized in the form of Sufi orders. Sufi orders are also considered to have played a role in the propagation of Islam in South Asia (Ahmed, 1999, p. 214). According to Lings (1975, p. 16), 'by being totally dependent upon one particular Revelation, Sufism is totally independent of anything else. But while being self-sufficient it can, if time and place concur, pluck flowers from gardens other than its own.' This description of Sufism is quite relevant for the current chapter and is taken into account at several levels.

Theosophical Sufism: The cultural-pluralist approach

Theosophy is defined as the divine wisdom that 'seeks divine knowledge through esoteric gnosis or divine illumination' (Ayoub, 2004, p. 149). Sufi theosophy is said to have gradually adopted other traditions existing in different contexts. The principal influences came from 'Neoplatonism, the Hellenistic world, Gnosticism, and spiritual philosophies of Iran and areas from the eastern Mediterranean to Iraq' (*Encyclopædia Britannica*, 2006). Theosophy can be considered a vehicle of Sufi expressions related to intellectual and spiritual knowledge and experiences.

The concept of peace viewed in the light of Sufi theosophy may be linked with a number of concepts. Here, we can explore a few of them.

The Sufi concept of *Wahdat al-Wujud* and peace

The concept of *Wahdat al-Wujud* ('the Transcendent Unity of Being') is strongly linked with pluralism especially if seen from the Sufi perspective. The Sufi concepts of *Wahdat al-Wujud* and *Tawhid* are largely inclusive since they, while accepting and honoring the diversity in God's creation, point to its inherent unity (Engineer, 1995) and the 'transcendent unity of religions' (Nasr, 2000, p. 26). The pluralistic view of Sufism is often explained through an ecological approach (Said et al., 2001). 'The Sufi tradition reminds human beings of their ecological function – that is, of their place within a greater, spiritual context which transcends and embraces all things' (Said et al., 2001, p. 254). The principal factor behind the harmony of relationships and the harmony of the universe is the concept of *Tawhid* and, if forgotten, 'relationships become unpeaceful' (Said and Funk, 2004, p. 248). Sufis are known to have made no distinction between human beings on the basis of caste, creed or religion (Nizami, 1999). It is the Sufi concept of *Wahdat al-Wujud* that, in the context of the Indian subcontinent, is said to be 'instrumental in promoting communal harmony by eliminating all formal differences of faith' (Engineer, 1995, p. 309).

Unity in diversity

The classic linkages between Islam and the concept of peace can be made through the concept of diversity mentioned in the Qur'an and how it advises to deal with it. The seemingly contradictory concepts of unity and diversity in Islam are actually two sides of the same coin. According to the Sufi definition of unity in diversity, all is part of the Whole and it is the Whole that is visible in everything.

Those who hold this belief claim to find its basis in the Qur'anic verses: 'Oh mankind! We created you from a single (pair) of a male and a female, and made you peoples (or "nations") and tribes that you may know one another' (49: 13). And that '[t]o every people (was sent) a Messenger' (10: 47).[11] The Islamic principle of unity 'is not premised on uniformity; rather, unity embraces myriad cultural and communal differences' (Said et al., 2001, p. 249). While elaborating the Sufi concept of pluralism and inclusiveness, some scholars argue that according to Sufism all created beings are inherently Muslim since all created things 'share in the existential condition of submission to the divine' (Said et al., 2001, p. 249).

Justice and peace

Being essential to Islamic faith, the concept of justice – everything being in its proper place – is a central concept within the Sufi cosmology. It is about the proper relationships between creation and the Creator. According to the Sufi concept of justice, every part of God's creation is bound to put the purpose of its creation in action. Each particle of the universe is turning around its orbit to the fulfillment of its purpose. As long as conditions are suitable for the creation to fulfill its purpose, there is peace in the universe and between its parts (Nasr, 2000). As long as every part of God's creation is conscious of its real identity with the divine, it experiences peace.

Inner *jihad*

Like the concept of peace in Sufism and other mystic traditions, the concept of war is also inherently spiritual. For example, spiritual writings in Muslim and non-Muslim contexts emphasize a spiritual battle which can be equated with the Sufi concept of inner *jihad* which, according to one tradition of the Prophet Muhammad, is the greater category than the one fought with arms.* The weapons used for the inner battle thus are also of intransigent character. As a twentieth century Sufi sheikh from Sri Lanka (who later came to live in the US and is buried in Philadelphia) propounds, '[i]t is our own satanic qualities that must be overcome with inner patience, contentment, trust in God, and giving all praise to God' (Muhaiyaddeen, 2001, p. 269). It is in the innermost heart where one experiences the presence of God, which is the ultimate condition of peace (Muhaiyaddeen, 2001, p. 269).

The concept of inner peace is a much talked about phenomenon within mystic traditions of diverse religious backgrounds. Buddhism's concept of inner peace and its disciplines of meditation and Hindu practice of yoga† are also reflected in the Sufi exercises. As for the practice of peace in the Sufi tradition, it is linked with the spiritual work that is mainly done by 'purification of the self, remembrance of the divine, and proper attention to relationships' (Said et al., 2001, p. 250).

The general principles of Sufism contained in its theosophic tradition are closely linked with its social roles. The theosophic Sufism later found its expression through organized institutions. These institutions served as centers of spiritual practices for Sufi adepts as well as social centers for the larger community.

Sufi orders and institutions: The cultural-pluralist approach

The early Sufi institutions or hospices established in the Indian subcontinent are said to be divided into three categories: *khanqahs* where the visitors and residents had individual accommodation; *jamaat khanas* or large halls that accommodated some disciples; and *zawiyas* or housing at smaller level where mystics lived in seclusion (Ahmad, 1969, pp. 35–36).

* Ed. Aurangzeb Haneef discusses the importance of Inner *Jihad* and its difference to the Greater *Jihad* in Chapter 8.
† Ed. Hindu yoga traditions are extensively discussed in Chapter 11.

Numerous studies have been done on Sufi orders that originated or operated in the Indian subcontinent (Trimingham, 1971; Ernst and Lawrence, 2002; Islam, 2002; Rizvi, 1978). Four main orders, namely *Chishtiyya*,[12] *Qadiriyya*, *Suhrawardiyya* and *Naqshbandiyya*, originated in areas between Iraq and Central Asia, were later established in the Indian subcontinent. These orders were afterward divided into suborders. Institutional models for the Indian Sufi tradition were *khanqahs* (hospices) established by the original Sufi saints. The early *khanqah* functioned as a simple 'dwelling taken over to house a *shaikh* and his dervishes' for practices such as prayer and meditation, among others (Trimingham, 1971, p. 166). Established 'on the outskirts of towns and villages' (Lapidus, 2002, p. 362) among the lower sections of the Indian population (Nizami, 1961, p. 261), these *khanqahs* performed social and spiritual functions for the locals. In order to successfully function in a complex Indian cultural and social environment, these *khanqahs* had to adopt features of the existing cultural and religious traditions, which alone could have made them win the trust of the local population (Nizami, 1961, p. 175). In this regard, *khanqahs* of the *Chishtiyya* order were most successful as 'people flocked to their hospices from every part of the country' (Nizami, 1961, p. 178).

Just as Sufi orders were significantly varied in terms of organization and functions (*Encyclopædia Britannica*, 2006), they also expressed varied attitudes towards local communities and their respective religious traditions. Several scholarly works describe the majority of saints belonging to the *Chishtiyya* order by their liberal and egalitarian attitudes and their generally unorthodox approach to religion. On the other hand, *Suhrawardi* Sufis were not as successful in winning the trust of non-Muslims mainly due to their 'emphasis on the external behaviour' (Nizami, 1961, p. 179), and their acceptance of pursuits such as 'accumulation of wealth' and 'participation in political matters' (Nizami, 1961, pp. 222–223), which separated them from the poor masses. *Suhrawardi khanqahs* were not open to all (Nizami, 1961, p. 227; Islam, 2002, p. 97). *Naqshbandis*, as Schimmel (1982, p. 12) remarks, drew 'a strict line between Muslims and non-Muslims' mainly on the basis of their emphasis on faith in the Prophethood of Muhammad. Later, *Naqshbandis* propounded the concept of *Wahdat al-Shuhud* 'unity of vision'[13] parallel to the concept of *Wahdat al-Wujud*. Sufis belonging to the *Qadiriyya* order were relatively more liberal (Ahmed, 1999, p. 215). *Chishti* Sufis did not emphasize on conversions of their non-Muslim following and let them 'taste the mystical experience' (Schimmel, 1982, p. 4) without having to assume Muslim identity.

An important feature of the early *khanqahs* and later *dargahs* was the presence of a *shaikh* whose role was central to the institution's life. A *shaikh* of such stature can be described in various ways. First and foremost, he was considered to be a 'deeply pious and learned' person who 'helped to cultivate spiritual discipline' in the lives of his followers (Islam, 2002, p. 444). According to Nizami (1957), the 'success of these *khanqahs* depended very largely on a *shaikh*'s ability to adjust and adapt himself to the mental climate of a particular region' (Nizami, 1957, p. 54). Important *Chishti* saints who, both in their lives and after death, remained sources of spiritual inspiration and guidance as well as of enormous support to the poor and marginalized sections of the society are Khwaja Mu'inud Din Chishti and Shaikh Nizam ud Din Auliya. Both are known to have extended equal treatment to Muslims and non-Muslims, which may be the principal reason for a large non-Muslim following with a predominant number of Hindus who venerate them to this day. These saints also adopted several Hindu rituals that are practiced to this day in their *dargahs* (Lewis, 1985, p. 80). Engineer (1995) argues that Sufis' willingness to accept insights from other faiths contributed to the communal harmony between the two main communities in the Indian subcontinent – Hindus and Muslims.

The *Chishti jamaat khanas* provided generous help not only to the poor and the downtrodden but also to mentally, psychologically and spiritually disturbed people who came to seek 'inner harmony' (Nizami, 1961, p. 210). Among others, these *jamaat khanas* were visited by scholars, government servants, business-people (Nizami, 1961, p. 210) and Hindu yogis (Nizami, 1961, p. 212). The Sufi ritual *zikr* was practiced in these early *khanqahs* and often attracted the non-Muslim following especially of low caste background who, in this way, could have access to religious ceremonies which had been earlier denied to them (Nizami, 1957, p. 64).

Role of *dargahs* in contemporary South Asia

Millions of people in the Indian subcontinent visit and venerate tens of thousands of tombs associated with Sufi saints. In the South Asian context, a Sufi tomb is called by terms such as *mazar, dargah, ziyarat gah* (a place of visit or pilgrimage), or *khanqah* (a hospice), etc.[14] The term *dargah* is derived from Persian, literally 'royal court,' where Sufi saints are believed to exercise spiritual and moral authority. Although not a part of mainstream Islamic tradition, Sufi *dargahs* are centers of popular beliefs and devotional life among Muslim and non-Muslim communities of South Asia. *Dargahs* in the South Asian context have also contributed to the linking of local traditions with the philosophy and principles of Islam (Gilmartin, 1984, p. 225). Some scholars argue that devotional beliefs practiced in the *dargahs* of South Asia today have a basis in the history of Islam going back to the veneration of Prophet Muhammad as an intercessor between God and his community (Schimmel, 1985, p. 82; Lewis, 1985, p. 25), and the Prophet according to the Muslim faith has been sent by God as a 'Mercy for the Worlds.'[15] The spiritual power of the saints, as popular beliefs describe, has its origin in Prophet Muhammad and Ali Ibn Talib, the Prophet's cousin and the fourth righteous caliph (Lewis, 1985, p. 28).

Sufi *khanqahs* and syncretic practices[16]

The *dargah* culture is said to be closely related to the local religious practices existing before the arrival of Islam in the area. The structure and organization of the South Asian *dargahs* are often a reflection of a 'fusion' of local Muslim and non-Muslim traditions, customs and cultural legacies (Saheb, 1998, p. 56). The historical *khanqahs* served as sources of 'syncretic forces which liquidated social, ideological and linguistic barriers between the various cultural groups' (Nizami, 1961, p. 262). This is particularly true of certain areas such as Bengal, where Sufis or 'cultural mediators' translated the Muslim mystic principles and traditions into the local cultural symbols (Roy, 1983, p. 122). Lapidus (2002, p. 363) shows that often the annual *'urs* festivals at the Sufi *dargahs* related to the veneration of saints corresponded with Hindu calendars and that the Sufi saints possessed the spiritual power which the Hindus usually ascribed to yogis.' The Muslim saints also had a large Hindu following and Hindu yogis had Muslim *chelas* (disciples) (Lapidus, 2002, p. 161).

Scholars locate similarities between Sufism and the Yoga tradition. In his recent article (2005a), Ernst points out that both Sufism and Yoga tradition had mutual influences on each other. Sufism adopted certain Yoga practices in its array of spiritual and meditative disciplines. Ernst locates a particular branch of Yoga, the *Hatha* Yoga, as being practiced by early Sufis of the Indian subcontinent. Nath Yogis are also said to have had close associations with early Sufi *khanqahs*. Carl Ernst remarks that the structure and the organization of Sufi tombs may have been close to the *lingham* shrines or *samadhis* set up for yogis (Ernst, 2005a, p. 23). The South Asian Sufi tradition shared with Hinduism and Buddhism the need for a spiritual master and belief in the intercessory powers of saints (Schimmel, 1982, p. 3). Studies have been done on Sufi shrines associated with saints who are commonly revered by Muslims, Hindus and Sikhs (Sila-Khan, 2004; Sikand, 2003; Dawani, 2002).

The egalitarian organization and open atmosphere of these *khanqahs* can be explained through the argument by Nizami (1999) that although the Sufis firmly adhered to their Islamic identity, 'they did not carry this difference to social relationships.' Sufis of particular orders also believed in the unity of the divine revelation. This marked their practices that helped in 'pulling down the barriers between various religious groups.' Sufis are said not to have indulged in criticizing customs and practices of the local people in the societies where they settled (Nizami, 1999).

Sufi *dargahs*: shared sacred spaces[17]

Sufi *dargahs* are built around the tombs of the saints who, though long deceased, are remembered and revered by the supplicants and devotees, and who also asked for intercession. Thus, they are also described as sacred places marked by intense devotional activity. These *dargahs* perform multiple functions among which an important one is linking the spiritual world with the mundane lives of the people (Schimmel, 1982). Built on the model of *khanqahs*, Sufi *dargahs* to this day serve as important sites for the distribution of charity to the poor and the needy (Gottschalk, 2006, p. 234).

Dargahs in South Asia provide an open and shared space for people of diverse religious, social and ethnic identities. Unlike 'orthodox religious gatherings, there is a great deal of tolerance for deviant behaviour' (Lyon, 2004, p. 215). South Asian Sufi *dargahs*, together with Hindu, Christian and Sikh shrines, have also, for centuries, served as ritual spaces where people of diverse religious backgrounds undertake devotional activities. The South Asian vow ritual[18] is one of these shared devotional expressions.

The inclusive nature of Sufism is also manifest from active participation of women (who otherwise have a rather limited access to Muslim public institutions) within various dimensions of Sufism. For example, women are an integral part of both institutional and literary traditions of Sufism. Female characters are frequently used in Sufi poetry and music. They perform active roles in stories and narratives and symbols used in the Sufi poetry. In their role of singers, women themselves become transmitters of the Sufi literary and music traditions (Abbas, 2002). Women form the majority of people visiting Sufi *dargahs*. In some cases, women hold high positions in the hierarchy of order within the institutional framework of Sufism. For example, they may perform roles of *pirs* or spiritual guides (Pemberton, 2006).

Sufi literary tradition in South Asia: cultural-pluralist approach

Sufi literature comprises a variety of genres of poetry and prose. Although original Sufi literature found in Arabic and Persian consists of excellent literary works, it was its 'popular cultural' element that made it known among wider circles of the societies (Ernst, 1997, pp. 148–149). This also owes to the adaptability of Sufism to multiple linguistic and cultural environments. Upon arrival in the Indian subcontinent, Muslims from Arab and other Middle Eastern countries with Persian and Turkish backgrounds brought respective literary traditions with them. However, in order to make their ideas understandable to the local population, they soon learnt their languages to express themselves. Besides, Sufis used the local cultural symbols for expressing their concepts of divine love. Nasr (2000, p. 172) remarks that through simple facts of life and folk tales, Sufi literature managed to express 'the profoundest truths.' Sufi poetry found excellent expressions in Hindi, Hindvi, Dakhani, Bengali, Gujarati, Punjabi, Sindhi and other local languages while the genres used for poetic expression also suited local contexts (Nasr, 2000, p. 162).

Sufi literature written by saints and poets continues serving as the source of guidance for the living Sufi masters as well as Sufi adepts and devotees. Sufi writings form a prominent part of shrine cults and *dargahs*. These writings are considered to provide links between the period when the Sufi saints – who may be long deceased – lived and provided guidance to their disciples, and the present times when the tombs of the same saints have become the source of inspiration and spiritual blessings for large numbers of devotees and pilgrims (Schimmel, 1980, p. 126). Sufi texts are also considered to have played a unique role in dissolving the barriers of time and space within the context of South Asian Sufism since it had originated elsewhere (Green, 2004).

Pluralistic poetry

For centuries, Sufi concepts of peace and cultural pluralism have found expressions through the Sufi literary tradition based on texts and poetry. The metaphorical usage of images and concepts in Sufi poetry not only satisfies the literary and intellectual minds, but also serves as vehicles of popular expressions of religiosity and folk culture in many parts of the Muslim and non-Muslim world. Scholars argue that Sufi literature is embedded in the Qur'an and the *Hadith* for its contents and form (Nasr, 2000, p. 155). The pluralistic character of Sufi literature, however, is manifest through its combination of Islamic imagery with the local customs and folk traditions (Eaton, 1974). This poetry to a large extent shapes the worldview of the local rural masses and acquires a sacred status, since it is linked with popular religiosity.

Main themes contained in the original Arabic and Persian Sufi poetry were divine beauty, God–love–intoxication, mystical love expressed through metaphorical or profane love, separation from the beloved, love for one's *Murshid* or spiritual guide, critique of orthodox attitudes and legal constraints, religious transcendence, etc. These themes later found fitting parallels in the literary traditions existing in the South Asian folk culture. For example, poetic themes contained in *Viraha Bhakti*[19] were later adopted in the Sufi poetry. Thus, parallel examples were found among the earlier mystic poetry of Sufi poets of the Middle Eastern or Mediterranean backgrounds and later Sufi poets in the Indian subcontinent. For instance, a famous poem[20] of Ibn al-Arabi's describing his adherence to the religion of love later found parallels in the poetry of the eighteenth century Punjabi Sufi poet Bulleh Shah, who rejects all religious and social associations, and instead focuses on his ardent spiritual love for his *murshid*. In one poem, Bulleh Shah wonders about his own existential reality.[21]

Punjabi and Sindhi Sufi poetry

The Sufi poetry of Punjab and Sindh shares most characteristics. Some scholars argue that 'it was in Sindh and Punjab where the mystical folk poetry developed most successfully' (Schimmel, 1980, p. 141). Punjabi poetry is usually linked with the Sufi tradition of the Punjab. In this context, the Sufi saint Shaikh Farid-ud Din Masud '*Ganj-i Shakar*' is known to have introduced the tradition of

Punjabi poetry. His poetry is considered an example of 'Hindu–Muslim synthesis' (Serebryakov, 1975, p. 22).

An important reason for the vast popularity of the Punjabi and Sindhi Sufi poetry may be that it includes genres of the old literary heritage that were present in the Punjabi and Sindhi cultures for centuries. There are frequent references to professional and domestic lives of the local population. Weavers, carpenters, farmers and features of rural life occupy a lot of space in the folk Sufi literature. Folk tales that are usually the subject of Punjabi and Sindhi poetry had been part of the historical popular literary tradition of these areas. Most frequently, tales used in the Punjabi and Sindhi Sufi literature are based on popular romantic legends such as *Hir-Ranjha, Sohni-Mahinval, Sassi-Punnu.* Common subjects of these tales are love, separation from beloved, and a longing for reunion. Sufi saints are said to have used these legends to metaphorically describe the love between human beings and their Creator while the female characters in these love-tales suffering from the pangs of separation from their beloved symbolize the longing of the human soul for its merger in its divine source.

Punjabi Sufi literature is mainly characterized by its folk subjects, love-legends and concepts and symbols from diverse religious backgrounds. These folk tales may be based on one religious tradition or the other but their popularity among Punjabis is often not bound by their religious background. Similarly, Punjabi Sufi saint-poets such as Shaikh Farid ud-Din *'Ganj-e Shakar,'* Khwaja Ghulam Farid, Sultan Bahu, Shah Hussain, Bulleh Shah, Waris Shah and others have to this day a common appeal to Punjabis of diverse religious backgrounds.

Sindhi and Punjabi literary traditions are closely linked. This may be due to their shared roots in the old Indus civilization. Schimmel (1974, p. 5) argues that the present Sindhi Sufi literature was built on the old Sindhi literature to which it gradually introduced new genres. Sindhi Sufi poetry, like its Punjabi parallel, has a popular character. It relies on the folk elements from the daily lives of the masses. Sindhi mystic poetry is said to be 'admired and memorised' by Muslims and Hindus alike (Schimmel, 1974, p. 14). This, some scholars argue, is due to the Sindhi culture that openly accepted mystic influences and thus welcomed the Sufi tradition in its fold.

Interreligious appeal of the Sufi poetry

An important characteristic of the Sufi poetry is said to be the universality of its message. In the context of Punjabi Sufi literature, *Hir-Ranjha,* a poem written by the eighteenth century Punjabi Sufi poet Syed Pir Waris Shah, is based on a Punjabi love-legend. Through his poetry, Waris Shah has painted a true picture of eighteenth century Punjabi life and its scenery (Serebryakov, 1975, p. 53). Waris Shah uses Hindu terminology and personages such as yogis in his poetry. *Hir-Ranjha* is said to be equally popular among the people of the divided Punjab (Narang, 1987, p. 164). Similarly, Waris Shah's contemporary Sufi poet Bulleh

Shah's poetry contains strong critiques of orthodox religious identities and the essential unity of religions.

Sufis of Sindh are considered to have equally adapted to the local traditions. Some Sindhi Sufi saints frequently make use of terminology from Hindu texts, personages and myths. For example, Shah Abdul Latif Bhitai, the eighteenth century Sufi saint-poet, mentioned Hindu sacred places and yogis in his poetry for describing the mystical path (*Sur Ramkali* Shah-jo-Risalo). Similarly, the poetry of a popular Sindhi Sufi poet, Sachal Sarmast, reflects his belief in *Wahdat al-Wujud* or transcendent unity among religions. The latter Sindhi poets as well as people in general have come to equate the Hindu terminology with Islamic beliefs.

Sufi Music or *Sam'a*

Sam'a is the old music tradition practiced in Persian Sufi *khanqahs*, which was transplanted wherever these *khanqahs* were established, also in the Indian subcontinent. While incorporating the local languages into their practices, the Sufis also welcomed the blending of the local poetry and musical traditions thus contributing to a unique mixture of poetic and musical traditions. Hindu mystical songs were also made part of the *Sam'a* gatherings (Rizvi, 1978, p. 326). In the context of the Indian subcontinent, the Sufi *Sam'a* included *Vaishnavite* themes especially in the Hindi-speaking regions (Rizvi, 1978, p. 359).

The status of Sufi music is controversial not only among mainstream Muslims but also among Sufis. Sufis belonging to certain orders may approve of certain practices while the same practices may be considered un-Islamic or undesirable by those belonging to other orders. The debates about the role of music in Sufism are related to the discussions on the ecstatic and sober expressions of spirituality within the Sufi tradition. Whereas *Suhrawardi* Sufis believed in sober practices (Schimmel, 1982, p. 4), *Chishti* Sufis did not see harm in *sam'a* (music) and *raqs* (dance), which made them a target for criticism from the *ulama* and the rulers who supported the *ulama* (Eaton, 1978, p. 48).

Despite the contentious nature of music among the Muslim and Sufi circles, its popularity is ever more on the rise[22] not only in Muslim societies but also in Western societies (Ernst, 1997, p. 179). The *qawwali* music tradition associated with the *Chishtiyya* order is the most popular form of Sufi music heard not only in South Asia but also in the Western countries. *Qawwali* combines elements of local music traditions. The lyrics sung in *qawwali* are usually borrowed from a variety of collections of Sufi poetry. These lyrics provide a mixture of Muslim, Hindu and Christian concepts. Through its different forms, *qawwali* not only makes references to Islamic beliefs, odes to the Prophet and Sufi saints, it also makes powerful references to common mystic themes such as unity of religions and unity of all creation. Other genres of Sufi music are practiced in varied geographical contexts. In the Sindhi Sufi context, most important genres of the Sufi music are *kafi, vai* and *ghazal*.[23] *Qawwali* is an integral part of rituals at some Sufi *dargahs*.

Conclusion

In this chapter, I have argued that the Sufi concept of peace is closely linked with cultural pluralism. In order to illustrate this, I used the theosophic, institutional and literary dimensions of Sufism. I have employed what I call a cultural-pluralist approach to explore the potential of Sufism for peacemaking. I used the case of Sufism in the Indian subcontinent in order to illustrate how the above Sufi dimensions are reflected in the lives of the South Asian Muslims as well as their relations with the broader society.

This chapter has identified themes that point to the Sufi concept of peace, which is linked with cultural pluralism. From its theosophic perspective, Sufism propounds a concept of transcendent peace through its concepts of *Wahdat al-Wujud* ('unity of being'), unity in diversity and inner *jihad*/peace. The popular institutional tradition of Sufism in the Indian subcontinent provides a link between various religious traditions by offering them shared spaces while it accommodated elements of local cultural and religious traditions. Through its literary tradition, Sufism propounds its pluralistic ideas and puts forward a universal message that love for the humanity and love for the divine are essentially one. It is through the above dimensions of Sufism that its concept of peace must be understood.

Although being an essential part of Islam, the Sufi tradition accommodates a wide variety of concepts and practices from contexts where it has established itself. It adapts to the local conditions. In this way, in each area where it has established itself, its association remains with the local contexts. In line with this pattern, we can say that Sufism neither alienates local cultures from its own framework nor likes to be alienated by them. Due to its adaptability to the local realities, the Sufi tradition deals with its immediate surroundings according to their needs through its transcendent view of cultural and religious multiplicity and an essential unity in cultures and religions.

In order to create a culture of peace, there is the need for finding common spatial and communal grounds where the peace activity may take place. Boulding (1998), in her elaboration of the term culture of peace, argues for certain 'zones of peace' or sanctuaries that may provide people safety and security from enemies (however one may define them). She talks about holy places and temples as zones of peace. Similarly, Sufi *dargahs* or historical *khanqahs* may be described as 'zones of peace' where people of diverse social, religious background are not only safe from outer enemies, they also find mental peace from the problems and anxieties attached to their daily life.

The concept of 'intercultural' peace, which forms the overall theme of the book, is also manifest through various dimensions of Sufism – theosophic, institutional and literary – practiced in the Indian subcontinent. The Sufi concept of peace linked with cultural pluralism is not different from 'intercultural' peace. In fact, the two concepts can be used interchangeably. 'Peace' according to this concept means a value shared by people coexisting in multicultural societies. The main lessons learnt from the Sufi experience are that through its various dimensions, Sufism practices a kind of peace that is intercultural based on a positive recognition of cultural pluralism. The Sufi concept of peace is a positive or 'interactive' peace that does not realize itself in isolation, rather it operates and flourishes in diverse cultural environments. It is a shared concept of peace based on mutual recognition and understanding.

The South Asian Sufi tradition is said to have adopted means from the local cultural contexts in order to convey its message to a widespread following. This has often resulted in a sort of religious syncretism among those following popular Sufi practices. The popular tradition within Sufism has allowed those with a Muslim background to have ample interaction with people from other religious traditions. At the same time it is the Sufi Islam which allows people to adhere to both mainstream Islamic tradition (as it provides them with an identity cover) as well as the popular tradition where religious barriers become rather irrelevant. The Sufi tradition in the Indian subcontinent seems to contribute to an intercultural environment.

The Sufi concept of peace linked with cultural pluralism suggests new ways of looking at religious traditions and a wide variety existing within each religious tradition. This calls for dispelling the monolithic notions of religious traditions. Religious traditions, as scholars have constantly warned, must not be viewed as closed systems that, by coming in contact, are bound to clash with each other. Sufi tradition, which is the inner dimension or mysticism of Islam, comprises varied systems based on its theosophic cosmology, its institutional structures, its literary, music and art traditions and its popular culture that have helped its various dimensions to flourish in new contexts. This is also how despite its ups and downs, the Sufi tradition has survived to this day.

Notes

1. For detailed information about Sufi orders and their transnational networks in various European and northern American countries, see Malik and Hinnells (2006).
2. The Holy Book revealed to the Prophet Muhammad in the early seventh century AD, in a gradual manner during a period of twenty-three years. The book contains historical events and stories of the Prophets shared by Jews and Christians, narrated on the pattern of the Old Testament as well as a body of principles and codes pertaining to religious, social, economic and spiritual aspects of the lives of believers and human

beings in general. The principal subject of the Qur'an is believed to be the 'human being,' 'the best of God's creation.'

3. A set of quoted traditions associated with the Prophet Muhammad that was later compiled by the Prophet's companions. These traditions of the Prophet form an important part of *Shariah*, the Islamic legal system.

4. Actions, customs and gestures ascribed to the Prophet Muhammad passed on to Muslims through members of his family, companions and their generations.

5. One must mention though that not all scholars agree to the role of Sufism in peacemaking. Some have called Sufis 'warriors' since they were engaged in militant activities against the non-Muslim resistance to the Muslim conquests in the northern part of India (Eaton, 1978, p. 19). Others contend that the early Sufis in the Punjab area were intolerant and orthodox (Sharda, 1998, p. xix). However, this discussion is beyond the scope of this chapter since it is the role of Sufism in peacemaking that I explore here.

6. Literary, 'divine wisdom.' The *Encyclopædia Britannica* refers to the substance of Sufi theosophy as explicit in the Prophet's holy tradition (which refers to direct words of God), 'I was a hidden treasure and wanted to be known.'

7. *Tawhid* is the principal foundation of the Islamic faith bearing the witness that 'There is no deity but God.'

8. The precept propounded by the twelfth century Andalusian Sufi mystic Muhiuddin Ibn 'Arabi based on *tawhid*, which means 'the knowledge that there is nothing existent but God, or the ability to see God and creation as two aspects of one reality, reflecting each other and depending upon each other.' See 'Sufism' in *Encyclopædia Britannica* (2006). The concept of *Wahdat al-Wujud* is compared with the Hindu concept of *Advaita*, implying 'existential monism' (Subhan, 1960, p. 145).

9. A more detailed account of Sufi institutions based on Sufi *khanqahs* and saints' tombs will follow in the chapter.

10. For a detailed study about the definitions of *Tasawwuf*, see Carl W. Ernst entry in *Encyclopædia of Islam* (Ernst, 2004).

11. Translation quoted from Said et al. (2001, p. 248).

12. *Chishtiyya* is the most widespread Sufi order in the Indian subcontinent that has several suborders and maintains its vigor to date. For a detailed study on *Chishtiyya* and its contemporary roles, see Ernst and Lawrence (2002).

13. '[A] subjective vision of unity, occurring only in the mind of the believer, not as an objective experience' (*Encyclopædia Britannica*, 2006).

14. For further definitions and functions of Sufi *dargahs*, see the Introduction in Troll (1989).

15. Also the title of the book by Q.M.S.S. Mansoorpuri cited in Schimmel (1985).

16. There are significant studies done on shared devotional practices in contemporary Sufi *dargahs* in the Indian subcontinent. Among these are Sikand (2003), Sila-Khan (2004) and Gottschalk (2000).

17. The term is used by Y. Sikand to explain holy sites in India that are commonly revered by people of diverse religious background. For reference, see Sikand (2003).

18. In a recent study on South Asian vows, the contributors explore the categories and meanings of the vow ritual performed in shrines and other sacred places of Hindu, Buddhist, Muslim, Sikh and Christian background. Contributors to this study argue that the vow ritual is one of the principal common features in South Asian religious and devotional traditions. For details, see Raj and Harman (2006).

19. For a detailed study on *Viraha Bhakti*, see Hardy (1983).

20. 'O Marvel! a garden amidst the flames.
    My heart has become capable of every form:
    it is a pasture for gazelles and a convent for Christian monks,
    and a temple for idols and the pilgrim's Kaa'ba,
    and the tables of the Torah and the book of the Quran.
    I follow the religion of Love: whatever way Love's camels take,
    that is my religion and my faith.' (Poem XI in Al-Arabi, 1911).
21. Poem by Bulleh Shah: *'Kih Jaanaan Main Kaun'* (I know not who I am) also available
    with English translation at the website of Academy of the Punjab in North America
    (APNA, 2008).
22. Recently, a documentary produced by William Dalrymple was shown on the British
    TV Channel 4 about the Sufi music in Turkey, Morocco and Pakistan (*Sufi Soul: The
    Mystic Music of Islam*, 2008). The documentary highlights a wide variety of Sufi music
    in different cultural contexts and attempts to dispel the common stereotypical
    notion of Islam as a monolithic phenomenon often found within the non-Muslim
    Western circles.
23. Genres of Sufi music practiced in Punjabi, Sindhi and Urdu.

Reference list

Abbas, S.B. (2002) *The Female Voice in Sufi Ritual: Devotional Practices of Pakistan and India*
    (Oxford: Oxford University Press).
Abu-Nimr, M. (2000/01) 'A Framework for Nonviolence and Peacebuilding in Islam,' *Journal
    of Law and Religion*, 15, 1/2, 217–265.
Abu-Nimr, M. (2003) *Nonviolence and Peacebuilding in Islam: Theory and Practice* (Gainesville:
    University Press of Florida).
Ahmad, A. (1969) *An Intellectual History of Islam in India* (Edinburgh: The University Press).
Ahmed, I. (1999) 'South Asia' in D. Westerlund and I. Svanberg (eds.) *Islam outside the Arab
    World* (New York: St. Martin's Press).
Al-Arabi, I. (1911) *Tarjuman al-Ashwaq: A Collection of Mystical Odes by Muhyi'ddin Ibn
    al-'Arabi*, trans. by R.A. Nicholson (London: Theosophical Publishing House).
Al-Hujwiri, A.I.U.A.J. (1953) *Kashf al-Mahjub: The Oldest Persian Treatise on Sufism*, trans.
    by R.A. Nicholson (Lahore: Islamic Book Foundation).
APNA (Academy of the Punjab in North America) (2008) http://www.apnaorg.com/, date
    accessed June 24, 2009.
Arnold, T.W. (1896) *The Preaching of Islam: A History of the Propagation of the Muslim Faith*
    (Westminster: Constable).
Ayoub, M.M. (2004) *Islam: Faith and History* (Oxford: Oneworld).
Boulding, E. (1986) 'Two Cultures of Religion as Obstacles to Peace,' *Zygon*, 21, 4, 501–518.
Boulding, E. (1998) 'Peace Culture: The Problem of Managing Human Difference,' *Cross
    Currents*, 48, 4.
Dawani, M. (2002) 'Shrine of Udero Lal: An Architectural and Symbolic Expression of
    Sindh's Cultural Past,' *The Journal*, 7, 1.
Eaton, R.M. (1974) 'Sufi Folk Literature and the Expansion of Indian Islam,' *History of
    Religions*, 14, 2, 117–127.
Eaton, R.M. (1978) *Sufis of Bijapur, 1300–1700: Social Roles of Sufis in Medieval India*
    (Princeton/Woodstock: Princeton University Press).
Eaton, R.M. (1997) *The Rise of Islam and the Bengal Frontier 1204–1760* (New Delhi: Oxford
    University Press).

Eaton, R.M. (2000) *Essays on Islam and Indian History* (New Delhi: Oxford University Press).

Encyclopædia Britannica (2006) 'Sufism', http://www.britannica.com/eb/article-68914.

Engineer, A.A. (1995) *Lifting the Veil: Communal Violence and Communal Harmony in Contemporary India* (London: Sangam Books).

Ernst, C. (2005a) 'Situating Sufism and Yoga,' *Journal of Royal Asiatic Society,* Series 3, 15, 1, 15–43.

Ernst, C. (2005b) 'Sufism, Islam, and Globalization in the Contemporary World: Methodological Reflections on a Changing Field of Study,' Paper presented at *Seminar on Islamic Spirituality,* Kuala Lumpur, May 24–25, 2005.

Ernst, C. and B. Lawrence (2002) *Sufi Martyrs of Love: The Chishti Order in South Asia and Beyond* (New York: Palgrave Macmillan).

Ernst, C.W. (2004) *Tasawwuf: An Entry from Macmillan Reference USA's Encyclopedia of Islam and the Muslim World* [HTML] (USA: Macmillan Reference).

Ernst, C.W. (1997) *The Shambhala Guide to Sufism* (Boston: Shambhala).

Galtung, J. (2003) 'Cultural Peace: Some Characteristics', http://www.transcend.org/t_database/printarticle, date accessed October 12, 2008.

Geertz, C. (1968) *Islam Observed: Religious Development in Morocco and Indonesia* (New Haven: Yale University Press).

Gellner, E. (1984) 'Doctor and Saint' in A.S. Ahmed and D.M. Hart (eds.) *Islam in Tribal Societies: From Atlas to the Indus* (London: Routledge and Kegan Paul).

Gilchrist, J. (1986) *Muhammad and the Religion of Islam* (Benoni: Jesus to the Muslims).

Gilmartin, D. (1984) 'Shrines, Succession, and Sources of Moral Authority' in B.D. Metcalf (ed.) *Moral Conduct and Authority: The Place of Adab in South Asian Islam* (Berkeley: University of California Press).

Gottschalk, P. (2000) *Beyond Hindu and Muslim: Multiple Identity and Narratives from Village India* (Oxford: Oxford University Press).

Gottschalk, P. (2006) 'Indian Muslim Tradition' in S. Mittal and G. Thursby (eds.) *Religions of South Asia: An Introduction* (New York: Routledge).

Green, N. (2004) 'Emerging Approaches to the Sufi Traditions of South Asia: Between Texts, Territories and the Transcendent,' *South Asia Research,* 24, 2, 123–148.

Hammarlund, A., T. Olsson and E. Özdalga (1999) (eds.) *Sufism, Music and Society in Turkey and the Middle East,* Swedish Research Institute in Istanbul (Istanbul: Svenska Forskningsinstitut).

Hardy, F. (1983) *Viraha-Bhakti: The Early History of Krsna Devotion in South India* (Delhi: Oxford University Press).

Hermansen, M. (2006) 'Literary Productions of Western Sufi Movements' in J. Malik and J. Hinnells (eds.) *Sufism in the West* (London: Routledge).

Hoffman, V.J. (1995) *Sufism, Mystics and Saints in Modern Egypt* (Columbia: University of South Carolina).

Islam, R. (2002) *Sufism in South Asia: Impact on Fourteenth Century Muslim Society* (Karachi: Oxford University Press).

Lapidus, I.M. (2002) *A History of Islamic Societies* (Cambridge: Cambridge University Press).

Lewis, P. (1985) *Pirs, Shrines and Pakistani Islam* (Rawalpindi: Christian Study Center).

Lings, M. (1975) *What is Sufism?* (Lahore: Suhail Academy).

Lyon, S.M. (2004) *An Anthropological Analysis of Local Politics and Patronage in a Pakistani Village* (New York: The Edwin Mellen Press).

Mahmoud, M. (1997) 'Sufism and Islamism in the Sudan' in E.E. Rosander and D. Westerlund (eds.) *African Islam and Islam in Africa: Encounters between Sufis and Islamists* (London: Hurst & Company).

Malik, J. and J. Hinnells (2006) (eds.) *Sufism in the West* (London: Routledge).

Michel, T. (2005) 'Sufism and Modernity in the Thought of Fethullah Gülen,' *The Muslim World*, 95, 341–358.

Muhaiyaddeen, M.R.B. (2001) 'Weapons for the Battle within' in A.Z. Said, N.C. Funk and A.S. Kadayifçi (eds.) *Peace and Conflict Resolution in Islam: Precept and Practice* (Lanham/ New York/Oxford: University Press of America).

Mujib, M. (1967) *The Indian Muslims* (London: George Allen and Unwin Ltd.).

Narang, C.L. (1987) *History of Punjabi Literature* (Delhi: National Book Shop).

Nasr, S.H. (2000) *Living Sufism* (Lahore: Suhail Academy).

Nizami, K.A. (1957) 'Some Aspects of Khanqah Life in Medieval India,' *Studia Islamica*, 8, 51–69.

Nizami, K.A. (1961) *Some Aspects of Religion and Politics in India during the Thirteenth Century* (Bombay: Asia Publishing House).

Nizami, K.A. (1999) 'The Contribution of Indian Sufis to Peace and Amity' in B. Sarasvati (ed.) *Culture of Peace* (New Delhi: IGNCA and D. K. Printworld Pvt. Ltd.).

Parrinder, G. (1987) 'Peace' in M. Eliade (ed.) *The Encyclopaedia of Religion*, 11 (New York: Macmillan), 221–224.

Pemberton, K. (2006) 'Women Pirs, Saintly Succession, and Spiritual Guidance in South Asian Sufism,' *The Muslim World*, 46, 61–87.

Raj, S.J. and W.P. Harman (2006) *Dealing with Deities: The Ritual Vow in South Asia* (Albany: State University of New York Press).

Rizvi, S.A.A. (1978) *A History of Sufism in India, Vol. I: Early Sufism and its History in India to 1600 AD* (New Delhi: Munshiram Manoharlal).

Roy, A. (1983) *The Islamic Syncretistic Tradition in Bengal* (New York: Princeton University Press).

Saheb, S.A.A. (1998) 'A "Festival of Flags": Hindu Muslim Devotion and the Sacralising of Localism at the Shrine of Nagore-e-Sharif in Tamil Nadu' in P. Werbner and H. Basu (eds.) *Embodying Charisma: Modernity, Locality and the Performance of Emotion in Sufi Cults* (London: Routledge).

Said, A.A. and N.C. Funk (2004) 'Sufi Prescriptions for World Politics: A Way to Global Community,' Paper presented at *The 'Shakir' World Encounters*, Marrakech, September 10–12, 2004.

Said, A.A., N.C. Funk and A.S. Kadayifçi (2001) (eds.) *Peace and Conflict Resolution in Islam: Precept and Practice* (Lanham/New York/Oxford: University Press of America).

Samson, F. (2000) 'Youth, Sufism, and Politics in Senegal,' *ISIM* Newsletter, June.

Schimmel, A. (1974) 'Sindhi Literature' in J. Gonda (ed.) *A History of Indian Literature*, III (Wiesbaden: Otto Harrassowitz).

Schimmel, A. (1980) *Islam in the Indian Subcontinent* (Leiden/Köln: E.J. Brill).

Schimmel, A. (1982) 'Islam in India and Pakistan' in T.P. van Baaren, L.P. van den Bosch, L. Leertouwer and F. Leemhuis (eds.) *Iconography of Religions* (Leiden: E.J. Brill).

Schimmel, A. (1985) *And Muhammad is His Messenger: The Veneration of the Prophet in Islamic Piety* (Chapel Hill: The University of North Carolina Press).

Serebryakov, I. (1975) *Punjabi Literature: A Brief Outline* (Lahore: Progressive Books).

Sharda, S.R. (1998) *Sufi Thought: Its Development in Panjab and its Impact on Panjabi Literature from Baba Farid to AD 1850* (New Delhi: Munshiram Manoharlal).

Sikand, Y. (2003) *Sacred Spaces: Exploring Traditions of Shared Faith in India* (New Delhi: Penguin Books).

Sila-Khan, D. (2004) *Crossing the Threshold: Understanding Religious Identities in South Asia* (London: Palgrave Macmillan).

Subhan, J.A. (1960) *Sufism, its Saint and Shrines: An Introduction to the Study of Sufism with Special Reference to India and Pakistan* (Lucknow: The Lucknow Publishing House).

Sufi Soul: The Mystic Music of Islam (2008) [Documentary] Directed by: Simon Broughton (USA: Riverboat).

Trimingham, J.S. (1971) *The Sufi Orders in Islam* (Oxford: At the Clarendon Press).

Troll, C.W. (1989) (ed.) *Muslim Shrines in India: Their Character, History and Significance* (Delhi: Oxford University Press).

Werbner, P. (2003) *Pilgrims of Love: The Anthropology of a Global Sufi Cult* (Karachi: Oxford University Press).

10
Salaam: An Alevilik Perspective

Alev Çakır

> The most valuable book that one can read is the human being itself.
>
> Haci Bekta Veli

Alevilik has survived through the years by cautiously transmitting, diligently transporting and indefatigably insisting on the protection of its religion, in order to endure permanent attempts to exterminate it by dominating empires in Asia Minor, especially during the Ottoman period. Alevilik has stood up for enlightenment of the religiously and religious-fundamentally cloaked minds, for self-reflection and for scrutinizing the strong religious norms by putting humans at the center of the religion, which proved especially difficult during the Ottoman Empire, a time where religious powers were strongly exercised.

The Alevis, a heterodox religious group in Turkey, formerly known as Asia Minor, do not attend mosques, do not possess established doctrines and have no shared liturgy. Their culture and religion have developed in rural Anatolia through hereditary holy figures who transmitted mystical religious thought through music, poetry and collective rituals (Shankland, 2003). Alevis reject the five pillars of Islam, which consist of: *Shahadah*, to believe that there is only one God, which is Allah, and Mohammed is his messenger; *Salah*, the rule to pray five times a day; *Zakah*, each year Muslims are supposed to give a fixed proportion of their savings for endeavors such as helping the poor; *Sawm*, to hold Ramadan; and *Hajj*, to take a pilgrimage to Mecca once in a life of a Sunni-Muslim (Nu`mān ibn Muḥammad, 2002, 2004).

Because of its ancient roots in Mesopotamia, some Alevi authors claim that Alevilik is a main source of the dominant religions of Christianity, Islam and Judaism. Others also claim that Alevilik is an unorthodox and liberal mix or mosaic of elements of the following: old Iran Zoroastrianism, esoteric-Christian Manichaeism, Christian Nestorianism and the antique Syrian Christianity; Cabbala Judaism, Islamic Schia and old Turkish Kam or Shamanism. In short, Alevilik combines or is the melting pot of various elements of different pre-Islamic religions and cultures in Mesopotamia and has elements of Sufism* or Islamic mysticism (Çınar, 2007).

Following the Sunnis, Alevilik is the largest religious group in Turkey, 'numbering some 15 million people, equal to approximately 25% of Turkey's current population' (Poyraz, 2006, p. 8). However, these numbers always have to be considered in light of the non-acceptance of Alevilik as an official religion. Therefore, Alevi spokespersons or Alevi people claim that Turkey's population is one-third Alevi or more than 20 million people (Schindeldecker, 1998), while others also estimate that between 30 and 40 percent of the total Turkish population is Alevi (Zeidan, 1999). The overwhelming majority of Alevis is composed of ethnic and linguistic Turks, descending mainly from Central and Eastern Anatolia (Zeidan, 1999). Alevilik is not an ethnic group, meaning that it is not demarcated by ethnicity and ethnic affiliation. Rather, it is a community that embraces all beings on earth regardless of their religion, national background, ethnicity and gender; insofar as their attitude is geared towards respecting other human beings, and they do not affect and interfere obstructively with other beings in their course of life and self-actualization.

In forgotten mountain villages under domineering repression within an atmosphere of deprivation, scantiness and persecution, if the Alevilik had not made serious unremitting and unflagging efforts to preserve the Alevi path, with the Alevi essence, this chapter would not have been possible. Alevilik is a rich, heterodox, syncretistic and ancient religion; it is a *path*. Due to its nature, it becomes highly challenging and difficult to describe Alevilik in words, because Alevilik starts where literature and words end, it is love, compassion and passion; it can be only felt. Therefore, my contribution through this disclosure is like a small drop in a wide ocean.

Sources of Alevilik

While many scholars and writers on Alevilik claim the scarcity of Alevi sources and therefore limited information about Alevilik, I find that there is enough knowledge traceable in sources of Alevi religion (Çınar, 2007). The key to gaining knowledge on Alevilik resides in finding an adequate way of understanding the available sources in which this philosophy is completely contained. 'Like the Torah for the Jews, the Bible for the Christians, the Quran for the Moslems are their books, oral traditions is the book of Alevis' (Çınar, 2007, p. 17 [trans. by author]), which are poems, folk songs, narratives, ceremonies and rituals.

The most important Alevilik source is the ritual *Ayin-i Cem*, also known in its short form as *Cem*, serving not only as the foundation of their ritual practice, but also of the whole religion itself. On the one hand, in this masterpiece the secrets

* Ed. Chapter 9 is dedicated to *Salaam* from a Sufi perspective.

of the cosmos are performed through symbols, present in ancient Alevi poems, and, on the other hand, the creation of the universe and the emergence of human beings are presented in the mystical ritual dance *Semah*, which literally means welkin. It represents the planetary system and the connection of the universe with life on earth. *Ayin-i Cem* is also the definition of Alevilik itself because, accompanied by music, ritual dances and poems, it explains the philosophy of Alevilik about the emergence of the cosmos, the earth, the planet system and the emergence of human beings. Of special significance is the connection between cosmos and human life on earth (Çınar, 2007), aiming to achieving harmony, which equals *peace*.

In the past, Alevilik could not express itself freely and was prevented from fully realizing itself because it has been permanently exposed to persecutions. As a result, this generated an identity of a 'secret belief'(Çınar, 2007) that drove the Alevilik oral tradition to be expressed in symbols and transmit its pillars through poems, sayings, folk songs, folk song texts and narratives as well as jokes and practiced rituals. Therefore, music is central to Alevilik, not only because Alevis had to survive by transporting their beliefs by music, but furthermore because of the meditative and transcendental effects of sounds and rhythm.

In this vein, the different forms of oral dissemination have to be understood in their deeper sense. In the face of being permanently threatened by measures and actions of extermination, Alevis had to veil their expressions as disguises and assimilate them in order to cope with harsh conditions characterized by Islamization during the Ottoman Empire (Çınar, 2007).

Etymological exploration of Alevi

Only until discovering the proper etymological meaning of the term *Alevi* by looking at it closer, unveiling it and examining it, can the roots and the essence of Alevilik be unearthed, to Alevilik itself. In other words, to understand Alevilik is a pre-condition to knowing the meaning of the term *Alevi*.

The stumbling block to discovering the real origin of Alevilik resides in binding the definition of the term *Alevi* in its etymological meaning to Prophet Alī ibn Abī Tālib. This thesis claims that the term *Alevi* derives from being followers of Prophet Alī ibn Abī Tālib. It starts with the caliphate dispute after Prophet Mohammed's death between the supporters of Ebu Bakr as caliph, referred as *Sunnis*, and the *Alevis*, who were in favor of Prophet Ali becoming caliph, as Prophet Mohammed announced during his lifetime (Yaman, 2007).

However, Alevilik is not an Islamic sect having only Prophet Ali at the center; rather it has been the 'religious property' of Anatolia since the time of *kadim* (Çınar, 2007), the period before Christ and the time of ancient civilizations (Çınar, 2007).

Luvi – Aluvi – Alevi

In order to perceive the bare nature of Alevilik, it is necessary to understand where the term *Alevi* actually derives from by switching off the overwhelmingly loaded assumptions imposed by both Islamic and Turkish nationalist views.

Alevi derives from the Turkish word *ulev* (Çınar, 2007). *Alev* is the name given to the incandescent light that exists in the source of fire, that is, the flame. It is understood as the symbol for *light*. Two thousand years before Christ, ancient people living in Anatolia referred to as 'Hittites,' established a kingdom in Hattusa, in north-central Anatolia or the central Anatolian plateau (Çınar, 2007; Akurgal, 2001). Hittites used cuneiform writings or letters (Çınar, 2007), and hieroglyphs to express themselves. The Hittites did so partly in their own Hittite language, which is part of the branch of Anatolian languages of the Indo-European language family (Akurgal, 2001) and, since they tolerated other religious or folk groups within their own empire (Çınar, 2007), they also used the language of the *Luvi*, another group that lived in Anatolia at the same time. In Turkish, this ancient term began to be used by placing the letter '*a*' at the front, turning the term into *aluvi* or *alevi*. *Luvi* was thus the name given by the Hittite for this folk group and meant, originally in their now dead language, *People of Light* (Çınar, 2007).

People of Light

Until the last quarter of the sixteenth century, in the Ottoman Empire's literature and language, Alevis were also referred to as *Işık taifesi*, 'People of Light.' In his research on Ottoman literature, Baki Öz highlights this thesis by pointing out how in speeches and declarations the term *Işık taifesi* recalled them as a group banned as 'troublemakers who should be caught and handed over to the security forces' (Öz in Çınar, 2007, p. 34 [trans. by author]). The Ottoman rulers accused the People of Light of leading Islam into *ungodliness* (Çınar, 2007, p. 35). In their own terms, Luvi or Alevi were 'worse' and more dangerous than 'profane' people were. Therefore, Alevi people were chased, hunted and massacred over the centuries. Alevis also used various word games in order to change the pejorative loaded term *Işık, Light* (Çınar, 2007, p. 35).

Even though until the last quarter of the sixteenth century the description of Alevi as *Işık taifesi*, People of Light, was used in the region of Anatolia, this term was completely forgotten (Çınar, 2007, p. 35). As Professor Süleyman Uludağ states in the *Dictionary of Terms of Mysticism*, 'Alevi, Bektashi, Hurifi and Rafizi tended dervish groups have been called *Işık, Işık taifesi*, light or People of Light' (Uludağ, 2001, p. 177 [trans. by author]). Alevi sought shelter and protection and tried to survive by creating word games and other terms that had a similar sound to *Işık taifesi*, like *Aşk, Aşık* and *Işık*.[1]

These terms were used during the Ottoman Empire in the Arabic alphabet, written with the same letters and having a very similar pronunciation. The poets, *ozans*, used the *Işık* pronunciation, although it was written on paper as *Aşık*. Hence, these word games became an important form in which the *Işık* people protected themselves from anger and violence arising from oppression and repression (Çınar, 2007).

That *Aşık* are *Işık* people is made evident in the very famous *nefes*[2] as follows:

> We are Aşıks we are Lights in fact we are poor
> We are mad we are passionately lovers exposed to the tyranny of
> the fate. (Çınar, 2007, p. 38 [trans. by author])

Yunus Emre, a popular Alevi poet from the fourteenth century, stresses regularly that he is a person of light, as follows (Çınar, 2007, p. 38 [trans. by author]):

> Fasting, Islam namaz,[3] hajj[4] are embarrassments for Aşıks
> [...] O Aşıks, O Aşıks Light denomination is the religion for me.

Hence, between the term *Alevi* and the name of the fourth caliph of Islam, Prophet Ali, there is a remarkable resemblance of sound. Alevis discovered the opportunity to hide themselves behind this similarity of sounds and, as result of their desperation, in this manner they could protect themselves from attacks (Çınar, 2007).

Peace in Alevilik

'The Alevi path presents an organization of the Alevi direction towards embracing all dimensions of Alevi societal life with an overwhelming participation based on love and peace, brother- and sisterhood' (Çınar, 2008). Alevilik considers itself a religion of friendship, respect, love and peace while combining both energetic as well as moral approaches to the notion of *peace*.*

Peace is perceived as achievable through prevailing or creating a harmonic flow among human beings, nature and the supernatural or cosmos. This is the more energetic character of their view on peace. However, peace is also perceived as moral approaches not yet understood in absolute and normative terms, but in terms of the relation, consideration and connection to the constellation of the Great Triad of human beings, nature and the supernatural or cosmos. Alevilik combines both philosophical streams of idealism and materialism. It is idealistic because it explains the world, nature and universe as a visible reflection or form

* Ed. Energetic and moral approaches to peace are further explained in Chapter 1.

of the divine and it possesses a materialistic nature because it places the capacity, potential and development of human beings at its center (Öz, 2005).

Alevilik perceive their entire existence as composed of unique particles, which are connected to each other and therefore *peace* is perceivable by maintaining these connections harmonically.

Alevis' notion of peace: energetic principle of the connection of human beings, nature and cosmos

Especially before the Ottoman Empire period, Alevilik had been based on the energetic understanding of existence. Such energetic perception is found almost in all continents and periods (Dietrich, 2006a). The basic attributes of this kind of perception are the relational and unconditional claim to truth. The appraisal of the so-called *good* and *evil* is made relationally between human beings and their situational conditions. Actions are set only in adjustment and consideration to others, to their contemporaries and their environment, and this way the dangers to harmony are recognized.

Within this framework, there exists no *bad* person as such, but a person can at best be ignorant by letting his/her mind be cloaked by dogmatic religious norms without questioning them. Consequently, Alevis value science highly. Alevilik sees science as a medium for the elimination of obstacles to *peace* that dominate between human beings, like greed, hate, jealousy and prejudices. 'A way without science ends in the darkness' (Gülçiçek, 1994, p. 16 [trans. by author]). Science is here perceived as a way of combining rationality with mystical experience by realizing the connection between human beings, nature and the universe. Even Prophet Ali claimed, '[h]uman beings are afraid of that, which they do not know' (Gülçiçek, 1994, p. 16) and 'every container becomes tightly packed with what is put in it, except for the container of knowledge, for surely it expands' (Gülçiçek, 1994, p. 16 [trans. by author]).

This perception creates preconditions where *peace* can develop itself naturally because there is no reason for fighting against any *evil* phenomenon or person, since the main essence is to create harmony without the concepts of *evil* and *good*. This creates a way of peace because everything is one and every aspect needs each other to exist harmoniously in this system of life. The cosmic energy is crucial here. For Alevis there exists no personified creator but there is a pantheist notion of the creator. They believe in the connection and similarities with the microcosmos – our bodily circulatory system and life on earth – and the macrocosmos – the universe, invisible phenomena or the supernatural. All actions and activities that are made happen in a closed system, so they have durable effects on everybody and everything. In this respect, energy never gets lost. Consequently, in this philosophy fear of death cannot appear because here an end in the rationalist way does not exist. All things that come to an end, which die, transform themselves into other beings until the stage of *insan-ı kâmil*, or *perfect human being,* is reached (Çınar, 2007). This stage symbolizes the highest reachable spiritual state of being. The concept of *insan-ı kâmil* is embedded in cosmological notions and stands as the symbol for the correspondence between microcosmos and macrocosmos. The main intention is to be in unity and harmony with the surroundings in which one lives, nature and the divine. This unity represents a harmonic flowing with all aspects, which leads to *peace* because every aspect is in balance and so creates a network of harmony.

At the stage of *insan-ı kâmil* the spirit returns and is dissolved in the divine. There is a reciprocal connection of all living and not living, thus in this notion of life everything is connected with each other. In this regard, there is a cross-linking and dependence between all creatures and human beings, their actions, non-actions, and with the non-living. Consequently, in this thinking and life system *peace* is connected with balance among all factors of existence.

The longing of Alevis for the unity of all beings is very clearly expressed in this *nefes*, taken from Krisztina Kehl-Bodrogi (1988, p. 243 [trans. by author]):

> Let the I and you aside, what is this anyhow
> It is about time, that I tell it
> Kurds, Turks and Circassian
> They all are sons and daughters of Adam
> [...]
> Is there any wrong and where
> Have a look to the Quran, the Bible
> All of these four books are true
>
> Discard and delete the you and I
> Go ahead the way, which you have chosen
> There should be no one who loses his/her way
> What is a Yezit, what is a Kızılbaş?[5]
> Are not we all brothers and sisters?
> Our fire burns all of us
> To extinguish is the only aim
>
> Who created the world is one
> He is the power for all the things
> What is Alevism, what is Sunnism?
>
> Each living derives from earth
> [...]
> Veysel, do not turn to one's right or left
> Ask Allah for the unity
> Because from the duality emerges all the evil.

Therefore, *peace* is understood in a wider manner. If *peace* were understood in terms of morality, with normative implications or rationality based on the criteria of *good* and *evil*, it would destroy the harmonic flowing of the constellation between cosmos, nature and beings on earth. It would mean to interfere and to provoke reactions by participating in *good* and *evil*, which goes against Alevilik philosophy and the meaning of an energetic understanding of life, world and cosmic circumstances, where every aspect of life and all human beings are part of the divine and therefore are necessary for having peace.

This concept is peaceful because it looks for harmonious connections between all aspects of life so that every living and non-living being flows in harmony and balance together, which creates a particular form of peace. According to Alevis, if there is peace it means that it is perceived through harmony. *Peace* results in that context through *harmony*; peace is harmony.

Three dimensions of harmony in Alevilik

Peace equals *harmony*, more precisely three dimensions of harmony are regarded as contributing to peace. First, it is about having harmony within oneself, second, harmony with fellow human beings, and third, harmony between cosmos, nature and human life on earth. All these dimensions are inherently connected, inter-dependent and interact with one other. They build on each other, meaning that if there is an imbalance in one of these levels, it will create imbalances in the other two dimensions as well.

The first face of harmony, peace within oneself, is realizable by being honest to oneself and transcending the Ego, the Self, in order to acknowledge the connectedness of every aspect of life and, therefore, to act in consideration of them in a *social*, i.e. in a *collective*, manner. In Alevilik, the existence of human beings would be useless if there is a judging God who would give directions and norms for every step in life. Human beings are looking for the truth in themselves in consideration to fellow beings and nature. Therefore, a ritual service aimed at an outlying object, distant from oneself, is not necessary for praying. Hence, Alevis have no mosque for praying but they pray when and where they regard as right. As Haci Bektaş Veli said: 'Do not pray with the knees but with the heart' (Gülçiçek, 1994, p. 58 [trans. by author]).

To understand the second dimension, being in harmony with human beings, it is necessary to comprehend the elemental role of human beings in Alevilik. Human beings are born with unknown properties and acquire everything, all their characteristics, here on earth. Hence, everything is in the hands of human beings and they are able to create conditions of *hell* and of *heaven* here on earth.

Human beings are in the center of reference for Alevis. Human beings are capable of making decisions without an exterior judging authority in the shape of God, they are rational but are also beings led by emotions and intuition. It is important to note that rationality on the one hand, and emotions and intuition on the other, do not take over human beings by themselves, but they are *balanced*. A human being is an independent creature who is able to lead his/her life without bans, and is able to continue life without having permanent fear of an exterior and judging God, for that, to lead life, the divine has given him/her reason, but also love, love to act in life out of love, love towards human beings and nature (Şener, 1996).

All Alevi sayings and poems demonstrate that love towards human beings is the main pillar of Alevilik, because the human being is the highest valued and admired being in the entire existence. It is part of the divine, it derives from the divine but it is even able to reach the stage of unison with the divine in the form of *insan-ı kâmil*, *perfect* or *mature human being* and, that way, human being is the divine. Therefore, in the third dimension of harmony, human beings are mediators between earth, cosmos and human life to create or maintain balance and so are responsible for peace on earth. Human beings are the key component, and they take the key role in the task of creating and maintaining peace.

Unison and harmony as peace

The *hurufi* concept of the manifestation of God or the divine in human being itself is combined with the concept of *Ibn al-'Arabī*, which means the *unison of being (vahdet-ı vücüt)*, and with the notion of *I am the truth (Enel Hak)*, by Ibn Mansūr al-Hallāğ. *Vahdet-ı vücüt* means the unison or unity with God, nature and human being. God manifests itself not in Qur'an, but in human being itself. *Dedebaba* Bedri Noyan interpreted the relation of the created, existent world to God in a *bātinī*[6] manner – as a mutual relation in correspondence: *The world is zāhir* (the outside, outward) *of Hak, Hak is the bātin* (the inner) *of the world. Enel Hak*, by al-Hallāğ, describes the condition of Unio mystica,[7] used by Alevis as a metaphor for the immanence of God. In the following poem, the concept of *Enel Hak* appears clearly by Kul Hüseyn (Dressler, 2002, p. 107 [trans. by author]) who lived in the seventeenth century:

> I am your palest, I am completely infatuated with you
> If you are searching the kıble,[8] kıble is in you
> My lord[9] has created your beauty from the light
> If you are looking for religion, the belief,
> The belief is within you.

This nefes obviously shows that the first step in life is to look in the Inner Self before taking any step or decision and to search for the answers and the *truth* in the Inner Self.

A second example for the concepts of *vahdet-i vücut* and *bātiniyya* is the next nefes by Derviş Rıza (Dressler, 2002, p. 110 [trans. by author]):

If the saz[10] is played, the whole spirit goes into raptures
It is longing to it, to get one in vahdet-I vücut
The eyes open for the world of bâtın...

In contrast to the transcendent-God understanding of Sunna, the immanent God-terminology leads to a strong adjustment to life on earth. From the notion of divine manifestation in nature and human being results a sacrilegious life on earth, which is not compatible with the differentiation between *holy* and *profane*, like a transcendent-God understanding implies (Dressler, 2002). Consequently, there is no concept of *heaven* and *hell* because human beings are one with the divine.

An example of the reconciliation of energetic and moral concepts of peace: Rıza S̗ehri – the city of harmony

Rıza Şehri, i.e. the city of harmony, with the deity will represent an idealistic or utopian Alevi society model (Dressler, 2002). In such society, there is no *conflict, jealousy and smugness*. There is even no circulation of money. Everybody has his/her own duty that he/she offers to society. The habitants of *Rıza Şehri* are three times in *harmony* (*rıza olmak*). Three levels of being in harmony or unison carry central Alevis' religious views. First, to be in harmony with yourself (*kendisi ile rızası*): there is a call for absolute honesty with yourself. 'If you are looking for something, look for it within yourself. Not in Jerusalem, in Mecca or on the pilgrimage' (Gülçiçek, 1994, p. 14 [trans. by author]).

Second, to be in harmony with society (*topluma rızası*): here the guiding theme of Alevis ethics is applied, namely to be a master of the hands, tongue and loin. Hands is the symbol for theft and violence; tongue for slander, lies, insult and divulging a secret; and loin stands for being master of sexual wishes. It simply means neither to live in hedonism nor in asceticism, to balance needs and wishes in adjustment to surroundings, like fellow human beings and nature. Alevis firmly act and decide in harmonious accord with fellow beings and nature.

Third, to be in harmony with the spiritual community (*tarikla rızası*): the spiritual way (*yol*) is entered without outside obligation or constraint, it is entered from the own realization and creed to its rules. The initiation in that way, which is constitutive of the integration into the rite community, takes place in acceptation of a way or path-brotherhood or spiritual brotherhood (*yol musahiplik*). Spiritual brotherhood is a symbolic union and a mutual commitment accepted by two unmarried men together with their wives. Both oblige themselves in a ritual commitment, which is classified higher than blood relationship, for standing mutually by and for the other one and his family, by taking legal and moral responsibility for the family of each other.

These three levels of *rıza olmak* are connected with each other – this connectedness is very clearly shown by the author Ali Adil Atalay (Dressler, 2002, p. 114 [trans. by author]):

If on the path brothers' harmony rules truly, then in the spiritual community harmony is ruling. If in the spiritual community harmony is ruling, then in social life harmony is ruling. If in social life harmony is ruling, then the individual is with his/herself in harmony. So the three kinds of harmony are unified together.

Here the *connectedness, unison* and *harmony* between all dimensions of life are outlined very clearly. It shows that in the Alevis' system, thinking everything or every aspect of earth and cosmos is inseparably connected. This connectedness provides a sense of *harmony* that leads to unison and ends in *peace*. In this model, the moral character of peace is combined with consideration of the energetic character of human being and the energetic nature of the entire existence.

Oath of peace, harmony and love[11]

Alevis organize their community or society according to the pillars of love and *peace*. The first step for entering the Alevis' is through an oral commitment, an *oath, a vow, or ritual* along with an *ikrar cem*, meaning acknowledgment *cem* or the promise to follow the rules of the Alevi community. The promise consists in adhering to the Alevi formula of being master of hands, tongue and loin.

Talip, the name given to the person who is under oath, participates in his/her villages or cities in the routine worship rituals, *Ayin-i Cem*, and is constantly under the holy power of the Dede. In this regard, Alevilik is spiritually and socially committed to a spiritual authority and obligated to live in love and peace with the society. If a person is mature enough to make his/her own decisions, this person selects a *musahip*, a path brother or spiritual brother. These spiritual brothers, together with their partners or wives, organize with the help of a *rehber*, which means *guide*, a vow ritual where they are accepted to the Alevi *path*. At this point, the Dede presents three *seals* (*eline diline beline sahip ol*)[12] for the ones who are under oath. The first one is concerned with the potential of the *tongue*. All the destructive potential that a person can create with its tongue, with the tool of language like lying or gossiping or issuing defamatory statements, is regarded as throwing the societal harmony out of balance. Second, the power of the *hands*, like killing and consciously endangering a living being, picking up a flower without any apparent reason and being interested in properties of others, or to steal is perceived as a threat to the society, and therefore to its harmony and *peace*. Third, regarding the balance of emotions this vow points to embracing the dimension of the *seed* or *loin*. Not being loyal or honest to one's partner, to destroy a family, to marry a man or a woman of a destroyed family or to engage in polygamy is also regarded as a danger to the balance in society.

There are two kinds of 'punishments' designated for those breaking this formula. *Düşkün* is a very hard 'penalty' because it means being excluded from the society; it is given to those who, for example, kill a person. A person who is *düşkün* is excluded forever and there is no reconciliation in sight because what this person did largely endangered the harmony of the whole society and, therefore, these actions are irreparable. The second is *Müşkül*; an Alevi saying goes as follows: 'His/her way is from our way, his/her property is from our property, his/her herd is from our herd separate.' In other words, *müşkül* is a 'punishment' that is reconcilable after a certain time, after this person has rebuilt that which it has destroyed. Hence, Alevis explain that 'Müşkül can be solved or reconciled, düşkün cannot be solved.' All of these 'penalties' are decided along a kind of 'public tribunal,' where the members of the society have influence because it is seen as a matter pertaining the whole.

Connectedness, mutual responsibility and collectivism are achieved also in the custom of spiritual brothers being responsible for each other in terms of social behavior. It is their duty to advise each other if one is deviating from the Alevi path.

Alevilik consider love and peace as their religion and this is regularly expressed in Alevi nefesler as follows: 'Love is our religion. We do not believe in any other religion.' According to the Alevi author Çınar Erdoğan (2008):

> Within Alevilik, which itself grounds on love and peace foundations, love and peace that are embedded in human relations and societal life are boundless. To love all living and non-living beings and to be in peace and harmony with nature are the elementary and most important pillars. To cut a tree in spite of having no apparent reason and against the objection of the villagers, a Dede surely will expose this person to a holy interrogation. To be in harmony, in peace with nature is permanently expressed in the book of Alevi, which is nefes.

Peace through humanity

In Alevilik, everything is hidden and concealed in the heart of the human being. Humanity, understood as the love towards human beings, is the pillar of the religion of Alevilik. According to Aleviliki, to look for *Hak*, meaning to look for the *divine* somewhere else than in human beings is absurd. The human being 'is *Hak*,' 'the human being is Kaaba,'[13] 'the human being is the position taken by prostrating oneself while performing *namaz*, it is the niche in a mosque wall indicating the direction of Mecca,' 'the human being is the speaking Quran' (Şener, 1996, p. 113 [trans. by author]). As the Sufi Ibn Mansūr al-Hallāğ stated, 'I am God,' which implies that a human being is the highest being and therefore the being who can or has to keep harmony in order to achieve peace. *Peace* is the 'love which makes the divine human, and the human divine' (Şener, 1996, p. 116 [trans. by author]). For Alevis, 'the most valuable book that one can read is the human being itself' (Gülçiçek, 1994, p. 14 [trans. by author]). All the time, Alevi poets continuously pronounce that 'my religion is love' (Şener, 1996, p. 116 [trans. by author]).

Humanity, or love towards human beings, and respect are the main pillars of Alevilik (Şener, 1996, p. 116). *Peace* in Alevilik means to shelter human kindness, to love and be compassionate to human beings in one's heart, for which respect for all human beings results and so facilitates *peace*. Respect of all religions composes in that way an elementary premise for *peace*.

Peace can be created by human beings through respecting people regardless of their language, religion, race and gender. Peace is realizable by placing a person as a human being, as a part of this planet, as a part of the existence and as a part of the divine, therefore as part of all human beings. At the center is human being because human being itself is part of the divine energy.

The role of human being is thus described clearly and precisely in one of the countless nefes in Alevi poetry as follows (Dressler, 2002, p. 110 [trans. by author]):

> I am the mirror of the universe,
> Because I am a human being
> I am the ocean in the essence of Divine
> Because I am a human being
>
> Human being is in Divine
> And Divine is in human being
> Are you looking for [him], look at the human being
> There is no insufficiency at the human being
> Because I am a human being
>
> I could write the Torah
> I could write the Bible
> I could write the Quran
> Because I am a human being
>
> So many wishes and desires,
> The fate is insignificant
> The angel has to bow before me,
> Because I am a human being.

Alevis consider the whole humankind as their 'community' and, based on it, the relations to fellow beings are the main concern and are perceived as the *key to peace*, by seeking harmony between the symbiosis of cosmos or the supernatural, earth or nature, and human beings, which is provided by *human beings*.

Peace means also *equality* of all human beings. Equality is generated through the perception of the unity between the creator and the created beings; creator and human beings are *one* (Çınar, 2007). Two principles and aphorisms of Aleviliki, which are used quite often in Alevilik to present their notion of *equality*, are the following: '*Kul kula kul olmazi*,' which means that '*Nobody can be the slave of no one*' (Çınar, 2008) and '*72 millete aynı gözle bak*' (Kaplan, 2009), which means to '*Look at 72 people with the same eye*,' while the number 72 equals *all* people on earth. These aphorisms show the understanding of *equality* for Alevis being that there is no justification of any human being to claim superiority over others.

Hence, the manifestation of the divine in nature and human beings leads to the sacralization of here and now and, consequently, no differentiation of 'holy' or 'profane' can be made. The notion of *equality* also derives from the view that there is no separation between the divine and the being. All human beings bear the divine energy and therefore are equal. All human beings are needed for the unison with the divine, because all make up essential particles of the divine.

All human beings have the same duties, to serve each other and to include all beings in their lives, who are needed to keep the harmony. Thus, respect is a precondition for peace. The highest imperative of Alevilik is love towards human beings and respect. In practice, this is experienced through dialogue between people and the inseparable empathy for fellow beings. A very important saying of Alevi, which presents this aspect, goes as follows: 'Accept the creatures for the sake of the creator' and as Haci Bektaş Veli explains '[e]ven if you get hurt, do not hurt still' (Kaplan, 2009). Moreover, in the thirteenth century the poet Yunus Emre (Kaplan, 2009) formulated it in this manner:

> They call us devoted,
> We have only one enemy, hatred
> We hate no one,
> We see all equal and one

In Alevilik, *peace* is perceived in a coherent, inclusive and entire manner because it embraces the entire existence by taking into consideration the connection of the universe, earth or nature and human life.

Peace as freedom, self-determination and plurality of religions under Seljuk rule and the Ottoman Empire

The period of Seljuk and the Ottoman Empire signified very hard and cruel times for Alevis. Alevi people were seen as *heathen* or *godless* and were persecuted, oppressed and even massacred by the rulers and their security forces (Çınar, 2007).

Therefore, *freedom of opinion* and *freedom of religion* were demanded by Alevis, just as well as the explicit right to *self-determination*. In this context, *peace* was transformed from a more energetic interpretation into having the *right* to practice their own cultural and religious thinking and rituals, to have *freedom of opinion* and *religion* as well as the right to *self-determination*. This *peace* understanding was formed by and is the result of the social and political conditions at that time. It is very helpful to understand the notion of *peace* always concerning the social and political context. In order to survive, this interpretation of peace formed itself as a necessary *reaction*.

Peace as understanding of Alevis from the foundation of the Republic of Turkey until today: Kemalist and Marxist Alevis

To address the issue of whom and what is an Alevi means to arrive at manifold different answers. *Everybody thinks his/her own Alevilik* (Ismail and Franz, 2000, p. 59 [trans. by author]) – according to Ali Balkız, even this expression published in one of the most popular gazettes of Turkey shows that there is no consistent identity of Alevis that makes every analysis as difficult and as fascinating. In the course of the foundation of the Republic of Turkey in 1923 by Mustafa Kemal Atatürk, most Alevis saw their chance to be present in politics, probably to have a voice in governance and the possibility to participate in the policy-making process (Dressler, 1999).

In today's Turkey, there are Marxist, Nationalist and Kemalist Alevis because Alevis see their only chance to survive by taking on an official and accepted way in Turkey. Especially, there is a widespread nationalist Kemalism, which additionally formally guarantees laicism, meaning that Sunni-Muslims cannot extend their religious influence into governance and oppress Alevis and their culture. Kemalism also abolished the sharia[14] and is the defender of secularism (Dressler, 1999), which for contemporary Alevis is one of the most important issues because beyond *securing* their political, social, cultural and religious views, it extends to their existential survival. *Peace* in this context is connected to being a follower of Kemalism and to realize its norms. *Peace* is to have *laicism*, to have *freedom of religion* and *opinion* and impart *secularism*. Therefore, Alevis take these concepts as plea and shield for protection, yet this is not a real alternative to their situation in Turkey because Alevis are still discriminated against.

There are also Marxist Alevis, who stand up for humanity, democracy and human rights in Turkey. They see in a social revolution the solution to their problems of still being discriminated against and persecuted by the Turkish government and its security forces. *Peace* here implies to *be free from the capitalist system* and *its oppressors*; it stands for living in a fully developed *freedom for all people*, especially for the *suppressed* ones in Turkey.

Peace as reconciliation between moral and energetic concepts of peace

Alevilik combines both *energetic* and *moral* notions of peace. An exclusively Western-rational epistemology, with ultimate truths and the duality of *evil* and *good* would be considered as insufficient and ineffective for perceiving the world and would present a danger to peace. An Alevi peace certainly acknowledges rationality or reason as a crucial capacity of human beings to perceive the world with its senses, but it completes it with a deeper dimension by combining it with the *energetic* character of individual and collective perceptions of peace. Their notion of rationality includes the energetic component of human beings and of their entire existence. Energetic peace equals the balance between human beings, nature and the universe or cosmos (the invisible phenomena) in which the human being has the role of mediation between these three aspects of existence. Peace does not only result from harmony, but is perceived as harmony in all dimensions of life. Alevilik believes in the cosmic and energetic character of human being, but it also believes in the rationality of a human being and appeals strongly to it. To see both in combination and in inseparable connection is a premise for peace.

The notion of peace of Alevilik transcends the one-dimensional narrowness of rational thinking, not by giving prevalence to rationality, but by neutralizing it (Dietrich, 2006b) while taking away the aggressive claim of truth and putting it at a higher or deeper level of human consciousness when recognizing the energetic nature of human beings and existence. Human beings are perceived as deriving from the divine, so that its energetic character prevails with all its connections; however, the human being is also seen as a rational being with moral attitudes. With the potential of their reason, human beings are able to perceive reality, although not completely. Such perception thus necessitates the deeper dimension of feeling and the awareness of being a human as composing a part of the entire existence. This is possible by perceiving the environment as an energetic constellation, which is not perceivable only through sensory perception, but calls on a *trans-rational* perception (Dietrich, 2006b).

Trans-rational perception is part of the mystical and esoteric interpretation of life by Alevis. It is based on being aware of the conditions of nature and the transgression of the consciousness of the Self or Ego by seeing oneself as a part of an entire amazing existence, nature and the universe. Such transcendence of the Ego is not perceivable (only) with the sense defined by rationalism, but necessarily entails transcending the Self's own definition and bounding to material goods that are fleeting and transitory, grasping that the spirit of human beings is part of eternity, part of the divine. Due to this combination of rationality and energetic concepts of peace, it can be understood as a *trans-rational* perception of peace

(Dietrich, 2006b). At this point, Alevilik achieves to combine both moral and energetic concepts of peace.

Consequently, for Alevis it is crucial to abandon the reductionist individualism in order to aim for the balance between the trio of human beings, nature and cosmos. Collectivism is one of the steps for creating conditions for peace, only in acting collectively, in solidarity and in correspondence to fellow beings can *peace* develop itself, because *peace* can only be perceived in a harmonic flow of all aspects of existence.

Conclusion

Alevilik, a heterodox religious group, is not the path to peace but the experience of *peace* or *harmony* itself. There exists no dogma, no prophecies, no holy books, no conversions and no feelings or justifications for superiority. Alevis see their *teachings* not as teachings of bans or fear of a judging outer existing God, but as a path of love towards human beings or humanity. For them, the purity and naturalness of existence is crucial. There exists the divine nature of humankind, instead of a God outside humankind. Alevilik is a pantheistic and mystic religion and interprets its religious assumptions in an inner form. From an Alevi point of view, there is the oneness of religions and the coalescing element of Mother Nature, which is loved and respected deeply by Alevis.

Social factors, like the respect of fellow human beings and all cultures, are part of their *peace* understanding because even by not understanding others' lifestyles, they respect human beings like members of their own culture because they consider the whole of humankind as their community when claiming that their 'religion is love.' To be an Alevi means to be a *human being*. Regardless of a person's origin, ethnicity, culture, religion or ideological view, as long as he/she is master of his/her *hands, tongue* and *loin*, as long as he/she sides with humanity, peace, brother- and sisterhood and friendship, as well as equality, freedom and equal distribution, this person is an Alevi (Şener, 1996).

In this view, the cycle of life represents a certain harmony in which all living and non-living are included. Therefore, all living and non-living beings are dependent on each other and need each other to be complete and to reach harmony. That phenomenon represents a way of peace because everything is connected in some way, and the more strongly and closely connected these aspects are, the more the whole life system becomes more harmonic and, thus, more peaceful. The energetic character of Alevilik, like the Great Triad, represents harmony between human being, nature and the divine and, hence, resembles ever more unity in diversity, being once more *peace* as harmony. Through this *connectedness* and *harmony, peace* appears.

Alevilik is a highly heterodox and complex religion, but in its main function, it is a *path* of life. On the one hand, the complexity and diversity of it makes it difficult to analyze the *peace* understanding of Alevis; on the other hand, its particular character makes it rich and multifaceted.

The original meaning of *peace* in connection with *harmonic flowing* of all aspects of life resulted in a change under the rule of Seljuks and Ottomans. In this first stage of transformation, *peace* changed to *freedom, self-determination* and *plurality of religions* as well as to *have the right to practice rituals*. This transformation was caused by the social and political context, namely persecutions and oppression of the Alevis for centuries. The second transformation took place through the foundation of the Republic of Turkey in 1923, where Alevis clung to concepts and theories like Kemalism, which was not developed by *them* and not for *them* – not for the solution of their social, political and cultural situation. Nevertheless, the Kemalist parties feed upon Alevi voters. Many Alevis in Turkey are Kemalist and see it as their only way out of persecutions or discriminations, instead of creating their own alternatives for themselves. Furthermore, Alevis are followers of Kemalism or Kemalist parties with the consequence of *Westernization* and *modernity*, as Mustafa Kemal proclaimed. Therefore, there is also the immense danger of *homogenization* or *assimilation* to the paradigm of a so-called *Western* lifestyle.

Kemalist Alevis also stand as supporters of a policy with a taste of military power, which has shown itself repeatedly in Turkish history as having a destructive potential against its own population. Hence, the current *peace* understanding of Alevis even goes against their own cultural wisdoms and existential *security* and endows *peace* with an increasing military influence. Accordingly, their centuries-long notion of *peace* as *freedom of thought* and *freedom of way of living* cannot be realized through borrowed ideas that are, furthermore, based upon militarism. Nevertheless, by Alevilik having its own character and nature, its own history and origin, by having preserved a wide range of sources, the efforts of bounding, reducing or constraining Alevilik to other religions are absurd.

In Alevilik, each aspect is connected with every other and needs every other to reach completion and perfection. Therefore, efforts are taken for creating and keeping a harmonic network, in which each particle of existence is in permanent interaction, penetrates every other and is dependent upon every aspect of life and nature. This way, to claim superiority, to suppress human beings, to exploit nature, and to have the urge to destroy or eliminate other beings or phenomena of life and nature, in order to satisfy *individual* desires, are all instances that have no place in Alevism. To respect each other, all cultures and religions, to perceive nature with its rich variety of plants and animals, and to perceive all human beings as necessary and *inseparable* parts of the entire existence, paving the way where different kinds of *peaces* can live side-by-side, means *peace*. That is *peace*.

Notes

1. *Aşk, Aşık* and *Işık* mean *infatuation, being infatuated* and *light.*
2. This kind of poem is called *nefes,* which literally means 'breath.'
3. *Namaz* is the Islamic way of praying.
4. *Hajj* is the Islamic religious pilgrimage to Mecca.
5. *Kızılbaş* has been used in Turkey as a synonym, mostly meant in a pejorative manner for referring to the Alevis. It means *readhead* and alludes to the Alevis red headdresses (Kehl-Bodrogi, 1988).
6. Inner meaning.
7. Mystical unison with oneself, nature and divine.
8. *Kible* means the direction of prayer, but in Alevilik refers to the residence of God and is used as metaphor for the spirit.
9. In this context, *Lord* is a metaphor for God.
10. *Saz,* an elementary instrument for the oral traditions of Alevilik, is a stringed instrument essential for the music of Alevis.
11. I have based this section on my interview with Erdoğan Çınar (2008).
12. The Alevi formula *Eline diline beline sahip ol* stands for being the *master of the hands, tongue and loin.*
13. In Islam, *Kaaba* is the central sainthood of Islam; it is the house of God.
14. *Sharia* is the Sunni-Islamic religious law.

Reference list

Akurgal, E. (2001) *The Hattian and Hittite Civilizations* (Ankara: Ministry of Culture of the Republic of Turkey).

Çınar, E. (2007) *Aleviliğin Gizli Tarihi* (Istanbul: Kalkedon).

Çınar, E. (2008) 'Alevilik as an Organization Based on Love and Peace,' interviewed by A. Çakır (December 20, 2008).

Dietrich, W. (2006a) 'A Call for Many Peaces' in W. Dietrich, J. Echavarría and N. Koppensteiner (eds.) *Schlüsseltexte der Friedensforschung/Key Texts of Peace Studies/Textos claves de Estudios para la Pazi* (Vienna: Lit Verlag), 140–162.

Dietrich, W. (2006b) 'Energetische und moralische Friedensbegriffe als paradigmatic Leitprinzipien der Friedensforschung,' *Innsbrucker Diskussionspapiere zu Weltordnung, Religion und Gewalt,* 12.

Dressler, M. (1999) *Die civil religion der Türkei: Kemalistische und alevitische Atatürk-Rezeption im Vergleich* (Würzburg: Ergon).

Dressler, M. (2002) *Die Alevitische Religion* (Würzburg: Ergon).

Gülçiçek, A.D. (1994) *Der Weg der Aleviten (Bektaschiten): Menschenliebe, Toleranz, Frieden und Freundschaft* (Köln: Ethnographica Anatolica).

Kaplan, I. (2009) *Richtziele der alevitischen Erziehung,* http://www.alevi-bielefeld.de/index.php/alevitischen-erziehung, date accessed June 12, 2009.

Kehl-Bodrogi, K. (1998) *Die Kızılbaş/Aleviten: Untersuchungen über eine esoterische Glaubensgemeinschaft in Anatolien* (Berlin: Klaus Schwarz).

Nu`mān ibn Muḥammad, A.H. (2002) *The Pillars of Islam (Volume I): Acts of Devotion and Religious Observances,* trans. A. Fyzee, completely revised and annotated by Ismail Kurban Husein Poonawala (New Delhi: Oxford University Press).

Nu`mān ibn Muḥammad, A.H. (2004) *The Pillars of Islam (Volume II): Laws Pertaining to Human Intercourse,* trans. A. Fyzee, completely revised and annotated by Ismail Kurban Husein Poonawala (New Delhi: Oxford University Press).

Öz, B. (2005) Alevilik *nedir?* (Istanbul: Der Yayınları).

Poyraz, B. (2006) 'EU Minority Perspective and the Case of Alevilik in Turkey,' *EUI Working Papers*, 2006/24, http://www.iue.it/RSCAS/WP-Texts/06_24.pdf, date accessed December 18, 2008.

Schindeldecker, J. (1998) *Turkish Alevis Today* (Istanbul: Sakhulu Sultan Kulliyesi Vakfı),

Şener, C. (1996) *Benim Kâbem insandır* (Istanbul: AD Yayıncılık AS).

Shankland, D. (2003) *The Alevis in Turkey* (London: Routledge Curzon).

Uludağ, S. (2001) *Tasavvuf Terimleri Sözlüğü* (Istanbul: Kabalci Yayınevi).

Yaman, D. M. (2007) *Alevilik* (Istanbul: Garipdede Türbesi).

Zeidan, D. (1999) 'The Alevi of Anatolia,' *Middle East Review of International Affairs*, 3, 4, http://meria.biu.ac.il/journal/1999/issue4/jv3n4a5.html, date accessed December 18, 2008.

Section III
Peace Concepts in South and East Asia

11
Shanti: An Indian Perspective[1]

Swami Veda Bharati

> Brahma Shantih – God is peace.
> The Vedas

Peace, like love, is experiential. We know experientially when we are in love. So do we know when we are at peace. Both love and peace are indefinable. But, for convenience sake, let us propose:

Peace is a state of consciousness and mind that is free of internal conflict(s) within an individual as well as collectively within, and consequently among, groups of individuals known as nations, religions or ethnic units and [the entities known by] such other terms. (Swami Veda Bharati, 2004, p. 2)

There are thousands of religions and spiritual traditions that arose within and from India in all their versions, and they further developed in other parts of Asia in their own local forms, for example in Indonesia, Thailand, China, Korea and Japan. It is not possible to take any one idea and examine it exhaustively as it is to be found in these various traditions and their innumerable versions. Nor is it possible to select just one tradition, say yoga or Mahayana Bauddha,[2] and examine the development of an idea within just that tradition. This is so because the traditions are interlinked and they share some of the ideas even in minor detail, having developed side by side throughout history, maintaining a continuous flow to and fro.

Only a question of peace

It would appear that in this presentation we are not addressing the question of war and peace (except when discussing two parts of Mahabharata). Indeed, so. Our mandate to ourselves is only to try to understand peace itself, *sui ipse*, not an absence of war. Peace here is seen in a very wide dimension extending from the tranquility of a saint to our choice of peaceable emotion and sentiments that extend into our relationships and communication. War, if it indeed needs to be defined, is simply a failure of this vast dimension of peace, which is a positive force; we repeat, a force that needs to be understood for the humanity and each individual to fulfill his/her very purpose.

Some of our discussion, quotations, narratives and stories may appear not to be connected to the definition of peace but their interrelations with each other as well as connections with the experience of peace will show themselves in our conclusions.

Unity of views in Indogenic traditions

To examine what peace is in the Indogenic[3] traditions, we are selecting here a broad spectrum of Vedic-Hindu dharma,[4] and Bauddha dharma. In the latter, we proceed with the understanding that on the question of peace there are no fundamental differences between the Theravada and the Indian Mahayana. The Tripitakas, the basic texts of Bauddha dharma are held in equal reverence by both Theravada and Mahayana. The texts that are exclusively Mahayana remain true to the ideas and ideals presented in the Tripitakas and are not at variance with Theravada on this topic. We may also briefly refer to some other traditions, such as Jaina, to demonstrate that the entire spectrum of Indogenic thought shares these ideas and ideals regarding the definitions and processes of peace.

Is war a defining referent for peace?

In the discussions on peace, the modern mind often juxtaposes the concept to war. Even though in the innermost interpretations of peace in the Abrahamic–Semitic religions, Hebraic, Christian and Islamic, the concept of peace is far wider, and deeply spiritual, it is not in that sense that the word is now commonly used. It is often used today as antonym to war.

Not so in the Indogenic traditions. There is no one word that may be viewed as a single antonym to war in Sanskrit, Pali or Prakrit. In the texts on polity, there are two words:

- *Saman*, conciliation or accord between two states, as a matter of policy 'calming, tranquillizing, (esp.) kind or gentle words for winning an adversary, conciliation, negotiation (one of the 4 *upaya*s or means of success against an enemy, the other 3 being *dana*, *bheda* and *danda*') (Monier-Williams, 1997).
- *Sandhi*, 'agreement, compact, (...) alliance, league, reconciliation, peace between (...) or with (...), making a treaty of peace, negotiating alliances (...)' (Monier-Williams, 1997).

The antonyms of these are

- *Vi-graha*, hostility, first as simply the absence of an alliance or normalcy, call it 'cold war,' leading to
- *Danda*, wielding the stick or the royal scepter which then takes the form of
- *Yana*, marching and attacking.[5]

The Sanskrit, Pali and Prakrit[6] words for peace, however, do not have war as a referent. Peace is certainly not a state between wars, for otherwise peace would become dependent on war in order to define itself. On the other hand, war is an aberration, a divergence from natural peace, a disturbance in the natural order, as we shall see.

Defining peace as interior state

Peace is an inner quest or an urge, not derived from external conditions. We seek peace because our mind seeks to be easeful, at comfort. Because, 'how can one not at peace [*a-shanta*] derive pleasure or comfort?' (BhG. 2.66). 'The very mind [becomes] a burden to one not at peace [*a-shanta*]' Mahopanishad (3.15) (*Upanishat-Sangraha*, 1996, pp. 427–453).

The words for peace are derived from the verb root √*sham* (pronounced *shum*). It is an intransitive verb denoting a state of consciousness, to be at peace, to become peaceful, to be pacified, to be tranquil, quiet or calm. It is a state of being. It cannot be expressed by a single verb in the English language. It may be translated in as yet non-existent constructions such as 's/he peaces,' 's/he has peaced.' We are strongly tempted to use such construction in translating the texts to be cited in this chapter but shall refrain from creating a new language!

There are some words derived from the verb root √*sham*, each with its own flavor containing different concepts. An understanding of these words will help us define as to what is peace in the Indogenic traditions. Some of these words are:

- *Sham* (not the verb root but an indeclinable derivative), used mainly in the Vedas as an invocation for peaceful conditions. Out of 174 occurrences of words derived from √*sham* in the Rg-veda, 141 are invocations using the indeclinable *sham*. Few of these invocations may be arbitrarily cited here:
  - Moon Ambrosia, fully drunk, be Thou *sham* for our heart – RV.8.48.41.
  - *Sham* for the bipeds and the quadrupeds in our settlements – RV.9.69.71.
  - Waft *Sham* to our field and expansive lights for our clear vision – RV. 9.91.61.

- *Shama*: tranquility of mind and character, first of the six prerequisites for the practice of the precepts of Vedanta such as intense desire for spiritual liberation, *moksha*.
- *Upa-shama*: pacification of (A) desires and agitations, (B) cycle of birth and death, (C) diffuse manifoldness of the multifarious phenomena of the universe and our consciousness thereof to merge into singularity of Spiritual Being.
- *Shanti*: the most commonly used word for peace. Originally, it meant pacification of natural calamities and disturbances caused by evil presences as well as mental distress. There is a large body of peace liturgies and peace chants (*shanti-pathas*). For example, before starting the recitation and study of each Upanishad, the master and the pupil recite a *shanti-patha* so that the study may be undertaken without disturbances, external or mental. Almost all Hindu prayer and ritual sessions end with three times recitation of the words *shantih, shantih, shantih,* that is, Peace, Peace, Peace. In the modern languages of India, influenced by Western mental associations, the word may be used as an antonym of war but not so in the classics that are of our interest here.

Let us look at some of the usages of the words derived from √*sham* in the Vedic, Yoga and Bauddha literature and arrive at some conclusions as to the definition or meaning of the word 'peace' in the traditions of our interest.

Yudhishthira, having won the war, enters his city with his retinue: first arranging his mind's peace (MB-SP 36.29).

It is not peace of mind with regard to a particular situation but rather a tranquil state of mind, free of excitations and agitations, neither celebrating victory nor fearing defeat.

[The highest realization comes] to the yogin who is living liberated, full of wisdom, tranquil (Shiva-samhita [SS] 3.77).

That [transcendental station, the highest] pedestal is imperishable, immeasurable, free of disturbances, tranquil (SS.5.252).

A noble one practices yoga that quenches the [burning] heat of the worldly existence (Goraksha-shataka [GS] 3).

Pacification [*upa-shama*] means conquest of all senses (SSP.2.32).

[A realized being] is neutral [staying above, *udasina*], always tranquil [*shanta*], in health [*svastha*],[7] illuminating the interior reflexive self (SSP.6.68.25).

[Meditate on] the Peace-being [*sham-bhu*] who dwells in the heart-space, with the fierce brilliance of a sun (Goraksha-paddhati [GP] 2.67).

The mind of one who has conquered the senses becomes tranquil [*shanta*] all by itself (Yoga-rasayana [YR] 135).

Having no object in the mind, being reduced, the gaze becomes peaceful and tranquil (YC. vol. II; Amanaska Yoga [AY] 2.68).

[One practices yoga] for the pacification [*shanti*] of the delusion created by the cosmic poison of the world's cycles (YC. vol. III; Yoga-taravali [YT] 1).

One absorbed in the practice of yoga, tranquil [*shanta*] attains Supreme Brahman (HPJ.4.15).

Preceded by *shama* and so forth [the six prerequisites], the intense desire for liberation is the first ground of yoga (HPJ.1.3).

Seeing the tranquil [*shanta*] contemplative ascetics [still, as though] in a painting, the mind goes into tranquillity [*shama*] (HPJ.1.13).

God is Peace-Being [*sham-bhu*] as He grants *sham* that is comfort to the devotees (HPJ.4.18).

[The Master] simply by the [power of] speech and by casting the glance of knowledge, generates tranquillity [*shama*] in a moment (YC. vol. IV; Bindu-yoga [BY] 77.6).

How is interior peace obtained?

All of these citations help us conclude that in the yoga texts peace is an interior tranquility, which is obtained through

- the acceptance that the trans-qualitative Divine Peace-Being, who is facing in all directions in one's interior space, grants all mental comfort,
- meditation and such yoga practices,
- conquest of senses,
- intense desire for the pacification of the poisons of worldly involvements and thus for spiritual liberation, and
- observation of those who are at peace because of these means.

When interior peace is obtained through these means, one develops the capability to calm one's own mind, the waves of the mind subside, the senses gradually calm down and no longer burn with uncontrolled and unchanneled desires and the glance and the very presence conveys peace. One who is thus at peace remains illuminated in his/her deeper self and awakens similar knowledge in others, leading them to an immeasurable, disturbance-free tranquil status.*

Identical view in Veda, Yoga and Mahayana

The most detailed text defining the pathways to such peace is the *Upashama-prakarana* (Section on Pacification) of the famous philosophical lyrical epic the

* Ed. For a European interpretation of inner peace, see Chapter 1 by Wolfgang Dietrich.

Yoga-vasishtha of Valmiki. This, the sixth canto in more than 4000 verses in ninety-three chapters, takes a reader through a journey of self-pacification in which one aspires to:

> Arriving at transcendental peace [*shanti*],
> with confusions of worldly whirl having vanished,
> like a maiden having found her lover,
> my intelligence[8] will seek no other.

> When will my mind
>   having lost all worldly curiosity,
>   with all conflicts [within] pacified [*upa-shanta*],
>   sinless, resting in spiritual self [*atman*]
> become purified? (Canto 2, verses 23, 24)

For the pacification of mind [*chitta-shanti*], the yogins practice the control of breathing and the *prana* energy (91.26).

Eventually they reach the state of *samadhi*, the perfect harmony, absence of the forces of contradictions and conflict within. They can then declare:

> I am ever enlightened.
> I am ever stainless, immaculate,
> I am ever the pacified [tranquil, calm, quiet] [*shanta*] spiritual self,
> I am ever dwelling in [interior] harmony (62.21).

Having arrived at that stage of self-pacification they ask, upon meeting another, not the mundane questions of health and wealth but:

> Do you dwell in *samadhi* which is
> free of intents,
> the supreme place of rest,
> the final beatitude which is the transcendental peace? (62.3)

All this quest for internal peace is in the context of an understanding of the cosmos as empty [*kham*] in the Veda-yoga, a zero sum as Stephen Hawking says, a transcendental Null [*shunya*] in the Bauddha tradition. This is elaborated in the Madhyamaka-shastra of Nagarjuna (MSN), the founder of the Mahayana philosophy, in his very first verse: 'non-cessation, non-birth, non-terminant, non-perennial, not having one end, not having many ends (...)' (1.1).

Compare Gaudapada's and Asanga's verses in our earlier footnote 7. These verses show the parallels and identities between the Vedic and yoga philosophy on the one hand and the Mahayana on the other. The texts in both traditions

view the forms and phenomena of the universe ontologically as well as episte-
mologically with the metaphor of a burning torch that is being whirled about.
It forms many shapes, real to our momentary perception but truly unreal. Of the
215 verses of Gaudapada's text, 100 are in the fourth chapter titled *alata-shanti*,
blowing out the torch. Here the word *shanti* defines itself by its other meaning,
blowing out like that of a torch. True peace will not be obtained until the illusion
of the phenomena of the cosmos is extinguished and their re-submergence into
the Noumenon of monistic unity is realized. The natural social dimension of
such monism is unity among religions and nations and all other component
groups of humanity. Peace is then defined in this context:

> An appearance of birth where there is no true birth as though [the person
> named] Theodorus[9] was ever born; (...)
>   The personal realization that [all this is] unborn, unmoving, insubstantial
> [and thus] non-dual is [what is meant by] pacified, or at peace [*shanta*].
> (Shankaracharya on verse 45 of *Alata-shanti-prakarana* of the *Karikas* of
> Gaudapada)

At such a lofty station of peace and transcendence, the problems like violent
crime and war among the 'less lofty beings' do not arise. Or, do they?

Peace, internal and external conflicts, resolution

In Veda-Yoga as well as Bauddha-Jaina traditions, a clearly defined philosophy
of daily life is developed in almost identical terms; it is based within the context
of transcendence but in very real terms of life and emotions. This guidance to
life is firmly rooted in the principles of transcendence whose ideals are applied
to the questions the living beings face daily.

The interpersonal conflicts and inter-state hostilities both have their origin in
the conflicts that are internal to each individual mind. The paths of meditation
and transcendence lead to the internal resolution (*samadhana*) of these conflicts
and thereby help to resolve the external hostilities.

The sciences of economics and polity are thus viewed in a fourfold scheme of
knowledge. To paraphrase:[10]

- *anvikshiki*, science of spirituality and metaphysics, the path of self-realization and final liberation, whose principles govern the three below,
- *trayi*, scriptural/textual knowledge,
- *varta*, economic sciences and polity, and
- *danda-niti*, principles of justice towards the populace within one's own state
  as well as justice to be meted out to other states in case of their transgressions. War of the last resort is an instrument enforcing this justice.

Peace during war

The words for peace are not juxtaposed to war and neither is peace defined as absence of war, yet it is also not the case that there is no discussion on the questions of war and peace. There is only one text in which peace may be regarded as in juxtaposition to war. In *Mahabharata*, the great epic,[11] there are at least two major sections constituting discussions over a choice between war and peace and there are many minor ones dealing with the same topic.

The first of these is the well-known *Bhagavad-gita* in approximately 700 verses divided into eighteen chapters. The other, introducing the *shanti-parvan* section of the *Mahabharata*, consists of nearly 1400 verses in thirty chapters; this is in preparation for King Yudhishthira receiving the teachings from Grandfather Bhishma[12] (in BhG). It is Arjuna who has serious doubts about the war that is to begin. Krishna allays these doubts through a very detailed argument that may at first reading appear to be meandering through many tangents, but all within the context of a cosmic vision of divine reality. Detailed studies of this text have been made by hundreds of scholars. But some points need to be brought into clearer focus here.

Even though Krishna the Incarnate Divine Being inspires Arjuna to war, in common with all the texts of Indogenic guidance to life and polity, he places strict restrictions on the attitudes and points out that:

1. All actions including the acts of polity such as alliance and war are to be understood within the context of (a) the path to spiritual elevation and liberation, for which (b) it is essential to develop a nonviolent mind that is peaceful (c) that is, meditatively tranquil. (d) All of the questions of ethics develop within such context only.
2. War is a duty only for the persons of a certain group whose *prakrti*, nature, dictates it to be their *dharma*, duty based on temperament. The purpose of such duty is to protect those whose *dharma* is total nonviolence.
3. Like all actions in life, war is to be undertaken with an equilibrium of mind, a state of equanimity in all emotions, holding victory and defeat as equal, with the satisfaction that one has done one's duty without attachment to or expectations of its desired effects.
4. '(...) not having hatred towards any beings, maintaining amity and being compassionate' are essential qualities to be maintained at all times (BhG.12.13). One must practice 'nonviolence [*ahimsa*] and forgiveness (...)' that is called knowledge (BhG.13.7.11). One must remain 'neutral towards both sides, the friend and the enemy' (BhG.14.25). It is with this attitude that Arjuna is advised to 'fight but after having vanquished the feverishness of the mind' (*yudhyasva vigata-jvarah*) (BhG.3.30).

Thus, it is against the duty of the majority of the population to fight in a war for national interests, and with a desire to destroy the 'enemy.' Even a person of the warrior caste must first work on purifying one's mind and cultivate the attitudes described above. This becomes clearer as we study other texts.

Dharma rules in war

Manu-smrti, the Law Book of Manu, is regarded as the foundation of Hindu law. It states:

> When fighting in the battle one must not attack the enemies with secret weapons, neither with barbed arrows, nor with the poisoned ones, nor with flaming ones.
>
> From a vehicle, one must not hit an enemy who is on the ground, nor a eunuch, nor one who is clasping his hands [in submission or greeting], nor one whose hair is in disarray, nor him who is sitting down [weary], nor who [surrenders] saying 'I am yours.' [One must not attack] a sleeping enemy, nor a naked one, nor one who is weaponless, or whose armour is broken, nor one who is merely watching without fighting.
>
> [Nor should one attack an enemy] whose weapons have broken down, or who is in grief, or is badly wounded, or is scared, nor one who is turning his back. (Manu-smrti 7. 90–93)

Here we come back to *shanti-parvan* of Mahabharata, referred to above. In the introductory chapters to *shanti-parvan*, it is the eldest brother, Yudhishthira, known as the son of very *dharma*, who is deeply hesitant to sit on the royal throne that has been won through the recent war. He not only expresses *vairagya*, disinterest in worldly powers and pleasures, he argues against taking up the throne that has been acquired through a fratricidal war. He further sees that royalty and the necessity for waging war are intertwined and for this reason he would rather take the vows of a forest dwelling ascetic than be consecrated a king. Here the very existence of the state is seen as dependent on one of its pillars, war.

Yudhishthira's brothers, wife Draupadi, sage Narada and the divine Incarnation Krishna all try to allay his fears and advise him to seek the teachings from grandfather Bhishma[13] as regards his duty.

Nearly one-fifth of the Mahabharata[14] consists of these teachings of Bhishma, especially in *shanti-parvan* and *anushasana-parvan*.[15] *Shanti-parvan* is divided into three major sections, namely

- *raja-dharma-parvan* (RDP), detailing the duties of king and the state, including the rules of war (4502 verses in Chapters 1–128),

- *apad-dharma-parvan* (ADP), explaining the duties in times of crises when the normal rules may not be operative (1560 verses in Chapters 129–167), and
- *moksha-dharma-parvan* (MDP), the path of spiritual liberation in which there is no scope whatsoever of transgressing the principles like nonviolence even in times of crisis (6794 verses in Chapters 168–353).[16]

The rules of war given in RDP are even more detailed than the ones in the Laws of Manu:[17]

One is not to fight against a kshatriya who is without an armour. A single [soldier] should battle another single one [challenging] '[shoot your weapon]' and 'I shoot [mine]'.
If [the opponent] comes armoured, one should become armoured; if he comes with an army, one could challenge him with an army. (…)
An arrow should not be poisoned or barbed; such are weapons only of the evil men. One should fight straight and should not get angry at [the enemy who] is trying to kill.
(…) [An enemy] who has already lost his vitality [is weary or faint] should not be killed, nor one who is without an offspring.
[An enemy] whose weapons are broken, who is in a state of helplessness, whose bowstring is cut, whose vehicle is destroyed [or mount is dead], should be given a [medical/hospitable] treatment in one's own realm, or should be escorted to his own home.
After the wounds have healed he must be released. This is the ancient law (…).
One feeling weak [*nish-prana*] should not be attacked, nor one who has no children [so his line may continue], nor one whose weapon is broken or bowstring is severed or whose vehicle is damaged nor one who is distressed. (RDP 95.7–14, 17–18)

Again,

If a brahmin [educator/priest] seeking to bring peace comes between two armies that are in battle array, the fight should be stopped.
If a so-called kshatriya were to break such a rule, he then no longer counts [as a soldier or a citizen] and cannot be allowed to take a seat in a council. (RDP 96.1, 8–10)

Did the authors of the Laws of Manu and Mahabharata perchance read the Geneva Conventions, or vice versa?

May we interpret these rules for our times to imply that if, for example, a council of philosophers for the European Union or the United Nations comes between two potential combatants and determines that a war is not moral (*dharma-yuddha*), the said war must not proceed. And, if anyone opposes the said ruling of the philosophers s/he must be barred from taking a seat in a council of power? And what about the rules against secret weapons, barbed arrows (cluster bombs?) and fiery weapons (napalm? fire bombs? atomic weapons?)?

MB states: 'The kshatriya who wins by immoral means [*a-dharma*], even though he has made promises to live by rules of morality [*dharma*], kills self by self; sinful, living in deception' (MB. 95.20).

War is illegal unless fought (1) only by those who are temperamentally inclined to such as a moral duty (2) within the rules laid down: 'When all citizens take to weapons [indiscriminately], they transgress their respective natural duties' [*dharma*] (MB.78.12).

It is stated implicitly and explicitly that a war, within these rules, is to be fought only to protect the right of others to remain free of involvement even within the limits of such a permitted act of well-controlled violence.*

Peace of relationships during war

When one embarks on a war, the warrior, commander, must not forget all other relationships.

After Arjuna's doubts have been allayed by Krishna in BhG., the war is to begin. Yudhishthira, the eldest brother, dons his weapons and walks to the enemy ranks. He approaches each one of his elder relatives who are on the opposite side, touches their feet and seeks their permission to fight, and their blessings to win. Each of the enemy elders gives him the blessing to win (MB Bhishma-parvan 41.6-82)! On the tenth day of the war, Bhishma himself tells the Pandavas the secret of how he, the otherwise invincible warrior, may be killed (Swami Veda Bharati, 2003).

Once an enemy is defeated, there are rules in the Laws and in the texts like MB as to how he is to be treated, generously and courteously and be honorably sent back to his own country (Manu 7.203–204).

After winning the war, Yudhishthira and the brothers enter the capital city. They ask Dhrtarashtra, the father of the defeated cousins, to lead the way to enter.

In another story, the king of Mithila defeats the king of Koshala country. His spiritual guide advises him: 'abandoning pride, false virtue, anger, excitation or fear, offer service to the [defeated] enemy, prostrating to them with hands clasped.'

The king of Koshala calls the defeated enemy and tells him: 'I have won by the fact of virtue (dharma), intelligence and strength, but, Oh best among the

---

* Ed. compare to the *ius ad bellum* in Chapter 2 by Karlheinz Koppe.

kings, you have won me by your good qualities. Do not have a low image of yourself; behave as though you have actually won (...).'

He then invites the defeated king to his home and gives him the honors normally given to a venerable one, and then bids him farewell with many gifts.

Peace as a goal, a goal for peace?

The discussions, statements and injunctions in the texts show that peace is to be understood as multidimensional reality, not merely a state to be aspired to. It has context and content. The context, as we have stated above, is spiritual liberation, whether defined in Bauddha, Jaina, Vedic-Hindu or any other Indogenic tradition. All the Indogenic traditions are agreed on spiritual liberation as the context for all human pursuit in virtue, ethics as well as meditation and such yoga practices.

Pursuit of peace produces certain states, virtues and emotional choices in our personality. Those states internal to us generate certain conditions in the society, in its rulers and citizens and in the surrounding nature as well. These conditions further ensure the presence and strengthening of peace, both internal and external. The purpose of such peace, for which the king or the state is as responsible as the citizenry, is to provide the optimum environment for all to be able to pursue the path of spiritual liberation. The conditions of such peace naturally generate physical health and material prosperity and harmony in all relationships among living beings (not only humans) and in nature. Let us look at the components of such a peace.

Peace through self-governance

The king or the state must follow certain principles for success and prosperity in peace. The following *sutra*s of Chanakya show us the progression in these principles:[18]

- The foundation of ease, comfort and happiness is *dharma* (virtue based in cosmic law).
- The foundation of virtue is the material means and polity (*artha*).
- The foundation of economics and polity (*artha*) is the statecraft/governance.
- The foundation of governance is conquest of the [governing persons'] conquest of [their own] senses.
- The foundation of sense-conquest is discipline.
- The foundation of discipline is service to the elders.
- By service to the elders [one obtains] personal experiential knowledge (*vi-jnana*).

- Through [such] personal experiential knowledge, let one perfect oneself [and thereby make oneself successful and prosperous].[19] (Chanakya-sutras 1–8)

Thus, self-governance is the best governance that ensures peace and prosperity for the governors and the governed.

What are the first principles of such self-governance? Echoing the entire Indogenic complex of traditions, the last three sutras of the text are:

- One attains heaven through ascetic endeavor (tapas).
- The ascetic endeavor of one who is endowed with forgiveness grows in multifarious dimensions.
- Thereby the works of all become fulfilled. (Chanakya-sutras 570–572)

Vrddha-Chanakya (VC), an old text on the philosophy of Chanakya states:

> What can a wicked person do to one who holds forgiveness as a weapon in hand?
> Fire falling where there is no dry straw extinguishes itself.[20] (VC 3.30)

Does not sound much like a modern text on polity but that is the point! Forgiveness in personal life and polity leads to success in all undertakings. (We thought it was the World Bank or the cruise missiles!)

Signs of peace through self-governance

What signs should we look for to see whether peace through the rulers and citizens' self-governance prevails? In the Ramayana of Valmiki there are twenty verses that begin with 'not in the State devoid of good governance [...].'[21] We may selectively summarize here some of the conditions that are stated to prevail in such a country:

- In a state without good governance
  - lightning-garlanded loud roaring cloud rains not on earth with celestial water;
  - handfuls of seeds are not scattered [to plant]; (...)
  - neither [performances of] happy dancers, performers, acrobats, nor festivals, gatherings – that commonly help the increase in a nation – [see any] growth; (...)
  - virgin girls wearing gold jewelry do not come to play in the parks in the evenings;

- the far travelling merchants, having earned much [wealth] meritoriously do not walk the paths safely;
- self-controlled mendicant, contemplating the self in the self, does not wander alone;
- scholars proficient in sciences do not sit discussing their subjects in the parks and groves. (Valmiki's Ramayana Canto 2, verses 9–28)

One may assume that opposite conditions prevail in a well-governed peaceful kingdom/state.

Qualities of leaders to ensure peace

In such a peaceful state that is to be run on the principles of self-governance, the king (leader? president? prime minister?) needs to be

[…] patient, tolerant, […] eager to listen, […] filled with sacred faith and devotion, […] giving a hand to the distressed, having wise ministers, […] not saying 'I', […] non-arrogant, always with a pleasant face, protector, […] non-angry, having a beautifully high mind, […] watching over the citizens' well being […]. (MB RDP.118. 28–33)

For the ministers to be appointed to ensure a peaceful state, run by those who practice self-governance, the qualifications are similar:

well educated, […] tolerant, […] grateful, powerful, forgiving, controlled, master of [one's] senses, not greedy, […] well wisher [for all], […] not arrogant, […] soft spoken, patient. (RDP.118. 18–25)

In relation to the economic management of the state, Bhishma asks Yudhishthira: 'Perchance, businessmen of your nation are not getting agitated, oppressed by [heavy] taxation, buying at great price and gaining little […]? Perchance, farmers – who bear the yoke of the kingdom and feed others – are not oppressed and leaving your nation?' (RDP.89. 23, 24)

Peace and natural phenomena

When a nation is run by the powerful who have not mastered the art of self-governance, the peace of nature itself is disturbed. This concept of a harmony and symbiosis between human affairs and nature is unique to the Indogenic traditions.[22] The mind of the rulers and the populace affects the 'mind' of nature and maintains or disturbs the nature's equilibrium. When Rama ruled the kingdom,

Then no widows lamented, and there was no danger from preying beasts nor from diseases [...]

The trees were ever-flowering, ever fruitful and wide in the trunks;[23] (VR 6. 98–102)

Thus, says Uchathya in MB: 'Clouds raining on time and the king reigning with virtue (dharma), this is the simultaneous prosperity whereby the citizens dwell in ease and comfort' (RDP 91.1).

On the other hand, when the king (leader, prime minister, president?) does not live by virtue, all nature becomes unbalanced;

It becomes cold when not winter,
in winter it ceases to be cold. (RDP 90.37)

In the commentary on 1.3 of Dhammapada is given a long story of Tissa Thera. In the story, to paraphrase in extreme brevity, one morning the sun does not rise due to the vagaries of a curse placed by a saint. So, the king of Kashi, Brahmadatta, examines himself: have I committed any wrong with my body, speech or mind that is adversely affecting the nature thus?[24] Just as the king's or the state's conduct brings adversity or prosperity through nature, so also 'whatever the king does, so the rest of the people follow' (avadana-kalpa-lata 53.22).

The entire Sanskrit, Pali and Prakrit literature is replete with such statements; we have given only an indication of the philosophy of the symptoms of peace as they manifest in nature. The equation is: spiritual tranquillity of mind > virtuous behavior of the state > virtuous behavior of the citizenry > balance in nature nourishing the living beings in turn.

It is in such philosophy of life that the teachings of the Buddha also show deep respect for nature. He says: '[...] Oh Monks, the monk Gotama [Buddha] refrains from causing harm, hurt or disturbance to any tree, plant (born of seed) or a living being [...]' (Brahma-jala-sutta[25] 2.10).

Buddha prevents a war: peace through character

In the Buddha's life, there were many occasions when he needed to help negotiate among the republics and monarchies. The story below will help demonstrate his technique for encouraging peace. King Ajatashatru of the Magadha country was planning for an invasion of the Vajji Federal Republic, to destroy the republican federation. He sent his chief minister, by the name of Varshakara, to the Buddha for his advice. To summarize a detailed story,

The Buddha asked his chief disciple Ananda who was fanning him from behind:

Have you heard that the Vajjis gather together in order to confer on matters among themselves?

Have you heard that the Vajjis sit in their councils fully united?

Have you heard that the Vajjis respect those who are elder to them in age or knowledge, give them honour, raise them high, and listen to their advice with due respect?

Have you heard that the Vajjis do not violate the women of others and do not force them into their own households?

Have you heard that the Vajjis protect and give honour to the visiting saintly and enlightened persons [*arhats*] hoping that these *arhat*s would keep coming back to their land to give spiritual advice?

The answer to all these questions was 'Yes, so have I heard. Indeed the Vajjis do so'.

The Buddha said: Once I was staying in the Sarandada shrine in the city of Vaishali for my spiritual practices [*sadhana*]. At that time I had given to the Vajjis the advice of these inviolable *dharma*s. So long as they will continue to follow these inviolable rules of conduct, they themselves will remain inviolable; they can look forward to progress and progress alone. No force can violate them or defeat them. So long as they follow even one of these principles they remain inviolable. So long as there is unity among them, they cannot even be bribed to betray their republic.

The chief minister Varshakara heard the Buddha and said: I better go; there is much to do.[26]

The Buddha's advice was not based on comparing the state of the treasury or the military prowess but simply on the strength of character. It is interesting to note that the king did not ask: How many [army] divisions have the Vajjis?[27] He called off the invasion, at least for the time being, simply because of the moral strength of the republican federation.

In MB RDP, Ch. 107 Bhishma is also asked the question about the treatment to be given to the republican peoples, *gana*s. Verses 6–32 of that chapter give advice identical to that of the Buddha cited above but we refrain from translating the same in full for constraints of space here.

Peace through renunciation

This kind of practice of the ethics of the state is firmly rooted in all Indogenic traditions because of the way the nature of reality and power is perceived. Let us here summarize the argument of peace through renunciation, repeatedly stated in all traditions and taken for granted as the truth of life:

- All phenomena (of nature and human power) are transient by the law of cosmic entropy.
- Involvement with them only leads to sorrow and disappointment.
- Being transient, sooner or later they terminate themselves, causing disappointment.
- Therefore one should undertake all one's worldly duties without attachment, maintaining an inner neutrality, without expectation of their fruit – only to perform the duties altruistically because 'the good must be done for its own sake.'
- At the end one should seek to renounce by one's own will and choice that the entropy and transience will automatically snatch from us any way.
- What one renounces of one's own will does not cause pain and disappointment, and
- prevents our indulging in excessive strife, struggle, contradictions (intrapersonal, interpersonal, interstate, inter-religious) conflicts and wars.[28]

It has been a tradition in India, not followed universally yet more widely practiced than is commonly recognized, that after living the life of a housekeeper one may enter the state of *vanaparastha*, the forest-dwelling (nowadays the 'Ashrams-dwelling') ascetic and finally take the vows of a *sanyasin*, a renunciate monk (Manu 6.2). The Law Book of Manu lays down that one should start thinking of renunciation when one finds his hair beginning to turn gray (Manu 6.1–32, 33–86).

Dasharatha, father of Rama the hero of Ramayana, turns sixty. He calls his council and suggests that he should renounce the throne and if the council members and the citizens (of the city and the countryside, *pauras* and *janapadas*) consider Rama suitable to be the king, he may be consecrated to the throne, or else they may suggest someone else (Valmiki's Ramayana 2.1–16).

Among such numerous examples is one found in Makhadeva-sutta.[29] King Makhadeva commands his hairdresser that the day he sees a grey hair in his head, he must let him know.

As the hairdresser obeys the command,

The king grants the hairdresser a village as a gift, summons the crown prince and tells him: Dear One, my angels from heaven have appeared. I have enjoyed all worldly pleasures and powers. Now it is time to think of the other world. Come, Prince, you now take up the duties of the State. I will now have my beard and moustache shaved, wear saffron robes and shall make myself a homeless [mendicant].

You, too, Oh Prince, when you see your grey hair appear, should likewise renounce and become a renunciate monk.

All the generations of the King Makhadeva followed that tradition of renouncing the kingdom whenever they saw their hair turn grey, because the one descendant who would break the tradition will turn out to be the last of the line.

The one who became the Buddha by renouncing his princely status was the King Makhadeva in that previous life.

One of the most elaborate examples of the renunciation of the power of the state and the kingdom to ensure peace is in the Jaina story of the brothers Bharata[30] and Bahubali.[31] Here is a brief summary.

Bharata is a *chakra-vartin*, universal ruler.[32] After his return from the customary tour of the empire, during which all kings would recognize his suzerainty over them, he prepares to enter the capital city, Ayodhya. The *chakra*, discus, hovers outside the gates of the city and does not enter. The ministers advise him that there is still one king who has not accepted him as the suzerain. It is his own younger brother Bahubali, the king of Podanapura.

A message is sent to Bahubali not to spoil the universal ruler's endeavor to unite all kingdoms under one parasol, imperial *chhatra*. The brother haughtily refuses and a war ensues.

Upon seeing the destruction being wrought by the potentially fratricidal war, the ministers suggest that the war be stopped and the two brothers engage in three kinds of duel:

- *Drshti-yuddha*, duel of the gazes, in which the two must gaze at each other without blinking. Bharata loses.
- *Jala-yuddha*, water fight, in which also Bharata loses.
- *Malla-yuddha*, wrestling match.

In the *malla-yuddha*, towards the end, Bahubali picks up Bharata and lifts him over his head to drop and smash him to the ground.

At that moment a transformation occurs; it is a moment of conversion. 'Why am I killing my own brother for the sake of a little kingdom?' He chooses to take the vows of renunciation. He pulls off his hair in five handfuls, the form of self-tonsure that the Jaina monks do when taking the vows to renounce. He tells Bharata to go rule over the entire earth including his own erstwhile kingdom.

He undertook a severe ascetic endeavor, standing motionless for a year in *kayotsarga-mudra*[33] but the final enlightenment, *kevala-jnana*, did not come to him.

Brother Bharata asks his father, *Tirthankara* Rishabhadeva,[34] why his brother was still not reaching final enlightenment. Rishabhadeva advised: Bahubali still has one astringent thought left in him, a thought of ego. He feels, 'I am still standing on my brother's land.'

Bharata reaches the spot where Bahubali stands and says: 'The land is also not mine. Whose land is it, anyway? I, too, renounce all claims to kingship and kingdom.'

At that point, Bahubali is freed of all past karma and was enlightened.[35]

Bharata also became a renunciate monk and bequeathed the kingdom to his son Arka-kirti.

This is a prime example of (1) peace, as stopping of war, through renunciation, and (2) that renunciation leads to eternal spiritual peace of enlightenment.

One of the contemporary examples of such renunciation is that of the Druk Gyalpo (Dragon King), Jigme Singye Wangchuk, the king of Bhutan, a Mahayana Buddhist, who has renounced the throne at the age of fifty-one in favor of his son Jigme Khesar Namgyal Wangchuk. The elder Wangchuk is also known for his theory of Gross National Happiness as juxtaposed to the more popular Gross National Product. This author knows of several Hindu princes (ex-Maharajas) who lead the life of renunciates in the Ashrams in the holy cities like Rishikesh where he is resident. So we are talking of a live tradition.

Peace through renunciation of favored ideas

Renunciation for peace and enlightenment is not only of kingdoms, power and wealth. One must also learn to renounce most dearly held ideas. That is the more difficult part. For example, the idea of nationalism about which Einstein[36] said: 'Nationalism is an infantile sickness. It is the measles of the human race [...].'

On the topic of not being able to change one's ideas, the Buddha gives the story of two seekers of fortune who went out looking for ways to enrichment. The travelers saw a heap of hemp and filled their sacks with it. In another village, they saw hempen sackcloth, which is more valuable than unspun hemp. One picked up a load of the sackcloth while the other carried on with just hemp. In this way, they saw in turn unspun cotton, cotton cloth, silk thread, silk cloth, copper, zinc, lead, silver, gold and so forth. One kept on renouncing the less valuable materials and picking up the more valuable ones whereas the first companion just carried on with the original load of unspun hemp. Naturally, when they arrived in their hometown, it is the wiser one who makes all his relatives and womenfolk happy and not the one who had stuck to his original load of hemp. Thus, should one renounce previously prejudiced ideas and accept new ones.[37]

Peace by renouncing religious exclusivity

This brings us to the question of peace through inter-religious understanding, where one needs to give credence to the ideas of others. This acceptance of others' ideas about religion is intrinsic to the Indogenic traditions. We have said above that there is no word for 'religion' in the Indogenic traditions. There are views, paths, ways of life, levels of realization. But no 'true or false' kind of religion.

As early as in the Rg-veda we recite how the One has become many forms:

One fire alone is kindled in many flames.
One Sun is sovereign over all the world(s).
One Dawn alone brightens all variety.
One alone indeed has become all this [universe of phenomena] manifold.
(RV.8.58.2)

Here are two verses[38] from the daily liturgy of the Hindus:

I do not know, Lord, of what form or nature you are;
Of whatever form or nature you are –
to that very one I prostrate myself.

We read from the Incarnation Krishna:

Do not create a confusion of opinions among people;
A wise person who practices yoga and practices right conduct
should help all to follow their own path of action. (BhG.3.26)

Again:

In whatever way people approach Me,
so do I respond to them.
In all paths it is My path that they
are following from all directions.
Whichever form or aspect of Mine
do they worship in faith,
towards that very form or aspect of Mine
I sustain their faith.
(BhG.4.11; 7.21.22)

It is difficult to state that all Indogenic traditions believe in polymorphous monotheism.[39] Since the Bauddha-Jainas do not accept a God as such, the best statement unifying the various Indogenic traditions would be that they all believe in multilateral polymorphous One Reality. In the Bauddha view it is clearly stated that no view is to be stated.

In Brahma-jala-sutta (BJS) the Buddha describes sixty-two different views of theology and cosmology and advises his disciples not to enter into discussion concerning these views (BJS 103–104). He also states:

Monks, if someone speaks ill of me, or of my teachings or of the monastic community, you should not feel hurt or dissatisfied or have mind's agitation thereby. If you were to react with hurt, dissatisfaction or mind's agitation, it will only adversely affect your spiritual pursuit and practice. You should only examine how much is the truth in their statements [...].

Monks, on the contrary, if someone praises me, or my teachings or the monastic community you should not feel joyous, happy-minded, exhilarated thereby. If you were to react with joyousness, happy-mindedness or exhilaration, it will only adversely affect your spiritual pursuit and practice. You should only examine how much is the truth in their statements [...]. (BJS 5–6)

To paraphrase further: 'You should refrain from boasting that you alone know the subject, that you alone have studied it well and the other disputant has not, that you alone are making statements based on dharma whether opposite views are not so based...you should avoid entering such disputes.' (BJS 18)

Numerous texts support the same view.

Nagarjuna, the founder of the Mahayana philosophy, especially the philosophy of the Middle Way (*madhyamaka shastra*), is a master of what is now called deconstruction. Make a simple statement like 'John has come' and he tears it to shreds; he employs this technique to show that all statements of theology, philosophy and so forth are illogical and there is no scope for insisting on a belief. By the same token, there is no scope for insisting on disbelief either. In such a Null-philosophy (*shunya-vada*) all that counts are spiritual practices that bring about total peace and tranquility of mind and an enlightenment-mind (*bodhi-chitta*).

In another text, Vigraha-vyavartani (VV), Nagarjuna states:

If I had presented a hypothesis, I could be challenged;
I have presented no hypothesis, therefore I cannot be challenged. (VV.29)

In these ways, the Bauddha approach refutes the establishing of doctrines as well as any refutation thereof. It seeks a non-involvement in disputes.

It is such view of dharma that made the emperor Ashoka (third century BC) issue the proclamation:

[...] The growth of the essence of the matter assumes various forms, but the root of it is restraint of speech, to wit, a man must not do reverence to his own sect or disparage that of another man without reason [...] the sects of other people all deserve reverence for one reason or another.

By thus acting, a man exalts his own sect, and at the same time does service to the sects of other people. By acting contrariwise, a man hurts his own sect, and does disservice to the sects of other people. [...]

Concord, therefore, is meritorious, to wit, hearkening and hearkening willingly to the Law of Piety as accepted by other people. For this is the desire of His Sacred Majesty that all sects should hear much teaching and hold sound doctrine. (Rock Edict XII, pp. 17–18)

This is not a proposal for peace through religious *tolerance* but rather acceptance of all paths as valid, depending on each person's mind and understanding of the divine Name and Form or formlessness. It is the view of polymorphous Ultimate Reality.

This validity of the multifarious paths is most reinforced in the Jaina doctrine of *syad-vada*, the theory of 'maybe so.' It is known as the doctrine of *sapta-bhangi*, seven components, as follows:

Any entity or proposition
syad asti: maybe is so
syan nasti: maybe is not so
syad asti nasti: maybe is or is not so
syad avaktavya: maybe undefinable
syad asti avaktavya: maybe so and undefinable
syan nasti avaktavya: maybe not so and undefinable
syad asti nasti avaktavya: maybe so, maybe not so, and indefinable.

There are voluminous texts by preceptors (*acharyas*) like Harishena Suri and Kunda-kundacharya that analyze and establish this doctrine, also known as *anekanta-vada*, 'doctrine of no single end.' It fits completely with the Jaina adherence to total ahimsa, nonviolence.

Another example is the Jaina version of the Ramayana story in which, unlike the more popular Hindu version, it is not Rama who kills Ravana but his less perfect younger brother Lakshmana. How could Rama, a perfect being, indulge in the act of killing even in a war? See, among others, Pauma-chariyu *sandhi* 75, song 22, where Lakshmana before killing Ravana also resolves, 'I shall forgive him, once Sita has been returned to Rama' (verse 5).

In this we have not dealt with the topic exhaustively.[40] We have not at all referred to hundreds of saints, teachers and guides who taught and sang their teachings in non-classical spoken languages of the people. For example, God is addressed by thirty-six names in the Guru Granth Sahib, the holy book of the Sikhs.

One needs to look into the history of the lands of Indogenic traditions in more detail to find how well this philosophy was applied, often successfully but many times those claiming to be adherents of the same also failed. The successful examples will show that with deep faith the philosophy can be a guide for establishing peace through recognizing the religious paths of others as valid.

Here we return to the scheme followed by the epic Mahabharata. After teaching the duties of the state in the first two, RDP and ADP, sections to Yudhishthira,

Bhishma devotes the major part of his precept to *moksha-dharma*, the guidance for spiritual liberation, in nearly 7000 verses. It is neither possible nor necessary to give a summary of all of these verses here. Suffice it to say that in this teaching the *raja-dharmas*, the duties of the state, are brought back into the context of spiritual liberation and in this there is no scope for violating the principles of nonviolence and forgiveness in any form. All the worldly means adopted so far had one simple goal, which is spiritual enlightenment. That goal is brought back into focus in MDP.

Personal peace, collective peace

In all Indogenic traditions, major and minor, *ahimsa*, nonviolence is the cornerstone of ethics. Ethics here begins with a state of mind. Only a nonviolent mind can practice nonviolence externally. Here we refer to the Yoga-sutras of Patanjali, the core text of yoga, as only illustrative of what is repeatedly stated in the texts like the Law Books, as that of Manu, Vedic and Yoga works, Bauddha-Jaina, all schools, scriptures like YV, BhG or MDP of MB, Tibeto-Chinese and Japanese translations of Indogenic texts, and so forth.

The concept of nonviolence extends to a wide spectrum covering a mind

- meditatively brought to peace,
- maintained as nonviolent, free of anger and vengefulness,
- filled with universal love for all living beings in all the cosmoses, therefore
- not given to indulging in violence, that is, inclination to harm or hurt, in any situation, by thought, speech and physical action.

This then is interpreted to mean also the meditative practices of universal love as well as gentle speech, total abstinence from anger, war or from killing for food, and all the degrees of nonviolence in between. Depending on each practitioner's spiritual station, many compromises are allowed until one reaches the perfection in the practice of *ahimsa*. Yogis may call this by the name *yamas* (rules of restraint) and *maha-vratas* (great vows). The Jainas may refer to it as *anu-vrata* (vows of subtlety), the Bauddhas may see it as part of the six *paramitas* (perfections). It makes no difference to the basic philosophy and the attitudes to be cultivated.

According to YS,

Nonviolence, truth, non-theft, sexual restraint and non-grabbing [of sense-experiences and possessions] [are the five] *yamas*.

[The *yamas* are] the universal great vows, to be practiced at all levels [of yoga] without delimitation of any conditionality as to species, locus, time or situation.

The *vi-tarka*s, [thoughts and attitudes that distract from the spiritual practice]
are [the opposite], violence etc., which may be
  committed by oneself,
  caused to be committed through others, or
  consented to,
preceded by greed, anger, and delusion;
whether mild, middling, or intense.
(YS.2.30, 31, 33–35)

On this, Sage Vyasa, the primary commentator, states:

[...] Ahimsa is [to be defined as] the non-intention to injure, pertaining to all
beings, in all ways, at all times. The following *yama*s [restraints] [truth, etc.]
and *ni-yama*s [rules of conduct] are rooted in that [nonviolence]; they are
expounded only for [the purpose of] promoting this, as [they are] intended
to bring about its perfection [*siddhi*]. They are undertaken only to spotlessly
refine and brighten its form. As has been stated:
  Indeed, as this child of God progresses and wishes to undertake many
[more] vows and observances, so gradually he turns away from the causes of
injuriousness that occur through negligence that would otherwise claim the
fruits of his ascetic endeavor [*tapas*]. He thereby affects the same nonviolence
of a bright and spotless form. (Vyasa on YS.2.30)

This bears out our earlier statement that nonviolence is the root of all Indogenic
concepts of ethics. In the Bauddha tradition, it is all part of *sila* (Sanskrit *shila*),
rules of conduct and character. Of the *Tripitakas* (Three Baskets of the Buddhist
Canon), the first one is *Sutta-pitaka*. One of its largest sections is *Sila-kkhandha-
vaggo*, the numerous chapters (*suttas*) on Conduct illustrated with long stories
and parables.
  Similarly, *Visuddhi-magga, the* text of Thera-vada meditation systems (which
includes the well-known vipassana) devotes important chapters to several sets
of five constituents of the principle of *sila*, and the contemplations/meditations
and observances in daily practice.
  The founder of the Yogachara school of Mahayana, Acharya Asanga, states:

Conduct is the foundation of all good qualities. Because it pacifies the
afflictions and [mental] burnings, it is a state of peace [*shanta*]. Because the
cognitions such as making [some being] lose [his] life[41] are prevented by
[these rules of] conduct, there ceases to be production of fear and unspeakable
hostility [etc., therefore the conduct *sila* is] a state of the freedom from fears.
(MSA 16.20)

Thus, there stands an equation of the principles of right conduct that is nonviolence that is freedom from fear that is peace. Within its realms also come parts of the Noble Eightfold Path, especially,

samma vaça: right speech, that is, truthfulness, not gossiping, not speaking harshly, not babbling falsely,[42]

samma kammanta: right actions, that is, refraining from violence, theft, licentiousness in sense pleasures,[43]

samma ajiva: right livelihood, that is, refraining from trading in weapons, living beings, meat (and such products obtained by violence), intoxicants, and poisonous substances.

The right livelihood as a component of right conduct for peace is so important that the phrase was found 269 times in sixty-six texts consulted. It is simply impossible to give full details of these principles as stated or implied in Veda-Yoga or Baudddha-Jaina traditions. A major part of the scheme of meditational conduct is the practice of the four *brahma-viharas* (literally 'frolics in divine consciousness'), given equal importance in YS and in the Bauddha tradition, both in attitudinal conduct and practice of contemplation/meditation. The four *brahma-viharas* are stated as follows:

By cultivating and impressing into oneself the sentiments of

- *maitri* [*Pali, metta*], friendship and amity,
- *karuna* [*karuna*] compassion,
- *mudita* [*mudita*] joyousness,
- *upeksha* [*upekkha*], indifference,

respectively towards those

- comfortable,
- suffering,
- virtuous, and
- non-virtuous,

the mind-field is made clear and pleasant. (YS.1.33)

This concept of *bhavana* means bringing these attitudes into being in oneself. The Bauddha literature describes in detail the qualities of the mind that has successfully cultivated these.[44] Further, these four help to raise one's consciousness to the upper four levels of *jhana* (Sanskrit *dhyana*) meditations.[45]

The concept of *maitri-metta* here, however, is not in the sense of common friendship. It is to be understood at least at three levels:

- *kalyana-mitra*, friend on the noble path. The Buddha called himself such a friend to his disciples;
- cultivating an attitude of universal amity in which any distinctions among living beings of all species and cosmoses are not permitted and no hostility from anyone is recognized; all thoughts, words and actions are based on such sentiment of amity towards all;
- a non-subject-specific method of meditation on universal love with appropriate mantras in Mahayana and without them in thera-vada.

What about one's enemies? Let us recognize them: 'Look upon these as enemies: miserliness, cunning, deceit, attachment to property, laziness, pride, sexual attachment, hatred, arrogance of caste, form, learning, youth and power' (NLG, p. 12).

It is these enemies that have to be vanquished in the mind. The source of comfort and ease is a mind that is clear and pleasant (*manasa ce pasannena* [...] Dhammapada 1.2). The definition of clear and pleasant mind has been given above in the context of the *brahma-viharas*.

Here then are some examples of the advice concerning enmity and anger:

He cursed me, he hit me, he defeated me, he ridiculed me –
Those who get knotted up in these thoughts, their hostility never comes to peace. (Dhammapada 1.3, 4)

Acharya Buddhaghosa, the commentator explains in his Attha-katha:

By not mentating on such thoughts (*a-manasi-kara*), not letting them make place in the mind, and by observing one's thoughts and such other practices, one conquers the anger that arises from 'he cursed me' etc.

Enmities do not come to peace through enmities, ever; they come to peace by non-enmity. This is the perennial law. (Dhammapada 1.5)

Unopposed to the opposed, neutral to those wielding a stick, not claiming where there may be claims – such a one I call a child of Divinity. (Dhammapada 26.23)

The Buddha taught to divert anger through skill in amiable communication. Here we shall refrain from giving stories in this regard but the literature is filled with numerous instances of the same. See, among others, the DP-AK story of Tissa Thera on 1.4.

One of the most powerful stories in the life of the Buddha is that of the bandit Angulimala, he who cut off the fingers of those he robbed and wore them as necklaces. Briefly:

Conversion to Peace:

One early afternoon, the Buddha proceeded out of his monastic camp towards the area where Angulimala was reported to be in a forest. All the cowherds and farmers and travelers along the way saw him heading in the direction of Angulimala's reported camp site. They all warned him: Do not go that way, Holiness; that Angulimala manages to capture even if fifty people try to go and confront him. It is not safe.

But the Buddha proceeded anyhow. The bandit saw him coming and he said to himself: even ten, twenty or fifty people together do not dare come my way and this monk is coming all alone! Anyway, I am going to kill him.

He prepared his bow and arrow and began to follow the Buddha. The Buddha was walking at a normal pace and the bandit was running full speed but somehow he just could not catch up with the Buddha.

He was baffled.

The bandit stood still and shouted: Hey monk, stop! Be still.

The Buddha replied: I am quite still, Angulimala; you try to be still!

The bandit wondered in his mind: these monks are normally truth speakers but he is walking and is telling me that he is still. What could that mean? Let me ask him.

So he asked him: Monk, you are walking away from me and telling me you are still; I am standing and you are telling me to be still!

The Buddha replied: Angulimala, having given up hostility towards all living beings, I have become still. You are unstable towards the living beings, that is why you are not still.

Hearing this the bandit pleaded: It is excessively late; so long have I not yet met a truth-speaking great sage. Today in this thick forest I have found you. I now wish to abandon the life of sin and live by dharma.

The Buddha's only response was: Come along, Monk!

That was the bandit's only ordination!

The Buddha followed by Angulimala the monk arrived at the city of Shravasti and stayed at his Jetavana monastery. At that time there was a big demonstration of citizens outside the palace of King Prasenajit of the Kaushala country, petitioning: Why don't you, Oh King, undertake some expedients to protect us innocent citizens from the bandits like Angulimala? So the King decided to organize an expedition against the bandit.

Before proceeding with the expedition, the king came to the Buddha to seek his blessing. The Buddha asked: King, what brought you? Is the king of the Magadha country becoming aggressive with you? Are the people of the Vajji-Licchavi republican federation in Vaishali causing you trouble? None of these, Holiness. It is a notorious bandit Angulimala who has devastated large parts of my kingdom and I am out to catch him to protect my people – replied king Prasenajit.

King! – asked the Buddha – If you were to see Angulimala in a monk's saffron robe, with his head tonsured, and having renounced violence, theft and untruth, eating once a day, celibate, performing good deeds and living by good conduct, what will you do with him?

The king honored the monk Angulimala with appropriate ceremonial and said to the Buddha: A wonder it is, Holiness, a miracle! The Blessed One brings under control even such uncontrollable persons; brings to peace who are not peaceable; liberates the unliberated ones. Those whom we cannot turn towards a peaceful life by the power of our weapons, you inspire them towards a life of peace without resorting to a stick or a weapon [...].

Mystic Power of Nonviolence:
One day Angulimala the monk went into the city of Shravasti to beg for alms at noon. He saw a woman who had had a miscarriage and was in great pain. A cry arose in his mind, 'Oh, how the beings suffer; how the beings suffer, alas!'

He came back from begging the alms, bowed to the Master, sat down in a corner and pleaded, 'Oh, how the beings suffer; how the beings suffer, alas!'

The Buddha advised him: go back to that woman and use your spiritual power. Stand before her and say in your mind, 'if, since my birth, I have not knowingly killed any living being, may by the power of that truth, this woman be healed.'[46]

Angulimala objected:

'Would it not be a gross untruth, since you know the kind of life of killing I lived before?'

Upon that the Buddha advised:

'Alright. Then make the mental declaration only by the power of truth, "since taking my vows I have not killed a living being knowingly," may by that power the woman be healed'.

Angulimala did so, and the woman was healed and happy.

The power of nonviolence continues:

One day Angulimala went to the city again to beg for alms. [Some people probably recognized the erstwhile bandit and] he was pelted with stones and sticks and pebbles. [In response he did not find any anger or fear in him] and returned to the monastery with bleeding head, damaged skull, broken begging bowl and torn garment(s).

The Buddha saw him and said:

Oh Brahmana,[47] the karmas the results of which you had to suffer for many hundred, many thousand, years in hell, you have [now] paid off right in this life.

Thus an important marker of peace is non-arising of anger where excitatory causes of such may be present.

Acharya Asanga, founder of the Yogachara School of Mahayana, quotes:

He fulfils the purpose of oneself and of another as well, who, seeing the other angry, puts himself to peace. (Mahayana-sutralankara on 16.22)

For the conquest of anger and 'killer inclinations,' there is an antidote commonly prescribed with a word that rhymes with *shanti*, that is, peace. The word is *kshanti*. It is third of the six *paramitas*,[48] perfections that are prerequisites for the Buddhahood. *Kshanti* and its synonym *kshama* are commonly translated as forgiveness or patience. Monier-Williams' *A Sanskrit-English Dictionary* (1970) explains its verb root √*ksham* to mean 'to be patient or composed, suppress anger, keep quiet.' This can be quite misleading. The verb root also means 'to be capable, to have a capacity.' The words are used in the Indogenic traditions as antonyms to anger, vengefulness and such negative emotions. It is explained by Asanga (Mahayana-sutralankara) immediately after *shila*, conduct, which is followed by *kshanti*. Briefly, it is at three levels:

- forbearance towards harm done to oneself by others,
- forbearance for one's own pain and suffering, and
- capacity for *dharma* (virtue) and *dhyana* (meditation). (Mahayana-sutralankara 16.20, 21)

Such *kshanti* is to be practiced 'towards all beings in all places and at all times without distinction' (Mahayana-sutralankara 19.7).

Kshemendra (Mahayana-sutralankara) gives the *avadana* story of a previous life of the Buddha to illustrate *kshanti*, to summarize:

The women wandering freely saw a sage (*rshi*), namely Kshanti-rati [One Whose Delight and Absorption is in the Practice of *Kshanti*], deeply immersed in high meditation and *samadhi*, sitting absolutely still, free of all attachments and mind-colorings.

Out of curiosity they stood surrounding and admiring him.

The king, burning with the fire of jealous anger, cut off the sage's hands and feet.

Even having been thus mutilated he found no trace of anger in him towards the king and prevented the groups of *gandharvas*,[49] *yakshas*, *nagas* and *devas* from inflicting even a more cruel punishment upon him [as they wished to do].

After the king had left the forest to return to his city, other sages gathered around and even though they had been practising *kshanti*, they were aroused to anger at the king.

As they were about to place curses at the king, the sage, saying 'one should always forgive', prevented them from casting the curses.

Then he, a being of clear and pleasant mind (*pra-sadi*), [did the *satya-kriya*[50]], saying:

If, I who have turned off anger, did not feel any rush of perturbation in me, then, by that truth, may my body become whole again.

Thus did the sage become whole, free of all wounds [...]
At that time, I was the sage Kshanti-rati [said the Buddha]. (Mahayana-sutralankara 38.8–20)

The most important text on the topic of *kshanti* is Bodhicharyavatara by the great Mahayana teacher Shanti-deva (eighth century AD). Here we may not give the entire argument given by Shantideva in the 134 verses of his sixth chapter. We urge the reader to read H.H. Dalai Lama's DL1, DL2 and DL3, especially the last, as commentaries on the said text. Shantideva begins his teaching on the subject with the statement: 'There is no sin like hate; no ascetic endeavor like forgiveness. Therefore, one should cultivate forgiveness with all different kinds of methods' (BCA 6.2).

The emphasis on the practice of *kshanti* is by no means limited to the Bauddha teachings. *Kshama* is second of the ten marks of dharma in the Laws of Manu. Elsewhere:

One who holds the weapon of forgiveness in his hand,
what can an evil person do to him? (Vrddha-chanakya 3.30)[51]

Furthermore,

If one has forgiveness what power have [others' unpleasant] words?
If one has anger, what other enemies [are there]? (Bhartrhari 2.18)[52]

The teachings advise all to practice an *anuloma-vrtti*, 'rubbing the hair the right way,' not in the opposite direction. To be in accord and concord with all, especially with those presumed to be one's enemies. It is also the best way of survival: this is explained by this example (summarized):

The ocean asked the rivers as to why they always bring him the trunks of the large trees but never cane or reeds. The rivers answered: when we flood the countryside, the trees with large trunks stand erect and proud and we easily uproot them but the canes and the reeds just bow down before our flood and we cannot find a way to uproot them. (RDP.113.1–11)

Thus the Sanskrit verb for humility also means 'to bend down,' a sure way to peace and the resultant true survival. Thus, freedom from anger and the practice of forgiveness can be undertaken only by one who has an enormous spiritual capacity. Such capacity is developed through the practices of meditation. Along with meditation, in the Bauddha tradition is the practice of *samatha* (Sanskrit *shamatha*), pacifying oneself, a twin of *panna* (Sanskrit *pra-jna*), wisdom. This pacification occurs through the twin paths of meditation and self-observation.

In the Bauddha tradition, both these are part of the practice of mindfulness, *sati-patthana* (Sanskrit *smrty-upa-sthana*). Here we shall not present a manual for these practices, as the teaching of these is easily available elsewhere. But, one very important part in obtaining peace within, which may then radiate to the surroundings, is a peaceful breath. Even though we quote from the most important thera-vada manual of meditation, VM, the system is taught with equal diligence and proficiency by the Himalayan yogis in Patanjali's tradition (see YPS-1 1.20, 34; 2.50, 51); it is also well known throughout the Mahayana world from Tibetan to Zen meditation traditions. Extremely briefly we read:

Further, Oh monks, the meditation (samadhi) of mindfulness of inspiration and expiration,
cultivated,
exceedingly practiced,
peaceful,
well guided,
not mixed [with extraneous thoughts] [...]
brings about pacification. (Visuddhi-magga 8.56)

The adjectival phrases here, 'cultivated,' 'peaceful,' etc. are interpreted to refer to the breath. The breath flow should be peaceful; such a breath brings about peace to the personality (*upa-sameti*; Sanskrit *upa-shamayati*).

Immediately after the chapter on mindfulness of breathing in VM is one on *upasamanussati*, the mindfulness of self-pacification in which 'the mind-field becomes easeful' (*uju-gatam*; Sanskrit *rju-gatam*) (Visuddhi-magga 8.78).

This is equated with *nibbana* (Sanskrit *nirvana*), the peace of transcendence.[53] It is a state of dispassion towards all that passes in the mind-field by way of attributes and processes (Visuddhi-magga 8.77 and MSP on 1.1). Here again, on pacification (*upa-shama*) the view of Veda-Yoga as propounded in the texts like YV and in Bauddha tradition coincide.

Peace: A summary

It will require another monograph to discuss and demonstrate the historical success of this approach to peace. Names like Gandhi* and the Dalai Lama† are

* Ed. For more information on Gandhi's life and philosophy, see Chapter 25 by Arun Gandhi.
† Ed. More on the Dalai Lama and his philosophy can be found in Chapter 12 by Karma Lekshe Tsomo.

well known, but there are numerous other examples throughout history where peace has prevailed through nonviolence.

As in a great many highly recognized theological systems of the world, the varieties of the universe emanate from the singularity of transcendence, so it is from the transcendent peace, that is, total self-pacification, which the lesser levels of peace emanate and radiate.

The persons who have attained this highest ideal and those who are practicing self-purification towards such an ideal become such beings of peace that their personalities become the focal points around which others may find peace of mind and personality.

Those practicing such pursuit of peace, and the attendant qualities such as non-anger and forgiveness, to whatever degree, then, generate peace in their surroundings, by their presence, language and body gesture. They do so in all their relationships and communications within the family, society and among religions and nations.

They earn their living without violence towards any beings. When in governing positions, it is their self-governance that serves as the model for all polity. In such a peaceful mind-field, the nature responds to love and remains in harmony, providing ease. The individual and collective consciousness in such a field is the true definition of peace. That is *shanti*.

Om shantih shantih shantih.

Non-Sectarian Meditation

Basic method

(1) Sit as straight as you can on an even, firm but cushioned surface
(2) Relax your forehead
(3) Relax your facial and physical musculature
(4) Bring your awareness to your breathing
(5) Breathe slowly, gently, smoothly, evenly; without jerk or sound in the breathing
(6) Now feel the touch and flow of the breath in the nostrils
(7) Let there be no pause between the breaths; as one breath is completed, begin to feel the next breath flowing and touching in the nostrils
(8) After a few breaths, choose

    (a) whichever name of God is your favorite according to your tradition or religion,
    (b) or a sacred but *short* phrase or prayer word from your scripture or tradition

Some suggestions are as follows:

(a) Those who wish to follow the Himalayan tradition may use the sound *so* (mentally pronounced sooooo) in the in-breath and *ham* (mentally pronounced huuuummm) in the out-breath, without a break in the cycles of *ham-so* with the breath

(b) The Sikhs may use: *Vaah-e-guru*, or *Sat-naam*

(c) Muslims may use the word *Allah* or any sacred phrase (such as *La-Ilah Illillah*, or *Allaho* or *Allahoo*), or one of the ninety-nine names of God

(d) Jews may use *Ha-shem*

(e) Christians may use one of these: *Jesus* or *Yeshu*, *Ave Maria*, *Hail Mary*, *Maranatha* (Aramaic), *Kyrie eleison* (Greek)

(f) Mazdayasnians (Zoroastrians, Parsees) may use any of these: *ahura mazda*, *ahuu va-iryo*, *esham vohu*. But for total beginners of the Mazdayasnian tradition the best recommendation is to use the phrase *vohu-mano*

(g) The Jainas may use *Om*, *Om hreem*, or *Hreem arham*

(h) Those who prefer total *nirguna*, transcendental, trans-qualitative divinity may use only *Om*

(i) The Buddhists may use the word *Buddho* to start with

(j) The Theravadin Buddhists may choose to use no word whatsoever, only practice mindfulness of breathing

(k) If you do not believe in a form of divinity or a divine Incarnation and so forth,

   exhaling, think Ooooonnnne (One)
   inhaling, think twwwooooo (Two) –
   without a break in this count with the breath

(9) Exhaling, think that phrase; inhaling think that phrase
   (a) The phrase is not to come in the mouth nor on the tongue;
   (b) it must be only a mentation

(10) Let there be no break between the breaths, nor between the incessant flow of the thoughts of the same phrase

(11) As soon as you become aware that you have lost the flow and other thoughts have begun to arise, restart the same procedure

(12) Sit for as long as you wish

(13) Let the quietness of the mind continue even after you rise

(14) If you practice this even for 2–3 minutes at a time many times in the day, you will notice subtle changes in yourself for the better

(15) Whatever you will do repeatedly with the mind, that will become the mind's habit; calming the mind repeatedly will return your mind to its original calm nature.

Notes

1. We ignore the correct rules of diacritical marks in Romanized transliteration of Sanskrit and Pali terms for the ease of our editors.
2. We choose to use the correct Sanskrit term rather than the Anglicized version, which has a different flavor.
3. Our neologism to express the traditions whose origin is in India.
4. We intentionally avoid incorrectly translating the word *dharma* as religion. The word dharma has no equivalent in the Western languages and the word religion cannot be translated into Indogenic languages. Like the word yoga (or Tao), it is best to borrow the word dharma outright into the Western languages.
5. We have chosen not to give textual citations as these expedients of state policy are commonly found in numerous texts on polity such as *niti-shastras*, *smrti*s and the *artha-shastra*.
6. Here our apologies for not being able to refer to the words in Tamil and the related languages.
7. The word *svastha*, literally meaning someone healthy or in good health, is defined: illumination, energy and stasis (*sattva*, *rajas*, *tamas*) are the three attributes of mind; it is the equilibrium of the three that constitutes the definition of '*svastha*.' MB, Shanti-parvan 16.13.
8. The words for intelligence, *mati* and *buddhi* in Sanskrit, are feminine, here personified.
9. The name used by Shankaracharya, Devadatta, has its literal translation in Theodorus, one given by God.
10. Chanakya's Artha-shastra 1.1.
11. To our knowledge, the fifth longest epic in world literature.
12. See Swami Veda Bharati, 2003.
13. See Swami Veda Bharati, 2003.
14. Using the critical edition by Sukthankar (1933–1966) for the count here.
15. For our purpose here, we shall ignore *anushasana-parvan*.
16. In addition, the *anushasana-parvan* consists of 6526 verses in Chapters 1–154.
17. Most of the quotations from Manu and Mahabharata given here were used by the author in an earlier article that was published under his pre-monastic name. See Arya (1975).
18. Chanakya, fourth century BC prime minister of the emperor Chandragupta (Sandrogottos of the Greeks), is often called the Indian Machiavelli. True, that his major text, the Arthashastra, is very realistic about the human condition. However, the principle of the fourfold knowledge starting from *anvikshiki*, metaphysical science, as shown briefly above, indicates that Chanakya's principles are far more fundamentally based in metaphysical ethics than those of Machiavelli and Sun Tzu. Furthermore, his sutras being quoted here serve as the foundation of his spiritual–ethical theory of polity.
19. For a more contemporary paraphrase of these sutras, see Swami Veda Bharati (2000).
20. SRB page 83.
21. Our paraphrase for '*arajaka janapada*' is the 'State without good governance.'
22. This statement about the uniqueness of the Indogenic traditions stands corrected. The Taoist philosophy of China is very emphatic on this point also.
23. These quotations from the Ramayana were formerly used by this author in Arya (1970, p. 22). For further depiction of the harmonious interrelationship between man and nature, see pp. 16–18 in the same publication.
24. Dhammapadattha-katha, Yamaka-vaggo, verse 3.

25. Sutta-pitaka, Digha-nikaya-Pali, 1 Sila-kkhandha-vaggo 1.
26. The ruins of the Vajji parliament building, the oldest republican parliament in world history (sixth century BC), can still be seen in the city of Vaishali in the Bihar state of India.
27. Echo here of the infamous question reported to have been asked by Stalin: How many divisions has the Pope?
28. The argument is so well known that it does not warrant using this space for lengthy quotations from texts and the exegesis.
29. Makhadeva-sutta in Sutta-pitaka, Majjhima-nikaya-pali, 2 Majjhima-pannasaka-mita, 33.
30. According to the Jaina tradition the present official name of India, Bharat, is derived from this Bharata.
31. The story occurs in many texts in different versions. Here we have summarized it from the epic in the Apabhramsha language (about eighth to ninth century AD), namely Pauma-Chariyu of the poet Tribhuvana Svayambhu.
32. *Chakra-vartin*, term used for a universal ruler; all kings are vassals under his suzerainty. It may also be used *honoris causa*. Some of the meanings of the term are: (1) one who turns the wheel of dharma, (2) one whose chariot wheels are always turning, (3) one who rules over the entire circular earth, a world-emperor. In the Buddhist and Jaina legends, there is a mysterious discus that hovers over a *chakra-vartin's* head or on his side. A Buddha is, however, a spiritual *chakra-vartin*. In *samudraka-shastra*, the science of reading the body (including palm reading), one whose ten fingertips have a whorl of subtle lines will be a *chakra-vartin*.
33. The position the Jaina yogis take is that of standing absolutely motionless but totally relaxed, in meditation. The forest creepers may rise and entwine around their legs and scorpions and other creatures may crawl but the yogi would not move until full enlightenment is reached.
34. Twenty-four *Tirthankaras* are in succession the founders of the Jaina religion. First of these is the legendary Rishabhadeva whose sons were Bharata and Bahubali. The epitome of enlightenment, Rishabhadeva had divided his kingdom between the two brothers and then renounced to retire at the holy Kailasha Mountain to live among the gods.
35. Bhahubali's statue, known locally as Gommateshvara, is a monolith 58'8" tall at Shravana Belgola. It is one of the holiest Jaina shrines in Karnataka, India.
36. Einstein (1981).
37. Paraphrased from Payasi-rajanna-sutta, 10th in Sutta-pitaka, Digha-nikaya pali. Mahavagga.
38. Coming from the mnemonic tradition of the Brahmanas (Brahmins) of India, this author finds it difficult to cite published sources for some texts memorized and recited since childhood. These two verses come under that category.
39. Belief in one God of many forms. For more details, see this author's *Unifying Streams in Religion* (2007) and *GOD* (several editions).
40. For more details, the reader is advised to see this author's book *GOD* (several editions).
41. The vows taken by every Bauddha lay person, novice or monk.
42. Digha-nikaya-pali, 2 Maha-vaggo, Sati-patthana-sutta 31.
43. Digha-nikaya-pali, 2 Maha-vaggo, Sati-patthana-sutta 31.
44. See, among others, Sutta-pitaka, Samyutta-nikaya-pali, 5 Mahavaggo, Bojjhanga-samyuttam 54ff.
45. Namely, *subha, akasananchayatana, vinnananchayatana* and *akinchannayatana* (Sutta-pitaka, Samyutta-nikaya-pali, 5 Mahavaggo, Bojjhanga-samyuttam 54ff). Restrictions

of space do not permit us here to give details of these levels of meditation but they may be studied from numerous texts such as *Visuddhi-magga* of Buddhaghosa.

46. Such a mental act is referred to in the Bauddha texts repeatedly as *satya-kriya* (Pali, *sacca-kiriya*), an act of truth, when one uses the mystical power of some secret meritorious act, one accomplishes a beneficial task. Some contemporary languages of India use the derivative word *kiriya* for 'taking oath.'

47. The Buddha often referred to his monks as *brahmana*s even though he condemned the caste system totally. He uses the term to mean a 'child of Divinity' and all forty verses of the twenty-sixth chapter of Dhammapada define a *brahmana* in this sense.

48. Lit., having crossed, having gone across.

49. Para-human races are very common in Indogenic legends.

50. See footnote 48.

51. As quoted in SRB, p. 83

52. As quoted in SRB, p. 83

53. *Vide* note 11.

Reference list and further reading

Primary sources

Arthashastra of Chanakya (2000) (AK) K.P. Kangle (ed.) (Delhi: Motilal Banarsidass).

Avadana-Kalpa-Lata of Kshemendra, Vols 1 & 2 (1989) (AKL) Parashuram Vaidya (ed.) Buddhist Sanskrit Texts series 22–23 (Darbhanga: Mithila Institute of Postgraduate Studies and Research in Sanskrit Learning).

Bauddha Paribhashika-Shabda-Kosha (2000) Dharmachandra Jain (ed.) (Delhi: Nirmal Publication).

Bhagavad-Gita (1988) (BhG) with Commentary by Shankaracharya (Delhi: Motilal Banarsidass).

Bodhicharyavatara of Shantideva (1993) (BCA) Paramanand Singh (ed.), transl. Hindi Ram Niwas Tiwari, Bauddha Akara Grantha-mala,Kashi Vidyapeeth (Varanasi).

Dhammapada Attha-Katha (2000) (DP-AK) (ed.) Paramanand Singh, Bauddha Akara Granthamala, Kashi Vidyapith (eds.), Hindi transl. Dwarika Das Sastri (Varanasi).

'Gaudapada-Karika' in *Ishadi-Dasopanisadah* (Ten Principal Upanishads) (IDU) Commentary by Shankaracharya (Delhi: Motilal Banarasidass).

Ishadi-Dasopanisadah (Ten Principal Upanishads) (IDU) Commentary by Shankaracharya (Delhi: Motilal Banarasidass).

Lalita-Vistara (1987) (LV) Parashuram Vaidya (ed.) 2nd ed. Shridhar Tripathi, Buddhist Sanskrit Texts – 1 (Darbhanga: Mithila Institute of Postgraduate Studies and Research in Sanskrit Learning).

Madhyamaka-shastra of Nagarjuna (1988) (MSN) with four commentaries re-translated from Tibetan into Sanskrit. Raghunatha Pandeya (ed. and transl.) (Delhi: Motilal Banarsidass).

Madhyamaka-shastra of Nagarjuna with *Prasannapada* of Candrakirti (1960) (MSP) P.L. Vaidya (ed.) Buddhist Sanskrit Texts No. 10 (Darbhanga: Mithila Institute of Postgraduate Studies and Research in Sanskrit Learning).

Mahabharata (1933–1966) (MB) Critical Edition, Vishnu S. Sukthankar (ed.) (Poona: Bhandarkar Oriental Research Institute).

Mahabharata (1991) (MB) T.R. Krishnacharya and T.R. Vyasacharya (eds.) (Delhi: Indian Books Centre).

Mahayana-sutralankara of Asanga (1970) (MSA) S. Bagchi (ed.), Buddhist Sanskrit Texts Series 13 (Mithila Institute of Postgraduate Studies and Research in Sanskrit Learning).
Manu-Smrti (1988) (MS) in Smrti-Sandarbha Vol. 1 (Delhi: Nag Publishers).
Milinda-Panha-Pali (1988) (MPP) Swami Dwarikadas Shastri (Hindi transl.) (Varanasi: Bauddha Bharati).
Nagarjuna's letter to King Gautamiputra (1978, 1996) (NLG) Lozang Jamspal, Ngawang Samten Chophal and Peter Della Santina (transl.) (Delhi: Motilal Banarasidass).
Pauma-Cariyu of Tribhuvana Svayambhu (1957, 1989) (PCTS) Vols 1–5, H.C. Bhayani (ed.), Devendra Kumar Jain (Hindi transl.) (Delhi: Bharatiya Jnana-Pitha).
Ramayana of Valmiki (1982) (RV) Shivram Sharma Vasishth (ed.) (Varanasi: Chowkhamba Vidyabhawan).
Ramayana of Valmiki with Commentaries Tilaka et al. (1990) Shastri Shrinivasa Katti Mudholakara (ed.) (Delhi: Parimal Publications).
Rg-Veda-Samhita (1995) (RV) (Delhi: Chowkhamba Sanskrit Pratishthan).
Subhashita-ratna-bhandagara (2002) (SRB) Narayana Rama Acharya (ed.) (Delhi: Chowkhamba Sanskrit Pratishthan).

Tri-Pitakas

— *Sutta-Pitaka, Digha-Nikaya-Pali, Sila-Kkhandha-Vaggo, Brahma-Jala-Suttam* (1996) (SP-BJS) Swami Dwarika Das Shastri (Hindi transl.) (Varanasi: Bauddha Bharati).
— *Sutta-Pitaka, Digha-Nikaya-Pali, Mahavaggo, Maha-parinibbana-sutta* (1996) (SP-MPS) Dvarikadas Shastri (Hindi transl.) Bauddha Bharati Series 35 (Bauddha Bharati).
— *Sutta-Pitaka, Samyutta-Nikaya Pali, Mahavaggo* (2000) (SP-MV) Swami Dwarika Das Shastri (ed.) (Varanasi: Bauddha Bharati).
— *Sutta-Pitaka, Majjhima Nikaya Pali, Majjhima-pannasaka-mita, Makhadeva-Suttam, Angulimala-Suttam* (1999) (SP-MDS, SP-AMS) Swami Dwarikadas Shastri (ed.) (Varanasi: Bauddha Bharati).
— *Vinaya-Pitaka Mahavagga-Pali* (1998) (VP-MP) Swami Dwarika Das Shastri (Hindi transl.) (Varanasi: Bauddha Bharati).
Upanishat-Sangraha (1996) (US) Pandit Jagadish Shastri (ed.) (Delhi: Motilal Banarasidass).
Vigraha-Vyavartani of Nagarjuna (VV) see MSP.
Visuddhi-magga of Buddha-ghosa (1995) (VMB) Tapasya Upadhyaya (ed.) Bauddha Bharati Series 12(B) (Varanasi: Bauddha Bharati).
Visuddhi-maggo Vols I and II (1969) (VM) Revata Dhammo (ed.) Pali-Grantha-Mala-3 (Varanasi: Varanaseya-Sanskrita-Vishva-Vidyalaya).
Yoga-Sutras of Patanjali with Sanskrit Commentaries of Vyasa, Vachaspati and Vijnana-Bhikshu (1992) (YS) Narayana Mishra and Bharatiya Vidya Prakashan (ed.) (Delhi).
Yoga-Sutras of Patanjali, Vol. I (1984) (YSP-I) Swami Veda Bharati (transl.) (Homesdale: Himalayan International Institute of Yoga Science and Philosophy).
Yoga-Sutras of Patanjali, Vol. II (2001) (YSP-II) Swami Veda Bharati (transl.) (Delhi: Motilal Banarsidass).
Yoga-Vasistha-Ramayana of Valmiki with Tatparya-Prakasha of Ananda-Bodhendra Sarasvati (1918, 1981) (YVR) Wasudeva Laxmana Sastri Pansikar (ed.) (Delhi: Munshiram Manoharlal).

Secondary sources

Arya, U. (UAH) (1975) 'Hinduism and Conscientious Objection to War,' *Studies in Comparative Religion*, 9, Summer, 146–154.
Arya, U. (UAM) (1971) *Man in Kavya* (Delhi: Motilal Banarsidass).

Dalai Lama XIV (DL1) (1999) *The Dalai Lama's Book of Wisdom* (New York: Harper Collins).
Dalai Lama XIV and Victor Chan (2005) (DL2) *The Wisdom of Forgiveness: Intimate Conversations and Journeys* (New York: Riverhead Books).
Dalai Lama XIV (1997) (DL3) *Healing Anger: The Power of Patience from a Buddhist Perspective.* Thupten Jinpa (transl.) (Delhi: Motilal Banarsidass).
Einstein, A. (1981) *The Human Side: New Glimpses from His Archives.* Banesh Hoffman and Helen Dukas (eds.) (Princeton: Princeton University Press).
Monier-Williams, M. (1997) *A Sanskrit–English Dictionary* (Delhi: Motilal Banarsidass).
Smith, V.A. (1992) *The Edicts of Asoka* (New Delhi: Munshiram Manoharlal).
Swami Veda Bharati (2004) *Education and Parenting for Peace* (Rishikesh: SRSG Publications).
Swami Veda Bharati (2002) *Introducing Mahabharata: Bhishma* (Rishikesh: SRSG Publications).
Swami Veda Bharati (several editions) *GOD* (Honesdale: Himalayan International Institute of Yoga Science and Philosophy).
Swami Veda Bharati (2003) *Mahabharata: Bhishma* (Rishikesh: SRSG Publications).
Swami Veda Bharati (2007) 'Unifying Streams in Religion' in Swami Veda Bharati *What is Right with the World: Human Urge for Peace* (Rishikesh: Ahymsin Publishers), 33–91.
Swami Veda Bharati (2000): *Yoga: Polity and Economy* (Rishikesh: SRSG Publications).
Yoga Concordance, Vols I–IV (2001, 2002, 2004) (YC) Editorial Board of Kaivalya Dhama (Pune: Lonavla).

12

Shi wa: A Vajrayana Buddhist Perspective

Karma Lekshe Tsomo

> The only true guardian of peace lies within: a sense of concern and responsibility for your own future and an altruistic concern for the well-being of others.
>
> H.H. Dalai Lama

A discussion of peace in *Vajrayana* warrants an exploration of the terms 'peace' and '*Vajrayana*,' and an examination of the distinctive features of the *Vajrayana* tradition. With this in place, it will be possible to trace the evolution of *Vajrayana* in relation to other Buddhist traditions and gain insight into how peace and *Vajrayana* are intrinsically intertwined. Although *Vajrayana* Buddhism is found in China, Japan and elsewhere, the focus of this analysis will be the Tibetan tradition.

Defining peace in *Vajrayana*

The phoneme *shi* in Tibetan appears both as *shi wa*, a noun meaning peace, and as *shi wa*, a verb meaning to pacify, calm, or quell. The phoneme *shi* appears in two important compounds in Tibetan, *shi de* and *shi ne*. The compound *shi de*, the most common term for peace, combines *shi* (peace) with the phoneme *de* (happiness). This close association of peace and happiness indicates both that the two states are inextricably linked and that peace is a desirable, happy state. The term *shi de* may signify a state of peace and happiness on a personal, communal, national or international level. On a personal level, *shi de* may signify peace from both a psychological perspective and a spiritual perspective, taking into account the fact that the two perspectives are so intimately connected as to be nearly indistinguishable. The goal of liberation is seen as the ultimate state of peace. A famous quotation from Buddha Sakyamuni explains the 'four seals' or axioms of Buddhist philosophy:

> All composite things are impermanent;
> All defiled things are unsatisfactory;
> All phenomena are empty of inherent existence;
> Nirvana is peace. (Buddha Sakyamuni)

The phoneme *shi* also appears in the compound *shi ne*, which may be translated as calm abiding or peaceful abiding, a specific type of meditation practice. Nine successive stages of meditation training are described for developing calm abiding: placement (focusing the mind on the object), continual placement, repeated placement, close placement, taming, pacifying, thoroughly pacifying, single-pointed concentration and equanimity.

The word *vajra* is translated variously as 'adamantine,' connoting indestructibility, and 'thunderbolt,' implying power. The word *yana* is glossed as 'vehicle' or 'conveyance,' i.e. the path that conveys one to liberation or enlightenment. As a compound, *vajrayana* refers to the branch of Mahayana Buddhism that employs *tantric* meditation practices. The term is used interchangeably with *tantrayana* and *mantrayana*. It is also sometimes referred to as esoteric Buddhism, based on the Chinese *mi cong* or Japanese *mikkyo*.

The word *tantra* literally means 'thread' and is interpreted as meaning lineage, the thread of continuity or transmission of the teachings. *Tantra* has a reputation for being antinomian, at odds with normative ideology and performance. Its rituals may make use of substances, such as meat and wine that are forbidden in mainstream religious practice.

Disputed histories

The Buddhist path turns out to be many paths: rational and devotional, colorful and austere, active and contemplative. Buddhism has been called a universalistic religion, not because it is concerned with converting others to the faith, but because it incorporates universal values like peace, compassion and honesty. People of different cultures, propensities, backgrounds, orientations and stages of spiritual development can seek the practice and approach they find most suitable.*

According to Tibetan tradition, Buddha Sakyamuni gave *tantric* teachings during his tenure on earth, but the teachings were too difficult for ordinary beings to comprehend, so they were transmitted secretly for hundreds of years. According to historians, the teachings date from around the fourth century in India. Although these teachings were eventually committed to writing, the notion

*   Ed. For a further discussion of this issue, see Chapter 11 by Swami Veda Bharati.

of transmission from master to disciple continues and is considered essential for verifying the authenticity of a particular text or teaching.

Tantric Buddhism was transmitted to China and Japan through different lineages and at different times from the fourth century CE up to the present time. Although some *tantric* Buddhist texts are extant in Sanskrit, the largest repository of *tantric* Buddhist teachings is preserved in Tibetan language. In addition to the texts, a vibrant tradition of Buddhist *tantric* practice has continued up to the present day, primarily in Tibet, but also in China and Japan, where it is preserved in the Shingon and Tendai schools.

The notion of peace

Attachments to identities and ideologies are major causes of violence in the world today. The Buddhist teachings on no-self examine the causes of ego-fixation, self-concern and the 'conceit of the I.' Understanding the lack of an unchanging, independently existent soul or self helps relax attachments to 'I, me and mine' that are at the heart of many conflicts. Human beings should be able to have philosophical, religious and sectarian differences without killing each other. Understanding the impermanence of ideas, attitudes and ideologies fosters flexibility, tolerance and non-reactiveness in encounters with those who hold views different from one's own.

Vajrayana Buddhist attitudes toward peace and violence share common ground with other Buddhist traditions. Peace and nonviolence are highly prized and Buddhist practices engendering ethics, wisdom and compassion are cultivated to advance these ideals. Buddha Sakyamuni's teaching that 'hatred ceases not by hatred, but by love alone' is frequently quoted as a maxim to live by. Followers are enjoined not to harm any living being, but instead to treasure each being as if it was one's loving mother or one's only child. Buddhists are taught that no living being wishes to suffer and therefore to protect life and protect living beings from harm, physical or emotional, is wholesome and meritorious.

Buddhist ethics are formulated to protect living beings from harm and from harming each other. In accordance with the theory of *karma*, actions give rise to consequences similar to the cause; that is, wholesome actions give rise to pleasant results, whereas unwholesome actions give rise to unpleasant results. In accordance with this theory, the Buddha taught along the lines of both the golden and silver rules, enjoining followers to treat others as they would like themselves to be treated. The development of mental balance and the cultivation of virtues such as loving kindness and compassion are believed to create conditions conducive to peace and happiness. The Buddhist texts contain myriad methods for cultivating these virtues, which then serve to prevent violent conflicts, resolve tensions, maintain equilibrium and automatically create inner peace. In this view, no specific techniques are prescribed for creating peace; rather, by being a genuinely ethical, compassionate person, one is naturally a peacemaker. One who cultivates peace in meditation* becomes more peaceful, less reactive, and more mindful in everyday encounters. In this way, inner peace extends to the surrounding community and the practitioner becomes a calming influence and natural resource for conflict transformation. This organic approach to conflict prevention and resolution sums up the Buddhist approach. All Buddhist practices can be subsumed into this schema.

The cultivation of virtue leads directly to a consideration of Buddhist ethics. Among the diverse formulations of Buddhist ethics, the Tibetan tradition enumerates three levels of precepts: *pratimoksa*, *bodhisattva* and *tantric*. These ethical values were to be cultivated by individuals, to create an ethical foundation for spiritual practice and for creating a peaceful society. The *pratimoksa* (*so tar*) precepts are the moral foundation for achieving individual liberation. Both, laypeople and monastics are enjoined to refrain from killing, stealing, lying, sexual misconduct and intoxicants. The *bodhisattva* (*jang sem*) precepts are a discipline for training to benefit and ultimately free sentient beings from suffering.[1] In addition, *tantric* practice requires a commitment to abide by a set of fourteen major and ten minor secret *mantra* (*sang ngag*) precepts. The *tantric* precepts are to be practiced in addition to the *pratimoksa* and *bodhisattva* precepts.

The Buddha's prescription for creating a peaceful society included ethical principles for ordinary individuals and for rulers. The ten qualities of a virtuous ruler include generosity, ethical conduct, self-sacrifice, honesty, self-control, friendliness, gentleness, compassion, humility and patience. The ideal ruler is one who governs with honesty, justice and compassion. With these principles as a foundation for governance, a country can achieve sustained peace and stability, creating conducive conditions for its citizens to be happy and prosperous. These qualities apply not only to rulers, of course; the qualities that serve as principles of good governance can be extended to other individuals as well.

The Buddha's guidelines for creating a peaceful society are no guarantee that the objective will be achieved, of course, since Buddhist societies are vulnerable to attack and corruption by outside forces as well as by unprincipled individuals within society. Despite their peaceful ideals, Buddhist countries have seen their share of brutal dictators and genocidal conflicts. These realities raise questions about the validity of peace as a governing principle, under any circumstances. Might forceful methods be justified in dealing with potentially violent situations and adversaries, analogous to the image of wrathful *tantric* deities who have the power to stomp out negativities? To what extent are assertive measures compatible with peace activism?

---

*   Ed. See Chapter 11 for an example of a basic meditation.

Violence and its consequences

A very practical consideration for all Buddhist traditions, including *Vajrayana*, is the futility of violence. From a normative Buddhist perspective, there is little to gain and much to lose by resorting to violence. The price of violence – the sufferings of death, injury, loss, property damage, financial costs, environmental destruction and psychological damage – far outweigh potential gains. In addition, in consonance with the law of cause and effect, there are fewer tangible costs. Violent actions sow the seeds for further hostilities, in the minds of both the perpetrators of violence and the victims and their families. Violence therefore represents an ethical lapse that can lead to a further erosion of values.

In accordance with the Buddha's Four Noble Truths, Buddhists in the Tibetan tradition investigate the causes of violence and recognize them to be the three poisonous delusions (*klesas*) of the mind: greed, hatred and ignorance. These three root delusions are regarded as the root causes of social problems, including theft, murder and domestic violence. These social problems are not simply personal or local, but can extend to the four corners of the earth. For example, greed and consumerism in one part of the world can be the causes of hunger, social injustice and political instability in other parts of the world.

Today human beings are connected globally and ever more closely through improved methods of transportation and communication reaching to remote corners of the planet. These increasing connections require greater understanding, respect and compassion than ever before to prevent misunderstandings that may lead to tensions and violence. The interrelatedness of all life is a teaching with great relevance in an increasingly connected world.

The Buddhist notion of peace is comprehensive, bridging inner development and activity in the everyday world. Beginning with acknowledging and transforming the seeds of violence in one's own mind, one extends this peaceful agenda from the individual level to the family, community, country and beyond to the entire universe. Buddhist texts describe an inclusive peace that encompasses social, political and interpersonal relations as much as individual hearts and minds. This holistic view of an inclusive peace may be seen as a means of both preventing and correcting structural violence. Buddhist ideals of cultural tolerance and inclusiveness may similarly be seen as a means of preventing and correcting cultural violence. As is well known, Buddhist tolerance and respect for a variety of religious and philosophical perspectives is recognized as a key element in the historical transmission of Buddhism and its successful adaptation in new and often vastly different cultural environments.

The notion of peace as structural nonviolence necessitates an assessment of all concepts and attitudes that are used to legitimate violence in all its forms. It therefore becomes necessary to analyze the relationship between gender inequity and violence, especially the structures that enable violence against women and children. It follows that gender discrimination in all forms is corrosive to peace on many levels.

Philosophical foundations of nonviolence

As a branch of Mahayana Buddhism, the goal and fruit of *Vajrayana* practice is Buddhahood. The prerequisites for *Vajrayana* practice are the 'three principles of the path' elucidated by the Indian monk/scholar Atisa (1983) in his *Lamp for the Path* (*Bodhipratipa*): renunciation, the enlightened attitude (*bodhicitta*) and direct insight into emptiness (*sunyata*). Renunciation is defined as the determination to renounce rebirth in cyclic existence (*samsara*). The enlightened attitude is the altruistic aspiration to achieve the perfect enlightenment of a Buddha in order to free all sentient beings from suffering. Direct insight into emptiness is the wisdom that understands the lack of true or inherent existence of all phenomena. Without these three prerequisites, *Vajrayana* practice is said to be impossible or even dangerous.

The logic behind the three principles of the path is integral to an understanding of the *Vajrayana* perspective on peace and violence. First, to achieve liberation or enlightenment, it is necessary to generate perfect renunciation. To generate perfect renunciation means to abandon all attachment to cyclic existence and to renounce all actions (*karma*) that lead to further rebirth, especially unwholesome actions that lead to rebirth in the 'unfortunate migrations,' or lower realms, as an animal, hungry ghost or hell being. Killing a sentient being (a being with consciousness) is regarded as a seriously unwholesome action that typically results in rebirth in a hell realm. Not only is rebirth in a hell realm torturous, but it can also last for an extremely long time, which poses a serious obstacle to the achievement of liberation.

Second, to achieve the perfect enlightenment, it is necessary to generate the enlightened attitude (*bodhicitta*). This enlightened resolve to become a fully awakened Buddha and work to liberate all sentient beings from the sufferings of cyclic existence was regarded by the Indian master Santideva as the essence of the 84,000 teachings of the Buddha. There are seven steps for cultivating the enlightened attitude, based on the understanding that all sentient beings have taken rebirth in cyclic existence time and again, and have therefore been related to each other in a multitude of ways.

The seven steps are: (1) recognizing that all sentient beings have been our mother at some point in time, giving birth to us and showering us with loving kindness an infinite number of times; (2) recognizing that we owe a debt of gratitude to all these sentient beings who have been our mother and cared for us so lovingly; (3) determining to repay the kindness of all these sentient beings; (4) generating loving kindness (*maitri*), the wish that all sentient beings achieve happiness; (5) generating compassion (*karuna*), recognizing that we are currently incapable of liberating sentient beings from suffering; (6) generating the special thought (*lhak sam*), the determination to take on oneself the responsibility to liberate all sentient beings from suffering; and finally (7) the actual *bodhicitta*, the aspiration to achieve perfect enlightenment, recognizing that only a fully awakened Buddha has the capacity to liberate all sentient beings from suffering. In order to become a fully awakened Buddha, it is necessary to avoid all unwholesome mental factors and unskillful actions, and to cultivate all wholesome mental factors and skillful actions. It follows that it is necessary to avoid all harm to sentient beings, including all violent acts, whether through actions of body, speech or mind.

Third, to achieve the perfect enlightenment, it is necessary to develop direct insight into emptiness (*sunyata*). The root cause of unskillful actions and therefore of sentient beings' involvement in cyclic existence is ignorance, or not understanding the true mode of existence of phenomena. Ignorant sentient beings misunderstand impermanent phenomena to be permanent, unsatisfactory phenomena to be satisfactory, and self-less phenomena to have a self, essence or true existence.

In the practice of *Vajrayana*, meditation is enhanced through *yogic* techniques such as meditation on the winds and channels of the body. The ability to gather the 72,000 winds (*lung*) or energies of the body into the central psychic channel is cultivated, so that, at the time of death, one may direct one's consciousness to the pure land of Amitabha. In each of the four classes of *tantra* – action, performance, *yoga* and *anuttarayoga* – the practitioner generates a vivid appearance of the visualized deity, then identifies as the deity with all its enlightened qualities, and finally generates the divine pride of being the deity.

The enlightened figure that is the focus of one's visualization may appear either in peaceful or wrathful form. The purpose is not to overcome mental defilements or even to transform them, but to encounter them and utilize them in the process of awakening. Like fertilizer for the fields, the afflictive emotions such as desire, if used skillfully, may be utilized on the path. For example, in all four classes of *tantra*, one consciously generates four types of bliss – expressed as looking, laughing, embracing and union – and utilizes them as tools for cultivating the path (Tsonghkapa, 1975). The male/female symbology is a code for the complementarity of skillful means (*upaya*) associated with the male and wisdom (*prajna*) associated with the female. The male and female deities in union (*yab/yum*) signify the non-duality of bliss and emptiness.

Skillful means of awakening

Mahayana Buddhism is characterized by a variety of philosophical schools, methods of practice and cultural expressions. Multiple interpretations of key teachings are common. In terms of method, Tibetan scholars typically classify

Mahayana practice into the Perfection Vehicle (*paramitayana*, also known as *sutrayana*) and the Mantra Vehicle (*mantrayana*, also known as *tantrayana* and *vajrayana*). A pivotal Mahayana concept is *tathagatagarbha* (literally 'womb of enlightenment'), the potential for enlightenment present within each sentient being.

Prior to embarking on the *tantric* practices, a practitioner is required to have a solid understanding of basic Buddhist teachings. A practitioner trains daily in the three trainings: ethical conduct (*sila*), meditative concentration (*samadhi*) and wisdom (*prajna*). Further, a practitioner cultivates the six perfections (*paramita*): generosity (*dana*), ethical conduct (*sila*), patience (*ksanti*), joyful effort (*virya*), concentration (*dhyana*) and wisdom (*prajna*).[2]

The third of the six perfections of the *bodhisattva* is patience, valued as an antidote to anger. The Fourteenth Dalai Lama likens the practice of patience by the *bodhisattva* to the patience a mother has when her baby 'kicks her, pulls her hair, and sticks a finger in her eye. She is patient, knowing how long her task will take. In the same way, a Bodhisattva is willing to spend an aeon to achieve one slight improvement in one sentient being' (Tsonghkapa, 1975, p. 177).

In addition, a practitioner is supposed to complete the preliminary practices (*ngondro*), 100,000 repetitions each of the refuge formula, prostrations, the 100-syllable mantra of Vajrasattva, the *mandala* offering and *guru yoga*. *Guru yoga* practices vary considerably, according to the *guru's* instructions, but each involves a visualization with the *guru* at the center of a lineage tree, surrounded by an assemblage that serves as an object of refuge. Through the power of visualization, one evokes the presence of these enlightened beings as a source of teachings and blessings.

After completing these preliminary practices, one seeks to receive an empowerment (*abhiseka*) from a qualified *tantric* master. This empowerment initiates one into the *mandala* of a specific realized being, popularly known as a meditational deity (*yidam*), who may be either a Buddha or *bodhisattva*, male or female, peaceful or wrathful in appearance. The rite entails receiving four successive empowerments: vase, secret, knowledge and word.

The aim is to realize the ultimately empty nature of all aspects of the practice, including the practitioner, the practice itself and the sentient beings to which one directs the merit of the practice. The meditational deity who is the object of one's visualization and the *mandala* that is the perfectly purified residence of the meditational deity are equally recognized as being empty by nature.

Simultaneous with the attainment of perfect enlightenment (*samyaksambodhi*), one achieves the two bodies of the Buddha: the 'truth' body (*dharmakaya*) and the form body (*rupakaya*). The truth body may be understood in two aspects: the omniscient nature of enlightened awareness (*jnana dharmakaya*) and the empty nature of enlightened awareness (*svabhavakaya*). The form body may also be understood in two aspects: the enjoyment body (*sambhogakaya*) and the emanation body (*nirmanakaya*). To achieve the truth body (*dharmakaya*), in meditative equipoise one cultivates wisdom or insight into emptiness (*sunyata*). To achieve the form body (*rupakaya*), one cultivates skillful means or method (*upaya*). The cultivation of wisdom results in the cognitive perfection of a Buddha, whereas the cultivation of method culminates in the physical perfection of a Buddha. The cause and consequence are similar by nature; that is, imprints of accumulated wisdom give rise to the *dharmakaya*, while the imprints of skillful means give rise to the *rupakaya*. Meditation on emptiness is essential, but meditation on emptiness alone is inadequate for the achievement of enlightenment. Meditation on emptiness needs to be conjoined with altruism and skillful means to alleviate the sufferings and bring happiness to all living beings.

Buddhist practices for cultivating peace

Buddhist *tantra* uses visualization as a means of transformation, thus transforming ordinary mental defilements like anger and desire to the path of enlightenment. The practice contains elements of visionary experience common to other spiritual traditions, but in the case of Buddhist *tantra*, the ability to control visual projections is key. The heart of the practice is called deity *yoga*, meaning to visualize oneself as an awakened being and ultimately to 'become' this being. Although some of these awakened beings have corollaries in Hindu *tantra*, they are not seen as ordinary gods, but as archetypes of one's own enlightenment. In other words, by visualizing and identifying with the enlightened qualities of an awakened being, one practices to embody those qualities and become fully awakened oneself.

To take on the identity of a deity for the attainment of enlightenment is therefore central to *Vajrayana* practice. The cultivation of the enlightened body of a Buddha through various practices, including deity *yoga* practice, culminates in a body (*rupakaya*) with thirty-two major and eighty minor marks at the time of perfect enlightenment (*samyaksambodhi*). The Buddhist *tantric* method of cultivation entails visualizing the meditational deity and then uniting one's body, speech and mind with the enlightened body, speech and mind of the object of one's visualization. All forms are perceived as the enlightened form of the deity, all sounds as the deity's *mantra* and all mental activity as the enlightened wisdom of the deity.

In the practice of deity *yoga*, one generates the 'divine pride' of embodying the meditational deity (*yidam*), which is said to expedite the achievement of Buddhahood. For this reason, *tantrayana* is known as the 'swift path.' While it charts a speedy course to this ultimate achievement, this path also entails responsibilities and risks. For this reason, it is also known as the 'dangerous path.' The activities of *tantric* deities include pacifying, increasing, empowering and destroying.

The representation of sexual union between two enlightened beings, male and female, is symbolic of the union of wisdom and compassion that are required for becoming a Buddha. The practice of *Vajrayana* begins by receiving empowerment from a qualified *lama* (guru or spiritual teacher), then honing one's ability to concentrate single-pointedly on complex visualized images of Buddhas and *bodhisattva*s, down to each hair of the eyebrows. For most practitioners, including all celibate monastics, *tantric* practices are accomplished through visualization; only a highly advanced *yogi* is qualified to practice with an actual consort.

If the meditational deity is shown in sexual union, the practitioner consciously generates successive levels of sexual desire in order to understand the true nature of desire. In Buddhist *tantra*, practice with an actual consort, as opposed to a visualized consort, was an option for a highly advanced practitioner, provided that the person was not under monastic vows and satisfied the prerequisites, which included perfect renunciation, the enlightened attitude of thorough-going altruism and direct insight into emptiness. Adherents of all Tibetan Buddhist traditions, including the *Gelugpa* ('Virtuous'), regard authentic practice of sexual *yoga* as virtuous, as long as these requirements are met. A person under monastic vows practices with a visualized consort rather than an actual consort.

In *Vajrayana*, visualization practice is used to transform perceptions and thereby the ways we respond to the world. The 'meditational deities' (*yidam*) that are used as the objects of concentration in *tantric* meditation practice are archetypes of enlightenment – Buddhas and *bodhisattva*s – that are understood to be empty (*sunya*) of true existence, just as one's ordinary physical body is empty by nature. The meditational deity or archetypes of enlightenment that is the object of deity *yoga* is understood to be generated by one's own mind and may appear in either peaceful or wrathful form. The deity that is the object of meditation practice is usually selected by the *lama* based on skillful means (*upaya*) and the inclinations of the practitioner. An understanding of the process of visualization requires an understanding of human consciousness and the way human beings habitually misperceive reality. Instead of perceiving phenomena purely and directly, the awareness of ordinary individuals is typically mediated and distorted by labels, concepts and judgments. The root cause of these distortions, the mental defilements, therefore obstructs one's perception of the true nature of phenomena. The process of visualizing oneself as an awakened being is a powerful means of cutting through mental defilements. As one becomes intimately familiar with the visualized being and identified with that being's enlightened qualities, one simultaneously gains insight into the true nature of one's own mind and one's potential for enlightenment.

By honing the ability to construct the meditational deity and environs, one becomes adept at understanding the mind's tendency to perceive mistakenly, distort and consciously project mental forms and content. Instead of remaining an unwitting victim of mental afflictions, misperceptions and mental projections, in *tantric* meditation practice, one gains mastery through a process of constructive projection, realization and mental transformation. One aspect of the process is nurturing the ability to control one's mind; another aspect is to construct an ideal universe and manifest an enlightened mode of perception that is wise, compassionate, effortless and spontaneous. The gamut of experience is grist for the mill. Not only archetypes of peace, generosity and loving kindness are utilized in the process, but also desire and other powerful thoughts and emotions, as a skillful means of effecting awakening.

The enlightened forms used as objects of *Vajrayana* meditation practice are intricate and enormously varied. As one progressively envisions, supplicates and embodies an enlightened being, one generates non-dual awareness of the ordinary (one's own unenlightened state of consciousness) and the ultimate (the enlightened realization of the meditational deity). This process is analogous to the non-dual status of *samsara* and *nirvana*, both characterized as empty by nature.

Calm abiding (*samatha*) and insight (*vipasyana*), the two primary streams of meditation practice, are used alternately, first, to analyze and, second, to fix the mind on emptiness. In *Vajrayana* practice, the enlightened form of the deity is understood to simultaneously be conventionally existent and ultimately empty. Just as *samsara* and *nirvana* are both ultimately empty, the conventional level of reality exists simultaneously with its essencelessness. So, while the ultimate aim of *tantric* practice is enlightenment, practical benefits may also be gained from the practice, namely, a capability to overcome obstacles, subdue negative forces, and enjoy long life and good health.

Tantric texts describe integrated ritual practices (*sadhana*) that integrate a variety of practices related to a specific meditational deity (*yidam*). A *tantric sadhana* begins with going for refuge and the generation of *bodhicitta*, the altruistic attitude that aspires to liberate all beings from suffering. Next, ordinary reality is consciously dissolved into emptiness and, in its place, a visualization of a meditational deity is constructed, to whom homage is offered, and supplications and offerings are made. Light rays are generated from the deity to remove all impurities and karmic obstructions, transforming the environment into the pure residence of the deity. The body, speech and mind of the practitioner and all sentient beings become identified with the enlightened body, speech and mind of the deity. All forms are seen as the form of the meditational deity, all sounds are the *mantra* and all thoughts are the enlightened wisdom of the enlightened ones. A *mantra* visualized at the practitioners' heart is then recited for as long as possible. The practice concludes with dissolving the entire visualization back into emptiness. Next, one meditates on the empty nature of one's own mind. Finally, one dedicates to all sentient beings the merit that has been accrued during the practice. The deity is visualized as abiding within an elaborate *mandala* and this is accompanied by the chanting of a liturgy that includes praises, requests, *mantras* (sound syllables) and *mudras* (ritual hand gestures). The form of the deity is visualized in the space in front or on the top of the crown, until eventually the practitioner is empowered to virtually embody the deity and become one with the deity's enlightened body, speech and mind. An example of a *sadhana* is the Avalokitesvara practice for cultivating compassion (Tsonghkapa, 1975, p. 233).

In the *Vajrayana* tradition, numerous Buddhas and *bodhisattva*s serve as meditational deities (*yidam*). The word 'deity' is used advisedly, since it has a wide range of denotations in religious studies generally and in *tantric* studies particularly. A deity may manifest in either peaceful or wrathful aspect and deities with multiple forms may appear in both peaceful and wrathful aspects. An example of a deity in a peaceful aspect is Avalokitsvara, the *bodhisattva* of compassion, whose face reflects serenity and benevolence. Examples of deities who appear in wrathful aspect are Yamantaka, Hevajra and Mahakala. The wrathful deities are not demons – a common misconception – but are manifestations of one's own mind that forcefully eliminate all inner and outer obstacles.

Some meditational deities have multiple forms, including both peaceful and wrathful forms. For example, Tara is an enlightened being in female form that manifests in twenty-one aspects, each in a unique pose with unique qualities. Tara is renowned for her power to swiftly remove mental defilements and to work ceaselessly for the benefit of all living beings. Once a suitable meditational deity is selected or received from a *guru* during an empowerment, the practitioner is authorized to engage in *tantric* meditation practice using the deity as the object of visualization. To generate the 'divine pride' of becoming the deity signals a shift of awareness from an ordinary unenlightened mode of perception and being to an enlightened mode.

Buddhist peaceful ideals and contemporary violent realities

The peaceful Buddhist ideal has of course not always been applied perfectly in Buddhist societies. Ordinary society is populated by ordinary, unenlightened individuals who are, therefore, still vulnerable to the afflictive emotions (*klesa*): greed, hatred and ignorance. Like any other skill, nonviolence requires training and meditation training requires time and strong commitment. Traditionally in Buddhist societies, this training was available primarily to monastics and to *yogis* dwelling in solitude. Even in societies that prize nonviolence, not all individuals are capable of perfecting a completely peaceful state of mind.

Does destroying negativity count as violence? The forcefulness of meditational deities who appear in wrathful form is regarded as useful and necessary for eradicating the powerful delusions of one's mind and removing the obstructions to spiritual practice. Can forceful means similarly be justified in overcoming the ills of society?

If the global economy were led by awakened beings whose motivation was purely to ensure the welfare of all the world's creatures, the results could be positive. But if the global economy is led by individuals seeking their own profit and motivated by greed, the modus operandi is likely to involve deceit, corruption, exploitation and the ever-increasing economic disparities that lead to tensions and violent conflicts.

Buddhist resources for peace

What resources does the *Vajrayana* Buddhist tradition have to offer for creating a nonviolent world? First, like other Buddhist traditions, it teaches insight into the three marks of existence: unsatisfactoriness (*dukkha*), impermanence (*anitya*) and no-self (*anatman*). Among other things, insight into unsatisfactoriness is a realization that things do not always go our way. Insight into impermanence brings home the reality that things do not last. Insight into no-self helps loosen the ego fixation and attachment to self-interest that Buddhists consider the root cause of conflicts and violent reactions. Reflection on no-self is also a tool for understanding the human person by recognizing its constitutive elements: form (*rupa*), feelings (*vedana*), perceptions (*samjña*), karmic formations (*sam.skara*),[3] and consciousness (*vijñana*). Contemplation of these five aggregates (*skandhas*) helps deconstruct habitual notions of the self, both the habitual notion of the self as a concrete, ongoing entity and the habitual notion of oneself as being intrinsically more valuable than other beings.

This process of analysis is used to look more deeply into the notion of self, dismantle patterns of self-centeredness and reverse the attachment to self that can lead to violent conflicts. This process of analysis nurtures insight into one's own true nature and acts as an antidote to self-grasping and self-cherishing.

A related practice is contemplating on the no-self nature of self and phenomena. This practice not only relaxes the hold on oneself as being truly existing, but also relaxes one's hold of grasping at other phenomena as being truly existing. Among the many practical benefits of the practice is the ability to let go of expectations, grudges, antipathies, disappointments and anger when one's expectations are not met. Another practical benefit is calling into question accustomed assumptions. Of relevance here are habitual assumptions about gender traits that lead to a view of human experience as either dominator or dominated. Through a process of questioning gender stereotypes of rugged men and passive women, it becomes possible to dismantle the hyper-masculinity that ferments dominion and destructiveness. The hyper-violence that is a steady diet for consumers of action films and video games can be seen as a product of social constructions of gender. Concepts of male as tough and aggressive, female as coy and submissive polarize and reify individuals into patterns that are unnatural and frustrating. The alienation and frustration borne of these stereotypes tend towards aggressive behavior, harm and militarism.

Buddhism has not been immune to the tendencies of government to harness religion for its own ends. Although Buddhism was a strong pacifying force after its introduction to Tibet, sporadic incidents of violence occurred, even in some instances between monasteries. According to historical accounts, the Fifth Dalai Lama, in league with the Mongols, sanctioned armed aggression to consolidate power in Tibet.

Buddhists would concur with Hobbes when he says that the cause of violence is not human nature, but a lack of imagination. Nonviolent solutions are available; they just need to be crafted and implemented. The international moral standing of the Fourteenth Dalai Lama and acts of civil disobedience by Tibetans both in exile and in Tibet proves that resistance need not be violent to be effective. Even in the face of heightened violence in the world today, the ethical integrity of peaceful resistance is still widely recognized and applauded.

Notes

1. In the Tibetan tradition, the eighteen major *bodhisattva* precepts are to refrain from: (1) praising self and belittling others; (2) not giving wealth and the Dharma; (3) not forgiving though someone apologizes; (4) abandoning the Mahayana; (5) stealing offerings to the Three Jewels; (6) abandoning the Dharma; (7) disrobing monks or nuns; (8) committing the five heinous crimes; (9) holding wrong views; (10) destroying towns; (11) teaching emptiness to the untrained; (12) reversing someone's aspiration for full enlightenment; (13) causing someone to abandon individual liberation; (14) disparaging the Hinayana; (15) falsely claiming realization of emptiness; (16) accepting property of the Three Jewels; (17) while meditating, giving one's belongings to others; and (18) abandoning *bodhicitta*. The *bodhisattva* precepts contained in the *Brahmajala Sutra* that are practiced in East Asia include refraining from: (1) killing; (2) stealing; (3) sexual misconduct; (4) false speech; (5) selling alcohol; (6) slandering the *Sangha*; (7) praising self and belittling others; (8) covetousness; (9) ill will; and (10) slandering the Three Jewels.
2. An alternative listing of ten perfections adds four more: skillful means (*upaya-kausalya*), aspiration (*pranidhana*), power (*bala*) and exalted wisdom (*jnana*). These ten perfections are emphasized respectively on the ten stages (*bhumis*) of the *bodhisattva* path to Buddhahood.
3. This term is also translated as 'non-associated compositional factors.' 'Non-associated' here signifies that items in this category (for example, *karma*, *dharma* and *sam.sara*) are neither material nor mental.

Reference list and further reading

Atisa (1983) *Lamp for the Path* (London: George Allen & Unwin).

Chagdud Tulku and Lama Shenpen Drolma (2003) *Change of Heart: The Bodhisattva Peace Training of Chagdud Tulku* (Junction City: Padma Publishing).

Chappell, D.W. (1999) (ed.) *Buddhist Peacework: Creating Cultures of Peace* (Boston: Wisdom Publications).

Jinpa, T. (2006) *Mind Training: The Great Collection* (Somerville: Wisdom Publications).

Kraft, K. (ed.) (1992) *Inner Peace, World Peace: Essays on Buddhism and Nonviolence* (Albany: State University of New York Press).

Moser-Puangsuwan, Y. (2000) 'The Buddha in the Battlefield: Maha Ghosananda Bhikkhu and the Dhammayietra Army of Peace' in S.S.J. Harak (ed.) *Nonviolence for the Third Millennium* (Macon: Mercer University Press), 121–127.

Rinpochen, K. (1999) *Vast as the Heavens, Deep as the Sea· Verses in Praise of Bodhicitta* (Somerville: Wisdom Publications).

Schlieter, J. (2006) 'Compassionate Killing or Conflict Resolution? The Murder of King Langdarma according to Tibetan Buddhist Sources' in M. Zimmermann (ed.) *Buddhism & Violence* (Kathmandu: Lumbini International Research Institute), 129–155.

Tsongkhapa (1975) *Tantra in Tibet: The Great Exposition of Secret Mantra*, 1 (London: George Allen & Unwin).

Tsongkhapa (2005) *Tantric Ethics: An Explanation of the Precepts for Buddhist Vajrayana Practice* (Somerville: Wisdom Publications).

13
He Ping: A Confucian Perspective

Kam-por Yu

遠人不服, 則脩文德以來之
When distant people are unsubmissive,
one should cultivate one's virtue to attract them.
Confucius [The Analects, 16.1]

This chapter aims to outline a Confucian account of peace. I shall begin with the etymology of some key Chinese terms, and then go on to introduce the Confucian views on war and peace as contained in mainline Confucian literature. A very important text in the Confucian tradition, the *Spring and Autumn Annals*, will be given a more in-depth examination, as it sets out normative principles of interstate interactions. I conclude with an analysis of the Confucian recipe for resolving conflicts, which represents a typical Chinese way of thinking.

The etymology of the Chinese terms

The modern expression for the term 'peace' in Chinese is 和平 (*he ping*).[1] The two words literally mean harmonious and fair. The etymology of the term implies that peace is not an order imposed by an authority, but a harmonious and contented state felt by the different sectors concerned. We shall first look at the etymological roots of the two characters that constitute this expression.

平 *ping*

The character 平 *ping* is made up of two parts: 于 *yu* (ease) and 八 *ba* (divide). The word 于 (also written as 亏) is again made up of two parts. The upper part is 一: meaning leveled or horizontal. The remaining part means exhale or exhalation. The whole word symbolizes leveled exhalation, which implies a peaceful mental state. The word 八 means *different* or *separate*. It pictorially represents the two (divided) parts of an object. The word 八 here is a simplified version of the world 分 *fen* (divide). The word 分 is made up of two parts: 八 (two parts) and 刀 (knife). It means dividing a thing into two parts. The component 八 (written as two dots

244

under the top line) in the word 平 means the same as 分 (divide), as the simplified version is used instead of the more complicated character.

To sum up, the word 平 is made up of two parts: 于 (ease) and 八 (分 divide). Together, the whole compound word signifies a distribution that people can accept calmly and with ease. It means a peaceful state of mind resulting from a fair distribution. Because of its etymological roots, the word 平 has the meaning of level, fair and calm.

In the Confucian classics, the term 平 (*ping*) is commonly used in association with the term 天下 (*tianxia*), which literally means 'all under heaven' and can be translated as 'the world.' The expression 平天下 (*ping tianxia*) means 'bringing peace to the world,' or 'pacify the world.' The expression 天下平 (*tianxia ping*) means 'there is peace in the world.'[2] Sometimes the expression 天下太平 (*tianxia taiping*) or 'grand world peace' is used.[3]

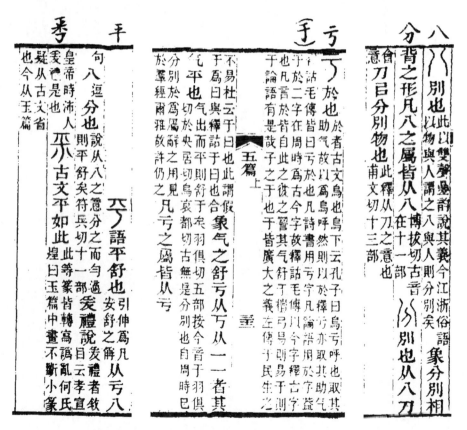

Illustration 13.1　Definitions and explanations of the words 平, 于, 八 and 分

Source: Shuwen Jiezi (說文解字) or *Explaining Simple and Analyzing Compound Characters*, the first Chinese dictionary compiled by Xu Shen in the first century AD.

和 *he*

The Chinese word for harmony is written today as 和 (*he*). The word is made up of two parts. The left part 禾 (*he*) indicates the sound of the word (the word should be pronounced as *he*). The right part 口 (mouth) indicates the meaning of the word, that is to say, the meaning of the word is related to the mouth. The whole character means 'echo' (as in singing). The word is borrowed to be used instead of 龢 or 盉.

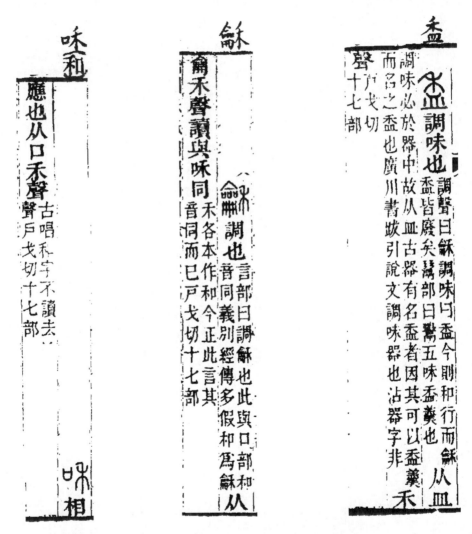

Illustration 13.2   Definitions and explanations of the words 和, 龢, 盉

Source: Shuwen Jiezi (說文解字) or *Explaining Simple and Analyzing Compound Characters*, the first Chinese dictionary compiled by Xu Shen in the first century AD.

We can find the meaning of harmony in the two original forms of the character: 龢 and 盉. The word 龢 is made up of two parts. The left part (龠) denotes musical instruments; the right part denotes the pronunciation of the word. This is the original Chinese character for harmony. It means harmony created by musical instruments.

The word 盉 also means harmony, but with special reference to cooking. The upper part denotes the pronunciation of the word (禾 *he*); the lower part (皿) denotes a container, which can hold different ingredients. The word is defined as 'mixing things to create taste.' Both 龢 and 盉 have the meaning that harmony is constituted by the mixture of different ingredients.

The Confucian views on war and peace

The Confucian tradition has been very consistent in holding that the function of governance is three-fold, all aspects directed towards the people: (1) survival, (2) prosperity and (3) education. The first and foremost duty of the government is to guarantee the survival of the people. The next stage is to enable the people not only to survive, but also to have a decent livelihood. Finally, it is to renew the people – to make them become civilized human beings.[4]

With regards to interstate relation, Confucius believes that there is some minimal ethics that is valid across culture: 'If in word you are conscientious and trustworthy and in deed single-minded and reverent, then even in the lands of the barbarians you will go forward without obstruction' (*Analects* 15.6 [trans. by Lau 1992, p. 149]). Confucius opposes the use of military force to coerce, but holds instead that a state should demonstrate its superiority to charm people in other states. When Confucius was asked about government, he replied: 'Ensure that those who are near are pleased and those who are far away are attracted' (*Analects* 13.16 [trans. by Lau 1992, p. 26]).

If foreign people remain unfriendly, then the first assumption to make is not that they are unreasonable people but that maybe our own morality is insufficiently cultivated. As Confucius said: 'When distant people are unsubmissive one cultivates one's moral quality in order to attract them, and once they have come one makes them content' (*Analects* 16.1 [adapted from Lau 1992, p. 161]).

The exposition of this position appears widely in the Confucian literature. The following is a notable one from *Zhongyong* or *Doctrine of the Mean*, one of the *Four Books*, four basic Confucian texts: 'By indulgent treatment of men from a distance, they are brought to resort to him from all quarters. And by kindly cherishing the princes of the States, the whole kingdom is brought to revere him' (Legge, 1971, p. 409). The two key terms from the above quotation, *huai* (cherishing) and *rou* (indulgent or soft), have been used to form the expression *huairou* (to cherish and to soften; appeasement), which is used to denote a mainstream foreign policy in Chinese history (Yang, 1968, p. 26).

But emphasis on the use of soft power does not mean belittling the importance and necessity of military force. As Confucius said: 'There must be civilized works on the one hand, and military preparation on the other' (Sima, 2000, Book 47). Force cannot be a substitute for reason, but neither can reason be a substitute for force. Force should only be used as a last resort and as a response to uncivilized acts. Ban Gu (32–92) sums up this position very nicely in his discussion of what the Chinese policy towards the Huns should be: 'To control the barbarians the sage rulers punished and resisted them when they came [to invade China], and prepared and guarded them when they left. [...] So that the blame of being crooked would always be on them' (Ban, Book 94).

Confucianism does distinguish between righteous and unrighteous wars.[5] A more sophisticated classification of wars was given by Wei Xiang (who died in 59 BC), a minister of Han Dynasty, in commenting on the idea of attacking Xiong Nu (the Huns). Wei Xiang classified wars into five kinds, some are justified and some are not. He criticized that the war against Xiong Nu was just stupid or irrational as it did not fall into any of the five types, and he could not find a name for that kind of war. The five types of military force are (Ban, Book 94):

1. 義兵 (*yibing* or righteous forces): Forces used to settle chaos and to punish the tyrannous;
2. 應兵 (*yingbing* or responsive forces): Forces used reluctantly for self-defense;
3. 忿兵 (*fenbing* or resentful forces): Forces used to release minor grudges or resentment;
4. 貪兵 (*tanbing* or greedy forces): Forces used to seize territory and wealth;
5. 驕兵 (*jiaobing* or arrogant forces): Forces used to display great power and numerical strength to awe the enemy.[6]

It is quite common for people today to associate Confucianism with the advocating central power and a single world order. However, it is actually highly doubtful how much support of this claim can be found in the Confucian classics. The feudal states had a lot of autonomy before China was unified by the state of Qin in 221 BC. The *Shi Huangdi* or the First Emperor, who unified China as one single empire ruled under one central government, was commonly regarded throughout Chinese history and especially by the Confucian scholars, as the worst ruler China ever had, because he only ruled China with military force and had no humanitarian concern.

The most important military emperor of Han Dynasty, Emperor Wu (140–87 BC), was also commonly regarded as an arrogant and bad emperor, mocked by the Confucians throughout the ages. Though he made Confucianism the orthodox teaching in the public examinations, he was disliked by the Confucians. In the book the *Debate on Salt and Iron* (*Yantie lun*), which recorded a debate on China's economic policy and foreign policy held shortly after the death of Emperor Wu, virtually all Confucian scholars attending the debates argued against Emperor Wu's policy of government monopolies on salt, iron, liquor and coinage of money, and the foreign policy of attacking the Xiong Nu (the Huns). Emperor Wu granted a high official status to Confucianism, yet his policies, in particular his economic policy and foreign policy, were quite at odds with the spirit of Confucianism.[7] The primary Confucian concern has always been about the well-being of the people rather than the might of the state. Unification, if it is ever desirable, is desirable only as a means, not as an end in itself.

For Confucianism, real peace is not an order imposed or maintained by an authority, but a state where different sectors can have their proper places and prosper in their own ways. It is said in the *Book of Changes*, 'each follows the right path of his true nature and mandate. The whole is then in grand harmony. This is conducive to benefit and perpetuation. The vital energy comes from myriad things, and the ten thousand states are at peace.'[8]

In the *Book of Rites*, Confucius talks about two orders of human society. The higher order is derived directly from the Confucian ideal of benevolence or humanity. It is a higher conception of peace, which is unlikely to be realized given the social structures and the human mindsets as they are. Anyway, this is the Confucian ultimate ideal:

> When the great Dao prevailed, the world was a common state (not belonging to any particular ruling family), rulers were elected according to their wisdom and ability and mutual confidence and peace prevailed. Therefore people not only regarded their own parents as parents and their own children as children. The old people were able to enjoy their old age, the young men were able to employ their talent, their juniors had the elders to look up to, and the helpless widows, orphans and cripples and deformed were well taken care of. The men had their respective occupations and the women had their homes. If the people had too much energy for work, they did not have to labor for their own profit. Therefore there was no cunning or intrigue and there were no bandits or burglars, and as a result, there was no need to shut one's outer gate (at night). This was the period of Datong, or the Great Commonwealth. (*The Book of Rites*, 1966, Chapter IX, p. 228 [quoted after Lin])[9]

Given that this higher ideal may be too good to be true, Confucius also talks about a lower ideal, which is a workable scheme based on the reality of Chinese society at least at one stage of human development. This is not just an ideal, but it has been actualized by the sage kings in the past.

But now the great Dao no longer prevails, and the world is divided up into private families (or becomes the possession of private families), and people regard only their own parents as parents and only their own children as children. They acquire goods and labor, each for his own benefit. A hereditary aristocracy is established and the different states build cities, outer cities and moats, each for its own defense. The principle of *li* (or forms of social intercourse) and righteousness serve as the principle of social discipline. By means of these principles, people try to maintain the official status of rulers and subjects, to teach the parents and children and elder brothers and younger brothers and husbands and wives to live in harmony, to establish social institutions and to live in groups of hamlets. The physically strong and the mentally clever rise to prominence and each one tries to carve his own career. Hence, there is deceit and cunning from these wars.

Yu, Tang, Wen, Wu, King Cheng and Duke Zhou[10] were the best men of this age. Without a single exception, these six gentlemen were deeply concerned over the principle of *li*, through which justice was maintained, general confidence was tested and errors or malpractices were exposed. An ideal of true manhood, *ren*, was set up and good manners or courtesy were cultivated, as solid principles for the common people to follow. A ruler who violates these principles would then be denounced as a public enemy and driven off from his office. This is called the period of Xiaokang or the Minor Peace (*The Book of Rites*, 1966, Chapter IX, pp. 228–229 [trans. by and slightly adapted from Lin]).

Shihlien Hsü identifies the following features in the stage of Minor Peace:

(1) family as the basis of social and political organization, (2) private property, (3) the national state and the necessity of national defense, (4) war, (5) selfishness, (6) worship of military heroes and cunning diplomats, (7) revolutions. In order to preserve possible harmony and obtainable order, the doctrine of rectification, the government of virtue, the principle of *li*, the institution of monarchical government, the theories of political democracy, punishment and justice, moral education, and the rules of benevolent politics are applied by the best governments. (Hsü, 1975, p. 236)[11]

The distinction of social roles, hierarchical social structure, a family-centered ethics, hereditary kingship – all these are important features of traditional Chinese society.* But the Confucian social ideal is not inseparably tied to these features. They only form the backgrounds of the lower order of human society known as *xiaokang* or Minor Peace, and they are not in any way the preconditions of the higher order of human society known as *datong* or Grand Peace.

The *Spring and Autumn Annals*

Our discussion of the Confucian account of interstate peace cannot be complete without an extended discussion of the *Spring and Autumn Annals*.

---

*   Ed. For a different perspective on this issue, see Chapter 11 by Swami Veda Bharati.

It is a book devoted to expounding the principles of good governance and interstate interaction.

The *Spring and Autumn Annals* as a book in political philosophy

The *Spring and Autumn Annals* is a history book written by Confucius (551–479 BC). The period covered by this history book is referred to as the Spring and Autumn Period (722–481 BC) by later historians. According to Confucius himself, the *Spring and Autumn Annals* is his most important work. He said: 'The future generations shall understand me through the *Spring and Autumn* and shall judge me on the basis of the *Spring and Autumn*' (*Records of the Grand Historian*, Book 47, 1966, p. 98 [quoted after Lin]).[12]

The *Spring and Autumn Annals* is a history book in form, but in essence it is a book in political philosophy. It states the principles of governance as well as the principles of international interactions. Confucius' aim in writing the book is to expound the principles of political philosophy. But he thinks that it is better to use specific cases to illustrate the principles rather than to state the principles in the abstract. When Confucius returned from his long travel, he realized that his political teachings had no hope of being put into practice in his lifetime, and he wrote down his teachings for future generations.

In his own words, the *Spring and Autumn Annals* has three components: facts, words and principles. The facts are what happened in history. The words or terms used carry special meaning and are part of a technical language used by historians at that time. He took over these two elements from earlier historians, but the third element, principles, is entirely his own invention or formulation. Confucius took full responsibility for introducing these principles. As Mencius quoted, 'the events recorded concern Duke Huan of Qi and Duke Wen of Jin, and the style is that of the official historian. Confucius said, "I have appropriated the didactic principles therein"' (*Mencius*, 4B21, 1984, p. 165 [quoted after Lau]). The story of the writing of the *Spring and Autumn Annals* is told by Sima Qian (145–90 BC) in the *Records of the Grand Historian* (*Shiji*) as follows:

Confucius said, 'This won't do! This won't do! A gentleman is ashamed to die without having accomplished something. I realize that I cannot get into a position of power to put into effect my governmental ideal. How am I going to account for myself in the eyes of posterity?' He therefore wrote the *Spring and Autumn* (Chronicles) on the basis of the existing histories, beginning from Duke Yin (722 B.C.) and coming down to the fourteenth year of Duke Ai (481 B.C.), thus covering the period of twelve Dukes (of Lu) [...]. He used different words implying approval or condemnation in criticism of the practices of his times, in the hope that should a great king appear in the future and open that book and adopt the principles implied therein, the unruly princes and robbers of power would be ashamed and restrain themselves. (*Records of the Grand Historian*, 1966, pp. 96–97)

Senior minister Hu Sui asked, 'Why did Confucius compose the *Spring and Autumn Annals?*' The Grand Historian replied, 'I learned from Mr. Dong Zhongshu [179–104 BC, an expert in *Spring and Autumn Annals*]: "When Confucius was the Grand Secretary of Justice, the feudal lords harmed him and the ministers frustrated him. Confucius knew that his words would not be used, and the way would not be followed. He gave positive and negative comments on the events that happened during this period of 242 years, in order to set standards for the world. He deprecated the Son of Heaven, dismissed the feudal lords, and disciplined the ministers, in order to accomplish the kingly tasks." Confucius said, 'I would like to convey the empty words, but it is not as profound and lucid as demonstrating them by actual affairs.' (*Records of the Grand Historian*, Preface [trans. by author])

Principles in interstate intervention

In the *Spring and Autumn Annals*, Confucius gives different degrees of censure to the following kinds of acts: Invading territory, destroying (conquering) a state, indiscriminate killing. Invading territory is an evil in interstate relation. Destroying a state is a major evil, but indiscriminate large-scale killing is an extreme evil. For example, in Year 2 of Duke Yin (722 BC), Confucius censured Zhan Wuhai, because he led an army to invade a neighboring state. It is explained in the *Gongyang Zhuan* (2000, p. 36): '[The reason for using the wording is to show] strong condemnation of the beginning of the destruction of another state.' In Year 7 of Duke Huan (705 BC), Confucius censured the use of fire by the state of Lu (Confucius' home state) in attacking a city of a neighboring state (*Gongyang Zhuan*, 2000, p. 104). In the words of He Xiu's (129–182) commentary: 'The way of punitive expedition is nothing but the use of military force. The force can retreat if the enemy submits. The force can advance if the enemy does not submit. Fire once spread wildly can no longer be stopped. So such an act is censured for its cruelty and inhumanity' (*Gongyang Zhuan*, 2000, p. 104).

Confucius has considered two opposite principles and rejected both of them. The two principles are *zhuan feng* (monopoly of territory) and *zhuan tao* (unilateral punitive expedition). According to the principle of *zhuan feng*, each state has absolute sovereignty, and military intervention of another state is always wrong. According to the principle of *zhuan tao*, as long as a state has a legitimate reason, it is justified for the state to send a punitive expedition. Confucius' position, as revealed in the *Gongyang Zhuan* of the *Spring and Autumn Annals*, is three-fold:

(1)   If there is a universal government (led by the Son of Heaven) then the expedition should be sent or approved by the universal government.

(2) If there is no universal government but a federation of states led by a hegemonic power, the expedition should be sent or approved by the federation. Even if the purpose of the punitive expedition is a good one, the expedition should go through the right procedure of being approved by the league of states, the leader of which is the hegemonic power. The expedition that has gone through the right procedure is called *ba tao* or hegemonic punitive expedition.

(3) If there is neither a universal government nor a federation of states to regulate, it is acceptable for a state to raise a war to revenge injustice that has been done. (*Gongyang Zhuan*, 2000, p. 144)

Confucius has laid down a number of principles for starting a war. First, the purpose has to be right. The purpose must not be for self-interest. To pursue national self-interest in the name of humanitarian intervention is wrong.*

In Year 2 of Duke Huan (710 BC), the joint force of four states Qi, Lu, Chen, Zheng settled the chaos of the state of Song. The *Spring and Autumn Annals* do not regard this as a good deed, but in contrast regards it as an evil deed. The military force was sent in the name of settling the chaos of Song, but actually it provided assistance to the usurper, gave legitimacy to the usurper and shared benefits reaped by the usurper (*Gongyang Zhuan*, 2000, p. 83). This is a classical case of 'using morality to serve self-interest.'

Second, the track record has to be good. The state that launches a punitive expedition must itself not be an evildoer. The principles proposed by Confucius are that an evildoer cannot correct the evil of another evildoer, but a doer of small evil can correct the evil of a doer of great evil. 'Carrying evil oneself and punishing others for being unrighteous – this is not acceptable by the gentleman' (Year 11 of Duke Zhao [531 BC], *Gongyang Zhuan*, 2000, p. 564). However, not all evils are equal. Some evils are greater than others are. It is quite unlikely that there is any state that can have a completely clean track record. It would be setting a standard that is too high if it is required that a state that has done some evil cannot do anything to correct the wrong of another evildoer. Confucius' principle is that one's own evil must at least be relatively small or quite disproportionate to the evil of one's enemy.

A further requirement is that there must be concrete evidence that a wrong has actually been done. An intention to do wrong is not by itself a sufficient justification. As pointed out by He Xiu's commentary:

The military action cannot be regarded as a hegemonic punitive action because the deed has not yet been done, and the crime has not yet been committed.

* Ed. Compare to the *ius ad bellum* in Chapter 2 by Karlheinz Koppe and 'just war' by Aurangzeb Haneef in Chapter 8.

Confucius says, 'Banish the tunes of Zheng and keep plausible men at a distance.' (*Analects*, 1992, p. 151 [quoted after Lau])

For those who have not yet committed the crime, what can be done is just to keep them at a distance. (Year 17 of Duke Zhuang, *Gongyang Zhuan*, 2000, p. 180)

Finally, it is necessary to go through the right procedure. The *Spring and Autumn Annals* distinguish between two kinds of punitive expedition: *Zhuan tao* (unilateral punitive expedition) and *bai tao* (hegemonic punitive expedition). As a rule, hegemonic punitive expedition is preferred to unilateral punitive expedition. The former is approved or supported by the federation of states while the latter is just the unilateral decision of one state. In some exceptional cases, a unilateral punitive expedition is justified. It is when great injustice has been done and there is no hegemony to appeal to.

It is also noteworthy that, according to the *Spring and Autumn Annals*, there is some minimal ethics even during war. One notable principle is that indiscriminate killing is unjust. The *Spring and Autumn Annals* disapproved of the use of fire in war. This is because fire is a weapon of mass destruction that kills indiscriminately. 'Even if one wants to surrender, it would not be possible to do so' (Year 7 of Duke Huan [705 BC], *Gongyang Zhuan*, 2000, p. 104). With the use of fire, civilians will be hurt or killed easily, and surrender is quite impossible. It is a kind of indiscriminate killing of civilians not in combat and of soldiers intending to surrender.

Dealing with the barbarians

The *Spring and Autumn Annals* outlines a code of conduct to be followed by the Chinese states or the civilized states. But the barbarians cannot be expected to follow the civilized code of conduct. So, the *Spring and Autumn Annals* allowed somewhat different standards to be applied to the Chinese states and the barbarians. However, there is still some minimal ethics in dealing with the barbarians.

In the *Spring and Autumn Annals*, the Chinese states and the barbarians are distinguished not by nationality, language or race. If the barbarians follow the civilized codes of conduct, then they are regarded as Chinese states. If Chinese states no longer follow the civilized codes of conduct, then they are demoted as barbarians: 'When Confucius wrote the *Spring and Autumn Annals*, the lords who acted like the barbarians were regarded as barbarians, and the lords who made an effort to follow the Chinese codes of conduct were regarded as Chinese' (Han Yu (768–824), *On the Dao*).[13] In the *Spring and Autumn Annals* there are instances of some former barbarian states being treated as Chinese states because they began to interact with Chinese states in a civilized way (for example, Year 23 of Duke Zhuang [671 BC], *Gongyang Zhuan*, 2000, p. 192). There are also some instances that the Chinese states are criticized by Confucius as behaving in a barbarian way. For example, in Year 33 of Duke Xi (627 BC), the State of Qin is criticized by the *Spring and Autumn Annals* as behaving in a barbarian way, for 'traveling one thousand miles to attack others' (*Gongyang Zhuan*, 2000, p. 315). Again, in Year 23 of Duke Zhao (517 BC), the Chinese states are described as 'the new barbarians' (*Gongyang Zhuan*, 2000, p. 595).

In general, the *Spring and Autumn Annals* regard the rejection of the barbarians as a good thing. The attack of a Chinese state by the barbarians is almost always regarded as a bad thing and disapproved by the *Spring and Autumn Annals*.[14] On the other hand, the defense of Chinese states from the attack of the barbarians is regarded, as a rule, a good thing. As it is said in the *Spring and Autumn Annals*, 'Rejecting the barbarians [...] is a kingly business' (Year 4 of Duke Xi [656 BC], *Gongyang Zhuan*, 2000, p. 249).

Of course, self-defense is justified and invasion is wrong. This applies both to the Chinese states and to the barbarians. But there is a notable difference in treatment with regard to self-defense. Among the Chinese states, preemptive attack is not unacceptable. One can respond to invasion only after the crime has been committed, and intention to invade alone does not constitute a real crime (Year 17 of Duke Zhuang, *Gongyang Zhuan*, 2000, p. 180). But in dealing with the barbarians, preemptive attack is acceptable. In Year 18 of Duke Zhuang (676 BC), the act of *yuyu*, which literally means 'advance defense' or 'preemptive attack,' is glorified (*Gongyang Zhuan*, 2000, p. 183). Preemptive attack has just been criticized in the entry for Year 17 of Duke Zhuang, but was commended in the entry for Year 18 of Duke Zhuang. The reason is that the preemptive attack in Year 17 was raised by a Chinese state against another Chinese state, but the preemptive attack in Year 18 was raised by a Chinese state against the barbarians.

However, there is still some minimal ethics even in dealing with the barbarians. In Year 30 of Duke Zhuang (664 BC), instead of writing Qi (the state of Qi) had a war with *Shan Rong* (mountain barbarians) Confucius wrote 'Qi executed the San Rong.' It is explained in the *Gongyang Zhuan* (2000, p. 312): 'Why is this not called a war? In the *Spring and Autumn Annals*, a war is between two rival states. With the barbarians, Duke Huan only needed to drive them away.' As pointed out by He Xiu's commentary: 'The barbarians are also born by heaven and earth, but they were forced to a dead end and killed. Sad indeed! So the term "war" is omitted, to give the event a negative judgment, so as to show the immorality of this act' (*Gongyang Zhuan*, 2000, p. 312). As shown in the above, the *Spring and Autumn Annals* formulate not only principles concerning when it is just to go to war, but also what cannot be done even in a war.

The Confucian recipe for resolving conflicts

War is a kind of conflict, and it is also a way of handling conflict. So, our discussion of war and peace can be put in the wider context of conflict and conflict resolution. The Confucian recipe for resolving conflicts is quite remarkable, as it represents a typical Chinese way of thinking and looking at the world.

When people have a dispute, it is very rare that one side is completely right and the other is completely wrong. It is more likely that both sides have their legitimate claims, to some extent. The secret to resolve disputes is to give due recognition to both sides, to the extent that the claim is legitimate or reasonable. Of course, one side may be more reasonable than another may, and it is sometimes justified to approve most of the claims of one side and reject most of the claims of another side. But even the side which is relatively unreasonable may still have some reasonable claims, and a dispute cannot be resolved satisfactorily if the reasonable part of a contesting side is not given due recognition.

The Confucian recipe to resolve conflict is to collect the elements of truth (or reasonableness) from the two conflicting views, and assert all the elements of truth (or reasonableness) contained in the two views at the same time. It is noted that if we simply take side with one of the two conflicting views, then the conflict will only escalate, but if we are able to derive an *in-between* view from the two conflicting views, then the conflict can be resolved.

It is said in the *Yi Zhoushu* or *The Lost Book of Zhou*: 'If there is an *in-between*, it is called *three*. If there is no *in-between*, it is called *two*. *Two* struggles with each other, and results in weakness. *Three* constitutes harmony, and results in strength' (*Yi Zhoushu*, or *The Lost Book of Zhou* [trans. by the author]). Here *two* refers to two opposite claims, and *three* is not another claim that competes with the *two*, but a synthesis of the *two*. The word 叁 means *in-between* (pronounced as *can* in pinyin), and it also means *three* (pronounced as *san* in pinyin). But it is not a *three* that is different from the *two*. On the contrary, this *three* is obtained by considering and accommodating the *two*. If the *three* is a *three* that is different from the *two*, then it will compete with the *two*, and conflict cannot be resolved. The *three* is constituted by the *two* – this is why the *three* is also called 'in-between.' Only when there is a *three* that is an *in-between* constituted by the *two* can the dispute be resolved and harmony be achieved. Hence, it is said, if we know how to identify an *in-between*, then there is a *three,* otherwise there are only *two*. The *two* compete and fight with each other. This will lead to weakness. Here two ways of dealing with conflict are identified. To exclude one by another is called struggle, and leads to degeneration. To accommodate both is called harmony, and leads to prosperity.

This approach to resolve conflicts is also put forward in *Zhongyong* (*The Doctrine of the Mean*), a very popular Confucian text. Confucius said:

> Great indeed is the wisdom of Shun! Shun likes to ask [*the views of all kinds of people*] and to investigate the words of those who are close to him. He omits the bad and propagates the good. He holds fast the two ends [*duan*] and uses the in-between for the people. This is what makes him Shun! (*Zhongyong* [trans. by author])[15]

Shun, the sage-king, is never self-righteous. He does not think that he already knows very well what is right in specific cases. When he listens to different opinions, he does not simply regard one as right and discard the others. He is willing to listen to diverse views, but he will also examine the views expressed to him. For every view he encounters, he is able to separate the justified part and the unjustified. He omits the unjustified part and combines the justified parts from different sources. He identifies the *in-between* on the basis of the two ends. It should be noted that the two ends are themselves one-sided. But the appropriate judgment is made by 'holding fast' to the two opposite ends at the same time. The *three*, which can resolve the conflict, is not constituted by denying the one-sided *two*, but by giving both of them due recognition at the same time.

The Confucian approach does not see value in the subjective opinions as such, but in the objective value that may be contained in the subjective opinions.[16] The reason for respecting different opinions is not that there is no objective truth, but that the truth is complicated and cannot be adequately grasped by a single perspective.[17]

It is a distinctive feature of Chinese thought to recognize the complementary nature of contrasting and competing values. The competing values are like *yin* and *yang* – they are different and competing with each other, but they also complement each other. Examples of such competing and yet complementing values in classical Confucianism include: filial piety and loyalty, personal commitment and social justice, decoration and substance, as well as leniency and strictness.

In *Zhongyong* (*The Doctrine of the Mean*), nine guiding principles of good governance (*jiu jing* or nine canonic principles) are identified (*Zhongyong*, 1971, Chapter 20, pp. 408–409 [quoted after Legge]). They are: (1) cultivate one's person; (2) honor the good and capable; (3) be devoted to one's kin; (4) respect the senior ministers; (5) understand the difficulties of the various officials; (6) love the common people; (7) attract the various artisans; (8) give preferential treatment to people from afar; (9) pacify the feudal lords. These nine aspects compete for our attention and resources. Although each aspect is important, it would not be right to concentrate on one particular aspect at the expense of some others. The right thing is not to do this or that, but to strike the right balance among all the relevant concerns.[18]

Ethical thinking involves not only a choice between right and wrong, but also a choice among different goods or conflicting values. Very often different goods are grasped by different points of views. The fair thing to do is not simply to decide which view is right and which view is wrong, but how to give due recognition to both sides of the conflicting views at the same time.

The Confucian insight is that it is very difficult for one side to see the whole picture, and it is also very rare for someone not to be able to see at least part of the picture. So in order to grasp the whole picture, it is necessary to learn from the perspectives of others and make use of them judiciously. The impossibility of monopolizing values or privatizing the right perspective forms the basis of the Confucian approach to resolving conflicts and achieving peace.

Notes

1. In Japanese, the expression is written as 平和 (*heiwa*).
2. For the expression 平天下 (*ping tianxia*) is best known through one of the most popular Confucian texts, *Daxue* (The Great Learning), originally a chapter from the *Book of Rites* but selected as one of the four basic texts of Confucianism known as the *Four Books*. The source of this expression can be found in the translation by James Legge (1971, p. 373). The expression of 天下平 (*tianxia ping*) is used, for example, in *Mencius*, 4A12, 7B32.
3. *The Book of Rites* (*Liji*), Chapter 28: 'The ruler who vigorously pursues these two things [the rites and music] may well stand with his face to the south [like the polar star, he just needs to stay where he is such that others can use him as a reference point], for thus will great peace and order be secured all under heaven' (Legge, 1986, p. 276).
4. *Analects* 13.9 and *Mencius* 3A3 illustrate this point very well.
5. According to *Mencius*, however, none of the wars in the *Spring and Autumn Period* was righteous (*Mencius*, 7B2, 1984, p. 287 [transl. by Lau]).
6. Ban Gu, *Hanshu*, Book 74, 'The Biographies of Wei Xiang and Bing Ji' states:

   Forces used to settle chaos and to punish the tyrannous are righteous forces, which will dominate all-under-Heaven. Forces used reluctantly for self-defense are responsive forces, which will win. Forces used to release minor grudges or resentment are resentful forces, which will suffer defeat. Forces used to seize territory and wealth are greedy forces, which will meet destruction. Forces used to display great power and numerical strength to awe the enemy are arrogant forces, which will meet extinction. These five are not only matters of man but also the way of Heaven. (Ban, 1968, p. 28 [trans. by Yang]).

7. As noted by the editors of the *Sources of Chinese Tradition*, the *Yanti Lun*, 'Wm. Theodore De Bary and Irene Bloom Wm.' shows clearly the struggle of the Confucian scholars to reverse the policies of the legalists installed by Emperor Wu' (Bary and Broom, 1999, p. 359).
8. *Yijing, qiangua, tuanci*.
9. I have changed Lin's transliterations into the pinyin system. See James Legge (1971) for an alternative translation.
10. The commonly recognized sage rulers according to the Confucian tradition.
11. Hsü also regards the stage of *datong* or the Great Commonwealth as having the following features: 'social ideals such as universal peace, universal brotherhood, absence of private property, absence of national states, moral perfection, and social communism' (Hsü, 1975, p. 239).
12. The same quotation can be found in *Mencius*, 3B9:

    When the world declined and the Way fell into obscurity, heresies and violence again arose. There were instances of regicides and patricides. Confucius was apprehensive and composed the *Spring and Autumn Annals*. Strictly speaking, this is the Emperor's prerogative. That is why Confucius said, 'Those who understand me will do so through the *Spring and Autumn Annals*; those who condemn me will also do so because of the *Spring and Autumn Annals*.' (Lau 1984, p. 129)

13. *Yuan dao*. This is a very influential piece of writing in Chinese intellectual history.
14. See, for example: Year 7 of Duke Yin (716 BC) (*Gongyang Zhuan*, 2000, p. 68); Year 10 of Duke Zhong (684 BC) (p. 170); Year 21 of Duke Xi (639 BC) (p. 283); Year 21 of Duke Zhao (519 BC) (p. 594); Year 12 of Duke Ai (482 BC) (p. 706).
15. For an alternative translation, see James Legge (1971, p. 388):

> There was Shun: He indeed was greatly wise! Shun loved to question *others*, and to study their words, though they might be shallow. He concealed what was bad *in them*, and displayed what was good. He took hold of their two extremes, *determined* the Mean, and employed it in *his government of* the people. It was by this that he was Shun!

16. The Confucian approach is quite unlike the 'politics of recognition' advocated by contemporary philosophers. The 'politics of recognition' aims at recognizing and including as many people as possible, as 'each of our voices has something unique to say' (Taylor, 1992, p. 30).
17. As a result, the importance of scrutinizing and screening opinions is emphasized. See, for example, *Analects* 15.28; 13.24.
18. A systematic discussion of the Confucian approach to multiple values can be found in my upcoming paper 'The Handling of Multiple Ethical Values in Confucianism' (Yu, forthcoming).

Reference list

Bary, T. and I. Broom (eds.) (1999) *Sources of Chinese Tradition*, 1 (New York: Columbia University Press).

Hsü, L.S. (1975) *The Political Philosophy of Confucianism* (London: Curzon Press).

Taylor, C. (1992) *Multiculturalism and 'The Politics of Recognition'* (Princeton: Princeton University Press).

Yang, L.-S. (1968) 'Historical Notes on the Chinese World Order' in J.K. Fairbank (ed.) *The Chinese World Order: Traditional China's Foreign Relations* (Cambridge: Harvard University Press).

Yu, K.-P. (forthcoming) 'The Handling of Multiple Ethical Values in Confucianism' in P.J. Ivanhoe, K.-P. Yu and J. Tao (eds.) *Taking Confucian Ethics Seriously: Contemporary Theories and Applications* (Albany: State University of New York Press).

Classic chinese texts

Ban, G. *Hanshu*, Book 74, 'The Biographies of Wei Xiang and Bing Ji' in *History of Han Dynasty*, Book 94, 'The Huns.'

Han, Y. 'On the Dao' in *Changlixianshengji 11.4b* (SBBY).

Sima, Q. (2000) *Records of the Grand Historian (Shiji)*, Book 47, 'The Biography of Confucius' *Chunqiu Gongyang Zhuan Zhushu* (Beijing: Peking University Press).

Translations of classic texts

Lau, D.C. (tr.) (1984) *Mencius* (Hong Kong: Chinese University Press).

Lau, D.C. (tr.) (1992): *The Analects* (Hong Kong: Chinese University Press).

Legge, J. (tr.) (1971) *Confucius: Analects, Great Learning, and Doctrine of the Mean* (New York: Dover Publications).

Lin, Y. (tr.) (1966) *The Wisdom of Confucius* (New York: Random House).

14
Haiwa: A Shinto Perspective

Ikuro Anzai

> Faith is like love: it cannot be forced.
> Arthur Schopenhauer

Introduction: *Shinto* and Buddhism

Shinto (sometimes written as *Shintoism*) and *Bukkyo* (Buddhism) are traditional religions of Japan. Most of the Japanese people follow the religion of their family, especially when they conduct the funeral service of their relatives in *Shinto* rites or Buddhist rites. Even if an individual does not adhere to a specific religion personally, he or she remains anchored to the religion of the family. For example, the religion of my family is *Shinto* and the funeral services of my father and mother were conducted in *Shinto* rites.

According to the 'Religious Yearbook' published by the Agency for Cultural Affairs of Japan, the number of Japanese people who believe in religion are 106 million in *Shinto*, 96 million in Buddhism, 2 million in Christianity and 11 million in other religions, making 215 million in total. In other words, the total number of believers in religions in Japan is nearly double the total population, which is approximately 120 million as of end 2008.[1] The sum of believers in only two traditional religions, *Shinto* and Buddhism, exceeds 200 million, which is a reflection of the fact that the Japanese people do not have a sense of incongruity to participate both in *Shinto* and Buddhism at the same time.

Again, in Christianity a person is regarded as a believer when he/she is baptized, but in Japan an individual is counted as a believer in *Shinto* or Buddhism when he/she participates in the ceremonies of *Shinto* rites or Buddhist rites, and so many Japanese people are accordingly counted twice.

Shinbutsu-Shugo: Fusion of *Shinto* and Buddhism

Shinto has no clear religious doctrine. Neither does it have a distinct qualification requirement for the believers. A large number of Japanese pay a newly born baby's first visit to the tutelary shrine,[2] celebrate a child's third, fifth and seventh birth year at shrines,[3] celebrate a wedding in *Shinto* rites, and make their first pilgrimage of the year to their favorite shrine. Residents in local communities popularly join and enjoy festivals of shrines in their hometown.[4] But all these people cannot be regarded as believers in *Shinto*. In fact, many of the people who habitually participate in the ceremonies cited above and in many others in daily life do not regard themselves as *Shinto* believers. Those who support and maintain their tutelary shrine for worshipping their ancestors peculiar to their clan or to the specific territory in which they live are called *Ujiko*, which means protégé of a patron deity, and they are usually regarded as *Shinto* believers. Those who have a family altar at home make offerings to the departed spirits and pray before the home altar in daily life – especially on the anniversary of their death, and hold wedding services and funeral services in *Shinto* rites – are also regarded as *Shinto* believers.

However, Buddhism in Japan is mostly Mahayanist Buddhism, but it does not have one absolute doctrinal system. There are so many different sects (schools) such as *Kegonshu* (*Todaiji* Temple in Nara),[5] *Hossoshu* (*Yakushiji* Temple in Nara), *Risshu* (*Toshodaiji* Temple in Nara), Tendaishu (*Enryakuji* Temple in Shiga), *Shingonshu* (*Kongobuji* Temple in Wakayama), *Joudoshu* (*Chion'in* Temple in Kyoto), *Joudo-shinshu* (*Higashi-Honganji* and *Nishi-Honganji* Temple in Kyoto), *Yuzu-nen-butsushu* (*Dainenbutsuji* Temple in Osaka), *Jishu* (*Yugyoji* Temple in Kanagawa), *Nichirenshu* (*Kuonji* Temple in Yamanashi), *Soutoushu* (*Eiheiji* Temple in Fukui), *Rinzaishu* (*Shokokuji* Temple in Kyoto) and *Oubakushu* (*Manpukuji* Temple in Kyoto), and each sect is often divided into several subsects.

It is sometimes said that there are thirteen traditional sects and fifty-six subsects in Japan. Buddhism was originally brought into Japan in the sixth century, and a number of time-honored temples, which were designated as UNESCO's World Cultural Heritages, remain intact in Kyoto and Nara. However, various famous monks including St. Honen (*Jodoshu*), St. Shinran (*Jodoshinshu*) and St. Nichiren (*Nichirenshu*) formulated their own doctrines in the *Kamakura* Period (1192–1333) and established new sects mainly to meet people's desire for spiritual awakening in the new era governed not by the Imperial Court but by the Warrior Class (*Samurai* Class). These traditional Buddhist sects in Japan are based fundamentally on the teachings of Gautama (Buddha) and the doctrines of the founder of each sect which are systematic interpretations of Buddha's teachings by the sects, but the believers are usually organized in accordance with rather generous precepts which are not so strict as to cause conflicting relations among the believers of different Buddhist sects or *Shinto* believers. Becoming a bonze or taking holy orders is the most fundamental religious way of living as Buddhists, but people are more loosely regarded as believers in Buddhism if they are found to be observing traditional Buddhist customs on the occasion of the deaths of their relatives.

Japan, as a matter of fact, has a long history of syncretization of *Shinto* with Buddhism,[6] and the boundary between *Shinto* and Buddhism is rather ambiguous today. It is not rare that a family has a Buddhist altar and a *Shinto* altar at the same time, and very many people do not feel a sense of incongruity to celebrate marriage in *Shinto* rites and to conduct the funeral service of relatives in Buddhist rites.

Again in *Shinto*, all things were thought to be created by *Kami* (divinity, *Shinto* God), and *kami* dwells in all things that exist in the universe. Usually, a shrine is built as a core of faith in *Shinto* and holy objects such as mountain, tree, land, etc., which have a special connection with the shrine, are worshiped as *Goshintai*, which literally means 'The *Kami's* Body.'[7] Furthermore, the shrine is decorated with sacred *Shinto* straw festoons, which indicate that the site is a holy precinct.

In the late seventh century, the state of Japan was firmly buttressed on the basis of emperor (*Tenno*)-centered ideology, and a hierarchy of *Kami* with *Amaterasu Omikami*,[8] the tutelary *Kami* of the emperor's family, and the people's faith was organized as a national religion to support the ruling system with the emperor in the center.

Even though a conflict between the pro-*Shinto* group and the pro-Buddhism group had already arisen since the introduction of Buddhism into Japan in the mid-sixth century, *Shoutokutaishi* (Prince Shoutoku) highly valued Buddhism and this subsequently became an important element to protect the nation from calamity.[9] At the beginning of the eighth century, *Jinguji* temples began to be built to protect shrines of national importance, and in some cases Buddhist saints were defined as *Goshintai* of shrines. From the eighth to the ninth century, *Shinto* gods in different regional communities manifested their belief in Buddhism in succession and *Jinguji* temples were often constructed by *Shinto* shrines to protect them. In those days, Buddhist monks chanted the sutras in front of the altars of *Shinto* shrines. In the tenth century, Buddhism proposed a unified interpretation of *Shinto's Kami* and the Buddha-named Theory of *Honji-suijaku*, which means 'original nature and provisional manifestation.' The theory was an attempt to relate the Buddha with the *Kami* (divinity) of the native *Shinto* by maintaining that the Buddha is the true nature of spiritual beings while the *Kami* is its provisional manifestation. However, the *Shinto* priests had dissatisfaction because they felt that *Kami* had been reduced to a mere expedient to set off Buddhism to advantage.

Formation of state *Shinto*

Thus, Buddhism* and *Shinto* were apparently in consistent harmony for many centuries until the *Meiji* Restoration of 1868. In that year, the *Meiji* government

---

*   Ed. For a broader picture of Buddha and his philosophy, see Chapter 12 by Swami Veda Bharati and Chapter 13 by Karma Lekshe Tsomo.

replaced the *Tokugawa Shogunate* under the slogan of 'Restoration of the Imperial Regime'[10] and adopted the reactionary *Shinto* ideology as a guiding political principle, by which the government was not only the executer of political power, but at the same time also the presider of national religious services.

In 1868, the *Meiji* government carried out a policy to strictly separate Buddhism from *Shinto*, which was an approach to make the *Shinto* a state religion of modern Japan. As a result, there arose a nationwide movement to demolish Buddhist statues, and deifying Buddhist statues as *Goshintai* (object of worship) of shrines was forbidden in order to completely wipe out the Buddhist tinge from the *Shinto* shrines. In the same year, and in accordance with the policy to nationalize the shrines, the government uncivilly suppressed the Christians in Japan. It also decided in the *Gozenkaigi* (Imperial Conference)[11] to exile 3394 Christians in Urakami Village, Nagasaki Prefecture, to twenty-two different districts in western Japan and ignored strong protests of the consuls from different countries.

In 1869, the *Meiji* government revived the institutionalization of the *Shinto* priest system that had existed in ancient Japan, and the following year, the Constitution of the Empire of Japan was promulgated.[12] Accordingly, *Shinto* was positioned as the national religion serving as a special moral norm and being exceptionally distinguished from other religions. In 1899, the Religion Bill was submitted to the House of Peers for the first time, but it was voted down. Similar Bills were proposed in the Diet in 1927 and 1929, but they were also put on the shelf. Finally, in 1939 when the Second World War broke out, the Religious Organization Regulation Law was enacted to provide a legal cover to comprehensively regulate religions in the Empire of Japan. This legal system continued to be valid until the unconditional surrender of Japan in 1945. From the beginning of the *Meiji* Era in 1868 to the end of the Pacific War in 1945, *Shinto* was especially called *Kokka Shinto* (State *Shinto*), and during this period the Japanese government put a special value on the utilization of *Shinto* for mobilizing people toward its war policy.

In the Constitution of the Empire of Japan, freedom of religion was admitted as a matter of form, but the government asserted that the State *Shinto*-led national policy did not undertake the invasion of freedom of religion by obstinately insisting that *Shinto* was not a religion. However, as a matter of fact, this State *Shinto* policy was vigorously pursued in close connection with militarism and nationalism, and it played an important ideological role in supporting imperial supremacy by interpreting the emperor as *The Living God*.

Since 1939, when the Religious Organization Regulation Law (or Religious Organization Law) was enacted, *Shokonsha* Shrine meaning 'shrine to invite the spirit of the deceased who died for the nation' was built in many parts of the country, and was later renamed *Gokoku Jinja*, which means 'shrines to protect the nation.' The Tokyo *Shokonsha* Shrine, built in 1869, was renamed *Yasukuni Jinja* (*Yasukuni* Shrine) meaning 'the shrine for national peace.' It was managed jointly by the Ministry of Army and the Ministry of Navy and the personnel was directly nominated by the Secretary of State for Home Affairs. In addition, *Yasukuni* Shrine was presumed to be the symbol of the State *Shinto*, and supported financially by the Ministry of Army. Religious rites conducted at *Yasukuni* Shrine were mastered by military and naval officers. During the so-called Fifteen Year War, which began on September 18, 1931 by the Manchurian Incident and ended on September 2, 1945 by the unconditional surrender of Japan, *Yasukuni* Shrine played a crucially important role as a spiritual engine to drive the whole nation toward aggressive wars.

Fifteen-Years War and State *Shinto*

From Edo Era to Meiji Era

In 1868, Japan experienced a revolutionary change from the *Edo* Era of 'Warrior Politics' (*Samurai* Class Politics) to the *Meiji* Era of 'Imperial Politics.' The Emperor *Meiji* announced the Five-Point Imperial Oath in the formality of vowing to *Kami* (*Shinto* God).[13] These were: (a) all things are to be discussed and decided in open meetings; (b) national orders must be strengthened by the cooperation of upper and lower ranges of society; (c) public officials, soldiers and commoners should set aims in life, never give up and never be idle; (d) people should get rid of old incorrect customs and conduct in rational ways; and (e) people should seek for new wisdom and knowledge from all over the world and activate the Imperial Nation. At first glance, the Imperial Oath seems to be 'democratic, rational and international,' but it was not. As such, there emerged social movements demanding freedom and people's rights. Eventually the Imperial Diet was established in 1890, and a great deal of effort was made to introduce Western cultures. However, the fact of the matter was that the Imperial Oath was announced in the form of the emperor's vowing, not to the people, but to the *Kami* and the construction of an emperor-centered political regime was promoted rapidly.

In 1869, the government ordered all the feudal clans to return their 'land' and 'people' to the Imperial Court, and established a centralized national regime. In the same year, an old social stratum of warriors–farmers–artisans–tradesmen was replaced apparently by an idea of equality, but there still remained a hierarchic stratum of peers–aristocrats–commoners and serious social discrimination against *buraku* people continued.[14]

In 1871, '*han*' (traditional feudal domain) were abolished, 'prefectures' were established and the government appointed the prefectural governors.[15] In 1873, the conscription system was legalized to be able to draft adult men by the order of the state.

Characteristics of the Meiji Constitution

The regime characterized by the emperor-centered absolutism was finally completed by the establishment of the Constitution of the Empire of Japan (*Meiji* Constitution) in 1889, which, however, was not established by the people, but was bestowed by the emperor on the people of Japan. The *Meiji* Constitution had two different faces, Constitutionalism and Absolutism. Although these two elements are not compatible, the *Meiji* Constitution tried to give the emperor absolute authority in the name of the Constitution thereby realizing the Constitutional Monarchy.

For instance, Article 1 of the *Meiji* Constitution stipulated that the emperor rules the Empire of Japan. In other words, sovereignty does not rest with the people but with the emperor. Likewise, Article 3 stipulated that the emperor is sacred and can never be violated, and the emperor was equated with *Arahitogami* (The Living God). This Article was the central element of the imperial regime based on State *Shinto*. Although Article 4 stipulated that the emperor rules the Empire of Japan by the Constitution, the emperor was given absolute authority including convocation, opening, closing and dissolution of the Diet (Article 7), issuing Imperial Ordinances when the Diet is not in session (Article 8), commanding armed forces (Article 11), declaring war, making peace and concluding treaties (Article 13) and imposing martial law to restrict people's rights when necessary (Article 14).

Of course, there are significant constitutional elements that project the constitution as visibly democratic. These include: (a) respective independence of the three institutions of governance–legislation (Imperial Diet), administration (ministers of state) and judiciary (court of justice); (b) public election system for the members of the House of Representatives; and (c) the Diet's authority to propose and approve the enactment of laws. However, as a matter of fact, the government did not adequately guarantee freedom of the people. In 1890, it issued 'The Imperial Message on Education,' which guided the people toward a way of living to sacrifice themselves for the sake of the emperor.[16] It became more and more difficult for the people to live liberally as independent individuals, and State *Shinto* symbolized by *Yasukuni* Shrine and *Gokoku* Shrine in regional communities played a crucial role in the promotion of such a self-sacrificing way of living together with a kind of nationalistic education, which was carried out in close relation to State *Shinto*.

The Imperial Message on education and the Sino-Japanese War

Here one may refer to the Imperial Message. The Imperial Message on Education is a set of messages addressed by the emperor to the people and these were fundamentally based on Confucianism and State *Shinto*, which valued filial piety, brotherly/sisterly affection, happy married life and requested people to bravely serve the emperor in case of national crisis and devote their lives to the prosperity of the emperor-centered nation. The Ministry of Education distributed this Imperial Message to the schools throughout the country, which were instructed to read out the message during school events. Next year, the Ministry of Education ordered every school to have custody of the Imperial Message and the photographs of the emperor and the empress, called *Goshin'ei*, which means 'The Genuine Figure.' Later, the government obliged each school to build a special building called *Houanden* for solemnly revering *The Goshin'ei*. The pupils were asked to make a vow when they passed by the *Houanden* to express their allegiance to the emperor.

In 1894, the Sino-Japanese War broke out and Imperial Japan sent troops to the Korean Peninsula to fight against the Chin Dynasty (China). It was in response to the request of the Korean government to suppress the large-scale riots in Korea caused by a new anti-Christianity religious group then growing to support the farmers in agony. Japan won the war, and in 1895 concluded a peace treaty named *Shimonoseki* Treaty with Chin Dynasty by which Japan obtained Liaodong Peninsula, Taiwan and Pénghú Islands in addition to China's consent of the independence of Korea. But, Russia strongly opposed the advance of Japanese military forces to Liandong Peninsula and demanded that Japan should return the Peninsula to China in cooperation with Germany and France. Japan finally accepted this demand and obtained approximately 300 million yen from China as reparations, which was later used for the establishment of the government-owned *Yahata* Steel Manufacturing Factory to modernize Japan's industrial capacity.

From the Russo-Japanese War to the First World War

The European countries advanced to China after the Sino-Japanese War, which triggered a resistance movement known as the Boxer Uprising, i.e. an anti-foreign and anti-Christian movement by the Society of Righteousness and Harmonious Fists (*Yihe tuan*). In 1900, the insurgent groups surrounded legations of European countries in Beijing and killed the German minister, but the revolt was finally suppressed by the troops sent by eight countries. Russia dispatched its legion to the Manchurian region, which considerably alarmed the UK and Japan. They became apprehensive of Russian expansion into the Korean Peninsula, and subsequently the Anglo-Japanese Alliance Treaty was concluded. In 1904 Japan declared war on Russia in the name of defending Japanese interests in Korea, and won the war. As a result, Japan obtained the southern half of Sakhalin, the South Manchuria Railway[17] and the Kwantung Leased Territory of Russia in China.

In 1910, Japan colonized Korea, and established its overall rule over the Korean Peninsula. Since Japan's national power and status was recognized by the developed Western countries, Japan began to develop its foreign policies with increasing interest in external territories and entered into competition with European nations.

Around this time the European countries, which had developed modern production systems after the industrial revolution, were expanding their colonies to profit from cheap raw materials and labor force, and competing with one another. The Sarajevo Incident in 1914 triggered the escalation of confrontation among European nations and consequently the First World War flared up between the Entente Powers initially consisting of France, the UK, Russia and their associated empires and dependencies, whereas the Central Powers initially consisted of Germany, Austria-Hungary and their associated empires. Later Japan joined the Entente Powers together with Italy and the USA, and attacked and occupied German territories in China and South Seas. The war ended in 1918 with the victory of the Entente Powers, and the Versailles Treaty was concluded in 1919 in Paris between Germany and the Entente Powers. Japan inherited German interests in the *Kiaochou* Bay and the *Shandong* Province in China and the South Sea Islands, and became one of the permanent members of the League of Nations, which was established after the termination of the First World War.

From the dawn of the Showa era to global economic panic

During the First World War, the people of Japan did not experience any war damage because Japan was so distant from the battlefields. As the war escalated, exports from Japan to European, Asian and African countries rapidly increased, and industries especially in the fields of steel manufacturing, shipbuilding and electric machinery prospered. But, after the war exports from Japan decreased as European economies revived from the ruin, and serious economic depression was rampant in Japan. Bankruptcy of enterprises and unemployment of workers gravely threatened Japanese society. Worse still, the damage caused by the Great Kanto Earthquake on September 1, 1923 was enormous. Some 100,000 people died and the damage amounted to about 6.5 billion Japanese yen (70 million US dollars).

In the field of politics, a 'Party Cabinet System' was established in Japan in which ministries other than the Ministry for War and the Ministry for Navy were occupied by the politicians from the political parties. At that time, voting rights were limited to adult men who paid a certain prescribed amount of tax. In 1925, the Universal Suffrage Law gave voting rights to all men older than 25 years of age, and the number of voters increased approximately four times, but women were not given suffrage. Moreover, the Privy Council, an advisory organ to the emperor, feared the growth of social movements, and pressed the Diet to enact the Maintenance of the Public Order Act (or Peace Preservation Law) to crack down on the activists demanding social change.[18]

In October 1929 the Wall Street stock market in New York crashed, causing an unprecedented financial panic, announcing the beginning of long-term global depression. The USA had prospered after the First World War owing to a rapid growth in the automobile industry and the expansion of export ties with

European countries, which were severely damaged by the war. But the gradual recovery of European countries reduced their imports from the USA, and US agriculture suffered overproduction. Meanwhile, the USSR had left the capital market and had become a socialist state, and the buying power of the capitalistic countries could not retrieve in such a short period of time. Additionally, investment in the stock market superheated and the US economy was reduced to a bubble economy. Within one week, the US stock market lost about 30 billion US dollars, an amount ten times larger than the US national budget and even larger than the war expenditure during the First World War. The collapse of the US economy caused the economic breakdown of the countries dependent on it. Germany, which was required to pay enormous amounts of reparations, was confronted with a social crisis due to an extraordinary inflation with a steep rise in commodity prices, and about six million people lost their jobs. In such a chaotic situation, the *Nationalsozialistische Deutsche Arbeiterpartei* was gaining power by raising the slogan of 'Reconstruction of Germany,' and Adolf Hitler, leader of the National Socialists, finally came to power. Undertaking a series of violent initiatives, Hitler excited the German people and embarked upon a program of territorial expansionism in the late 1930s.

Around this time, a large number of Japanese enterprises had gone bankrupt, and the streets were full of jobless people. Prices of commodities fell rapidly because of the decline in the purchasing power of the consumers. Damage to crops from the cold weather additionally brought malnutrition caused by shortage of food. These soon became very serious social problems. Workers and farmers earnestly cried out in pain, but the government changed the Public Order Act for the worse by introducing the death penalty as the heaviest punishment for those who negated *Kokutai*, the emperor-centered National Structure,[19] and reinforced control over the social movements by *Tokkou*, the Special Higher Police. The Manchurian Incident was ignited by the *Kanto* Army, the Japanese Imperial Army stationed in Manchuria, on September 18, 1931 under the slogan 'Manchuria is the lifeline of Japan.' Manchukou was founded on March 1, 1932 and the Japanese government gradually adopted an aggressive policy toward mainland China.

Fifteen Years War

Having been plunged into the depths of economic depression, Japan planned for a scenario to forcibly acquire natural resources by advancing into China, increasing exportation and stabilizing national life. The foundation of Manchukou was not accepted internationally, and Japan withdrew from the League of Nations in 1933. The country thus became more and more isolated from international communities.

Gradually, the party government system decayed and the military grew more and more powerful. In 1935, a book entitled *Emperor Organ Theory* authored by

Tatsukichi Minobe was criticized as clearly treasonable, and the government banned the sale of the book.[20] According to Minobe, even the emperor was no sacred power beyond the state but only an organ of the state. This theory was regarded as dangerous for maintaining the emperor-centered absolute monarchy, and the government began to ruthlessly suppress the freedom of speech. On February 26, 1936, young army officers executed a coup and killed political leaders including the Finance Minister, Lord Keeper of the Privy Seal and Inspector-General of Military Education, which resulted in the expansion of the political influence of military authorities.

On July 7, 1937, the Marco Polo Bridge Incident, a military conflict between Japanese and Chinese troops, occurred in the suburbs of Beijing, China. Since the Boxer Uprising in 1900, Japan had sent troops to mainland China for the ostensible purpose of guarding Japan's legation. The situation worsened and developed into an all-out war between Japan and China. Japan dispatched massive military forces to China, but was tenaciously resisted by the people of China. As a result, the war protracted for many years with tragic consequences for combatants and non-combatants alike. In December 1937, the Nanjing Massacre Incident, caused by Japanese military forces, killed a large (but unknown) number of Chinese people. The incident, one may note, is still one of the most controversial and sensitive issues between the peoples of the two countries.[21] One year later, in 1938, the Japanese government enacted the General Mobilization Law calling for the involvement of the whole society into the war efforts and optimum utilization of all resources including natural resources, industries and human resources. The State *Shinto* played an essentially important role in strengthening the war regime and in drumming up war hysteria.

In 1939, Germany invaded Poland, triggering large-scale military conflicts in Europe. Japan hurried forward to construct a powerful national system for the war to come, and *Taisei-Yokusan-Kai* (Imperial Rule Assistance Association/ Imperial Aid Association) was organized in 1940 to remove sectionalism in the fields of politics and economics and to bring together different political groups to mobilize the whole nation for war. Rapidly enough, the Empire of Japan was converted into a single political party state. It then entered into a military alliance with Germany and Italy by concluding the Tripartite Pact, which meant the formation of Axis Powers opposing the Allied Powers. As a step for establishing the Great East Asia Co-Prosperity Sphere, Japan further advanced military forces to the Indochina Peninsula to exploit natural resources such as petroleum and rubber needed for fighting wars, but it was strongly objected to by the USA, the UK and the Netherlands.

In October 1941, Hideki Tojo was appointed as Prime Minister of Japan. Already in the previous year, he had issued 'The Instruction for the Battlefield' called *Senjinkun*, in the name of the then War Minister, which forbade surrender and plainly suggested to the Imperial soldiers that surrender was a disgrace and it was worse than death. The instruction listed a number of exhortations about military regulations, combatants' preparedness, esprit de corps, etc., among which was veneration of *Kami* (*Shinto* God).

On December 8, 1942 (Japan standard time), Japan assaulted Pearl Harbor, Hawaii, after the attack on the Malay Peninsula, and opened hostilities against the USA and the UK. Prime Minister Tojo then concurrently held the posts of Minister of Foreign Affairs (1942), Minister of Education, Minister of Commerce and Industry, Minister of Munitions (1943) and Chief of the General Staff (1944). The people were exhausted by the long-ranging wars, suffering from extreme shortage in supplies for daily life and experiencing intolerable difficulties in making a living. Having been almost completely deprived of their freedom, separated from their blood relatives and compelled to endure the poorest life under the slogan of 'Luxury is the enemy,' 'We want nothing until victory,' 'Sacrifice yourself for the nation at sacred war,' etc., people were driven to colossal hardship because of the National Spiritual Mobilization Movement. Japan's defeat in the Battle of Midway in 1942 drastically changed the tide of the Pacific War and finally cornered Japan into difficulties even in securing the Absolute National Defense Sphere prescribed in the war direction scheme in 1943. On Saipan Island, approximately 30,000 Japanese Imperial soldiers 'died in honor' (*Gyokusai*) in 1944. *Gyokusai* is a glorified word meaning 'being fragmented into gem-looking beautiful pieces,' but the reality was undoubtedly 'deaths in vain.' The US military forces occupied Saipan, Tenian and Guam Islands, and constructed airbases to make direct air raids to mainland Japan.

Japan's defeat and the collapse of the State Shinto System

Japan was comprehensively and mercilessly destroyed by air raids and bombardments by warships. Indiscriminate bombing on the non-combatants escalated especially during 1945. The bombing of Tokyo on March 10 killed some 100,000 people overnight. US troops landed on Okinawa Islands in April 1945 and resorted to fierce bombardments. Often described as 'Typhoon of Steel' or 'Iron Storm,' the bombardment caused the death of friend and foe amounting to more than 200,000. After the victorious operation in Okinawa, the Allied Powers sent the Potsdam Declaration to Japan on July 26, urging unconditional surrender, but Japan did not respond positively. The USA used two nuclear weapons for the first time in human history, one on Hiroshima (August 6, uranium bomb) and the other on Nagasaki (August 9, plutonium bomb) which killed more than 300,000 people. About 240,000 A-bomb survivors are still living, and many of them are suffering from physical, mental and social difficulties.[22]

On August 15, 1945, the Emperor of Imperial Japan made an announcement over the radio about the acceptance of the Potsdam Declaration (so called 'The Imperial Rescript on the Termination of the War'). During the last twenty days from the issuance of the Potsdam Declaration by Allied Powers to Japan's acceptance, at least 380,000 Japanese people lost their lives due to the hesitation of Japanese leaders in power who had a strong apprehension about the preservation of the emperor's status, the preservation of *Kokutai* (Emperor-centered National Structure). The Imperial Rescript of the end of war also began by referring to the preservation of *Kokutai*, belief in immortality of *Shinshuu* (God's Land or Country of Divinity) and the full activation of the essence of *Kokutai*. This was almost the ultimate destination of the emperor-centered modern Japan firmly based on the spirit of State *Shinto*. On September 2, 1945, Japan officially signed the Instrument of Surrender on the US battleship *Missouri* at anchor in Tokyo Bay, which was the final moment of the end of the Pacific War and the Second World War.

The General Headquarters (GHQ) of the Allied Powers immediately initiated the war termination process and took a series of steps to deal with Japan after its defeat. It adopted an indirect governing system, in which the Japanese government carried out the policies ordered by the GHQ. Considering Japanese leaders' aspiration for the preservation of *Kokutai*, the GHQ did not abolish the *Tenno* System (Emperor System), but made use of the emperor as a centripetal force for ruling postwar Japanese society by giving the emperor a status of 'the Symbol of the Unity of the People,' an idea propounded by a Japanese jurist.[23]

A public opinion poll carried out in December 1945 showed that 95 percent of the Japanese people supported the Emperor System. There was a strong opinion in the USA that the Emperor of Japan was a war criminal, and the Gallup Poll in June 1945, shortly before the termination of the war, revealed that 33 percent of US citizens were in favor of the execution of the emperor, 11 percent favored life imprisonment, 9 percent exile and 17 percent were in favor of putting him on trial. The predominant viewpoint in the US government was not for supporting, but for making use of, the emperor.

In December 1945, the GHQ ordered the abolition of the State *Shinto* and put an end to the subjects in school education such as *Shuushin* (Morals), Japanese History and Geography, which were taught in close relation with the State *Shinto*. In 1946, the emperor issued 'The Imperial Rescript on the Construction of New Japan' and 'The Imperial Rescript on National Revitalization.' Popularly known as the Humanity Declaration, it was essentially a sort of assertion that the emperor was not the Living God but a human being. Soon afterwards, the State *Shinto* disappeared institutionally and *Shinto* shrines protected by Imperial Japan became ordinary shrines having the same legal status as religious places of other religions.

The *Yasukuni* Shrine in the contemporary context

As mentioned earlier, the *Yasukuni* Shrine was established in 1869 as Tokyo *Shokonsha* Shrine meaning 'shrine for inviting the spirit of the deceased who died for the nation.' It was renamed *Yasukuni* Shrine in 1879. The Shrine was under the joint control of the army and navy, and enshrined those who sacrificed themselves for the emperor and the Empire of Japan as *Gunshin* (God of War). One of the members of the special attack corps popularly known as *Kamikaze* (Divine Wind) wrote a *tanka*, a thirty-one-syllable Japanese poem, when he made a sortie for Okinawa Land Battle, referring to his soul blooming fragrantly in *Yasukuni* Shrine.

The Shrine played a very important role in preparing and mobilizing the whole nation for aggressive wars, and it is often called a 'War Shrine' in Western countries. As is well known, the *Yasukuni* has also been enshrining military leaders who were declared Class-A war criminals by the International Military Tribunal for the Far East (IMTFE). Although there may be room for further discussions about the fairness of the IMTFE, cabinet members' official visits to *Yasukuni* Shrine may have significance beyond the question of religious freedom, and may be a sort of litmus test regarding the official attitude towards the past wars conducted by Japan.

Since the cabinet system was first established in 1885, fourteen out of fifty-nine prime ministers have visited the *Yasukuni* Shrine as of February 2009. No prime minister before the end of the Pacific War ever visited the Shrine, but fourteen out of thirty prime ministers (47 percent) in the postwar period (1945–2009) have paid visits to *Yasukuni*. The people of the neighboring countries have strongly criticized the visit of Japanese cabinet members to *Yasukuni* Shrine on the following grounds: (a) *Yasukuni* Shrine was the source of spiritual motive force to propel aggressive war policies; (b) *Yasukuni* Shrine is not the facility to remember the memories of war victims, but the facility to enshrine the war dead as heroes; (c) *Yasukuni* Shrine does not seem to admit aggressiveness of Japan during the Fifteen Years War. According to its website, 'All the enshrined divinities in *Yasukuni* Shrine are those who gave their lives to the nation to defend Japan with the sincere hope to attain everlasting peace just as His Majesty the Emperor hoped' (Yasukuni Jinja, 2009). 'War is truly sorrowful. Yet to maintain the independence and peace of the nation and for the prosperity of all Asia, Japan was forced into conflict' (Yasukuni Shrine, 2009). The museum *Yushukan* also displays artifacts, photos and panels based on the viewpoints that the museum is the facility 'where visitors can touch the spirit of dead soldiers who confronted national crisis to defend their mother country, hometown and family' (Yasukuni Shrine, 2009). The museum is internationally regarded as a social facility for popularizing the *Yasukuni* view of history that contradicts globally recognized historical views on the aggressiveness of Japan's wars.

Concluding remarks

The story of the State *Shinto* in modern Japan is a typical example of national abuse of religion. Japanese political leaders converted traditional *Shinto* into a state religion, and improperly used it to mobilize the whole nation towards aggressive wars by institutionalizing the emperor as the Living *Shinto* God never to be profaned. Politics and religion were inseparably combined, and political messages were sent to the people in the name of the institutionalized Living *Shinto* God. The rightless people of the Empire of Japan could not effectively push back such structural violence, because they were totally isolated from the international communities and could not find a road to access the people beyond the borders, to develop solidarity and cooperation for wisely overcoming difficulties. The results were horrible. Tens of millions of people were killed. Cities, towns and villages were devastated. Peaceful relations between nations were thoroughly destroyed. Grudge and hatred were deeply implanted and still prevent people from developing partnership, for realizing a more peaceful community in which human rights – including freedom of religion – will prosper. It is expected that we should share lessons from our histories in a most frank way and tax our ingenuity for finding solutions to a number of serious questions we now confront.

Needless to say, *Shinto* itself is not militant in its nature, just like science is not either. Science can be used for peace and at the same time for war. The Japanese people know about the tremendous destructive power of atomic bombs that were developed by science, but the evilness of nuclear weapons cannot be attributed to science itself. Science and religion have often been used for evil purposes; therefore, we must always be careful about the value to be pursued in all human activities, including science and religion. For Japanese militarists, it was valuable to utilize State *Shinto* for mobilizing the whole nation for aggressive wars, and for the US military authorities it was important to develop nuclear weapons that had unprecedented power to destroy Japan in retaliation for the surprise attack on Pearl Harbor.

Finally, I would like to narrate two experiences regarding the role of *Shinto* in contemporary times.

In 1995, I was asked to supervise the renewal project of the Nagasaki Atomic Bomb Museum. The City Mayor of Nagasaki expected me to exhibit not only the facts resulting from the explosion of a plutonium bomb at 11:02 a.m. on August 9, 1945, but also the historical background prior to the atomic bombing on the city. A small corner named C1 was set up in the museum for briefly sketching the course of the so-called Fifteen Years War: from the Manchurian Incident in 1931 to Japan's Unconditional Surrender in 1945, including the Nanjing Massacre Incident of 1937. Then, the citizens' group *Hinomaru-kai*[24] (The Rising Sun Flag Association) headed by a *Shinto* priest of a well-known shrine in Nagasaki[25] found fault with the reliability of a photograph regarding the Nanjing Incident, and filed a lawsuit against the city to demonstrate the unreasonableness of paying a reward to the supervisor. I was called to the court in testimony, and the city finally won the suit. But this was one scene of the reactionary movements carried out by the revisionists in Japan to deter peace museum workers from displaying the facts of aggression by Japanese military forces.

On the other hand, I know a number of *Shinto* Shrines that have been making efforts for peace and nuclear disarmament. I have often been asked to send a peace message to the memorial gathering held in August at *Ueno Toshoguu* Shrine, which has been preserving 'The Flame of Hiroshima and Nagasaki.' The flame was lit in 1990 in this Shrine by combining the two flames originating from the A-bombed areas in Hiroshima and Nagasaki, and has been maintained as a symbol of a wish to abolish nuclear weapons.[26]

Shinto preaches that *Kami* (divinity) dwells in every being. People's veneration for divinity dwelling in all creatures can play a role in spreading a philosophy to hold a high regard for lives, together with the Buddhist way of thinking which highly values harmonious coexistence with all living creatures.

Notes

1. According to the CIA World Fact Book, 84–96 percent of the Japanese population adhere to *Shinto* and Buddhism and only 4–16 percent of the population believe in other religions or have no religions to believe in.
2. In Japanese, the word *hatsu* means 'first' and *mairi* 'visiting a shrine.' *Hatsu-mairi* is 'the first visit to a shrine' after the birth of a baby.
3. *Shichi* means 'seven,' *Go* 'five' and *San* 'three.' *Shichi-Go-San* is the celebration for boys turning five years old and girls three and seven years. For this celebration, people generally visit a shrine on November 15. In the Chinese culture, odd numbers are said to be lucky. There are other reasons behind these numbers, which are peculiar to Japanese culture of the older times.
4. *Hatsu-moude* is the celebration of visiting a shrine or a temple for the first time of the year, usually between January 1 and 3. The number of visitors to a famous shrine or a temple during these three days normally exceeds two million.
5. The name of the temple shown in parenthesis is an example of a typical temple of each sect.
6. Syncretization of *Shinto* with Buddhism or fusion of *Shinto* and Buddhism is called *Shin-Butsu-Shuugou*. *Shin* is connected to *Kami*, the *Shinto* God, *Butsu* means Buddha and *Shuugou* means 'reconstruction of a system by syncretizing or fusing different elements.'
7. *Goshintai* is 'the object for worship:' *go* standing for 'the honorific prefix, *shin* meaning *Kami* and *tai* the 'body.'
8. *Amaterasu-OmiKami* means 'Great God lightening the heaven:' *Ama* is 'heaven,' *Terasu* means 'to lighten' and *OmiKami* the 'Great God.'
9. Shotukutaishi is also known as Prince *Umayado* (573–621), who was a regent and also a politician of the *Asuka* Era. Besides being known as a proponent of Buddhism, he is also famous for the promulgation of the so-called 'Seventeen Article Constitution.'
10. 'Restoration of the Imperial Regime' is called *Ousei-Fukko* in Japanese: *Ousei* means 'Imperial regime' and *Fukko* the 'returning to the old times/restoration,' a political

change achieved by a declaration of 'Direct Government by the Emperor' and schemed by the Anti-*Shogunate* Group (January 3, 1868).

11. The literal translation of *Gozen-kaigi* is 'the conference in front of the noble face (the Emperor):' *Gozen* means 'before a person of high ranking' and *kaigi* 'conference, meeting, congress.' The *Meiji* government made decisions about daily affairs by the prime minister-headed cabinet system, but decisions concerning critical affairs such as declaration of wars were formally made in the conference attended by the emperor, the *Gozen-kaigi*, which was extra-constitutional. The conference was usually attended by the Prime Minister, Minister of Foreign Affairs, Minister of Finance, Minister of the Army, Minister of the Navy, President of the Planning Board, Chief of the Army General Staff, and Chief of the Navy General Staff.

12. 'The Constitution of the Empire of Japan' is often simply called '*Meiji* Constitution' or 'Imperial Constitution.'

13. 'Five-Point Imperial Oath' is *Gokajo-no-Goseimon* in Japanese: *Gokajo* meaning 'five articles,' *no* meaning 'conjunction (of)' and *Goseimon* 'Oath.' It is sometimes translated as 'Oath in Five Articles' or simply 'Charter Oath.' It was promulgated at the enthronement of Emperor Meiji on April 7, 1868.

14. The word *buraku* originally meant 'village, community or hamlet,' but in Japan the word has often been used as 'socially discriminated community' or 'community that has not been liberated yet.' Although *buraku* was legally liberated in 1871 by the abolition of the feudal caste system, violation of human rights such as social prejudice and discrimination against *buraku* persisted until recent years.

15. *Han* was the traditional feudal domain ruled by the feudal lord (*daimyo*). The Imperial *Han* System was replaced by the 'Prefecture System' in 1871 by the Imperial Government in order to introduce centralized government authority. All feudal lords had to return their authority to the Emperor Meiji.

16. 'The Imperial Message on Education' was called *Kyoiku-chokugo* in Japanese. *Kyoiku* means 'education' and *chokugo* 'words spoken by the emperor.' The role played by *Kyoiku-chokugo* to obtain the loyalty of the Japanese people for the emperor was immense and immeasurable.

17. The South Manchuria Railway was often called *Mantetsu* which is the abbreviation of *Minami-Manshuu-Tetsudou*: *Minami* means 'South,' *Manshuu* 'Manchuria' and *Tetsudou* means 'railway.' The South Manchuria Railway Company was established in 1906 after the Russo-Japanese War (1904–1905) in Japan, but it actually operated in China in the South Manchuria Railway Zone controlled by the Empire of Japan.

18. 'The Maintenance of the Public Order Act' or 'Peace Preservation Law' is the literal translation of the Japanese term *Chian-iji-hou*. *Chian* means 'peace, security, order,' *iji* 'maintenance, preservation, keeping' and *hou* 'law.' The translated words give an impression of 'peaceful and orderly' rule, but the actual role played by the law was tremendously violent, never peaceful. More than 70,000 people were arrested between 1925 and 1945, and it is said that some 194 captors died during interrogation and lynching and more than 1500 captors died of illness in prison.

19. *Kokutai* was one of the most important keywords to explain the politics of the government of Japan during the war periods. *Koku* means 'nation' and *tai* 'body, structure, system, form,' hence *Kokutai* originally means 'national structure.' But when this word is used, it strongly means 'emperor-centered national structure on which the Empire of Japan exists.'

20. 'Emperor Organ Theory' by Tatsukichi Minobe (1873–1948) was first published in 1912. Minobe was a scholar of constitutional law and entered the House of Peers in

1932. One year after his resignation, he was seriously injured by a ruffian who had felt outrage because of Minobe's 'Emperor Organ Theory.'

21. The number of people who were massacred by Japanese military forces in Nanjing is still controversial. On the wall of the Nanjing Massacre Museum, the number 300,000 is resolutely displayed. See *Definition of Peace, Peace Museum and Museum for Peace with Reference to Peace-Related Museums in Asia* (Anzai et al., 2008).

22. The author of this paper, Ikuro Anzai, is originally a scientist majoring in radiation protection, and has been supporting A-bomb survivors (*hibakusha*) for more than thirty years. About 300 *hibakusha* have been bringing lawsuits against central government for demanding official certification of their disorders as A-bomb diseases. As a specialist of radiological health science, the author made testimonies for *hibakusha* before the court five times within twenty years.

23. Yasuzo Suzuki (1904–1983), researcher on constitutional law, greatly contributed to drafting a new constitution of Japan which was highly evaluated by the GHQ. Regarding the emperor's legal status, he wrote in his draft 'The Emperor administers national rites by the people's trust.'

24. The word *hinomaru* consists of *hi*, meaning 'the sun' and *maru* 'circle,' which is the national flag of Japan. *Hinomaru* was the symbol of the Empire of Japan together with *Kimigayo* (the national anthem). Many people who had hard war experiences were not able to get over the bitter memories in connection with *Hinomaru* and *Kimigayo*. On the contrary, many people who still admire the emperor-centered Ruling Regime highly value *Hinomaru* and *Kimigayo*, and sometimes cling to the use of these two elements in school ceremonies. For example, the Board of Education of Tokyo Metropolis punished more than 300 teachers who did not stand up when *Kimigayo* was played at graduation ceremonies. The Governor of Tokyo, Shintaro Ishihara, is in favor of *Yasukuni* Shrine and once made a commemorative speech in a ceremonial assembly held at *Yasukuni* Shrine on August 15, the anniversary of the Imperial Rescript on the Termination of the War.

25. *Suwa-jinja* (*Suwa* Shrine) is very popular in Japan as a presider of a festival named *Kunchi* or *Nagasaki Okunchi*. It was started in the late sixteenth century for celebrating autumn harvests and became a festival of *Suwa* Shrine in the seventeenth century. Another purpose of this *Kunchi* was to check the so-called 'hidden Christians.' *Kunchi* takes place during October 7–9, and was designated as a national intangible cultural asset in 1979. The festival is also known as 'Dragon Dance,' originally performed by the Chinese residents there. *Suwa* Shrine is included in the list of relatively higher rank shrines provided by the Association of *Shinto* Shrines, an organization overseeing approximately 80,000 *Shinto* Shrines in Japan.

26. 'The Flame of Hiroshima and Nagasaki' was later transferred to the Peace Flame Garden in Wellington, New Zealand, conveying a hope for a nuclear weapon-free world. As is described in the text, this flame was originally derived from Hiroshima and Nagasaki. An A-bombed Japanese soldier found a fire smoldering in an air-raid shelter of his uncle's house on August 6, 1945 immediately after the atomic bombing, and brought the flame to his home village in Fukuoka. This Hiroshima Flame was preserved with care in the Commemorative Tower established by the village, and later transferred to *Ueno Toshoguu* Shrine in 1990. On the other hand, the Nagasaki Flame was ignited by rubbing A-bombed roof tiles gathered in the devastated area. It was transferred to *Ueno Toshoguu* Shrine and integrated into one flame with the Hiroshima Flame.

Reference list

Anzai, I., J. Apsel and S.S. Mehdi (2008) *Museums for Peace: Past, Present and Future* (Kyoto: The Organizing Committee of the Sixth International Conference of Museums for Peace, Kyoto Museum for World Peace and Ritsumeikan University).

Yasukuni Jinja (2009) http://www.yasukuni.or.jp (Japanese home page), date accessed June 28, 2009.

Yasukuni Shrine (2009) http://www.yasukuni.or.jp/english (English home page), date accessed June 28, 2009.

15
Buddhism and the World Peace

Johan Galtung

Peace: An introduction to peace theory

Whenever the relation between X and Y is to be explored, it may be a good idea to present some thinking about X, then some thinking about Y, and then some ideas about compatibility or conflict, harmony or disharmony or simply irrelevance, between X and Y. I shall follow that format, and take them in the opposite order of the title, starting with peace then proceeding to Buddhism. And this I shall do at a fairly high level of abstraction, the present chapter being in the field of social philosophy rather than concrete contemporary politics.

Thus, I do not intend to discuss balance of power theories particularly prevalent in the Occident, or power center theories, particularly prevalent in the Orient. To a large extent these are peace theories of the elite, reflecting the interests of elites in monopolizing and wielding their power. They are not necessarily peace theories. Rather, I shall have as a point of departure one very simple insight: that peace has something to do with entropy, here taken in the sense of 'disorder.'

However, that term does not quite connote the idea of peace. Disorder sounds like something messy. The basic point is not messiness in any pejorative sense, but high complexity of the system: many and diverse components and many and diverse ties of interaction between them. The underlying thinking would be that the moment the system tends to crystallize, and becomes more orderly, the number of social types (such as nations, blocs, alliances) gets smaller. The concentration on one point gets more pronounced, and the links of interaction no longer fill the total space or possibilities but tend to connect certain types only, and often mainly in a negative hostile way. At that point, the system may look very orderly, but is in fact poised for destructive battle. In conflict theory, this state of affairs is known as polarization, when two alliances are pitted against each other. Most of the interaction takes place between the leading powers (super-powers), and actually mainly between the leaders (super-leaders). A 'summit meeting' is the typical example outcome of that type of social pathology, even if it produces a disarmament agreement. The structure producing that agreement is so false – meaning low in entropy – that we have all reasons to be skeptical of the outcome. Could it be that the agreement is a veil, a *maya*, disguising an armament agreement?

Against that image of 'unpeace' or peacelessness, I would like to sketch, very briefly, an alternative image. This image presupposes immediately willingness to consider that peace has to be discussed and understood not only as peace among nations, but also as peace within societies, among and within human beings and certainly also with nature. It has to be understood in nature space, human space, social space and world space. In all four spaces there seem to be two common factors that are necessary conditions for peace: diversity (between the parts, types, actors mentioned above) and symbiosis (the interactive links mentioned above).

In nature, diversity and symbiosis would lead to ecological balance. In human beings, diversity and symbiosis would lead to rich, mature human beings, to persons, capable of developing several dispositions within themselves and letting them play together. At the social level, diversity and symbiosis would lead to pluralistic, even fascinating societies, not fragmented into different parts but with the parts interacting with each other, constantly evolving. And at the world level diversity and symbiosis would lead to active peaceful coexistence between several systems, not only between two as Soviet theory has it. And they, in addition, do not practice that excellent theory inside their own society; they gamble on only one social type, 'Socialism' – even if seen as highly dynamic under glasnost conditions. Let it be added that we assume symbiosis, or interdependence, to be equitable, 'horizontal,' with no part dominating, exploiting the other. This is certainly not always the case in nature; predator/prey relationships being symbiotic but not equitable and consequently no model for human, social and world space.

It is easily seen how different this image of peace is from current reality. Even at the level of theory, both East and West today think about peace as if it were compatible with war with nature, destroying the ecological balance which has diversity and symbiosis as its basis; at the same time bringing forth simple-minded, often dogmatic and materialistic human beings; at the same time trying to have one system, their own, dominate the whole world. There is no delight that others are different; no appreciation of the value of diversity; little sense that it is unnecessary and even harmful if one social type dominates society and even the world, alone. Both social and world spaces can evolve so much better through symbiosis between diverse parts, e.g. by 'Socialism' and 'Capitalism' cooperating and coexisting together, not assuming that any one of them will 'win in the long run.' But that is not mainstream ideology, neither in the East nor in the West.

With significant diversity and symbiosis deficits, our world becomes a warlike system, with efforts to control violence through balance of power monopoly policies. However, when such policies are based on offensive arms (arms that can take the battle to the enemy and be used to destroy the other side, not only to defend one's own country), the outcome seems always to be arms races because the other side cannot possibly know for certain whether the assurances that the arms are for 'defensive purposes only' are true. And arms races almost invariably lead to war, if not directly between the two contestants, then indirectly, using third and fourth parties.

And that is our situation, our predicament – as briefly told as possible. We all know that a war with arms of mass destruction of any proportion is something that simply must not take place. Hence our prospects are not too bright, to put it mildly. We are building war structures, not peace structures, very low on diversity and symbiosis; very low entropy. This is the trend that has to be reversed.

Buddhism and peace: twenty strong points

I then move on to the second part: Buddhism. In the world as a whole, Buddhism is the major system of belief that, to my mind, comes closest in its way of looking at the world to the type of dynamic, highly complex peace theory just indicated. I shall try to explore this point by dividing it into two parts: twenty strong points in Buddhism, highly compatible with active pursuits of peace, and six weaker points, to be developed in the next section, which may stand in the way. At the end, then, I shall try to draw a balance, relating the images presented of peace and Buddhism to each other.

(1) Very basic in Buddhism is the *anatta* doctrine of no individual, permanent soul or self. I take it that this does not rule out something impermanent, ever-changing that might correspond metaphorically to an occidental soul concept at a collective level: a collectively shared empathy with sentient others all over, in all spaces. What is ruled out is the strong, occidental emphasis on individualism, and the individual self as something unique, specific and detachable, guaranteed 'eternal life,' i.e. permanence. The *anatta* doctrine certainly does not rule out a sense of a transpersonal 'soul' – in short unity with all humans and other sentient beings wherever they are, transnationally, across any kind of borders (by age, gender and race; by nation and class) and with nature, and not necessarily only the biosphere, nor only with animals. One might perhaps say that in Christianity the quest for unity points upwards from individuals here and now, via Jesus Christ to a transcendental God (more or less mediated by the Church, depending on the type of Christianity). In Buddhism, the quest for unity extends in space to everybody, downward (if one may use that expression at all) to non-human nature, and backwards and forwards in time through the principles of *karma* and rebirth, as distinguished from the Hindu concept of transmigration where an individual and permanent soul is involved.

Thus, the *anatta* doctrine makes for a very high level of empathy with everything alive in past, present and future, even unity as something immanent. There is that of me in everybody and that of everybody in me. 'I' am a process, continuous with other processes in minds, bodies and matter elsewhere in past, present and future; conditionally caused by and causing others. The *anatta* principle rules out borders, counteracting fragmentation, uniting individuals that otherwise may be pitted against each other in a competitive fight for God's attention and grace as each individual sees him, translated into more secular causes if/when God starts waning; a phenomenon only too well known in the Christian world. Christians and other theists seek union upwards, with God; Buddhists try to unveil a unity that is already there with Others, in space and time. Christianity may divide. Buddhism, because of the *anatta* principle, can only unite.

(2) A consequence of the *anatta* doctrine is the *ahimsa* doctrine, nonviolence towards all forms of life,* certainly including animals (a reason why Buddhists tend to be vegetarians). *Ahimsa* should not be seen in terms of egoism or altruism. These are concepts that already presuppose individualism with the egoist being the individual only trying to maximize his own benefits, even at the expense of others and the altruist being the individual trying to maximize the benefits of others, even at the expense of himself. Within the *anatta* doctrine, the *ahimsa* doctrine should be understood as a norm not to hurt others because hurting others is the same as hurting ourselves since we are all of the same, including that part of the processes-in-continuity-with-each-other that is associated with me, here and now. For Gandhi† this thought was absolutely essential, his unity-of-man (actually unity-of-life) doctrine being the pillar on which his construction rested. Needless to say, a strong nonviolence doctrine is highly peace-building, but problematic if some parts of the world are nonviolent and others are not. Hence the argument for at least a transitional strategy on the way towards a more enlightened world: a concept of defensive defense.

(3) *Metta-karuna*, compassion. *Ahimsa*, nonviolence, is nevertheless a negative formulation. It means a (not) *himsa* (violence), although in Sanskrit it comes out less negatively. The formulation is taken from the *pancha shila*, with five precepts, all of them negatively formulated (in addition to abstention from taking life, one should also abstain from stealing, from adultery or sexual misconduct in general, from lying and from intoxicating drinks). The *pancha shila* should be seen in conjunction with the *pancha dhamma*, the five deeds that are formulated positively. One of them is *metta-karuna*, translatable as 'compassion.' In other words, one should not only abstain from violence but also develop compassion

* Ed. For more discussions on nonviolence in Buddhism, see Chapter 11 by Swami Veda Bharati and Chapter 12 by Karma Lekshe Tsomo.
† Ed. See Chapter 25 by Arun Gandhi to find more about Gandhi's life and philosophy.

towards all beings, everywhere. The other four deeds are 'good vocation,' which would exclude the sale and making of weapons and liquor; 'positive control of sexual life and passions,' 'telling the truth' and 'mindfulness, carefulness' – in the sense of abstaining from negligence, carelessness. From the point of view of peace theory, this is important. In the very center of Buddhism, there is a basis not only for negative peace, but also for positive peace, not only for absence of war, but also for positive relations. Not only *pancha shila*, but also *pancha dhamma*.

(4) Symbiosis. A basic idea of Buddhism is the collective ethical budget, the idea that Buddhahood is something we reach together. The goal is not self-realization of the individual, permanent self or soul, *natta*, but self-realization of all, because we are so strongly coupled together by conditional causation.

This thinking could not also be applied to world space. The well-being, development and security of other countries are also well-being, development and security for my country. If I hurt and harm the other party at the individual or collective level we can no longer develop together, not even reach each other. I may triumph alone, but that is also all. In principle this type of thinking should lead to a new kind of trade theory where I always try to build up the other party (and thereby all of us) through cooperative arrangements, instead of only trying to maximize my own short-term profit. National accounting, e.g. in terms of trade deficit/surplus and gross national product (per capita or not) become meaningless as they fail to recognize the interconnectedness of the world. They are expressions of a *natta* doctrine in world space, seeing the nation-state as separate and eternal. A collective ethical budget points toward symbiosis and equity.

Another consequence would be a theory of not only common security (the Palme Commission) but cooperative security. Some of this might take the form of world institutions such as the United Nations Peace-Keeping Forces. More important today are perhaps efforts to build one's own security without reducing that of the others, for instance through defensive rather than offensive weapons. In short, the collective nature of this thinking would in peace theory take the form of 'my security is your security and vice versa,' leading to a concept of additive rather than subtractive security. This points far beyond a simplistic focus on disarmament alone as the road to peace.

(5) Diversity. Basic in Buddhism is tolerance with the famous dictum of the 84,000 sects, a history practically speaking with no 'holy office' to protect doctrine, no inquisition and no intra-religious wars. But there is also tolerance of other systems of belief, making it possible to combine them with Buddhism to a large extent, or at least to coexist with Buddhism. There is pluralism rather than singularism, even the idea of helping other religions. There is unity in diversity; but also diversity in the assumed unity. And there is a symbiotic use of this diversity as witnessed by the ability of Buddhists to integrate other types of thinking in their

own approach. In peace theory this is the condition of diversity of social types, including diversity of human attitudes and behavior as conditions for resilience in the system; if enacted in symbiotic relations; highly compatible not only with Buddhist thought and practice. Sharp lines of confrontation are avoided. There is a search for unity in compatible ideas and actions.

(6) The doctrine of the middle road is a concrete approach to life. The basic point is 'neither too much nor too little,' an approach that will tend to make Buddhists non-fanatic. In the field of attitudes and belief, this would also imply a tendency to stay away from extreme positions which could, in turn, make Buddhists, like Quakers, useful as bridge-builders. Buddhists serve easily as contacts between the extremes, perhaps pulling the extremes towards a more 'pragmatic' Buddhist position, conceiving of their extreme views as partial insights only.

(7) The policy of the middle road is a concrete manifestation of the point above. In material life this means neither too little – the basic needs have to be satisfied – nor too much – accumulation of excessive riches should be avoided. In spiritual life, it means neither self-torture, nor self-indulgence. One implication would be relatively egalitarian societies, less concerned with exploitative and acquisitive materialism, and great care in economic life so that others are not deprived of the possibility of a middle of the road life. The unity of man principle would play a basic role in this connection. What is here seen as a social doctrine could also be a world doctrine among countries: no country should consume too little; no country should consume too much. More particularly, no country should consume too little because others consume too much; no country should consume too much because it is taken from others that consequently consume too little. Again, from the point of view of peace theory this obviously gives a strong basis for positive peace policies based on equality, on equitable forms of exchange so that equality is not destroyed, on cooperative (symbiotic) behavior. From the point of view of Buddhist philosophy, a doctrine of equity could also be anchored in an extended definition of theft, closer to the concept of exploitation. But that is controversial.

(8) Small is beautiful;* if we accept that the type of cooperation needed to move forward towards Buddhahood, with human beings constantly interacting, helping each other, can only be meaningful in smaller units. Even a Buddhist mass movement like the *Soka Gakkai*, with its famous mega-manifestations, seems to be at its best in the small, face-to-face groups. In general this type of thinking might be more typical of *hinayana* than of the *mahayana* Buddhism

---

* Ed. Compare to Leopold Kohr and his notion of 'small is beautiful' in Chapter 1 by Wolfgang Dietrich.

of which *Soka Gakkai* may be said to be an example. From the point of view of peace theory, small social units seem to be more peaceful in all four spaces (nature, human, social, world), among other reasons because there will be more steering mechanisms, people telling each other when something goes wrong, suffering the consequences of conflict, enjoying the benefits of cooperation. In mass societies of mutually fragmented individuals, kept at a considerable distance from the power elite, such mechanisms are less available. In general, Buddhism would tend to favor smaller units of social organization, and smaller units – by and large – are less belligerent than the larger ones, if for no other reasons than having fewer resources for destructive activity. Small groups give a better basis for brotherhood and sisterhood as conditions for personhood – on the road to Buddhahood; a good example of compatibility between peace theory and Buddhist practice.

(9) Holism. Buddhism will have no difficulty thinking and acting in terms of all four spaces, not accepting divisions, man-made, artificial, of the great unity of sentient life. However, of all the four spaces it should be pointed out again that Buddhism is at its strongest as a philosophy and as a practice, in human (and nature) space, and less developed as a canon of thought and practice for social and world space. But the relative lack of social and world doctrine in Buddhism could easily be overcome with more active contributions from contemporary Buddhists, including philosophers. Basic conditions are present. A holistic orientation draws no borderline in principle between the spaces, saying 'this is not our concern.' Then, Buddhism is non-metaphysical. It is a moral philosophy to be tested empirically, with no room for divine revelation as something separate from human beings. Buddha had the deepest insight, but he was also human. Where occidental religions would develop a theology as a science of the divine, Buddhist philosophy ('Buddhist theology' being a *contradictio in adjecto*) is freer to focus on this world and as holistically as the problem would require. It is strongest in the field of philosophy, psychology, health and nutrition; weaker as sociology, economics or international relations. But there is nothing in principle impeding Buddhist thinkers from making great strides forward also in these fields.

(10) Historically, Buddhism tends to be a populist religion, or system of belief, for the people, the broad masses, rather than for the upper classes and the power elite. Thus Buddhism was expelled from India for being incompatible with the *varna* (caste) aspects of brahminic Hinduism. In Japan, leading elites adapted the much more nationalist and regressive (state) *Shinto* as their basic orientation,* in addition to Christianity. In Korea, and to some extent also China, the power

* Ed. Ikuro Anzai discusses State *Shinto* at length in Chapter 14.

elites embraced Christianity, and its secular off-springs, Liberalism/Conservatism and Marxism.

Thus, in Korea today, one finds aggressive Christianity in the South and aggressive Marxism in the North, among the elites, on top of widespread Buddhism among the people – presumably also in the North. This represents a great potential for peace politics if only the leaders could either step back or reconcile themselves with the general Korean urge for unification. With Buddhism as guidance, a joint Korean peace policy based on Buddhist thinking would have a solid foundation in terms of the masses of the countries involved. But Buddhism was too weak, possibly also too corruptible, to withstand the Japanese (*shinto*) conquest of Korea,* one possible reason why the elites embraced hard versions of Western thinking as a response. Western thinking† tends to be more self-, less Self-oriented – more self-assertive on behalf of the believers (Christianity), the nations(s) (Liberalism) and/or the class (Marxism).

(11) In Buddhism there is no division between creator and created – an essential point in the Buddhist unity-of-all (and not only unity-of-man image of the world). From a peace theoretical point of view, this means that we have only ourselves to rely upon. A Buddhist does not hope to get peace in return for obedience to a transcendental God, as part of his grace. Nor would he be deterred from hard work by ideas like 'if the Creator wished there to be peace He would have created peace.' Peace has to be of our own making, as a part of the ongoing creation of the world as made by all sentient beings past, present and future. Peace is not a gift, but the possible result of conscious, deep and collective action.

(12) Closely related: In Buddhism there is less of a subject-object distinction. There is not only us watching the world – the world is also watching us. We are in it, but also of it. Concretely this means that there is an ongoing dialectic where we influence the world and the world influences us. Peace is not something we make by shaping the world; peace is also something the world shapes in us in the process. It is our task to use that dialectic positively. And this is not done by asking occidental questions like 'Where do we start, by changing the world or by changing ourselves?' but by promoting all those processes so that changes in nature, human, social and world spaces can go hand in hand.

(13) According to Buddhist thinking, there is impermanence in everything, the *anicca* doctrine. The world and everything in it is ebbing and flowing, not a rigid structure of global architectonics – but rather like a process based on diversity

---

* Ed. For more detail on Japanese *Shinto* wars, see Chapter 14 by Ikuro Anzai.

† Ed. More on the Western perspective can be found in Chapter 2 by Karlheinz Koppe and Chapter 4 by Nigel Young.

in symbiotic interaction. It does not make any sense to try to freeze the world in a form or a structure once and forever. Whatever plan one might make for peace, it has to be a process plan, not a structure plan. From a peace theoretical point of view, this is much more realistic than any structural blueprint that lays down for eternity what peace should look like, not taking into consideration the evolving nature of the four spaces in general and the interaction, within and between them, in particular.

(14) According to Buddhist thought, this interaction is always two-way. My consciousness is working on the world; the world is shaping my consciousness. To achieve anything we should never try to proceed in a linear manner, pushing a lever forgetting that there is a *reactio* to every *actio*. Nor should we try to find one lever that can be used to move the rest of the system, but rather work from all corners at the same time. Much better than a major one-dimensional push are many small but coordinated efforts along several dimensions at the same time, starting in all kinds of corners of material and spiritual reality, remembering that the system will react in a complex web of interrelations. Not only is peace indivisible; peace, development, enlightenment and eco-balance are indivisible. The whole logic of the system has to be changed for the *actio/reactio* processes to be more peace-building.

(15) According to Buddhism the world is filled with contradictions, the whole approach is highly dialectic. Thus, current Chinese thinking in terms of 'one country, two systems' – meaning that there can be both Socialism and capitalism within one country, the People's Republic of China – is fundamentally Buddhist and Daoist. It is certainly not Marxist, which is a much more linear, one-sided, occidental system of belief. From a peace theory point of view, an implication would be not to fight all contradictions, trying to make systems pure. Diversity with contradictions is possible, and even desirable. This is particularly important, as we shall always live in a mix of systems with different logic. To strive for a contradiction-free reality would be meaningless in a Buddhist philosophy that sees causal forces flowing in all directions.

(16) Buddhist thought is organized like a Buddhist wheel. It is not pyramidal and deductive from first principles. Of the various ideas mentioned above none would be seen as more fundamental than the others would. Rather, they could be seen as organized around a wheel where all possible lines are drawn between the points as connections to be explored (with the danger that this image would lead to bilateralism, always looking at only two points at a time, rather than three, four, many). There is no unbroken core of fundamental and final articles of faith; and that the system as a whole is open to new points, meaning new approaches. As the Buddhist wheel rolls through time, new points are spun into an ever-tighter

web of thought and action. Ultimately, it is the totality of all of this that matters, the whole approach being fundamentally holistic and dynamic – as opposed to a deductive pyramid tying together atomistic insights or 'findings.'

(17) Buddhist thought is profoundly optimistic. There is a Buddha nature in all of us if we only realize it and exert ourselves. Nobody is left outside. But there is a difference between the *hinayana* approach perhaps more emphasizing how to avoid *dukkha* (suffering) and the *mahayana* approach perhaps more emphasizing how to obtain *sukha* (bliss, happiness). Thus, it stands to reason that from the *hinayana* school more emphasis might be expected on negative peace and from the *mahayana* school more in terms of positive peace. Since both are parts of a dynamic peace concept, a Buddhist gift to the world would be to combine the *hinayana* and *mahayana* approaches, see them as examples of diversity, and let them interact more symbiotically with each other. A challenge to Buddhism!

(18) The Buddhist view of process tends to be cyclical, not linear. There is neither any definite guarantee that things are going well, nor that they are going badly. There are ups and downs in all four spaces, and that which has come up may come down again just as that which has come down may come up (as opposed to heaven and hell in Christian theology that are seen as end states in human evolution, as points of no return). From a peace theoretical point of view, the cyclical view may inoculate Buddhists against being too optimistic when things go well, or too pessimistic when things go badly, opening for a middle of the road position also in this regard. On the other hand, there is also – particularly in the *mahayana* school – a basic optimism which would imbue the cyclical perspective with an element of linearity, somewhat like a spiral moving forward and upward.

(19) In Buddhist philosophy, the focus is on continued striving, self-improvement and Self-improvement being not only necessary but also possible, and – in the longer run – sufficient. Neither acts of faith, of submissiveness nor acts of Grace from divine quarters (except in *amida* Buddhism, if this is Buddhism) are to be expected, to be hoped for or would in any sense be useful. Much striving and hard work is needed – a type of thinking entirely compatible with peace theory. Moreover, peace is not a final state at the end of the road, stable and reliable once obtained, but the possible continued striving.

(20) And finally, there is the ultimate goal of Buddhism in human space: *nirvana*, which can be seen as some type of maximum entropy. It should not be translated as 'extinction' or similar metaphors used in Western presentations. It might rather be seen as some kind of realization of the unity-of-all doctrine, a Self-realization where the *anatta* doctrine is fully realized in a state of constant *sukha*. This would be highly compatible with the idea of peace as expounded above, in

the mini-peace theory already indicated at the outset. *Nirvana* is entropy, peace is entropy – hence, in a certain sense, peace is *nirvana* and *nirvana* is peace. Boundaries have been eliminated; unity has been obtained. And the preceding nineteen points are concretizations of this point number 20.

Buddhism and peace: six weak points

But Buddhism also has weak points that contribute to explaining why it does not play the great role as a peace-building factor Buddhism certainly has the potential for doing. Six such points will be briefly touched upon. Those living in Buddhist countries may see many more.

(1) Tolerance is good. But Buddhism may also have been led to become too tolerant, for instance of highly violent systems of militarism – as in the case of Japan where Buddhists too easily also embraced *Shintoism* and combined the two with *Confucianism** in a highly dangerous way most useful for Japanese militarism (the *kamikaze* suicide expeditions being a good example). Another case in mind may be Buddhist support for military regimes, as in Thailand.

(2) Tolerance is good. But Buddhism may also have been too tolerant of systems practicing structural violence, for instance in their economic policies, so that the middle way doctrine becomes a structural impossibility. The result is extreme misery on the one hand and extreme wealth on the other, without Buddhists necessarily standing up, fighting the system, possibly in an effort to practice middle way policy. Again, Japan is an example of such economic policies, inter-nationally speaking, itself accumulating riches while periphery countries in the Japanese economic sphere experience extreme poverty, even misery. But then, at the same time, it should also be mentioned that the income distribution of Japan is among the most egalitarian in the world. And the index of equality varies little over time, meaning that rises and declines come in a parallel fashion for the elite and for the people. Both factors are probably to some extent attributable to the influence of Buddhist thought and practice within the country. In a sense, this might be taken to indicate that there is more of a social doctrine than a world doctrine in Buddhism, even if there is less of either than the important doctrines structuring behavior in the nature and human spaces, at the micro rather than macro levels. As often mentioned above, these are the strongest points where the spaces are concerned. And that may lead to blindness, compatible with excessive tolerance of violent behavior in the other spaces. The officer sharing risks and treating his soldiers well while doing his best to rout the enemy; the company

* Ed. See also Chapter 13 by Kam-por Yu to read more on Confucianism.

manager sharing salary, power and privilege with the workers, exploiting sub-contractors abroad and foreign markets mercilessly.

(3) The idea of working in small groups, next to the temple and the tank, in the village, under the guidance of the *bhikkhu* (monk), is beautiful. Of the *Triple Gem*, the Buddha and the *Dhamma* (the teachings of Buddha) are available to all. But the *Sangha* (the order of the monks) becomes marginalized from the rest of society, having its own existence in splendid, micro society isolation, meaning both that it is isolated and that it is splendid, practicing *ahimsa* and *metta-karuna* among themselves. Buddhism becomes privatized, not in the sense of being individualized, but in the sense of belonging, collectively to small groups on their cooperatively engineered road to Buddhahood. The impact on macro society is negligible or even negative by taking individuals far on the road to Buddhahood out of social circulation.

(4) Buddhism may too easily accept that the leadership of a country practices the opposite of Buddhism as long as it gives in return freedom of worship. In other words, Buddhists like others may too easily accept a concordat with the powers that be, and are of course not immune to the fringe benefits, the emoluments that such a concordat might carry in its wake. Where Buddhism becomes a state religion, this danger is very apparent; Thailand being one, Sri Lanka possibly another.

(5) The idea of cyclical as opposed to linear processes accommodates a high amount of fatalism, accepting defeat too easily even if there is no inner capitulation. According to the cycle perspective decline is inevitable. However, it is not too dangerous since according to the same cycle idea there will also be an upswing, in due time. Since this will come anyhow, no real effort is needed. In short, there is some truth to occidental prejudices about the fatalism of the Orient and vice versa, of course.

(6) Given the five conditions just mentioned, Buddhism may easily become ritualistic, ornate, embroidered and very beautiful like in the countless temples in Southeast and eastern Asia. But this may also be all there is to it. The focus may be on the Buddha as an object of idolatry and on the *gasho*, pressing the hands together, bowing lightly to the image of the Buddha in any position. The focus may be on the *Dhamma*, on his teachings as something to be learned by heart, even in quaint languages (for instance in *Pali*, which is the same to Sinhalese as Sanskrit to Hindi, or in very classical Chinese and other languages). And the *Sangha* may be something admired but at a distance, not to be imitated. In other words, Buddhism may become an object rather than something subjective entering the life of the person as an almost inexhaustible reservoir of insight into

human life; a psycho-philosophy *sans pareil*. And that is the recipe for stagnation – which is another way of saying that a religion is dying.

Conclusion

Looking through the 20 + 6 points just made the balance is obvious. Buddhism has a tremendous potential as a source for active peace politics, to a large extent untapped. But Buddhism has to be revived and kept alive in order to escape the corruptive influences of a world replete with direct and structural violence. No doubt, there are such peace potentials in all religions. But Buddhism differs from many of the other religions (for instance from Judaism, Christianity and Islam). By no stretch of imagination can Buddhism be used to justify direct and structural violence, war and exploitation. When Christianity turns its ugly side up, it spells war; when Buddhism turns its ugly side up, it spells retreatism, ritualism. It is our task to have both of them turn their beautiful, soft sides up, and those beautiful sides may actually be quite similar in their action consequences.

It might be useful to remember that the Lord Buddha practiced his doctrine, but also a social and political doctrine for the social and inter-social formations of his time. So maybe that is what we are missing: a higher level of consciousness as to what Buddhism could mean in practice, with more exercise of inspired leadership to implement the insights.

Of course, there are such inspiring and important examples of Buddhist leadership as the late UN Secretary-General, the Burmese *U Thant*; the *Soka Gakkai* international leader, the Japanese *Ikeda Daisaku*; or the *Sarvodaya Shramadama* international leader, the Sri Lankan *Ariyaratne*. The challenge is certainly there. And all over the world there are efforts to build more peace-like structures – but they are often missing in ethos. Buddhism is such an ethos, perhaps in search of a concrete structure. Maybe the two could meet, and maybe this could also be a very concrete example of a meeting of East and West, very much overdue?

Section IV

Maori and Native American Peace Concepts

16
He Taura Whiri: A Maori Perspective

Peter Horsley

Dialogue in relationship is a pre-requisite for seeking the multitude of cultures of peace. It takes place across all dimensions and domains – the inner and the outer, the diversity of peoples, and the living world of nature. But the essential weaving, if it is to have enduring value, has to embrace the open and common heart.

Introduction

Over the last thirty years, New Zealand has begun the painful and contentious process of revisiting its colonial history. It involves a truth and reconciliation process that is being carried out in the public realm and involves a wide array of political, social and cultural initiatives. A central issue for debate is how the culture can revisit its founding ideals (a treaty that promised a relationship of mutual benefit between the indigenous Maori and British settlers), deal with contemporary issues of democratic coexistence, immigration, and identity, and see if these threads can be woven into a deeper set of interrelationships that lead to a more harmonious and peaceful future.

In his introductory chapter *Beyond the Gates of Eden: Trans-rational Peaces*, Wolfgang Dietrich stresses the need to destruct the myth of a single and universal normative peace founded on the notion of one order, one truth guaranteed by power, and in its place to construct a multitude of cultures of peace that embody harmonious relations and the practice of energetic peace. These concerns are particularly relevant to societies that have been subjected to the violence – intellectual, structural, cultural – of colonization. While Aotearoa New Zealand's colonial past contains the usual legacy of domination and subjugation of the indigenous Maori people by European settlers, the last thirty years have seen a wide array of political, social and cultural initiatives that have at their roots a quest for peace and conflict resolution. This chapter will critically examine some of these in an attempt to see how insights into the nature of peace can assist the peace-building process that this distant South Pacific nation has tentatively begun.

From an international peace perspective, Aotearoa New Zealand is often held out as a small beacon of resistance and hope. It has maintained an independent foreign policy since the 1970s with various Labor governments ignoring American and other Western policy demands. Its pacifist-based anti-nuclear policies reflect a strong stance held by the vast majority of residents irrespective of political affiliation, and its opposition to nuclear weapons is formally recognized in legislation passed in 1987 (the New Zealand Nuclear Free Zone, Disarmament and Arms Control Act). It has challenged nuclear weapons testing carried out in the South Pacific at the International Court of Justice, and by direct protest action – like sending frigates into test zones and supporting flotillas of protest yachts – it has forcefully argued in the international arena that nuclear weapons are illegal and immoral; and it has been a driving force in establishing nuclear weapon-free zones in Antarctica and in the South Pacific. These actions can be considered as useful steps towards 'energetic peace' – ethical actions prompted by a determined citizenry that, over time, generate a political response which, when supported by sound leadership, becomes part of a strong cultural identity.

While these initiatives are viewed as powerful statements in international peace movement circles, they can also be seen as gestures that touch only one component of international militarization. The initiatives have not been 'exported' to other countries; the super-powers have accommodated the nuclear-free policies as a minor irritant held by a relatively insignificant, small and remote country; and New Zealand defense forces still join their colleagues in troublesome international conflicts, although usually under UN mandates with a focus on civil reconstruction and peace-keeping. A sharper lens reveals further contradictions. A highly sophisticated US military-based intelligence system operates out of New Zealand without formal democratic control; a significant portion of the annual government budget is still being directed at building up defense force capability; and there are ongoing calls from civil society for more funding to engage effectively with communities of need in the South Pacific, Africa and Asia. Internally, the picture is also troubling: violence within families and communities is common; the culture exhibits all the 'shadow' trademarks of a modern materialistic, technological society; and in the midst of a bountiful land, a significant number of New Zealanders struggle socially, culturally and economically.

Peace is a deep aspiration. It embodies the multidimensional elements highlighted by Panikkar (1995). In *Cultural Disarmament: The Way to Peace*, peace is a political problem that makes the fullness of human beings possible in human society; it requires intercultural reflection based on equality and collaboration of all cultures.* Peace embodies harmony, freedom and justice; pathways to peace involve reconciliation and dialogue and opening to the depth of the 'other;' and at a philosophical level, peace is a fruit of contemplation, a gift from the very structure and depth of reality. In the current volume, Dietrich† adds to these insights: difference is a key concern of peace studies; peace is the state in which each culture blooms in its own unique way; we need to open the door for relationships and the recognition of mutual and intercultural respect; and every normative concept of peace comes from an energetic ground of interrelationship and spirituality.

With this in mind, it is useful to examine how the multifaceted quest for peace is being explored in New Zealand's public and cultural life. Over the last thirty years, the country has begun the painful and contentious process of revisiting its colonial history. After years of protest by Maori, the indigenous people of the land, successive governments have provided formal legal and political opportunities for Maori to seek redress for breaches by governments of the guarantees and promises set out in the nation's founding document, the Treaty of Waitangi signed by Maori tribes and the English Crown in 1840, and to reclaim their status as *tangata whenua*, the first people of the land. At its core, this process involves a truth and reconciliation process that is being carried out in the public realm. It has enabled Maori to tell their stories, to reassert some of their customary authority and to gain entry into the institutions of power after 150 years of deliberate exclusion. Maori have begun a major cultural renaissance that embodies language revival, education from preschool to tertiary level, art and sport, rebuilding tribal and Maori-owned assets, establishing Maori communication channels (radio and TV), and increasing political representation through MPs and the establishment of a Maori Party.

These initiatives strike at the heart of the country's history and identity. They highlight the predicaments faced by all colonized countries – how to respond to a past that contains deeds that are unjust, illegal or immoral; how to make amends for these actions knowing that a return to the past is impossible; and how to lay the foundations for a national identity that can embrace respect for diversity, plurality and sustainable pathways. For many *Pakeha*, the Maori term for European New Zealanders, the picture is confusing and filled with uncertainty, particularly as Maori gain greater authority and influence in their expression of cultural identity. Maori on their part wish to keep asserting their uniqueness by weaving it into the fabric of an Aotearoa New Zealand identity that was promised when the nation-state was established in 1840.

* Ed. Gustavo Esteva, in Chapter 31, considers in depth Raimon Panikkar as peace thinker and discusses in detail the mentioned work *Cultural Disarmament*.
† Ed. See Chapter 1 'Beyond the Gates of Eden: Trans-rational Peaces'.

This chapter examines how a multitude of cultures of peace that embody the potential for harmonious relations and the practice of energetic peace are being constructed and debated in Aotearoa New Zealand. Given the summary set out above, the nuclear weapon-free *external peace* history will not be further examined. However, issues surrounding the Treaty of Waitangi, essentially an internal *political peace* response, will be explored as will Maori aspirations that embody a quest for *cultural peace*. These two concerns share a common heritage of cultural interaction and involve interrelated issues of how Maori and European (as descendents of the two parties to the initial interaction formalized by the Treaty of Waitangi) are exploring new political and social arrangements that reflect the country's bicultural foundation; and how the worldview of the indigenous Maori people is opening up new areas of dialogue and debate. Lastly, these initiatives will be viewed through the lens of a possible *trans-rational peace* to see if there are prospects for strengthening cultural processes that promote dialogue in the debate about honoring the country's founding ideals and its link with contemporary issues of immigration, interculturality and identity. The central element in this task is how challenging issues can be woven into a deeper set of interrelationships – *he taura whiri*[1] – relationships that could lead to a more harmonious and peaceful future.

Setting the scene

Aotearoa New Zealand[2] is one of the most recently settled major landmasses. The first settlers were Eastern Polynesians who came to New Zealand in a series of migrations between 800 and 1300 AD. Over the next few centuries, they developed a distinct culture, now known as Maori, and the population was divided into *hapu*, subtribes and larger *iwi* (tribal) groupings. European explorers made contact in the seventeenth and eighteenth centuries, and after increasing numbers of settlers began to arrive in the early 1800s, the British government sent an envoy to New Zealand to claim formal sovereignty and negotiate a treaty with Maori to pave the way for European settlement. The Treaty of Waitangi was signed in February 1840 by the British Crown's representative and Maori chiefs. It was written in English, translated into Maori and contained three articles that dealt with English sovereignty, Maori self-governance and the application of British citizenship to Maori. Over 500 chiefs signed the Maori version. Because the two versions of the Treaty are not the exact rendering of the other, there remains a wide and often contentious variation in interpretation.[3]*

---

* Ed. The tensions between native populations and settlers played out in formal treaties, the untranslatability of these commitments and the power relations at stake are also main topics of discussion in Robert Vachon's Chapter 18. In this chapter, Vachon explores the notion of peace from a Mohawk perspective.

From 1840, migrants from the British Isles streamed into New Zealand. At first Maori were eager to trade with Pakeha, but as settler numbers grew, conflicts over land increased and eventually led to the New Zealand Land Wars of the 1860s and 1870s. The wars, subsequent confiscations and the imposition of British law led to massive loss of Maori land and cultural cohesion. While there were some attempts by governments in the 1920s–1930s to deal with the grievances of *iwi* whose land had been confiscated or fraudulently obtained in the previous century, the response was, at best, minimal. The intellectual and structural violence of previous government actions was further cemented in the 1950s when broad assimilationist policies were imposed that negated any place for Maori to express their cultural values and aspirations.

During the 1960s and 1970s, the Treaty of Waitangi became the focus of a strong Maori protest movement, which rallied around calls for the government to 'honor the Treaty' and to 'redress Treaty grievances.' Maori expressed their frustration about continuing violations of the Treaty in legislation and government policy, as well as unsympathetic decisions by the courts that provided no means for legal redress and further alienated Maori land from its traditional owners. The government was eventually forced to respond and in 1975 established the Waitangi Tribunal as a commission of inquiry tasked with researching breaches of the Treaty by the Crown or its agents, and suggesting means of redress.[4] In 1985, the Tribunal's powers were extended to allow it to examine government actions dating back to 1840. The number of claims quickly rose, and during the 1990s, when the government began to negotiate settlements with Maori, the Office of Treaty Settlements was established to develop government policy on historical claims and carry out negotiations with Maori.

Successive governments began to include references to the principles of the Treaty of Waitangi in legislation and acknowledged the status of the Treaty as the nation's founding document. The Waitangi Tribunal and the courts formulated Treaty principles, which could be applied to practical concerns and stated that the Treaty should be interpreted as a living document based on a covenant or partnership between Maori and the government. The overarching principle was 'reciprocity-exchange' – Maori ceded sovereignty in exchange for reciprocal government protection of *tino rangatiratanga* (traditional tribal authority). Other principles referred to 'partnership' – Maori and Pakeha are required to act towards each other reasonably, in mutual cooperation and trust and with the utmost good faith; 'active protection' – government has a duty to actively protect *rangatiratanga* rights (a fiduciary relationship arises when one side is weaker and more vulnerable than the other); and the principle of 'autonomy' – the authority of Maori to manage their own affairs according to their cultural preferences, and to work through differences with the state as equals (Maaka and Fleras, 2005).

Since the 1980s, Treaty of Waitangi claims and settlements have become a central feature of New Zealand race relations and politics. While a number of longstanding grievances have been settled, the complexity of the issues involved means that progress is slow. The process is not without contention – there is criticism from those who believe that the redress is insufficient to compensate for the scale of Maori losses and that the state-determined process is not an appropriate plural response. Others see no value in revisiting painful and contentious historical issues. Despite these differences, there is a recognition that positive elements are emerging out of the process. These include the way the Waitangi Tribunal has provided a forum and release valve for Maori who want their history recognized, their experience recorded, some compensation offered and their *mana* (standing) restored, and the rewriting of New Zealand's history, a task shared by Tribunal historians and academics – both Pakeha and Maori. The courts have also played a pivotal role in setting out working Treaty principles that successive governments have been able to shape to their political color (Sneddon, 2005). These steps have all helped build a degree of cross-cultural confidence that, to date, has defused conflicts that could have led to violence and bloodshed.

As cultural awareness of Maori dimension expands, the interrelationship with Pakeha continues to evolve in a number of ways. At the symbolic level of national identity, it seems to be developing smoothly – most Pakeha are happy to embrace some rudimentary elements of Maori culture such as words of greeting and the *haka* (traditional war dance). It also functions well at the interpersonal level in daily life where both races intermingle, marry and share common experiences (Liu, 2005). Problems arise, however, when Maori set out their aspirations for sovereignty based on the Treaty promise of *rangatiratanga*. Their struggle against the legacy of colonization includes the articulation of new culturally based governance models. Some of these are already in place in the education and health sectors. But limits have been placed on these aspirations by successive governments who have asserted a 'principle of non-assimilable difference' – government's sovereignty is built around the basic right of Maori to practice, maintain and promote their distinctive culture but they do so under a national Westminster (British-based) political structure. While there is acceptance that Maori culture should not be the target of assimilation and can be lived without interference and celebrated as an aspect of national culture, notions of a shared sovereignty have not been countenanced.

The focus on developing a working Treaty relationship between the two groups contains a tension between two narratives – one liberal democratic, the other Maori bicultural, and it shows no sign of abating. Maori continue to assert their political aspirations, while the state tends to respond in ways that do not unsettle the Pakeha majority. Between these two poles, a range of other responses is emerging. Some of these suggest that if New Zealand is to have a secure future, its two founding peoples (each with their different histories and cultures) need to live together in peace and justice. Coexistence – 'peaceful existence side by side' – is one concept that encapsulates this need in what has been termed the 'just accommodation of two peoples in one country.'

A democratic plurality as the basis of political peace?

A number of academics have suggested that if a 'just accommodation' of the two peoples is to be achieved, a new shared understanding between Pakeha and Maori is necessary to transcend the in-built tensions between them.[5] This requires reconceiving what has been referred to as the 'competitive and sometimes antagonistic Maori/Pakeha paradigm.' Instead, inclusive processes are required that acknowledge both cultural realities and that enable a new shared understanding to emerge by transcending the difficulties that both positions represent. For Maaka and Fleras (2005), the focus must be on 'living together differently' and 'rethinking citizenship' to create 'innovative patterns of belonging.'

A number of models of engagement have been developed by both Maori and Pakeha to revitalize relations and foster new understandings. There is agreement that in this undertaking the greater commitment must be made by the dominant party (Pakeha), which effectively controls the means by which change can be affected. Some of the models are summarized below to illustrate components of pluralism that are currently being debated. They include the 'Two Cultures' model, constructive engagement and collaborative management.

The 'Two Cultures' model (also known as the '*Raukawa* Model')[6] proposes a new national constitutional structure for decision making where Maori and Pakeha are required to find, together, mutually acceptable solutions. Three constitutional 'houses' are proposed – one Pakeha, one Maori and one Treaty house. It is based on the recognition of the distinctness of the two peoples, and signals that both peoples must continue to foster and develop their own cultural identity, each drawing strength from its own culture. The partnership between Maori and Pakeha of necessity requires a shared space (the 'Treaty house') that allows new understandings to emerge. It is suggested that this space (what one commentator has called 'the child of the relationship') might liberate Maori and Pakeha from the antagonistic paradigm that has constrained relations thus far.

Constructive engagement: *he putahitanga* – a true partnership

Another reconceptualization of Crown–Maori relations that seeks to move beyond the 'unproductive engagement' to a true partnership – *he putahitanga* – is 'constructive engagement.' Developed by New Zealand sociologists Maaka, Fleras and Spoonley (Fleras and Spoonley, 1999; Maaka and Fleras, 2005), its purpose is to create a meeting ground for negotiating a broader framework of cooperative coexistence. To free the two peoples from interacting exclusively within the parameters that have shaped their relationship in the past, the focus must be directed toward 'a future orientation, and a living and ongoing relationship.' This requires 'rethinking the basis for living together differently, in part by emphasizing the importance of the 'differently' without reneging on a need for the 'together.' It also requires developing 'innovative patterns of belonging,' and as part of this, a thorough transformation of the current con- stitutional monoculture into a 'new social contract' and a 'new constitutional order' is required. The new ground, Maaka and Fleras propose, can emerge with an emphasis on: 'engagement over entitlement, relationships over rights, inter- dependence over opposition, cooperation over competition, reconciliation over restitution, and power-sharing over power-conflict' (Maaka and Fleras, 2005).

Recognizing that the legacy of colonization places the onus on government, this model is largely directed to affirming the status of Maori as sovereign, indigenous peoples, and requires the government to acknowledge this and engage with Maori as such. Other aspects enjoin both parties to commit to productive modes of interaction in which their differences are not 'antagonistic' but 'deeply interconnected and existing in a state of creative tension with potential opportunity.' Reconciliation is key. According to Maaka and Fleras (2005), reconciliation must involve:

> the righting of historical wrongs by way of reparations; new partnerships as a basis for interaction; full and equal participation in decisions that affect them; working through differences rather than closing doors when things do not proceed smoothly; and taking indigeneity seriously by taking it into account for recognition or rewards.

Collaborative management

A further contemporary approach that offers new ground for Maori–Pakeha relationships in the environmental area is collaborative management or co-management. It sets out a process that is inclusive, pluralistic, consensus and community based and has the aim of promoting sustainability in human– ecological relationships through collective and cooperative effort. Its components include recognition and power-sharing with *tangata whenua* in resource management, an evolving partnership between Maori and government under a core Treaty platform, and engaging local and indigenous forms of knowledge and participation. Given the extent of environmental problems in New Zealand and the concern for protecting and restoring land and ecosystems – a common ground for both cultures – collaborative management initiatives are being actively debated and implemented at national, regional and local levels and are the subject of Waitangi Tribunal consideration in claims brought by Maori over national park lands.

These models all highlight the potential of 'living together differently,' the first steps required for developing plural pathways appropriate to New Zealand conditions. Regrettably, the possibility of exploring innovative local or regional expressions of autonomy by Maori have not been taken up by governments in a creative way and, given the climate of opinion, the more challenging governance possibilities are unlikely to be considered in the short to medium term. However, the focus on coexistence is a theme that continues to be explored in the debate about a shared future.

Durie (1995) notes:

What is needed is a commitment to seek out agreements within which Maori and Pakeha can advance, without any assumption of a single truth or a common starting point, but in the belief that the goals for grandchildren and their children are essentially the same – good health, a share in the country's wealth, justice, a right to cultural development and an expectation that as individuals and groups they will be valued by each other, by their people and by the collective state.

On the Pakeha side, King (2003) argues that Pakeha do not want to see anything taken *away* from Maori, just to ensure that the measures of protection and respect extended from the one culture embrace *both* cultures – asking for a 'mutuality of respect.' Sneddon (2005) also notes that Pakeha are nervous about what they may lose, forgetting for a moment the enormous lift to their *mana* secured as a just and open people through their support of the Waitangi Tribunal process.

Liu (2005) is even more direct:

My advice to Pakeha would be not to shrink from the gaze of others who seek to define you. It is a rare majority group member who gets to see him or herself in the light of a less powerful group's gaze. The humility that brings, combined with a confidence in one's own fortitude, will go a long way in dealing with the difficult points of the relationship with Maori. A good partner is someone who acknowledges when he has done wrong, but also stands up for what she believes is right. Everyone should be marginal sometimes; no one should be marginal all the time. These two things together are good because they define a shifting centre for the soul.

The biculturalism debate is complicated by a richly diverse migrant population that is making New Zealand its home. The 2006 census identified the following national ethnic categories: Pakeha/European 68 percent, Maori 15 percent, Asian communities 9 percent, Pacific Island communities 7 percent, with 23 percent of New Zealanders being born overseas. The flow of migrants continues to grow rapidly and Auckland, New Zealand's largest city, is becoming one of the most ethnically diverse cities on the planet. The projected ethnic mix for Auckland in 2016 is: European 51 percent, Asian 23 percent, Pacific Islander 15 percent, and Maori 11 percent.

Needless to say, many migrants are unfamiliar with New Zealand history and the place of Maori as *tangata whenua*. As a means of meeting their needs for identity, meaning and belonging, they tend to coalesce in ethnic groups in self-selected urban areas. New Zealand's adoption of the non-assimilable principle (something that can be attributed to the force and expression of Maori aspirations) means that government accepts the place of difference and diversity in New Zealand society, but to date there has been no consensus about adopting a particular model for nation building. Two approaches offer themselves – biculturalism and multiculturalism. While the biculturalism focus of the relationship between the two Treaty parties is being actively explored at the legal and political level, it can sideline the place of the growing ethnic minorities in the debate about a wider identity. Similarly, if multiculturalism becomes the focus of public policy concerns, it can reduce Maori culture to just one among many. Metge (2004) suggests that lateral thinking is needed to develop a new model of nationhood that is inclusive and positive about our relations with each other, hence her call for *he taura whiri*.

Others suggest that – if the bicultural relationship can be restored and nurtured over time, the experience gained in making space available for positive and affirming cultural initiatives could be applied in developing similar positive relationships with other communities and ethnic groups. Patterson (2004) argues that Pakeha can adopt core elements of Maori thinking (particularly *mana* and *manaakitanga*) to build better peaceful relationships between all people and with Nature. *Mana* can be gained through success in any culturally sanctioned enterprise. It is ultimately dependent upon giving *aroha* (affirmation, love, cooperation, support) to the other, and the reciprocal nature of the relationship that is generated raises the *mana* of the all parties involved. Sneddon (2005) adopts a similar stance.

The issue of how to build a deeper peace across all the necessary domains – political, social, cultural, environmental and spiritual – can be assisted by probing further into the Maori worldview and how it is being articulated in contemporary times.

Cultural peace: the quest for authentic being

The debate about biculturalism has its most visible focus on Maori aspirations at the external level of power and politics. However, a profound worldview has always motivated Maori in their struggles against colonization and their associated quest for social justice, the achievement of authentic being and the restoration of *mana*. The knowledge that flows from the Maori worldview is traditionally held by *tohunga*, people trained in *wananga*, the ancient schools of learning. Over time, traditional *wananga* have waned but some of the knowledge has been opened up for a wider purview and is now being applied in a contemporary mode across a wide spectrum of cultural activities including art, Maori educational institutions and political initiatives.

Marsden (2003) notes that the Maori worldview can be characterized as a cosmic process, unified and bound together by spirit. At its centre – the highest or deepest level – is the non-material, inseparable, metaphysical linkage of everything. Rhythmical patterns of pure energy are woven through interconnected realms and provide an integrative element across the whole spectrum of life. Ultimate reality is *wairua* (spirit); the universe is 'process;' and spiritual power is ubiquitous, immanent in the total process; upholding, sustaining, replenishing, regenerating all things by its *hau* or *mauri* (breath of life principle). As a corollary, the All-is-One is interlocked together and humans are both human and divine and an integral process of the natural order. The Maori approach to life is holistic, and there is no sharp division between culture, society and their institutions.

Marsden speaks of the *tohunga* who safeguard *whakapapa* (genealogy) and understand the power of relationships: 'reciprocal living' is the essential nature of all reality. The ethical act of the *tohunga* is the fostering of relationships – to weave people and all things into a fabric of *whanaungatanga*. The word *whanaungatanga* is the basic cement that holds Maori people together in bonds of association and obligation. Out of this emerge social values of loyalty, generosity, caring, sharing, that serve one's extended self. The resulting holistic approach to life serves to unify its diverse elements and allows people to achieve a balance and harmony conducive to life abundant.*

The interrelationships woven through Maori thinking are seen in the creation stories and their *atua* or gods, all born from the union of *Papatuanuku* (Earth Mother) and *Ranginui* (Sky Father).

Table 16.1   Nga Atua Maori: Guardians of the environment

Atua	Domain	Resource Interests
Tangaroa	the seas and waters	fisheries and fish
Rongomatane	kumara (potato)	cultivated crops
Haumiatiketike	fern roots	forest undergrowth
Tane Mahuta	the forests	trees and birds
Tawhirimatea	the elements	wind, rain
Tumatauenga	humankind	human exploitation

Source: Durie (1998) p. 22.

Tumatauenga is the god of war. *Rongo-ma-tane*, the god of cultivated food and the god of peace, and *Haumia-tiketike*, the god of forest foods, provided the

---

* Ed. For a diverse understanding of the holistic view, see Chapter 23 by Belachew Gebrewold.

means of land sustenance. The practical link between their domain and human interaction is clear: the food supply could not be sustained during continuous fighting, an activity that was commonplace in early Maori society, much of it centered on disputes over land.

The land, central to Maori existence, is termed *whenua* (the name also used for placenta). To speak of the land is to speak of the spiritual relationship, the union, the bond that exists between the Maori people and the *whenua*. Land was not an economic commodity to be bought and sold; it was a sacred gift, a heritage passed down from the tribal ancestors, a possession that could never be sold, bartered or alienated. (Durie, 1998).

Kaitiakitanga (loosely translated as a duty of 'guardianship' of the *whenua* according to *tikanga* Maori) comprises a set of responsibilities and entitlements that spring from the rights to the land, although Durie (1998) emphasizes that *kaitiakitanga* is a duty 'more frequently associated with obligation rather than authority.' *Kaitiaki* duties include the protection and enhancement of the *whenua* and resources. Those who are appointed as *kaitiaki* are accountable both to their *whanau, hapu* or *iwi*, to their forebears, future generations and to the *atua* and must take their duties seriously. Proper fulfillment of *kaitiaki* duties relies on an intimate knowledge of a place and the *tikanga* governing its use and application. Such knowledge is generated by stable occupation of the *whenua* by a *hapu or iwi*, the use of *whakapapa* to organize that knowledge and its transmission from one generation to another.[7]

All cultural activities are grounded in basic Maori values, emphasizing particular respect for the spiritual dimension (expressed in *karakia* – prayers, and in the observance of *tapu* – the sacred), ancestral connections (expressed in *whakapapa* and *whanaungatanga*), attachment to the land (*whenua*), generosity (*aroha*) and care for others (*manaaki ki te tangata*), peace (*rangimarie*) and unity (*kotahitanga*) (Metge, 2001).

The focus on living according to traditional values is integral to all aspects of the Maori renaissance. Huge social, economic and cultural challenges face all Maori communities, but the positive energy that has been released since the establishment of the Waitangi Tribunal continues to challenge, change and transform negative stereotypes imposed by colonization. Given the centrality of balance and harmony in the Maori worldview, the need to resolve conflict and to make peace with the past is a constant concern. Maori communities and groups follow formalized processes established by *tikanga*, and their insights are now being picked up and being used by some non-Maori groups (Metge, 2001). There are also Maori peace stories that have a well-known history, a high national profile and have been explored through books and films and public events that have received widespread public interest and acclaim. Two prominent examples are Parihaka, and the Moriori people of the Chatham Islands:

Stories of peace: Parihaka

From the mid-1860s Parihaka, a Maori settlement in the Taranaki tribal area of the North Island, became the centre of a peaceful resistance movement. The movement involved Maori from a number of tribes around the country. Its leaders, Te Whiti-o-Rongomai and Tohu Kakahi, were both from Taranaki. Throughout the Land Wars of the 1860's the Parihaka leaders forbade the use of arms and condemned violence and greed. The confiscation of land then became the central problem faced by Taranaki Maori, and under Te Whiti's leadership a new approach to this issue was developed: that of resisting European settlement of the confiscated land through nonviolent methods. In 1879, when the government started surveying confiscated land in the vicinity, followers of Te Whiti began disrupting surveys and ploughing and fencing land occupied by settlers. Many were arrested and held without trial in the South Island, but the protests continued and intensified. Finally in November 1881, the government sent a force of over 1500 troops to Parihaka. Its inhabitants offered no resistance, were arrested or driven away, and the village was later demolished. Te Whiti and Tohu were imprisoned without trial until 1883. In their absence Parihaka was rebuilt and the ploughing campaigns continued into the 1890s. In recent times, Parihaka has become an icon for peace and a number of initiatives (including a 2000 exhibition: 'Parihaka – The Art of Passive Resistance', and annual Parihaka Peace Festivals) and has been successful in creating art, music, dialogue, education and healing between Maori and other races. In 2003 the Parihaka leaders were recognised posthumously by an international delegation of representatives of Martin Luther King Jnr, Mahatma Gandhi and Daisaku Ikeda for their foundational work and sacrifice as fathers of nonviolent action. (Parihaka, 2009)

Stories of peace: Moriori

Hundreds of years ago the Moriori Maori of the Chatham Islands (500 km to the east of New Zealand's South Island), took a solemn vow of peace known as Nunuku's Law. In 1835, twenty-four generations after the Moriori chief Nunuku had forbidden war, Moriori welcomed 900 people from two Maori tribes on New Zealand's North Island. They had voyaged on an overcrowded European vessel and arrived severely weakened, but were nursed back to health by their Moriori hosts. However, they soon revealed hostile intentions and embarked on a reign of terror. Stunned, Moriori called a council of 1,000 men to debate their response. The younger men were keen to repel the invaders and argued that even though they had not fought for many centuries, they outnumbered the newcomers two to one and were a strong people. But the elders argued that Nunuku's Law was a sacred covenant with their gods and could not be broken. The consequences for Moriori were devastating. They were slaughtered, enslaved, and dispossessed of their lands. Nevertheless, the

Moriori people survived. In the 1990's, a Waitangi Tribunal hearing clarified their position as rangata hunu (people of the land) of the Chatham Islands, and its 2001 report recommended compensation for cultural and material losses. After years of difficulties, the two competing groups finally achieved unity in 2001, forming the Hokotehi Moriori Trust with the aims of seeking redress for past injustices, reviving the language, customs, and traditions of the Moriori ancestors, building a sustainable economic future for the Chathams, and broadcasting a message of tolerance and peace to the world. A newly coined Moriori greeting is used in all written communications – me rongo, meaning 'with peace'. (Davis and Solomon, 2009)

A notable feature of the Maori renaissance is that modern initiatives (e.g. Te Wananga o Raukawa, a Maori tertiary institution, and the Maori Party, set up in 2004 to represent Maori people in New Zealand's Parliament) are basing their structures and philosophies on the Maori worldview. Under this approach, a set of principles and values (*kaupapa*) derived from the worldview are given expression through *tikanga* (processes and policies aligned to the *kaupapa* or philosophy). For example, the Maori Party's (2009) principles include:[8]

Manaakitanga: behaviour that acknowledges the *mana* of others as having equal or greater importance than one's own, through the expression of *aroha*, hospitality, generosity and mutual respect.

Rangatiratanga: the expression of the attributes of a *rangatira* (weaving the people together) including humility, leadership by example, generosity, altruism, diplomacy and knowledge of benefit to the people.

Whanaungatanga: underpins the social organization of *whanau*, *hapu* and *iwi* and includes rights and reciprocal obligations consistent with being part of a collective. It is inter-dependence with each other and recognition that the people are our wealth.

Kotahitanga: unity of purpose and direction demonstrated through the achievement of harmony and moving as one, and promoting harmonious relationships between all people.

Wairuatanga: reflected in the belief that there is a spiritual existence alongside the physical that is central to the wellness of people in their everyday lives. It is expressed through the intimate connection of people to their *maunga*, *awa*, *moana* and *marae*, and to *tupuna* and *atua* (i.e. mountains, rivers, sea, homelands, ancestors and gods).

Mana Whenua: that which defines Maori by the land occupied by ancestral claim. It defines [...] the places where you belong, where you are important, and where you can contribute. Once grounded to the land and home, Maori are able to participate in society in a positive and productive manner.

Mana Tupuna/Whakapapa: that which defines who Maori are as a people. It is the bridge, which links us to our ancestors, which defines our heritage, gives us stories which define our place in the world.

Te Reo Rangatira: the cornerstone of all that is Maori [...] it is the medium through which Maori explains the world.

Kaitiakitanga: embraces the spiritual and cultural guardianship of *Te Ao Marama* (the world of light), a responsibility derived from *whakapapa*. It entails an active exercise of responsibility in a manner beneficial to resources and the welfare of the people.

The force and scope of Maori aspirations and the growing confidence in the deep insights that the Maori worldview presents will continue to define new cultural initiatives and the Pakeha New Zealand response. The potential for greater cross-fertilization is being explored quietly and tentatively in many arenas but there is as much uncertainty as there is confidence about the direction that possible paths may take.

How to build a deeper peace?

A reality check is necessary at this stage. Some innovative thinking on the margins, and a powerful indigenous tradition that reaches deep into the nature of relationships (albeit one that is not widely understood) is not representative of the body politic at large. New Zealand's society experiences all the *anomy* of modern civilization. There is much angst and confusion about the predicaments and complexities of modern life. Despite twenty-five years of ongoing public debate, the Treaty is still a source of dissention with perspectives ranging from blame to grievance to resentment. Many New Zealanders are still ignorant of their history and when major controversial issues arise (for example, a court decision that would allow Maori to seek ownership of parts of the coastal foreshore and seabed), governments invariably opt for status quo decisions that favor the European majority.

But there is also acceptance and celebration of the recent stories that are becoming part of the country's identity. To be nuclear-free is firmly cemented in public consciousness; the bicultural Treaty Settlement process is becoming accepted as a means of healing the past and building for the future; Maori confidence in defining themselves as *tangata whenua* continues to grow; the country's strong sustainability focus and being 'clean and green,' paradoxically, an image born of sophisticated marketing rather than environmental reality, is integral to being a 'kiwi;' more urban dwellers are seeing cultural diversity in a positive light; and there is an ongoing and underlying public debate about identity and the place of difference.

These are all tentative first steps towards building cultures of peace as Panikkar's and Dietrich's insights reveal. The central issue is: how to further open these doors so that people can see the necessity for building multifaceted 'cultures of peace,' cultures that embody harmonious relations and the practice of energetic peace? What is needed to build on this energy, these interesting stories of human aspiration? Clearly, there is no prescription for what has to be done, but there are some useful signposts that can offer insights for the journey ahead. More elucidation from Panikkar is helpful.

Panikkar's intercultural dialogue

One of the profound insights of Panikkar's *Cultural Disarmament* (1995)[9] is that people and human traditions, whether religious or secular, are capable of growth and change through their interaction with the 'other.'* The process requires mutual sharing with, receiving from, and critiquing of themselves and the 'other' in dialogue. In order to recognize our own myth we need the contribution of other cultures: interculturality is a source of intelligibility for all concerned, and the necessary dialogue requires a deep human honesty, intellectual openness, trusting the other and a willingness to forego prejudice in the search for truth.

Panikkar stresses the deep commitment and desire required to understand another tradition. This means being open to a new experience of truth since 'one cannot really understand the views of another if one does not share them.' Dialogue 'is primarily the meeting of persons; the aim is convergence of hearts, not just coalescence of minds.' Both partners are encouraged to 'cross over' to the other tradition and then 'cross back again' to their own. In so doing, they mutually integrate their testimonies 'within a larger horizon, a new myth' of understanding.

This process is central to the quest for peace, which, according to Panikkar, requires interculturality – the collaboration of all cultures.

> Only forgiveness, reconciliation and ongoing dialogue lead to peace [...]. Reconciliation comes from *concilium*, denoting the convocation of others. Reconciliation means convoking everyone, speaking with others. [...] Peace is the synthesis of three primordial experiences of the human being – harmony, freedom, justice [...]. Harmony is tantamount to saying 'balance' [...] nothing to excess [...] each element should have its place [...] a space in which there is room for all [...] harmony implies totality, something comprehensive. [Freedom means] absence of determination from without, from dependency [...] it consists in doing, thinking, acting in conformity with what one is [and can be equated] with an acknowledgement of the dignity of the person [...];

---

*   Ed. Likewise, the book *Cultural Disarmament* is singled out by Gustavo Esteva in Chapter 31 as being one of Raimon Panikkar's most crucial pieces in order to comprehend his contributions to peace thinking.

[while justice is] an essential ingredient of peace [...] a fundamental relation [...] our relations with others. [...] We are all set in relation and are interdependent. (Panikkar, 1995)

What then are the prospects and possibilities for deepening the stream of experience in New Zealand to advance the quest for peace? Three areas of encounter underpin the experience of the last thirty years and lay out guiding ropes that could be used to weave a richer foundation for building stronger cultures of peace. They can be summarized as: the value of the other in our midst; new stories of relationship; and rediscovering the universal system of relations.

The value of the other in our midst

Opening to the other

The forceful expression of the Maori renaissance is one of the defining features of contemporary New Zealand culture. The creative tension between the Maori challenge and the Pakeha response illustrates the value of having a strong 'other' in a society that acts as a prompt to push people to explore and understand elements of relationship and interculturality. This interaction is particularly beneficial when there are social mechanisms that link the 'other' into a wider framework that enables people and cultures to come together in an open and respectful way. Maori welcome rituals (*powhiri*) on *marae* have particular value in this regard. They are a regular part of cultural events on *marae*, but in recent times, *powhiri* are becoming commonplace in public ceremonies and meetings. Young people also experience the rituals as a part of their educational curriculum.

The *powhiri* enables participants to come together in a formal process of encounter and embrace, and its focus on identity, connection, community, hospitality, acceptance and belonging heightens the awareness of 'living together differently' by allowing people to experience Maori cultural values in a non-threatening way. A key factor of the ritual is the acknowledgment of the visitors (*manuwhiri*) and the home people (*tangata whenua*), both of their ancestors, the spiritual realm, the land, the mountains and the waterways.

The requirement for space to reconceive and reencounter the other

The invasion of cultural space by colonization requires a cooperative response by the Pakeha majority to symbolically step back and create a space for the flowering of cultural traditions, in ways that reflect the quest for authentic being. The emergence of these spaces includes regeneration of *marae*, language revival (Maori is an official language), education initiatives (Maori immersion from preschool to tertiary levels), art and performance activities, and accommodation of Maori values and processes in legal and political institutions. Cultural space is also required for people to reconceive and reencounter the other. One of the important elements of the Treaty Settlement process has been the role of the Waitangi Tribunal (supported by the courts) in acting as critic and conscience of society (Liu, 2005). These bodies have reaffirmed the values of good faith, respect and inclusion, and in so doing have helped generate greater cultural awareness. The acknowledgment by governments of breaches of the Treaty has also been pivotal in acknowledging the pain of the past. Treaty settlements take place on *marae* and involve an apology read to the affected tribe by senior political leaders (often the Prime Minister), which is a powerful experience for all concerned.

These bicultural processes have the potential to be extended into other shared encounters of difference. The value of learning from other traditions by 'looking across the fence' and seeking mutual illumination is now being understood and helps affirm positive possibilities for the world.

New stories of relationship

Generation of dialogue

Dialogue is a means of promoting conversations where previously there was silence, suspicion, fragmentation and domination by the voices of the powerful. The Treaty process has given Pakeha and Maori the means of finding a 'common language' of coexistence, paradoxically born of assertions of difference. The Treaty principles require both parties to engage in dialogue and for Pakeha to consult Maori and discuss options with open minds. The call for partnership is still a contentious one but because of its status in the public policy realm, innovative approaches are being developed across a wide range of administrative spheres. As an underlying theme, consultation and its constituent processes are now being applied to many areas of interaction, and are helping to promote a stronger capacity for building relationships and trust.

Defining centers of identity that express connection and belonging

Liu (2005) notes that biculturalism has created alternate centers for New Zealand's society located on *marae* and rivers and mountaintops, and these draw energy into spheres of cultural rather than economic creation: 'it behooves a nation to know what things it holds sacred and what things it cannot afford to compromise.' This focus on the power of the land and ocean is a key expression of New Zealand identity for Maori and Pakeha. There is a strong mutual interaction: the Maori dimension highlights the centrality of the sacred and spiritual realm, and Pakeha talk openly of being affected by the dynamic natural world and the abundance of light, clear air and big skies. A constant theme of the poets is the spirit of the land – 'upon the upland road, ride easy stranger. Surrender to the sky your heart of anger' – while the songwriters make pleas for connection – 'anchor me in the middle of the deep blue sea.' Maori speak of *turangawaewae* – being rooted in the tribal homelands, having a place to stand that provides identity, depth, breadth, a sense of continuity and promise, and Pakeha have built a strong peace movement and a powerful environmental presence that continues to push for visionary sustainability goals. The land and its layers (Maori embeddedness, the deepening connection of Pakeha and the growing interaction of migrant groups) is thus one component of an emerging shared identity.

Language is another. A growing number of Maori words have been absorbed into New Zealand English, e.g.: *mana, whanau, hapu* and *iwi, karakia, powhiri, hui, marae, mauri, kaitiakitanga, kaumatua, kohanga reo, kuia, koha, rangatiratanga, waka, mokopuna, whakapapa* (Metge, 2004). They represent a wider cultural understanding and can offer new insights into the nature of reality. For example, *mauri* (life force) can be a more apt way of describing states of ecosystem health or degradation; it has both a qualitative and depth dimension that can capture the essence of ecological interrelationships. However (and needless to say), its use needs to be placed in a cultural context and discussed in dialogue with appropriate *tangata whenua*.

Relationship building is arguably easier when a country is small and where the consequences of actions are seen and felt in personal ways. People living in a relatively remote island culture cannot easily escape interactions and the consequences of actions. They know the quality of relationships both by their negation, and by experiencing them in their fullness. The energy of social movements is vital in this respect as it keeps building horizons of understanding and fosters public debate.

Rediscovering the universal system of relations

Embracing depth traditions

Underpinning all these encounters is the quest to find greater meaning in life and to reach out to people and ideas 'in relationship.' The quality of the relationships in question can best be seen when placed in a context of fundamental origins. For example, Marsden's (2003) understanding of the Maori worldview can provide a measure of how a Maori person or group is achieving 'balance and harmony conducive to life abundant.' His insights also have relevance to the call to rediscover the universal system of relations by providing a powerful lens into a cultural perspective that continues to evolve and adapt to meet contemporary demands. But what is the place of this worldview in the intercultural exchanges that are now occurring in New Zealand?

Panikkar (1995) stresses that cultures continue to intertwine historically so that self-understandings and symbols are in a constant process of mutual influence and growth; only by cross-fertilization and mutual fecundation can the present problems be overcome; and the ground for understanding needs to be created in the space between the traditions through dialogue.

The Maori worldview, at its core, has an elegant understanding of interrelationship that can accommodate other perspectives when the dialogue takes place in conditions of equality. How Pakeha respond to a call for deeper engagement is still a matter of uncertainty and debate. A recognition that 'depth prompts depth' in the quiet spaces of dialogue may encourage participants to go deeper into one's own culture as well as experiencing the insights of another culture, and this interaction is beginning to occur. One response to the strong Maori assertion of *whakapapa* has been to set out an 'ancestors (or whakapapa) of the mind' (Traue, 1990) that celebrates the extraordinary passion and creativity and power of Western thought. This type of exchange can encourage a greater expression of reciprocity and balance that is an embodiment of any lived relationship. Other Pakeha writers and artists (along with their Maori kin) are portraying these islands as a place of spirit (e.g. Morris, 2002, 2004) and energy that nurtures human creativity and the telling of powerful stories of struggle and accomplishment.

The metaphor for these emerging encounters – *he taura whiri* – is particularly apt. But it is crucial to reflect that the path for a deeper understanding of reality and peace lies in the higher realms of consciousness and awareness. Because this terrain is an 'upland road,' it is sacred, open to mystery, and given the New Zealand context (islands with a backbone of mountainous terrain), well-woven ropes and themes are needed to guide the dialogue. On one side of the path lies the Maori *taura*, on the other side Pakeha, and they both link back to the best of their respective cultural traditions. Each side has the capacity to develop new possibilities in ways that express authentic being, generosity of spirit, expanded spheres of care and concern, courage and aspiration. And in the space between, rooted in the land, the multiple stories of creating connection and belonging and acceptance can be carefully constructed and laid out.

Opening the common heart

The beauty of interculturality is that insights can emerge from many traditions and coalesce in ways that inform and affirm the core potential of human experience.

> The higher stages of consciousness have an inherent openness and non-judgmental element woven into them. They can accommodate beginnings, openings, limitations, trends. The focus is on affirmation, compassion and insight for the human endeavors, limited though they are. (Dietrich, 2006)

> The aim of dialogue is 'convergence of hearts, not just coalescence of minds.' (Panikkar, 1995)

[...] across different cultures and religions, meaningful human communication and agreement can and does occur, especially when the heart is silent and listens with respect; [you are] on a journey into your very own heart, a common ground that is timeless and therefore eternally present, spaceless and therefore infinitely open [...]. (Wilber, 2006, pp. pxii, xiv)

Wisdom is a thing of the heart. It has its own thought processes. It is there that the knowledge is integrated for this is the centre of one's being. (Marsden, 2003)

The old people talked about the heart of the mind and the mind of the heart. The heart of the mind is headstrong and is often too powerful. The mind of the heart opens to balance and insight and harmony and peace. (Richards, 2005)

Dialogue *in relationship* is a prerequisite for seeking the multitude of cultures of peace. *He taura whiri* take places across all dimensions and domains – the inner and the outer, the diversity of peoples, and the living world of nature. But the essential weaving, if it is to have enduring value, has to embrace the open and common heart.

Notes

1. The term comes from the title of a lecture 'Ropeworks *He Taura Whiri*' on nation-building by a distinguished academic, Joan Metge (2004). She explains the term:

   The Maori word *'taura'* means a rope and *'whiri'* means 'to plait', the technical process used in rope making. *'He taura whiri'* is a 'plaited rope', a metaphor much loved by Maori orators. They commonly use it to describe the way middle-sized descent groups – *hapu* – are plaited together in the *iwi [the tribe]* by common descent and the diplomatic skills of the *rangatira [traditional leaders]*. They also apply it to any situation where disparate elements are combined in a unity. [...] Making ropes in the traditional way, Maori twisted and rolled strands [...] together to make [...] ropes [...]. The strands might vary in thickness and color, and new ones were easily spliced in. A rope thus made was many times stronger than any of its strands alone. All of us have experience of ropes in our everyday lives, so we should readily understand how this metaphor could be used to inspire a new model of nation-building [...]. Such a model would begin with strands representing the two parties to the Treaty of Waitangi, Maori and Pakeha, splice in the diversity of other ethnic groups, and plait them all together into a strong and effective whole, creating a sense of belonging to each other, of national identity.

2. In modern Maori usage, Aotearoa ('the long white cloud') is the name for the country. 'New Zealand' originated with the Dutch explorer Abel Tasman, who called the islands 'Nova Zeelandia' in 1642, after the Dutch province of Zeeland. The British explorer James Cook, who landed in 1769, subsequently anglicized the name to New Zealand. In recent years, the term 'Aotearoa New Zealand' is being used to denote the country's bicultural heritage, but the official name is still New Zealand.

3. The Treaty had both an English and Maori version and consisted of three Articles. In the first Article, the English text states that Maori ceded sovereignty to the English Crown. Under the Maori text, Maori gave up *kawanatanga* or the right of governorship to the Crown. Under the English text of the second Article, the English Crown guaranteed to Maori the undisturbed possession of their properties including their lands, forests and fisheries as long as they wished to retain them. In the Maori text, Maori were promised their absolute authority (*tino rangatiratanga*) over their lands, settlements and other treasures (*taonga*). The third Article, which promised Maori the rights of all British subjects and the benefits of the Crown's protection, was unusual for nineteenth century treaties. In essence, the Treaty gave the new European settlers the right to live in New Zealand in exchange for according Maori people specific rights and privileges. From the beginning, the two signatory parties interpreted the Treaty of Waitangi with very different intentions. The British saw it as an eventual step towards the establishment of a colonial government, while Maori chiefs saw it only as morally binding with no real transfer of traditional authority over their tribal areas to British interests (the population mix in 1840 was 2000 Europeans and over 100,000 Maori).
4. The process involves Maori lodging claims, research being carried out by Tribunal historians, public hearings conducted by the Tribunal (made up of Maori and European members) on *marae* (tribal homelands) and in cities, and the writing and release of a report that sets out the historical record together with recommendations to government. Settlements (which consist of an apology by the government, financial reparations and recognition of specific cultural matters) have been made to a number of Maori, and there is broad agreement among all political parties that the settlements are appropriate within the confines of government policy.
5. The following points are summarized from a 2007 unpublished thesis 'The Culture of the Land,' written by Stephanie Howard at the Victoria University of Wellington.
6. The *Raukawa* Model is named after the tribal affiliation of the model's architect – W. Winiata.
7. These issues are of increasing concern because New Zealand's environmental legislation includes *kaitiakitanga* and the Maori relationship with the environment as a central principle of sustainability, the main purpose of the legislation. The challenge of recognizing spiritual values is now being dealt with regularly in resource use conflicts.
8. These principles are summarized from those set out in the Maori Party's Constitution. The Maori Party currently has four MPs in Parliament, and its approach to political life has won widespread approval from both Maori and non-Maori (Maori Party, 2009).
9. The quotes and comments that follow are taken from this source.

Reference list

Davis, D. and M. Solomon (2009) *Moriori: The Impact of New Arrivals*, http://www.teara.govt.nz/NewZealanders/MaoriNewZealanders/Moriori/4/en, date accessed June 20, 2009.

Dietrich, W. (2006) 'A Call for Trans-Rational Peaces', *Virtual Peace Library of the UNESCO Chair for Peace at the University of Innsbruck*, http://www.uibk.ac.at/peacestudies/downloads/peacelibrary/transrational.pdf, date accessed June 13, 2009.

Durie, M.H. (1995) 'Beyond 1852: Maori, the State, and a New Zealand Constitution,' *Sites*, 30, 31–47.

Durie, M.H. (1998) *Te Mana, Te Kawanatanga: The Politics of Maori Self-Determination* (Auckland: Oxford University Press).

Fleras, A. and P. Spoonley (1999) *Recalling Aotearoa: Indigenous Politics and Ethnic Relations in New Zealand* (Auckland: Oxford University Press).

Howard, S. (2007) 'The Culture of the Land,' unpublished thesis (Wellington: Victoria University of Wellington).

King, M. (2003) *The Penguin History of New Zealand* (Auckland: Penguin Books).

Liu, J. (2005) 'History and Identity: A System of Checks and Balances for Aotearoa/New Zealand' in J. Liu, T. McCreanor and T. McIntosh (eds.) *New Zealand Identities, Departures and Destinations* (Wellington: Victoria University of Wellington).

Maaka, R. and A. Fleras (2005) *The Politics of Indigeneity: Challenging the State in Canada and Aotearoa New Zealand* (Dunedin: University of Otago Press).

Maori Party (2009) *Constitution of the Maori Party*, http://www.maoriparty.org/index.php?pag=cms&id=133&p=constitution.html, date accessed June 20, 2009.

Marsden, M. (2003) 'God, Man and the Universe: A Maori View' in C.T.A. Royal (ed.) *The Woven Universe: Selected Writings of Rev. Maori Marsden* (Otaki: The Estate of Maori Marsden), 2–23.

Metge, J. (2001) *Korero Tahi, Talking Together* (Auckland: Auckland University Press).

Metge, J. (2004) *Rope Works. He Taura Whiri*, http://www.firstfound.org/Listen%20to%20Ropeworks%20by%20Dame%20Joan%20Metge.htm, date accessed June 20, 2009.

Morris, P. (ed.) (2002) *Spirit in a Strange Land* (Auckland: Godwit Press).

Morris, P. (ed.) (2004) *Spirit Abroad: A Second Selection of Spiritual Verse* (Auckland: Godwit Press).

Panikkar, R. (1995) *Cultural Disarmament. The Way to Peace* (Louisville: Westminster John Knox Press).

Parihaka (2009) *The History of Parihaka*, http://www.parihaka.com/About.aspx, date accessed June 20, 2009.

Patterson, J. (2000) *People of the Land: A Pacific Philosophy* (Palmerston North: Dunmore Press).

Richards, C. (2005) *Ngati Rangi* Aotearoa, personal communication.

Sneddon, P. (2005) *Pakeha and the Treaty: Why It's Our Treaty Too* (Auckland: Random House).

Traue, J. (2006) 'Ancestors of the Mind: A Pakeha Whakapapa' in R. Brown (ed.) *Great New Zealand Argument: Ideas About Ourselves* (Auckland: Activity Press).

Wilber, K. (2006) 'Foreword' in N. Miles-Yepez (ed.) *The Common Heart: An Experience of Interreligious Dialogue* (New York: Lantern Books).

17
Skennen: A North American Indian Perspective

Pat Lauderdale

Indigenous knowledge, which emerges from a symbiotic relationship between nature and underlying transformations, continues to help us learn more about restoration and peace. This restoration includes all of our relatives, that is, all living things. An examination of many indigenous societies shows us that struggles to achieve equality before efficiency is crucial and egalitarian policy solutions are essential.

Before humans assumed their present form, the Holy People had their own problems to address. During that time, Lightning and Horned Toad had a dispute. Horned Toad was walking on some land, when suddenly Lightning confronted Horned Toad and asserted that he, Lightning, owned the land and Horned Toad must leave immediately. Horned Toad replied, 'My brother, I don't understand why you should have possession of this land, and I certainly don't lay claim to it.' He continued along. Again, Lightning asserted his claim, and he threw a bolt of lightning as a warning. Horned Toad said, 'I am very humble, and I can't hurt you as you can hurt others with your bolt of lightning. Could we talk about this tomorrow? I'll be waiting to talk with you on top of the refuse left there by Brother Water.' Lightning agreed. The following day, Horned Toad arrived, wearing his armor. Lightning announced his arrival and asserted his power by throwing more lightning bolts at Horned Toad.

Horned Toad sat atop a pile of driftwood, which was left behind after a storm. From atop that pile, he discussed the matter with Lightning. Horned Toad said, 'You are very powerful; you can certainly strike me down with a bolt of lightning.' 'I certainly can,' said Lightning. 'That's not what we are here about,' said Horned Toad. 'We are here to discuss the land ownership issue, and we must talk.' 'There is nothing to discuss; the land is mine!' Lightning got angry and threw another bolt of lightning, which hit Horned Toad. 'Brother, you did not hurt me,' he said. The bolt bounced off Horned Toad's armor. 'Brother,' he said, 'this armor was given to me by the same source as your bolts of lightning. Why is it we are arguing over the land, which was also loaned to us?' (Retold by Bluehouse and Zion, 1993)

North American Indians and peace

Power, status, authority, money and property are intimately related to the absence of peace in our world today. How does a traditional North American Indian framework respond to the absence of peace? Is an emphasis on decentralized, i.e. the deconsolidation of power by grassroots government, an important factor in explaining the relatively peacefulness of North American Indians? Should we pay attention to the emphasis on equality before efficiency? How can you have peace without modern law and prisons? Can you ignore the lessons from nature?

You cannot have peace without understanding nature and all of the rest of our relatives. Most contemporary non-indigenous individuals have been taught that the environment is external to them, that it lies outside of them and that the human animals have the right to control the environment solely for their ends. This anthropocentric perspective attempts to control and dominate nature, that is, people and all forms of environment (Nader, 2002). Recent social controls, for example, in the form of new laws and related social regulations that intend to protect the environment are usually shortsighted and fragmented, and often focus upon modern notions of 'developing' the environment. Ostensible developers attempt to control and dominate nature and then define this process as progress. Rather than learning the diverse lessons of nature, the modern linear, univariate, so-called development plan is one of controlling and dominating nature – whether it be rainforests, animals/humans or natural technologies (Harris and Lauderdale, 2008).* Controlling and dominating nature is a path that will not lead to peace.

Different indigenous peoples living in quite diverse cultures and speaking many different languages found lessons about peace from learning about the interrelatedness of nature. Are prisons, for example, a lesson learned from nature? Most scientists remain perplexed by the fact that they have not uncovered or discovered jails or prisons where indigenous people lived and who explored the diversity of life in North America. North American Indians traditionally did not have police or prisons, and created complex yet clear paths to peace.† These paths did not lead to simple social techniques or punitive moral standards for

---

* Ed. Chapters 1 and 7 further discuss the ideas and problems posed by a linear understanding of time/progress and its assumption on the domination of nature in regard to peace.

† Ed. In Chapter 7, Munir Fasheh also deals with the question of imprisonment as punishment and the need to find creative ways of community healing.

a nation. They included respect for diversity and interdependence of all living things, rather than simply tolerance, and did not lead people down the path of homogenization or sameness. And, they now stand as a useful foundation for a critical examination of fundamental concepts such as individual responsibility, group rights, time, peace, diversity and nature. We also need to consider the deep problems with rigid social hierarchies if we truly want to embrace diversity and peace (Lauderdale and Oliverio, 2005; see also Dietrich on virtue, 2006).

Respect for diversity seems central to civil law and peace, especially in the early history of contact between indigenous peoples and Europeans. Cooperation, respect, kinship and the fundamental role of spiritual values and ceremonies were embodied within education and caring for indigenous youth. In the 1600s Le Jeune had his work cut out since he did not know how to respond to indigenous people who did not punish children, encouraged women's independence and decision making, and were horrified of authority imposed from the outside. People who, in Le Jeune's words, could not 'endure in the least those who seem desirous of assuming superiority over the others, and place all virtue in a certain gentleness or apathy [...]. They have reproached me a hundred times because we fear our Captains, while they laugh at and make sport of theirs' (Le Jeune, 1633, p. 242).

Despite numerous attempts to destroy indigenous people in North America, some and important parts of their traditional knowledge have persisted. This knowledge includes information on cultural values and social organization based on learning the lessons of nature, which appear central to making or keeping the peace. While issues concerning the relatively small size of most indigenous nations and their homogeneity are important considerations, it is crucial to note that despite comparable size and homogeneity of numerous modern subcultures or similar groups, they typically do not possess the social organization or cultural values of the indigenous peoples who lived symbiotically with nature. Another important issue concerns the kinship structure of many indigenous cultures. Ideas emerging from this structure are not used as a simple social technique or as a punitive moral standard for a nation. The ideas include a respect for diversity rather than simple tolerance, and a critical examination of fundamental concepts such as individual responsibility, group rights, time and nature.

The path that traditional North American Indians also still follow leads through the oral transmission of knowledge. The (often-ignored) precision of oral knowledge partly is created by carefully telling the stories over and over again. We are all here today because our ancient ancestors were precise in orally recounting those stories. If nothing else, this tradition will help remind us of the increasing problems in the written forms of law, especially those aimed at peace, but where legal specialists are in conflict over contradictions in legal statutes or the exact meaning of written law.

Many traditional North American Indian peacemaking processes are grounded in a 'horizontal' system of justice in which parties are not labeled as adversaries, and the peacemaker is not presumed to be neutral, but is selected from within the community based upon her or his abilities to restore peace. Although you rarely find the word justice in traditional Indian languages, it seems apparent that traditional peoples knew that you could not have peace without something such as justice or fairness. Contemporary restorative justice perspectives share with peacemaking a focus on restoring relations and community. However, there are key distinctions because mediation is often a one-time service, while peacemaking is a way of life. Mediation often ignores cultural values while spirituality it is central to peacemaking. Mediation is based on the decisions of one decision maker, yet peacemaking is based on consensus. The Navajo peacemaking process, for example, is one where community members related to both parties are frequently involved in the search for peace. It is strikingly different from US legal programs that are based on a 'vertical' and adversary system, where participants are treated as 'plaintiff' and 'defendant' or 'offender' and 'victim,' and a presumably neutral arbitrator metes out decisions in an adversary system of modern law that is narrowly concerned with procedural matters rather than substantive issues of justice.

Recently, many Navajo peacemakers have been attempting to reincorporate more traditional cultural values into peacemaking (Nielsen and Zion, 2005). They try to engage in a 'teaching' process during peacemaking in an attempt to reach a new conception of shared reality and responsibility that 'gets beyond excuses.' Justice is viewed in these cases as akin to a 'ceremony' in which the peacemaker tries to help offenders understand their current circumstance in light of interconnections, traditional values, mutual respect and community well-being. We might learn invaluable lessons from considering the wisdom of the elders, rather than leaving their knowledge on the shelves of our bookcases or minds. And when a traditional person discusses beauty in the peacemaking process and points out that it means harmony, we might see that some useful New Age ideas often emerge from old age wisdom.

Most traditional North American Indian laws (or law-ways) focus upon problem solving, community participation and sharing of resources. US law too often concentrates on punishment by the state rather than providing space for victims and offenders to give voice to their concerns. Peacemaking processes usually are perceived as more open than the larger criminal justice system because the experiences of participants are afforded more value. The peacemaking process can be viewed as a version of restorative justice that provides an alternative to models of retributive justice.

Among the diverse North American Indians, there also is a tradition of a community-healing program. The Hollow Water Ojibway Community, for example, created a community circle-healing program. They wrote:

The use of judgment and punishment actually works against the healing process. An already unbalanced person is moved further out of balance. What the threat of incarceration does do is keep people from coming forward and taking responsibility for the hurt they are causing. It reinforces the silence, and therefore promotes, rather than breaks, the cycle of violence that exists. In reality, rather than making the community a safer place, the threat of jail places the community more at risk. (Ross, 1995, p. 19)

The dominant American justice paradigm furthers imbalance and disrespect, for it does not seek to restore or heal the offender, the immediate family, friends who are also victims, or the entire community that is unbalanced by the transgression (Ross, 1996). A common practice for most traditional indigenous peoples is living in accordance with traditional teachings and retaining balance by respecting and protecting each other and the rest of the natural world (see Krech, 1999, for a divergent perspective).

These circles of justice consist of interrelated structures and socialization practices that provide a multidimensional system of checks and balances that work in unison to retain diversity and harmony within communities and nations. The preventative mechanisms for conflict are found within the traditional teachings, for example in ceremonies, songs, dances, stories, kinship relations and healing and warrior societies. Despite the cultural diversity among North American Indian nations, most traditional practices emphasized civil rather than criminal sanctions. The goal of indigenous justice is to promote peace, heal the network of relationships, and eradicate political, spiritual and emotional injustices (Lyons, 1992, p. 38).

North American indigenous jurisprudence, which emerged from a symbiotic relationship between law and underlying transformations, grants predominance to sanctions that were restitutive or basically of a civil law character (Lauderdale, 1997). The majority of the known collections of ancient law and legal systems is characterized by a feature that distinguishes them from systems of contemporary jurisprudence. The proportion of civil to criminal law is striking. One of the distinct characteristics of most indigenous cultures, especially prior to colonization, was the lack of repressive punishment as the mode of control or domination.

Civil law is not a revolutionary concept emerging in 'modern,' post-industrialized nations or post-modern discourse. An examination of many indigenous societies shows us that struggles to achieve equality before efficiency are not unique nor are egalitarian policy solutions a modern invention. Indigenous confederations and nations in North America, such as the Iroquois, Cheyenne and Laguna, had flexible leaders who possessed policymaking power that led to the implementation of what modern states claim to be social justice. There is increasing evidence, for example, that the Iroquois confederation, which included the Mohawk, Onondaga, Seneca, Oneida, Cayuga and later the Tuscarora nations, was the primary model for civility in modern political forums such as the United Nations. The Haudenosaunee (Iroquois) confederation is noted for a major characteristic, the absence of punitiveness and the presence of discipline as the mode of social control. The people who created this confederation focused foremost upon the welfare of the young, and the complementary nature of all life forms was central.

Even by the early twentieth century, Smith and Roberts (1954, p. 121) note that '[i]mprisonment is not a usual form of legal sanction at Zuni, and it is imposed only for the purpose of holding an offender temporarily pending trial or for the purpose of compelling him to perform labor in situations in which he is unable to pay a fine or damages.' They also mention that except for witchcraft, the premeditated killing of another human 'seems originally to have been, in our terms, a "civil" rather than "criminal" matter' (Smith and Roberts, 1954). The perpetrator was to be held liable for damages to the family of the victim but not for any kind of retribution at the hands of the body politic. Spirituality and ritual remain central to traditional North American Indian cultures, not separate from practical everyday life. The relationship with spiritual forces is a primary idea, and the creation of the world as related to childbearing and both genders is represented by their belief system as well as by the shamans and healers.

Indigenous Indian culture embodies a practical as well as sacred symbiosis, reflected by interpretations of the spiritual in everyday lives, relationships and social institutions. The kinship of traditional indigenous North Americans emphasizes the welfare and education of youth. The raising, educating and training of youth is an intrinsic part of tribal life. In contrast, most 'modern' contemporary education of youth is dominated by formal, external social institutions such as schools, day-care centers, juvenile prisons or orphanages. Paula Gunn Allen (1986) notes that young women and men are trained according to their individual interests and inclinations without resort to bureaucratic instruments of 'higher education' that claim to measure fundamental human characteristics. Young people learn useful skills not only for themselves but also for civil society. The leaders of society, for example, are often those who demonstrated an early competence for work and had leadership qualities.

Gender-specific roles, behaviors and rituals are also taught; however, in most North American indigenous societies, the division of labor between women and men is more practical in that people's inherent inclinations and abilities are encouraged rather than suppressed. This understanding is reflected in how the youth were trained. The constitution of the Iroquois League, for example, has become part of the vision of human liberation movements around the world. In nations such as the Cheyenne, as well as the Iroquois confederacy, the selection of leaders and/or the system of governance was a central role of the Matrons. Allen (1986, p. 213) maintains that:

[F]eminists too often believe that no one has ever experienced the kind of society that empowered women and made that empowerment the basis of its rules of civilization. The price the feminist community must pay because it is not aware of the recent presence of gynarchical societies on this continent is unnecessary confusion, division and much lost time.

Allen also notes that men learned to cook since they were often away hunting or fighting and there were also girl warriors. There were girls who were raised as boys; if, for example, a family only had daughters. The relevant point here is that despite the great differences among the Indian nations, most of them did not have a sharp division of roles, and the diffusion of hierarchy appears to be a central part of learning and teaching in the traditional manner.

Barbara Kanatiiosh points out that Haudenosaunee traditional teachings are found within the *Kaienerekowa* (Great Law of Peace), the words of *Karihwiio* (The Good Message), *Ka'shatstensera* (The Power) and *Skennen* (The Peace) (Kanatiiosh and Lauderdale, 2006). The teachings of the Great Law of Peace help people understand the concepts of love, unity, peace, equity, coexistence, cooperation, power, respect, generosity and reciprocity. The teachings include reaffirmations of the kinship system, duties, ceremonies and societies that promote *Karihwiio*, the good mind, which is necessary to heal the body, the spirit and to maintain diversity and harmony. Haudenosaunee traditional teachings explain how peace is maintained by preventing injustices to the natural world and by protecting the future generations yet to be born.

Kanatiiosh notes that restorative justice is dependent on the foundational traditional preventative structures and practices that work together to create justice and prevent injustice. Focusing only upon the restorative aspects of justice without incorporating the preventative mechanisms, creates injustice, for it breaks the Circle of Justice and leaves individuals and the community without the necessary cultural foundational structures to heal and prevent conflicts. Colonization has, for many peoples, destroyed or displaced these essential foundational traditional teachings (Lauderdale, 2008a, see also Baogang and Goldsmith, 2008). Traditional teachings are preserved in a 'tribal encyclopedia' that is maintained by 'keepers of the tribal encyclopedia.' The Keeper, who is a traditional civil leader, is called a *naat'aanii*. The word describes someone who speaks wisely and clearly. A *naat'aanii* is someone who is respected for her or his ability to solve problems. A Keeper can help identify and provide invaluable insights concerning the traditional teachings found within ceremony, prayer and in the foundational narratives and stories. Frank Pommersheim (1995) emphasizes the importance of narratives by suggesting that stories are not extrinsic niceties, but are basic life forces needed to establish and to preserve communities and develop a common culture of shared understandings and deeper, more vital ethics.

The Haudenosaunee, for example, follow narratives that contain foundational principles, norms, practices and structures: (1) The *Tsi kiontonhwentsison* (Creation Story), (2) the story about the creation of clans, (3) the *Ohen:ton Kariwatekon* (Thanksgiving Address), and (4) the *Kaienerekowa* (Great Law of Peace). Their Great Law of Peace contains traditional laws, political and spiritual principles, and the spiritual/political structure of the Haudenosaunee confederacy (Kanatiiosh and Lauderdale, 2006). The duties and responsibilities of each person in the society is given and reaffirmed when the people come together for ceremonies and social activities. The Great Law also reaffirms the sacred ceremonies, songs and dances and the clan system. It contains a system of checks and balances that depends not only on people not wanting to commit a transgression, but on people understanding and having the will to prevent others from breaching the peace.

The kinship or clan system is one example of an important structure that contains duties, protocols and practices that function to maintain justice. Chief Tom Porter (1993, p. 7) states that '[t]he clans are extremely important, and in fact without the clans we would have almost nothing as a society of people. Like the human body, the bones are what gives the body structure and the ability to function, so the clans serve the same purpose in the societies of the *Rotinonhson:ni* (Haudenosaunee) people.' This kinship functions to maintain justice in many ways. Kanienkahake Doug George-Kanentiio (2000, pp. 70–71) writes:

A clan in former times took care of all of its members from the time they were born until they died. Housing, food, health care, education, and employment were administered by the clans. Criminal acts and family disputes were also adjudicated by the clan elders. Clans controlled marriages and ceremonial activities, and they selected political representatives.

Many concrete practices suggest the reasons for the absence of internal violence. For the Haudenosaunee, the practice of the new husband moving to live in the house of his ever watchful and present mother-in-law is a practical deterrent to not committing domestic violence. Some North American Indian nations still have wedding ceremonies where young couples are instructed in the importance of marriage to the nation, as well as appropriate behavior, which includes not abusing each other. Among the Haudenosaunee, a traditional marriage is more than the combining of two people, for it brings together clans and their extended family. Everyone who is present at the joining of the couple is reminded of these acceptable norms and their duty to ensure that they are not broken.

These indigenous justice practices are multidimensional and contain a balancing process dependent on numerous practices and social structures that function as both preventative and restorative mechanisms for maintaining justice. A synergistic, recursive model reminds us that the comparative and historical analysis of theories and practices of justice and its relationship to peace is a relevant alternative to most philosophical treatises and jurisprudence on what justice should be, rather than how it is practiced (Lauderdale, 2008b).

Imposed forms of government and laws via colonization, the loss of lands and policies to assimilate North American Indians have caused many of the traditional indigenous-justice mechanisms to become lost or damaged. Today, numerous tribal courts exist that only replicate the Western-imposed beliefs and practices of an adversarial system of justice, instead of using traditional indigenous-justice methods and values. Such tribal courts and forms of governance can be a form of internalized colonialism. These types of courts cause disharmony within the community, as they do not preserve cultural traditions, nor do they heal the community. This type of replication of imposed laws, practices and ideas has seeped into many aspects of North American Indian governments. Many tribal codes currently are merely restatements of federal and state law and devoid of indigenous knowledge, values and norms. Such tribal codes suggest that the Great Circle of Justice needs to be restored within American Indian communities before other people try to borrow and implement ostensible Indian restoration practices. An important part of traditional codes is their grounding in tradition and an intimate connection with nature.

Traditional teachings, socialization practices and organizational structures that once worked to prevent social injustices can be replanted. Some of the traditional indigenous teachings contain the seeds of how people can once again live in *skennen* (peace) or *Hozho* (balance and harmony). Prior to colonization, 'law' in North America was relatively direct and accessible to indigenous North Americans, since it was based on concrete notions of the individual and collective good rather than on a modern abstraction imposed by the nation-state as the ideal (largely for political purposes) to which people must conform (or be punished) in order ostensibly to have security and private property. It is critical to remember that for most North American Indians 'law' was accessible to everyone since the oral tradition allowed it to be carried around as part of themselves rather than confined to legal institutions and inaccessible experts who largely control the language as well as the cost of using the law.

Social diversity, the recognition that humans are part of nature (not separate from it), and harmony are essential to peace and justice. From the indigenous perspective, justice requires a communal approach in that preventative, as well as, restorative mechanisms and practices need to be restored throughout the community for there to be healing and justice. Alfred Taiaiake (1995, p. 144) writes that 'the goals that flow from our traditions demand an approach based on undermining the intellectual and moral foundations of colonialism and exposing the internal contradictions of states and societies that promise justice and practice oppression.'

Communal restorative justice has the potential to reduce social and economic injustice and it can continue to limit the impact of imprisonment, especially imprisonment that is directly related to unemployment, debt, suicide and innumerable diseases (Kanatiiosh and Lauderdale, 2006).

In general, traditional indigenous law contains the norms, mores, values and responsibilities, duties and appropriate behavior for the maintenance of unity and harmony, including an individual's relationship to a particular nation and nature. Traditional indigenous law is taught from birth and continued throughout life. Traditional teachings are reinforced, and cohesion and social order is maintained, for example, via active participation in important ceremonies. Most such traditional law also emphasizes the principle of equality. A nation's harmony is maintained through a system of checks and balances that insures against any individual or group having too much power or control. Most indigenous law is sensitive to the lessons of nature.

Life, for traditional Indians, is more about learning than receiving a 'formal education,' life is more about healing and peace than war or conflict. Gustavo Esteva notes that within many traditional perspectives no one can learn for you or heal you (Esteva and Prakash, 1998).* Taking charge of learning instead of being educated, or of healing instead of being cured, reflects the continuous exercise of dignity and autonomy that characterizes most traditional indigenous peoples.

Randel Hanson (2001) notes that for contemporary developers and most business people, time is money; however, for indigenous people time may be more relevant for consensus. Consensus often is more important than material gains. In his work with Prairie Indian Dakota, he also notes that they see and learn that everything comes from the earth and only recently was something invented (nuclear weapons) by the human animal that threatens everything living on this earth (Hanson, 2001). Those indigenous peoples point out that related nuclear threats were created by a society that claimed it was quite civilized and not primitive. Hanson (2001, p. 19) stresses that for many indigenous peoples the contemporary problem may be how to 'embrace the tar baby of new global capitalism as a means of economic self-determination but not let that step become the thing itself, not let economic development become the predominant justification.'

Indigenous peoples have been resisting the negative phases of globalization in the Western hemisphere for centuries, and for millennia in Africa and Eurasia. Globalization is a process that is deeply connected to the first invention of states, at least over 5000 years ago (Lauderdale, 2008a). This process includes a series of economic, cultural and political changes typically viewed as increasing

---

* Ed. Gustavo Esteva and Arturo Guerrero co-authors of Chapter 19. Their discussion on Zapotec notions of peace echoes the arguments by Lauderdale in terms of healing and learning as well as the obstacles posed by experts and institutions to peace as harmony. On this topic, see also Chapter 7.

interdependence, integration and interaction between people and organizations throughout the world. Globalization claims to increase peace, yet the claims are couched in abstract and indirect terms, and the empirical data are a conundrum. It often is touted as bringing an increased standard of living and prosperity to poor countries and further wealth to rich ones, yet, another perspective suggests that globalization often perpetuates the long history of plundering and profiteering. This experience is very familiar to indigenous peoples, since it focuses upon forced cultural assimilation, the export of artificial wants both material and symbolic, and the destruction or inhibition of local and global democracy along with the erosion of community, ecology and cultures (Shenandoah, 1987).

The majority of traditional indigenous ideas for peace are relatively direct and accessible to indigenous peoples since they are based on concrete notions of the individual and collective good, rather than modern abstractions imposed by the nation-state as the ideal to which people must conform (or be punished) in order to have stability, security and material goods. The laws of peace are accessible to everyone because the oral tradition allows them to be carried around as part of oneself, rather than confined to legal institutions. Oral traditions in indigenous life can stimulate, develop, protect and deliver knowledge in a systemic manner. Jurisprudence based on oral traditions has continued to preserve much of the diversity and respect for nature. Vine Deloria (1992) suggests that the guidelines for preserving life and the future of all nature can be found within the traditions, beliefs and customs of the peoples. We are instructed to learn from nature rather than try to control and 'develop' it for various ends. In contrast, modern claims of progress and civilization, as part of the domination of nature, pose a conundrum, as is the imposition of labels such as backward and primitive to nature. In this context, the term primitive is a result of different types of anthropocentrism and ethnocentrism. Nature has never been backward.

In general, contemporary philosophers, however, continue to emphasize 'the state of nature' from which humans must separate themselves in order to dominate nature. The issue of nature becomes unduly narrowed to the concept of human nature, which often turns into questions about race or utopian naturalism. Pseudospeciation, the human animal invention that leads people to define their own species as different in order to dominate others and often to extinguish life for narrow political and economic purposes, is not a lesson taken from nature. Deloria (1992, p. 298) stresses that 'if all things are related, the unity of creation demands that each life form contribute its intended contribution. Any violation of another entity's right to existence in and of itself is a violation of the nature of creation and a degradation of religious reality itself.'

The care for and examination of nature provides the lessons that can demonstrate the relevance and importance of peace through diversity. A deep understanding of diversity and the importance of all of our relatives yields ideas and methods to practice responsibility and ensure the existence of future generations. Traditional indigenous knowledge of peace through diversity is useful for adapting to change. The old saying that the only thing that is constant is change can be deeply understood from such a perspective.

Indigenous knowledge, which emerges from a symbiotic relationship between nature and underlying transformations, continues to help us learn more about restoration and peace. This restoration includes all of our relatives, that is, all living things. An examination of many indigenous societies shows us that struggles to achieve equality before efficiency are crucial and egalitarian policy solutions are essential.

Despite the varied attempts to destroy indigenous peoples, important parts of their traditional knowledge have persisted. Cultural values and social organization based on learning the lessons of nature are central to this persistence. Issues concerning the relatively small size of most indigenous nations and their homogeneity are important considerations. Peoples who lived symbiotically with nature still have important lessons, which we can learn. Again, it is a significant finding that scientists remain perplexed, for example, by the fact that they have not uncovered or discovered any jails or prisons in indigenous places in North America. Different indigenous peoples living in quite diverse cultures and speaking many different languages did not find such a lesson from learning about the complexities of nature.

One of the most interesting features of indigenous peoples is their substantive reliance on the interrelatedness of nature. Today's call for global diversity and acceptance of diversity is severely limited when it is built within the constraints of modern nation-states, which often view diversity as deviance if it does not conform to modern norms and definitions, especially those connected to markets and money. This is not to suggest that traditional indigenous knowledge can provide all the answers to current problems; however, it can provide us with ideas on how to improve our questions and, therefore, improve our potential to provide more equitable, less oppressive structures from which to approach problems that fracture or destroy peace (Dietrich, 2005).

While United Nations (UN) Secretary General Boutros Boutros Ghali welcomed indigenous people from across our earth for the 'International Year of Indigenous Peoples' in 1992, and the UN officials wrote many good words on paper, we might consider turning every year into a time for learning the lessons of peace contained in diverse forms of indigenous knowledge. The words from the UN remain on paper, on those old leaves, and the issue now is how to make those words on paper become reality.

Law in books never seems to be the same as law in action (Inverarity et al., 1983; Fitzpatrick, 1992; Lauderdale, 2008b), yet words about peace have the potential to become peace in action. In contemporary terms, it also seems important to note that the following comment is not a cliché, but a declaration gained from long, traditional experiences, which were often attempts to prevent genocide: if we want peace then we have to work for justice.

Reference list

Alfred, T.G.R. (1995) *Heeding the Voices of Our Ancestors: Kahnawake Mohawk Politics and the Rise of Native Nationalism* (Oxford: Oxford University Press).

Allen, P.G. (1986) *The Sacred Hoop: Recovering the Feminine in American Indian Traditions* (New York: Beacon Press).

Baogang, H. and B. Goldsmith (2008) 'Letting Go Without a Fight: Decolonization, Democracy and War, 1900–94,' *Journal of Peace Research*, 45, 587–611.

Bluehouse, P and J.W. Zion (1993) 'Hozhooji Naat'aanii: The Navajo Justice and Harmony Ceremony,' *Mediation Quarterly*, 10, 4, 328–331.

Deloria, V. Jr. (1992) [1973] *God is Red* (Golden: North American Press).

Dietrich, W. (2005) 'A Call for Trans-Rational Peaces,' *Virtual Peace Library of the UNESCO Chair for Peace Studies at the University of Innsbruck*, http://www.uibk.ac.at/peacestudies/downloads/peacelibrary/transrational.pdf, date accessed September 19, 2006.

Dietrich, W. (2006) 'Peaces – an Aesthetic Concept, a Moral Need or a Transrational Virtue?' *Asteriskos Journal of International and Peace Studies*, 1/2, 25–47.

Esteva, G. and M.S. Prakash (1998) *Grassroots Post-Modernism: Remaking the Soil of Cultures* (Boston: Zed).

Fitzpatrick, P. (1992) *The Mythology of Modern Law* (London: Routledge).

George-Kanentiio, D. (2000) *Iroquois Culture & Commentary* (Santa Fe: Clear Light Publishing).

Hanson, R.D. (2001) 'Half Lives of Reagan's Indian Policy: Marketing Nuclear Waste to American Indians,' *American Indian Culture and Research Journal*, 25, 1, 21–44.

Harris, R. and P. Lauderdale (2008) 'Introduction to the Light of Andre Gunder Frank,' *Journal of Developing Societies*, 24, 1, 2–12.

Inverarity, J., P. Lauderdale and B. Feld (1983) *Law and Society* (Boston: Little, Brown, and Co.).

Kanatiiosh, P.G. and P. Lauderdale (2006) 'The Great Circle of Justice: North American Indigenous Justice and Contemporary Restoration Programs,' *Contemporary Justice Review*, 9, 4, 1–19.

Krech, S. III. (1999) *The Ecological Indian: Myth and History* (New York: Norton).

Lauderdale, P. (1997) 'Indigenous North American Jurisprudence,' *International Journal of Comparative Sociology*, 38, 131–148.

Lauderdale, P. (2008a) 'Indigenous Peoples in the Face of Globalization,' *American Behavioral Scientist*, 51, 12, 1836–1843.

Lauderdale, P. (2008b) 'Introduction: Critical Issues in Law and Justice from an Evolutionary Perspective' in L. Gsell (ed.) *American Justice: Ethical Foundations and the Evolution of Modern Law* (Phoenix: Coast Aire Publications), 1–21.

Lauderdale, P. and A. Oliverio (2005) (eds.) *Terrorism: A New Testament* (Ontario: De Sitter Publications).

Le Jeune, P. (1633) *The Jesuit Relations and Allied Documents Travels and Explorations of the Jesuit Missionaries in New France 1610–1791* (Ottawa: National Library of Canada).

Lyons, O. (1992) 'The American Indian in the Past' in O. Lyons, J. Mohawk and V. Deloria Jr. (eds.) *Exiled in the Land of the Free: Democracy, Indian Nations, and the U.S. Constitution* (Santa Fe: Clear Light).

Nader, L. (2002) *The Life of the Law* (Berkeley: University of California Press).

Nielsen, M. and J. Zion (2005) *Navajo Nation Peacemaking: Living Traditional Justice* (Tucson: University of Arizona Press).

Pommersheim, F. (1995) *Braid of Feathers: American Indian Law and Contemporary Tribal Life* (Berkeley: University of California Press).

Porter, T. (1993) *Clanology* (New York: Native North American Traveling College).

Ross, R. (1995) 'Aboriginal Community Healing in Action: The Hollow Water Approach' In R. Ross (ed.) *Dueling Paradigms? Western Criminal Justice versus Aboriginal Community Healing* (Saskatchewan: Native Law Centre of Canada).

Ross, R. (1996) *Returning to the Teachings: Exploring Aboriginal Justice* (Toronto: Penguin).

Shenandoah, A. (1987) 'Everything has to be in Balance' in J. Barreiro (ed.) *Indian Roots of American Democracy,* special ed., *Northeast Indian Quarterly,* IV, 4, 4–7.

Smith, W. and J.M. Roberts (1954) 'Zuni Law: A Field of Values,' *Peabody Museum of American Archeology and Ethnology,* 43, 46–121.

Taiaiake, A. (1999) *Peace, Power, Righteousness: An Indigenous Manifesto* (Oxford: Oxford University Press).

18

Kayanerekowa: A Mohawk Perspective

*Robert Vachon**

Listening together with gratitude to the Cosmotheandric Pluralism
of Reality

The Mohawk nation is one of the six nations of the historically famous Iroquois
Confederacy in North America. The Mohawks are presently a nation of some
25,000 people living inside and outside of seven communities distributed in the
upper states of New York and in the Provinces of Quebec and Ontario (Canada).
While these people are customarily called 'Mohawks' by outsiders, a name given
to them by the Algonquian tribes/nations, in their own language the Mohawk
call themselves Ganienghehaga, literally meaning 'People of Ganiengheh' (the
land of the Flint). The French, following Huron practices, used to call them 'les
Agniers.' The Six Nations Confederacy, of which the Ganiengheh have always
been a constituent member, is still called the Iroquois by outsiders; in their own
languages, however, the Iroquois call themselves the Haudenosaunee: 'People
of the Longhouse' or 'People of the Great Peace' (or 'Of the Cosmic Kinship'
(*Kayanerekowa*).

Besides signifying primarily the Great Harmony and the Peace Messenger's
message, *Kayanerekowa* (The Great Peace) also refers secondarily to two historical

* This text is an abridged and revised version of a series of studies on the Mohawk nation
and the Haudenosaunee (Six Nations Confederacy), named People of the Longhouse
or People of the Great Peace. The series on the Mohawk communities was written and
published by R. Vachon in the Intercultural Institute of Montreal's International journal
Interculture in two separate English and French editions (Vachon, 1991, 1992, 1993a,
1993b). All issues were written with the help of two highly respected Mohawk elders
namely: Kaientaronkwen (Ernie Benedict) and Sakokwenonkwas (Tom Porter). Our focus
in this present study limits itself only to the notion of peace in the Mohawk nation
and among the Haudenosaunee, without reference to the already dealt with origin and
history of their Dynamics of Peace from the beginning to our time. We are also leaving
aside here our further studies in the *Interculture* series 'Guswenta or the intercultural
imperative: towards a re-enacted peace accord between the Mohawk nation and the
North American nation states (and their people)' (Vachon, 1995a, 1995b, 1995c).

forms that it has taken in Iroquois and Mohawk history. I shall now describe briefly each of these four meanings.

The great harmony or cosmic kinship

Introduction

I once asked the respected elder Sakokwenionkas (Tom Porter) of the Mohawk nation: 'How would you translate in English the word *Kayanerekowa*?' He thought briefly and said: 'The closest I can find is simply: "The Great Nice", i.e. the Great Splendor, the whole cosmos and all its life forms, humans, animals, earth, sun, moon, planets, galaxies, rivers, mountains, trees, winds, etc. seen and expressed in terms of the Great Kinship. [The Great Kinship refers to] Grandmother the moon, the grandfather the sun, uncles the winds [and] each human clan be expressed in terms of the bear clan, the turtle clan, the wolf clan, etc. And it is the "Law of Peace" not because somebody legislated and announced it one fine day, but because of the way things are. It is the proper nature of everything.'

The Great Peace is not primarily the Peace Messenger's message or any message about something called the Great Peace, but the message is the Great Peace and Kinship of all beings. It is the Great Peace that speaks. It is important to distinguish between the Great Peace as the Peace messenger's message (see below) and the Great Peace itself as the source of the Messenger's message. The Great Peace is not primarily the Peace Messenger's message or any message *about* something called the Great Peace, but the message *is* the Great Peace of Cosmic Kinship that reality is. The Peace Messenger is simply an emissary, a voice of that Peace. It is the Great Peace and Cosmic Kinship that primarily speaks, not the messenger. It is the Great Peace that makes itself known through him and is realized as well through the clan mothers, the council of Rotiianeson, the words, the symbols.

In this fundamental sense, the Great Peace is not Iroquois or Mohawk, although it has found an Iroquois interpretation and expression. No Iroquois would claim that the Great Peace or Cosmic Kinship is Iroquois property or the exclusive creation of the Iroquois, although their interpretation and expression of it is bound to be unique and Iroquoian.

The words that come before all else: the thanksgiving address

It is customary for Mohawks and Haudenosaunee – who still claim to follow the *Kayanerekowa* – to start every meeting in their own languages with 'The words that come before all else,' namely giving thanks to the *Kayanerekowa*, i.e. to the Great Nice, to the grand Splendor of it all, thus inviting everyone to enter into 'the good mind' or into the spirit of the Great Peace and Cosmic Kinship as they come together to deliberate and to do whatever they are doing. It is a spirit of thanking 'The Great Nice' and listening to it. This is done by all, even the young in school and elsewhere, before any important meeting. The *Kayanerekowa* is not written but oral, it is not a repeated formula but it is each time spelt out differently in eloquent and poetic words that are left to the inspiration of the one who gives thanks and who invites all to be 'of the good mind.'

As illustration, after an introduction in the Mohawk language, Sakokwenionk-was (1993) pronounced the following 'Mohawk Welcoming Ceremony' opening address at the International Colloquium 'Living with the Earth: Cross-cultural perspectives on sustainable development; indigenous and alternative practices:'

First, I have asked the Creator for permission to speak in a language that he did not give me in the beginning when the world was made. I asked the Creator that I may use the English language, for as we gather here, there are many people who have come from all over the world. The English language is a language that is understood throughout the world. For that reason, I asked the Creator for permission to use that language, so that many people from all over the world will know the mind of the Creator and what he has told us here in North America.

Before I begin, I would like to ask for your attention. In Mohawk, we have an expression. When we begin to speak, we say *Ensewatehonsicoste*. In English it means literally: I ask that you stand your ears up straight to catch all the words that are spoken.

Also, I am going to be speaking today of the Creator. When I say 'Creator,' I am not describing a Creator or God, like the image that appears in your mind or in many people's minds. I mean a Higher Power that has no definition. It is so powerful that there can't be any definition.

It is our belief that when we were made, our life was predestined. The number of days we will live here on the earth was marked on a counter-stick when we were born, and no one, man or woman, has the power to change what the Creator has made. Sometimes the Creator may give us one hundred years to stay here on the earth. He makes a mark on the stick as each day passes, and when we come to the last mark, then we'll journey from this world to the next world.

When this occurs to our loved ones, we never seem ready, even though we have a lot of experience with grief. We never seem to be comfortable with it. It is for this reason that I ask you 'to stand your ears up straight' for the many human brothers who have journeyed here from all over the world. In some parts of the world, there is great turmoil and there is sadness. And I say these words before we really begin the ceremony because among the human beings that are here, it could be that somebody has recently lost a loved one who has journeyed to the next land. And when that is the case, the eyes are filled with tears, and this blurs their vision of Reality. And such a person needs help. When a loved one has passed, the ears become obstructed by dust, the dust of death. You cannot hear properly when your children, or your cousins, or your uncle talk to you, nor can you hear the birds when they sing. If any of you has lost a loved one, it is for your benefit that I say this. If this is the situation that you are in, I ask you now to listen, because you are a human brother.

From the very beautiful blue sky, from the blue clear sky, I will take the eagle's feather. And I will use this eagle feather in a spiritual way to remove the death dust that obstructs your ears from hearing. And I will push the death dust away so that your hearing can be restored, so that you can hear your little children when they speak to you, so that you can hear the song of every bird as he sings to you and so that you can, in fact, again hear the life that the Creator has given us. And then, my fellow brothers, in your sadness, in your grief, in your heaviness, I take a glass of medicine water from the very beautiful blue clear sky and ask the Spirit to remove what has stuck in your throat, obstructing the food from passing through and obstructing the words that come from your thoughts. I offer from the very beautiful clear sky this fresh glass of medicine water. I offer it to you now, so that whatever obstructs the passage in your throat will now go through to your stomach. The knots will be untied and you can eat again properly, and you can again speak properly to your kids, to your young ones, to all that live.

And now I take from the very beautiful sky a beautiful cloth that is white, made out of deerskin as soft as cotton. And my brother, if your mind is heavy with sorrow, I will use the cloth of the deer that is so soft. From the clear blue sky I'll wipe the tears, so that your vision will not be blurred again tomorrow, so that you will see the beauty that the Creator has made, so that you will see your fellow human beings and your nephews and nieces, your sons and daughters. They need you to see in a correct way. And so it is, fellow brothers, if your mind is grieving for some loved one who has passed, I lift up your mind so that you may walk again in a correct way.

And now, I would like to begin with this ancient 'prayer.' I don't know if prayer is the correct word. The reason I mention this is because I thought I knew how to speak English very correctly. That was what I thought for many years. And for many years, I spoke it as if I was a master of it. But did you know, until two weeks ago, I always thought that prayer meant an individual relationship or communication with the Creator Power? That was what I thought it was. And then I picked up the big *Webster's Dictionary* two weeks ago, and I looked it up. It says 'to request something.' For almost half a century, I was saying the wrong thing! English is a very tricky language. I have been tricked for 40 years or more. So, bear in mind that this is the language that we have for this meeting and that we come from all over the world. We need to take care so that we don't get tricked or misinterpreted, by no fault of our own.

I am going also to ask you to help me with this opening ceremony, this special spiritual moment. You know that when the teacher writes on the board all day, it is all smudged. Then at the end of the day it is all wiped clean. You take a white cloth and you clean it all off, and it becomes crystal clear, like a beautiful lake. And then when you next mark on it, it is very visible, very clear. That is what I am going to ask that we do in this group, in a symbolic way – that we wipe everything away to make room for the Creator and for all the spiritual things in the world before we can begin this wonderful gathering.

Now this is what Mohawk people do each time we mention a sacred thing. At the end of each spiritual statement, I will say our minds are one, then I will ask if you will show agreement in your language, for instance in English say 'Yes,' or in Mohawk we will say 'Tho,' which means 'Yes, I agree.' In French, this will be 'Oui,' I suppose. We will participate together. I have heard this spiritual talk since I was a child. It is the same spiritual speech that opens all official meetings and also closes each meeting. It opens all ceremonies. Even when people marry, it is the most important part. When two or more people come together to discuss something of human life, they say this prayer too. See, here I go saying 'prayer' again! You'll understand why 'prayer' is incorrect when I have finished. We begin, now, brothers and sisters.

As we are gathered here, in this very beautiful place, with the trees and the hills, and the birds and the animals that live around here, we are their visitors. And as we are gathered here and I look around, and we look around at each other, it seems that everybody is handsome and beautiful. Some even have flowers on their chests like roosters with beautiful feathers. And as I look around, it appears that no one had an accident on their journey here. No one has a crutch or cast because their leg is broken. And we are fortunate. As we look around, we see and we feel tranquility and peace, at least as much as can be expected. And that's very wonderful. And we will do as the Creator said. We will gather our minds together and think in one way. And then, in a symbolic way, we will pile up our 'thank-yous,' layer after layer, and then we will pile our greetings on the same pile, layer after layer, and then we will wrap and tie those 'thank-yous' and greetings with our love, each of us. And we will offer this one to another, to our fellow human beings, our brothers and sisters. And we say 'thank you' and we give our greetings to one another and our love. Our minds are one. (*All: Yes!*)

And now, we will turn our attention to our mother, the earth. For in the beginning of the world, our Creator used his hands and his body and he created the earth. And then, when he created the earth, he turned the earth into a woman, into a mother. This is why we call our earth our mother.

And then, when he touched her, her whole body became spiritual, her whole body became sacred. And then he told mother earth: you are going to be the mother of all human beings: you are going to be the mother of all the bears and the deer and the animals, and the birds and the insects. You are going to be the mother of all life. You will give birth time and time again, for evermore.

And after you give birth to all those lives, mother earth, your job is not done yet. You have to nourish them. You have to grow the food that will feed them so that they will have a good life. And so now, fellow human beings, men and women that are gathered here today, I am asking that our minds be gathered and come together as one mind and one thought. The reason is because we have one of the most steadfast, one of the most consistent mothers in all the world. It is our mother earth who carries the weight of our bodies as we walk upon her, who gives birth and feeds us every single day. And she's been doing it since the beginning of mankind and before. What a wonderful mother!

And so, I ask for that reason, that we, the children that are gathered here, bring our minds and thoughts together as one. And in a symbolic spiritual way, let us pile up our 'thank-yous' again, layer after layer, and then our greetings, layer after layer. And let's tie it up with our love, those greetings and thank-yous, and let's gently pick it up and say: mother earth, we children today thank you for our birth, for our nourishment and for our life. Mother earth, your children say 'thank you' and give you our love. Our minds are now one. (*All: Yes!*)

And then we turn to our beautiful Creator who has no face and no body, and whose appearance nobody knows. All we know is that it is the Great Power of the universe. And when our Creator made mother earth, he made the grass that grows so that deer and elk and buffalo can eat. He planted the medicines in the valleys, in the mountains, in the great plains, in the woods, in the deserts. And when he planted those medicines of all kinds, our Creator spoke to those medicines, and he touched each medicine. He gave each a spiritual meaning and he told those medicines: whenever the animals and the humans get sick and there is discomfort, and there is no peace in their life because of sickness, they will come to you. And you, the medicines will doctor them and remove their sickness; you will restore their peace and tranquility and comfort.

For every sickness known to mankind or animals, there is a plant growing out there somewhere that can take away that sickness if only we communicate to it in a spiritual way. And the medicines wait every day for the great privilege of being asked to help us feel better. But we don't ask enough. And if we don't ask, they feel abandoned and then, there is more sickness. All the plants are growing, the grass is growing, there is life. And so I ask this fine gathering of fellow human beings: can our minds come together, and our thoughts line up as one thought, and can we pile up our 'thank-yous' again? Yes, we can. Pile up again our greetings. Let's pile up again our love. Then, in a symbolic spiritual way, let's distribute those piled-up 'thank-yous,' and greetings and love to every grass, to every medicine plant in the valleys, the mountains, the forests, everywhere. And we say 'thank you' for bringing health and power to us, for helping us. We thank you, medicine plants of the world. Our minds are now one. (*All: Yes!*)

And then, our Creator made the rivers and the waters that flow upon the mother earth. And when our Creator made the streams and creeks, our Creator used his hands and his body and the water became a power, a spirit. And then our Creator spoke to the waters and the creeks and the rivers and he gave them a soul, he gave them a spirit. And he said: now, waters of the world, your job will be this: you will go and move in the rapids, in the Niagara Falls and the Grand Canyon. You will go to the villages of the animals, the villages of the humans and you will quench their thirst. You will purify. You will help them prepare their food so that they may have life. And so the rivers are indeed a living entity. And if one day they should disappear, so that we cannot drink the water from the streams and the rivers, we will perish. We will dry up and we will have no life.

But the rivers are still running, the oceans are still making waves the way their Creator told them to do since the beginning of time. And so, because of that, when we drink a cold glass of water each day, we think: what a peaceful feeling and what assurance that there will be a tomorrow. What strength that cold glass of water gives to us. For that reason, our minds should come together again as one. And we will pile up our 'thank-yous,' our greetings and our love together. And we will give it to every river, every lake, every ocean, every stream, every spring. And we talk to the spirit of the water and we say to the spirit of the water: we, who are the human beings and who are your relatives, thank you today. We are giving you our greetings and our love for the quenching of our thirst, on behalf of our children, our nephews and nieces. Water spirit of the world, we say 'thank you' for following the plan that the Creator gave in the beginning of the world. Our minds are now one. (*All: Yes!*)

And then our Creator made the trees that grow everywhere, all kinds of trees. Some trees are tall and big, some are skinny and tall, some are short and big, just like human beings you know. And he made female trees and male trees, who make little babies together, almost like humans. And then each baby becomes a sapling, which is a little kid, and then a teenaged tree, until it becomes a grandpa tree, and completes the cycle. To the trees, the Creator said: you will help the human beings, and the bears, and the wolves. He told the trees that.

And from the trees will come the apples, the oranges, the plums, the cherries, and on and on. From those fruits, we will be nourished; our children, our elderly will have the strength and power to live. From the trees, you will gather boards to make a shelter over your head. But make your shelter humble enough for you, your wife and your children and no more. If there is no excess, life will be everlasting. You will use the boards to make a little house so when the cold rain drops come, you will have comfort. When the hot summer sun comes, you will seek shelter within. And when the cold winds bring the big snow of the winter, your children will not freeze. From the trees, we may take rest and in their shade, we find comfort in the hot summer days.

The trees will make the wind that we breathe from day to day and night to night. And of all the trees that the Creator made, he chose the maple tree to be the leader. Now the trees are starting to get buds, and soon the leaves will live again to maturity. Again there will be cherries, and peaches, and plums and apples. And our life will be sustained the way their Creator intended in the beginning of time. Just a few weeks ago, our people had our maple tree ceremony, because the maple is the leader of all the trees of the forest.

And so now, I ask this fine group of people to let our minds become one, and let us pile up our 'thank-yous,' our greetings and our love and let us throw it to the universe so that every tree and every bush receives an acknowledgment of our love, our 'thank-yous' and our greetings. To the trees of the world, we say 'thank you' for following the Creator's plan so that we have life. Our minds are one. (*All: Yes!*)

In the beginning, when the world was new, when our Creator finished making all the animals and every creature, then the very last one to be made was the human being. And when he noticed the human being was the last to be created, he gave us so many days to live. And he did the same with the bears and the deer – they only live so long. And he said: there is a likelihood that the humans, the bears and the deer may become bored every day that they live. They may become lonesome for lack of something to do. And so, do you know what the Creator did? He began to create what they call 'birds,' and he put wings on them of beautiful colors. He let them go into the air so that they would zoom by where the human beings walk, so the minds of the people would not become bored. And then, our Creator gave them each a song, and he told the birds of the worlds: every morning, without fail, just as the sun begins to rise in the east and the dawn breaks, all the birds will begin to sing their multitude of tunes and songs. And they will make a chorus, a beautiful song of life. Every morning, without fail. And this morning, I heard them again, just as they did yesterday, and since the beginning of mankind's memory, because the Creator told them to do that. They shake up our mind so that we will not be bored and we will enjoy our visit on this earth. And, of those birds, our Creator chose the eagle to be their leader. So the eagle is our guardian bird.

And so I ask now that our minds become one and that we send our 'thank-yous,' our greetings and our love to every bird. And we, your human relatives, thank you, the bird life, for the past days' songs. They are very beautiful songs, with which you follow the Creator's way. We acknowledge you with our love. Our minds are one. (*All: Yes!*)

And then, our Creator made the four winds of the universe. When mother earth had given birth and was working to produce the food to feed this life, she got very tired. And so our Creator made the east and the north winds, to bring a white blanket of snow to cover mother earth. Then mother earth can rest. And when mother earth has rested, then, the brother winds of the south and the west will take away the white blanket of snow and all the flowers will start to sprout. And everywhere there will be blossoms of all colors, and life will be reborn. And that's the time now, it's coming. And so to the four winds that bring us the changes of the seasons, that we may have life – we the people are now of one mind. And again, we will pile up our 'thank-yous,' our greetings and our love. We will throw it into the universe, so that the four sacred winds will bring the season changes. They will be acknowledged with thank-yous, greetings and love. Our minds are now one. (*All: Yes!*)

Our Creator made two suns in the sky. First there is the daytime sun that shines. Our Creator said we will call him our eldest brother. You and I will be the younger brother and sister. And like an old brother, he will watch over his younger brother and sister. And our Creator said: every day you will shine so that the humans, the bears, the deer and the birds will see one another with the light. When they walk upon mother earth, they won't collide and cause injury to each other. He told the elder brother sun that he should bring the warmth so mother earth will give birth and growth. And our elders told us that the old brother sun starts in the east, and he goes across our sacred land to the mountains and the valleys until he gets to the great Pacific Ocean. And there the Creator waits for a report from the old brother sun, on how his younger brothers and sisters are doing, and what they are doing.

And so now, I suggest again, because we are people of logic, people of kindness and compassion, that we bring our minds and our thoughts together again. And in this room, if we can imagine it, we will pile up all our 'thank-yous,' layer after layer, in a big pile. And then we will pile up our greetings and our love. We will wrap it up, and we will pile it on in one big concerted effort. Let us pick it up, this parcel of thank-yous, greetings and love, and throw it up into the universe to our old brother, this sun. We thank the old brother sun for today's miracle of day and for the warmth that he brings and the life that he secures and guarantees us. We say 'thank you,' old brother sun, from your human relatives. We are now of one mind. (*All: Yes!*)

And the second sun, which we call the moon, is our grandma. We call her in Mohawk *Ietisotha osontenneka karakwa* our grandmother, the moon, the night-time sun. Our Creator made her and he told her: you are going to be the grandma, the great-grandest one of them all. Every 28 or 30 days, you will have a cycle. And in that cycle, you will orchestrate the movement and the birth of children to the mothers of the world. And so that's why every month, the women clean their body and their blood, so that new blood can be made and a new human being can be born with the privilege to live on this earth. And the moon, our grandmother, orchestrates that. It makes no difference what women they are, how rich or how poor, what color they are, when grandma moon says: ladies, get ready, it is time for you to give birth to a human being. And that's what the Creator told her her job would be. My children were born. My grandchildren are born. What a wonderful gift.

And so I ask now that in this fine group our minds come as one. Let us pile up our thank-yous, our greetings and our love. Let us pick it up and throw it up high into the universe, to the grandmother moon. And we say: grandma moon, we are your grandchildren and we are of one mind. We thank you for all the births of our children and our grandchildren, and for the babies that were born to every nation of the world. Grandmother moon, thank you for the birth of those children. Our minds are one. (*All: Yes!*)

And now, to the stars of the sky world, the multi-millions of shining stars. Our grandma and grandpa say each of us has a star that shines for us. In days long gone by, when the world was new, it is said that the stars talked to the people, that we communicated. They told us what was coming next year, whether there would be an earthquake, or a drought, or a wet season that would drown the crops. The stars would tell us, a year ahead of time, for that is their job. When the Creator made the sacred earth, he didn't abandon us there without any facilities. Everything is there to help us live. But our elders told us the day would come when human beings would forget how to read and talk to the stars. And I think that that has come now. Most people of the world, our elders said, would become like little children, and they would not know how to read the stars. They would not have full warnings. And even though that is the case, and we've forgotten we know something, yet in a dry season, it is the stars that bring the fresh water, the morning dew, to each blade of grass that grows. And even though we may have forgotten the other things that the stars help us with every night, there is one thing that we cannot forget, and that is that the stars are of great beauty when they fill the sky at night. Even the greatest artist of the entire world could not paint a more beautiful picture than the stars of the night. That alone is sufficient to be grateful for. So, let us pile up our 'thank yous,' our greetings and our love again, and throw it up high into the universe so that every single star is acknowledged by you and me. On behalf of our children, we say 'thank you' to the stars of the sky world for following the Creator's way. Our minds are one. (*All: Yes!*)

And now, we turn to the four sacred beings whom we call the sky dwellers, the four mysteries of the universe. These are the ones who do not have a body, and who are like the wind. They are the ones who protect us when we might destroy ourselves. For after the Creator made all of creation, and his last creation was the humans, he looked at the humans as they walked and said: I made a little bit of a mistake when I made humans. For it is the human beings who are the only ones who forget who they are and why they are here. The wolf who walks the earth never forgets he is a wolf. The eagle who flies in the sky never forgets he is an eagle. But the human being goes only a little way and then he forgets who he is, for the human is the weakest of all the species of the creation.

For that reason, the Creator created four sacred human beings called the 'mysteries of the universe,' the protectors of humans. Whenever the human race goes in the direction of complete destruction, then one of those will be born as a human being. He will be a prophet or a teacher and he will re-instill and renew our instructions so that we will be able to find the road again. These are the great 'messiahs' that are born throughout the world. And so, to the four sacred beings who have helped us to survive since the beginning of time, whoever you are, wherever you are and for everything you are, we the humans say 'thank you' today. Our minds are one. (*All: Yes!*)

And now, to our Creator, the maker of all the universe. When our Creator made this universe, he did not make it complicated. He did not make the program on the IBM machine too detailed and complex. All he did was to say: all I want you to do is to be born and to walk on the earth for so many days. And all I ask is that every time you will drink a glass of water, you say 'thank you' to me and to the power of the water. When you eat food, all I ask is that you be grateful for the food that you eat and not take more than you need. And when you build a home, build it only big enough for your wife and your children and no more, no excess. If you do that, there will be enough in the world for all, and all will have everlasting life.

So don't forget to say 'thank you,' simply 'thank you.' No great religion, no great complexity. Just humbly, honorably 'thank you' to all that is life. Our Creator made the most perfect world. And so I ask now that in the most powerful, humble way, we fill this room up here. Imagine it in our spiritual minds, our symbolic minds. Let us pile up our 'thank-yous' in a hundred layers. Let us lift the ceiling with our greetings, and then let us tie it with a big rope of love that we will get from here, and then let's pick up this big pile with one effort, in a symbolic way, and let's gather up that big pile of love, 'thank-yous' and greetings and send it high into the universe, to make sure that our Creator hears and feels our 'thank-yous,' our greeting and our love. Our Creator, who is our maker – your children today simply thank you. Our minds are one. (*All: Yes!*)

And now, I have officially opened this gathering in a spiritual way. And with such words, I have made a spiritual rope to tie everyone, to bring our minds together. You come here from all over the world. These words that I have said come from ten, twenty, forty thousand, fifty thousand years ago. They are the original spiritual words of the native people of North America. On these grounds, I welcome you here, to North America, in the original way, you who come from all over the world.

And our concerns are the same here. How do we enjoy this life, in a proper, humble way, without exploiting it? How do we honor our mother the earth that the Creator made, so that our children and their children will have a chance? That's the most honorable reason to come together – as intellectual and rational people from every color, like a beautiful garden of many flowers. Let the rain fall on it, let the wind give it nourishment, so that even 'the powers that be' may know how to appreciate the beauty of the bouquet. And in that way, we have now opened officially. So be it. Our minds are one. That's all. (*All: Yes!*) (Sakokwenionkwas, 1993)[1]

The peace messenger's message or constitution

The legend of the peace messenger

Long before Europeans first came to this country, a man, a Huron (it is sacrilegious to name him), came to Iroquois country as an emissary, a symbol, a messenger of the Great Peace, i.e. he claimed that the Great Peace spoke through him. But he carried also a message of peace, an interpretation of that Great Peace to offer and to establish in concrete form. 'I plant the Tree of the Great Peace – a great White Pine and bury all implements of war under it,' he said. All nations and individuals are welcome to take shelter under its spreading branches. It has spreading and ever growing branches and white roots that extend to the four quarters of the earth. He came to reconnect the Iroquois and all the nations to the Great Peace.[2]

The nature of the message[3]

Weapons of war were buried under the Tree of Peace, forever. Warriors and War Chiefs were eliminated forever. The Great Law does not contain the word warrior but *Rotisenrake:te*, meaning 'braves' – just 'young men,' nothing else. The War Chiefs and head warriors were replaced with fifty Peace Chiefs[4] (*rotiianeson*: the good men), who could never go to war and were not to order anyone around. It also elevated assistants, deputy or subchiefs, runners for the Peace Chiefs (good men). The women were made into clan mothers who were to name and raise the Peace Chiefs and watch over them.

Besides signifying the Great Harmony/Cosmic Kinship and the Peace Messenger's message or Constitution, *Kayanerekowa* – the Great Peace – also refers to the two historical forms that it has taken in Iroquois and Mohawk history (Vachon, 1993a, pp. 19–35). I shall now describe briefly the nature of these two forms.

The League of Six Nations, the Grand Council of 50 *Rotiiane* (*Rotiianeson*)

This is now called the Six Nations' Confederacy, and is the only form of 'government' detailed in the Great Law of Peace. The Great Peace here refers to the alliance between the five Iroquois nations (six since 1714) past and present, namely Onondaga, Mohawk, Seneca, Oneida, Cayuga and Tuscarora. These nations allied themselves into one League, one Longhouse, where each nation had and has its own Fire, and where all formed and still form one 'family' consisting of elder and younger brothers. Each kept their own languages, customs and national differences, yet they forward and still form one body, one mind, one heart linked together in a loose confederation rather than a unitary state, each of them retaining full independence but bound by kinship ties rather than by the relationship of estate or real property. All were and are based on the 'Constitution,' namely the Great Law of Peace.

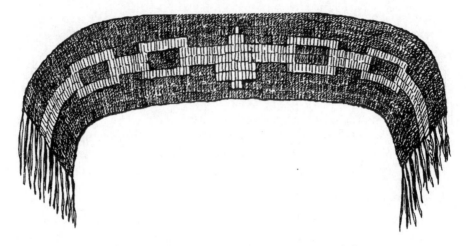

Illustration 18.1   Aionwatha: The Five Nations belt

The center symbolizes the Onondaga nation, flanked by the Mohawk and Seneca nations, then by the Oneida and Cayuga. The two extremities remain open for other nations to join in.
Source: Vachon (1993a) p. 19.

The Great Peace may refer also to the past and present Grand Council of the fifty *Rotiiane* (*Rotiianeson*), which is today often called the government of the Confederacy, or simply the Confederacy. This government is not a central, statist, coercive government in the Western sense. Each one of the five (now six) nations are physically distant from each other. Each has a distinct homeland and is profoundly independent from the others, although they all constitute one Longhouse and are bound together as a single bundle of arrows. They each have as well their own Longhouse, their own Fire, their own Peace Chiefs, but the latter also sit together in a common Longhouse, each with their respective functions, yet with no king or commanding chief. None of the Peace Chiefs either alone or together are commanders. It must be made crystal clear that these Peace Chiefs are named by the Iroquois people through the Clan Mothers of clans abiding by the

Great Law of Peace, of which the *Rotiiane* are held to be the official interpreters, in consort with Clan Mothers, elders, faith-keepers, ancestors, etc. Hence, such a 'government' can never form a self-perpetuating body, which would continue to exist over against or in spite of the people.[5]

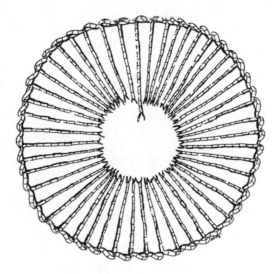

Illustration 18.2   Tekentiohkwahnhakstha: What binds the people together

The sacred circle is composed of fifty strings, each symbolizing a *royaner* (an entitled leader); the longest string symbolizes Atotarho of the Onondaga nation. Their arms are intertwined, in a role where the political and the spiritual are never separated. It also symbolizes the people and the cosmic kin.
Source: Vachon (1993a) p. 20.

This alliance or League or Confederacy and its Constitution are still very much alive and active today. So is the Council of the fifty *Rotiiane*. Both the League and the Grand Council (as well as the Constitution) – although undeniably ancient – have been relatively unchanging in their elaborate structure. The internal structure of the Grand Council has remained 'relatively unaffected' by interaction with Europeans during the colonial era. It is equally very much still 'in charge' today, that is, unimpeached in its authority, all rumors to the contrary throughout history (and even today) notwithstanding. Its function has always been and remains 'to prevent a disuniting of the minds' not only of the League but also between the League and other nations. But it could never and cannot today enforce peace. It was and it remains a matter of good thoughts, of Good Mind. This it brings about through ceremonies and condolence rituals, restraint, wampum and the exchange of gifts. The fact that the League and the Grand Council are still with us today is eloquent testimony to the Iroquois people's loyalty to the Creator's instructions as given in the Great Law of Peace.[6]

Extended family alliance system between the Six Nations Confederacy and other nations

The 'linking of arms' in a kinship alliance (*Tehona – tenentshawā:kon*) was intended by the Confederacy to function with either other Native Nations or with European nations (Druke, 2003, pp. 29–39). In practice, these both were kinship alliances set up to last forever, needing only to be periodically reaffirmed and ceremonially refined. The system did, however, tend to work differently in each of the two cases.

With other native nations

Alliances were forged before and after European contact, and the system is still practiced today. Westerners have called it 'intertribal tributary alliance.' This is not correct. The idea of paying tribute has always been foreign to the sharing traditions of the Great Law of Peace. It was and it is, rather, an alliance of communitarian or extended family reciprocity, where the Confederacy and other Native Nations committed each other to share hunting grounds, counsel, foods, furs, flint, wampum, etc. There could and can be a mutual non-aggression pact, whereby the implements of war were and are symbolically buried. There could and can be mutual assistance pacts, either by coming to each other's help in case of outside aggression from other nations, or through trade. *This alliance was and is a parental relationship – as brethren, cousins, uncles, nephews, grandfathers, women, etc. – but never one of subordination, subjection, or sovereignty over subjects.*

Few studies have been made of these alliances before and during contact. It is not within the scope of this chapter to do so. Suffice it to say that the oral traditions of the Iroquois do transmit valuable information. For example, there is a long Cayuga tradition which affirms that the Delaware (or *Lenni Lenape*) were considered generally, by all nations, Iroquois included, as the 'Grandfathers of the Algonkian family of Nations' and were respected as such by the Iroquois, who also called them 'grandfathers' and even 'women.' The Iroquois oral tradition also narrates the first battles initiated by the Algonkians and Mohicans against the Iroquois, and how these two conflicts were settled according to the principles of the Great law of Peace. For example, a peace alliance (or treaty) was made between the Iroquois and the Algonkins (northern Algonkians), where the war clubs were buried in a hole and a peace belt was given by the Algonkins, which still exists today, and which opened the Saint Lawrence valley to Iroquois settlement (Blanchard, 1980, p. 97).

Sometimes, other Native Nations even sought and got a seat and voice inside the Grand Council of the Five Nations Confederacy. One entered the Confederacy through one of the Five Nations, usually the one in whose vicinity one was living. Then one spoke through that nation. This is, for example, still the case today with the Tuscarora nation, which speaks in the Grand Council through the

Oneida nation. The southeastern Susquehannocks entered through the Mohawks, the seven Christian nations of Canada through Onondaga, the western Native Nations through the Senecas, etc. A consensus had and has to be reached, for example, between the Oneidas and Tuscaroras for the Tuscarora to be heard in the Grand Council. After contact, as we shall see, many of the Native Nations used the latter method to enter into kinship alliances with the British, although they felt free to proceed to such alliances with the British without going through the Confederacy Channel.

With European nations

The Confederacy also practiced the 'linking of arms' and kinship alliances with the first European nations whose members came to Turtle Island – also always based on the Great Law of Peace. But such alliances were designed to deal specifically with Confederacy/European relations. What characterized them was that they explicitly acknowledged the unique and irreducible ways or paths of life of each culture, accepted the differences and intended to respect them, from both sides. They were based in other words on the two-row (or two paths) wampum treaty, called by the Mohawks, the *Tekeniteyoa:te* (Two Paths) and by other Iroquois, *Kashwen:ta* (sometimes spelled *Guswenta*, their word for *wampum*).

The very first such alliance was made by the Mohawks with the Dutch, and later ones with the English, the French and the Americans. They were to be the basis for peaceful Confederacy/European relations through all history – and are still considered so today, despite the triple betrayal of these sacred alliances by the French, English and Americans during the eighteenth century and thereafter. This linking of arms and kinship alliance was first called a rope, then an iron chain, then a Silver Covenant Chain.

The British were the first to use the name 'Covenant Chain,' in 1677. But for them it meant the British/Iroquois chain, called the Silver Covenant Chain, and it excluded the French. The French called theirs the Friendship Alliance, for they never accepted being part of the 'Covenant Chain.' For them, the latter was the British Chain. For the Iroquois, it was *Tehonatenent-shawá:kon* (the 'linking of arms' or 'clasping of hands for peace'). When speaking to Euro-Americans, they still refer to it as the Covenant or Friendship Chain. Unlike their Western 'allies,' they never had any problem including both the French and the English in its embrace.

Twofold understanding of the 'Covenant Chain'

It must be clearly stated at the outset that the Iroquois and European understandings of this system were radically different, in spite of the fact that both spoke of the 'Covenant Chain' or 'Friendship Alliance' (or Chain). To put it briefly, it was for the Iroquois a kinship alliance of brothers for protection and peace. For

Europeans, it was a kingship and friendship-based alliance with 'subjects and allies' for their own self-protection and to facilitate further conquest.

From the Iroquois' viewpoint, it was an institution based on the extended family or kinship relationship of brothers, uncles, nephews, women, etc., to which they were accustomed in the Iroquois League of Nations. It followed the spirit of the Great Law of Peace and its protocol. It was founded also on the Circle of non-governance, where no one nation is higher than any other, although there may be – and was – a *diplomatic* Central Fire and Head of the Circle (the latter being the Mohawk nation within the Confederacy, and the Confederacy itself within the Covenant Chain). I call it a 'diplomatic' center or head, in the sense that it was not a 'power' center, a head that governs, orders or makes subjects of others.

The Iroquois always refused, either as a Confederacy or as nations, communities and people, to be kings or 'subjects' of anyone outside or inside the Confederacy. They never tried to turn other nations – whether European or native – into subjects. From their point of view, therefore, the Covenant Chain was not based on any notion of kingship. Notions of kings and subjects were completely foreign to their language and their philosophy. So, indeed, was the notion of friendship – they accepted the European word 'friendship' to express the linking of arms, but they understood it as kinship.

Furthermore, this Covenant was not based on any notion of ownership, territory, territorial expansion, transformation and expansion, or conquest and empire, as would be the case in European political philosophy. The 'Covenant Chain' was never an Iroquois empire, nor was it ever intended to become one. There was no question of tribute or tributaries.

Finally, for the Iroquois, this institution was neither one nor two (or more) covenant chains, but a pluralistic chain of covenants, in the sense that kinship alliances might take very different forms according to the nations (native and/ or European) it linked. The Iroquois – contrary to the French, English and Americans – had no problem making alliances with very different European or Native Nations, even with those currently at war with one another, as was the case, for example, between the French and the English, the British and the Americans, Canada and the USA, during various epochs.

The Covenant Chain was, in principle, neither exclusive of any nation – European or native – nor omni-inclusive, i.e. imperialistic. In fact, Native Nations and European nations (specifically British, French and American) were all part of that Chain, the *Tehonatenentshawā:kon*.

Another characteristic of the Covenant or Friendship Chain – this extended-family alliance with European nations – was that many Native Nations would ally themselves with European nations by going through the Iroquois Confederacy, as the diplomatic 'head' of the system of alliances, whenever they found this procedure useful. But none were obliged by the Confederacy to do so in order to establish alliances with European nations.

From the European point of view, the 'Covenant Chain' or 'Chain of Friendship' was understood and presented in a radically different light.

It was seen, first, as a *kingship alliance* between the European king, on the one hand, and his loyal subjects, the Native Nations, on the other; the king being the father, and the native subjects his children. It was also viewed as an alliance between friends, i.e. allies, not between kin. And all this was according to the best traditions of kingship (as fatherhood) and friendship in the Western traditions.

De facto, however, these noble European traditions had somewhat deteriorated. By the time they reached the shores of the New World, they were invariably adulterated with elements of conquest and territorial expansion. At first, when the Europeans were unable to dominate the Native Nations, they confederated with some of them as formal peers and allies in order to gain advantages over other Europeans and their native allies.[7] Later, when they were more powerful, they sought to conquer and subdue these native 'peers and allies' themselves. So their alliances with Native Nations were forged as if between independent nations, but the Native Nations were in fact seen as (and even called) subjects in order to please the European kings and impress European powers. In the final analysis, however, the Europeans sincerely believed that the Native Nations were subjects, or at least had to become so. Indeed, from the European point of view, they could be nothing else.

Now, since the Mohawks – Keepers of the Eastern Door, Head of the Iroquois Confederacy – seemed to the Europeans eminently successful in 'controlling' the corridors to the West, to the north (from the south) and to the south (from the north), they were – in European eyes – a 'power' not only to reckon with, but primarily with which to be allied in order to make headway in conquering the continent. The Mohawks had been so successful in making alliances with the Dutch and eastern Algonkians that they were seen by the British as possible strong allies for British penetration, or as a buffer to protect the British from the French up north. The French thought likewise, but saw the Mohawks and the Iroquois at first as a danger to their northern fur trade and yet also as a buffer protecting them from British incursions into New France and the rich northern fur trade.

Brief history of the Covenant Chain

The first official 'linking of arms' or 'clasping of hands' with European nations happened between the Mohawks and the Dutch in 1643 at Fort Orange (now Albany, NY). This is where the first Two-Row Wampum Treaty took place. In 1645, the Mohawks, on behalf of all the Iroquois, made a treaty of friendship with New France, its Algonquin and Huron allies. In 1663, they entered into another Friendship Alliance, solely with the French.

The English phrase 'Covenant Chain' first appeared in the Maryland Mohawk agreement of July 1677. In 1677, the first 'Silver Covenant Chain' was made between the Iroquois, on the one hand, and the New York, Massachusetts and

Connecticut colonies, as well as the River Indians of the Hudson Valley, on the other. In subsequent years, the alliance was gradually extended to all the colonies and other Indian nations, south, east, north and west, and was constantly renewed. As Jennings (1984, p. xvii) puts it: 'The Covenant Chain is the reason there was peace during the long period from 1677 to 1755.' Finally, for the British, it was a British chain that excluded the French. Since the Iroquois had become British allies, the British started presenting the 'Iroquois Confederacy and its Native Allies as the Iroquois Empire dependent on the Province of New York' (Colden, 2005), and the Confederacy's Native Allies as their 'tributaries.'

Jennings has shown that the Iroquois Empire did not exist. It was a creation of the British imagination employed in order to eventually appropriate their lands. The British used their alliance with the Iroquois (and *their* allies) to argue the dependency of these nations on the British Crown and, hence, British sovereignty over all of known North America. The Iroquois 'depended' on New York, which was in turn a dependency of the British Crown. If the Iroquois therefore had tributaries and an empire, it belonged to Britain. What belonged to the Iroquois belonged to Britain. All very convenient. As early as 1688, the British were saying: 'We have thought fit to own the Five Nations as our subjects and resolved to protect them as such.' As Jennings (1984, p. 11) has written, '[l]acking a reasonable alternative until the French could be forced off the Continent, the British donated an empire to the Iroquois in order to claim it for themselves.'

In 1701, a separate Alliance and Covenant was established in Montreal between the Iroquois, the French and the latter's allies, because the French refused to join the Covenant Chain which was considered by them (and the English) as an exclusively British/Iroquois (plus native allies) Chain – although never so by the Iroquois, as noted above.

For the British, the Covenant Chain was an instrument of conquest. Its purpose was to extend the British Empire. This was the hidden agenda. When the western Native Nations left the Iroquois Confederacy in the mid-1700s, and thus were no longer seen by the British as tributaries of the Iroquois, the British really thought that the Iroquois Empire – the Confederacy itself, and thus the Covenant Chain – had collapsed. In fact, for the Iroquois, there had never been an Iroquois Empire. There had always been and still was a Confederacy or League of Five Nations, an extended kinship alliance with some other Native Nations, and still a Covenant Chain alliance with the Dutch, the British, the French and the Americans, based on the *Guswenta*.

There was, further, still an 'official' European Covenant Chain, which was being 'officially' betrayed by the very French, British and American nations that had 'officially' signed it. The betrayal had, however, taken place long before. Kelsey (1984, p. 16) puts it well: 'In all their negotiations with the Indians, both British and French authorities behaved toward the Confederacy as though they considered it an independent nation. [...] But the truth was that both the French and the British considered Indians, whether within or without the Confederacy, as subjects [...].'

At first, the natives had not understood what the word 'subject' meant. When they did, they categorically refused – all along – to be considered the subjects of any king, European or otherwise. Some accepted being called children of the French father Onontio,[8] but they made it clear what they meant by father. Today, nothing much has changed. The words children and subjects of the kings are not used, but their modern equivalents are: citizens of the United States and of Canada, subject to the laws of the United States and of Canada. And the Mohawks and Iroquois are still saying: 'We are not citizens of your United States or your Canada. We are not subject to your laws. We are brothers and sisters who long ago made an eternal kinship and friendship alliance, based on the Two Row Wampum, where we welcomed you to share this land with us in mutual respect for each other's cultures: you staying in your boat and we in our canoe, and linking arms forever.'[9,10]

Conclusion

A note on some of the major Mohawk-Haudenosaunee peace symbols

These peace symbols, whether it be (1) the *Guswenta*, also known as the two-row wampum belt that underlines the mutual respect for the differences between the Handenosaunee and the newcomers from Europe, as they travel together on the same rivers of life, one in its canoe and the other in its boat without trying to have one foot in the one and the other foot in the other, or whether it be any of the other below, they should not be understood as being one of exclusive relationship, because for the Haudenosaunee it is a kinship alliance which respects the different kinships.

It is definitely not a kingship relationship. This is further emphasized by another peace symbol, namely (2) *the rope or belt of friendship* 'which is understood' by the Haudenosaunee also as a relationship of kinship, which goes beyond Western friendship and which must be renewed periodically. It is expressed also (3) by the *symbol of both holding hands and arms together in a circle around the Tree of Peace* so that the Tree of Peace may not fall, and (4) by asserting that all implements of war have been thrown in the hole under the Tree of Peace, so that there should never be warriors nor war between us all.

Furthermore, (5) the symbol *'One bowl, one ladle'* or *'One dish, one spoon,'* is one of the many traditions of mutual understanding with regard to the use of land, meaning the mutual promise that there should be no knife of property or of exclusion with regard to Mother Earth, so that everything should be in common. The Haudenosaunee in their presentation to the Royal Commission on the Aboriginal People of Canada (1993–1994) reminded the Commission: 'All

Nations will eat from the same bowl and dish, being careful that there be no knife near the dish in order to avoid confusion and shedding of blood.' According to the Six Nations Confederacy itself, the emphasis is on 'relationship' more than on formalities of a treaty between powers and their respective subjects. The very notion of 'subjects' is foreign to them.

Finally, all these extremely important peace symbols are only a part of the Great Peace so that the Great Peace should not be reduced to them, for together we must listen ever more to the Great Peace and abide together by its pluralism, which cannot be reduced to any one single definition of it. Hence the words that come before all else: those of the good mind, thanks to the *Kayanerekowa*, the Great Harmony of it all, keeping in mind the seven generations to come.

Notes

1. I remember Tom porter saying to me laughingly once: 'God must cringe when he hears the words that come before else, in English and not in Mohawk.'
2. For a brief history of the legend, see Vachon (1993a).
3. Taken from 'The Mohawk Dynamics of Peace' (Vachon, 1993a, pp. 16–18).
4. See further down the preliminary note on the English word 'chief' as a translation of *Roiane Rotiiane*.
5. A note on the words chief and *royaner* (pronounce *loyané* which is the singular, and *rotiianeson* which is the plural and pronounced *lodianeson*): to avoid misunderstandings, it is very important to know and understand what is meant by the words chief or peace chief, which is an English translation of the word *roiane* (singular) and *rotiane/rotianeson* (plural), which literally means the 'good/kind/peaceful men' that are named by consensus by the clan mothers who watch over them and can correct or even depose them if they do not act properly. The word chief in English usage connotes commander, head or 'subjects.' Not so the word *roiane* which, according to elder Sakokwenionkwas, means the good, kind, peaceful man who does not command but is an entitled mirror of the Great Peace and Cosmic Kinship in his behavior.
6. For a brief history of the League and Grand Council, see R. Vachon (1993a, pp. 22–26).
7. Allied and peer nations, since it is not in the European tradition to make treaties with groups who do not have a status equivalent to nations. Europeans in general, however, had trouble recognizing native peoples as nations since they did not have many of the trappings of European nation-states. But it can be argued that they did treat them officially as nations, at least temporarily, to further their own colonial interests.
8. The Mohawk title given to the French king or to his New France governor. The word means 'beautiful mountain.'
9. For a brief descriptive overview of the Mohawk kinship diplomacy with regard to European nations and to United States and Canada's assimilation policies from 1600 until today, see Vachon (1993a, pp. 36–82).
10. A short bibliographical note: it must be remembered that the Kayanerekowa is primarily an oral tradition, although much has been written about it; this must be kept in mind as we write this text and refer to texts written even by the Mohawks and the Haudenosaunee. Finally, for a first-hand, more detailed official account of our topic by the Haudenosaunee themselves, which was presented to the Royal Commission on Aboriginal Peoples 1993 and 1994 (445 pages) and published by the latter, see William and Nelson (1997).

Reference list

Blanchard, D.S. (1980) *Kahnawake: Apercu Historique* (Kahnawake: Kanien'kehaka Raotitiohkwa Press).

Colden, C. (2005) [1747] *The History of the Five Indian Nations of Canada Which Are Dependent On the Province of New York in America 1747* (Whitefish: Kessinger Publishing).

Druke, M.A. (2003) 'Linking Arms: The Structure of Iroquois Intertribal Diplomacy' in D.K. Richter and J.H. Merrell (eds.) *Beyond the Covenant Chain: The Iroquois and their Neighbors in Indian North America, 1600–1800* (Pennsylvania: Pennsylvania State University Press).

Jennings, F. (1984) *The Ambiguous Iroquois Empire: The Covenant Chain Confederation of Indian Tribes with English Colonies* (New York: W.W. Norton).

Kelsey, I.T. (1984) *Joseph Brant 1743–1807: Man of Two Worlds* (Syracuse: Syracuse University Press).

Sakokwenionkwas (1993) 'Mohawk Welcoming Ceremony,' *Proceedings of the International Conference* 'Living with the Earth: Cross-Cultural Perspectives on Sustainable Development; Indigenous and Alternative Practices' (Orford: Intercultural Institute of Montreal), 17–26.

Vachon, R. (1991) 'The Mohawk Nation and its Communities: Some Basic Sociological Facts,' *Interculture*, 113.

Vachon, R. (1992) 'Western and Mohawk Political Cultures: A Study in Contrast,' *Interculture*, 114.

Vachon, R. (1993a) 'The Mohawk Dynamics of Peace: The People of the Great Peace,' *Interculture*, 118.

Vachon, R. (1993b) 'The Mohawk Nation: Its Seven Communities. A Brief History,' *Interculture*, 121.

Vachon, R. (1995a) 'Intercultural Foundations of Peace between Mohawk Nation and North American States: Towards a Common Language,' *Interculture*, 127.

Vachon, R. (1995b) 'Intercultural Foundations of Peace between Mohawk Nation and North American States: A Common Horizon,' *Interculture*, 128.

Vachon, R. (1995c) 'Intercultural Foundations of Peace between Mohawk Nation and North American States: A New Method,' *Interculture*, 129.

Willlam, P. and C. Nelson (1997) 'Kaswentha,' Research Reports, Treaties, Project Area 1: Early Treaty Making in Canada, January 1995, in *For Seven Generations: An Information Legacy of the Royal Commission on Aboriginal Peoples* [CDROM] (Ontario: Libraxus Inc.).

19
Guelaguetza and *Tu Chha'ia*: A Zapotec Perspective of What Others Call Friendship

Gustavo Esteva and Arturo Guerrero *

> Each people's peace is as distinct as each people's poetry.
>
> Ivan Illich

In the house in Mexico City where Gustavo Esteva was born, his grandmother could not enter through the front door, because she was an Indian. Like many other people of her generation, his mother assumed that the best she could do for her children was to radically uproot them from their indigenous ancestry, in order to avoid the exclusion and discrimination she had suffered. But Esteva adored his grandmother and spent many holidays with her in Oaxaca, in her Zapotec world.

Like many other people of his generation, Esteva reclaimed his own cultural roots late in his life. In his early 40s, when he was suffering the collective frustration with development and he was trying to discover his own path, he began to remember his experiences with his grandmother and such memories reconnect him with his people at the grassroots. He now lives in a Zapotec village, near the place where his grandmother was born.

Arturo Guerrero has a very different story...but it follows similar lines of alienation and rediscovery.

This chapter is about the Zapotecs, the largest Indian pueblo[1] of Oaxaca and one of the most important and numerous indigenous groups in Mexico and even the American continent. There are at least half a million people who are known

---

* We are particularly grateful for the contributions of Melquiades Cruz, Zapotec from the Rincón, who guided us along these explorations and in particular who shared with us the inspiration of his grandfather, Don Pablo Cruz, from Santa Cruz Yagavila. We have used in this text modified fragments of the article 'Els zapoteques: L'harmonia com a justícia' (Esteva, 2004).

to speak Zapotec. Perhaps another half a million consider themselves Zapotec, but have lost mastery of the language. Many Zapotecs are part of the indigenous diaspora: there are more Zapotecs living out of Oaxaca than in Oaxaca.

We will refer to the Zapotecs here, but we have the impression that the Zapotec[2] pueblo never existed, does not exist at the present and will probably never come into existence, in the sense that they are not a 'group of people who share a history, culture, territory and project.' Zapotec intellectuals suggesting today the 'reconstitution' of the Zapotec pueblo are applying to the Zapotecs a nineteenth century ideological construct arbitrarily projected on people who, in their majority, have no interest in such a political initiative and ideology. While colonial domination certainly had a disjointed impact, no fragmentation occurred. The Spaniards did not fragment something that was united, which formed a unit, which had some form of organic integration, economic, political or cultural. On the other hand, what can currently be said about all Zapotec communities is irrelevant, superficial and inaccurate. These are generalizations without much substance or empirical basis. The assumptions common to all of them, their horizons of intelligibility, which perhaps could characterize a Zapotec culture common to all who are considered Zapotec, have not been subjected to systematic exploration. We do not know if there really is such a level of communion. Apparently, they have formed what would more precisely be called multicultural configurations on a regional level.

If there is not a 'Zapotec pueblo'[3] and none of the Zapotec languages have a word for peace (or war), how can we address the question of the meaning of peace among the Zapotec people?

Words are the symbolic expression of the real world, the way in which reality is manifested in us (through a symbol). With them, we build concepts, which are the ways in which we imagine and represent the patterns of what exists and its passing. Words and concepts are always culturally ingrained: they belong to a place. Only there, in a specific cultural territory, do words and concepts acquire their meaning, in their interconnection with the semantic constellation to which they belong.

To explore the meaning of peace among the Zapotec, who lack an equivalent word, is not merely a linguistic problem. Many of our Zapotec interlocutors speak Spanish fluently. They know what the word peace means 'out there' in the larger society. In conversation between Zapotecs, one can insert the Spanish word, *paz*, with the contemporary meaning derived from the *pax romana* and updated in the *pax americana* as a contract of domination. It is a meaning that the Zapotecs have directly suffered under for more than 500 years. This very reality underscores the difficulty of expressing this concept in Zapotec. Whenever we raised the question with Zapotecs it produced bewilderment. An initial response seems to coincide with other traditions. *Chiirula* or *chhiz*, in the Zapotec of Sierra Juárez, means 'to choose not to confront,' 'to leave in peace', 'to not make noise,' 'to not get to you,' alluding primarily to those from outside, to the government, for example. Generally, it means to be in a situation free of external pressures. It is a notion to which Illich* had made reference: 'At the center, the emphasis is on "the maintenance of peace"; at the margin, people hope "to be left in peace"' (Illich, 1981, p. 1). The confusion arises when the term is applied inwardly or alludes to a condition that not only relates to what the other does (who chooses not to confront one, who leaves one be), but to the relation itself, to the state of things existing in this relation, which seems to lead to multiple directions and which is only understood, from outside, through appreciation of the context.

In everyday practice, the peoples of the Sierra, the Zapotecs, Chinantecs and Mixes of the Northern Sierra of Oaxaca, speak of being well together, of sharing, of giving a hand to each other. But the contemporary concept of peace does not seem to relate to this. Illich himself warned that 'the peace of every nation is as different as the poetry of every nation. Hence, the translation of peace is as arduous a task as the translation of poetry' (Illich, 1981, p. 1). This chapter deals not simply with translation, but with the search for homeomorphic equivalents that yield a plurality of ideas: the search does not give primacy to a specific concept of the dominant culture, but seeks to identify equivalent conditions for a social function that seems to exist, with multiple variants and meanings, in diverse cultures.

Only through unbearable distortions can the practices which occupy the homeomorphic equivalents of that social function in all Zapotec communities be reconciled. In order to give the appropriate context to the exploration, we will refer to ways of being that seem common to the majority of Indian communities in Mesoamerica, not only to the Zapotec, and ways of being that seem common to the regional and cultural configuration of Sierra Juárez of Oaxaca, where Zapotecs, Chinantecs and Mixes coexist. However, our elaboration concentrates on a small region of Sierra Juárez: our interpretations as to the meaning of 'peace' can only be strictly applied to this small region. While we are confident that they could also apply to other regions, and perhaps even to other Mesoamerican pueblos, to do so would require many qualifications and distinctions that cannot be made here.

To be Zapotec

According to identified archeological evidence, the first human settlements in the territories of what are now the Mexican states of Oaxaca and Puebla appeared nine or ten thousand years ago. Other evidence indicates that four or five thousand years ago the family of Zapotec languages that are spoken today emerged. There are profound variations between them. Even among those who speak Zapotec,

* Ed. For more on Ivan Illich contributions as peace thinker, see Chapter 28.

the variations are not mutually comprehensible. But these languages have some common patterns that scholars can detect.[4]

Those who spoke these languages lived for a long time in small, independent villages, often forming regional communities. Within the regional communities, one of the villages was assigned the function of being the ceremonial center, although apparently this did not imply an administrative or political role. Two thousand five hundred years ago, some of these regional communities seem to have formed a type of confederation, which preceded the establishment of an urban lifestyle in what is now known as Monte Albán. Here in the first part of our era, between the years 200 and 750 CE, a large human settlement flourished, perhaps one of the largest cities of the world in its time. In the eighth century, it began its decline and for centuries suffered continuous deterioration, while other centers consolidated.

In 1521, the little resistance that the Spaniards encountered in Oaxaca ended. Although there were skirmishes with Zapotecs from different regions, alliances were soon arranged. During the colonial period, the Zapotecs suffered forms of political, economic and religious oppression characteristic of this regime, often with the intermediation of their own political and religious authorities. At the end of the period, almost all regional structures had been dismantled and the Zapotecs survived in relatively isolated rural communities.

At the end of the colonial rule, among nearly all of the Zapotecs, as within other groups as well, a communal reaffirmation of the relationship with the earth as both a sacred and worldly place was consolidated. This communion was shared by all members of the community even when they were no longer living on this land – an attitude that is still maintained in most communities that are considered Zapotec and which experts call residential identity.

The current way of life in these communities perhaps provides historic continuity to ancient traditions, in which the rooting to a particular place stimulates diversity. Even today, every community maintains a distinct way of life that defines its existence. This unique vision may surface in the neighboring communities with which there is frequent interaction. In some cases, a common cultural sphere is recognized with other communities in a small area and a form of fraternity is recognized with the larger regional community.

In any case, from both within and outside of the community people tend to distinguish between the Zapotec communities of the central valleys, of the Northern and Southern Sierra and of the Isthmus. The areas occupied by these communities represent almost half the land area of the state of Oaxaca and constitute the Zapotec territory. In recent years, this territory has extended to other parts of Mexico and the United States. In addition to the Zapotec communities that may be found in urban neighborhoods, 'transnational communities' have also emerged, in some of which the same group of people may in turn reside in two countries (Kearney, 1996).

To be Zapotec today is an attitude and a state of mind that only acquires full meaning, rigor and exactness within rural communities and some urban neighborhoods, which maintain their own fitting cultural rule of life.

The pursuit of harmony

The shared life of a 'Zapotec' community is based on dynamic customs embodied in changing behaviors. One or another community shows such differences in form and substance, that generalizations imply reductions or unacceptable distortions. The terms and concepts available, even those that have already entered into this text despite the authors' resistance, 'habits' and 'behavior,' seem inappropriate for discussing the issue that we want to address. How do you talk of 'peace' in communities where the word is unknown and in which the notions of law and rights that could give context to it are not only unknown but irrelevant?* Communities where the ideas of 'justice' and 'social order' are entirely foreign or have radically different meanings than the conventional understanding? The differences are not just procedural, but of substance. They are based on different presuppositions.[5]

The traditions associated with certain words illustrate the difficulty. For those who read this text, legality is associated with law and justice, jurisdiction is an area of authority, a jury is a judicial body. But legality and jurisdiction were born under circumstances in which the word was law. They are derived from *dicere*, 'to say' and *dictio*, 'the action of saying, statement,' associated with *jus*, *juris*, what relates to the law. The jury comes from swear, 'to make a solemn declaration invoking a deity.' In many Indian communities, what we call 'legal' has some resemblance with what the origins of these words mean, but not what they mean today. Despite its gradual subjugation to the kingdom of the alphabet, the oral way of being still defines their life.†

In 1997 in Oaxaca, intense discussions took place concerning a new law on indigenous pueblos and communities, which, among other things, sought to recognize their 'internal normative systems' in positive law and bring them under formal regulation.‡ In those discussions, Zapotec and Mixe lawyers vigorously defended the oral nature of their rules of conduct. They strongly resisted any attempt to enclose them in a text. They knew well the consequences

---

* Ed. For more on the impossibility of translations of key words, such as peace, see Chapters 7 and 21.

† Ed. In this book, manifold chapters underline the importance of oral traditions to comprehend, experience and grasp peace. To find discussions on this topic in other cultures, i.e. in non-Native American cultures, see especially Chapters 7 and 10 on the Middle East.

‡ Ed. A thorough discussion on legal systems and the differences between restorative and retributive justice, oral processes of healing and their difference from the punitive positive system in regards peace can be found in Chapter 17.

of subordinating their lives to the straightjackets imposed through written legislation on various themes, such as agricultural property and agricultural property rights. They did not want these restrictions to continue expanding. In support of their argument, they cited numerous cases as proof of the vitality, dynamism and flexibility of their oral 'legal culture' and of the conflicts created by the written word.[6]

Defending the oral form of 'internal normative systems' signified the protection of a way of being and living and the prevention of the scourge of written rules being extended to other areas. A couple of features of these 'systems' can illustrate this style of functioning.

Differential treatment

'Each theft of a turkey is different,' said Hugo. 'Why treat them as if they were all alike?'

Among the Zapotecs there does not appear to be egalitarian obsessions and manias of uniformity. What seems correct, what is right, is not associated with the idea of giving everyone the same treatment or of applying the rule in the same way in all cases. The Zapotecs are aware that they are persons, knots of nets of relationships; below every individual skin is a bearer of these nets, who is recognized as such and treated accordingly, as the distinct person he or she is, not as the homogeneous atom of an abstract category.* The circumstances of each event are also different and should be carefully taken into account. Although the same person commits the same offence, he does so in different circumstances that must be weighed. These attitudes often cause great concern among the state authorities and human rights activists who are convinced of the universal validity of the ideal of equality and individual rights.[7]

Each case is different, just as each person is different. There are no written rules or uniform definitions. And yet, even the children know what to do when someone commits an offence. If the case goes to an authority, social control is exercised in the observation of the person who is involved: all are attentive to what the authorities will decide. The deviation from what is considered appropriate would have serious consequences.

'Westerners represent the figure of justice as a blindfolded woman,' Marcos said one day. 'We want her with her eyes wide open, so that she can see, with care, all the circumstances of each case and consider well the differences between people.'

Consolation and compensation

The immediate reaction to the person who has committed an offence is to meet his need for help, perhaps consolation. It is assumed that such a person is in distress. For many, it is likely that they require supernatural assistance.

---

* Ed. For the problematization of autonomous subject and individual and how it can be viewed as relational, see Chapters 1 and 7.

In some Zapotec communities, the person who has committed a serious misconduct, a crime for example, is immediately tied to a tree, to the great displeasure and concern of human rights activists. He is not being punished. It is to allow time for the elderly to come and talk with him. They will try to bring him back from the delirious state that assumedly took control over him. Only out of his mind could he have committed the offense. Once they have heard him, and he has been able to explain himself and they have been able to fully understand the matter, he regains complete freedom.

From that moment on, what is important is the compensation to the victim of the offense. In most cases, the result is known by all. Sometimes it is simply to repair the damage, for example covering for the value of a damaged cornfield, providing a number of turkeys or goats equivalents to those that were stolen or abused, and so on. Other times, the offense generates a permanent, or at least prolonged, responsibility. The person who committed a crime, for example, is now economically responsible for the family of the dead person. As a result of the burden of the two families, he may have to migrate to the United States regularly, to earn some dollars. For him, escape would be worse than prison or death. Usually he becomes a hard-working, complying citizen. The community recognizes and appreciates his effort and responsibility. Many times no stigma is laid upon him, but in the case of a serious crime, the person is not allowed to have important *cargos* in the community since he has lost his moral authority.

Governing bodies which resolve conflicts

The intense vitality of communities, the density of their relationships and interactions and the splendid differentiation between the people, favors the proliferation of conflicts, which have worsened with the broadening and deepening of the relationship with other cultures and the larger society. Conflicts are appearing which, until recently, were entirely unheard of, such as those related to the economy.

Most of the conflicts are resolved between those directly involved or with the intervention of their immediate or extended families. Some cases, however, do not achieve resolution there and are taken to the local authorities, which have different levels and areas of responsibility, and sometimes even other governing bodies.

In many communities, the agents of the solution can have a supernatural nature. In the same way that the offense or the conflict can be attributed to them, their help can be sought to resolve it. A witch, a healer or a priest can be an effective intermediary for this purpose and can directly contribute to the solution, including, in its appropriate place, the phase of atonement.

Mayors, municipal presidents and communal judges deal with different types of offenses and proceed conforming to the recognized rules, which, in various jurisdictions, primarily serve to define the gravity of the offense. Written records of the trials are known to exist, as it is customary to maintain them in many communities, but the 'trials' themselves are conducted as conversations induced by the authorities as they try to discover the root causes of the conflict and at the same time guide the inquiry to the expected outcome: through their intervention, they seek to lead to the reestablishment of harmony between the parties.

In general, it is thought that to maintain a grievance is bad for the health of both the person and the community. It is necessary to release it, although this does not need to happen immediately. Sometimes the injury can wait until one of the large fiestas in the village, which are spaces that are suitable for airing old and new grievances and settling them within the general festive spirit, conducive to conciliation.

Exceptionally, when all these mechanisms have proved futile and the grievance persists, the person who still feels the grievance can turn to other governing bodies, whether they be regional, which have the same character – to the head of the administrative district, for example – or the state or federal governing bodies, which apply conventional legal procedures to which have recently been incorporated the obligation, rarely fulfilled, to rigorously take into account the indigenous condition of plaintiffs and defendants.

The path of atonement

Very diverse communal mechanisms try to encourage the balancing of all involved (without equalizing or standardizing) and to continually adjust the norms, both in terms of ideas and behavior, so that everyone can fulfill them and avoid conflicts. But inevitably some conflicts arise. People deviate from the norms. They commit errors that affect everyone else.

The overall dedication that is seen in everyone, from families to the authorities and the courts, reflects a deep concern for the harmony that was lost. Attempts are made to reestablish it. This is what is considered truly important. We already indicated that they do not seek to punish those who committed an offense. If the offense is severe, an attempt is made to provide support, natural or supernatural. They arrange the compensation to the victim. But all this has to be at the service of the most important thing: the cultivation of harmony among the people in conflict. It is something that moves beyond forgiveness.

In these villages, gossip is an act of introspection. People belong to the community and the community belongs to them, but perhaps the reality is not reflected in these terms. All of them *are* the community. The settling of issues between them, after a conflict, is like confronting oneself and fixing the disorder that is produced internally. It is a question of being internally calm, of dealing with one's own demons in order to keep them under control. It means to live in peace.

The oral form of existence

Orality is the technology with which the distinct We of the community maintains the homeostasis, the balance, of the world. To recreate with the spoken word a present in precarious equilibrium, always in relation to the external Other, separates those memories which are no longer relevant and begins to consider and create new hopes. The present requires a fitting forgetfulness. It is in the concrete reality of the situation where the words acquire their meaning. Each time the speaker accommodates himself to a different audience and confronts new situations: the art of the oral tradition is rooted precisely in the daily play between memory and hope.

In everyday conversation, the repetition of stories and cultural formulas is evident. Everyone knows them. They know the gestures. They have seen and heard all this again and again, and, every time, enjoy the same story or cultural formulas, woven into recent or new stories. Thus they participate in the communion, the everyday sharing, with 'established' phrases infinitely repeated, in which what matters is precisely the celebration of the common experience and the reaffirmation of Us in front of the external Other.

The oral tradition does not contain the complex categories found in writing. In the oral tradition, thought and expression relate to what is one's own, people to which one is close to, the street and the flower, the known and recognized of our living environment, the everyday reality. In general, everyday communication is a story that describes the personal relations between Us and the Others.*

The *serrana* community is a zone of verbal challenge. Proverbs, riddles, jokes, insults, the evasion of direct answers, beating around the bush and responding with other questions are some manifestations of this daily combat, a battle of wits where you can seek to wound the adversary, but also pursue favor and kindness, grace (see below).

Unlike what occurs in writing, established, linear and reversible, in the oral tradition there is nothing to return to in order to confirm what was said, because once said, it disappears. But to repeat what was just said, continually engaging in redundancy, is a way for those speaking to remain in tune with one another. The speaker must repeat the same thing or something similar several times for it to be understood (there is always someone who will not understand); to continue and insist upon certain ideas, creating what might be called 'contingent formulas,' relevant only within a particular discourse or way of speaking.

The communal experience of social relationships

Displacing the exploration of peace to the exploration of harmony, as we do in the preceding paragraphs, does not completely resolve the difficulty. Between the

---

*   Ed. In Chapter 18, Robert Vachon brings to his chapter a centuries-old ceremonial oral traditional 'prayer,' offering a practical example of the arguments put forward here by Esteva and Guerrero.

people of the Sierra, there is not any word that uniquely expresses the meaning of the term harmony. There appear a number of expressions, meanings and practices that are organized and recreated every day. To identify equivalencies there remains the need to explore generalized principles, such as *guelaguetza* and reciprocity, together with other components of communal life that give substance to the 'harmonious condition' and allow others to begin to see the communal horizon. As we move closer to the everyday experience, in the morphology of Santa Cruz Yagavila, in the Rincón of the Sierra Juárez, we seem to find in the notions of *tu chh'ia* and *waka lenbëchi luuzaro* a concrete form of the communal principles of reciprocity and *guelaguetza*, in what would be a local way of naming the conditions which create harmony, as we will discuss below.

In order to appreciate the mental space that operates as a framework for the communal experience, we need to appeal to the notion of communality:[8] the all-encompassing myth of the communal Oaxacan world, the horizon of intelligibility derived from the movement and the interpenetration of two juxtaposed spirals.

First, the spiral *outward*, formed by relations with the other since the Conquest, in which the communal We is constructed into a subordinate position. As each external imposition generates resistance, it constitutes an adaptation: it introduces into the communal world an innovation that is deemed necessary in order to endure, because without it a confrontation would be produced that would lead to destruction. And second, the spiral *inward*, whose root core is (i) the communal territory, in which (ii) authority fulfills an organizational function beginning with (iii) communal work and (iv) fiestas, creating a world through (v) the vernacular language. These five elements are the foundation of communality. To share the myth, the horizon of intelligibility, is to create a territory, as a realization of everyday politics. This is not merely a discourse: it is expressed in the form of making decisions and of carrying out collective work; in the encounter of action, word and creation; in the conviviality between us, with others, the world and the unspeakable, with a disposition of service for the common good.

In searching on this horizon for a common understanding, between different communities, pueblos and languages of the Northern Sierra of Oaxaca, which may represent a homeomorphic equivalent of harmony, the dual order of the *guelaguetza* and reciprocity appears.

The *guelaguetza* is the aesthetic beginning of the communality: the celebration of sharing, the experience of being together and sharing a common feeling. It is kinship, friendship, what it is to be neighbors, the fact of belonging to a community, the fact of being close and being a fellow human being. According to Andrés Henestrosa, Zapotec of the Isthmus, '*guelaguetza* means that spirit of service between men, in the certainty that all joys and misfortunes can occur within a given moment appropriate to each' (Henestrosa, 2001, p. 16). It is the disposition and the act of walking with another at my side in the key moments of life. Mutual help among relatives, friends and godparents in the community, municipality, in celebration or in ill health.

The *guelaguetza*, the shared and joyful experience, is, ultimately, the shared realization of the communal, whose generating ethos is reciprocity, the imperative that weaves the Us. Reciprocity appears as a commitment and obligation among people close to one another, which establishes a complex system of material, symbolic and emotional exchanges of mutual aid, where a sense of community ownership and personal freedom is forged. It is the normative framework of the movement that again and again weaves the interdependence between *serranos*, creating new links, between them and the gods and the dead, and thus recreating the communal territory.

Reciprocity appears, therefore, as the ethical principle of communality. If a person dies in the community, the people close to him will take coffee, wood or anything else to the family for use during the wake and the rosaries. This family will do the same at the next opportunity, not necessarily for another death. Even more, the service one offers to the community through *cargos* appears as a duty woven into the very reciprocity by which the community exists.

The *guelaguetza* and reciprocity are basic complementary principles and practices among the pueblos of Oaxaca. They are known as *guendalizá, mano vuelta, guetz, gozona* and other names, and form part of the secret of the resistance. Jaime Martínez Luna, Zapotec of Guelatao, has attempted to update in Spanish the concept of *guelaguetza* with the neologism *compartencia* (the sharing), which means 'an activity that involves respect, dedication and consistency' (Martínez, 2003, p. 38). It is comprised of sharing life willingly and participating the grace fully in the festive celebration of Us. In this sense, the verbs participate (reciprocity) and share (*guelaguetza*) define the ontology of community. In the very movement from the ethical to the aesthetic that they generate lies the art of communal proportion, the way in which harmony is cultivated in this world.

With the *guelaguetza* and reciprocity, the social fabric is woven and the territory is re-created each day. This creative act requires the free decision that may be exercised from the foundations of the myth by the communal authority, through the two institutions with which this authority is made concrete in the structural dimension of the world: the assembly and the *cargo* system. The assembly will ultimately determine the validity of the *guelaguetza* and reciprocity in the communal space; it gives them practical application and ensures, as far as possible, their continuity and permanence.

The assembly is the highest forum of reflection, discussion and communal decision making. It is the constituent We. Every We within the fabric – family, godparents, neighbors, neighborhoods, committees, music bands, religious fraternities, brotherhoods and a long list of other knots within networks of relationships – has its assembly. But only the general assembly of citizens and community members determines how to share the territory and maintain the *guelaguetza*. The assembly embodies the communal power: its dignity. At its center, decisions are made by consensus, often the result of lengthy discussions. Every citizen has the right to have their say on the issues of community interest and is obliged to hear the positions of others, until, through complex and subtle mechanisms, the whole group is able to reach a consensual decision.

In the assembly, the face-to-face encounter between citizens is assured and appointments are made for those who will occupy different *cargos*, from which the agreements which were reached will be implemented. These appointments may be revoked at the moment that the assembly considers it necessary.

There, in the assembly, the two main types of relations are regulated and defined, the two spirals of communality: the inward (between us) and the outward (with the Other, both regional and extra-regional). Thus, in the assembly authorities are appointed, the governing bodies which are necessary for the functioning of the community are generated (such as committees) and work for the common good is organized (the *tequios*). Therefore, the assembly is the method of confronting together the problems of all, although this may imply an injury to a person, family or group. Communal well-being, harmony, is largely a result of the work fulfilled in the assembly. There, conflicts are recognized and measures to resolve them are decided upon, both of which are mechanisms for maintaining order. The communal is a world so convulsed by the tensions inside/outside, that it must be recreated every day.

In the assembly it is decided who will organize the fiesta for the patron saint; the destruction with hammers of a local food vendor located on communal territory off the road, by considering its operation outside of the norms of conviviality; or the decision to use the resources from a communal forestry in a remote community in the Sierra, to build a giant gymnasium, a decision that may seem foolish but that has a clear logic: the community's needs are covered by remittances from migrants, and the money that was produced through the sale of the trees might create discord. It seems better to build the most incredible basketball court in the region, which will distinguish the image of this community in the regional system of power and, above all, with such up-to-date facilities from the 'first-world,' will create a bridge between the traditional community and the recreation of that same community among migrants in the United States.

In intercommunity relations, the general assembly of citizens from each community plays a cardinal role in determining the ways in which each community will satisfy the *guelaguetza*. In general, when there are differences at this level of the social fabric, it is not a problem between individuals, but of the affairs between communities. Intercommunity conflicts are confronted from the assembly of each community in conflict. In these cases, decisions are made in the presence of the enemy, the friend and the neighbors, for example when problems concerning territorial limits between neighboring communities arise.

If there is the need to take extreme measures, the assembly determines such measures by consensus and assumes the responsibility for the decision itself and the consequences of the decision. The same principle applies when the music band from the village participates in the fiesta held by the neighboring population, or in the case of the siege imposed by one community on another, in the turbulent second decade of the twentieth century.

Harmony in regional, sectorial, micro-regional and municipal spaces involves a complex give-and-take in the communal assemblies. 'Better a bad settlement than a good lawsuit' is a saying that applies widely in the region, to underline the importance of agreement among different groups.

Work, another foundation of communality, is made concrete in the *tequio*, which is both a collective creation for the common good and one of the main mechanisms to facilitate processes of communal identification and differentiation. The *tequio* is the free and compulsory service that all members of the community provide, so that everyone can help meet the community's needs and solve the problems of everyday life. The call to perform *tequio* originates from the assembly. The authority is responsible for coordinating and organizing the effort that the assembly calls for. The assembly oversees and sanctions the performance of everyone in the *tequios*.

The value of the service is the gift itself, the personal fulfillment which occurs when each person gives his best in the shared *tequio*, or in the assigned *cargo*. We suspect that *tequio* and service are largely the instrument and the mindset that construct communal harmony. In both, the recognition of the other being in Us and of a shared destiny is completed for and with the other, and gratuitously realizes their very existence in this exchange, in this sacrifice. The counterpart of work is the fiesta and the counterpart of service is grace.

The fiesta is closely related to communal harmony: it is one of its foundations. Its liberating force, its excesses, its encounters and departures, which in the fiesta recreate the communal, are well known. The living and the dead reunite and commemorate, mutual promises are made; the life that everyone shares is celebrated, despite the sorrows; and in the fiesta an economic balancing mechanism is practiced within the community: it is common for those with greater revenues to assume a larger responsibility for the expenses of the celebration. The fiesta is a way of recreating communal land in distant territories, in a context of migration. In the fiesta the Us acquires an immediate and visible reality; relatives, friends and godparents are reunited, and everyone lives the *guelaguetza* and renews their hopes. They worked throughout the year for this moment, when the designated provisions are consumed and the best dress clothes worn. Those who normally stay in their homes and on their grounds go out on the streets or in the square, and there they dance, eat, chat, drink and laugh. In communality there is sacrifice, but joy is just as inherent to life as work.

Grace represents the value of the encounter and assumes that someone realized a full service: it is the radiance that is produced between the one who gives the best of himself and those who receive this gift. Grace is receptivity, the recognition of the gift that the other gave, or the recognition on the part of the other for what one provides. Nobody can give himself the gift, but it is possible to receive it from another – God, people who one is close to, or the supernatural – and enjoy it together. If one has the appropriate disposition, one will capture the spark that exists in what the other gives, will recognize the abundance of the world, will judge out loud or in silence that this person, action, saying, contains the grace in the moment of joy. Grace is a briefly shared illumination. In acknowledging the gift, given by the other, one appreciates what was received, literally, with pleasure – thus, one reciprocates it –, a personal pleasure, which rebinds the collective in the sparkle of the *guelaguetza*.

We need the other so that life may pass with grace. One or the other fosters grace, so that all can enjoy it. Grace is the value that we attribute to the actions of others, or that they attribute to our actions, when this gesture, word or maneuvering has, in addition to its meaning in a particular context, to its truth or falsity and its practical utility, a singular sense of beauty that reunites people and makes life more enjoyable for Us.

One's behavior, work and commitment are recognized; it is acknowledged that this vital exchange creates a better world. For this reason, grace is a double demand, because it is hoped, within the myth, that one fulfills a certain dose of grace in what one does and gives to others. It is not enough to get things right, not enough to simply fulfill your obligations. It is necessary to give it a flavor: a soup prepared reluctantly, without pleasure, may be very nutritious, or be ready just in time, but will not taste good, will not have grace. It is the receiver who qualifies, but the server, the giver of the gift, will have to work hard to ensure that his creation is fresh and powerful. It is not for him to decide or to judge if what he provides has grace, because grace is not in him or in what he does, but rather emerges in the joyous encounter with the other, if it is in the server to dedicate all his efforts, so that his work is also a subtle blessing for all. But it is also a requirement for the person receiving the gift. Finally, it is he who judges whether grace has occurred. This means being open to looking, listening, being prepared to feel. The receiver gives himself in the very act of receiving and shares in the received. Without an attitude of listening, no word is of value: the speaker can give his maximum, but grace will not occur, because there is no one to embrace it.

In morphological terms, grace emerges when one misses it. It is easier to name it in its absence. Such as when one observes an indolent attitude and thinks, 'they do not have even a little grace....'

The manner in which the principle of complementarity is related to harmony can be observed in three cases: the two spirals, inwards and outwards, of the all-encompassing myth; the three dimensions, mythical, structural and morphological, of the communal world; the five fundamentals of communality: territory, authority, work, language and fiesta. In all three cases, the items are related in solidarity with one another, collaborating in the creation of reality. The spiral inward is different from the spiral outward, but cannot be separated from it: both rotations accomplish the communal. The myth, the structure and the morphology of the world are not hierarchical or progressive levels; they appear as the sides of a cube, simultaneous, distinct and indispensable to each other. The territory only exists when a community exercises its authority through work and the spoken word, and thus finds the conditions in which to celebrate.

The isolation or the sovereignty of any of the elements is unthinkable: whether it be a relationship between two, three or more components, the logic of the relationship is that of complementarity. While each element of the relationship is different and one cannot be reduced to the other or confused with it, in themselves each element contains the other, just as the other contains it, which implies movement. This does not mean that the pieces go quietly into a totality, but rather that the relationship is recreated in every moment in an undivided reality, in which elements can be distinguished with analytical eagerness, but that in their actuality do not exist separated from the rest, nor are they independent, but form a single movement. Complementarity is a communal dynamism; it defines the co-participation in the search and the ongoing construction of balance.

The principle of communal integrity is the condition of possible complementarity. Reality is movement, without fragmentation, and everything is interdependent. The world cannot be composed of autonomous spheres, whether they be subatomic particles or the legal field as separated from religion, but rather a flow that binds together natural and supernatural beings, the world and the unspeakable. The linguistic distinction that names an element separates it from the framework in the analysis, but it should be immediately remembered that this condition does not exist in the integrated reality of the communal horizon.

One consequence of this principle is that *serranos* establish dialogues and exchanges not only in the realm of the human and the natural, but also with the very distinct Other and the ineffable, that is born of the Earth and whose emissaries acquire peculiar forms, the spirits of the mountains and forests, or the Holy Cross. The hill or the field, for example, can provoke punishments (accidents, illness, the loss of the soul or the harvest) upon those men and women who are disrespectful in their relationship with the natural world.

The world is not divided into subject and object. The plurality of people linked to one another is recognized, plants like corn (which have a heart), or animals such as bulls (which have a soul), are recognized as linked, woven in a single movement with Us. Communal integrality establishes interdependence between the simple or unexpected everyday events and the transcendental. As in the case of the loss of a bull, the family conducts a *limpia*, sweeping the bodies with a candle and praying, in order to open it up to the sacred and make propitiation that will allow the bull to find its way back.

In conformity with the principle of integrality, the legal is not separated from the communal world: it includes the civil, the sacred and the supernatural. The vernacular language and the territory are the sediment of the communal myth, but local norms, the oral tradition and communal work are its concrete morphological realizations and define what is the communal. The *tequio*, oral tradition and the *milpa*[9] are technologies of Us.

The celebration of everyday listening and speaking, the face-to-face encounter, fosters what is the communal and reorders the communal experience. It is what is said, powered by how it is said. In practice, work and the joy of words and the listening between everyone is more important than what is actually said and its grammar. The rationalization that legitimates a discourse weighs much less than the grace put into it: its truth lies in the *guelaguetza* it generates.

By linking harmony with the principles of *guelaguetza*, reciprocity, complementarity and integrality; with the fundamentals of the authority, work and fiesta; with the institutions of the assembly and the *cargo* system; and with the concepts of service and grace, what is harmony, the harmonious condition, appears in the communal world as something desired and desirable, which is the result of the full relationship between men and women and with the complete reality.

The incarnation of harmony

To give concreteness to the expression of harmony within the myth of communality, we focus now on the Zapotec pueblos located in the Rincón of the Northern Sierra of Oaxaca, particularly in the community *Bëni xidzai*[10] of Santa Cruz Yagavila, derived from talks with Don Pablo Cruz, a man who by virtue of living in relation with others became wise.

To consider and experience harmony in Yagavila also starts with the distinction of two matrix movements, an inward and an outward. Communal harmony, or the lack thereof, is based on the not necessarily coherent or kind rotations of these spirals. For Don Pablo the conflict is somewhat encouraged by the ideas that come from outside and which disrupt an inside which he believes to be stable, the Outside that since the Conquest is also inside and contributes to the formation of Us.

In Yagavila, inside, among the people, *tu chh'ia* flows, 'what is all right and has no face, the energy, the word.' The *Bëni xidza* do not consider *tu chh'ia* a substance but rather a shared well-being, a full empathy that consumes Us. It is the joint vibration of the living: the encounter, the coexistence and the exchange of human beings with other beings through the positive energy that they themselves promote in their way of acting together with the other; a *compartencia*. *Tu chh'ia* would be one way to achieve the principle of *guelaguetza* in this community in the Rincón of the Sierra in Oaxaca.

Tu chh'ia is not the product of spontaneous generation or an unassailable decision of the gods. Harmony is built on the logic of reciprocity, beginning with a vigorous process of mutual hospitality. The *Bëni xidza* say: *waka lenbëchi luuzaro*, which can be translated as 'let the other enter into my heart, while I'm in theirs.' This hospitality and self-acceptance rebind us in grace and define the person in community with others. It is the ethical and historical disposition that stems from the recognition of foundational diversity (inward and outward, we and the other, natural and supernatural...) and the need for it to be complemented in reciprocity in order to reintegrate the world. 'We host death in our lives and we must learn to recognize it,' warns Don Pablo. *Waka lenbëchi luuzaro* is the path towards the emergence of *tooyía* – a realization of the principle of communal reciprocity between the *Bëni xidza*. Again, the momentum from the ethical to the aesthetic. These two notions indicate how harmony is procured in Yagavila.

The flow of *tu chh'ia* is the experience of the totality, but it is not a permanent state, on the contrary, it is always a provisional union that people must maintain and, when appropriate, restore. The vital flow stops, hospitality ends, the Us is diluted and everything is broken when selfishness appears. The I singular is placed before Us. The private mutilates the communal. The desire to accumulate and compete – instead of participating and sharing – changes the attitude towards life. The person or group thinks from the position of 'masters of reason.' Nobody is hospitable to anyone else and a radical separation from the other is experienced. From there, the person – a knot in a net of real, concrete relationships – is reduced to the individual – an atom of abstract categories, which leaves aside its unfathomable singularity and is instead simply compared and equated with the other, such that the dissolution of diversity, for a supposed homogenizing equality, opens the way to conflict.

For the *Bëni xidza*, 'the selfish believe that the earth belongs to them and does not host death. He has a dirty heart.'

The basis for well-being among the *Bëni xidza*, according to Don Pablo, would be to acknowledge at the same time unity and difference with the other, *tula pas nakaro*: 'We are alike and we are different.' The tension is constant, the movement incessant in the formation of Us. It is work, this perennial yes, to create territory. Not for nothing, when one speaks of recreating the life and sowing the earth in *didza xidza*, the language of the Zapotecs of the Rincón, one uses the same verb: *gaazaro*.

How does one restore the flow of *tu chh'ia* when it has been broken by selfishness? Ideally, how does one solve a conflict and renew a mutual sense of hospitality? Don Pablo says, 'with what out there they call friendship.' And this would be, finally, the name of peace in Yagavila.[11]

Notes

1. Neither in academia nor in the United Nations system exists a generally accepted definition of the term *pueblo*. One school of thought considers it a sociological category: it is applied to groups that share certain identifiable characteristics. Others accept it as a political and legal concept, which applies to all residents of a territory or a state, regardless of its features. Often the word pueblo, or nation, is used to describe a group of people who share a history, culture, territory and project.

   The term is bounded in connection with the so-called Indian pueblos, a term that remains the subject of intense controversy. Almost all the groups which this term makes reference to refer to themselves in their own terms, different for each group and generally reject any denomination that seeks to encompass them all. The expression *pueblos indios* is commonly used to refer to communities and villages that existed before the formation of nation-states in the American continent, who have maintained until now their own forms of cultural existence distinct from those used by the dominant societies within which they are found inserted, and who continue affirming themselves in these forms in order to orient their thoughts and behavior and reclaim their autonomy.

2. According to one version concerning the origin of the word Zapotec, it was derived from a Náhuatl word, *tzapotecatl*, related to the *zapote*, a tree that abounds in some of the land that is considered Zapotec. It is said that the Mexicas used this generic term to refer to different groups, all of which used different words, in their different languages, to refer to themselves. There is no common term, in the current languages of those groups, which distinguishes all the so-called 'Zapotecs,' a term that arose, like the term Indian, from the desire to attach, from the outside, an abstract label on very different realities that were supposed to form a union. The words that, in the different 'Zapotec' languages, are used to recognize themselves, can be translated as 'real people,' 'people of the true word,' 'people of the wise word,' 'people who speak a language,' 'people of the Sierra mountains' (or another region) and so on. These are words that generally identify a specific way of speaking...with the result that there are multiple forms.

3. We are not discovering the wheel. Studies of the Zapotecs almost always record this impression. Some time ago, Julio de la Fuente (1960) expressed it this way: 'Notwithstanding the lack of data on the Zapotec group, what is known of its culture allows for the proposal of the hypothesis that we are not faced with one culture but rather several.' In recognizing the differentiated current status of these different human groups and their antecedents, anthropologists now argue that the 'current ethno-linguistic groups' (such as the 'macroetnia' of the Zapotecs) are 'polisegmentary configurations without political integration, within which a variable number of ethnic group organizations are registered' (Barabas, 1999, p. 19). We have the impression, however, that scholars do not derive the logical consequences of this realistic perception. After planting this warning at the beginning of their work, they proceed to describe the whole Zapotec union, at most separating it into some subsets. The analysis, therefore, tends to stay at the level of abstract generalizations that appear to be increasingly far from a diversified and changing reality.

4. An analogy could be drawn to the romance languages in saying that the Zapotecs are as similar to each other as Romanian, French, Spanish, Italian and Portuguese. As in the case of the romance languages, a short period of interaction may allow for intelligibility between speakers of various Zapotec languages, 'because many words have common roots.' Intellectuals of the different Zapotec linguistic groups argue 'that

the variations, though significant, can be unified in order to form a single language' (Barabas, 1999, p. 61).

5. We note with fascination the increasingly intense debates that have been conducted at the heart of the so-called field of legal anthropology, but we did not find in them a way to escape the modern occidental legal ethnocentrism, which still continues to infect it. We believe that the most that can be done, in the tradition of legal pluralism which has been opening itself up to new paths in recent years, is to identify some homeomorphic equivalents, that is, concepts and practices that seem to have an analogous or similar role in different cultures. See Krotz (2002) on legal anthropology. On legal pluralism, see Panikkar (1979, 1993, 1995) and Robert Vachon (1990, 1992a, 1992b, 1993).

6. If we arrive at a remote community, and we start to talk about an agrarian conflict, there will be a moment when the oldest of our friends will go to his hut and display the title that the Spanish Crown gave to his ancestors, recognizing his right to the lands that he still occupies. It is possible that no one in the pueblo can read this document, but they are forced to refer to it in case of conflict. In many communities the relationships between neighbors and their mutual confidence still defines issues associated with the occupation and use of land, which in its design cannot be owned. They still employ rituals in order to regularly ratify *colindancias* (the territorial limits of a community) mutually agreed upon. They still honor the word transmitted from father to son that alludes to a type of relationship with the cosmos, prominently including the Mother Earth and her children. Increasingly, however, interaction with others requires that they refer to documents, even among the illiterate, in order to defend their existence and traditions. With the proliferation of documents, agrarian conflicts also multiply, which often end in violence.

7. The positive law used in almost all countries, recognizes the differences among individuals and the circumstances of each case through the construction of abstract categories in the population (children, women, etc.), for whom the law is applied differentially, and through the legal definition of aggravating or mitigating factors in the crimes that judges should take into account in each case. These distinctions, which are established within the framework of the formal treatment based on the application of the law, remain within the fundamental assumption that there exists an absolute similarity between individuals and that they must all be treated in the same way: they are all human beings, all are individual atoms of abstract categories, all should be considered equal in the eyes of the law, which must not show any preference. And so, an ancient metaphysical definition – all souls are equal in the eyes of God – and a specific historical struggle against the privileges of the nobility, found the occidental obsession with the equality of individuals, which not only reduces them in abstract uniformity but also legitimizes real injustice, based in illegitimate hierarchies such as money. The current prototype of this exercise is the case of O.J. Simpson. The person who led his team of lawyers, Alan Dershovitz, made visible the reality that they are obliged by the law to use the law for the benefit of their clients, who are often criminals. It is no longer a question of 'delivering justice' but rather of completing an efficient professional exercise that can be translated, in practice, as freedom for criminals and death for innocent people.

8. The term was coined, simultaneously and independently, by Jaime Martínez Luna, Zapotec of Guelatao, in the Sierra de Juárez, and by Floriberto Díaz, Mixe, to share with others the communal way of being. See, among others, Maldonado (2002), Robles and Cardoso (2007) and Jaime Martínez Luna (1995).

9. The traditional combination of corn, beans and squash, cultivated together in the same field and usually accompanied by more than a hundred different plants, growing wildly in the *milpa* and usually called *quelites*.

10. This expression means *'people of the Rincón,'* the name that the communities of this area of the Sierra gave to themselves; it is what in anthropology is called an ethno-linguistic group.

11. Bibliographical clues; The work of A.M. Barabas (1999) and the one she published with M. Bartolomé in Millán and Valle (2003) contains the best ethnographic documentation on the Zapotecs. Bibliographies of these texts and of the book by Whitecotton (1984) (still considered a classic) are very comprehensive. See also Carmagnani (1988), Newbold Chiñas (1992), Ríos (1994), Pérez García (1996), Bennholdt-Thomsen (1997), Stephen (1998) and González (2001). Michael Kearney (1996) has published the results of his research in California concerning Zapotec, Mixtec and other indigenous pueblos in the United States in California. Laura Nader (1990) has conducted numerous studies on the social structure, ways of resolving conflicts and regulatory systems in various indigenous areas and particularly among indigenous Zapotec of the Sierra. As for the debate on the legal issues, see Krotz (2002) and the work of Panikkar (1979, 1993, 1995) and Vachon (1990, 1992a, 1992b, 1993). In the case of Oaxaca and the Zapotecs, see, in particular, Carmen Cordero (1982, 1995, 1996, 1997). On the ongoing struggle for autonomy and its connection to Zapatismo, see, among many other texts, Esteva (1994, 1998, 2002).

Reference list

Barabas, A.M. (1999) 'Gente de la palabra verdadera: El grupo etnolingüística zapoteco' in A.M. Barabas and M. Bartolomé (eds.) *Configuraciones Étnicas en Oaxaca: Perspectivas Etnográficas para las Autonomías* (Mexico: INI / CONACULTA-INAH).

Bennholdt-Thomsen, V. (ed.) (1997) *Juchitán, la Ciudad de las Mujeres* (Oaxaca: IOC).

Carmagnani, M. (1988) *El Regreso de los Dioses: El Proceso de Reconstitución de la Identidad Étnica en Oaxaca. Siglos XVII y XVIII* (Mexico: FCE).

Cordero, C. (1982) *Supervivencia de un Derecho Consuetudinario en el Valle de Tlacolula* (Oaxaca: FONAPAS).

Cordero, C. (1995) *La Justicia en el Derecho Consuetudinario en las Comunidades Zapotecas del Valle de Tlacolula* (Mexico: Comisión Nacional de Derechos Humanos).

Cordero, C. (1996) *La Justicia Indígena en una Sociedad Pluricultural: El caso de Oaxaca* (Mexico: UNAM).

Cordero, C. (1997) *La Vara de Mando: Costumbre Jurídica en la Transmisión de Poderes* (Oaxaca: Ayuntamiento).

de la Fuente, J. (1960) 'La cultura Zapoteca,' *Revista Mexicana de Estudios Antropológicos,* XVI, 233–246.

Esteva, G. (1994) *Crónica del Fin de una Era: El Secreto del Zapatismo* (Mexico: Posada).

Esteva, G. (1998) 'Autonomía y democracia radical: El tránsito de la tolerancia a la hospitalidad' in M. Bartolomé and A. Barabas (eds.) *Autonomías Étnicas y Estados Nacionales* (Mexico: CONACULTA/INAH).

Esteva, G. (2002) 'Sentido y alcances de la lucha por la autonomía' in S.L. Mattiace, R.A. Hernández and J. Rus (eds.) *Tierra, Libertad y Autonomía: Impactos Regionales del Zapatismo en Chiapas* (Mexico: CIESAS).

Esteva, G. (2004) 'Els zapoteques: L'harmonia com a justícia', *Avui – Dumenge*, Dossiers de Cultures del Món, www.unescocat.org/ct/p6/pdf/zapoteques.pdf.

González, R.J. (2001) *Zapotec Science: Farming and Food in the Northern Sierra of Oaxaca* (Austin: University of Texas Press).

Henestrosa, A. (2001) *Mágica y Hechicera Oaxaqueña* (Mexico: Miguel Porrúa).

Illich, I. (1981) 'Desvincular la paz y el desarrollo,' *Tecnopolítica*, 6.

Kearney, M. (1996) *Migration, the New Indígena, and the Formation of Multi-ethnic Autonomous Regions in Oaxaca* (San Diego: International Studies Association).

Krotz, E. (2002) *Antropología Jurídica: Perspectivas Socioculturales en el Estudio del Derecho* (Barcelona: Anthropos/Mexico: UAM).

Maldonado, B. (2002) *Autonomía y Comunalidad India* (Oaxaca: CONACULTA/CEDI).

Martínez Luna, J. (1995) '¿Es la comunidad nuestra identidad?' *Ojarasca*, 42–43.

Martínez Luna, J. (2003) *Comunalidad y Desarrollo* (Oaxaca: CONACULTA/Campo).

Millán S. and J. Valle (eds.) (2003) *La Comunidad sin Límites. Estructura Social y Organización Comunitaria en las Regiones Indígenas de México* (Mexico: INAH).

Nader, L. (1990) *Harmony Ideology: Justice and Control in a Zapotec Mountain Village* (Palo Alto, CA: Stanford University Press).

Newbold Chiñas, B. (1992) *The Isthmus Zapotecs: A Matrifocal Culture of Mexico* (Fort Worth: Harcourt Brace Jovanovich College Publishers).

Panikkar, R. (1979) *Myth, Faith and Hermeneutics* (New York: Paulista Press).

Panikkar, R. (1993) *Paz y Desarme Cultural* (Santander: Editorial Sal Térrea).

Panikkar, R. (1995) *Invisible Harmony* (Minneapolis: Augsburg Fortress).

Pérez García, R. (1996) *La Sierra Juárez* (Oaxaca: IOC).

Ríos, M. (ed.) (1994) *Los Zapotecos de la Sierra Norte de Oaxaca: Antología Etnográfica* (Oaxaca: CIESAS/IOC).

Robles, S. and R. Cardoso (eds.) (2007) *Escritos de Floriberto Díaz: Comunalidad, Energía Viva del Pensamiento Mixe* (Mexico, UNAM).

Stephen, L. (1998) *Mujeres Zapotecas* (Oaxaca: IOC).

Vachon, R. (1990) 'L'étude de pluralism juridique: une approche diatopique et dialogale,' *Journal of Legal Pluralism and Unofficial Law*, 29.

Vachon, R. (1992a) 'Ontogestión y desarrollo: La tradición autóctona contemporánea de autogestión y solidaridad cósmica,' *Opciones*, 3.

Vachon, R. (1992b) 'Derechos humanos y dahrma,' *Opciones*, 6.

Vachon, R. (1993) 'Las solidaridades del círculo,' *Opciones*, 51.

Whitecotton, J. (1984) *The Zapotecs: Princes, Priests, and Peasants* (Norman: University of Oklahoma Press).

20
Thaq: An Andean-Amazonian Perspective*

Grimaldo Rengifo V.

> When I think about Fitzcarraldo and his mercenaries, when I think these genocidal maniacs were men, I feel like becoming a member of the nation of snakes.
>
> Ino Moxo†

Introduction

In the Peruvian Andes, we have been hearing the word peace with renewed persistency. This is because of the conflict our country went through in that regrettable decade that we, the Peruvian people, suffered during the 1980s and early 1990s. Peace was then associated with the end of war and the end, once and for all, of the genocide that knocked at the doors of Peruvian homes. Peace demonstrations multiplied in the streets and towns, involving schoolchildren, young university students and a great number of union, peasant and urban-grassroots organizations; that is, the social conglomerate that today we call the civil society. We all wished for the climate of insanity to cease, and there was not

---

* This text, which is just an initial approach, is the result of a *minga* that has been possible thanks to the collaboration of the participants in the Diploma Course on 'Intercultural Education and Sustainable Research' that PRATEC (Andean Project of Peasant Technologies) executes in agreement with the Postgraduate School of the Universidad Nacional Agraria de la Selva (National Agrarian University of the Jungle), particularly the attendants to the II Workshop that took place in Urubamba, Cuzco, from January 10 to 25, 2007. They contributed short texts about the understanding on peace and conflict in the communities they represent and work with. Any errors in the translation and comments are the full responsibility of the author.

† Ed. The original quote in Spanish reads: 'Cuando pienso en Fitzcarrald y en sus mercenarios, cuando pienso que esos genocidas eran hombres, me dan ganas de nacio-nalizarme culebra' (Calvo, 1981, p. 305).

one person, except for the merchants of war, who wanted that order of things to continue. We all wanted to return to a tranquil life in our country and homes.

Today almost nobody speaks of peace, even though, curiously, the language of war is starting to be heard again among the highest spheres of power with the term 'death penalty.' The demonstrations, the thousands of dead counted by the Truth and Reconciliation Commission and the great amount of ink wasted by the communication media apparently have not been enough to quench the thirst for revenge and the agitated hearts of many of our fellow countrymen who now take to the streets demanding capital punishment as a remedy for the evils engendered by the genocide we lived through.

All the reflections, all the actions, have not been enough to dissolve the disease, and it is requested that each of us examine what we have lived through so that, with our remaining strength, we may explore new possibilities for living together that will prevent it from taking over our body once again. We require renewed reflections and actions, particularly from rural and peasant social groups that have profound ethnic roots, such as the Quechua and Aymara peoples, who suffered and carried upon their shoulders the heaviest weight of the conflict.

All this leads us to suppose that we have pending obligations and unapproved issues; among these is that which refers to peace, as it is understood by the indigenous peoples and the popular sectors in general; today more than ever we require their contributions for the renewal of the national debate about the future of our country. It would seem that the visions of peace and reconciliation that were ventilated towards the end of the twentieth century were not sufficient.

The following pages are an invitation issued to those sectors in Peru and the Andes in general, which are committed to peace, to jointly explore in each of our regions the issue of peace, as the Andean–Amazonian peoples understand it.

'Peace' in the Andean–Amazonian culture

The Andean conception of peace

In the Andean–Amazonian culture, there are words that evoke a kind of peace that is understood as a state of serenity and tranquility. In the Quechua tongue of Lircay, Huancavelica, they speak about *hawkalla*, a word related to calm and tranquility. *Hawqa* (or *Qawka*, both are read *jauqa*) is said of a tranquil person who respects and does not disturb the community, celebration or ritual. *Hawqa yachay* means knowing how to live in tranquility without fostering conflicts in the community. It is common, for example, for people to say *Hawqalla kawsasun* ('we will live in tranquility'). In Auquilla, Ayacucho, the same as in the Quechua (or Quichua) of Ecuador, the word for someone who is tranquil, peaceful, who does not look for trouble, who is not a provoker and who gladly receives and assumes his or her commitments is *Kasilla*, so that *kasilla kawsay* means 'to live in tranquility.' In Agato, Ecuador, *fangalla* is said of a light, tranquil person.

In general, the Quechua words *kasilla* or *hawqalla* are associated with the Quechua word *kawsay*, and they mean 'to live in a tranquil and relaxed manner.' The expression *allin kawsay* means 'to live well,' and better still if you add the adjective *sumaq* – nice, pleasing – to the expressions *hawqallu kuwsay* and *allin kawsay*. In this case, these phrases would mean 'to live in harmony, nicely, without problems or difficulties.' In the Quechua of Ancash, in northern Peru, there is the expression *mana ajanashqa*, which means 'without difficulty, to be well, without conflict.' Alternatively, there is another: *Mana piñashqa, mana chikinakushqa*, which is translated as 'we are not in situations of bitterness, wrath or hatred, we are tranquil.'

Thaq, a Quechua word from Cuzco, in southern Peru, is another Andean expression that can be related to peace. In English, among other aspects it means 'tranquil; to be well, serene, sharing what you know, in peace, just living nicely,' for example *thaq kunanka tiyaychi* ('now live in tranquility, in peace'), *thaq kani* ('I am in peace, tranquil'), or *thak kay*, which means 'in tranquility.'

In the Aymara tongue, to be tranquil in peace can be said with the expression *ph'ajtata* or *phajtatawa*, and to say that everything is tranquil, in calm, in peace, you would say *Ph'ajtatakiwa*. Ms. Victoria Panti Espillico (2007), from the village of Queruma, Juli, in Puno, says, for example, *Yapu irnaqawita juttha chuymaja wali phajtatawa* ('my heart is tranquil because I have finished harvesting in my entire farm').

This feeling of calm, serenity, tranquility and joy can be observed when, during the celebration of carnival, the *comunero* (joint holder of a tenure of lands) appraises his crops in full bloom, when the fruits have been gathered, when there is food for everyone (in Quechua expressed by *mikuylla kachunqa thakllan tiyakusun*, 'we will live in tranquility if there is food'). Also, these circumstances are experienced when the corn is softly caressed by the wind, or when the sunset is windless and tranquil, the morning is sunny, when there is an intense experience of being at the moment of a ritual, or in the calmness of the countryside after a storm.

Tranquility is also related to the circumstances in which the rains fall when the plants need it, and when the children respect their parents. This calm and joy in the heart of the *runa* ('human' in Quechua) is also experienced when the *Pachamama* (mother nature/universe) rejoices in seeing the children play and be joyful in the fields, when a gathering has taken place in a serene and tranquil manner, when the animals increase, and when cooking and gathering firewood. The *thaq* also reposes in deities, such as the *Pachamama*, and in nature; it is then not a concept that is solely centered on human beings.

Tranquility lives and rests in the heart of the Andean dweller when there are no arguments between parents and children (*thaqmi tiyakuyku*), when there is tranquility in the house (*thaq kawsay wasinchi*, 'let there be tranquility in our house'), when the peasant families have finished sowing on their farmlands, or storing their products after the harvest. It is common to hear the peasants say *chacrata tarpuytatukurushparaqmi thaq kachkan* ('I am tranquil after I have finished working in my farm'), also when a mother says *wawaypaq p'anchanta ruwayta tukurusparaqmi thaq kachkani* ('now that I have finished knitting my newborn child's garment – *chompa* – I am joyful, tranquil, in peace').

Modesta Challco, a teacher from Sicuani in Cuzco, tells that her grandmother, after participating in the great labors in her village, would say *Hay thak kunanqa karusun* ('now I will be tranquil'). When roads are being fixed, after the *comuneros* have fulfilled their labor, they also say, joyfully, *Hay hananay kunanqa thak karusun* ('now we are tranquil'). In these examples, *thaq* is associated with the fulfillment of obligations, a kind of being happy, well and in harmony with the community, such as when the task of authority has been fulfilled. Alejandro Choccelahua Quispe, from the village of San Juan de Dios, Lircay, says about this:

> When you are an authority [*autoridad vara* – *alwacer*], during the period of your post [*cargo*], you worry about the fields, because you are watchful of the weather [climate], of hailstorms and frost. This is why, when we are councilmen or *alwacer*: 'Even night does not feel like night, nor is the day a day'. Because you have to be watchful of the frosts, to serve the mountain deities [*Apus*], and this must be done until we have passed our post [*cargo*]. Once we have passed our post [*cargo*] as authority, then we reach tranquility [peace]; then we can say we have fulfilled our duty in caring for the crops, in taking care of the *Pachamama* or Mother Nature. (Zevallos, 2007, p. 2)

As mentioned above, the word tranquility is related to the Quechua expression *allin kawsay* (good life) or *miski kawsay* (sweet life). For a Quechua *comunero*, tranquility is also a permanent wish. They say *Allin kawsay kachun ayllunchiskunapi* ('let there be a good life for our community'). Thus, tranquility is associated with good living in your place (*pacha*) of reference, as the Quechua from Ancash say *Shumaq purwakusqa kaway mana ajanashqa* ('when you live in community there are no problems and difficulties').

In this sense, life is tranquil when the person is in harmony with his/her community, when the *aynis* and *minkas* (forms of mutual aid) are developed with the participation of everyone, when the whole community is present in celebrations and ritual ceremonies, when the human being remembers his/her deities. As we are reminded by Ms. Eustaquia Huanca from the Aymara village of Tutacani, in Juli, Puno:

> Before it is time for the celebration of the Trinity, I must worry about lighting the candles for the saint to care for my cattle, so that they won't get sick, so

that they can have their offspring each year. I ask the *Pachamama* to care for them; when I do that, I feel tranquil, knowing that my animals will be taken care of. (Atahuachi and Apaza, 2007, p. 3)

Brigida Layme, teacher from the village of Labraco in Cuzco, has found this expression that circumscribes tranquility to experience in the local *pacha*: *Wasillaykipin thakpa tiyawaq runaq wasimpi tiyayqa sasan* ('Only in your house or in your *ayllu* you can live in peace, it is problematic to live in somebody else's house or in other villages'). This is because in your house or *ayllu* you have learned to become attuned to any circumstance. The *thak* or *thauj* – in the Quechua of Ayaviri, Puno – is a circumstantial experience rather than something permanent; it is experienced intensely during certain moments of the agricultural celebration cycles of the community, be it in the rainy season or in the dry season. As Zenón Gomel and Wilber Ramos (2007, p. 2) point out, '[a]fter the storm, there is calm, or after the labor of plowing that is pretty agitated, a time of calm comes; in the Quechua of the Northern region of Puno we call this *thauj*.'

As Atahuachi and Apaza express, tranquility for the Aymara *jaque* (human being) is related to doing things well, in their due moment and place.

Almost all rural families are worried about the cattle, the farm, the deities, the children, or when an activity was not finished in due time; but when it is all done you feel tranquility because you have finished in time, when the animals or the farm are producing, you feel tranquil, unworried, because we'll have food. (Atahuachi and Apaza, 2007, p. 2)

In the Andean world, words can generate tranquility or conflict, between the word and the fact there is no intermediate representation. In oral cultures, there is identification between the word and the reality the word refers to.* In this sense, words give rise to harmony in the same way in which they can produce disharmony. As Campos, Mendoza, Alarcón and Ticona warn us:

Human harmony is preserved and nurtured by our words. When people have two words, that is, when they say 'I will come' and do not come, 'I will give' and do not give, 'I will do' and do not do, this generates disharmony. People who have two words are two-faced, like a coin [*iskay uya* in Quechua], because they have two or more talks and one or more of them are false and, thus, untrue. These are the persons who generate conflict, and it is said of them that you cannot talk to them; neither can you trust them, or give them any importance because they will only lead you to conflict. In the Andean world, words are used sparingly and with prudence, nothing can be added or

---

* Ed. On the topic of language and reality, see Chapter 19.

subtracted when you narrate events or impart knowledge, amongst others. You say things as they are (*kaqllata rimakuna*) without detracting from them. You also laugh only what you must, only what is needed, because if you laugh exaggeratedly and uncontrollably you are sure to cry. Everything is balanced and moderate. When these values are broken, unbalance is generated in the nurturing of human beings, farms, animals, plants and everything that forms a part of our Andean family. (Campos et al., 2007, pp. 5–7)

Just as tranquility is not only human, but also of deities and nature, it is said of the *ayllu* that to be in effect it implies respectful and constant conversation between all members of the *ayllu*. As Carrillo points out: 'The Andean world is a world with elevated conversation and attunement. When there is a lack of conversation, there is agitation, movement, punishment. Harmony is sought through rituals' (Carrillo, 2007, p. 1).

Disruption

However, tranquility is not a permanent state. Andean life is always subject to disruptions (*kuti* in Quechua), which disturb serenity and calmness and give rise to conflict and tension, be it because they represent problems between human beings, between human beings and nature, or between human beings and deities. It is common that problems arise in the homes between parents and children, between the parents themselves, or among relatives. This happens when the youngsters who go to school adopt the *jatsi simi* or *q'ayma simi*, speaking with harsh and tasteless expressions instead of the *miski simi* or the sweet talk of their grandparents. When these forms of expression invade dialogue, verbal fights arise that later become physical confrontations that could easily be overcome by passions and emotions. In this case, they would say among them '*sapa kutilla chiknikuwanqi*,' a Quechua phrase that may be translated as 'You despise me greatly, your affection has been greatly "disrupted" or "overturned".'

There are Quechua expressions to name disharmony. The Quechua word for conflict is *ch'aqway*. To fight with everything – hands, feet and even in groups – is *maqanakuy*. To disharmonize is *chharqusqa*. Exchanging insults and jibes is *kaminacuy*. These words suggest anger, enmity, annoyance, harm, irritation, injury, quarrel and disorganization. In the Quechua of Cuzco, a conflictive person is called *chiqmi*, and *chiqminacuy* means to live for a long time among quarrels and conflict. The person has felt that a word or action has hurt him or her deeply. In Aymara, *Juchaqipt'anjiwa* means that they have fought or are fighting; *nuwjapjiwa* means they have hit him or her. In the Ancashino Quechua, a fight is translated as *maqanakuy, tsaktanakuy*.

In the Andean–Amazonian tradition, the origin of a conflict is considered to be that the members of the *ayllu* 'have surpassed our measure,' that 'we took the wrong road' or that 'we were disrespectful.' The man has his measure, the woman has her measure, the children as well as the rivers, the *apus* and the winds. When a member of the human, natural or sacred collectivity surpasses 'his/her measure,' does not fulfill his/her duty or does not walk down the path he/she must take, conflict arises. When a deity in charge of bringing rain, for example, does not fulfill his obligation, the human community brings him out of the temple and flogs him. The same occurs with the toads that are in charge of calling the rain, if they do not do so, they are put in the sun and are made to 'cry' until the deities take pity on them and the rain comes. The same happens with the children who have to cry for the rain to come to the farms, etc.

Disharmony must not be prolonged; it must be dissolved for life to follow its course. Usually, the return to tranquility, to the good life, takes the form of rituals where all the members of the collectivity participate.* As Don Crecencio Poma from Juli, Puno, points out, 'when the hail, the frost and the diseases come, it is because we have been disrespectful of our *pacha*, and then immediately we become worried, because adversity may come; then with an *aytu* we must heal the earth again so that we can all be well' (Atahuachi and Apaza, 2007, p. 7).

Some of these rituals, which to foreign eyes might be seen as violent fights between factions, persons or families, and that in certain regions have disappeared under official orders, aim to dissolve the conflict. In the Andes, there are still instances of *tinku* (encounters), *alucheos* (fights between factions) and *waraqanacuy* (the exchange of 'insults' between persons, neighborhoods and communities from a region in certain celebrations).

Many of these demonstrations such as the *chiarajes*, which take place in the highlands of Canas in Cuzco at the time of the carnival, or the *tinku* that take place at the beginning of the harvest in the village of Acacio (Potosí, Bolivia), are considered by the official and educated worlds as acts of cruel savagery, for sometimes during these encounters one or more people die or end up injured because of the use of stones, fist blows or kicks from the participants. Current bullfights are also expressions of this same conflict-solving ritual in some communities. However, these deaths or injuries, which deeply sadden the families and the community, are also seen as offerings to the *Pachamama* and the deities that protect the communities, and they are said to predict a good harvest.[1]

However, we must not forget that the word *tinku* also means place of communion, joining, encounter and it does not always serve to solve disputes but also to share. These 'account renderings,' as we could call them, are named *Hakanacuy* in the Quechua of Ecuador and they have appropriate moments and places. They normally coincide with ceremonies of profound agricultural celebration content, like sowing, harvests, *aporques* and the drawing of boundaries, and they are performed in certain places before the whole communities, with

---

* Ed. Diverse rituals for restoring harmony in a communal manner are also discussed in Chapters 18 and 19. For a discussion of the differences between such rituals of healing processes and positivist retributive justice, see Chapter 17.

charismatic authorities watching over to prevent the emotions of the conflicting persons or parties from overflowing. These actions ritually and communally dissolve conflicts that arise during the year and facilitate the recovering of the lost harmony. The community waits for the propitious moment to do this, to reunite, to gather the harmony that the moment demands.[2]

In the community, respect is associated to the expression that 'everything must be done in its moment and place.' This happens in Lamas, San Martin, in the high Peruvian Amazon, where the resolution of conflicts takes the form of a ritual called *carahuasca* (ritual whipping) that is performed in ceremonial events and also at home. This ritual binds together several moments. It begins when the offenders and the offended narrate their experiences of the conflict. The participants listen patiently to the reasons of all parties. Then they proceed with performing the punishment and, later on, the corresponding council concludes the ceremony with an embrace among all, so that the life of each will 'go well.' The punishers must 'have a good hand' at this, because the person and the whip are one and the same. They are respected persons (*pampa shunqu kaway* in the Ancashino Quechua meaning 'a kind person, who lives with his heart,' or *llampu sunku* in the Quechua from Ayaviri, Puno), who confer their kind hearts to the fighters when they whip them.[3]

Thus, harmony returns to the punished person and his/her integration to the family and the community occurs with no resentment. At the end of the punishment, all ask for forgiveness, and tranquility returns to the heart. The Quechua-lamas consider that you must never give out punishment if your heart is restless or worried, because you transfer that condition to the person who is in conflict and he or she will not recover the desired harmony. This is why the moment, the place and the person must coincide in a situation of *thaq* or tranquility.

When major conflicts that alter and place at risk the life of the community itself arise, the first question a Quechua or an Amazonian asks him/herself is what caused the disharmony. Usually, the first answer is from the person or the community itself; it is not originated from the outside. The *comuneros* ask themselves when and under what circumstances I have exceeded or we have exceeded the measure or gone out of the way to produce such a disruption of tranquility. A hailstorm, for example, that affects a farm, is not caused, as anyone might suppose, by temperature changes and atmospheric pressure. The origin is not outside the subjects, but rather it is sought in a human action or actions that have caused such an unusual phenomenon.

Brígida Layme, a teacher from the community of Labraco in Cuzco, uses the following expression related to the presence of a hailstorm on a farm: *Qayna p'unchawmi Timoteo ch'aqwayun wawanwan papa muyuy chawpipi chaymi chichi papaman haykumuy* ('Don Timoteo and his son had a fight amidst a potato farm yesterday; this is why it hailed on the potatoes'). This means that if there is a discussion or fight between humans in a sown field, the hailstorm comes and does harm.

The origin of any disharmony is always endogenous, either to the person, the family or the *ayllu* (community integrated by humans, nature and deities); the idea is to know what the humans have or have not done to produce such a situation. The presence of an illness, the visit of a plague, an earthquake, a river overflowing, have as first reference an oversight in our nurturing of each other.

However, ills such as drought or hailstorms come 'announced,' there is a series of signs that life gives us and that we must know how to read. The signs warn us if we are in disharmony, in distress, and they point out what circumstances might occur in the near future. The songs of certain birds, certain dreams, the appearance of the moon or sun, certain droughts or unusual amounts of rain, let us know that the time has come for us to harmonize ourselves for the person-illness is approaching. Espillico et al. (2007, p. 3) say that when conflicts occur in the Aymara communities there are signs that appear as premonitions. Some of them are:

> To dream of a dogfight is a premonition of a possible fight in the community. Also when they dream of the 'gringos' arriving at the community, this announces possible violent deeds. A fight between large birds (condors) implies serious conflicts, when it is a fight between smaller birds (kestrel, eagle), it means there will be conflicts within or between families. In other occasions, you can see whirlwinds gathering dust in the roads; they are signs that there is disharmony in the surroundings, and it is necessary to heal and cast it away.

In the Andes and Amazon a plague, the same as a conflict, is experienced as if it were a person, and as such it does not just arrive suddenly, but rather it announces itself. This is how the violence that devastated the Andes during the 1980s was experienced. 'We did not know how to read the signs in our lives back then,' says Marcela Machaca (2003), whose village of Quispillacta in Ayachucho went through terrible violence. 'When the violence came to our community, we deserved it.'[4]

This is a very harsh sentence, because to the eyes of the world this community took care of its agrarian and cattle raising activities in a tranquil and serene manner and it shows us the Andean outlook. 'Something was wrong in us so we did not know how to see what was coming and we did nothing to prevent it... then, we deserve it because we were careless' (Machaca, 2003). This would be more or less the sentence that summarizes their reflection after going through the plague of violence in Marcela's community.

This outlook on life offers us indubitable lessons. One of them is that these types of expressions do not give rise to the notion of an 'enemy' and thus there is also no concept of a victim. (If what happens happens, it is because we deserve it. We caused the hailstorm because we argued on the farm.) In the absence of this concept, we do not give the plague a role of victimizer, the invader the statute of a colonizer, that is 'I do not feel like a victim; I do not feel colonized or invaded.' The other may decide to present himself as a colonizer, a victimizer or a warrior, but I do not grant him that role. This way of being renders null the relationship the invader is attempting to establish, even if the plague occurs with unusual violence. This attitude dissolves the duality of the colonizer/colonized, victimizer/victim, conqueror/conquered, war/peace.

Another lesson is that such an attitude prevents the appearance of dichotomies, of contradictions, and thus it also prevents the practice of the law of retaliation or *Lex talionis* ('an eye for an eye, a tooth for a tooth') and so deters revenge as a way to reestablish lost harmony. It is not about denying conflict, but rather it is about finding ways to solve it so that life may return to its serene course, to tranquility.[5] In rituals, whatever form they take, the Andean peoples find a way to overcome conflicts. Through the ritual, they solve and get over conflicts and with that *qawqalla*, *thaq* return to the hearts of each of the members of the *ayllu*.

To return to *thaq* is returning to an experience of calm and serenity, as it is expressed in this Quechua phrase: *qhariyki maqarqasunki kunan ripuqtin thakchu kashanki* ('now that your husband who beat you is gone, tranquility has returned to you'). After conflicts, when harmony has returned to their hearts, people are heard to say: *chayraqmi thaq karuni*, which can be translated into something like 'I am finally tranquil.' Likewise, they usually say *khunanqa chayraqmi thaq karuni* ('now at last I am tranquil'). This means that tranquility is also a state of living that must be nurtured. *Thaq* is not a gift, but rather it is the result of a nurturing relationship between human beings, and between them and nature. The *thaq* is nurtured and it nurtures us.

Reconciliation: empathy between humans, nature and deities

After the decade of violence of the 1980s that ravaged the Andes, the first thing that the relatives of the official victims requested from the Truth and Reconciliation Commission set up by the Peruvian transition government at the end of 2000 was that they be allowed to bury their relatives. The relatives of the approximately 70,000 disappeared persons wanted their return and, if they were known to be dead, their exhumation, so that they may be given a proper Christian burial. This was particularly the request of the Andean peoples, for it is calculated that 80 percent of the disappeared population were Quechua peasants.[6] Economic and moral accountability was a question of what came afterwards. Very few people asked for the death penalty for terrorists and soldiers.

In the first place, what they wanted was reconciliation. It seems that this reconciliation took place in many Andean communities with much weeping and crying, for many *comuneros* – particularly young people – were forced to participate in this genocidal wave by one or the other factions in conflict. After the conflict was over, many of them returned to their communities to regenerate the life and harmony in their *pacha*, and they did it in due time, because as Carrillo (2004, p. 15) points out:

> Before seeking 'reconciliation', the Andean *comuneros* seek the permanent recreation of balance in their *pachas*. There is no resentment in their hearts, everything is faced and 'fixed in due time'. If they have to fight against the deities for the love of a maiden, they do it, they do not wait or they might be killed. The *abio* comes when the plague 'pesters', not afterwards, or the community too may disappear.

There are common expressions in the villages that state their desire always to live in tranquility. They say 'to just have a nice life,' which is expressed in the Quechua phrases *sumaqlla tiyakusunkiq* ('we just have to live nicely'), *allinllata causakusunchiq* ('we must live well'), *Ama pilyaspa causakusunchiq* ('we must not fight') and *Allinllata tiyakusuk kay pacha mamapi* ('we must just live nicely here with the sacred earth'), which reveal an emotion of love for life, a desire again to have a clean heart (*Chuya sonqo*).

For an Andean community, the prolonged absence of rain may have its origin not in meteorological phenomena, but rather in the wrongdoing of some of its members. It is not rare to hear that the rains have returned after the person who caused disharmony has been expelled from the community. At this moment, the *qawqalla*, the serenity and tranquility return to the community. Thus, *qawqalla* must be preserved, cared for and nurtured like a fire in the hearth so that it may remain in the community. This implies opening and deepening the ability to listen and perceive the signs of nature and the deities; it entails acting in accordance with the moment.

Yet it could also be that after the corresponding rituals to solve the conflict endogenously have been performed, the conflictive situation continues. When this happens, there is also a ritual procedure; if the plague has installed itself in the community, a 'dispatch' is performed for it to leave. This happened, for example, in the community of Sarhua in Ayacucho, when the plague of cholera arrived. For them, the death of *comuneros* was experienced as a person-disease who was eating human beings. When they considered its hunger had been satiated, ceremonies were performed to send it along its way in a good manner, so that it might continue its journey.

This also occurs when there are plagues of locusts, foxes and mice; that is, when the presence of some of the members is so excessive that it hurts the tranquility and harmony in the community. When they eat beyond 'their measure,' they prevent others from eating, thus harming the tranquility of the *pacha* or Andean local microcosm. It may also occur with some human beings who, for example, continue stealing in the community or have reiterative conducts that cause the anger of the deities such as abortion or incest, that this implies their expulsion from the community and, eventually, their death. This occurred in central Peru, at a certain time, in the relationship between communities and the rebel columns.

Human beings have the desire, more so when we go to school and start being educated on freedoms, to become individuals; in consequence, this breeds separation, isolation, and we become deaf to the sounds of nature, to the links that unite us to our communities, and to our links with the deities.* We become blind and deaf to the signals and we annul our relationship with mother earth. It then happens that we embark ourselves in manufacturing contrivances that no longer have any correspondence to time and place. As the Aymara say, we begin 'to do anything out of time and place.' We begin playing the music for sowing in harvest time, and dancing to rhythms that do not correspond to the time and place. We begin to do what has now become spread among many communities: to disrespect. Disrespect is the new illness that has been installed in the Andean world that is asking from all of us to 'go back to respect,' so that we may recover tranquility.

Beyond what might have happened to one or the other community, the prolonged and profound violence in the Peruvian history of the twentieth century that we have lived through, violence has questioned the survival of Peru itself, its destiny as a people. Violence showed how wrong, how sick the country was. In spite of that, after the wave of violence, we as citizens have not yet reconciled with our own selves. This is why the signals, the warnings, continue to show that at any moment any kind of plague or sickness will arise among us. The discussion of the death penalty in our country is one of them. We must be prepared for this, as the *comuneros* say: 'We must return to respect,' to tranquility, let the *thaq* return to our hearts and let the *allin kawsay* set in so that we may once and again live in the harmony of the *ayllu*.

Notes

1. As Don Antonio Pineda Peláez from the village of Corani in Ayaviri, Puno, points out: 'When we wear the clothes of those who perform the *waraqanaquy*, an *anima* (energy) enters us that changes our personality, we are another, we are not ourselves; it seems that *anima* is from all the *apus* of our community, all our farms. When we are exchanging blows, we do not feel pain, we do this so that later on we may have hands to work our farms. I have gone through *waraqanaquy*, after that I have become more of a farmer. It seems the farms love you more when you go through the *waraqanaquy*. Many get hit in the head, in the jaw and joints (knees, elbows); it hurts later, but then you like the farm more' (Pineda in Gomel and Ramos, 2007, p. 4).

* Ed. In Chapter 7, Munir Fasheh also develops the idea of the institutionalization of education and the professionalization of expert knowledge as deriving in a blindness and deafness to community relations, indeed turning into an obstacle to peace. For more on this discussion of differences between learning and education, see Chapter 17.

2. Here there is a link with the concept of peace. As we know, the term peace comes from the latin *pax* (genitive *pacis*) and it is related to the verb *pacisci*, which means 'to agree' or 'make a deal' (the word 'pact' stems from its participle *pactum*). The word comes from the Indo-European *pag*, meaning 'to fix, unite' (*Etimología de la Lengua Española*, 2006).

3. About this ritual of punishment with the whip, let us hear the version of Don Antonio Pineda Peláez from the community of Chimboya, Ayaviri, Puno: 'Respect is the *yupaychanaquy*, it can be present anywhere, for example my father has taught me that respect is also in the *werlincha* (flogging cord), he would punish us with it, but with much serenity. He would call me nicely and when he was very calm, he said: "let's have a chat with the *werlincha*", he would lock me up in a room and there, praying, he knew how to hit me. He would say: "It is not I who punished you, the *werlincha* has punished you, I just appealed to it, and I thanked the whip with faith and let go of myself and only because of it, I was in *thauj* (in peace)". Later, he would embrace me caringly telling me about all the things they had taught me to respect. This is how we knew we had to respect the *werlincha*. My father said: "This whip is the lord, our father", and he would talk to it, and make us kiss it three times when we misbehaved, he wouldn't punish us every time. This *werlincha* was like a person, when we did our *qhoyasqas, jaywarisqas, churaqusqas*, he would place it beside his *istallas* (ritual robes) and cover it in some *untu* to give it a smell of passivity. When we kissed it and saw it hanging in a sacred place, we felt *yupaychay* (respect) and we all remembered that everything that exists must be respected, and so we would walk correctly, this is how it was' (Pineda in Gomel and Ramos, 2007, p. 5).

4. Eduardo Grillo, in reference to the word 'plague,' said: 'Just like in our immanent world all that occurs flows from the inside, we feel this plague has appeared here amongst us. We feel that the plague has occurred because we have become careless in the everyday nurturing of the harmony that is convenient for us and even because some weaker symptoms that our animal world had been showing us in the growing alteration of their harmony have passed unheeded. Because we have been blind and deaf to these symptoms, the alteration has been growing until it became this great plague. This is why for us it is clear that we truly deserve it. This is how we feel this here in the Andes, in conformity with our way of being' (Grillo, 1996, p. 75).

5. In the Peruvian Amazon, the name Fitzcarraldo evokes the exploitation of rubber (*Hebea brasilensis*), the destruction of the forest and genocide. Precisely the opening quote to this chapter by Ino Moxo, an Amazonian healer, in reference to this period of ethnocide renders void the contradiction established by the colonizers, placing the dealing of the conflict in its cultural dimension.

6. The Truth and Reconciliation Commission (TRC) has concluded that the most likely number of fatal victims in these two decades (between 1980 and 2000) is over 69,280 Peruvian men and women, dead or disappeared in the hands of either subversive organizations or government agents. Three of every four victims were peasant men or women whose native language was Quechua. Ayacucho was the region that concentrated the greatest number of dead and disappeared as reported to the TRC (over 40 percent). Together with Ayacucho, in the regions of Junin, Huanuco, Huancavelica, Apurimac and San Martín the TRC has registered nearly 85 percent of the victims reported in the testimonies (CVR, 2004, pp. 9–10).

Reference list

Atahuachi, R. and E. Apaza (2007) 'Sunma jakawia: Saranaqawisa.' Presented at Minga on Intercultural Education and Sustainable Research, Juli, May 2007.

Calvo, C. (1981) *Las tres mitades de Ino Moxo y otros brujos de la Amazonía* (Iquitos: Proceso Editores).

Campos, N., A. Mendoza, M. Alarcón and R. Ticona (2007) 'El secreto para recuperar el *Qawqa Kawsay* o el vivir tranquilo' (Andahuaylas: Centro de Estudios Andinos Vida Dulce).

Carrillo, P. (2004) 'Digiriendo "onqoy tiempos": Con todos se convive hasta que haga daño' (Ayacucho: APU).

Carrillo, P. (2007) 'Paz.' Presented at Minga on Intercultural Education and Sustainable Research, Ayacucho, April 2007.

CVR (Comisión de la Verdad y Reconciliación) (2004) *Hatun Willakuy: Versión abreviada del Informe Final de la Comisión de la Verdad y Reconciliación* (Lima: Comisión de Entrega de la CVR).

Espillico, V. et al. (2007) 'Violencia en el mundo andino.' Presented at Minga on Intercultural Education and Sustainable Research, Juli, May 2007.

Etimología de la Lengua Española (2006) 'El origen de nuestras palabras: "Paz",' http://etimologia.wordpress.com/2006/11/20/paz/trackback/, date accessed April 24, 2007.

Gomel, Z. and W. Ramos (2007) '¿Paz? o yupaychanaquy y allin kawsay.' Presented at Minga on Intercultural Education and Sustainable Research, Ayaviri, March 2007.

Grillo, E. (1996) ¿Desarrollo o Afirmación Cultural en los Andes? in E. Grillo (ed.) *Caminos Andinos de Siempre* (Lima: PRATEC).

Machaca, M. (2003) *Contribution at América Profunda*, Mexico D.F., December 2003.

Zevallos, B. (2007) 'La paz en las comunidades de Lircay, Huancavelica.' Presented at Minga on Intercultural Education and Sustainable Research, Lircay, March 2007.

21
Nengelaasekhammalhkoo: An Enlhet Perspective*

Hannes Kalisch
Nengvaanemkeskama Nempayvaam Enlhet

¡Lheep nak! It's you.
Eehe, ko'o. Yes, it's me.
Enlhet greeting

This chapter will discuss a conceptual construction generated by the Enlhet people.[1] Although we identify this conceptual construction as corresponding to the European–Western concept of 'peace,' such an identification implies a certain danger for our discussion: it lends itself to the simple projection of a Western conceptualization onto a different universe of symbols.† For this reason we initially question the orientation towards a comparative procedure, proposing that during all approximations to alternative dimensions the description from within must be of primary importance. Once this point has been made clear, the main part of the chapter is dedicated to a description of the Enlhet's conceptual construction and to pointing out its transformation during recent decades. First, however, we begin with a brief description of the Enlhet.

* The present chapter is based on the accounts of Enlhet elders and its writing was aided by constant discussion with Ernesto Unruh. Manolo Romero made suggestions relating to the Toba-Enenlhet world. I thank them for their support in carrying the responsibility that the development of a new approach always implies. I am also indebted to Enrique Amarilla und Dorothee E. Kalisch for their comments on earlier versions of the text. However, I remain solely responsible for any deficiencies or incoherencies. The original text was written in Spanish; I thank several translators for the English version and Nicholas Regan for the final revision.
† Ed. Several chapters in this book deal with the difficulties of 'translating' words and concepts in local cultures to the English 'peace.' For diverse etymological investigations that discuss this issue and different terms that could connote 'peace' in vernacular languages in local cultures, see Chapters 6, 7, 10, 17, 18, 19 and 20.

Contextualization

The Enlhet lived, and still live, at the center of the Paraguayan Chaco, at the center of the South American continent. With approximately 7000 members (DGEEC, 2003), the Enlhet form the largest people within the Enlhet-Enenlhet nation, which also includes the Enxet, the Angaité, the Sanapaná, the Guaná and the Toba-Enenlhet (Unruh and Kalisch, 2003b).[2] Traditionally, the Enlhet lived from hunting and, where possible, fishing, from fruit collected in the forest and from horticulture, which was particularly important for the organization of their protracted celebrations. Enlhet society was composed of small relatively mobile units living within a certain area, which formed their respective 'home space.' The social and political life in this society was not stratified beyond the generational-family structures and was characterized by a fluid relationship with neighboring groups that was formalized through the cycle of celebrations. Simultaneously, the celebrations were an important frame for the intense interethnic relationships which are characteristic of almost all of the Chaco peoples[3] and which have facilitated a symbolic–cultural construction widely shared between the Enlhet and the neighboring peoples. Therefore, although our consideration will mostly refer to the Enlhet and occasionally to the Toba-Enenlhet, it is *mutatis mutandis* valid for those neighboring peoples as well.

White settlement of the Paraguayan Chaco began only during the last decades of the nineteenth century and came from its eastern side, the Paraguay River. Initially settlement affected the eastern peoples of the Enlhet-Enenlhet nation in particular. The Enlhet (particularly their northern groups), who lived in the interior of the Chaco, had no significant contact with white people until the end of the 1920s, just before the so-called 'Chaco War' (1932–1935) between Bolivia and Paraguay, which established the final subordination of Enlhet territory to a nation-state. The preparations for war, and the war itself, with all its physical violence against the Enlhet, coincided with the arrival of Mennonite immigrants from Canada and Russia who from 1927 settled in very large numbers in the midst of Enlhet territory.[4] In conjunction with the physical and economic impact that both events had on Enlhet society, the migrants developed a marked religious and cultural proselytism (Klassen, 1991). This proselytism legitimized and organized the exclusion of the indigenous universe from the construction of the new geographic, economic and ideological spaces, which were gaining more and more importance. After approximately thirty years, the constant increase of territorial, economic and ideological pressure on the Enlhet had led to almost all Enlhet people being baptized (Regehr, 1979, p. 274). Because of the way in which these sudden mass baptisms took place, they may be interpreted as the surrender of the Enlhet in the face of a new world and of a new logic that disabled the continuing development of their own way of being (Unruh and Kalisch, 2008). This surrender has determined not only the current way of life and social interaction of the Enlhet people. It has simultaneously had a strong influence on their understanding of their own being and future and, thus, on their processes of reflection which, at first sight, appears to have a bias against everything that comes from their own tradition.

However, the situation is ambiguous. At the level of official discourse as well as at the institutional and formal level in general we observe an unconditional surrender to that which comes from white people. And yet, in their everyday and family life the Enlhet ignore virtually all external propositions. This articulation between, on the one hand, their own daily practice, and on the other, *reflexive parameters* fundamentally oriented towards another system of ideologies and ways to live, produces highly specific interferences: namely, that the Enlhet's reflexive access to their own conceptual categories, which continue to construct and define their daily lives and to determine the foundation of their values, is increasingly overwritten by categories deriving from a foreign logic. While the possibilities for continued development of their own categories have become fewer, these foreign categories, grounded in another tradition, do not fit the practices of their daily life, and are consequently of little use in their functioning. Rather, they tend to disarticulate them (Kalisch, 2000, 2005, 2006).

This situation has an effect on the Enlhet concept of peace. Within the dominant local context, peace is thought to reign when those who are excluded assume their own exclusion.[5] Concomitantly, to question the exclusion is considered destructive and disruptive. Projecting this logic onto their conceptualization, the Enlhet's own *conception* of peace has been inverted and perverted. They are losing a *vision* of peace and, thus, the concrete *possibility* of constructing it. But before arguing this statement in more detail, we must clarify some methodological points related to the description of the Enlhet construction which would correspond to the European–Western concept of 'peace.'

Approaching the subject

The search for an Enlhet equivalence to the concept of 'peace' of European–Western origin is no trivial matter in itself. In the first place, the linguistic perspective is of no help: Enlhet offers no linguistic variable that would intuitively correspond to the English word 'peace.'[6] Clearly, the meaning of words derives from their conventionalized usage in order to talk about – that is, refer to – *concepts*, which in turn can be understood as mental constructions that connect the concrete–experiential sphere to the symbolic sphere.[7] So, in fact, we are not searching for corresponding linguistic variables. At best, we are searching for a correspondence of the concepts that are expressed by them.

This continues to be a difficult task. For even when we perceive a correspondence between concepts that belong to different cultural constructions, it is never more than a partial correspondence (we are talking, after all, of markedly distinct contexts). The respective spheres of the concrete–experiential never correspond directly, and neither do those of symbols; less still, the specific interrelation between the spheres of the concrete–experiential and the symbolic.[8] The *common* perception of the European–Western concept of 'peace,' for example, is maintained by philosophical, legal or political terms, which are extremely abstract insofar as they have little impact on personal conduct. Concomitantly, there is no clear common understanding of the concrete attitudes necessary to obtain this particular 'peace.' In Enlhet life, however, philosophical, political and experiential spheres form an integrated totality, which is reflected in daily life. Therefore, if we hastily identify equivalences between the two universes, we run the risk of comparing concepts deriving from life contexts that do not correspond.

Given these considerations, and so as not to become mired in methodological complications, this chapter does not address the comparative issue. This implies, specifically, that the present chapter does not refer to the European–Western school of thought and its concept of 'peace' in order to describe those Enlhet concepts which concern harmonious social interaction and, therefore, an idea of 'peace' (Dietrich, this volume). Instead, we will try to approach the Enlhet's conceptual configuration from the context of their own classifications. Such a description 'from within' the Enlhet's construction implies that the assumption of possible relationships between experiences, actions, attitudes and symbols has to arise from the Enlhet conceptualization itself. It upholds the need to first achieve an understanding of the Enlhet conceptualization that is as independent as possible from external conceptual constellations, before being able to compare it with different conceptual constructions.[9] Such a comparison is beyond the scope of the present chapter and would require its own methodological considerations.

Therefore, the next section begins with the description of an Enlhet *social practice*, which builds a harmonic community and serves, at the same time, to minimize conflicts. This social practice, which the Enlhet refer to as *nengelaasek-hammalhkoo*,[10] is located among a set of other expressions of the spheres of the symbolic and the concrete–experiential, which it simultaneously interacts with and is integrally combined with. This set of practices will be discussed below. We call the totality of these expressions the 'conceptual complex' to which we will refer with the term 'Enlhet peace.' This terminology serves to indicate a possible correspondence between the Enlhet's conceptual complex and the European–Occidental concept of 'peace.'[11] However, it should not be read as a simple equation of the two.

A description 'from the inside' refers to a methodological procedure that attempts to reduce the distortions produced by any descriptive act. In no way does it claim that a pure Enlhet conceptualization exists. In fact, the Enlhet's original universe of concepts has been significantly reconfigured due to contact with the world of the *sengelpaalha'vay'*, 'those who have appeared among us.' Through a process affected by the discrepancy between life practice and reflective penetration mentioned above, different readings of the *nengelaasek-hammalhkoo* have emerged which are related to different experiences of life and which are linked, in part, to different generations. As a consequence, today the linguistic variable *nengelaasekhammalhkoo* simultaneously refers to different concepts. Such a coexistence of readings, such an ambiguity, is repeated in the case of other words, and accentuates the usual impossibility of understanding the present solely through contemporary reflection. That is to say, in order to understand how the different readings are interrelated it is indispensable to address the original understanding of those Enlhet concepts that continue to motivate current life. However, the reconstruction of those concepts implies a methodological difficulty: current references to such concepts are overlaid by several decades of a life with strong external interference, while at the same time there are no written historical documents. However, accounts of past situations constitute a useful source to gain access to traditional conceptualizations: they point to social practices now disappeared and allow us to grasp something of their original meaning.

In response to the situation of ongoing change, this chapter now begins a reconstruction of the original understanding of 'Enlhet peace.' This reconstruction also answers the need for a construction of proven practical use to serve as an alternative to (since uninfluenced by) the European–Western concept of 'peace.'[12] Recent transfigurations of the conceptual complex of the 'Enlhet peace,' which clearly have been influenced by Western concepts, are discussed in the second part of this chapter.

Nengelaasekhammalhkoo: The original reading

A constant element of Enlhet accounts is the description of the openness that people showed one another with the explicit intention of excluding nobody. Again and again, old Enlhet men and women tell of how they would call together everybody from the village after having cooked game or prepared the fruits of the forest. Nothing was too small to share with others (Ortiz, 2005), and in a spirit of 'Do they have enough to eat?' they would take food to their neighbor, since everyone cared for each other. The elderly, in particular, maintain this practice even today, making clear that what they describe in their accounts is more than the creation of a myth from the past (which they are accused of locally): they speak of a way to build community.[13] In the same vein, the Enlhet elders tell over and over again how actions were never performed alone. The Enlhet informed each other of their plans. They invited one another to accompany them on their errands. They discussed what should be done. Nobody departed without saying their goodbyes to the others. In summary, they remained in a constant dialogue (Savhongvay', forthcoming).

The essence of these actions is ***sharing****.* Sharing characterized the Enlhet's social interaction: People shared food, shared time, shared their whole lives so that everybody would feel equally well fed and satisfied, equally included and equally participative in the commonly constructed happiness. The Enlhet refer to the manifestation of this sharing with the term *nengelaasekhammalhkoo*. In linguistic terms, *nengelaasekhammalhkoo* is the reciprocal form of the verb *nengaasekhay'oo engmook*,[14] and means 'making each other *nengaasekhay'oo*' – 'to mutually respect each other.'[15] According to the attitudes and actions described above, it refers to the objective of relating well to one another. The concepts that it comprises will be elaborated throughout this chapter. They are reciprocity in the initiative of the construction of shared life and responsibility for it, equilibrium as an objective in the shared life and harmony as a result of that equilibrium. They are combined with the attitudes of openness towards the other, determination to maintain personal freedom, respect for the other and discipline in the relationship.

As is highlighted by the reciprocal linguistic form itself, *nengelaasekhammalhkoo* refers to a practice based on ***reciprocity***. Reciprocity in this case does not primarily concern being treated equally in respect of material things. It refers to equality in terms of the initiative and responsibility of every Enlhet in and for the construction of community through sharing (this understanding does not exclude the material dimension, but rather relativizes it). It is the willingness to make one's own contribution, instead of living at the other's expense. Further, it implies including the other; it means approaching shared life from the point of view of the other. In this way, reciprocity lived through *nengelaasekhammalhkoo* guarantees ***equilibrium***, *akmoo mook*, 'one like the other.'[16] The construction of equilibrium is the central objective of *nengelaasekhammalhkoo*. The achievement of this objective in turn is reflected in the term *akpayhaeklha' engva'lhok*, which denotes the result of participating in a situation of such socially constructed equilibrium: It refers to the 'harmony felt by somebody' or the 'happiness of somebody.'[17] Thus, there is a terminological differentiation between the practice of reciprocity, which is attained by sharing its objective, the construction of equilibrium, and its result, effective participation in a situation of ***harmony***. Simultaneously, it is important to note that from the perspective of the conceptualization of the Enlhet, the term for equilibrium and equilibrium, *akmoo mook*, 'one like the other,' denotes a *situation* conceived through a relational concept. The term for 'harmony,' *akpayhaeklha' engva'lhok*, in turn, implies a *perception* and is, therefore, conceived from the viewpoint of a single actor. In the following, the terms 'equilibrium' and 'harmony' will be used in this manner.

The concept of reciprocity is not sufficient to describe the practice of *nengelaasekhammalhkoo*. To include the other, to approach relationality from

*   Ed. Because the words in Enlhet are written in italics, those expressions that the author wishes to emphasize appear both in italics and bold for the reader to identify them more easily.

his[18] point of view, implies a willingness to be open with the other. With reference to equilibrium, this **openness** to the other does not mean the denial of self, but rather building the self jointly with all others. Thus, a predisposition to openness is inseparable from a determined self-definition: *nengelaasekhammalhkoo* is linked to a clear **determination** to maintain personal freedom (that is, the freedom to be oneself, not the freedom to do whatever one wants).[19] This determination is the attitude, which causes one person to react when the other takes advantage of his openness. It is complemented by another attitude, which prevents one from taking advantage of the other's openness: **respect** for the other. Respect for the other implies taking the other seriously and giving him space. As far as possible, respectful behavior intends that the other does not have to defend himself, seeking an equilibrium that is mainly preserved through a reciprocal and shared construction rather than restauration after a transgression.[20] Thus respect is a constituent aspect of *nengelaasekhammalhkoo*; in fact, there is no word for 'respecting the other' apart from *nengaasekay'oo engmook*. It is only in its negation that 'respect for the other' is linguistically separated from *nengaasekay'oo engmook* through the term *nentavaskama engmook*, 'treating the other without due respect' and, thus, 'acting against her or his integrity.'[21]

This observation can be generalized: the transgression of *nengaasekay'oo engmook* is terminologically differentiated, whereas its positive counterpart is not.[22] Several terms negatively highlight the intrinsic aspects of *nengelaasekhammalhkoo* discussed so far, namely, sharing, inclusion of the other, openness towards the other and respect for the other. In addition to *nentavaskama engmook*, mentioned above, these negative terms are most importantly *nengmasma x*, 'not sharing x'; *mongelaaney'oo engmook*, 'not looking at the other, not looking after the other;' *nengyetnakhaameeykam' engmook*, 'avoiding the other;' *nenga'ankeem engmook*, 'rejecting the other;' *nengyeekahay' engmook*, 'ignoring the other;' and *nentamhaeklha neeten*, 'to make oneself more important than the other.' As they destroy the equilibrium in a relationship – that is, as they destroy the *nengelaasekhammalhkoo* – these attitudes are perceived as clearly negative.

There is one further term that, via a negative definition, describes an attitude inherent in the concept of *nengelaasekhammalhkoo*: **discipline** in the relationship. This is *nengloom*, which refers to an uncontrolled or angry behavior.[23] That is, it refers to a form of confronting the other which is inappropriate, through which one seeks to impose oneself and which therefore destroys *nengelaasekhammalhkoo*.[24] *Savhongvay'* (personal communication) concurrently specifies that the absence of *nengloom* – that is the presence of discipline – enables a generalized state of *nengelaasekhammalhkoo*, since it enables a state in which all remain in mutual communication with one another. Consequently, if a person does not obviously act against the *nengelaasekhammalhkoo*, if he does not violate it, then he will not be labeled as *nengloom*.[25]

In summary, *nengelaasekhammalhkoo* refers to a complex of attitudes that broadly encompasses sharing, reciprocity, openness towards the other made manifest in strategies for including him, respect for the other – taking him seriously and giving him space – and a determination to preserve equilibrium. These attitudes and their symbolic complements form a conceptual complex – elsewhere called the 'ideology of relationship' (Kalisch, 2005) – which revolves around a conception of equilibrium.[26] Therefore, this conceptual complex relates to a concept of harmony or of 'peace.' Importantly, however, it does not refer to an *idea* of 'peace,' but rather to a *practice* of 'peace.' It does not *define* 'peace,' but it serves to *produce* 'peace.'[27]

Nengelaasekhammalhkoo forms part of the Enlhet universe. It is an intrinsic, unquestionable part of the Enlhet being. Nonetheless, this condition does not relieve the Enlhet from ethical decision making, that is, from individual personal responsibility, as is illustrated by the very fact that discipline is required to develop appropriate related attitudes. Congruently, *nengelaasekhammalhkoo* is also legitimated by, and overseen from, a spiritual perspective that argues from outside the human sphere. However, before we approach *nengelaasekhammalhkoo* from the spiritual point of view, it is necessary to examine contexts in which the concepts related to *nengelaasekhammalhkoo* are manifested – concepts that allow the individual to live, and to continually restore, equilibrium.

Nengelaasekhammalhkoo: Its manifestation

As a social practice, *nengelaasekhammalhkoo* is in use in every context where people live together. It is the everyday task of each Enlhet to carry it out in the forms summarized above: sharing, dialogue and joint action. During lengthy celebrations[28] these attitudes were formalized so that the celebrations became a ritual expression of *nengelaasekhammalhkoo* in which being together and harmony were brought together. Toba-Enenlhet provides a term that vividly portrays this conception of harmony as the result of a socially constructed equilibrium underlined by these celebrations. It is the term for 'celebration' itself, *taqmelaikama·lhma'*. *Taqmelaikama* is the extensive[29] form of *taqmalma*, 'healthy, good,' meaning 'good in different intensities or in different ways at different moments and/or places.' *Alhma'* in turn means 'space.' The expression *taqmelaikama·lhma'*, then, means something like: 'movably good space.'[30] The connection of *taqmelaikama·lhma'* with *nengelaasekhammalhkoo* illustrates that 'Enlhet peace' is a 'peace' within movement. The life practices of the Enlhet demonstrate that it is in fact a 'peace' of laughter. It is a 'peace' with many voices.[31]

Thus, 'Enlhet peace' is clearly distinct from other concepts of harmony currently dominant in the Enlhet world and orientated towards conceptualizations of the white man. It opposes the concept of harmony contained in the term *alveenama·lhma'*, 'silent space,' and promoted by the discourse of the local

Christian church as synonymous with 'peace.' 'Enlhet peace' corresponds still less to that alleged peace, *nengvanmaykeklha'*, 'to become silent,' which is proposed by the surrounding society but which is an imposed silence. As with so many of the spaces left to the Enlhet nowadays, celebrations take place within these new dominant categories. Given these different conceptions, it is unsurprising that Enlhet celebrations were once completely different from today's celebrations, which are, depending on the context, either boring or violent. The core of those celebrations was the people; the celebrations built life. The person who builds life, who brings 'peace' – the 'prince of peace' in the new world symbolism introduced by the immigrants' proselytism – can, in the Enlhet's understanding, never be the *kelvehensaeklha·lhma'*, 'he who silences space,' or the *sengvanmeessaeklha'*, 'he who makes us be silent.' They await the *sengaasekhay'oo*,[32] 'he who actively and concretely demonstrates respect for us and gives us participation.'

We have shown how the *nengelaasekhammalhkoo* is conceived out of respect towards, and inclusion of, the other. However, individuals do not always nurture respect towards another person or group – thence the term *nentavaskama engmook* – thereby inducing that person or group to react: a conflict arises. Without discussing in detail the strategies for conflict resolution in a social system built and molded by *nengelaasekhammalhkoo*,[33] the following sets out responses to conflict which clarify the relationship between determination to preserve equilibrium and respect towards the other as intrinsic parts of *nengelaasekhammalhkoo*.

The great potential for mobility inherent in traditional Enlhet life facilitated the recombination of the groups before serious conflicts arose. Simultaneously, there were means by which to admonish the other (*nengeltemnaaskeklhoo engmook*). In the case of a serious transgression, the person responsible for the deterioration of the relationship was punished (*nengyekpelkaskeskamoo engmook*),[34] and the death penalty could even be applied (Metyeeyam', forthcoming c; Grubb, 1911). And yet, whenever possible the Enlhet would try to reintegrate whoever had caused the disturbance.[35] Haatkok'ay' Sevhen (forthcoming), for example, tells of a woman who was disrespectful towards other women and assumed more importance than was due to her; she behaved *ayaasennaummalhka'*, 'as if she alone were sufficient for herself.' The other women punished her for disturbing the community. In her defense, her father, in turn, acted without self-restraint – that is, with *aploom* – towards some of the men of the group.[36] To calm him, they invited him to hunt. Afterwards, they gave him the largest share of the prey so that he might recover his *akpayhaeklha·pva'lhok*, his happiness, his personal equilibrium. With this *nengaasekhay'oo*, 'respect for him,' which re-included the wrongdoer, they simultaneously expressed the restoration of *nengelaasek-hammalhkoo*, of the relational equilibrium. Similarly, after a war, the Enlhet did not impose tributes on the defeated enemy in order to subjugate or punish them. Rather, after one side surrendered, gifts were exchanged, just as was done during celebrations (Metyeeyam', forthcoming c; Melietkesammap, 2007). This bidirectional action expressed the restoration of equilibrium in the relationship.[37]

It is not always possible to restore a relationship. This is evident in the war of the Enlhet with their northern neighbors, the Ayoreo. In the 1920s, before the large-scale arrival of white people, some Ayoreo groups were displacing the northern Enlhet groups, the *koonamaalhek*, from their territory because of the pressure they felt from Bolivia (Fischermann, 2003). The resulting conflict caused several battles and a prolonged state of war between the border groups of both peoples.[38] There are different Enlhet interpretations of the start of this war, but all agree that it began with an act of disrespect (*nentavaskama engmook*) on the part of one of the two sides, which ignited the 'unquenchable fire of war' (Haakok Aamay, 2005). Haakok Aamay explains how the determination to defend what is one's own must be dynamic in order to remain able to restore *nengelaasekham-malhkoo*. To link determination with respect for the other is vital to maintaining the balanced relationship of *nengelaasekhammalhkoo*. To renounce the will (or the possibility) to reestablish respect for one another leads to entrenched conflicts which make the recovery of *nengelaasekhammalhkoo* impossible. Respect for the other without the determination to preserve one's freedom, in turn, leads to submission.

Another interethnic relationship, that with the *sengelpaalha'vay'*, 'those who have appeared among us,' illustrates how this determination to preserve personal freedom was renounced. The sudden invasion by Mennonite immigrants and the Paraguayan army at the end of the 1920s occurred without physical resistance from the Enlhet. Indeed, such resistance would have made no sense considering the scale of the intrusion. On the contrary, when the Enlhet were seriously threatened by one part of the invading force, the Paraguayan army, they sought refuge among the other part, the Mennonite immigrants (Unruh and Kalisch, 2008). They subsequently developed an attitude of thankfulness towards the immigrants. This attitude made it difficult for the Enlhet to determinedly state their case in the face of the dispossession they suffered and made it easy, in turn, for the immigrants to overlook Enlhet attempts to make themselves heard (Kalisch, 2003). The Enlhet were left with no means by which to build a balanced and reciprocal relationship with the immigrants. In contrast, the newcomers advanced their settlement into Enlhet territory in a completely unilateral fashion. The Enlhet, with no possibility whatsoever to determinedly assert their freedom[39] within the relationship, could only assume dependency: they surrendered.

Today, the Enlhet face a situation of interethnic coexistence which, having not been built reciprocally, is unbalanced and unequal. Inevitably, this has had an effect on the conceptual complex of 'Enlhet peace.' However, before describing the transfiguration of this complex, we will explore its spiritual dimension.

'That which lies beyond the human'

The concept of *nengelaasekhammalhkoo* is exclusive to the social sphere, to the world of human beings. Nevertheless, as the concept of *taqmelaikama·lhma'* refers to a 'movably good *space*' and, thus, to a universal totality, it indicates that the Enlhet conception of equilibrium and harmony is not limited to the relationship between human people, that is, to the *social dimension*: it equally concerns the relationship between human beings and what may be described as 'that which lies beyond the human.' This relationship is what we call the *spiritual dimension*. The social dimension and the spiritual dimension are not discrete; they rather constitute complementary expressions of the Enlhet world. It is important to consider what this means, first in general and then in relation to the conceptual complex of 'Enlhet peace.'[40]

Many entities that in the Western world are things, plants or animals were, in the Enlhet world, beings with specific attitudes.[41] To fail to give due attention to the characteristics of each one could have negative, and even dangerous, consequences. Deer, for example, had *apaskok*, a master who watched over them, the *yammeeme* bird. To kill the deer, one had to be on good terms with this bird. Offending it, on the other hand – by not appreciating the meat of the prey, for example – would lead to it withholding further potential prey; the hunter would find no more deer, or his shots would miss their mark.

This fate was not seen as punishment applied due to the transgression of human or divine law. It was the inevitable consequence of not remaining aware of the conditions of living in a shared world, just as there are consequences of failing to pay attention to the laws of the physical world: if you touch fire, you get burned.[42] In keeping within this logic, the Enlhet knew no prohibitions, but rather maintained a living consciousness of appropriate behavior and actions: whatever was not appropriate was a *moosee'*, a 'dangerous' action. To commit a *moosee'*, to fail to pay attention to the conditions of the world and to disrespect – *nentavaskama* – the specific characteristics of the entities that exist in it, is called *mongya'askaalhma'*, 'not to know the space,' that is, not to know how to act appropriately.[43] It produces the *senselhnanangkama*, 'something that brings us into trouble and harms us,' which makes tangible the consequences of the destruction of equilibrium caused by each act of *nentavaskama*. Viewed from the opposite perspective, the situation of equilibrium is preserved by respecting the rhythm and characteristics of the world and the entities that inhabit it by attending to natural, social and spiritual dimensions in an integrated way. It is only possible to preserve equilibrium if there is respect for every entity – that is, an absence of *nentavaskama*, and so too, therefore, of its consequence, *senselhnanangkama*.

However, people did not live impotently, simply waiting for that which lies beyond the human to react. They acquired influence over certain beings, which they called *nengmovaan*, 'their power.' These beings enabled them to build a concrete relationship with that other world. The *metnaha-pketkook*, in particular, the elders of the community who held power, knew how to bear positively upon that world so that, for example, the *yammeeme* bird would offer prey generously. They could prevent the consequences of a potentially dangerous but inevitable action. They knew how to restore equilibrium when it had been violated. For example, they could restore friendship with the master of the deer or appease the anger of water incurred by contamination with blood. They knew how to cure many diseases (both physical and non-physical in Western terms).[44] Again, what makes harmony possible is a relationally built equilibrium.

In fact, although the term *akpayhaeklha' engva'lhok*, which denotes the feeling of harmony, refers primarily to the social dimension, it encompasses a perception of harmony resulting from the spiritual dimension, and there are several ways in which harmony is determined by both dimensions. First, when one fears the spiritual dimension, it is impossible to experience harmony. *Akpayhaeklha' engva'lhok* implies the absence of fear. Second, harmony can be perceived in the positive responses of nature, such as in a bountiful harvest in consequence of a balanced spiritual relationship. It can be produced, finally, through the restoration of the spiritual equilibrium expressed, for example, in a recovery from sickness. Both the harmony in the spiritual dimension and the harmony in the social dimension are based, therefore, on the same logic: they are the expression of a balanced relationship with an 'other' which has specific characteristics of its own that must be respected.

The analogy between the two contexts of equilibrium is reflected in a wide terminological parallelism that allows us to postulate a conceptual complex of 'Enlhet peace,' which simultaneously includes social and spiritual dimensions. The terms *nentavaskama* and *senselhnanangkama*, for example, are used to describe both a transgression of the *nengelaasekhammalhkoo* and a transgression of the equilibrium in the spiritual relationship in the same manner. Also, the manner in which one must conduct oneself wisely (*nengya'askamkoo·lhma'*) and with discipline (*nenta'melsammalhkoo*) in social relations, must be transferred to the spiritual dimension. Indeed, it is not surprising that the two contexts of equilibrium are unified in a single conceptual complex, since in the Enlhet universe the human world and the world of that which lies beyond the human form a united whole. To briefly sketch how the link between them manifests itself:

- Celebrations – such as *yaanmaan*, the initiation of women; *na'teymaykam'*, the initiation of young men; the rainmaking celebration, and *yaaskama-kaaya*, the expression of joy in response to an abundant harvest – were the manifest connection between the spiritual and the social dimensions. They served to give shape to shared human life in its relation to that which lies beyond the human. In this manner, they built and restored

- – even guaranteed – equilibrium in the social and spiritual dimensions simultaneously.
- Spiritual transgression, that is, transgression in respect of that which lies beyond the human, has consequences for the whole group. The *senselh-nanangkama* is not limited to the wrongdoer. If, for example, a menstruating woman comes close to the watering place, she provokes the water's anger, which brings a dangerous storm that harms everyone. In the same way, if a woman is careless with meat and it spoils, the hunter will no longer be able to find animals, which once more harms the whole group.
- Therefore, it is everybody's responsibility to preserve equilibrium. On the one hand, the *metnaha-pketkook*, the elders, knew how to take care of their people through the use of their special powers. By resolving unresolved issues with non-human beings, they preserved or restored equilibrium in spiritual relationships. On the other hand, every Enlhet knew how to act wisely and correctly (*nengya'askamkoo·lhma'*) in order to avoid harmful consequences (*senselhnanangkama*). The elderly insist again and again that, when each person assumed his responsibility, they were not afraid of the world beyond the human, although it was potentially dangerous. This reflects again the perception of harmony based on equilibrium.
- Maintaining social relationships is an important means to control that which lies beyond the human, as there are non-human beings that watch over social relations. For example, the *enlhet-neeten* can become offended when a person makes a habit of speaking badly to others. They haunt him until he is driven mad (Haakok Yenmongaam, forthcoming).
- At the same time, the power of the elders constitutes a potential danger for the community. Therefore, it is particularly important not to offend powerful elders, so that they will keep their power under control. The prototypical offense is to neglect sharing, that is, to overlook the *nengaasekhay'oo engmook* as each person's contribution to the *nengelaasekhammalhkoo*. In this manner, fear of the elders constitutes an important motivation to maintain the discipline of the *nengelaasekhummalhkoo* in Enlhet society.

Given that well-being and harmony require simultaneous attention to social and spiritual dimensions, the conceptual complex of 'Enlhet peace' can be summarized thus: it is a set of attitudes and symbols, which have the objective of constructing an equilibrium in the relationships among the beings of the world, so that these can preserve their specific caracteristicas within these relationships without harming others. The task of preserving this equilibrium is understood as the responsibility of everyone; it is not a demand that one person makes on the other.

This description provides an, albeit brief, account of the spiritual dimension of 'Enlhet peace.' The next section will discuss the transformation of the conceptual complex discussed above since the appearance of white people in the Enlhet world about eighty years ago.

Nengelaasekhammalhkoo: The transformation of readings

Since the arrival of the *sengelpaalha'vay'*, of the white people, in Enlhet territory, there has been strong interference in the conceptual complex we have been describing. The *sengelpaalha'vay'* have stripped the Enlhet of their own world by continually constraining their options for action (Kenteem, forthcoming; Metyeeyam', forthcoming b). At the same time, they have excluded the Enlhet from the construction of a new multi-ethnic Chaco, thereby creating an imbalance of power and imposing vertical relationships.[45] However, this chapter does not seek to focus on current constellations of power. It rather traces the transformation of the basic concepts of *nengelaasekhammalhkoo* as it derives from contact with a dominant alien world that has refused to build a balanced relationship. In the next section, the interferences between the old and new readings will be outlined.

One Enlhet response to the new framework of vertical relations has been the attempt to retain the equilibrium–harmony concept inherent to the *nengelaasekhammalhkoo* by adapting the term *nengaasekhay'oo engmook* to the changing situation: The Enlhet began to classify the relatively less aggressive among the newcomers as *sengaasekhay'oo*, 'they respect us' (Haatkok'ay' Akpaasyam', 2003), without evaluating whether those immigrants utilized the relationship or even exploited the Enlhet,[46] that is, without considering the existence of structural violence. Such a relativizing adaptation has turned the *nengaasekhay'oo engmook*, which previously was the description of an attitude, into a characterization of a way of appearing. It also has meant a renunciation of the notion of reciprocity. Concurrently, the use of the term *nengelaasekhammalhkoo*, which makes reciprocity explicit – to mutually perform *nengaasekhay'oo engmook* – has clearly decreased in everyday life. Today the predominant term is *nengaasekhay'oo engmook*. Although this refers to the same attitude and practice as the former, it implies a unidirectional orientation: someone applies *nengaasekhay'oo* to somebody else. That this latter term is preferred nowadays (both terms exist originally in the Enlhet language) indicates a new premise in relationships: With the loss of the concept of reciprocity, relationality is reconceived as basically unidirectional. This means that the notion of equilibrium is abandoned. This new vertical model of relationships has become manifest in different ways in relationships both within and outside Enlhet society in different ways.

In the relationship outside Enlhet society, with the *sengelpaalha'vay'*, 'the newcomers,' the transfigured use of *nengaasekhay'oo engmook*, 'respecting the other,' is reflected when, for example, *nengaasekhay'oo sengelpaalha'vay'*, 'respect for the newcomers,' is sometimes paraphrased as 'we have to trust the newcomers.' Such an expression indicates an uncritical acceptance of the submissive posture within the new power constellation. It is the acceptance of subjugation on the part of the subjugated; the acceptance of dependency in order to preserve harmony. This amounts to a new concept of harmony, no longer one which results from equilibrium: Harmony is now a situation in which everyone remains silent. Concurrently, conflict no longer arises from a transgression of equilibrium, but rather from the report of a transgression.[47] It coincides with the dominant discourse in the Chaco that describes the context of life as peaceful despite the fact that a great part of the population is excluded from all constructive participation (Kalisch, 2005). This dominant discourse speaks of a 'peace' which is in practice unilaterally functional for the interests of the *sengelpaalha'vay'* insofar as it allows them to build a Chaco for themselves.

In relationships within Enlhet society itself, the vertical re-reading of *nengaasekhay'oo engmook* assumes more complex nuances. The surrender of the Enlhet in the face of a new world, which made it impossible for them to continue developing their own universe, manifested in the form of a conversion to Christianity and the simultaneous adherence to a political–cultural model imposed by the immigrants through the so-called 'missions.' Under these conditions, attendance at church – the symbol of this model – is still understood as a favor preformed by the Enlhet to those involved in the organization of the church, that is, to Enlhet pastors and immigrant society. The resulting lack of serious commitment to the church translates into the expectation of the Enlhet that church leaders indulge them unfailingly. They are quick to take offence at any statement or attitude they perceive as going against them, because such gestures make them feel uncomfortable.[48]

In general, Enlhet society shows a profound lack of commitment to the new direction of its political life with its specific social and cultural objectives. Consequently, the attitude of waiting to be pleased by leaders in order to remain loyal to them[49] has fully impregnated Enlhet social interaction. It has given rise to the understanding of *nengaasekhay'oo engmook* as a right: the attitude of *nengaasekhay'oo engmook* – respecting and addressing the other – has become the claim to *sengaasekhay'oo engmook*, the demand that 'the other respect and address me.' Thereby, an inversion of the direction of the initiative has occurred: initiative is expected from the other, instead of oneself being proactive.[50] This means that maintaining *nengelaasekhammalhkoo* is no longer understood as the responsibility of the individual, but the responsibility of the other. This inversion symbolizes the definitive loss of the approach of reciprocity and, thus, of equilibrium.

The inversion of the original dynamic not only excludes the notion of reciprocity. It also facilitates the utilization of the traditional ethics that motivated attention to and inclusion of the other, since it enables a situation in which an individual makes himself dependent on another with the intention of obligating the other to attend to him in the manner suggested by the Enlhet's traditional ethics. That is to say, the inversion of the original dynamic suggests a type of vertical relationality in Enlhet society that tends towards submitting oneself to another in order to take advantage of him. This is successful because the other is still rooted in traditional Enlhet ethics, so that he fears the reproach resulting from a supposed violation of those ethics if he resists the attempted submission.[51] Thus, another inversion is apparent: the original ethics advocate including the other if he excludes himself through inappropriate behavior; the exploitation of these 'ethics of inclusion,' the act of submitting oneself for the sake of submission, engenders the exclusion of the other.[52]

Linguistically, this exclusion is reflected in the transfiguration of the term *nengloom*. Originally, *nengloom* referred to an attitude or action without discipline (Seepe-Pta'heem-Pelhkapok, forthcoming). Today, however, the term is used to describe any determined act, even if it is carefully considered. Nevertheless, it retains the traditional connotation of strongly negative, despicable; to be called *nengloom* is still a great dishonor.[53] It is therefore easily used to invalidate an attitude or expression that one does not like in the other, without reference to criteria orientated towards the construction of shared life. Thus, together with the re-reading of *nengaasekhay'oo engmook*, the re-reading of *nengloom* is functional in the strategy of self-submission: the re-reading of *nengaasekhay'oo engmook* inverts the direction of the initiative, and the re-reading of *nengloom* simultaneously eliminates the possibility of a determined and constructive reaction to *sentavaskama*, to the attitude of disrespect produced easily by the exploitation of traditional Enlhet ethics and keenly felt by those affected.

In spite of these transfigurations, traditional concepts have not yet disappeared completely. There are various forms of interference between the traditional and the transfigured conceptual sphere in the current ideological universe of the Enlhet.

Nengelaasekhammalhkoo: The coexistence of readings

Beyond all that has been said in the previous section, contemporary Enlhet society has not renounced the conceptualization it was originally shaped by and of which it continues to be the product. It is certain that the strategy of submission for the sake of subjugation suggests a type of action that contradicts the traditional conceptual framework. Furthermore, this new frame of action tends to expand throughout society. Nevertheless, it is not applied by all members of the community at all times; the practice of inclusion remains relatively valid. In fact, the concept of *nengaasekhay'oo engmook* still maintains the connotation of a profoundly good and desirable attitude, of a determining value – it is precisely because of this that its utilization is possible. In summary, in contemporary Enlhet society, two mutually exclusive conceptual frameworks coexist: an ethic of inclusion, and its inversion.

This coexistence constitutes a strong contradiction within current Enlhet life. This contradiction, however, is difficult to grasp, since the very fact that both conceptual frameworks are expressed by the same term, *nengaasekhay'oo engmook*, creates ambiguity. It is, in fact, more than just a simple ambiguity, as today the potential reference of the term *nengaasekhay'oo engmook* (and of *nengloom*) includes concepts which traditionally were mutually exclusive. It is, in fact, a sub-differentiation, a lack of distinctive terms,[54] which hinders, and even paralyzes, reflective penetration of the corresponding concepts, as the reflective process is simultaneously supported by distinct conceptual frameworks that interfere in ways that are not immediately obvious.[55]

While a terminological subdifferentiation is apparent, a process that strives for the elimination of the ambiguity of the corresponding terms is also at work. However, this process is not directed towards a terminological differentiation, but rather towards the reduction in the diversity between real life and symbols. Today the attitudes corresponding to traditional conceptualizations are steadily decreasing and so the practical use of words corresponds less and less to their original reading. Thus, younger generations increasingly interpret the terms according to their changed concepts, and grasp the original concepts with ever less insight. Therefore, although the attitudes that correspond to the traditional conceptualization are still present in everyday life, they are accompanied less and less by a shared present-day construction of symbols. For that reason, the building of life with these attitudes is ever less the natural option using current shared ethics. Rather, it increasingly requires a determined personal decision. In this way, the transfigured conceptualization acquires even more weight, while the traditional one loses integrating strength – and so the cycle continues.

Because of the interrelation between the realm of tangible experience and that of symbols, the loss of conceptual configurations not only entails the simple loss of historical information about Enlhet cultural constructs. Rather, this loss reflects the loss of a concrete and lively awareness of the mechanisms that build Enlhet society, mechanisms that propose shared life as a common value oriented towards equilibrium and the inclusion of others. In consequence, it creates a loss of access to the society's constructive and corrective potential. In the current clash of universes,[56] such a loss is especially serious as it gives disproportionate importance to an externally generated gravitation. This external pull causes the existing mechanisms for social cohesion to disintegrate, but it does not generate equivalent alternatives. In fact, the vertical re-reading of the terms *nengaasekhay'oo engmook*, *nengloom* and others defines an ideological construction that makes it extremely difficult to maintain the equilibrium within relationships. It facilitates the imposition of one's own interests, and allows a small group of individuals to take advantage of the rest. It corresponds to the dominant meaning of 'peace,' which makes the use of the word impossible by declaring it offensive in itself. It gives rise to the domination of those who know how to act without addressing themselves to others. It destroys communication.

The vertical re-reading of relationality is produced, then, by the interaction of several factors. It is related to surrender in the face of a system that has not been embraced, and to ways of interacting with the newcomers. But the system is not destroyed by inequality alone. The destruction stems above all from the lack of capability to act: outside pressure decreases the Enlhet's options for action and leads them to project the vertical model onto their own society. The next section illustrates what it means for the Enlhet to live between mutually exclusive conceptualizations corresponding to irreconcilable social practices.

Enlhet society today

It is the senior members of Enlhet society who continue to demonstrate an experiential knowledge of the autochthonous dimension as it existed when the Enlhet were fully responsible for themselves. This is why they are in a position to criticize the current situation; their critique is expressed through accounts of a way of life that is *concrete* and *approved*. They attest to the banishment of their traditional places and the destruction of their territory. They point out that the Enlhet's own forms of subsisting are being lost.[57] They talk about the abandonment of celebrations and the subsequent loss of the joy and happiness they produced. They talk about the disappearance of the *metnaha-pketkook*, who had the power to preserve or restore equilibrium with that which lies beyond the human, thereby protecting their people. They talk about an increase in *mongya'askaalhma'*, that is, 'not knowing how to behave in accordance with the characteristics of the world,' which today frequently means 'not *being able to* live adequately.'

But although it is the elderly who have the most reasons to speak, there are many Enlhet who say and feel the same. They are aware that life in a generalized state of *mongya'askaalhma'* has negative consequences.[58] These consequences, however, are no longer measurable or avoidable, which is why having to wait for them produces uncertainty, doubt and fear.[59] Concurrently, the Enlhet observe that nature itself is unbalanced. Recently, for example, an Enlhet woman became seriously ill after eating an armadillo. The Enlhet attributed her illness to the fact that, because of the destruction of the forest, the armadillos had turned against their nature and were starting to eat the bones of the dead. It is clear to all the Enlhet that such a violation of life can only have destructive effects. Again, this consciousness increases uncertainty and raises fear, while simultaneously inducing people not to eat armadillo any more, and thereby limiting even further the possibilities for nourishment beyond that which can be obtained with money – so hard, itself, to come by.

The perception of a loss of equilibrium is not limited to the spiritual and natural dimensions; it also affects the social dimension. This is the case not only because equilibrium can easily be destroyed by some individuals, who thereby hold sway over others. It is destabilized by the very fact that it is no longer conceptually normal to think about shared life from the other's point of view and to direct oneself to him on one's own initiative. In consequence, the feeling of harmony, *akpayhaeklha' engva'lhok*, diminishes, and social interaction becomes more difficult. At the same time, a widespread perception among the Enlhet maintains that there is no longer any respect for the other, a perception revealed in the statement that *nengelaasekhammalhkoo* no longer exists. However, rather than recovering it reciprocally and on each individual's initiative as a dimension of shared life, the Enlhet are trapped in the unidirectional reading which is nowadays given to *nengaasekhay'oo engmook* and which requires one to always wait for the other to take the initiative. In this way, they estrange themselves further and further from the equilibrium and harmony they seek. Haakok Vaetke-Ta'lelhkapok (2006) expresses this with a cry of despair: 'Where did *nengelaasekhammalhkoo* go? Where is it? In our hearts? In our heads? In the streets? In the fields? In the woodland? Where did it go?'

Existing social, economic, territorial and other constellations make it a highly complex task to recover the equilibrium of shared life. There are no longer spaces for dispersion and retreat in case of conflict as there were before. On the contrary, people live crowded together in communities (Seepe Pta'heem-Pelhkapok, forthcoming) and the subtle forms of structural violence sustained in the perversion of traditional concepts become even more discouraging, and generate fear of the other. Simultaneously, however, even though the community is a prison, it is still perceived as a place of refuge, since there is a pervasive distrust and fear of whites among the Enlhet, which leads them to perceive the world they live in as clearly dangerous.[60] Faced with these conditions, the Enlhet find it extremely difficult to see the need or possibility to look for alternatives to the space to which they are reduced – where they are, in fact, to keep them from becoming a nuisance.[61] They feel that their only option is to pursue the offers of the newcomers, despite the fact that they cannot manage these offers independently and are required to proceed at a pace that is not their own. All of this paralyzes Enlhet society. It tries to resist this paralysis, as is evident in the joy the Enlhet continue to maintain in their daily life. Nevertheless, their joy does not liberate them from the ambiguity of their situation: from their own point of view, they live in a somber world that does not offer them a defined and comprehensible place. They live in a state of generalized exhaustion, anxiety and fear, while the prospect of harmony fades further and further away from Enlhet society.

This statement should not be understood solely as the impossibility of *experiencing* 'peace.' It simultaneously expresses the difficulty of *living* 'peace' in its traditional Enlhet manifestation. But, above all, it refers to the elimination of a *vision* of 'peace.' Beyond all the social, political and ideological difficulties, the conceptual sphere of 'Enlhet peace' in effect has disintegrated, without having been substituted by a conceptual complex equivalent in terms of social integration, shared rootedness and reflexive–conceptual penetration. This is why new generations no longer know an alternative to today's life which would point them to a concrete and socially anchored understanding of a 'peace' that fits *their* context. They are only vaguely aware that they are living without harmony, and at the same time do not have the conceptual tools to express this perception. To the young generations, even hunger seems normal.[62]

End and beginning

In this description of the transformations of the conceptual complex of 'Enlhet peace,' two distinct domains emerge which coexist and crystallize around the same terminology. Both conceptual fields are the Enlhet's own creation, but they are not equivalent: They differ in their functionality for the aims of the Enlhet society,[63] as, while one implies equilibrium and inclusion, the other legitimizes and promotes the neighbor's exclusion. In other words, the latter responds to parameters opposed to those which Enlhet society is built and shaped by and which it has not renounced. At the same time, although both conceptual complexes coexist, they are not consciously recognized and are not applied in the same manner. That is to say: in its present stage of development, Enlhet society is only partly nourished by the constructive forces which derive from its specific tradition and which still exist at its core. Rather, the current line of development is functional for the ideologies of subjugation, with their expansionist objectives, which exist in the environment in spite of their not offering any convincing proposals as to how to achieve and preserve social cohesion constructively and harmonically. In consequence, the disintegration of social and personal life is ever more perceptible.

Conclusions about the conceptual complex of 'Enlhet peace' seem somewhat pessimistic. What is left for the Enlhet to build? Together with the conceptual background, the attitudes that have guaranteed 'Enlhet peace' have been lost to a great extent. Because of this, and in the face of current social, economic and territorial constellations, the identification of ways in which to achieve the equilibrium proposed by this concept of 'peace' is hugely problematic. However, the older Enlhet, who bear witness to a different life, may make the younger generations aware of the fact that they live in a prison. They can help them to recover visions that are from within and provide clues as to how to recommence their own construction beginning from the place they find themselves in today. For this reason, their testimonies constitute seeds of concrete hope; they may be joined with the treasure of daily joy that the Enlhet have succeeded in keeping alive.

Notes

1. Concerning the pronunciation of the Enlhet words, two equal letters indicate germination. <lh> represents the lateral fricative [ɬ]. <'> represents the glottal stop [ʔ]. All further letters correspond roughly to the phonetic value that is associated with them in Spanish.
2. For an exhaustive bibliography of the Enlhet-Enenlhet nation, see Fabre (2005).
3. The Ayoreo, northern neighbors of the Enlhet, are excluded from this statement, as they lived in a state of war with the Enlhet. Enlhet accounts indicate that these tensions could be relatively recent. They might have been the result of pressure exerted by Bolivian Creoles on the Ayoreo, which caused their displacement to the south. A worsening of interethnic relations for analogous reasons was observed in the south of the Enlhet-Enenlhet space, which borders the territory of the Toba-Qom.
4. The Mennonites are an Anabaptist group that separated from the Reformist movement in the sixteenth century and migrated to Eastern Europe. Some of them arrived in the Chaco via Canada; another group migrated directly from Russia. This latter group's traumatic experiences in Stalinist Russia were turned to a marked missionary fervor towards their new neighbors in the Chaco. The Chaco Mennonites speak a so-called 'German dialect,' but form a separate ethnic group rather than a German community (Klassen, 2001).
5. Because relatively little blood has been shed (and even though it began during a cruel war), the contact with the immigrants has frequently been described as a peaceful encounter.
6. This has frequently been felt and expressed by the translators of the Bible into Enlhet. They have interpreted the linguistic incompatibility of the two universes of symbols as deficiencies in Enlhet, ignoring the fact that the word does not equal the concept (as already noted by de Saussure). Consequently, a substantial discussion of concepts between white society and indigenous people has never taken place (Kalisch, 2005). However, such a discussion is crucial if an 'inter-universal' communication is to achieve more than just tiptoeing around a few miscomprehended linguistic variables, as is still typical of much local interethnic dialogue.
7. If we are talking, then, about concept x, we must understand this mode of speaking as an abbreviated way of saying: the concept to which we refer with the word x.
8. In two different cultural landscapes, corresponding experiences do not interrelate to other experiences in a parallel way. We can see this, for example, in the case of grieving for the dead, which in European cultures is related to constructions concerning guilt, while in the Enlhet world they are related to those concerning fear. Thus, the same experience belongs to conceptual complexes that are barely compatible, and generates extremely different reactions.
9. Approaching an indigenous conceptualization from the hegemonic conceptualization's point of view subdues it to dominant categories and, in fact, colonizes it.
10. Enlhet terms are also normally translated in the body of the text. However, a translation of the term *nengelaasekhammalhkoo* is not offered here, as its meaning must be discussed further.
11. This is reflected at a linguistic level: the words *nengelaasekhammalhkoo* and *peace* cannot be considered equivalent in translation, for they refer to highly different conceptualizations. The first, for example, concerns a practice, the latter a state. In fact we have never heard anybody intuitively relate the Enlhet word *nengelaasekhammalhkoo* to the Spanish word *paz* (peace).

12. Our interest in traditional expressions recognizes that due to their weight and function in everyday life, their understanding and inclusion is essential in order to work with the present. This acknowledgment makes it possible for the Enlhet to make use of the latent potential of their properly Enlhet being without thereby implying that they should set aside their current reality.

13. Although the Enlhet themselves attest to a great reduction in such sharing, for outsiders it is still a marked characteristic of their social interaction. Kidd (1999), for example, describes Enxet sharing.

14. The arguments of Enlhet verbs induce a co-referential reading: *Nengaasekhay'oo* means 'we respect it.' In consequence, *nengaasekhay'oo* cannot be cited by itself, for such a use would not satisfy the evoked co-reference. Thus, this chapter uses the form *nengaasekhay'oo engmook*, which means, literally, 'we respect it; it is the other.' The same is true for all other verbs that have a type of 'object' (in the case of the correspondent 'subject' the co-reference is saturated by the mark of the prefix *neng-*, 'we').

15. *Nengaasekhay'oo engmook* is difficult to translate. In Unruh and Kalisch (2003a, 2005, forthcoming) it is frequently translated using the German term *wohlgesonnen sein* ('well-disposed'), although this is not completely accurate. The translation 'respect for the other,' which is used in the present text, is not satisfactory either. Still less acceptable is the common practice of translating it as *love* (Kidd, 1999, 2000 *inter alia*), as this might denote anything from an emotion to a sexual act, while *nengaasekhay'oo engmook* is not related to emotions, and still less to eroticism: it refers to an attitude.

16. The Enlhet term *akmoo mook*, 'one like the other,' is often translated as 'equal, equality.' However, in the occidental world, equality is a right that can be claimed; it is not conceived from the point of view of concession to the other, as the Enlhet's conceptualization implies. Because of this observation, we prefer the term 'equilibrium' to 'equality.'

17. Literally, *akpayhaeklha' engva'lhok* means: 'the interior of somebody expands.'

18. For reasons of concision alone, this chapter refers to the individual as generically masculine, thus avoiding tedious repetition of such phrases as *himself or herself, he or she*, etc.

19. The need to preserve personal freedom during this state of openness towards the other, as well as respect for this freedom by the other, is an old Enlhet theme, which is found, for example, in Metyeeyam' (forthcoming a) or Melietkesammap (forthcoming).

20. Several authors have discussed the egalitarian character of the Enlhet and the Chaco peoples in general (from Grubb, 1911, to Kidd, 1999, in the case of the Enxet), insisting that it is inseparable from a marked 'personal autonomy.' Importantly, the orientation of this personal autonomy is inverse to the orientation found in the Western conceptualization: it is an autonomy granted to the other, not an autonomy imposed upon the other (Kidd, 2000). Although there may be situations in which it is necessary to defend this autonomy, it is not conceived from a defensive point of view. In order to avoid the connotations of occidental conceptualizations we therefore prefer the term 'personal freedom' to that of 'personal autonomy.'

21. It is worth noting in passing that *sengelnavaam* – 'having scruples' – is an attitude that is crucial in guaranteeing respect for the other. It also regulates how to act with determination in dealing with the other.

22. This is probably related to the fact that such a transgression signifies an existential danger. That is why it is necessary to specify different ways of avoiding it.

23. *Nengloom* can also be understood as 'being dangerous.'

24. Naturally, the labeling of a specific action as corresponding to *nengloom* or not depends on many factors and is not always unambiguous, even among the people involved in the situation.

25. In contrast to the majority of the negative terms introduced so far, *nengloom* is not linguistically conceptualized as relational. That is to say, it does not project the respective attitude as an action on the other, but characterizes the subject of this attitude itself.

26. In Toba-Enenlhet accounts, *nengelaasekhammalhkoo* – and together with it the description of the formalized attitudes of sharing – does not have a special place. This is probably due to the fact that even the eldest of present-day Toba grew up near Creole centers. There are no surviving Toba narrators who remember a time when the Toba led an independent life, or, as they say, the time when the Toba were responsible for themselves. Even so, Toba narrators emphasize concepts related to what we call 'ideology of relationship.' Melietkesammap (2007), for example, refers to equilibrium with the term *mamma·kiekammalhka'*, 'not to surpass each other.'

27. Most abstract Enlhet concepts appear to refer to an attitude more than to a feeling. This fact clearly distinguishes Enlhet conceptualizations from European–Western conceptualizations.

28. These celebrations constituted a central space for interethnic encounters, which were not limited to related peoples with relatively intelligible languages. Along the western side of the Enlhet territory, for example, the Enlhet maintained close relations with the Nivaclé, which became manifest in widespread bilingualism.

29. The 'extensive' is a verbal category of the Enlhet-Enenlhet languages (Unruh et al., 2003, p. 176). These languages can be described as polysynthetic and omnipredicative (Unruh and Kalisch, 2003b).

30. The corresponding Enlhet term is *ta'malma engneenyek*, 'the celebration.' Again, *ta'malma* means 'healthy, good.' It can be understood from other conventionalized terms that in ancient Enlhet, *engneenyek*, 'the chest,' was the seat of the will and the force of life. *Ta'malma engneenyek*, 'the celebration,' is, then, the manifestation of the 'healthy will of life.' Although this term refers only to people and not to the whole of the *alhma'*, in its conceptual context it must be read as grounded in, and functional for, social life.

31. Manolo Romero (personal communication) proposes an intuitive relationship between the concepts of *taqmelaikama·lhma'* and 'peace,' and translates the Spanish *paz*, 'peace,' as the Toba-Enenlhet word for 'celebration.' Conversely, Haakok Amay (2001) translates *ta'malma engneenyek* with *paz*.

32. While the prefix *neng-* indicates the direction away from the speaker, *seng-* indicates the direction towards the speaker.

33. Not all conflicts originate in a lack of respect. Relative unanimity in life projects greatly reduced possible conflict sources in comparison to life today. But, above all, the current external pressure on Enlhet society produces conflicts that tend to erupt internally.

34. This word means, literally, 'to make her or him recognize.' It describes the fact of deliberately entering into the destructive logic of the other so that he might feel the effects of his actions. It is this word which Haatkok'ay' Sevhen (forthcoming) uses in her account referred to below; there it is translated as 'to punish.'

35. Like many of the things summarized here, this strategy remains current.

36. *Ap-* (in *aploom*) is a prefix that indicates that the actor is male. *Neng-* (in *nengloom*) marks the first person plural or generic actor.

37. It may be argued, then, that the Enlhet are a peaceful people, not because of an absence of conflict or because of a general decision to avoid it, but rather because a basic feature of their being is to preserve or restore equilibrium.

38. Situations such as these shape people, and in fact it is said of the *koonamaalhek* that they were *apkelloom*, quick to react. With this characteristic one becomes fearsome, a potential danger to the equilibrium.

39. Here, the term 'freedom' is preferred to 'rights,' as the common reading of individual rights is of rights in opposition to others and as a value *per se*. However, for the present discussion, 'rights' would be understood as the indispensable condition for the preservation (or restoration) of equilibrium. That is, they would be rights that one shares with others.

40. In light of the complexity of the Enlhet's perception of that which lies beyond the human, the treatment of this topic must necessarily remain rather rudimentary. It is also important to clarify that we are reconstructing a traditional conceptualization that continues to affect the present, but whose categories are no longer actively available to the younger generations.

41. These are not simply *things* that are animate or that have a soul, they are beings. On the other hand, social units that are ascribed independent life, such as a 'legal entity' that is entitled to impose its own laws on natural human law, do not exist in the Enlhet universe.

42. The Enlhet universe acknowledges the existence of physical, social and spiritual laws. However, it holds that these different dimensions overlap.

43. Such a conceptual constellation determines the Enlhet understanding that transgression is not of a moral nature. In consequence, the words *sas* and *akta'mela*, 'good,' have no ethical or moral connotations, in contrast to what is proposed by the European universe of symbols. This conceptual difference leads to a great communicative misunderstanding in the relationship between the white man and indigenous peoples. For example, if a missionary speaks the native language, he projects his European concepts of 'sin' and 'good' onto the words *mongya'askaalhma'* and *sas*, while an Enlhet performs the inverse projection when speaking Spanish. Neither of them realizes that they are talking about very different things.

44. The Enlhet made a distinction between physical and non-physical diseases (Haakok Yenmongaam, forthcoming). A physical disease is always understood *also* as a hint of a disturbance in the spiritual dimension, that is, as sign of a problem of *nengvanmongkama*, the spiritual face of human nature. In consequence, a purely medical or clinical treatment never completely cures the Enlhet, because it does not make them feel healthy.

45. In the Chaco, white–indigenous relations develop along axes such as employer–employee, missionary–pupil, counselor–counseled, project coordinator–beneficiary, etc.

46. It is still a widespread practice in the Chaco to use friendship as a strategy for the construction of interethnic coexistence: The *sengelpaalha'vay'*, the newcomers, show friendship (*sengaasekhay'oo*), but they do it within the framework of a unidirectional relationship, since they are the ones who determine the conditions of life and coexistence. Thus, be it deliberate or not, the apparent demonstration of friendship functions as a strategy for pacification and submission.

47. Stahl (in Klassen, 1991, p. 274) refers to this reading when he asserts that the indigenous peoples are not opposed to dependency as long as there is harmony in the relationship, that is, as long as there are no open conflicts.

48. Discomfort constitutes an important constructive motivation for many social dynamics. For this reason, when one's own discomfort can, in principle, be interpreted as aggression on the part of the other, and when the person causing the feeling of discomfort can therefore be rebuked, society loses a central motor for innovation. At the same time, a very subtle form of aggression evolves which undermines social cohesion.

49. As was noted above, traditional Enlhet society was not stratified. That is, there were no generalized forms of coercion; rather, loyalty towards a leader was subject to a constant reestablishment. To the extent that Enlhet society lacks a common and clearly defined social and cultural objective, it is *de facto* impossible that its people will follow leaders simply on their own initiative.

50. Another effect of verticality is that today during bartering it is frequently necessary to demand the goods agreed in exchange from the other. It is no longer the other who takes the initiative by providing the goods and thus acting in reciprocity and preserving the equilibrium.

51. This threat is strengthened by the discourse of the church, which censures non-submissive actions.

52. There are several Enlhet terms to describe attitudes that follow the logic of exclusion. One example is *nengyelhanmaeklha' engmook*, 'to hide oneself behind the other in order to use him' (derived from *nengyelhanmoom*, 'to hide oneself'). Another example is *nengelyepvaataeklha' engmook*, derived from *nengelyepvaateeykam' x* which means 'to defeat someone or something without encountering resistance, to overwhelm someone easily because of his inability to defend himself.' Its derivation means 'to use the other's willingness, harming him in this way.'

53. The undifferentiated use of *nengloom* is clearly linked to Christian life. Non-baptized individuals can act with determination in the original sense, without being called *nengloom* (or without the term having a derogative connotation). That is to say, conversion to Christianity implies the assumption (at least theoretically) of the new logic of submission.

54. This deficit is quite natural, as the new concepts form slowly while departing from the traditional concept. At the beginning, then, there is no need (or possibility) to reveal ambiguity. To detect this ambiguity is precisely the beginning of a new process of reflection.

55. Kidd (1999) argues that autochthonous ethics are not eliminated, as the application of coercion or direct verticality in relationships is still unacceptable. Departing from this observation, he puts forward an opposition between assimilation and distinction in the face of the dominant society. However, this opposition does not capture what is happening: The assimilation that takes place does not turn the indigenous people into whites; nor does it eliminate most of their distinctive elements. Rather, it constitutes a process of interference on the indigenous society that breaks up and disintegrates its ethics. The process is negative in that it is, above all, a reaction and an adaptation to imposed limitations; it does not allow the constructive expansion and appropriation of new spaces based on the Enlhet's own logic.

56. In fact, the new readings are empowered because they are much more compatible with the dominant discourse than the original readings. They are, so to speak, co-designed by this same discourse, which claims to represent '*the* true content' and simultaneously permeates all official spaces (church, radio, institutions such as schools and hospitals, meetings and assemblies, etc.).

57. This abandonment did not take place deliberately; rather, it occurred because of the gradual exclusion of the Enlhet from most of their territory and their subsequent

concentration in highly limited spaces, and because of the great destruction of the natural resources on which the Enlhet used to live.

58. Although it may seem contradictory, this statement is valid also for the Enlhet who nowadays laugh at the world of the elders and defend the demystification of the world promoted by the missionaries and development agencies – that is: the assimilation of 'white' categories – which has made the Enlhet's world materialistic and secularized (Loewen, 1969): They feel that the traditional universe is still related to current times, yet simultaneously they know that its healing and recovering mechanisms have been destroyed.

59. An important argument of the Enlhet in favor of participating in the church is precisely that this participation will help to prevent such consequences and to calm the doubts caused by waiting for them to materialize.

60. This statement might surprise many non-indigenous inhabitants of the Chaco, who define themselves as markedly peaceful. However, it is a common feeling among the Enlhet.

61. About the motives of the immigrants for settling the Enlhet see Klassen (1991, p. 156ff.). From an Enlhet point of view, the process of building the current Enlhet communities, the so-called missions, is described in Unruh and Kalisch (forthcoming): While the mission was initially perceived as a place of peace (Unruh and Kalisch, 2008), today 'there is no peace in the mission' (Ernesto Unruh, personal communication) that the Enlhet might feel.

62. The young Enlhet who are imitating the newcomers' way of life are constantly told by them that they are progressing when, in fact, their people's quality of life continues to deteriorate. It seems it is exactly this loss of understanding of their own world that is taken for progress, and progress comes to be synonymous with 'to be led by the newcomers.'

63. It should be emphasized that when evaluating the new constructions, it is unimportant whether there have been interferences with European–Western conceptualizations. Rather, the key parameter by which to determine their coherence is the degree of functionality for the Enlhet's own purposes.

Reference list

Enlhet names are not expressed as first and family name. They appear in the bibliography as they are quoted in the text.

DGEEC (Dirección General de Estadística, Encuestas y Censos) (2003) *II Censo Nacional Indígena de Población y Viviendas 2002: Pueblos indígenas del Paraguay. Resultados finales* (Asunción: DGEEC).

Fabre, A. (2005) 'Los Pueblos del Gran Chaco y sus Lenguas. Primera Parte: Los Enlhet-Enenlhet del Chaco Paraguayo,' *Suplemento Antropológico*, 40, 1, 503–569, http://www.tut.fi/~fabre/SA_Junio_05_Enlhet.pdf, date accessed December 8, 2008.

Fischermann, B. (2003) *Historia de Amotocodie* (Filadelfia/La Paz: Script).

Grubb, W.B. (1911) *An unknown People in an Unknown Land: An Account of the Life and Customs of the Lengua Indians of the Paraguayan Chaco* (London: Seeley).

Haakok Aamay (2001) 'Ta'malma engneenyek,' *Nengvaanemkeskama Nempayvaam Enlhet – Programa de Radio*, 2.

Haakok Aamay (2005) 'Das Zusammenleben wurde schwierig' in E. Unruh and H. Kalisch (eds.) *Sie wissen nicht, wie sie es zu Gehör bringen sollen*, Jahrbuch für Geschichte und

Kultur der Mennoniten in Paraguay, 6, 214–221, http://www.menonitica.org/2005/8. pdf, date accessed December 8, 2008.

Haakok Vaetke-Ta'lelhkapok (2006) 'Nengelaasekhammalhkoo,' *Nengvaanemkeskama Nempayvaam Enlhet – Programa de Radio*, 137.

Haakok Yenmongaam (forthcoming) *Apkeltemnaykam' Haakok Yenmongaam* (Ya'alve-Saanga: Nengvaanemkeskama Nempayvaam Enlhet).

Haatkok'ay' Akpaasyam' (2003) 'Er war uns wohlgesonnen' in E. Unruh and H. Kalisch 'Er war uns wohlgesonnen,' *Mennoblatt*, 74/1, 3–4, http://www.enlhet.org/pdf/05.pdf, date accessed December 8, 2008 [to be reprinted in Unruh and Kalisch (forthcoming)].

Haatkok'ay' Sevhen (forthcoming) 'Streit' in E. Unruh and H. Kalisch (eds.) (forthcoming) *Wie schön ist deine Stimme: Berichte zur Geschichte der Enlhet aus Ya'alve-Saanga* (Ya'alve-Saanga: Nengvaanemkeskama Nempayvaam Enlhet).

Kalisch, H. (2000) *Hacia el Protagonismo Propio: Base Conceptual para el Relacionamiento con Comunidades Indígenas* (Ya'alve-Saanga: Nengvaanemkeskama Nempayvaam Enlhet), http://www.enlhet.org/pdf/01.pdf, date accessed December 8, 2008.

Kalisch, H. (2003) '"No escucharon," decían y se rindieron: Una crítica a la actuación unilateral que quita protagonismo indígena,' *Acción: Revista Paraguaya de Reflexión y Diálogo*, 240, 27–30, reprinted in Kalisch (2005), http://www.enlhet.org/pdf/08.pdf, date accessed December 8, 2008.

Kalisch, H. (2005) 'La convivencia de las lenguas en el Paraguay: Reflexiones acerca de la construcción de la dimensión multilingüe del país,' *Revista de la Sociedad Científica del Paraguay*, 17, 47–83, http://www.enlhet.org/pdf/08.pdf, date accessed December 8, 2008.

Kalisch, H. (2006) 'Educación indígena – ¿Educación o aprendizaje?' *Acción: Revista Paraguaya de Reflexión y Diálogo*, 265/267, 25–27/13–15, http://www.enlhet.org/pdf/nne23-aprendizaje.pdf, date accessed December 8, 2008.

Kenteem (forthcoming) 'Wir müssen unsere Art aufgeben' in E. Unruh and H. Kalisch (eds.) (forthcoming) *Wie schön ist deine Stimme: Berichte zur Geschichte der Enlhet aus Ya'alve-Saanga* (Ya'alve-Saanga: Nengvaanemkeskama Nempayvaam Enlhet).

Kidd, S.W. (1999) 'The Morality of the Enxet People of the Paraguayan Chaco and Their Resistance to Assimilation' in E.S. Miller (ed.) *Peoples of the Gran Chaco* (Bergin and Garvey: Westport), 37–60.

Kidd, S.W. (2000) 'Knowledge and the Practice of Love and Hate among the Enxet of Paraguay' in J. Overing and A. Passes (eds.) *The Anthropology of Love and Anger: The Aesthetics of Conviviality in Native Amazonia* (London: Routledge), 114–132.

Klassen, P.P. (1991) *Die Mennoniten in Paraguay, Band 2. Begegnung mit Indianern und Paraguayern* (Bolanden-Weierhof: Mennonitischer Geschichtsverein).

Klassen, P.P. (2001) *Die Mennoniten in Paraguay, Band 1. Reich Gottes und Reich dieser Welt* (Bolanden-Weierhof: Mennonitischer Geschichtsverein).

Loewen, J.A. (1969) 'Los Lengua y su Mundo Espiritual,' *Suplemento Antropológico de la Revista Ateneo Paraguayo*, 4, 115–133.

Melietkesammap (2007) *Halhema-Teves. Apkeltennaikamaha Melietkesammap aktemakha' nelvetai'a takha'*, Biblioteca Paraguaya de Antropología, 59 (Ya'alve-Saanga: Nengvaanemkeskama Nempayvaam Enlhet).

Melietkesammap (forthcoming) *Yettelev'. Apkeltennaikamaha Melietkesammap aktemakha' apkenmopvana enenlhet apkelietemo taqmelakha' apkeliaihekamaha* (Ya'alve-Saanga: Nengvaanemkeskama Nempayvaam Enlhet).

Metyeeyam' (forthcoming a) 'Warum hast du bloß deine Schwäger getötet?' in E. Unruh and H. Kalisch (eds.) (forthcoming) *Wie schön ist deine Stimme: Berichte zur Geschichte der Enlhet aus Ya'alve-Saanga* (Ya'alve-Saanga: Nengvaanemkeskama Nempayvaam Enlhet).

Metyeeyam' (forthcoming b) 'Das letzte Fest' in E. Unruh and H. Kalisch (eds.) (forthcoming) *Wie schön ist deine Stimme: Berichte zur Geschichte der Enlhet aus Ya'alve-Saanga* (Ya'alve-Saanga: Nengvaanemkeskama Nempayvaam Enlhet).

Metyeeyam' (forthcoming c) *Nengko'o·yka' nengeleyvaamak hay'* (Ya'alve-Saanga: Nengvaanemkeskama Nempayvaam Enlhet).

Ortiz, R. (2005) 'Der Busch war unser Supermarkt' in E. Unruh and H. Kalisch (eds.) *Sie wissen nicht, wie sie es zu Gehör bringen sollen*, Jahrbuch für Geschichte und Kultur der Mennoniten in Paraguay, 6, 197–205, http://www.menonitica.org/2005/8.pdf, date accessed December 8, 2008.

Regehr, W. (1979) 'Die lebensräumliche Situation der Indianer im paraguayischen Chaco: Humangeographisch-ethnologische Studie zu Subsistenzgrundlage und Siedlungsform akkulturierter Chacovölker,' *Basler Beiträge zur Geographie*, 25 (Basel: Wepf).

Savhongvay' (forthcoming) 'Sie sind ganz weiß' in E. Unruh and H. Kalisch (eds.) (forthcoming) *Wie schön ist deine Stimme: Berichte zur Geschichte der Enlhet aus Ya'alve-Saanga* (Ya'alve-Saanga: Nengvaanemkeskama Nempayvaam Enlhet).

Seepe-Pta'heem-Pelhkapok (forthcoming) *Apkeltemnaykam' Seepe-Pta'heem-Pelhkapok* (Ya'alve-Saanga: Nengvaanemkeskama Nempayvaam Enlhet).

Unruh, E. and H. Kalisch (2003a) 'Er war uns wohlgesonnen,' *Mennoblatt*, 74/1, 3–4, http://www.enlhet.org/pdf/05.pdf, date accessed December 8, 2008 [to be reprinted in Unruh and Kalisch (forthcoming)].

Unruh, E. and H. Kalisch (2003b) 'Enlhet-Enenlhet: Una Familia Lingüística Chaqueña,' *Thule: Rivista Italiana di Studi Americanistici*, 14/15, 207–231.

Unruh, E. and H. Kalisch (2005) *Sie wissen nicht, wie sie es zu Gehör bringen sollen*, Jahrbuch für Geschichte und Kultur der Mennoniten in Paraguay, 6, 195–221, http://www.menonitica.org/2005/8.pdf, date accessed December 8, 2008 [to be reprinted in E. Unruh and H. Kalisch (forthcoming)].

Unruh, E. and H. Kalisch (2008) 'Salvación – ¿Rendición? Los Enlhet y la Guerra del Chaco' in N. Richard (ed.) *Mala Guerra: Los Indígenas en la Guerra del Chaco (1932–35)* (Asunción and Paris: Museo del Barro, ServiLibro and CoLibris), 99–123.

Unruh, E. and H. Kalisch (forthcoming) *Wie schön ist deine Stimme: Berichte zur Geschichte der Enlhet aus Ya'alve-Saanga* (Ya'alve-Saanga: Nengvaanemkeskama Nempayvaam Enlhet).

Unruh, E., H. Kalisch and M. Romero (2003) *Enenlhet Apaivoma. Nentengiai'a nengiangvaiakmoho neliateikamaha enenlhet apaivoma: Guía para el aprendizaje del idioma materno toba*, Biblioteca Paraguaya de Antropología, 43 (Ya'alve-Saanga: Nengvaanemkeskama Nempayvaam Enlhet), http://www.enlhet.org/pdf/13.pdf, date accessed December 8, 2008.

Section V
Peace Concepts in Africa

22
Asomdwoe: A West African Perspective

Kofi Asare Opoku

In order to understand the African perspective on peace, it is necessary to look critically at African life and culture and the principles that undergird them. For the perspective on peace that is found in African societies is not based on theory, but is borne out of the experiences and reflections on life in all its multifarious dimensions, as well as in the daily lives of the people. As humanity's ineffable and greatest gift, life is fully lived and realized, and a state of peace is achieved, when life is without let or hindrance, constraints, impediments and threats, and when all that is required to make life happy, prosperous and meaningful is attained. This state of peace is not limited to the presence of material things alone, for there are essential non-material things that go to make life happy, prosperous and meaningful. In other words, peace has its material and non-material aspects and is understood in the traditions of Africa to be a totality with spiritual, moral, material and physical aspects. The state of peace represents all that goes to make life ideally complete and unencumbered.

A Gikuyu[1] prayer for peace, recorded by John Mbiti (1975, pp. 162–163), provides a broad view of the African perspective on peace that goes beyond the narrow limits of 'absence of conflict' to include: serenity in the country; an increase in the human and flock population; good health for both humans and animals; harmony in nature as well as among people, the banishment of all that causes strife and the consignment into the deepest recesses of the forest of all ill words.

> Praise ye Ngai (God) – Peace be with us
> Say that the country may have tranquility – Peace be with us
> And the people may continue to increase – Peace be with us
> Say that the people may continue to increase – Peace be with us
> Say that the people and the flock and herds
> May prosper and be free from illness – Peace be with us
> May peace reign over the earth,

May the gourd cup agree with vessel – Peace be with us
May their heads agree and every ill word
Driven out into the wilderness, into the virgin forest,
Praise ye Ngai – Peace be with us.

The prayer is addressed to *Ngai*, the Gikuyu name for the Supreme Being, regarded as the source and giver of peace and the origin of the harmonious order and equilibrium of the universe, which is each person's responsibility to maintain by his or her life in the community.

Peace and community

Though there are many diverse societies and cultures on the African continent, a careful and meticulous examination reveals a striking commonality that characterizes them all, and that is the emphasis on community and communal living. This emphasis stems from an awareness of the limitation or lack of self-sufficiency on the part of each person and the consequent need to overcome this by cooperating with others in order to realize each person's full potential. A lesson from the human body provides imaginative insights into this matter in the form of an African proverb: 'The left hand washes the right and the right hand washes the left' (Opoku, 1997, p. 17). Each hand has a limitation in the sense that it cannot wash itself, but when the hands wash each other they become clean. In the same manner, each person has a limitation in the sense that he/she cannot meet all his/her basic needs single-handedly, but requires the assistance of others. Through cooperation and mutual helpfulness, individual limitations are overcome and human welfare is enhanced, and each person can fulfill his or her potential.

Society exists to promote life in its fullest dimension, which can be described as a state of being at peace, but this cannot be achieved without the cooperation of others and therefore cooperation and mutual helpfulness are necessary to bring about peace. Communal living is based on the harmonious interrelationships between the members of the community, as its *sine qua non*, for in the African understanding life is not possible without community. Society is the context of human existence and the Akan of Ghana say: 'When a person descends from the heavens, he/she descends into a town inhabited by human beings' (Akan proverb),* which means human society. But this society is understood to include not only the visible members, but also invisible members: the Overlord of the community, the Great Spirit or Supreme Being; the ancestors, who are forbears and predecessors of the community; the divinities, regarded as agents of the

---

* Ed. Many of the African proverbs referred to in this article were and are passed orally; hence, for some quotes there is no written source to include as conventional biblio-graphical reference.

Supreme Being; and those who are yet to be born. The society also includes animals and nature, regarded as an integral part of humankind's world order; and life is at its best and peace is attained when a state of equilibrium prevails, and when there is a state of undisturbed, harmonious relations between humans, the spirit world, animals and nature.

A way to create peace is sharing, and common etiquette demands that strangers be welcomed into homes. As Malidoma says, 'It is the task of him who is not a stranger to turn the potential enemy in the stranger into a friend' (Malidoma, 1994, p. 96). The Ibo (Nigeria) do this in their communities through the ritual of splitting *kola*, praying over it and sharing it with the guest and those present, to indicate that the guest is genially welcome. Likewise, in Akan communities, guests are given *Bresuo*, literally water against weariness; since tiredness is one of the most common signs of dehydration, the guest is cooled by the water, which is shared with him and prevents him from becoming mentally fuzzy and enables the guest to feel at ease and welcome.

The community is based on peace as its inescapable foundation and the moral obligations imposed on members of the community have as their goal the securing of a state of peaceful living so that each person can live his/her life fully. This goal is achieved through education.

Peace and traditional education

Traditional education has as its main thrust the inculcation of the values that make people uphold the principles that make life livable. It aims at producing human beings who will uphold the society's values and promote peace and harmony that supports life and its fulfillment, and shun all that which threatens the best interests of the society, namely, peace and harmony.

Generally, the children's naming ceremony is also the occasion for society to impart its values to its newest members. Children are told to be truthful, hardworking, obedient and respectful and to avoid all that leads to a disruption of peace – lies, laziness, disobedience, wickedness, selfishness, greed, violence, etc., which cause trouble for others and for the society at large. As the children grow into young adulthood, they enter the initiation schools where the ideal of manhood and womanhood are taught to them. The idea is to make the young adults conscious bearers of the values of society and become acutely cognizant of themselves as responsible adult members upon whose shoulders rest the peace, harmony and happiness of the society. Camara Laye's account of his initiation ritual among his people, the Soninke in Guinea, is worth noting:

> The teaching we received in the bush, far from all prying eyes, had nothing very mysterious about it; nothing, I think, that was not fit for ears other than our own. These lessons, the same as had been taught to all who had

preceded us, confined themselves to outlining what a man's conduct should be: we were to be absolutely straightforward, cultivate all the virtues that go to make an honest man, to fulfill our duties toward God, toward our parents, our superiors and our neighbors. We must tell nothing of what we learned, either to women or to the uninitiated; neither were we to reveal any of secret rites of circumcision. Women, too, are not allowed to tell anything about the rites of excision. (Laye, 1954, pp. 128–129)

At the stage of marriage, couples are advised not to deceive each other or inflict undeserved hurt on the other or treat each other unfairly. By giving such advice, the couple is being shown the conditions that bring about peace, for it is assumed that peace in the society at large begins with its realization in the homes of its people. This idea is expressed in the Akan proverb: 'The fall of a nation begins in the homes of its people.'

Finally, the dirges and utterances to the deceased found in death rituals that usher deceased people into the ancestral world urge the dead to go and become good ancestors. Good ancestors fulfill their obligations to society by protecting and guiding members of their families, and people in society in turn fulfill their obligations by remembering, honoring and feeding the ancestors and also upholding the traditions bequeathed to society by the ancestors. The symbiotic relationship between the living and the ancestors brings about peace.

In the political processes of electing traditional rulers, the most eligible ones are those who have intelligence, humility, generosity, manliness and physical fitness. Oaths are taken by prospective rulers to affirm their commitment to values that bring about peace and justice in the society, by cautiously shunning behavior that is disruptive of that high ideal. The Akan chief-elect is told:

> Do not go after women. Do not become a drunkard. When we give you advice, listen to it. Do not gamble. We do not want you to disclose the origin of your subjects. We do not want you to abuse us. We do not want you to be miserly; we do not want one who disregards advice; we do not want you to regard us fools; we do not want autocratic ways; we do not want bullying; we do not like beating. Take the Stool. We bless the Stool and give it to you. The Elders say they give the Stool to you. (Busia, 1968, p. 12)

The chief-elect is also confined in what is called *apatam* for a period of six weeks during which the elders instruct him in his duties, responsibilities and, above all, comportment that brings about peaceful and harmonious relations between the chief and the people and ensures amity, stability and tranquility in the state. As a model of peace who assiduously avoids actions that bring about untoward unrest and turbulence in society, the chief is described in royal appellations as 'the big tree on whose branches birds take shelter, and in whose shade animals rest' (Sarpong, 1989, p. 358).

The mechanisms of traditional education express the understanding that peace does not fall from the sky, but that human beings have a role to play in its realization as a lofty and desirable end. Education is therefore a tool or a means to an end in the search for peace.

Peace and symbols

In the search for peace, African people look to the natural world for symbols to represent the much-cherished ideal of peace. In many societies in Africa, the snail and the tortoise are regarded as peaceful creatures, who do no harm to other creatures in the forest, and who are featured in proverbs, folk tales and art. 'Not a gunshot would be heard in the forest, if the tortoise and the snail were the only creatures in the forest,' says an Akan proverb that alludes to their peaceful nature. The tortoise as a peaceful creature has encased himself in a hard shell, not wanting to harm or be harmed by anyone; as another Akan proverb says: 'Because the tortoise wants no part in trouble, he has encased himself in his shell' (Sarpong, 1989, p. 359). And when a seemingly weak or powerless person cannot be harmed by a powerful person, this proverb is cited: 'The leopard prowls through the forest in vain, [for] the tortoise is the owner of the forest [because it walks freely through the forest without fear of the leopard of whom many animals are terror-stricken]' (Opoku, 1997, p. 128).

Two crocodiles with a common stomach, often referred to as the Siamese Crocodiles, is the Akan symbol for society. The saying that goes with the symbol is that although the two crocodiles have a common stomach, they tend to fight over food, as if the food were going into different stomachs, indicating the futility of social conflicts. Human society is made up of individuals with different tastes and desires, hence the two heads and two tails of the crocodiles. Common observation shows that the conflicts arising in society are largely due to the individuality of its members. But the symbol takes the observer beyond the individuality of members of society to point

Illustration 22.1   Funtummireku:
The two-headed crocodile

out the common stomach shared by the crocodiles. Members of society have something in common that sustains them all; the interest of members of society is convergent rather than divergent and the cooperation of each member of society ensures the prosperity of all.

Water and rain are symbols of peace and when droughts inflict harshness, excessive heat and hunger, people await the soothing presence of rain and the restoration of the parched earth to life again. Particularly the ability of water to quench fire, the symbol of danger, violence and intense heat, is regarded as its sacred attribute. A Yoruba incantation to effect healing puts it thus:

> Water quenches fire,
> Fire does not quench water.
> No fire traces the course of a river,
> Any fire that dares trace the course of the river,
> It will be quenched completely. (Murphy and Sanford, 2001, p. 199)

Heavenly bodies, especially the moon and the stars, provide salutary and instructive lessons in peaceful living, constancy, fidelity, loyalty and guileless trust. Seeing the moon and the stars always going together, the ancestors of the Akan considered them as a married couple, and their example worthy of emulation in human society. They gave the name *Kyeye pe aware* to the symbol of the moon and the star, and it stood for the encouragement to learn from the enduring togetherness of the moon and the star, which – like marriage – is based on trust, love, kindliness and compassion. The cultivation of these values, it is believed, will lead to the creation of a harmonious and peaceful society that duplicates the harmony of the heavenly bodies.

Illustration 22.2   Osrane Ne Nsoromma:
The moon and the star

Illustration 22.3   Ese Ne Tekrema:
The teeth and the tongue

The human body provided many lessons and out of this came the symbol of the teeth and the tongue. The symbol states: if the teeth, which are sharp, are able to live peacefully with the tongue, which is very soft (how often does a person bite his/her tongue?), then all of us must learn to live together harmoniously in society in spite of our differences (Opoku, 1997, p. 117). The upper and lower lips also provide a lesson in cooperation, which leads to peace and the achievement of tasks whose completion would otherwise be difficult but which become achievable because of cooperation. This idea is expressed by the proverb: 'If anyone thinks that cooperating with each other is not useful, let him/her hold his/her upper lip, and see whether the lower lip alone can speak.'

Illustration 22.4   Obi Nka Bi:
Do not bite one another

The symbol, *Obi Nka Bi*, one does not bite one another, expresses the value of peaceful and harmonious living among human beings in society. The symbol is sometimes made up of three fishes, each with the tail in each other's mouth, and it suggests that people in society are all intimately connected with each other and one must not bite or hit the other just because their two bodies happen to touch each other. The symbol goes on to suggest that every person must be respected as an individual and protected from harm. Individual integrity, respect for the individual person and his or her body are an important cornerstone for peaceful, societal living and no one should be used as a means for the satisfaction of the unbridled appetite of others.

Peace and proverbs

In the proverbial lore of Africa, ideas about peace are embedded. Making or searching for peace is not a sign of cowardice, and the Ibo say: 'If a person loves peace, it does not make him/her a coward' (Ibekwe, 1998, p. 141). It is within an atmosphere of peace that the fullness of life can be achieved, hence a Swahili proverb says: 'It is better to build bridges than walls' (Ibekwe, 1998, p. 141). To avoid conflict, an effort must be made to take into account the interests and preferences of all and to make an effort to bring about peace, as a Malagasay proverb puts it: 'One does not like heat and the other does not like cold; make it tepid and still remain friends' (Ibekwe, 1998, p. 142). The commitment to peaceful living in society makes it obligatory for all members, as an Akan proverb puts it: 'When two people fight, the third one is the peacemaker' (Ibekwe, 1998, p. 141). And harmonious living in society is so important that it is considered wise to let go of personal grievances in the interest of future peace, as the Yoruba proverb states: 'If we do not forget yesterday's quarrels, we will not have somebody to play with tomorrow.'

The acknowledgment of the fact that all people have equal social, economic and political rights, a fundamental recognition that leads to peace in human societies, finds expression in the Akan proverb: 'When the parrot eats, the toucan also eats [some of the food]' (Opoku, 1997, p. 103). This basic sense of egalitarianism also characterizes Ibo social relations as Achebe (1994) writes in his novel *Things Fall Apart*: 'We shall all live. We pray for life, children, a good harvest and happiness. You will have what is good for you and I will have what is good for me. Let the kite perch and let the eagle perch too. If one says no to the other, let his wing break' (Achebe, 1994, p. 19). Peace and justice are inseparable, indeed justice creates peace for its absence leads to an irreconcilable breach of peace; and the person who wants peace must not trample on other people's rights, as the Akan proverb puts it: 'If you trample on another person's property in looking for your own, you will never find your own' (Opoku, 1975, p. 26).

Peace and African traditional religion

Traditional religion is an integral part of African life that links every aspect of life into a coherent system of thought and action and gives poignant significance and meaning to life. It links human beings with each other and with the spirit world – the Supreme Being, Ancestors and Divinities, as well as with nature. This linkage brings about harmony, equilibrium and peace which are believed to originate from the Creator, and which African traditional religion strives to uphold. It draws its strength and orientation from African wisdom by not laying claim to absoluteness or universality, by recognizing that truth is not an exclusive possession already in human hands, rather as the proverb says: 'Truth is like a baobab tree, and one person's arms cannot embrace it.' Truth is not within the grasp of one religious tradition alone, but if we are to succeed in surrounding the baobab tree of truth, we virtually have to hold hands. This insight leads to openness towards other religions, an attitude that leads to peace instead of conflict, and the avoidance of costly and disastrous inter-religious conflicts.

African traditional religion has put several rituals in place for ensuring that life at its best, that is in peace, can be attained here on earth and that a person can receive the tangible blessings of the supernatural in the form of a good life and a good death and an eventual return to life.

Through prayers, sacrifices and offerings, which are means of communication, human beings can remain in harmony with the spirit world. But human misconduct can also attract the punishment of the spirits, and so sacrifices give the community a way of making peace with the spirits to ensure that harmony and peace may prevail. It is believed that suicide or the spilling of human blood on the soil defiles *Mother Earth* and that the consequences of such defilement goes beyond the offender to affect the entire community. In such instances, sacrifices of appeasement are performed to restore normal relations between the people and *Mother Earth*, so that peace may prevail. Other ways of relating to the earth include not tilling the soil on certain days of the week and observing periods of peace before the farming season to honor *Mother Earth*. During this period, people are expected to live so peacefully with each other to the extent that a harsh word to a neighbor is a dreadful and unpardonable violation of a sacred custom. When this happens, sacrifices are made to appease the spirit of the earth in order to restore peaceful and harmonious relations with the people; and when this happens, *Mother Earth* will bless the crops during the farming season.

Many festivals whose basic rationale is a quest for peace are celebrated in African societies. These festivals bring the people and the spirits together and also strengthen social bonds. Some festivals, such as the Akan *Odwira* festival, cleanse the people and the community from the stains and pollutions of the past year as they usher in the New Year. The reason for the celebration of the *Apo* festival in the Brong Ahafo region of Ghana is given by an informant:

> You know that everyone has a *sunsum* (soul) that may get hurt or knocked about or become sick, and so make the body ill. Very often, although there may be other causes, e.g. witchcraft, ill health is caused by the evil and hate that another has in his head against you. Again, you too may have hatred in your head against another, because of something that person has done to you, and that, too, causes your *sunsum* to fret and become sick. Our forbears knew this to be the case, and so they ordained a time, once every year, when every man and woman, free man and slave, should have freedom to speak out just what was in their head, to tell their neighbours just what they thought of them, and of their actions, and not only their neighbours, but also the king and chief. When a man has spoken freely thus, he will feel his *sunsum* cool and quieted, and the *sunsum* of the other person against whom he has now openly spoken will be quieted also. (Opoku, 1978, p. 97)

The festival creates peace among the people when everyone in the community is regenerated once a year and community life is characterized by a series of regenerative rituals that keep peace both at the individual and the community levels.

A peace ritual, *Asafosa* (Communal Drink), preceding the annual *Ohum* festival of the people of Mamfe in the Akuapem District in the Eastern Region of Ghana, ensures that the community is at peace before the celebration of the festival. Before the festival, every attempt is made to resolve all outstanding disputes between individuals in the families as well as any others relating to other clans. After this, each head of household sends a pot of palm wine that is poured into a big pot in the chief's palace. After all the households have sent their pots of palm wine, the entire community gathers to drink from the common pot. This ensures that the people are united and are at peace with each other before the celebration of the annual *Ohum* festival to thank the ancestors and divinities and renew the balanced relationships among the people and between the people and their spiritual counterparts.

Peace and the indigenous African judicial system

An Akan proverb says: 'Conflicts are resolved best with the tongue and not with an axe' (Opoku, 2005, p. 14). This principle underlies the traditional African emphasis on the resolution of conflicts through peaceful rather than forceful or violent means, in order to promote social harmony and peace. And, from the level of the family to that of society, those charged with the task of the resolution of conflicts, who are considered to be impartial and fair in their dealings – elders, family heads, chiefs and rulers – endeavor to use persuasion, discussion and established procedures for settling cases instead of force. Traditional courts, charged with the task of settling disputes, maintained this principle and they functioned to reconcile the aggrieved parties with the aim of ensuring or restoring good and harmonious relations in society. Punishment is given, but its limitation of not being able to solely create social harmony is countered by other more effective means.

It is no wonder that in the modern nation of post-apartheid South Africa, this traditional African principle undergirded the establishment of the Truth and Reconciliation Commission. The Commission, in adherence to African traditions of reconciling disputing parties in arbitration procedures instead of administering punishment, was bent on healing the reeking wounds of the society so that all people could live harmoniously in a new nation, rather than merely administering punishment to the perpetrators of apartheid. The Truth and Reconciliation Commission has had its problems and its deliberations and decisions have not been without criticism, but its total orientation of pursuing justice with a much broader objective – that of achieving social harmony by the attempt that it hoped would reconcile the people of the nation, is truly in line with the African search for peace.

Conclusion

The quest for peace in its multifarious dimensions in African societies, as discussed above, does not mean that conflicts and wars did not occur in the past or in the present; nor does the discussion portray African societies as havens of peace. On the contrary, Africans searched for peace because they understood that conflicts, disputes and misunderstandings were very much part of the human experience and they therefore had to employ all the resources at their disposal to effectively deal with them. They used their community life, traditional education, symbols and art, proverbs, traditional religion, jurisprudential traditions and other means to express their understanding of and desire for peace. All these means have yielded a vast array of extensive knowledge about peace in African societies; but the distance between knowledge and praxis is long and arduous, as human experience everywhere attests, and it takes an undaunted will to travel it. Catholic Archbishop Peter Sarpong wrote: 'If the question is asked: Why, in view of this impressive system of moral values, Africans can still do wrong and, indeed, fight among themselves, the answer is that in the realm of moral value, more than anywhere else, mere knowledge is not power' (Sarpong, 1989, p. 365).

Peace in African societies is regarded as the good *sans pareil* in life for human beings and the African ideas of peace cannot be overlooked in any discussion of world peace, as our ancestors advised us: 'Hunt in every forest, for there is wisdom and good hunting in all of them.'

Note

1. The Gikuyu form the largest ethnical group in Kenya.

Reference list

Achebe, C. (1994) *Things Fall Apart* (New York: Anchor Books).

Busia, K.A. (1968) *The Position of the Chief in the Modern Political System of Ashanti* (London: Frank Cass & Co. Ltd.).

Ibekwe, P. (1998) *Wit and Wisdom of Africa: Proverbs from Africa and the Caribbean* (Trenton, NJ: Africa World Press).

Laye, C. (1954) *The Dark Child: The Autobiography of an African Boy* (New York: Hill and Wang).

Malidoma, P.S. (1994) *Of Water and the Spirit: Ritual, Magic and Initiation in the Life of an African Shaman* (New York: Penguin/Arkana).

Mbiti, J.S. (1975) *The Prayers of African Religion* (London: Society for Promoting Christian Knowledge).

Murphy, J.M. and M.M. Sanford (eds.) (2001) *Oshun across the Waters: A Yoruba Goddess in Africa and the Americas* (Bloomington: Indiana University Press).

Opoku, K.A. (1975) *Speak to the Winds: Proverbs from Africa* (New York: Lothrop, Lee and Shepard Co.).

Opoku, K.A. (1978) *West African Traditional Religion* (Singapore and Accra: Far Eastern Publishers).

Opoku, K.A. (1997) *Hearing and Keeping* (Pretoria: UNISA Press).

Opoku, K.A. (2005) 'Introduction' in J. Halperin and H. Ucko (eds.) *Worlds of Memory and Wisdom: Encounters of Jews and African Christians* (Geneva: World Council of Churches).

Sarpong, P. (1989) 'African Traditional Religion and Peace (with Special Reference to Ashanti),' *Studia Missionalia*, 38, 351–370.

23
T'ùmmu: An East African Perspective

Belachew Gebrewold

> Mannu manna ihanohu manninet. A person becomes person through fellow persons.
>
> Kambaata aphorism

Introduction

The peace concept of the Kambaata is characterized by ecological and sociological necessities and facts. This chapter tries to show that the concept, etymology and context of peace in Kambaata culture are influenced by their cosmological (holistic) understanding. What is the term 'peace' used for, in which context and for what aim? How is peace feasible and what is the role of the individual and the community in making peace? These questions help us to understand the meaning and the socio-political relevance of peace in the Kambaata culture.

This chapter attempts to discuss the Kambaata understanding of peace. My main method of analysis is discussing the etymology of peace. However, I do not claim that my analysis of the Kambaata concept of peace is *the* most comprehensive analysis. Given that so far nothing has been written in this field on the Kambaata culture, this is the first attempt to introduce the Kambaata peace concept academically. My aim is not to idealize the Kambaata culture as a peaceful and harmonious one. For example, the low social status of women, potters, tanners, smiths and the slave-holding tradition* of the Kambaata shows us that there are social groups that are marginalized, although the Kambaata culture consists of very interesting concepts of peace in a holistic way. Notwithstanding all these social injustices and cultural shortcomings, the focus of this chapter is to discuss how the Kambaata without any written constitution deal with their conflicts, what their peacemaking process looks like and why the process is more efficient for them rather than one which is a 'modern' state with

---

* Ed. For more information on slavery and peace in Africa, see Chapter 24 by Amadou Lamine Sarr.

its own written constitution. This is a key problem in the modern project of state building. Different peoples with different understandings of peace are 'pathologically homogenized' (Rae, 2002) in the state-building project. The Ethiopian state, which consists of about eighty-five cultural and ethnic groups, is in the process of modernization, which means the formation of a political structure according to Western cultural patterns. One of these cultural elements is the concept of peace, which is being universalized all over the world because it is considered the most efficient one. But on the local level its universalizability is not that self-evident. In spite of various attempts by the central government and its political elites, traditional cultures like the Kambaata keep to their methods of dealing with conflicts. This means that there exist two political cultures side by side: the formal 'modern' one and the informal 'traditional' one. Since the Kambaata concept of peace is part of the whole culture structure (political, economic, social, religious), the task of peacemaking is the duty of the communities, not of the political elites or political professionals.

According to the Kambaata, peace and politics are the way of life of the people, which rules out alienation of peace and *professionalization* of politics. When politics is a construct of the elites, it becomes professionalized and peace is alienated from the people; it ceases to be the way of life and people become mere consumers of peace, which is hammered out by politicians or experts. Ultimately, it becomes security rather than peace.

What is politics? In the Western or Westernized world the creation of centralized authority, representative democracy, state building, power monopoly, separation of legislative, executive and judiciary authorities, etc. led to the *professionalization* of politics. Through modernization, politics began to be professionalized. Politics became a profession like any other, run and manipulated by 'experts,' and in extreme cases resulting in violence and war. The socio-cultural setting of peace, according to the Kambaata, de-professionalizes the concept and the process of peace, as the etymology of peace shows us in this short analysis of the peace philosophy of the Kambaata.

The Kambaata etymology of peace

Peace is called *t'ùmmu* in Kambaata language. There is an etymological and phonological relationship between *tùmmu* (peace), *tùmu* (good, well, kind, generous) and *tùmat* (goodness, justice). *Tùmmu* is not only absence of conflict (in a political sense). *Tùmmu* is also something economic and sociological. Scarcity of livelihood, death of a relative, of a neighbor can be considered as some kind of absence of peace. Therefore, peace does not only mean absence of conflict but also of everything that disturbs the life of human beings. The shortage of cattle fodder is absence of peace, likewise a conflict between two individuals.

The opposite of peace could be helpful to understand the meaning and context of peace in the Kambaata culture and language. The only political and military concept of absence of peace (war) is called *òlu*, whereas conflict is called *ba'ànchu* or *ba'ànchat*. Etymologically, it is derived from the verb *bà'u*, which means 'not to be' or 'to cease to be.' This implies not only the non-existence of peace, but also the disorientation of the individual as well as of the community. The concrete manifestation of this *bà'u* is called *hàwu*. *Hàwu* (suffering) is the summary of all that disturbs the social, economic and political order such as the consequences of war, drought, poverty and other calamities. *Hàwu* means literally to suffer or suffering. As *hàwu* is the summary of all that is bad, *t'ùmmu* is the summary of everything that is good. Therefore, peace is not only the absence of war or a micro- or macro-sociological disagreement. It is rather a socio-political functioning of the society of the Kambaata. In my opinion, this is the reason why the language of the Kambaata has the same etymological background for substantive *t'ùmmu* (peace) and adjective *t'ùmu* (good, kind, well).

Socio-cultural settings of peace

There are two major ways of maintaining or creating peace: through greetings and feasts. In the Kambaata language to greet is called *t'ùmmisu*. It is derived from *t'ùmmu* (peace) and literally means to pacify. Hence, to greet means to pacify. This means any greetings are acts of pacification. Why?

To greet a guest* means to maintain and declare the good relationship between the guest and the host and to renew the covenant of peace (continuous pacification). Not to greet means to declare the non-existent relationship between the individuals and/or the groups, or it means to point to the obliterated good relationship between the individuals and/or groups. Moreover, *t'ùmmisu* points out that there is a hidden conflict potentiality between the guest and the host. Therefore, this potential conflict has to be transformed by *t'ùmmisu*. To greet means, hence, to renew and maintain the covenant of peace. The word guest (*koichu*) itself has two different meanings: something that is new and someone who comes to visit relatives or friends. To greet means, therefore, to remind one of the possibility of non-peace (entailed in something new and unusual) on the one hand, and to transform the distance between the guest and the host on the other hand.

The process of maintaining and creating peace through feasts makes it an important aspect of social life. Peace as pacification is a ritual act. Even the greeting itself has a ritual significance. It is the re-actualization of the former peaceful atmosphere. Re-actualization means temporal re-presentation of a happening. It is a temporal transcendence or transformation that interlinks the

---

*   Ed. On the same issue of hospitality, see also Chapter 22 by Kofi Asare Opoku.

temporal sequences as one and the same. Re-actualization or re-presentation aims at continuously remembering the unwritten religious and cultural covenant that connects generations. The covenant is manifested by daily acts that remind us of the togetherness of the members of the cultural group.

According to the Kambaata culture, the coffee ceremony, the birth of a child, circumcision, wedding, heavy sickness or funeral ceremonies have a strong significance in relation to peace. All these events result in the coming together of friends, neighbors and relatives. The degree of participation in these events has direct proportionality to the intensity of friendship, kinship and neighborhood. This means that peace depends on the active material and immaterial participation in and sharing of the joys and sorrows of the individuals and groups (Stanley, 1970, p. 220). This is especially important because the economic or environmental hardships of the Kambaata make the interdependence absolutely important. However, this interdependence has to be demonstrated. Through active participation during the time of needs, such as by helping neighbors or relatives during big feasts or in death by bringing firewood, fetching water, pitching a tent for the guests or coming from distant places, the intensity of community participation is demonstrated.

This is the only social security of the Kambaata. To be for the Kambaata means to remain part of the community. However, the objective of being in the community as part of the community is not only because there is no alternative system of social security. It is not only because of the material instrumental rationality that Kambaata emphasize the importance of being in the community. Even if someone has all necessary material wealth to be self-sufficient, she is not a complete human being as long as she is not an active actor of the cultural rituals within the community. To be means to be in the community and to be in the community to be in peace.

As we have seen above, peace presupposes being in the community. Even the so-called *internal peace* of the individual is dependent on the social members. However, no peace can be possible if it is taken out of the ecological context. This becomes obvious in the way of greeting of the Kambaata. The Kambaata greet interrogatively, saying: *'baadu t'ùmman?'* Baadu literally means country, village, area, people. The interrogative greeting is saying: Are you all peaceful? The 'all' here not only means those present or the relatives of the greeted person, but also all that makes the person. This includes the neighbors, relatives, cattle, the peace of land, farm or harvest. Even if the person addressed is only one person, the questioning greetings are addressed to many people and beings that are not present during the greetings. The being and becoming of the greeted depends on the situation of the cattle, harvest, farm, etc.; this means the whole environment and living beings. For example, another interrogative greeting implying these aspects is *irù tumman* (is the piece of land, region peaceful?), *bòku t'ùmman* (is the village, kinship peaceful?), etc. The word *t'ùmmu* is used here to inquire about the state (*goodness, wellness – t'ùmat*) of the subject and everything that belongs to it. The inquiry is about the peacefulness of the greeted person as well as those beings that enable the peace of the greeted person. 'Peacefulness' does not imply the opposite of aggressiveness or alike, instead the integrity of that person as well as of those beings which the being and becoming of the greeted person depend on.

Hence, peace means social, economic and psychological wellness and integrity of the human, spiritual and ecological environment that human beings are dependent on. This means that the ecological and sociological facts are essential parts of the interpersonal greetings. But this is not enough if the spiritual world is not integrated and re-actualized as an acting agent on the being and becoming of human beings, on their material possessions and on the environment. In other words, the peace (*tummù*) of the individual is dependent on the *t'ùmat* (*kindness, wellness* and *goodness*) of the society, spiritual world and environment and on their *t'ùmu* (undisturbed, good, kind, just, well) attitude. This holistic approach is based on justice towards the co-humans, environment and the spiritual beings; and there is no peace without justice.

Peace as justice

We have seen above that *tùmat* is translated as kindness, wellness and goodness. If, however, the being and becoming of the human being is dependent on the community, as the aphorism (*mannu manna ihanohu manninet*) shows us, peace presupposes justice towards the community. Further, the peace, being and becoming of the individual as well as of the community depend on the justice towards the spiritual world and the environment, this is why the Kambaata concept of justice is related to *t'ùmat*, which etymologically derives from *tummu*, which means peace. However, justice entails two concepts with two different etymological origins. First, as we have seen so far the concept of justice (*tùmat*) derives from *tummu* (peace). The second concept of justice as truth derives from the verb *gàru*; its abstract form is *gàrit*, which means truth, justice and right. *Gàru*, in its simplest translation, means, first, to win a competition, second, to convince someone in an argument. Hence, *gàrit* means: possession of truth, defending the right, defending justice.

Peace in the context of justice implies one important cultural setting. In the predominantly agricultural society and culture of the Kambaata, embedding peace in the cultural institutions is a very important aspect of guaranteeing the peaceful coexistence of the social members. As I have hinted in the introduction, Kambaata is a highly populated agricultural society. The piece of land for growing crops is demarcated by certain symbols such as shrub or trees. The symbol of demarcation is called *gabala*. *Gabala* means delimitation as well as demarcation. *Gabala* is delimitation in the theoretical or abstract sense, and it is demarcation in the sense of positive (given, real) boundaries. *Gabala*, taken from this material world (economic context) is applied to the immaterial abstraction of cultural institutionalization. In the ceremonies of peacemaking, therefore, the expression *gabala higissot* (do not trespass the boundary) is one of the common expressions which the peace facilitating eldest of the village utter. The *gabala* as boundary demarcation or delimitation is not necessarily meant in the context of territorial delimitation and demarcation, but in the ideational or institutional abstraction. Therefore, for the Kambaata, peace depends on the maintenance of the delimitation of their cultural institutions that comprise justice, right and truth of the community, surrounding nature, spiritual world.

T'ùmat as justice has two judicial connotations: the *benevolence* of nature and of society (rewarding for the compliance with nature and society); and the *punishing justice* for misdeeds and violating the rights of the others (like Nemesis, Goddess of the punishing justice, in Greek mythology). The twofold nature of the same *t'ùmat* is manifested in the acts of blessings and curses. In blessing rituals of the Kambaata, for example, the blessing statement *t'ùmat kesaan ikku* or *t'ùmat korabbohe* (may the *t'ùmat* be with you, may the *t'ùmat* protect you) the rewarding nature of the *t'ùmat* (justice) is at work; whereas in the curse *t'ùmat tuddohe* (literally: may *t'ùmat* look at you and judge you) the goodness/justice manifests its punishing nature – because someone did not comply with the norms and expectations of nature and community. For the Kambaata peace is not just a state of being and living without hostilities, instead it is a procreating power. It is an abstraction of the power emanating from the nature, human community and the spiritual world. Because of this creative power, peace is a real being. Peace is something that works, creates and strengthens the community and enables the growth of the person. Peace can go away as well as come back, die as well as create, can be given to as well as taken away. This depends on the degree of the individuals' participation in the comprehensive community (human beings, nature and spiritual world). For the Kambaata the concept of justice emerges from this ambivalent nature of peace.

Above we mentioned that *tùmat* could be understood as justice in the form of Nemesis. I tried to show that justice is intrinsically connected to right and truth. According to the 'modern' interpretation of 'right' and 'truth,' one would say that if there is justice in a community every member of the community is supposed to have the same 'amount' of 'right,' and 'truth' should be absolutely independent of the social status of the individual. The Kambaata understanding of right and justice differs considerably from this modern concept of justice and truth. The degree of justice and right depends on the social status (age, gender, clan). According to the cultural institution of the Kambaata, for example, the fact that children, women or those from lower clan status have a relatively less 'portion' of right and justice does not mean that they are disadvantaged. Justice in this context does not mean that each individual is entitled equally to all material and immaterial goods of the society; instead, each individual gets them according to its social status. Even the spiritual power is distributed according to this social status. Eye, for example, is one of the main sources of spiritual power, especially regarding the punishing aspect of justice. The eye of an adolescent has more spiritual power than the eye of a child. Furthermore, even among the elderly people, the eye of the eldest has more power than those of the younger ones, even if all of them are adolescent. Old age is directly proportional to the spiritual power of the individual. The claim for a bigger portion of justice and right is substantiated by age. Peacefully living together is based not on the objectively equal distribution of justice, but because it is proportionally equal.

For example, regarding the punishing nature of justice (*t'ùmat*), to look at someone means to exert power on her/him. This is why according to the Kambaata culture, during a conversation, the younger partners of the discussion are not allowed to look at the eyes of the elders; otherwise this would contradict the socio-cultural hierarchy. According to this cultural understanding, eyes are the source of the good as well as of the evil. The eyes of the elders can yield more good or evil than those of the younger ones. The elders as full members of the community have a legitimate authority, and because of their maturity in the community they have a special relationship with spirits that grant them this authority.

As already mentioned above, the environment or nature is an important aspect of the being and becoming of the individual. The being and becoming of the person in the community depends on the nature that brings forth life and enables the reproduction of human beings. Moreover, the nature outside is the dwelling place of the spiritual worlds that play a decisive role in initiation of the youngsters, in the peacemaking, or other cultural rituals. This means the relation to nature implies the relationship to the spiritual beings and indirectly to the community itself. Even if the Kambaata have a proverb, *mannu manna ihanohu manninet* (a person becomes person through fellow persons) explicitly specifies the role of the community, it implicitly includes the ecological as well as spiritual world. To be means to be in the community. Accordingly, peace is the principle of being and becoming. Hence, peace means enabling the becoming of a person while the becoming and along with it the personality can be lost whenever the person loses communality.

The cultural embedment of peace is especially important for the Kambaata because of the peculiar political system and because of the comprehensive (cosmological) concept of peace that comprises the spiritual as well as the ecological world. This cosmological comprehensiveness is especially experienced when the Kambaata elders invoke the spirits of their ancestors during the peacemaking ceremonies. This invocation of the ancestral spirits makes it quite difficult for the conflicting parties not to accept the solutions proposed by the elders. The solutions are presented as the will of the ancestors to accept the suggestions to forgive and forget even the injustices done unto one or both parties. Not accepting the suggestions would mean violating the *gàrit* (right, truth and justice) of the spirits of the ancestors, which is called *ayyàna*. *Ayyàna* means fortune, spirit or feast. The basic concept of *ayyàna* is that the fortune of the individual is dependent on the spirit of the living and of the dead (the communal spirit) which is usually experienced during feasts. Through this communal *ayyàna*, the past (spirit of the dead) and the present are in the feasts of all community rituals. This getting together is the most important act of peacemaking.

In the community rituals, the exchange of greetings demonstrate the state of peace in the community. 'To greet' or *tùmmisu* for the Kambaata signifies temporal re-presentation of the communality founded on collective covenant whose aim is to point to the significance of peace for the future living together. Greetings and reconciliation ceremonies of the community renew the founding peace covenant to which everyone obeys through the active membership of the community.

The individual is not only a beneficiary of peace but also its actor and creator. This action and contribution depends not only on the physical participation of the individual. Even those who are not yet born have a very essential role in the creation and maintenance of peace. This becomes obvious when one observes some names of the Kambaata. The Kambaata give names to their children according to the respective sociological, ecological and economic state. Names are the abstraction of the personality and the role and position of the individual in the cosmos. Names that are related to peace are a good example of this. When a child is born at a time of peace agreement, it will be called: *T'ùmmebo* (boy) or *T'ùmmebe* (girl) which means you who brings peace; *T'ùmmiso* (boy) or *T'ùmmise* (girl) which means you who pacifies. These names are not randomly chosen. They are a living memory of the necessity of peace and its constitution (Braukämper, 1983, p. 227). This implies that according to the Kambaata cosmology the present is the meeting point of the past and of the future. The present is not only the product of the past happenings, of the spirits (*ayyàna*) of the ancestors and of the community, but also the *ayyàna* of the future and of the unborn, which plays a role in forming the present. The peace of the present is the product of the past and of the future. This cosmology of time and peace also has an impact on the political system of the Kambaata.

Peace as politics

Another very important aspect of peace in the Kamabata language and culture is its interdependence with the concept of politics. In the concept of the Kambaata politics is *gàltit*, which is the abstract form of the verb *gàlu*, which means to pass the night. It is interesting to see why the Kambaata analogize the terms *politics* and *passing-the-night*. Politics and peace are embedded here in the cosmological context. By keeping this cosmological context in mind, the Kambaata interrogatively greet in the morning as follows: *tùmma galténta?* Which means: did you spend the night peacefully? The sociological, economic and cosmological background of this question or way of greeting has the following reasons: it is during night that the thieves come and plunder; it is during night that wild animals threaten human beings; and it is during night that the evil spirits frighten the living.

To have not been confronted with these evil powers means to pass the night in peace. Therefore, every greeting is a question of the past, not a wish for the future. Only while departing do people wish each other a peaceful day or night.

Politics (*gàltit*) means the skill of human beings to effectively organize this collective 'passing-of-the-night.' The analogy of passing the night in the temporal sense means to overcome the socio-political dangers that destabilize the life of the individual as well as of the community. These dangers are inter-individual, intra-clan and inter-clan conflicts that obstruct the being and becoming of the individual and the peace of the community.

Politician (*gashánchu*) – derived from the verb stem *gàshu* – means *he* who enables the passing of the night. However, *gashánchu* is not the one who makes politics. He does not enact laws. He does not reward those who comply with, nor does he punish those who trespass. He just watches the transgression as well as the compliance. It is the task of the community itself to punish (through excommunication) or to reward (through inclusion of the social members into the community feasts, funerals, etc.). Therefore, the aim of politics is maintaining and making peace. This is why Kambaata conceive peace as a way of life of the community, not just as part of the political event.

All positive qualities such as good, kind, well, just (*tùmu*) are represented in peace (*t'ùmmu*). Peace is the state of creative action of these adjectives. When these adjectives are at work peace emerges as a communal dynamic power. When the Kambaata say *t'ùmmu daqansunne* (may peace bring us together), they wish each other a good and happy reencounter. *T'ùmmin mar* (go with/in peace) or *t'ùmmu qorabohe* (may peace protect you) means: may peace be your companion. This shows that peace is personified. It is not only a state of nonviolence or nothingness, but is a being, a personified or reified good. It is not a state wherein nothing happens. It is the state in which everything good happens, the religious rituals are performed, the joys and sorrows of neighbors, friends and relatives are shared.

According to the culture of the Kambaata, 'politics' is a way of life that comprises culture, politics and economics.

During a ceremonial chanting, which is called *gifata* (Yacob Arsano, 2002, p. 54), those who dance sing a verse '*Kambata galtit tummando?*' (Kambata, is *galtit* peaceful, safe?), or '... *beto galtit tummando?*' (son of...is *galtit* peaceful, safe?). In both cases *galtit* implies the state of the 'family,' 'cattle,' 'relatives,' 'agricultural products,' 'village,' 'hera' which is cultural, religious, political subdistrict, etc. It is interesting to see that just one word has so many different connotations. The idea behind this concept is to imply the cosmological comprehensiveness, the inter-connectedness of all material and immaterial, human and non-human worlds. This shows that politics, economics and culture are inseparably intermingled. Prosperity is possible only if there is peace, as a proverb says '*ollé tummin ozita itenno*' (literally: only if the village is peaceful, you can enjoy your meal, which means you can live in peace).

Proverbs and aphorisms convey an essential political concept of the Kambaata.* The aphorism *mannu manna ihanohu mannienet* (a human being becomes human being through fellow human beings), for example, is one of the most important political aphorisms. The word *ihanohu* ('that it becomes' derived from the verb *ihu* – to become) has a deep philosophical meaning. According to the Kambaata, a person is in the process of becoming as far as she is in the community. To exclude someone from the community or ostracize means to stop her becoming. If the intensity of the life of the community decreases, the 'humanness' of the human being decreases too. As Sundermeier witnesses, exactly the same aphorism is to be found in the Zulu language (Sundermeyer, 1988, p. 208).

Peace as security or way of life?

In the process of the so-called nation building, the collision of cultures within the state territory characterizes one of the central problems of colliding peace philosophies. This collision of philosophies is becoming obvious in the process of so-called modernization of the political systems through state building or nation building. In this process of homogenization of culture, 'out of practical reasons,' the modern culture is replacing the mosaic of cultures within the state territories that are agreed to be maintained since the decolonization era. The Kambaata culture within the Ethiopian state is a good example here.

Whereas according to the Kambaata peace is conceived as a culturally, religiously and ritually maintained way of life, the modern state system of Ethiopia understands peace and security as absence of war. In the current Ethiopian constitution – formed according to the concepts that prevail in the modernization process of state and politics – the nation is in peace when there is security. According to the Ethiopian constitution (Art. 26, 3) national security and public peace are interchangeable. In the same way the government, state and the law become the protectors of peace (Art. 27, 5; Art. 52, 2(g)). On the international level, the Ethiopian government conceives as its objective to seek and support peaceful solutions to international disputes (Art. 85, 6). In case of state of emergency, the Council of Ministers shall, in accordance with regulations it issues, have all necessary power to protect the country's peace and sovereignty,

---

*   Ed. Compare the proverbs in Chapter 22 by Kofi Asare Opoku.

and to maintain public security, law and order (Art. 93, 4(a)). According to this article of the Ethiopian Constitution, sovereignty, peace, security, law and order are guaranteed by the martial state, whereas the people are just passive consumers of this martial peace. They are not its active makers and bearers. Since the understanding of security is based on secret services, spies, police, military and martial coercion, which are decisive factors that try to balance power by deterrence and violence, peace is just a violent security and a suppressed war.

The New Shorter Oxford English Dictionary (1993) defines peace as 'freedom from, or cessation of, war or hostilities; or a state of a nation or community in which it is not at war with another. [...] Freedom from civil disorder, public order and security.' In the same way, the Western tradition of peace is reflected in the definition of peace in *The Oxford Companion to Politics of the World* (Krieger, 1993). In the international law that reflects the Western political tradition, peace is interpreted as the absence of warfare, i.e. organized violence, between groups defined by country, nation (culture, ethnicity, race, class or ideology) (Galtung, 1993). Further Johan Galtung (1993) says that, according to Western tradition 'international or external peace is the absence of external wars: inter-country, inter-state or intercultural. Social or internal peace is the absence of internal wars: ethnic, racial, class, or ideological groups challenging the central government, or such groups challenging each other.'

According to Art. 1.1 of the United Nations Charter, the purposes of the United Nations are among others: 'To maintain international peace and security, and to that end: to take effective collective measures for the prevention and removal of threats to the peace, and for the suppression of acts of aggression or other breaches of the peace.' Furthermore, international law becomes the guarantor of this peace. An important constituent element of international law is territorial integrity and sovereignty of the state. Sovereignty is a concept about the way of exercising political power. Further, sovereignty is associated with the notion of national interest, national independence, the capacity of the state to impose its will on its citizens as well as on other states, and national security (Camilleri and Falk, 1993, p. 11). This means that ultimately the state becomes the guarantor of peace. However, the state cannot guarantee peace without resorting to its various martial elements such as arms, police, military, spies, secret services, which can be subsumed as security or violent peace. Peace here becomes an artifact of martial experts. This is one of the striking differences between the Kambaata peace concept and the modern state's understanding of peace, which Ethiopians try to materialize in their attempt at state building.

In the Kambaata culture, peacemaking is accompanied by traditional and semi-religious rituals. In the peacemaking process, the living and the dead, the parties to the conflict as well as the whole inhabitants of a village are directly or indirectly involved in the peace as well as conflict process. Based on the cultural–philosophical principle of the Kambaata that 'human being becomes human being through fellow human beings,' a conflict is not a dissonance or violence just between two groups or individuals, instead it is a disturbance of cultural community including those who are not directly involved in the conflict. This is the main reason why any reconciliation process tries to involve as many members of the village or community during the peacemaking. At the end of the reconciliation process, all those who were present during the ceremony embrace each other, not just the main parties of the conflict. The central reason for this comprehensive reconciliation is that if there is a conflict in a community, there is always a danger to side with one or the other party. This would undermine the cultural order, which the Kambaata consider as the principle of their being and becoming. In the modern conflict resolution process (judicial system) in Kambaata introduced by the central state, however, the whole reconciliation process is reduced to arbitration and adjudication. Since the modern Ethiopian institutions of peacemaking lack the above-mentioned dimension of recon-ciliation, the Kambaata still prefer to solve their problems according to their traditional ceremonial procedures rather than through governmental institutions or court systems (Singer, 1980, pp. 546–547).

Any peacemaking process for the Kambaata happens from the background of cultural and social philosophy of being and becoming. Reconciliation between two individuals as conflict parties is a kind of renewal of the reconciliation process of the whole community or village. This means that what is being solved is not only a conflict between two individuals. The reconciliation process is at the same time a sign of warning to the whole community. This is especially relevant because the socio-economic situation obliges the Kambaata to value and cherish the importance of being in the group. For example, since the health centers are very far from most of the villages in the region, in the case of sickness the sick person will be carried to the health center by the male members of the village, whereas the women of the village prepare food for those carrying the sick and bring it to the family of the sick when the sick person is brought back from the health center. Almost all members of the village gather at the family of the sick person and chat. This coming together signifies the repeated renewal of their consciousness of belonging together. In the same way, burial ceremony, circumcision feast, wedding, harvest time and birth of a child have all decisive peacemaking relevance by bringing as many members as possible together. All these events intensify the sense of belongingness of the members by minimizing the chances for intra-group dissent.

Conclusion

Not only is the fact of peacemaking important for the Kambaata, but also how peace is made is decisive. Peace is a semi-religious ritual, a covenant. Through peace ceremony, the Kambaata come together, drink coffee, embrace each other, pray, etc. It is the combination of *tùmmu* (peace) and *tùmat* (kindness, goodness, wellness and justice) that guarantees the dynamic life of the individual and of the community by transcending the mere concept of peace as absence of war, which the modern state system is trying to guarantee. This demands, according to the Kambaata, not necessarily the so-called *pacta sunt servanda* (treaties must be observed). This concept of peace would make the treaties a kind of an isolated entity, which exists by itself. For the Kambaata, the community itself is the reification of the treaties. Therefore, for the Kambaata the best way of observing treaties is to be in the community. Moreover, instead of the Roman legacy of *si vis pacem, para bellum* (if you want peace, prepare for war),* the Kambaata political philosophy seems to maintain that *if you want peace, be in the community*. Of course the question is: What about the freedom of the individual in this very community-oriented society like the Kambaata? This question has to be answered within the general context of the social structure of the Kambaata.

Without idealizing the Kambaata cultural understanding of peace, the impacts of cultural globalization and the challenges of the modernization process to the Kambaata culture have to be underlined. In the face of cultural globalization and homogenization, many traditional societies like the Kambaata are submerging into a cultural inferiority complex. They know that their cultural values would not be considered to contribute to the global culture. But the painful experience for them is that what they have believed so far as a sign of cultural identity and pillar of peaceful living together is being discarded by modern cultural and political understanding. They are losing their confidence in their own cultural and political initiatives in the comprehensive cosmological setting. There cannot be global peace if the global peaces are not given due consideration and respect. This is a global learning process.

Reference list

Arsano, Y. (2002) '*Seera*: A Traditional Institution of Kambata' in B. Zewde and S. Pausewang (eds.) *Ethiopia: The Challenge of Democracy from Below* (Uppsala/Addis Ababa: Nordiska Afrikainstitutet/Forum for Social Studies).

Braukämper, U. (1983) *Die Kambata. Geschichte und Gesellschaft eines südäthiopischen Bauernvolkes* (Wiesbaden: F. Steiner Verlag).

Camilleri, J.A. and J. Falk (1993) *The End of Sovereignty? The Politics of a Shrinking and Fragmenting World* (Aldershot: Elgar).

Galtung, J. (1993) 'Peace' in J. Krieger et al. (eds.) *The Oxford Companion to Politics of the World* (New York: Oxford University Press), 688–689.

Krieger, J. (1993) (ed.) *The Oxford Companion to Politics of the World* (New York: Oxford University Press).

* Ed. Regarding this notion of peace, see also Chapter 2 by Karlheinz Koppe.

Singer, N. (1980) 'The Relevance of Traditional Legal Systems to Modernisation and Reform: A Consideration of Legal Structure' in J. Tubiana (ed.) *L'Éthiopie modern: De l'avènement de Ménélik II à nos jours* (Addis Abeba).

Rae, H. (2002) *State Identities and the Homogenisation of Peoples* (Cambridge: Cambridge University Press).

Stanley, S. (1970) 'The Political System of Sidama,' *Proceedings of the Third International Conference of Ethiopian Studies*, 3 (Addis Abeba).

Sundermeier, T. (1988) *Nur gemeinsam können wir überleben* (Gütersloh: Gütersloher Verlagshaus).

24
African *Salaam*

Amadou Lamine Sarr

I proclaim: only through peace is it possible
to uphold religion, human dignity
and also the ideal of tolerance.

El Hadj Omar Tall

Introduction

Without doubt, Islam has currently become an explosive topic. At least since 2001, the Islamic religion has fallen into such disrepute that it is almost impossible to engage with it without offending somebody's feelings. Terms like violence and terror are associated with Islam without differentiation. Nevertheless, just for this very reason it should be a concern for all of us to deal with this explosive package of problems. The main focus of this chapter will be centered on Islam in Western Africa and especially in Senegal. Already during the tenth century, in the wake of Islamic expansion, African societies got in contact with the religion of the Prophet Mohammed. This was the beginning of the process of Islamization, which was completed in some regions already before the beginning of the European politics of domination on the continent. Although Islam had become a religious, economic and social as well as political factor in Africa during the course of more than ten centuries, it still remains for the most part neglected in research and news.[1]

Humanity is currently living through a unique phase of development in the field of technology. The media possess capacities for broadcasting unknown to the world before. Due to the high intensity and regularity of reports, we receive information about disasters from all regions of the world, information that we can no longer even 'digest.' This feeling of powerlessness surfaces each time pictures of attacks with exploding vehicles and dead bodies lying around flicker through the screens. For viewers and outsiders it is not always easy to understand the manifestations of violence transported by suicide commandos in the 'right' way. In this plethora of events, Islam and the whole Arabic world take up an impressive amount of space. Islam, Iraq, Saddam Hussein, Al-Qaeda and, most recently, terrorism have become the most used words in Western societies since the fall of the Berlin Wall. In fact, this gives the appearance of two completely different cultural concepts clashing with full force. When on September 11, 2001 two passenger airplanes exploded in the towers of the World Trade Center in New York and caused the death of more than 2000 people, the high point of a seemingly 'Islamic' terrorism was reached. It seems as if the attack on American soil constitutes the attempt to violently create an anti-pole against the Occident.

When Samir Amin points out that the hostile reaction of some Islamists towards the Western world might be related to the effects of capitalism, he so affiliates himself with a widely held opinion in many Asiatic and African countries. He formulated this hypothesis already before 9/11, and seems to have interpreted the political situation correctly:

Il nous paraît réaliste de partir de cette constatation crue que le développement capitaliste et la conquête impérialiste ont créé la situation que nous vivons. Qu'on le veuille ou non les problèmes qui se posent à nous sont ceux que ce développement a engenders. (Amin, 1986, p. 326)

As regards a renaissance of fundamentalism in relation to problems, Samir Amin speaks about an answer to the US hegemonic politics and about a fundamentalist renaissance in relation to problems and options of our time. Questions that thus invariably emerge are: Based on which questioning do fundamentalists act and at which kind of societal formations do they aim? In the opinion of this author, fundamentalists do not allow for an economic–political debate, because they remain fixed in their much simpler but nevertheless rigid point of view. In their perception, the whole Islamic world is faced with a choice: an Islamic society or a non-Islamic society.

What can be deduced is that the fundamentalists' actual goal consists of ousting from the Islamic world all influences coming from non-Islamic societies and, in particular, from the capitalist and materialist West. This should be achieved through all means necessary and – in the last instance – also through acts of violence. Such a belligerent and uncompromising stance has become manifest since the 1980s.[2] Thus, the world public is continually confronted with the religious doctrine of *Jihadism*, a phenomenon that rests on strict principles and the use of violence, but also has eschatological tendencies.

Are the means they choose legitimate and adequate for the political battle? Can those means be matched with the Islamic understanding of peace or, rather, with the different traditions of peace within Islamic societies? The problem of representativeness furthermore highlights a valid question: In the name of whose Islam are the 'acts of resistance' carried out? This is a particularly important question since the Islamic world under no circumstances must be reduced to only the Arabic area.*

Arabic expansion and the spread of Islam in Africa

The point of departure for the Islamic expansion in Africa was Egypt. After the Muslim Arabs had conquered Persia and Syria, between 639 and 642, they invaded Egypt in order to use it as staging ground for entering northern Africa. This first phase of conquest ended with the death of the Caliph Utman and the resulting civil war between Mu'awiyas and the followers of Ali. Only in 661 could the politics of territorial expansion be resumed under Mu'awiyas rule, after the Umayyad dynasty had taken over power. This second wave of conquest ended with the integration of the Maghreb into the Arabic realm and the occupation of Spain.[3]

The Arabs were so able to build a mighty empire about a century after the death of the Prophet Mohamed. As already mentioned, Africa was thus not 'spared' from the Islamic campaigns. In the north of the continent, the Arabs first had to finish the process of conversion of the Berber people, before a further expansion of the new religion could be conducted south of the Sahara.[4]

Although Islam is carried by a strong sense of mission, it is not certain that the conversion of western African societies was the result of wars of conquest. The development of the first conversions should much rather be related to the close connections between Islam and trade in the southern Sahara. It is known that the most dynamic trading peoples like the *Dioula*, *Hawsa* or *Dyakhanke* let themselves be converted fairly soon. It can be assumed that the traditional commercial spirit of those societies made it possible to establish contact without many problems. The reason could be common commercial interests, especially since Arabian traders are considered canny and effective precursors of Islam. Ivan Hrbek (1990) relates the process of missionizing with economic and social factors and points towards the important role of the economy for the Islamic history of origin and development.[5] Very often, the combination trade/Islam was so interconnected that both concepts seemed to be synonymous:

> Ainsi l'Islam apparut-il tout d'abord non comme une frontière mouvante de conversion des masses dans une zone continue, mais plutôt comme une série d'enclaves urbaines dans les centres de commerce et de pouvoir politique, tandis que les populations rurales étaient peu touchées. Ces établissements, le long des routes commerciales et dans les grands centres urbains, devaient constituer les bases de la propagation future de l'Islam. (Hrbek, 1990, p. 97)

* Ed. For a discussion on a different Islamic group, the Alevites, see Chapter 10 by Alev Çakır.

However, the importance of traders within the process of Islamization has to be seen within a general context. They were actors focused on economic matters, who had to pay attention to their own businesses. Although they played a decisive role in the process of conversion, due to their specific interests they still had their own priorities, which barely allowed them to take over a complete missionizing function. Thus, they had to leave this role to other scholars of Islam.

The real missionizing work was carried out by the *Marabouts* who, in contrast to the traders, added more weight to the religious aspects. They were *professional missionaries* whose main function consisted of bringing Islam to other peoples. The new religion so reached the African traders first, but subsequently already came to the leading strata and thus the sovereigns and courtesans. The Muslim annalists themselves might have interpreted this phase as a success, since it is only from this time that they started to document in more detail the process of Islamization in the ruling families and aristocracies. So far the assumption is justified, that the Arabian annalists had counted on a faster and more continuous spread of Islam; even more so as the conversion of a ruler to Islam could foster greater acceptance of the new religion also within the affected societies. It is generally known that the missionizing successes effectuated by the traders did barely draw the attention of the annalists; but the conversions within the ruling classes acted like a signal for more elaborate and exact 'reports.' Historians and researchers today are able to glean important insights from those precious records. Thus, we know, for example, that it was War Jaabi, king of the Takrur Empire, who became the first sovereign to convert to Islam in the tenth century (Hrbek, 1990, p. 98).[6]

Ultimately, the intensification of the process of Islamization would take place only a century later. When the Sanhaja-Berbers between 1039 and 1049 founded the Almovarid movement, they at the same time built the foundation for the establishment of Islam as a cultural factor in western Africa. From the eleventh century onwards, the big empires like Ghana, Mali or Songhay could no longer elude the growing influence of the new religion. This fact can be illustrated very well in the example of the Mali Empire. There the processes of conversion had progressed so far that the pilgrimage to Mecca became one of the most important duties of the *Mansa* [sovereigns]. Furthermore, a regional clergy developed in some economic centers like Djenne, Gao and especially Timbuktu, where central religious functions (Kadi, Imam, Katib) were performed by African scholars:

La naissance d'une classe de savants et de clercs musulmans érudits d'origine soudanaise fut un événement important de l'histoire de l'islam dans l'Afrique au sud du Sahara. Elle signifia en effet que l'islam serait dès lors propagé par des autochtones connaissant les langues, coutumes et croyances locales. (Hrbek, 1990, p. 104)

The takeover of the missionizing work through a new class of African theologians in fact constituted a decisive phase in the process of Islamization, for those local *Ulamas* were perfectly suited to successfully continue the Islamization of the Mali Empire. The discovery of old manuscripts – in part dating from the thirteenth century – in Mali, Mauritania, Senegal and Niger confirms the assumption that during that time Timbuktu was an important center for commerce and university life. Through new insights it can be ascertained that in the fifteenth century the city had a population of about 100,000, among which about 25,000 were researchers and students (Djian, Aug. 2004, p. 16).[7] The phase of the introduction of Islam to western Africa lasted about four centuries and was completed with the rise of Timbuktu. At this point, Islam finally stops being a uniquely Arabic religion and also takes on specifically African characteristics.

Political and social importance of Islam

Islam as a religion has become a central part of African spirituality. In most African Muslim countries, Islam is not perceived as an imported religion or even a foreign element but on the contrary as a denomination that has been permanently integrated into the societal structure. It is therefore not only the religious leaders who are occupied with the Islam problem, but also the common strata of society, as well as all political organizations whose program contains an ambition to take over power. Due to the fact that Senegal gives the impression of a typically Islamic country, I will try to deal especially with the Senegalese example.

Already in the second half of the seventeenth century, Islam started to emerge as an important power factor. The puritanism of a belligerent Islam first became noticeable with the *Tubenan movement*. It was the beginning of a long series of religious wars (*Jihad*), which have entered the historiography of the region under the name of *Guerres des Marabouts* (Barry, 1988). Boubacar Barry defines Islam as an ideology of change, which had to develop as counterweight to the European hegemony in order to be able to continually guarantee the profits from the trans-Sahara slave trade (Barry, 1988, p. 69).[8]

> Dans son foyer d'origine le mouvement de Nasir Al-Din es tune tentative de régler la vie politique et sociale selon les enseignements de la Sharia dans son orthodoxie la plus pure, en mettant fin au pouvoir arbitraire des guerriers Hassan par l'instauration d'une véritable théocratie musulmane. (Barry, 1988, p. 89)

The action of Nasir Al-Din, a *Marabout* hailing from southern Mauritania, was without doubt economically motivated. Nevertheless, the proclamation of a 'holy' war was simultaneously based on religious as well as on political motivations. Thus, it can be assumed that the catastrophic consequences of the transatlantic human trade have induced the Tubenan movement to act against the European economic monopoly. Nasir Al-Din's death in 1674 and the defeat of his troops implied an intensification in the confrontation between local sovereigns and their own population. As seen from the point of view of the societies within the region, Islam provided a social and political force that could sustain the struggle against the arbitrary rule of the aristocrats.

Another proponent of a belligerent Islam, El Hadj Omar Tall (1794–1864), tried in the middle of the nineteenth century to continue the works of Nasir Al-Din. [9] With him, religious militancy reached a new climax. He was probably the most important resistance fighter against the colonial penetration and simultaneously the leader of a messianic movement. In face of French predominance in western Africa, he tried to establish new relations of power. His project to found a theocratic state was not only part of the Islamic tradition, but it should also free the Muslims in the region from the ligatures of a 'Christian' colonial system. Thus, El Hadj Omar had to fight his *Jihad* on two fronts: on the one hand against France and on the other against the 'pagan' African rulers, insofar as they were not willing to fight colonialism in the name of Islam. El Hadj Omar so challenged the colonial order and tried to instill a new religious drive into Islam. The French administration immediately reacted to the actions of the *Marabout*, because his 'holy' war at the same time meant a territorial expansion. In 1857, he could not avert military defeat[10] and had to evade the French colonial troops.

El Hadj Omar, who conducted the pilgrimage to Mecca three times in a row (1827, 1828 and 1829), was given the opportunity to study the theological writings of the famous Islam exegete Al-Ghazâli (1058–1111) and so introduced Sufism to the whole of western Africa.[11]

This political culture invariably bears the seal of a militant Islam that for centuries had been able to mobilize Islamic societies against European presence, but also against the despotism of local sovereigns. The Senegalese variation of Sufism[12] has always taught a rigorous mistrust against all kinds of secular power. The Sufi spirituality demands an orientation according to the Sunnah or tradition, which means an orientation according to those norms (statements and actions) which characterized the life of the Prophet. That is why Sufism has to be interpreted strictly according to the principles of the Sunnah, because only the Sunnah is able to guarantee the harmony between the secular and the divine. Senegal, like most Islamist African states, is a country where the people explicitly avow themselves to the Sunnah.[13] Because of its social engagement, Sufism has a sustained resonance in public opinion. Therefore, it has become possible for the *Marabouts*, as teachers of the Sufi doctrine, to occupy an essential political role.

The colonial administration's fear of subversive activities of the *Marabouts*, or a 'deterioration' of the relations between France and its colonies, manifests itself in the overly strict observation of religious figures through the police and simultaneously indicates the social and political importance of Islam. Documents from the *Archives Nationales du Sénégal* (*ANS*, 1913) are proof of the existence of a colonial commission for the supervision of militant Islam as well as for the creation of an index documenting the missionary zeal of the *Marabouts* in French West Africa. In this respect, Governor General William Ponty (1860–1915) writes to the Lieutenant Governors on January 15, 1913:

> Plus que dans tout autre pays, musulman, l'Islam affecte en Afrique Occidentale la forme de l'anthropolâtrie. C'est toujours, en apparence, la religion d'Allah, mais c'est surtout le culte du maraboutisme. Ici donc, plus que partout ailleurs, la surveillance politique de l'Islam est avant tout une surveillance de personnalités musulmanes... L'Islam est aussi une constitution sociale et un corps de droit. Quoique son succès dans ce champ ait été des plus relatifs, on ne saurait nier que son action, par la force même des choses tend chaque jour à se faire sentir plus intensément, sauf exception, dans les antiques institutions coutumières du pays, restées vivaces même chez les noirs islamisés. Il n'est pas enfin jusqu'au domaine économique qui, du fait de connexité des phénomènes religieux et sociaux, n'ait, dans certaines Colonies, ressenti les effets des doctrines islamiques. (Ponty in ANS, 1913)

French officials had the task of gathering precise information about any religious figure to better keep the *Marabouts* under control. Due to their spiritual power, the *Marabouts* were able to exert a great influence on the public, which is why their freedom of movement within the French colonial Empire was restricted to a minimum. A further reaction to Islam was the introduction of French schools and the expansion of French language and culture, which implied a radical intensification of the politics of assimilation. In the Archives (*ANS*, 1913), the following is written on the *Situation générale de l'Islam en Afrique occidentale Française*:

> [I]l est utile de retenir que l'islam africain, encore à demi fétichiste, ne parait pas mettre sérieusement en danger notre souveraineté, que notre devoir est de guider nous-mêmes son évolution vers des conceptions philosophiques et sociales favorables à notre action, enfin que l'expansion ininterrompue de la culture française dans nos possessions africaines, fait social de haute importance, amènera peu à peu l'islam soudanais à se renfermer dans une sphère d'action purement spirituelle, en dehors de tout idéal politique panislamique.

The confrontation between Islam and the West actually is not a phenomenon of modern world politics and thus cannot be seen as the result of the end of the conflict between capitalism and communism. The letter of the US Vice and Deputy Consul, Raymond P. Dougherty, in Freetown (Sierra Leone) dating from

March 25, 1913, as well as the subsequent answer of the French Governor General Joseph Clozel from April 26, corroborate the assumption that the hostile image of Islam cannot be seen as new either in Europe or in the USA.[14]

Thus, there exists certain continuity in the interpretation of Islam as a manifestation of a classical political, economic and social ideology. Although prominent religious leaders like Nasir Al-Din or El Hadj Omar in the end did not prevail militarily, they are nowadays perceived as pioneers of the 'orthodox' Islam established in Senegal. Basically, they are the architects of a Muslim civil society which – at that time as well as currently – is permanently taking care to articulate its social and political interests. To that end, this civil society works through the brotherhoods which have existed for a long time and which present themselves as the voice of the Islamic general public.

Islam of brotherhoods: Qadiriyyah, Tijaniya, Muridiya

With the end of the colonial conquests, Islam was no longer able to expand in large parts of Africa because the European 'competition' would not allow it.[15] Therefore, it could only expand in regions where it already had been established. This process made it possible for some religious systems to consolidate themselves in the form of strongly hierarchical orders. Hence, Islam in Africa currently shows itself as a religion dominated by *Marabouts* and brotherhoods. The Qadiriyyah, Tijaniya or Muridiya are all Sufi brotherhoods, which had taken hold in northern Africa since the thirteenth century and in western Africa since the eighteenth century. Without a doubt, they have strongly characterized the process of Islamization.

Brotherhoods are religious collectives that, under the guidance of a teacher, try to walk the mystic road to the awareness of God. In this manner, every member refrains from the individual search for God and declares his willingness to submit to the teaching and the ritual method of the community. The mentor should furthermore be a charismatic personality and possess *Baraka*,[16] in order to be able to command absolute authority. Usually the conditions within brotherhoods surpass simple religious matters and express themselves in social, economic or political activities.

Due to their adaptability, the brotherhoods were able to dynamize people's belief and especially their confidence in Islam. As a haven for the suppressed and weak members of the Islamic community, they have been able to gain a real popular dimension. The Muslims of the African continent – contrary to the unreceptive attitude towards the European hegemony – only rarely encounter the need to live outside of the Islamic world. Christoph Marx takes note of a real feeling of togetherness among Muslims:

The Sufi brotherhoods took care that the African Muslims remained connected and in contact with the international currents of the worldwide Islamic community, the Umma, an undertaking which has been helped in no small degree by the pilgrimages to Mecca. (Marx, 2004, p. 88 [trans. by ed.])

The Qadiriyyah, founded close to Baghdad in Iraq, counts as one of the oldest western African brotherhoods and has been named after the Iranian theologian and lawyer Abd Al-Qadir Al-Jilani (1077–1166). Besides northern Africa, the Qadiriyyah tradition is also present in most other African countries. Followers of the Qadiriyyah can be found in Nigeria, Côte d'Ivoire, Benin, Gambia, Ghana, Kenya, Niger, Senegal, Sudan, Western Sahara, Zaire, but most of all in Guinea and Mauritania.[17] Coming from northern Africa and the Sahara, the Qadiriyyah needed about five centuries, from the fourteenth to the nineteenth, before it could efficiently spread in all of western Africa. The doctrine of the brotherhood is based in the first instance on an absolute submission before God. Furthermore, intensive charity, rigorous devoutness and – not least of all – spiritual humility are demanded from all members. This orthodoxy expressed itself also in spiritual ceremonies including recitations from the Qur'an usually ending in a form of mystic ecstasy. Today, the Qadiriyyah has suffered the loss of most of its traditional influence, since it continues to be called the religion of the Mauritanian slave traders. It was unable to fend off especially the competition of the Tijaniya and Muridiya both of which, owing to their 'youth,' are not associated with the negative circumstances (slavery and house raids) of Islamization or Arabization. This claim especially concerns Senegal, where about half of the Muslims avow themselves to the Tijaniya brotherhood, about 30 percent to the Muridiya and where the Qadiriyyah has to content itself with about 15 percent. Here one also needs to point out the special character of the Senegalese example: the Tijaniya brotherhood remains, despite its numeric superiority, in economic and political importance far behind the Muridiya.

Compared to the Qadiriyyah, the Tijaniya is a very recent phenomenon. In reality, an Islamic reformist sets a simple and liberal teaching for his disciples. Through abstaining from the rigorous Sufi mysticism, he was able to present a doctrine mainly focused on missionizing and economic activities. Thus, the brotherhood could favor the vulgarization of its own dogma and at the same time further the continuing Islamization of the African societies in a sustained manner. It is a central commandment of the Tijaniya that every Muslim can design his own path on the basis of personal meditation and advocacy through one's religious teacher. The Tijaniya became, under the guidance of the theologian and researcher on Islam El Hadj Malick Sy (1855–1922), one of the most important co-creating forces of social and political life in Senegal and has remained so until today. El Hadj Malick Sy's credo was to enable a peaceful coexistence between all people living in the country. He rejected any kind of exclusion and was active for an efficient politics of integration. This is why he demanded that the Senegalese Muslims thankfully accept the French hegemony because the colonial politics of 'pacification' were a guarantor of peace:

Les Français avaient été choisis par Allah pour nous protéger, nous et nos propriétés… Avant la conquête française, nous vivions dans un monde où régnaient la captivité, le meurtre et le pillage, un point sur lequel les musulmans comme les infidèles seront d'accord. (El Hadj Malick Sy in Marty, 1917, p. 208)

This quasi-uncritical recognition of the French authority brought El Hadj Malick Sy the reputation of a *Realpolitiker* trying to woo the sympathies of the colonial administration at any price.[18] The nationalists on the other hand called him a 'collaborator' and architect of a program for the upkeep of the colonial system, even more so as he was not able to question the concept of the *Mission civilisatrice*. What can be deduced is that he was neither a nationalist nor a patriot in the ideological sense of the terms. He was much rather a Tijaniya leader whose religiosity surpassed manifold political ambitions. Moriba Magassouba (1985, p. 43) also writes that the love of religion in El Hadj Malick Sy was more intense than his love of patriotism, and that this made him into an objective ally of the colonial system. This hypothesis does not seem unfounded if one takes into account the existence of a militant wing within the Tijaniya brotherhood.

It is this militant tendency that, in contrast to the reform, oriented the Tijaniya of El Hadj Malick Sy to the *Jihadism* of an El Hadj Omar Tall, founded in its communal form in the year of 1936 in Madina-Gounass (in southern Senegal). This community was ruled by its initiator Tierno Mamadou Seydou Bâ with an iron fist and functioned like a 'small Islamic republic' in which the secular structures of the Senegalese state were prohibited.[19] This rigid interpretation of Islam did not allow any innovation or relations to the modern state, which was seen as a symbol of Occidentalization and representative of the capitalist system. As seen from the perspective of its founder, Madina-Gounass represented an ideal Islamic society in which concepts like social solidarity, inner peace, integrity, the study of the Qur'an and, of course, God had an important role to play. It was also a politics of disconnection which should have culminated in the constitution of an autarkic Tijaniya brotherhood. Within Madina-Gounass, Islam took over a rigorous organizational function in order to build a certain framework to save the old religious tradition and free the Islamic community from the ligatures of the 'decadent' modern state. This fundamentalist position of the *Marabout* Tierno Mamadou Seydou Bâ remained more or less isolated until the 1980s, because it corresponded to neither the social and political concept nor the religious understanding of the reformist Tijaniya brotherhood. Only the Muridiya resembles a community, which partly follows a similar doctrine.

The Muridiya brotherhood was founded in Senegal in 1866 by Cheikh Ahmadou Bamba (1853–1927). In the beginning, he was a member of the Qadiriyyah before he decided to build his own community. The Muridiya is characterized by a strong feeling of togetherness and an extraordinary energy. The rigid mechanisms of organization,[20] but also the absolute submission of the members to the *Marabout*, bestow on this movement an almost perfect coherence. Cheikh Ahmadou Bamba, a great mystic, was always searching for the 'absolute' and so reached a religious ecstasy of unimagined proportions. The originality of his doctrine consists of an ideology of work, which is not to be found in any other brotherhood. Discipline, work and solidarity have attained a holy meaning with the *Murides*. This is why Paul Pélissier writes:

> Se faire mouride, c'est accepter une terrible soumission mais c'est aussi adhérer à un corps social solidaire, s'assurer que l'on ne mourra jamais de faim et qu'en toutes circonstances on trouvera auprès de son marabout non seulement le réconfort spirituel mais, de manière immédiate, la sécurité matérielle. (Pélissier in Magassouba, 1985, p. 29)

The community, having become a real economic power in the meantime, is taking care of all its members. It invests the necessary energy to cultivate the fields of the *Marabouts* or to fill the financial coffers of the brotherhood. Therefore, it develops the feeling of having contributed substantially to the welfare and prestige of the whole organization. Due to its economic potency and especially its capabilities for mobilization, the *Muridiya* is also able to play a special role in the social and political realm. Cheikh Ahmadou Bamba was practicing certain anti-colonialism,[21] even if he never declared his struggle against the colonial administration explicitly. For their part, his successors developed a clever strategy of political cohabitation and arranged themselves with the Senegalese state.

Tolerance and peace from the perspective of Muslim societies in Africa

Slave trade and colonialism are two historic periods that without doubt have influenced the social, economic and political evolution of the African continent.[22]* Existing social structures, especially the daily lives of people, were destabilized by foreign domination, violence and raids. It was under those conditions and under an atmosphere of fear and uncertainty that the Muslim leaders saw themselves forced to intervene on the political scene. Subsequently, Nasir Al-Din as well as El Hadj Omar Tall started to question the European predominance and the position of power of African sovereigns. Latter day Muslim leaders have remained true to

* Ed. More on this topic can be found in Chapter 23 by Belachew Gebrewold.

this militant tradition and still play a central role in their respective societies. The widespread popular success of Islam can be traced back to the fact that this religion was always capable of satisfying the social aspirations of Islamized peoples through its political engagements.

During the course of centuries and via the activities of the Sufi brotherhoods, Islam has been able to establish itself as a religious and cultural system in Africa. Therefore, the leaders had to distance themselves from the belligerent Islam of past centuries, more or less arrange themselves with the European colonial power and, most importantly, take over already existing elements of African social life. For despite the military character of its conquests, Islam in Africa is largely based on tolerance towards people of different faiths. This is why Islam could become the new denomination for many Africans almost without force and violence. Even more so because the monotheist Islam was able to properly address the local forms of religion.[23] Islam's abilities to adapt were also linked to the certain willingness of the affected populations to compromise on their part. Thus, a religious environment could bloom in which an important value was placed on tolerance and compatibility.

Senegal in this respect portrays an ideal example of an Islamic country, which – despite a strong syncretism – offers a practically harmonious religious coexistence. It is very likely that this can be traced back to the old social mechanisms of the Senegalese society. Due to the diversity of its ethnic groups, Senegal has developed a societal tradition based on interethnic mixing. The different ethnic groups really correspond to different cultural areas, but they also have a common cultural basis. The system-immanent method of conflict prevention and conflict solution is successful because there have existed ties of kinship between the different groups of the population since the ninth century. That is why social and political conflicts in Senegal only very rarely acquire an ethnic character. It is, for example, often mentioned that the first president of the state Léopold Sédar Senghor (1906–2001) was *Sereer* and Roman Catholic and had a French wife, but that those facts were never made a political topic. His enemies knew that with such arguments they could never have mobilized the population against the regime because the Senegalese place a high value on ethnic and religious cohabitation.

Acceptance, consensus and proportionality invariably characterize the social life in Senegal, a country where the ethnic factor cannot be separated from the religious. Political harmony has to be seen in combination with religious harmony, with the kinship between the different ethnic groups as foundation of social peace. The existence of different Sufi brotherhoods in connection with the manifold ethnic groups or independent denominations is commonly perceived as cultural diversity. This is why it is also consistent with society if Muslim families declare their willingness to celebrate Christmas and New Year's Eve with

Catholic neighbors or friends, and nobody is subsequently accused of having committed a sin.

On a different level, the social coherence is also guaranteed through an alliance between the official authorities and the religious brotherhoods.[24] The state in a certain way is able to buy the sympathy or neutrality of the *Marabouts* by supporting the economic activities of the brotherhoods and sometimes also giving financial aid to scholarships for students of Islam. This form of clientele relations between state and Islam is actually a manifestation of mutual respect, but also (on both sides) an expression of a certain fear of losing the respective privileges. It is towards this purpose that the brotherhoods also work as a transmitting link between civil society and state:

> Cette pratique de l'échange de services eut en quelque sorte son âge d'or entre 1960 et 1970. Contrôlant chacun des 'ressources' différentes mais complémentaires, les marabouts et la classe dirigeante s'unissent pour maintenir le statu quo...ce schéma clientéliste demeurera en toile de fond, comme une sorte de 'type idéal' des relations entre le pouvoir musulman et le pouvoir politique. (Coulon, 1981, p. 233)

It is definitely a case of political opportunism. The strategy of the *Marabouts* thus aims at bringing institutions of the state under their control, while the politicians[25] are interested in asserting their legitimacy with the help of religion. This makes the Senegalese brotherhoods very powerful. The omnipresence of religion (in almost all segments of society) furthermore bestows a conflictive element on the status quo and this is how grave situations of conflict can also arise.

Nevertheless, each time the situation demands it, the religious and political leaders signal their willingness to defuse the impending conflict. Christian Coulon (1981, pp. 253–255) mentions in this respect the example of a political confrontation between the government and the Tijaniya, which brought the country to the brink of a severe crisis in 1963. In this crisis, Cheikh Tidiane Sy, the nephew of the *Caliph* of the Tijaniya brotherhood, played an important role. Two years after his nomination as Senegalese ambassador in Cairo (Egypt), he was ordered to return to Dakar under the suspicion of financial embezzlement. Subsequently, he went into opposition and allegedly tried to found an Islamic party (*Union Progressiste Musulmane*). The month of September 1963 culminated in violent riots in the wake of which Cheikh Tidiane Sy was arrested by police forces. The danger of an escalation was imminent when his followers commenced an operation to free him. In the end, the *Caliph* of the Muridiya decided to intervene in order to defuse the crisis:[26]

L'Islam, religion de paix, de fraternité et de concorde, ne saurait cautionner aucune entreprise susceptible de mettre en cause le calme et la tranquillité de notre paisible pays, de retarder son développement et de nuire à son crédit extérieur. (Unité Africaine, 1963)

A religious leader as a pragmatic and a *Realpolitiker*. The intervention of the *Marabout* furthermore shows the whole ambiguity of the accommodating relation between secular and spiritual power. For although the religion tries to keep the state under its control, it still needs to hope for a strong force of the state which is able to guarantee the territorial integrity of Senegal, its economic development policy, its presence in foreign politics and thus also the capability of the whole country to survive. The words of the *Muridiya-Caliph* furthermore clearly express the privileged position of peace, solidarity, concord and tolerance within Senegalese society. Seen from his view, the Islamic religion incorporates a whole range of positive values from which the whole population might profit. It still may be added that the premises for a politics of conflict prevention and conflict solution clearly are based on the link between traditional societal structures and the Islamic concepts of morals.

The mystic Sufi doctrine is in principle a well-established tradition in Senegal. The brotherhoods were also very successful in bringing about the social impact of Islam. Through their two great personalities, El Hadj Omar and El Hadj Malick Sy, the Tijaniya was able to effect a fusion of the Islamic values with the social values of many African societies. If the *Caliph* of the Muridiya calls upon the traditional spirit of tolerance within the Senegalese population, he is following the moral–theological and political footprints of the militant Islam exegete El Hadj Omar. During his time (in the middle of the nineteenth century) and through his attempts to create a theocratic state, the latter had without doubt tried to effect the conversion of non-Islamic peoples and had been eager to create an Islamic missionary vision. Therefore, he concluded in his theological writings that an essential dogma of Islam would be to do 'good' and simultaneously 'avoid evil' (Ly-Tall, 1991, p. 110). In 1831, El Hadj Omar issued a historic appeal for peace (Gerresh-Dekais, 1977),[27] in which he imperatively made it clear that every exponent of Islam was forced to honor human life, because it would be God's creation. El Hadj Omar highlighted, at the same time, that it would be a religious commandment for all humanity to work for peace. In his interpretation of the writings of El Hadj Omar, Madina Ly-Tall (1991, pp. 111–112) writes:

L'argumentation est organisée autour de deux idées: la portée exceptionnelle de la fraternité religieuse et le caractère sacré de toute vie humaine. Selon une vue chère à de nombreux Suufi et basée sur des versets du Coran, tous les musulmans sont des frères, parce qu'issus d'un même père qui est l'Islam. Cette fraternité à vocation éternelle est portée à un très haut niveau par les

Tijane qui la tiennent pour plus importante que la fraternité biologique, qui est éphémère.

Traditional societal norms in Senegal are also based on similar values. The successful combination of Islamic provisions with Senegalese circumstances continues to show a positive effect for the social cohabitation and leads many Senegalese to call their religion the 'other Islam' or the 'peaceful Islam.' Still they should not forget that the Islamic militancy, which has continually grown since the end of the 1980s, could unhinge the social equilibrium.

Islamic renaissance and Occidental hegemonic politics

Since the time of the religious wars of the *Marabouts* in the seventeenth century, Islam has remained a constant social, economic and political factor. In northern as well as in western Africa, it has led a struggle of resistance against European colonial expansion and especially against France's doctrine of cultural and political assimilation.[28] Since the wave of independence in the 1960s, 'modern' nation-states (with Muslim majorities) decided to continue the old politics of collaboration with the brotherhoods, even more so because they were interested in making use of the religious importance of Islam. For this purpose, the 'reformists' had to be marginalized. This strategy led to the emergence of a generation of oppositional Islamists, which advocated a more militant Islam as well as a radicalization and acceleration of the process of politicization.[29]

Two historic episodes played an important role in the process of renovation of Islam in Africa: the Iranian revolution and the breakdown of real existing socialism. From the perspective of the African Islamists, the victory of Ayatollah Khomeini (1979) marked an effective signal that Islam could develop into a dynamic and potent factor in world politics.

Une opinion musulmane s'est forgée depuis les années 1980 qui défend l'idée selon laquelle l'Islam n'est plus apparu comme une formule dépassée, mais comme un outil pour sortir le continent de son isolement, investir l'espace public et concurrencer l'Etat sur ses propres terres. C'est la consécration d'un Islam politique qui devient un instrument de conquêtes d'espaces et défend un autre système référentiel basé uniquement sur le sacré, à l'inverse de celui imposé par les Etats depuis les indépendances. (Gomez-Perez, 2005, p. 13)

The 'African' Islam, which up to that date could be called a comfortable religion, but which most of all had been well integrated into the pro-Western world order, started to question the classical cooperation between the established brotherhoods and the modern state. Today, the Islamists have become harsh critics of the African governments for their unwillingness to free themselves from the dominance of the West. The new Islam militants simultaneously claim ruling positions in their respective societies. Furthermore, they demand the installation of the Qur'an as a legitimate means for adequately governing a state. This is why they strictly reject secularism and ground this rejection in the argument that secularism would be an Occidental 'invention,' which does not reflect the realities of African societies.

This belligerent and at the same time uncompromising phase of the politicization of Islam is fundamentally connected to the breakup of the Soviet Union and the end of the Cold War. After the Soviet counterpower ceased to exist, the US administration (first under Bill Clinton and then George W. Bush) has been able to politically and militarily engage in Africa. Therefore, the ACRF (African Crisis Response Force) was founded in 1996 as a military unit conceived to counter interventions. Since then, it has been replaced by a more efficient formation – the ACRI (African Crisis Response Initiative).[30] Africa currently plays an important role in the global strategy of the USA, which since 2001 fights a dogged battle against the so-called Islamic terrorists. In Washington, one is convinced that 'terrorists' would be able to build up new bases of operation in the Sahel area or the Maghreb if the US military pressure in Afghanistan and Iraq becomes unbearable. In this regard, George Bush remarks: 'The USA will not allow terrorists to threaten the African peoples, or to abuse Africa as base to threaten the whole world' (Bush in Abramovici, July 2004).

From this, it can be deduced that the logic of the Bush administration will invariably imply a militarization of American–African relations. It is in this light that in many (and not only the Islamized) countries in Africa the concept of the *New World Order* is perceived as Occidentalization or Americanization. From the ranks of Islamic organizations, the argument arises that the whole continent would now have entered the era of 'fighter jet politics,' after the classical gunboat politics of the former colonial powers had ended. Parts of the Islamic world are thus reacting with estrangement and rejection to the aggressive US hegemonic politics and their almost unchecked wars in Iraq (twice) and Afghanistan since 1990.[31] In reality, this factual situation is nothing new, even more so since the USA with their expansionist politics gradually present themselves as a world empire. History teaches us that mighty empires are often confronted with political crises and social revolts. In each case, the intra-systemic factors invariably lead to the resistance of the periphery against the center. The system so carries its own contradictions inside itself and produces the forces capable of fighting it. This is why it may be deceiving to perceive the confrontation between the capitalist West (USA and Europe) and the Islamic organizations (Hezbollah and Al-Qaeda) or states (Iran, Iraq and Syria) as a war of civilizations. In addition, the rhetoric of some actors ultimately is not conducive to peace and the course of events may well bring further dangers.[32]

It is especially alarming when the struggle is conducted in the name of religion. The US administration now officially speaks about 'criminal terrorists' and proclaims a battle in which 'Good' and 'Evil' are opposing each other, whereas the Islamists try to argue that it would be a struggle for freedom. The latter defy the USA as 'Satan' and thus also use a religious discourse. Of course, the question needs to be asked whether terror as means of political combat should be allowed, or if terrorist attacks, like the one on September 11, 2001 can be legitimized through US arrogance. The strategy of the Islamists obviously consists of committing terrorist attacks in order to be able to hit the enemy everywhere. This guerilla strategy can ultimately be traced back to their military inferiority.[33] Due to the asymmetric character of the power relations, the Islamists are not able to lead a conventional war and willingly take in their stride the death of innocent people. It has to be pointed out, however, that the US strategists also speak of the unavoidable collateral damage of their military operations.

Universal recipes for the fight against terrorism unfortunately are not available; and probably do not exist. The USA, as well as Europe, in principle could make an important step if they would start to revise the relations of dominance that are so beneficial for them. Thus they perhaps could also give the 'Others' the possibility to fashion their societies according to their own images and realities. During times of colonialism, Europeans had the intention of 'pacifying' the dominated peoples. The USA, with help from Europe, is currently trying to 'democratize' and 'pacify' the rest of the world through an attempt to determine the economic and social criteria of extra-European societies. It is at least problematic if Euro-American offices, in a quasi-immediate reflex, depoliticize any attempt at resistance against their hegemonic position and simultaneously try to define the norms and principles of conflict according to their own values – while presenting those values as universal. The complexity of the relations between the capitalist West and the rest of the world makes it – on the one hand – possible for the USA to manipulate democratic principles to their advantage while – on the other hand – it provides a welcome pretext for the radical Islamists to present themselves as proponents of justice and thus also as revolutionary avant-garde of a political Islam.

Conclusion

It can therefore be assumed that the desire for a politics of integration and the striving for solidarity among the Muslim states, but also the attempt to build an Islamic block, ultimately all are responses to Western hegemony. Due to its immense potential for mobilization, Islam has become a fascinating power factor within world politics. During the course of the Iranian revolution, Ayatollah Khomeini had been read by many African Muslims as spiritual leader and as a symbol for the resistance against the West. In the end, he was successful in giving Islam a proper international format. Since that moment, most African countries (with Muslim majorities) have become enthralled by an extraordinarily vital Islam. Everywhere on the continent, there is an inflation of Islamic organizations and the religious fervor is able to overcome many borders. In the 1980s, even the proselytizing rate in many countries (Senegal, Mali and Côte d'Ivoire) rose slightly.

This new generation of militant Islamists usually takes over those social areas that have been left underfocused by the state (politics of supply, family politics and religious education) and so tries to build a broad frame of action for the political Islam. The Islamic world, especially Saudi Arabia, conducted an intensive religious propaganda up until the 1990s and has financed the construction of schools, mosques or social institutions. Since the events in New York in September 2001 and the second war in Iraq, those subventions have been massively reduced. A new and interesting phenomenon is becoming noticeable with many women (Cameroon, Senegal) now showing a dynamic engagement in social and political as well as economic areas.[34] This implies that a hitherto disadvantaged societal group is now able to use the Islamic religion in order to obtain a central role in the design of communal structures. Further explicit mutations of Islam in Africa can also be observed in the religious behavior of the people and the steadily growing number of Mosques. The well-known cliché according to which people without financial means tend to compensate for their poverty with the help of religion seems to have lost much of its validity. African Muslims from diverse strata of society and from all professions are discovering their religiosity, building houses to the Lord (which they also frequently visit), are politically engaged and evaluate all possibilities for further missionizing work.

And although the displacement or substitution of the modern and 'unsuccessful' state apparatus through the Qur'an is proclaimed, the religious struggle is nevertheless largely concentrated on the spiritual realm. The ideological indoctrination, which turns believing Muslims into suicide attackers, seems to be ineffective in the case of Africa. There is an absolute necessity for a large proportion of fanaticism and readiness to sacrifice in order for young Muslims to declare their willingness to die for a religious idea. The current degree of sensitization in this respect probably might still be rather low for African Muslims. So far, there have been no suicide attacks in the name of Islam anywhere on the continent.[35] This does, of course, not imply that Africans would be incapable of choosing the martyr's death – especially since the human being is easily manipulated. But most Islamist movements in Africa are still led by personalities who are not inclined to accept international terror as a means of political combat. Despite a common Islamic identity and the always-proclaimed Islamic solidarity, the use of violence is still rejected. The reasons are, on the one hand, of a pragmatic nature (the cooperation with the West creates privileges) and, on the other, they are closely connected to the mystic interpretations of the Qur'an and to the traditional religious mechanisms according to which African societies function. The desire for tolerance and peace can, in principle, enable a harmonic encounter between different denominations. For that, it is worth living!

Notes

1. This observation concretely regards sub-Saharan Islam.
2. The Soviet invasion in Afghanistan (1979–1989) brought an adequate cause. The Mujaheddin (guardians of religion and the Islamic space) subsequently began a war of resistance, which has been characterized with the term *Jihad*.
3. Besides the thrust towards the northeast, Arabic troops also pushed until Poitiers (France) where they were stopped in 732 by Charles Martel.
4. Other groups reached the coast of eastern Africa either via the Red Sea or from the southern part of the Arabian Peninsula.
5. Economy always played a central role in the Islamic world. Ivan Hrbek (1990) does not consider this a coincidence, even more so because Islam originated in the economic circles of Mecca and Mohammed was a trader by profession, before he turned Prophet.
6. See also Barry (1988, p. 30).
7. The existence of manuscripts in Arabic and Fulani serves to challenge the myth of an oral continent and bestows on Africa a solid historical foundation that it unfortunately has very often been denied.
8. The Tubenan movement was therefore a reaction to a crisis situation provoked by European Mercantilism. The intensification of the transatlantic slave trade triggered an economic, political and social process of destabilization within the region, which the Islamic leaders tried to stop.
9. The political engagement of religious leaders had become a reality at the latest by the seventeenth century. After El Hadj Omar other *Marabouts*, for example Maba Jaaxu, Amadu Seexu or Cerno Brahim, tried to keep up the spirit of *Jihad* and to counter the expansionist politics of France.
10. Between April and July of 1857 El Hadj Omar failed in trying to take a French fort located at the Senegal river. Prior to his death in 1864, he therefore focused on the east (French Sudan).
11. This Iranian theologian and philosopher was a prominent exponent of Sufism. He decisively influenced the development of Islamic thinking and was called the 'proof of Islam.'
12. Sufism can be defined as the most important mysticism within Islam. The central message of Sufism insists that a Muslim is constantly engaged in an active search for the divine absolute, and thus can encounter God here on earth. For more detailed information see Lory (2005, pp. 74–83).
13. Islam in Africa is definitely of a Sunni orientation. However, only two (Maliki and Shafi'i) of the four Sunni schools of law are represented (the other two are Hanafi and Whahhabi). Furthermore, the Sunnites in Senegal belong to the Maliki school of law.
14. Raymond P. Dougherty wrote: 'Sir: I have the honour to write you with reference to the extent and economic value of Mohammedanism in your colony and shall be pleased to receive answers to the following questions' (Letter from March 25, 1913). In his response, Joseph Clozel called the Islamic question a very complex topic (Letter from April 26, 1913). See *ANS* (1913).

15. For example, in Nigeria the English tried to arrange themselves with the Muslim leaders and made use of the principle of indirect rule to place power partially in their hands, whereas France insisted on the principle of secularism.

16. *Baraka* is not directly comparable to charisma. It becomes recognizable through manifold attributes like spirituality, devoutness and leadership qualities. *Baraka* is a God-given grace and manifests through the capability to work miracles.

17. In both Guinea, where about 70 percent of the population is Muslim, and in Mauritania (96 percent) the Qadiriyyah tradition represents the strongest brotherhood (Ende et al., 1996, pp. 136–140).

18. As a reward for his loyalty, El Hadj Malick was given financial aid from the French administration for the construction of a Mosque in his city of residence, Tivaouane.

19. The rule of the Sharia means among others: total ban on the consumption of alcohol and of leisure activities (cinema, dance evenings, etc.). Furthermore, there were no state-run schools, no post offices, no civil registry office and no police. Only the commercialization of the peanut production and the tax policies of the government were allowed.

20. The Muridiya has its own order (Baay Faal) for organizational questions and police work.

21. In 1895, he was deported to Gabun, where he had to spend seven years. He also was in exile (four years) in Mauritania, before he was allowed to return to Senegal in 1907.

22. There is no doubt that the African societies had also not been free of conflict: wars had been conducted there regularly and many violent events occurred. Still, this potential for conflict was to reach a completely new dimension through the transatlantic slave trade and the beginning of European colonialism.

23. The principle of polygamy was gratefully taken over by most African Muslims.

24. The collaboration between state and the Muslim religion is, in principle, nothing new. Prominent *Marabouts* cooperated with the colonial administration already before independence. The Muridiya, for example, could subsequently monopolize the production and commercialization of peanuts.

25. Most of them, of course, are Muslims, members of a brotherhood and sometimes even the disciples of a *Marabout*. In this manner, also personal relations between politicians and *Marabouts* can arise.

26. Cheikh Tidiane Sy was released in April 1964 after the intervention of the Tijaniya-Caliph (the uncle of the arrested).

27. The cause was the conflict between two African sovereigns, Mohammed Bello (Sokoto) and Shaykh El Kanemi (Bornu). El Hadj Omar's attempt to mediate was an expression of his conviction that Muslims have to develop an extraordinary sense of solidarity.

28. The *Association Musulmane des Etudiants d'Afrique Noire* (with a seat in Dakar) in the 1950s criticized the Tijaniya's and Muridiya's politics of collaboration with the colonial administration. This organization furthermore tried to found its own schools in which subjects like mathematics, history, geography or Arabic grammar were offered. The members of the organization were mostly francophone students, who were not always willing to engage in studies of the Koran but wanted to be active in the cultural and also the political realm. During the Algerian war of independence, they took on a nationalistic position and proclaimed their solidarity with the Algerian people.

29. Followers of a radical and revolutionary reform of Islam demand a new but still rigorous and fundamentalist interpretation of the Qur'an. Prominent 'reformers' are especially active in Senegal, Côte d'Ivoire, Burkina Faso, northern Nigeria and seem to have excellent contacts to the Arabic world (Iran, Kuwait, Saudi Arabia or Libya).

30. The official goal of the ACRI is the training of African special forces for peacekeeping or humanitarian aid. Between 2001 and 2002, it had a budget of more than 30 million dollars. Since July 2001, about 400 Senegalese soldiers have been trained for psychological warfare. The ACRI is furthermore responsible for the organization of Battalion-sized units (800 to 1000 soldiers) in Senegal, Mali, Ghana, Côte d'Ivoire, Uganda as well as Malawi and Benin (Abramovici, July 2004, p. 15).
31. Armed organizations like Al-Qaeda or Hezbollah have frequently signaled their readiness to fight the West with military means.
32. Current examples are the conflict between Israel and Palestine or the crisis between the USA and Iran.
33. Since September 2001, the USA have admitted to themselves that the guerilla war has reached a new dimension, namely through the possibility of Islamists' staging terror operations outside of crisis regions and outside of the Arabic world.
34. Many colloquia with cultural, religious or political topics are organized by women. Women also have obtained the possibility to visit different courses (for example, tailoring workshops).
35. Uprisings with a religious background have taken place in Nigeria and have demanded a high death toll. Nevertheless, there is still a substantial difference between the Nigerian events and the Islamic suicide attacks, which have a more global dimension.

Reference list

Abramovici, P. (July 2004) 'Activisme militaire de Washington en Afrique,' *Le Monde Diplomatique*, 14–15.

Amin, S. (1986) *La déconnexion: Pour sortir du système mondial* (Paris: La Découverte).

ANS (Archives Nationales du Sénégal) (1913) *Dossier sur L'Islam*, 19 G 1 (Dakar).

Barry, B. (1988) *La Sénégambie du XVe au XIXe siècle: Traite négrière, Islam et conquête colonial* (Paris: L'Harmattan).

Coulon, C. (1981) *Le Marabout et le Prince: Islam et pouvoir au Sénégal* (Paris: A. Pedone).

Djian, J.-M. (Aug. 2004) 'Les manuscrits trouvés à Tombouctou,' *Le Monde Diplomatique*, 605, 16.

Ende, W., U. Steinbach and G. Krüger (1996) (eds.) *Der Islam in der Gegenwart: Entwicklung und Ausbreitung, Kultur und Religion. Staat, Politik und Recht* (München: C.H. Beck).

Gerresh-Dekais, C. (1977) 'Al Hajj Umar Al Fûti: Tadkirat al-Ghafilîn an Qubh ikhtilâf al Mu'minîn,' *Bulletin IFAN*, Série B, 4.

Gomez-Perez, M. (2005) (ed.) *L'Islam Politique au Sud du Sahara: Identités, Discours et Enjeux* (Paris: Karthala).

Hrbek, I. (1990) 'La diffusion de l'Islam en Afrique au Sud du Sahara' in *Histoire Générale de l'Afrique*, III (Paris: Unesco/Nouvelles Editions Africaines), 92–116.

Lory, P. (2005) 'Le Soufisme, Mystique de l'Islam' in C. Golliau (ed.) *Islam: Avicenne, Averroès, Al-Ghazâlî, Ibn Khaldoun. Les textes fondamentaux commentés* (Paris: Tallandier).

Ly-Tall, M. (1991) *Un Islam Militant en Afrique de l'Ouest au XIXe siècle: La Tijaniyya de Saïku Umar Futiyu contre les Pouvoirs traditionnels et la Puissance coloniale* (Paris: L'Harmattan).

Magassouba, M. (1985) *L'Islam au Sénégal: Demain les Mollahs?* (Paris: Karthala).

Marty, P. (1917) *Etudes sur l'Islam au Sénégal: Les personages*, I (Paris: Ernest Leroux).

Marx, C. (2004) *Geschichte Afrikas: Von 1800 bis zur Gegenwart* (Paderborn: Ferdinand Schöningh).

Unité Africaine (1963) 64.

Section VI
Peace Thinkers

25
Mahatma Gandhi's Concept of Peace: A Grandson's Perspective

Arun Gandhi

> We must become the change we wish to see in the world.
>
> Mahatma Gandhi

Early influences

Mohandas Karamchand Gandhi was born on October 2, 1869, in a very ordinary Hindu home where he had a very simple, unpretentious, upbringing in a small town called Porbandar, on the west coast of India. In his autobiography, Mohandas repeatedly claims that his childhood experiences were in no way more exceptional than the experiences of any other child born during the same period under similar circumstances. Nor was he an exceptional student.

As a child, he was in awe of his father who was always firm and aloof and, therefore, not exceptionally close to his children. Mohandas narrates the poignant moment when he felt compelled to apologize to his father for stealing money and other valuables to indulge in bad habits like smoking and eating meat. Mohandas did not have the courage to make a vocal apology so he wrote a letter and handed it over to his father who upon reading it began to cry. The distraught father embraced his son and, as Mohandas describes the scene, allowed 'our tears to wash away the guilt.' This was Mohandas' first encounter with the power of truthfulness and the need to forgive. Mohandas had expected some form of physical punishment but instead got love, understanding, forgiveness. As a result, he developed a deep desire never to hurt his parents, or anyone else, again.

Mohandas was also greatly impressed by his father's sense of loyalty to his employers and a strong sense of righteousness and self-respect. Mohandas once witnessed the bold stand taken by his father against a British officer who publicly insulted the regent of Porbandar state. In those days of colonialism taking a self-righteous stand against a British officer, however just one's cause, was fraught with grave consequences. His father was insulted, arrested and bound like a common criminal and made to stand in public all day. In spite of this his father would neither apologize to the British officer nor would he beg for mercy. This was a lesson for young Mohandas on morals and values and the need to remain staunch when you know you are right. However, later as a young adult, Mohandas was harshly critical of his father's 'carnal desires' that led him to marry again after the death of each wife.

The reason why Mohandas stressed repeatedly the ordinariness of his upbringing was to convince people that anyone with the same commitment to self-improvement and conscientiousness in the pursuit of truth could also achieve greatness. He emphasized that he was not endowed with any special gifts or talents. There were enough examples in daily life, then and now, to show how we human beings tend to elevate people with exceptional qualities to sainthood and then worship them. Towards the end of his life, Mohandas made a poignant comment about Indians who will 'follow me in life, worship me in death but not make my cause their cause.'*

There were three women involved in Mohandas' spiritual growth. At first, he was influenced by the broad-minded liberal thoughts of his parents. Both were spiritually inclined, but not dogmatic in their outlook. Their friendly curiosity towards different faiths resulted in periodic dinner meetings involving different religious leaders talking about their different ways of worship. This early exposure to diversity surely had an impact on Mohandas and probably roused his curiosity more as he grew up. Much later in life he declared that a friendly study of all the scriptures was the sacred duty of every individual.

The first of the three women who influenced Mohandas as a child was his mother, Putliba. She did not only pray regularly but often took vows that meant – for a period of time – giving up something that she loved the most. Taking of vows is a common practice among Indian women. Sacrificing food and doing it cheerfully instills in one discipline and humility. The vow that vexed young Mohandas the most was his mother's decision not to eat any food until she saw the sun. What was most galling was that she took this vow during the monsoon season when the overcast skies would make it impossible for the sun to make an appearance, sometimes for several days. What was truly noble was that she shouldered cheerfully all her household responsibilities, cooked meals and fed the family always with a smile on her face. Mohandas said his mother never lost her composure or her temper. Often the young Mohandas would sit at the window praying to God for the clouds to part so his mother could see the sun and eat a meal. Sometimes his prayer was granted and the sun did peek out of the clouds and Mohandas would call his mother urgently to the window but often before she could leave what she was doing and come to the window the sun would

---

* Ed. The quotes mentioned in this article follow an oral tradition within the Gandhi family, hence they do not originate in written sources.

disappear behind the clouds again. At such times, Putliba would smile and tell her son: 'God does not want me to eat today so don't fret over it.'

This extraordinary commitment and sacrifice remained imprinted on Mohandas' mind forever. His mother could well have broken the vow anytime she wanted to but she never did, despite the arduous tribulations. She would say to Mohandas: 'I made a promise to God and I will have to live with the disgrace if I break it.' The importance of being true to your word was deeply instilled in the young boy.

Then there was the spiritual lesson taught by his nanny, Rambha. She was appalled that Mohandas, as a young boy, was so fearful of darkness, robbers and snakes that he would not enter – or sleep in – a dark room. Rambha taught him that Lord Rama always protected the believers and that all he had to do was chant the name of the Lord whenever assailed by fear or distress. This became a daily practice and it not only helped him overcome his fear but awakened in him the realization that full faith in one's belief was very important. It was this faith in a higher power that sustained Mohandas through the trials and tragedies of an intense political life.

Since Gandhi effectively used nonviolence as a strategy to win India's independence philosophers have focused more on *satyagraha* as a strategy rather than *satyagraha* as a way of life. Indeed, the point that we have all missed is that nonviolence is not as Gandhi put it, a jacket that one can wear today and discard tomorrow.

The reason why Gandhi expressed this thought is because he realized that humans respond to a conflict in the way they are taught. Over centuries, human beings have allowed themselves to be dominated by an oppressive culture of violence. Indeed, violence is so deep rooted that we truly believe conflict is an integral part of human life. The sad consequence of this belief is that our emotions, attitudes, relationships, responses, in fact, every aspect of our life are governed by negative feelings and thoughts. Suspicion, hate, prejudice, dislikes, discrimination, greed, selfishness are some of the many negative thoughts, feelings and attitudes that determine our relationships leading inevitably to conflict. We have created a highly combustible world of exploitation and the best analogy to describe our situation is that of a family living in a highly combustible home with a penchant to play with matches. There are only two options available to the family, either let the conflagration consume the home or attempt to douse the fire with buckets of water. What should one do when neither seems to work well? Learn to stop playing with matches.

Gandhi's *satyagraha* has many facets to it. The first is that to practice *satyagraha* one has to make a sincere attempt to replace the culture of violence with a culture of nonviolence. It means replacing the negative thoughts, attitudes and emotions with positive thoughts, attitudes and emotions. Love, understanding, respect, compassion and more are essential feelings to enable oneself to practice *satyagraha,* or nonviolence. One cannot practice nonviolence with anger, hate and prejudice in one's heart just as one who is trained as an engineer cannot perform a medical procedure.

The second aspect of *satyagraha* is the recognition that injustices have many facets. There are social, economic, religious, cultural, gender, race and many other forms of injustice in the world, each requiring a different approach. Unlike violence, which teaches us to fight and destroy 'our enemies,' *satyagraha* teaches us to change our enemies into friends and change injustice into justice.

While involved in the struggle for India's independence from the British Gandhi recognized the existence of other conflicts. Children were given inadequate education, women were tormented and denied equality, and the oppressive caste system had relegated millions to the status of slaves, to name a few. Gandhi had the ability to recognize the abilities of volunteers and entrusted them with the responsibilities of conducting *satyagraha* in different fields. Opening schools to educate children in a holistic manner, educating conservative adults to give greater freedom and equality to women and liberating the low caste and bringing them into mainstream Indian life. Thus, *satyagraha* was fought at many different levels.

Mohandas' childhood curiosity ignited by his experiences as a leader led him to study the scriptures of all the different religions of the world. Mohandas recognized the fact that a country as diverse as India could be ruled either by dividing the various factions and letting them fight among themselves, or by teaching each other respect for diverse beliefs and living with respect. He was not a protagonist of divide-and-rule so he studied the scriptures to speak to each religious group with authority. Gandhi's study revealed that no religion was perfect and none could claim to possess the whole truth.

Mohandas believed a philosophy, whether religious or intellectual, must keep changing just as *truth* does so that it can remain vibrant and meaningful. Change does not necessarily mean throwing away the core and replacing it with something totally different. What it needs to change is the chaff that engulfs the core values, otherwise a great philosophy can be quickly reduced to a meaningless dogma. There was, according to Gandhi, a distinct difference between rituals and religion. Rituals are often meaningless. It is not how often we pray that counts, but how sincerely that prayer makes a difference in our lives and our relationships with one another. We cannot fill our hearts with hate, violence and disgust and profess love for God. All religions of the world, as understood and practiced today, Gandhi believed, have been interpreted by imperfect human beings often leading to grave misunderstandings. Since *truth* itself is ever changing, we can begin to comprehend its meaning only if we have an open mind. At one stage, Gandhi proclaimed that he would like his mind to be like a room with many open windows allowing the breeze to flow in from every direction but refusing to be blown away by any one of them. The conflict today is that the world is divided unequally between those who believe we 'possess the *truth*' and those who believe that we can only 'pursue the *truth*.' Possession of truth indicates a closed mind while an honest and sincere pursuit of truth reveals an open mind. Mohandas was convinced that God can only be manifest in goodness, truth, love and respect and other such positive attributes and values. No God can ever profess or condone hatred, prejudice, violence and such negativity.

The third woman to teach Mohandas the most significant lesson was his child bride, Kastur. They were both 13 years old when they were married. As the relationship developed Mohandas was confused about who laid down the rules and enforced them. The only model Mohandas had to go by was that of his father who always played the role of the master of the house. Was that right? Or is there another form of relationship? Gandhi wanted to be perfect. Mohandas sought books from Western culture to determine the ideal relationship between a husband and wife. Alas, the books he found were written by male chauvinists who advocated the husband be the master, lay down strict rules and enforce them vigorously.

The Gandhis, like traditional Indians, lived as a 'joint family' where several generations and several branches of a family lived in one house with the eldest becoming the *de facto* head of the household. In such families, during the day the men were either out at work or spent their time in the outer precincts of the home with visitors, while the women attended to household chores and nurtured relationships with friends and other families. Each functioned independently of the other for the most part.

Armed with what he considered to be the gospel of Western rectitude Mohandas decided he was going to change the rules and become the master. He would ensure strictly that his wife obeyed his orders. One day, in the privacy of their bedroom, Mohandas brusquely declared: 'From tomorrow you will not step out of this house without my permission. That is my order and I will entertain no arguments.'

Unschooled, yet wise beyond words, Kastur considered this remark to be unworthy of a response. She did not retort nor did she indicate in any way that she disrespected her husband's wishes. She simply went to bed without saying a word. She knew that none of the other women of the Gandhi household ever asked their husbands before going about their business inside or outside the house so Kastur decided to follow suit. Mohandas realized that his wife was being 'defiant' and he was going to have none of this. Once again, in the privacy of their bedroom, Mohandas confronted Kastur: 'How dare you disobey me? Did I not tell you not to go out without my permission?'

Kastur realized she could not ignore Mohandas this time and decided to express herself in a manner that did not seem defiant or arrogant. She simply asked: 'I was brought up to believe that we must always obey the elders in the house and

I believe that your mother is the elder I should be following. Do you want me to tell her that I will no longer obey her but obey you instead?'

Mohandas did not anticipate this question. He had no answer. Obviously, he could not tell Kastur to disobey his mother. The matter was settled without anyone getting angry or straining a relationship. It was not only an outstanding lesson in anger management but, Mohandas proclaimed later, it was the most profound lesson in nonviolent conflict resolution. Under similar circumstances, one would be tempted to retort in anger which could escalate and even break up a relationship. Later, when Mohandas developed his philosophy of nonviolence he realized that anger management was the first and most important step in the practice of nonviolence.

A victim of prejudice

In 1893, at the age of 24, Gandhi received an unexpected invitation to South Africa. The contract between him and an Indian merchant was for one year of legal advice. The desire to earn money and help the family pay back the enormous loan taken for his education in England was so compelling that he accepted this offer without hesitation although it meant, once again, a prolonged absence from his wife and children. At this point, nonviolent public action or the philosophy of nonviolence was not even remotely on his radar screen. However, it was one defining moment when extreme insult evoked extreme anger. He remembered the wisdom with which his wife responded to a similar situation and came to the conclusion that he had to channel his anger into positive action. Nonviolence was the response that ultimately took birth.

It was that fateful moment in South Africa when he decided he was important enough to travel in a first class railway compartment that changed not only one man's life, but the way the world would look at conflict resolution. Gandhi became a victim of vicious prejudice and was physically thrown off the train because his skin was of a darker shade. This incident enraged him and, typically like most of us, his first reaction was to seek vengeance. When he called upon his Indian friends to mobilize a strong opposition he was mortified to find out how they preferred to meekly submit to injustice and indignities heaped on them by the white community in South Africa.

Where is our self-respect and dignity, he asked. How can anyone submit to such prejudices? What can we do? Are we really so helpless? We do not have the weapons or the power to fight the establishment, the Indians replied. Until this moment, 'fight' was construed to mean physical violence or war. People appeared to be unaware that there was a peaceful choice. Should self-respecting people become helpless victims of injustice, Mohandas wondered.

The more Mohandas analyzed the evils of prejudice the more convinced he became that there was more to violence than human beings realized. Violence was daily being committed not only in the form of physical violence but more in the form of 'passive' violence. He defined passive violence as the kind of violence where no physical force was used but, nevertheless, one's actions or inactions, one's words or the lack of them, one's attitude or ineptitude hurt someone directly or indirectly. The more he contemplated this thought the more he realized that humankind practiced passive violence on a much larger scale and often without even realizing it. The result was that passive violence generated anger in the victim and since the victim knew of no other way of expressing their anger they resorted to physical violence to get justice. It became clear to Gandhi that it was passive violence that fueled the fire of physical violence. Anger management thus became the first step in learning to practice nonviolence.

Anger and electricity, Gandhi realized, had something in common. Both could be powerful and useful if channeled intelligently – or deadly and destructive if abused. Anger used intelligently was also liberating. On another occasion when Gandhi became a victim of physical abuse and the police invited him to the police station to file charges against his tormentors he went to the police station but declined to file charges. Punishing them, Gandhi argued, would serve no purpose. Gandhi told the perpetrators of violence that he preferred to forgive them and hoped they would learn a lesson that prejudice and violence are not for civilized human beings. Besides, Gandhi realized, by punishing those who do wrong we punish ourselves because we are never happy with the amount of punishment meted out. It weighs on our minds leading to unhappiness and even anger and frustration. Forgiving his tormentors, on the other hand, was calming and released him from violent thoughts. All of these experiences made it clear to Gandhi that human society everywhere was inexorably dominated by a 'culture of violence' that seeped into every aspect of life from language to relationships. It was greed and selfishness that fueled violence in every sphere of life. Violence seeks to control through fear, which means to acquire greater control the level of fear must keep escalating. It is only when humankind can be liberated from fear and greed, Gandhi said, that civilization will become more meaningful. The concept of nonviolence thus began to expand and acquire new dimensions.

The more Gandhi practiced nonviolence, the more convinced he became that just as darkness cannot be dispelled by darkness violence cannot be quelled by violence. It is only light that can destroy darkness and therefore only respect and understanding – nonviolence – can overcome violence. Gandhi's experiences with racial prejudice in South Africa compelled him to stay there for twenty-one years during which time he organized many civil disobedience campaigns against injustice. It was during his first incarceration in South Africa that he found a copy of Henry David Thoreau's book *Civil Disobedience* and, after reading it, Gandhi proclaimed that he felt vindicated that such a great philosopher as Thoreau also expressed the same thoughts on nonviolence as he did.

Later, Gandhi discovered books by Count Leo Tolstoy who advocated passive resistance as a viable nonviolent way to resolve conflicts. By then Gandhi began to be disillusioned by both civil disobedience and passive resistance because he saw nothing 'disobedient' or 'passive' in seeking justice and fair play. Gandhi decided nonviolence was not only an active force, but a far superior weapon than anything produced by the culture of violence. For too long the word nonviolence represented the opposite of violence and had therefore acquired a negative connotation. Gandhi saw it differently. By removing the hyphen nonviolence became a word on its own besides, to practice nonviolence one has to be in a positive frame of mind totally immersed in love, respect, compassion, understanding and other such positive emotions and attitudes while to practice violence one has to be angry, hateful, prejudiced and senseless. This brought to the fore the question: Can nonviolence be practiced as a strategy or, to rephrase it, is nonviolence just another weapon in the armory?

Gandhi found it more and more difficult to accept nonviolence as a coat that can be worn today and discarded tomorrow. For nonviolence to succeed humankind had to break from the culture of violence that dominates every aspect of life. Unless one begins to think nonviolently and behave nonviolently, Gandhi was convinced, one cannot act nonviolently if a situation requires it. This line of thought gave rise to a search for a term that best described the expanded philosophy. When the constraints of the English language made it difficult for Gandhi to find a suitable word, he launched a competition and his nephew, Maganlal Gandhi, came up with a combination of two Sanskrit words: *satya* meaning truth and *agraha* meaning pursuit of. Thus was born a comprehensive movement called *satyagraha – the pursuit of truth*. Since Gandhi believed that truth is God and since life is about a search for God or salvation, *satyagraha* was an appropriate name for a philosophy of life.

To practice *satyagraha* effectively one must relinquish the culture of violence. Otherwise, we could be caught in an endless struggle of putting out fires only to find them raging again and again. In some ways, our present disposition with regard to conflict resolution is like trying to put out a blaze with a tanker full of water and a tanker full of gasoline with both liquids being poured into the conflagration simultaneously. It is for this reason that we find conflicts flaring up over and over again. What exactly did Gandhi mean by transformation to a culture of nonviolence?

The first step is to learn what is anger, what are the issues that provoke anger within you, how can you stop yourself from reacting in a moment of madness and how can you channel the energy generated by anger into positive action. For those of us who ignored this training the result is that we abuse anger and cause violence – physical, emotional or passive. According to Gandhi, it is just as violent to express anger verbally as it is to express anger physically. There is an interesting episode in Gandhi's life that illustrates the point appropriately. In

1913, just before Gandhi decided to leave South Africa forever, he launched one final nonviolent campaign against racial injustice. As always, everything that Gandhi did was transparently open to the public. He kept no secrets. When his plans were made, he informed everyone from the Prime Minister, General Jan Christian Smuts, to the local police precinct and through the media he made the public aware of what would happen and when. After Gandhi announced his plan, the workers of the South African railways decided to strike for better working conditions. Gandhi considered this to be an important issue for the public and considered it 'unfair' to put added pressure on the government in a moment of crisis. Gandhi withdrew his campaign. The railway workers pleaded to make common cause since we 'are fighting a common enemy.' Besides, a strike is a legitimate nonviolent strategy. But Gandhi responded that he did not have any 'enemies' and although a strike is a nonviolent strategy he did not wish to take the responsibility of associating with people who were not adequately trained in nonviolent action.

The strike took place but there was considerable pent-up anger that manifested itself in the body language and the slogans shouted by the strikers. This atmosphere gave the police the opportunity to infiltrate the ranks of the strikers, cause an incident and unleash extreme violence to crush the strike. After four days, the workers called off the strike and went back to work without gaining any of their demands. Later, Gandhi launched his campaign and several weeks later Prime Minister General Smuts invited Gandhi to discuss a settlement. At the talks, General Smuts confessed to Gandhi that he did not know how to deal with someone who was so considerate and compassionate while he had no problem dealing with angry railway workers with violence. The lesson is obvious: anger in any form in a nonviolent campaign is detrimental to its success.

Anger is an emotion that one must work to control on a continuous basis. It is unfortunately widely believed that anger is evil and that it should either be suppressed or, at best, expressed harmlessly. Gandhi disagreed with this line of thinking. He was convinced that it is not anger *per se* that one should be ashamed of but the way one abuses anger. We need to learn how to use this energy intelligently.

The second step is to be committed to *truth* just as Gandhi was. He insisted on examining all issues from every different perspective and only after he knew all the details would he begin a dialogue or launch correspondence with the adversary. If dialogue reaches a stalemate only then would he launch a protest campaign. At no time would he embarrass or take undue advantage of his opponent. It is for this reason that Gandhi vehemently opposed dehumanizing anyone with such words as 'enemies' or 'adversaries.' An opponent to Gandhi was just a misguided 'friend' who needed to be shown the *truth*.

The third most important aspect of Gandhi's philosophy is relationship building. All living creatures and, especially, all human beings must be treated with utmost respect. The idea of dehumanizing people, something that is so widely done in a culture of violence, is totally rejected by Gandhi. In fact, he insisted, that relationships must be built on the positive foundations of respect, understanding, acceptance and appreciation as against the current practice of building relationships based on self-interest. It is only when we respect each other and all of creation that we understand who we are, what we are and why are we here on earth. The advent of human beings on earth is not an accident. There is a purpose that we cannot fathom because we are so immersed in the culture of violence and the resultant greed and selfishness. So, respecting one's opponent is very important.

It is also important that we look at Gandhi's definition of *peace*. It does not mean the absence of war or the absence of violence, but peace must mean the creation of harmony in society, in the nation and between nations. As long as human society is determined to be exploitative – whether individually or internationally – peace will remain elusive. Gandhi attempted to build harmonious communities by setting up ashrams and invited anyone who wanted to live a nonviolent lifestyle to participate. The idea was that those who were trained in the ashrams would go out and influence others in society and a ripple of change will begin from the bottom up. Some have done what was expected but for the most part those trained just went back into society and merged into the tide of violence. Does this mean that Gandhi's philosophy of *satyagraha* is unrealistic? I don't think so. The fault lies with human beings who believe that material possession is all that matters in life. It is only when humanity realizes that materialism and morality have an inverse relationship, that the growth of one leads to the demise of the other, that we will learn to give morality the importance it deserves and be successful in establishing a nonviolent society.

26
Ghaffar Khan:
Gautama Buddha of Hashtnagar

Syed Sikander Mehdi

> Tomorrow is always too late. But it is never too late for peace. That is
> why we must make a start in writing a historical record that is different,
> one that, for the time being, we can only describe.
>
> Federico Mayor

My visit to the Khyber Pass[1] in September 2006 was not for the first time. I had
been to this place before. However, the experience this time was unique in the
sense that I was overwhelmed not by the usual historical narratives of the armies
marching through the Pass, but by the glimpses of another past, a past which
was scattered all over the place, which was always there and which is nowhere.
It was here at the Khyber Pass on that windy, chilly September afternoon where
the other past came running to me and whispered: 'History is not a war museum
only. It is also a peace museum. You are welcome to the peace museum on the
lands of the proud Pathans.[2] This is the museum where Khan Abdul Ghaffar
Khan – Gautama Buddha of Hashtnagar – lives. Have you ever heard of him?'

Born in 1890[3] in Hashtnagar, now known as Asghatnager or 'eight towns' in
the village of Utmanzi, Ghaffar Khan is perhaps the greatest Pathan of all times.
Undoubtedly, he is the most prominent apostle of nonviolence after Gandhi in
modern India and one of the outstanding nonviolent leaders of the twentieth
century.* However, awareness about his life, nonviolent struggle and sufferings
is still rather limited and his remarkable contribution to peace is still widely
unrecognized. It is only in recent years, and the protracting war and violence
in Afghanistan since the invasion of Soviet troops in Kabul in December 1979
and the unending upheavals and acts of terrorism especially in the Pakhtun
belt cutting across the Afghan–Pakistan borders, that the post 9/11 panicky
world is turning to him for salvation. Due to the upsurge of Muslim anger and

---

* Ed. For more on Mahatma Gandhi's concepts of peace, see Chapter 25.

militancy around the world, the concerned power centers, leading international research institutes focusing on Islam, Muslim societies, terrorism and on peace and nonviolence are now looking at Ghaffar Khan as the savior of the future.

They are also looking at him with amazement and disbelief: How can a Muslim be an apostle of peace and nonviolence? How can someone from among the Pathans – a people widely known for centuries for valor, warriorism and savagery – be nonviolent? How could he raise the soldiers of faith and nonviolence in a region frequently trampled by the armies passing through the Khyber Pass? Is it not all mythology woven around the Khan?

These queries are important and need to be attended to, because the misperceptions are widespread and there is a dearth of historical account throwing light on the other past, which was always there and which is nowhere. For instance, it should be noted that the history of the events taking place at the Khyber Pass and in the adjoining areas is not merely a history of the Aryans descending upon the fertile northern plains in 1500 BC and overwhelming the native Dravidian population; the Persians under Darius crossing into the Punjab in the sixth century BC to annex yet another province of the Achaemenian Empire; the armies of Alexander the Great marching through the pass in 326 BC to reach the plains of the Indus; the Scythians, white Huns, Seljuks, Tartars, Mongols, Sassanians, Turks, Moghuls and Durranis making successive inroads into the territory beyond the Peshawar valley and the Indus (*Afghan Network*, 2006).

The history of the Khyber Pass and beyond is clearly much more than all this. The region can really boast a grand heritage of peace and nonviolence. Banished from history for centuries, the narratives of this heritage need to be recalled not only to explain the disinheritance of intolerance and violence by Ghaffar Khan, a pious and practicing Muslim and a Pathan to the core, but also to strongly suggest that a peaceful Muslim society, even a peaceful Pakistani society, is possible.

History, in fact, whispers at every nook and cranny of Hashtnagar, the birthplace of Ghaffar Khan, and a tract in Charsadda Tehsil of the Peshawar District, comprising a strip of territory that extends ten miles eastward from the Swat River and stretches from the hills in the north to the Kabul River in the south. The archeological site having a cluster of imposing mounds in Charsadda, 30 kilometers north east of Peshawar, is identified with Pushkalavati (the Lotus City), the ancient capital of Gandhara during the days before the Kushan emperors transferred the seat of government to Peshawar. During the Ghandhara period, one may point out, Charsadda, Taxila and Swat were the main centers of culture, trade and learning and Taxila also had a grand university attracting students and scholars from near and far away places including China.

Hashtnagar and its adjoining areas stretching to Charsadda, Takhtabai, Dir, Swat, Shehhaz Garhi, Jamal Garhi, Chota Lahore, Hund, Attock and Taxila and comprising Peshawar valley was the seat of various flourishing civilizations and was comprehensively influenced by Buddhism in particular. A culture of peace was there and it flowered in these territories and beyond, and flourished for centuries.

One also may be dazzled by the images of the gentle and peaceful reign and rule of King Asoka – the Peace King of India – as governor of the land, the mushrooming of the monasteries teaching and preaching love, and the tolerance and peace in the areas where the Gandhara civilization once flourished. Then there are the images of the dancing, laughing, colorfully dressed women and children and the wandering and singing Buddhist monks and their followers that blink and glitter like neon signs in the darkness of historical narratives of wars and warriorism woven around the Khyber Pass and beyond. History whispers to me again: 'These monasteries, stupas, trading, dancing, learning places are not mere images. These are real things. Just have a feel of these. Move around with me in the peace museum and see for yourself this world of peace which Ghaffar Khan had inherited.'

And I move around with the past, which was always there and which is nowhere, and with great amazement I look at a gigantic stupa emerging from behind the Khyber Pass, from just outside the Ganj Gate in the old city of Peshawar, a stupa built by the great Kushan King Kaishka I to house the relics of Buddha, a stupa which was probably the tallest building of India at that time (*Audarya Fellowship*, 2009). In amazement, I also see the four statues of lord Buddha at the base of an enormous peepal (banyon) tree on the bank of River Bara, near the confluence where today stand Bazar-i-Bazzazan (cloth market) and Batair Bazar (bird sellers' market) in the heart of Peshawar city (Ishaq, 2006). Moreover, I see hundreds of colorful monasteries and stupas preaching peace and nonviolence and numerous monuments and rock pillars jeweled with Buddhist teachings, principles and codes of conduct. For centuries, the religion of the people of this region was Buddhism. Little wonder that Ghaffar Khan emerged from the shadows of these monasteries, stupus and other learning places as a remarkable apostle of nonviolence.

His unshakeable adherence to nonviolence may also be understood in the light of his family background. He was the fourth child of Behram Khan, a rich landlord and a highly respected Khan of his village. Writing about his father, D.G. Tendulkar (1967) observes in his excellent biography of the Khan:

He had neither pride nor vanity of being a Chief Khan of Hashtnagar, of Muhammadzai clan. He was humble, God-fearing and self-restrained. He was so trustworthy that the poor people would come and leave all their savings in his keeping, for his word was as good as his bond. He had many friends and no enemies. He had no feuds – a unique distinction for a Khan – because he had forgiven all his enemies. He knew no revenge. He believed that there was no dishonour in being deceived, it lay in deceiving. He was a man of his word and was so transparently truthful that none dared to disbelieve or contradict him.

He never told a lie, he had not known how to. When there was any village feud he took the side of the underdog. He never believed in dancing attendance upon those in authority, but they held him in awe. (Tendulkar, 1967, p. 13)

Tendulkar adds:

Both the father and the mother were unlettered, they lived more in the world of the spirit than of the flesh. The mother would often sit down after her namaz to meditate in silence. She cooked food in a big pot and distributed it among the poor neighbours. Though there was a retinue of servants in the house, the father would insist on carrying a basketful of nan on his head and a platter of cooked vegetable to his village Hujra for travelers passing through. 'The traveling visitors, unknown and uncared for, are veritable guests of God' he would say, 'and that is why I like to carry the food for them.' (Tendulkar, 1967, p. 14)

The influence that the family exercised on the religious thinking and practice of Ghaffar Khan was doubtless crucial. Equally significant was the influence of political thinking and action of his forefathers. Nonviolent activism was an important feature of family tradition and despite belonging to the privileged and political elite of the region, the elders and leaders of the family espoused the cause of the poor and challenged the power of the powerful. Though not unfriendly with the British officials, Khan's father, Behram Khan, was critical of the Pathans' crossing all limits to seek the favor of the British and 'not without a sense of shame, he used to recall how his elder brother served the British by commanding the military guard of the Charsadda Treasury' (Tendulkar, 1967, p. 14).

Ghaffar Khan learnt the early lessons of history and politics from his father and learnt more from the narratives of the heroics of his forefathers. The very fact that his grandfather, Saifullah Khan, always sided with his oppressed brethren whenever the British had any clash with the tribes or tried to subjugate them had a profound impact upon him. What also made him proud and prepared him to endure all kinds of sufferings and not to compromise on principles was the shining example of his father's grandfather, Obaidullah Khan, who was hanged by the Durranis, the rulers, for his enlightenment and patriotism (Khan, 2004, p. 8).

Later, Ghaffar Khan's involvement in Indian politics, his closeness to and emotional attachment with Gandhi, his courageous nonviolent movement against the British Raj, his fierce and relentless struggle for democracy, justice, equal rights and equitable power and resource sharing among all the provinces and peoples of Pakistan and his enormous capacity to suffer for the causes important to him, steeled him into a fearless non-compromising crusader of nonviolence.

How relevant is Khan's nonviolent struggle for the contemporary world and especially for the Muslim world where violence abounds? This question came to my mind when I was wandering in amazement in the peace museum of history. The museum was glimmering with the narratives of his life and struggle and highlighting the importance he attached to education, peace potentials of religion, place of women in society, freedom and honor and peace and nonviolence in his struggle during the British Raj and after.

To begin with, by any calculation or criterion, Ghaffar Khan was a man of the future. He was the son of unlettered parents and he himself had a rather modest formal education.[4] But he strived to promote literacy in the Frontier province in extremely challenging circumstances. These were, indeed, very difficult times. Very modest educational facilities were available on the eve of the twentieth century. There was no university in the province and the only college, Edward Mission College at Peshawar, was affiliated to Punjab University at Lahore. The number of matriculates in the whole province was only fifteen in 1891 and seventy-one in 1903, in hardly a dozen schools. Worse still, the obscurantist religious forces were then deadly opposed to mission schools and the teaching of English in particular. 'Any parent sending his son to the Mission Schools will be excommunicated' was the *fatwa* of the *Mullahs* when such schools were opened. Later the position was somewhat modified: 'Let the boys go to school but beware lest they learn English, for English is the language of infidelity and will certainly destroy their souls.' And still later: 'Let the boys read English, so long as they do not read the Christian scriptures, for the Christians have tampered with these books and it is no longer lawful for the Muslims to read them' (Tendulkar, 1967, p. 18).

Fearing their loss of political clout, the *Mullahs* opposed the opening of modern schools and ferociously campaigned against the promotion of critical temper and creative thinking. They encouraged their *Madressah* pupils and others to recite the following verses loudly and ardently in open areas and market places:

Sabaq de madrase wai – Para de paise wai
Janat Ke bae zai navi – Dozakh Ke bai ghase wahi

In English, it translates as 'Those who learn at school, they do for money. They will have no place in heaven and will find themselves in hell' (Tendulkar, 1967, p. 17).[5]

In this context, critically damaging was the unholy alliance between the British colonial government and its agents in the NWFP (North West Frontier Province) and the *Mullahs*. Being apprehensive of the liberating effect of modern education upon a restive and defiant population, the British discouraged and resisted the opening of schools in the province, and encouraged the *Mullahs* to vilify modern education on a religious pretext.

The government became far more ruthless with the arrival of Lord Curzon as the new Viceroy of India in 1897. In swift succession, a series of measures were taken by Delhi to spread fear and force obedience. The Frontier was put directly under the Viceroy's control so that crucial decisions could be taken swiftly; hill tribes were compulsorily separated from those living in the settled districts to complete the vivisection of the Pathans; a standing army of 10,000 men was kept to guard the province along a 200 mile perimeter, from Malakand in the north to the southern tip of Waziristan on the Indian border; more forts were built and railway lines and roads were laid down for the swift movement of the army to disturbed areas; a 6000 man police force was to maintain peace; a series of restrictive laws known as Frontier Crimes Regulations were enacted, which could be applied to 'transport' or send a man to a foreign penal colony for life without court or trial; and justice was put in the hands of the political agent or pro-British landlords invited to hear the cases (Easwaran, 2001, p. 65). On November 9, 1901, the North West Frontier Province was created and reduced to a virtual armed garrison or police state.

Such were the conditions of the NWFP when Ghaffar Khan opened a school in his village Utmanzai. 'Neither he nor Curzon could have imagined that someday the small school would help to undermine the Viceroy's plans' (Easwaran, 2001, p. 66). The opening of the school in Utmanzai in 1910 proved to be a turning point in the Frontier's politics. The village of the Khan soon became the center of nonviolent action and a seat of people's power. It grew into a sort of political academy teaching and preaching peace and nonviolence and stressing the importance of modern education. Utmanzai also emerged as a challenger to the British government in the Frontier and the *Mullahs* and other collaborators in the region. Subsequent developments further alarmed the British and the collaborators.

The Khan was not content with the opening of only one school. He wanted to open more and moved around the length and breadth of the province campaigning in favor of establishing schools and enhancing political consciousness of the downtrodden masses. His candid discussions with the powerless gave a direction to the people. Not much later, he began campaigns for the empowerment of women, for equal rights for all and for building up a nonviolent army of God and directly challenged the power of the colonial lords, the local feudal lords and the *Mullahs*.

The British responded by unleashing a poisonous propaganda against the Khan and his mission, threatening and coercing him, putting restrictions on his movements from place to place, bribing the teachers to leave the schools or threatening them of dire consequences if they continued to serve the schools, and frequently throwing him into prison. But Ghaffar Khan, like the mountains under whose shadows he had grown up, remained undaunted and did not bow down. He went on with his movement for freedom, spread of literacy, enhancement of political and social awareness and for equal rights for all including women.

Ghaffar Khan was a great champion of women's rights. He urged upon his people to recognize the value and importance of women as human beings and as equal partners in the society and fought against the traditions, customs and laws that discriminated against women. He openly expressed his displeasure about the Pathan custom of accepting money in return for giving the hand of their girl in marriage. He often referred to his own marriage. Almost a century ago, in 1912, he got married, but his wife's father did not demand any money. Ghaffar Khan often praised his father-in-law in public for being 'the first Khan not to accept money for the hands of his daughter' and also for making a will bequeathing a full share of inheritance to his female relatives. Besides projecting the modernistic approach of the Khan towards social issues including women's issues, such examples clearly impacted upon the social and political consciousness of the male-dominated Pathan society (Muhammad, 1989). The approach, moreover, had a transformative effect as he often referred to Islamic teachings in this context.

He, for instance, criticized gender discrimination and said: 'Inferiority and superiority depend on deeds and not gender. [...] God has created men and women to be partners in the development of civilization. They are the two wheels of humanity's carriage which cannot run on one wheel alone' (Khan in Muhammad, 1989). Again, addressing a large gathering of women at Bhaizai, he declared:

God makes no distinction between men and women. If someone can surpass another, it is only through good deeds and morals. If you study history, you will see that there were many scholars and poets amongst women. It is a grave mistake we have made in degrading women. [...] In the Holy Koran, you have an equal share with men. You are today oppressed because we men have ignored the commands of God and the prophet. Today we are the followers of custom and we oppress you. But thank God that we have realized that our gain and loss, progress and downfall are common. (Khan in Easwaran, 2001, p. 133)

The Khan strongly advocated female education and bravely confronted the centuries-old hardened male attitude towards the issue. He relentlessly fought for a change in such attitudes and often pointed out that Islam had made learning obligatory for men and women alike. He also saw to it that his daughter not only went to the school, but also traveled to Europe for higher studies. He, in fact, faced opposition within his own family for sending his daughter to school. This was in spite of the fact that the school to which she was going was in the house of a local Khan and his own wife taught there.

Besides advocating female education, Ghaffar Khan openly encouraged the Pathan women to step out from the medieval world behind the veil and take an active interest in public life, and the women actively and positively responded to the call of their liberator. They began attending his public meetings and the number grew with the passage of time. In such meetings, they could be seen seated on the roofs and around the venue and taking an active interest in the proceedings. At a special meeting of women held at Lundkhawar near Mardan, the female participants presented a letter of appreciation to Ghaffar Khan, which among other things included the following verse: '*Should young men not keep up with you, Fakhr-e-Afghana, don't worry, we girls will see you through victory*' (Muhammad, 1989).

The women actively supported the *Khudai Khidmatgars*'[6] struggle. 'It made,' the Khan recalls, 'a big impact on young and old, men, women and children alike. Girls had also made themselves red clothes [color of the dress of *Khudai Khidmatgars*] and learnt poems by heart, which they recited to other women-folk. They read *Pakhtun* [Khan's monthly journal] with eagerness. When *Pakhtun* arrived, girls would gather around. One girl would read it aloud, while the others listened. In this way the *Khudai Khidmatgars* aroused interest in reading newspapers' (Muhammad, 1989).

Indeed, so profound was the impact of *Khudai Khidmagars*' movement on women that they were no more afraid of death for their cause. Highlighting the point, Ghaffar Khan writes in his autobiography that once the colonial police opened fire on a public meeting of the *Khudai Khidmatgars* held at Utmanzai. The firing was so intense that men began running in all directions for their life. At such a time, a young Pathan woman, sister of Rab Nawaz, ran towards the place where firing was incessant and intense. The men in flight from the meeting called her to stop, not to go where the firing was taking place and asked as to why was she going towards the place where firing was incessant. The young woman shouted back that she was going into the jaws of death because the male Pathans were so cowardly that they were running away to save their life and they had no consideration for the honor of the Pathan. Tremendously moved because of the valor of the woman, the men in flight stopped running and then moved towards the meeting place. They were no more afraid of police firing and death. They encircled the British police and dictated it to accept their demands (Khan, 2004, pp. 113–114).

Such was the power of the Pakhtun women, who were encouraged by Ghaffar Khan to fight for their equal rights and fight with the Pakhtun men to achieve freedom from colonial yoke. Since the rise of the *Taliban*[7] in Afghanistan and Pakistan in the 1990s, these very Pakhtun women faced the grim prospect of their forced return to the medieval world of degradation, disempowerment, ignorance and gross neglect. Once again, they were (and still are) ambushed by the dark forces of religious extremists. Also under assault today is the nonviolence-teaching and peace-promoting religion of Islam. The fully armed *Taliban* and their supporters near the Khyber Pass and beyond refuse to see the giant figure of the Gautama Buddha of Hashtnagar emerging out of the stupa built by the great Kushan King Kanishka I at Peshawar.

But standing at the Pass, I see him and hear him clearly; he tearfully says that violence and terrorism committed in the name of Islam by the *Taliban* and other terror-striking forces and their warlords has nothing to do with the faith of Islam and the glory of the faith cannot be achieved through human killing and violence.

'A devout Muslim,' observes Easwaran in his excellent biography of the Khan, 'he showed in his life a face of Islam which non-Islamic countries seldom see, proving that within the scope of Islam exists a noble alternative to violence' (Easwaran, 2001, p. 12). The Khan was, indeed, a devout Muslim. Languishing in jails or under house arrest during the British Raj and in independent Pakistan for over thirty years, attending and addressing numerous political meetings, conversing with fellow Pathans, with the opponents, with Pakistani officials and others, moving for days, months and years in the villages, towns and cities, he remembered to say his prayers five times a day and performed other obligatory commandants as well. He also used to read the Qur'an regularly. However, he never hated other religions or the followers of other faiths. He knew Islam as a faith of love and tolerance. He said:

> One great weakness amongst us people of Hindustan is that we are unable to tolerate in others something that is forbidden according to our own creed. We hold the same expectations of others as we do of those of our own faith. We do not think – if something is forbidden in our religion, it is forbidden for our co-religionists, not for others, who share the same faith. (Khan in Bult, 1989)

He added:

> The truth is, all revealed religions have come to us from God. They have come in order to bring unity, love and amity to the world, so that people should make life easy for others and serve God's creatures. It is incumbent upon followers of religion to rid the world of hate and intolerance. They should imbue God's creatures with a spirit of love and mutual regard, so that they may offer one another a helping hand. (Khan in Bult, 1989)

Ghaffar Khan was not only a preacher of religious harmony and co-flourishing; he practiced what he preached during the times when communal conflict and religious hatred was already spreading in British India. Way back in 1930, when he was in Gujrat jail, he worked to promote inter-faith harmony and requested the jail authorities to arrange for the teaching of Qur'an for the Hindus and Gita for the Muslims. He used to give lecturers on the Qur'an there and a Hindu Pandit Jagat Ram Haryanni used to give the lessons of Gita (Khan, 2004, pp. 100–101). He himself often used to read Gita. Throughout his life, he paid respect to all the religions including Hinduism. Little wonder that when he was with Gandhi at Wardah, he used to join the latter in daily prayers and also in Tulsi Ramayan reading every morning (Korejo, 1994, p. 77).

As a matter of fact, Khan Abdul Ghaffar Khan, a very devout Muslim, was of the view that though different religions pursue different paths, they approach the same and only God. As such, all religions are the religions of the same God, who is also Muslims' God. He therefore belonged to all religions and had absolutely no problem in identifying himself with all of them and strived to promote religious harmony during very difficult times. His relevance to the contemporary times, when inter-faith mistrust and conflict are on the rise, is clearly very much there. Rajmohan Gandhi observes:

> We saw that Ghaffar Khan the Muslim thought that 'prayer in whatever language or form was addressed to one and the same God'. His daily life demonstrated this belief in the unity of humanity. We noticed the joy with which he showed the Buddha statues of Bamiyan to Kamaluayan Bajaj and Madalasa Agarwal, statues that the Taliban would later destroy. Comfortable with his Hindu friends, comrades and colleagues, Badshah Khan we saw, also loved westerners and Christians like the Wigram brothers and was even able to forgive a white political foe who had blocked some of his plans, Olaf Caroe. (Gandhi, 2004, pp. 275–276)

Besides his universalist approach toward religion, his application of Islamic values into the making of a nonviolent Pakhtun society and in his struggle against the ruthless oppressors in British India and later in Pakistan are highly relevant for the transformation of the contemporary world, especially that of the Muslim societies. The approach is all the more relevant in the sense that it was not merely conceptualized and theorized, but also fully applied when Ghaffar Khan introduced the *Khudai Khidmatgars* in his nonviolent political action against the British and transformed a scattered, somewhat disoriented and rather violent people into well-disciplined, courageous, nonviolent political activists. The task was not easy. The Khan was aware of the difficulties. He once said:

> The history of my people is full of victories and tales of heroism, but there are drawbacks too. Internal feuds and personal jealousies have always snatched away the gains achieved through vast sacrifices. They were dispersed only because of their own inherent defects, never by any outside power – for who could oppose them on the battlefield? (Khan in Easwaran, 2001, p. 35)

Furthermore, there were the Pathan customs and traditions glorifying warriorism, bloodletting and revenge and confusing peace seeking with shameful acceptance of defeat. Referring to these features of Pathan society, Abdul Ghani

Khan, a renowned Pakhtun poet and philosopher and the eldest son of Ghaffar Khan, writes about the Pathan:

His violent nature, strong body and tender heart make a very unstable combination for living, but an ideal one for poetry. One day he goes out and never comes back. He has laughed his way into a bullet that was fired by another of his own blood and race. His wife inherits from him a moment of joy, two sons, and a lifetime of sorrow. She hangs up his rifle and sitar for his sons. She learns to hide her tears when she hears a love song in the evening. And when the son grows up, 'He must shoot. He has no alternative. Revenge and Death. Death and Revenge… always and forever'. 'The Coward dies', the boy's mother tells him, 'but his shrieks live long after'. So the boy learns not to shriek. He is shown dozens of things dearer than life so that he will not mind either dying or killing. He is forbidden colourful clothes or exotic music, for they weaken the arm and soften the eye. He is taught to look at the hawk and forget the nightingale. It is a perpetual surrender…an eternal giving up of man to man and to their wise follies. (Kahn in Banuri, 1990)

A Pathan himself, Ghaffar Khan knew that such customs and traditions were promoting a culture of violence. He was also aware of the fact that deep down, every Pathan was very religious and could be very easily provoked into any sort of violent act in the name of Islam. He therefore worked for the spread of literacy and promotion of enlightened thinking and told his people about nonviolent Islam, which Islam really is. Frequently referring to the Qur'anic verses and *Hadith* and Islamic traditions, he pointed out that 'the Quran teaches Jihad, which in its real sense means to struggle for the welfare and advancement of its follower' (Khan in Banerjee in Lynch, 2004). 'The Holy prophet Muhammad (PBUH),' he told his people, 'came into the world and taught us that man is a Muslim who never hurts anyone by word or deed, but who works for the benefit and happiness of God's creatures. Belief in God is to love one's fellow men' (Khan in Majeed, 1991).

Again, he made it abundantly clear that his concept of nonviolence was directly derived from Islam and observed: 'There is nothing surprising in a Muslim or a Pashtun like me subscribing to the creed of nonviolence. It is not a new creed. It was followed 1400 years ago by the Holy Prophet (PBUH) all the time he was in Mecca, but we had so forgotten it that when Gandhi placed it before us, we thought he was espousing a novel creed' (Khan in Majeed, 1991).

Standing at the Khyber Pass and listening to the voice of the unheard past, a past which was always there and which is nowhere, I wondered why only the armies of violence led by the Aryans, Greeks, Persians, Seljuks, Mongols and others have a prominent space in our history and in our memory and why the torch bearers of nonviolence were banished. After all, many of these invading armies that rattled around conquered territories, murdered innocent human beings, enslaved people and trampled and destroyed the colorful sites of peace once blooming in the Lotus City *Pushkalavati* – ancient capital of Gandhara before the capital was transferred to Peshawar. The heritage of peace is housed in the peace museum of history, which also proudly displays the colorful images of the army of nonviolence singing love songs, reciting verses from religious books, chanting freedom slogans and marching around like clusters of red roses on the move.

This was the unarmed and harmless army of nonviolence, popularly known as *Khudai Khidmatgars* or servants of God raised in 1930 by Ghaffar Khan. It was not a kind of godless, Bolshevik army. Neither was it a prisoner of rituals, even when it was firmly rooted in religion and derived strength from Islamic teachings and tradition. It was a unique movement against slavery and colonialism and was a living embodiment of Islam as a powerful but peaceful mass movement for political and social change. It called upon its adherents to take an oath that is unique in the context of Pathan history and tradition. Any Pathan aspiring to become a *Khudai Khidmatgar* had to declare solemnly:

I am a *Khudai Khidmatgar*; and as God needs no service, I shall serve Him by serving His creatures selflessly.

I shall never use violence, I shall not retaliate or take revenge, and I shall forgive anyone who indulges in oppression and excesses against me.

I shall not be a party to any intrigue, family feuds and enmity and I shall treat every Pakhtun as my brother and comrade.

I shall give up evil customs and practices.

I shall live a simple life, do good and refrain from wrongdoing.

I shall develop good character and cultivate good habits.

I shall not lead an idle life.

I shall expect no rewards for my services.

I shall be fearless and prepared for any sacrifice.

It was not an ordinary oath to be broken when so wished. It was an extraordinary oath as it was meant for the feuding Pathans. 'For a Pathan' Easwaren (2001, p. 112) points out, 'an oath is not a small matter. He does not enter into a vow easily because once given, a Pathan's word cannot be broken. Even his enemy can count on him to keep his word at the risk of his own life. Non-violence was the heart of the oath and of the organization. It was directed not only against the violence of the British rule but against the pervasive violence of Pathan life.'

Furthermore, while the oath clearly suggested that the *Khudai Khidmatgars* were more concerned in transforming the Pakhtun members into good Muslims, good Pakhtuns and good human beings, the organization was meant to be much more than a mere social advocacy agency. It could not have been otherwise. For its founding father, nonviolence was far more than a mere passive creed. Ghaffan Kahn made it clear when he said:

People have an extraordinary idea about what is meant by nonviolence. A lot of propaganda is made about this principle and there is a great deal of misunderstanding amongst people regarding what is meant by it. Some said that it involves turning the other cheek when you have already been slapped on one cheek. Some said that it means one must lie down and let others walk over you, or remain lying down and let others beat you up, without moving your hands or feel in the process. Some remarked that the Pakhtuns are a brave and powerful people, but Ghaffar Khan wants to turn them into cowards. They used to say all sorts of things. The fact of the matter is that nonviolence is a great force in itself, just as violence is a force. Non-violence has its own army, in the same way as there are armies of violence. The difference is that the weapon of nonviolence is preaching (*tabligh*) while the weapon of violence is the gun. Nonviolence breeds love, endeavour and valour in people whereas violence engenders hate, fear and cowardice [...] There is no defeat in nonviolence but there is in violence [...] Violence is an easy path to follow, but it is extremely difficult to tread the path of nonviolence. It is easy enough to return a slap with a slap but it is very difficult to control oneself when one has been slapped. (Khan in Bult, 1989)

With firm belief in the power of nonviolence, Ghaffar Khan launched the *Khudai Khidmatgars* organization as a powerful movement of the powerless against the ruthless oppressors to achieve freedom, equality and dignity. His was a nonviolent political action projecting itself as Islam in action. Led by a fearless political leader who was a pious and practicing Muslim, who was not at all interested in small political or material gains and who was always prepared to suffer imprisonment, banishment and hardships for the sake of the causes he espoused, the movement rapidly grew in strength. The Pakhtuns joined this movement in thousands and following their leader exhibited tremendous courage, spirit of sacrifice and willingness to suffer. Indeed, they suffered the terrorism of the powerful with great dignity. Their dwellings were frequently burnt down, the members of the movement were often beaten, tortured and sent to jail; their properties were seized; and many were shot in cold blood. They, however, remained true to their vow of nonviolence and never resorted to violence, which the British often desperately desired.

The history of the *Khudai Khidmatgars* movement is full of events and situations where the powerless triumphed over the powerful, but the limited space of this chapter does not permit an enumeration of all of them. Here, however, the encounter between the violent and nonviolent forces at Qissa Khawani Bazaar in Peshawar in 1930 may be discussed in some detail. This was the time when India was in ferment. The All India Congress Party, the dominant political party led by Gandhi, had launched the civil disobedience movement against the British. By picking up a pinch of salt from the Dandi beach and breaking the law restricting the making and selling of salt to the government monopoly, Gandhi had inaugurated on April 1930 the great salt *satyagraha* in the presence of thousands of cheering Indians surrounding him. Soon after, the whole of India – including the NWFP – was convulsed in a revolutionary situation.

The Frontier, under the leadership of Ghaffar Khan, rose in revolt against the British who ruthlessly used power to break the resistance and arrested a number of *Khudai Khidmatgars*. The Khan was arrested on April 23 and when news of his and others' arrest reached the already agitated public of Peshawar, the city exploded – nonviolently. A procession was spontaneously formed. The police responded by arresting some of the leaders and carried them towards the police station in a jeep. The vehicle, however, broke down and then the arrested leaders offered to go themselves on foot to the police station. Their peaceful walk to the police station was followed by the agitated but disciplined procession of people.

When the procession reached Kabuli Gate police station, three armored cars carrying government troops appeared and drove into the crowd. The motorcycle of an English man who was following the cars collided with one of the armored cars and he was crushed to death. Soon after and rather suddenly a machinegun began firing on the crowd at the Qissa Khawani Bazaar. The firing continued for three hours. The crowd set one armored car on fire. The Bazaar was literally littered with the dead and the wounded. At this time, the commander of a Gadwali regiment of Hindu Rajput, Chandar Singh, refused to step into the military van taking the sepoys from cantonment to Qissa Khawani Bazaar. When the sepoys, without their commander, reached the scene, they were ordered to open fire. But soon after someone shouted: 'Don't open fire, the unarmed people are your brothers' and all the soldiers of the regiments put down their arms. Some of them joined the crowd. A British battalion then rushed in, and the Gadwali were taken to the police stations. They were finally given different prison terms (Malik, 1990).

Describing the firing at Qissa Khawani Bazaar, Gene Sharp in his study on nonviolent movements says:

> When those in front fell down wounded by the shots, those behind came forward with their breasts bared and exposed themselves to the fire, so much so that some people got as many as 21 bullet wounds in their bodies, and all the people stood their ground without getting into a panic. A young Sikh boy came and stood in front of a soldier and asked him to fire at him, which the soldier unhesitatingly did, killing him. The crowd kept standing at the spot facing the soldiers and were fired at from time to time, until there were heaps of wounded and dying lying about.

The Anglo-Indian paper of Lahore, which represents the official view, itself wrote to the effect that the people came forward one after another to face the firing and when they fell wounded they were dragged back and others came forward to be shot at. This state of things continued from 11 till 5 o'clock in the evening. When the number of corpses became too many the ambulance cars of the government took them away and burned them. (Sharp in Easwaren, 2001, p. 123)

However, the mass resistance in Peshawar and elsewhere in the Frontier continued despite British atrocities. A couple of days later, both the police and the military left the city, leaving it in the hands of the *Khudai Khidmatgars*. But they returned after a few days, took control of the city, declared the *Khudai Khidmatgars* illegal and closed down their offices. Repression was also let loose in the village of the Khan, Utmanzai, but the spirit of the people remained unbroken. The movement had a liberating effect upon the rest of India and the British were stunned. They provoked the Pathans and very much wanted them to retaliate violently so that their ruthless military and police action could be undertaken and justified on moral and other grounds and the movement be crushed for ever. But the Pathans remained nonviolent and this unnerved the British. Commenting on their despair, Ghaffar Khan said: 'The British feared a nonviolent Pathan more than a violent one. All the horrors the British perpetrated on the Pathans had only one purpose: to provoke them to violence' (Khan in Easwaren, 2001, p. 125).

The British feared the two Gandhis most – Mahatma Gandhi and Frontier Gandhi (Ghaffar Khan). Both almost completely dominated the nonviolent struggle for freedom for a united India and played a crucial role during the last phase of the British Raj from 1930 to 1947. However, freedom at midnight in August 1947 brought no reprieve for the two Gandhis. India was then seized by the worst kind of communal violence and the divided Bengal and Punjab were affected most. Both the Gandhis directed all their energies towards the protection and rescue of the victims of violence. But then Mahatma Gandhi was assassinated in 1948, and Ghaffar Khan found himself hounded by the newly created state of Pakistan.

The going was, indeed, very tough for the Khan and the *Khudai Khidmatgars* in the new state. His preference for a united India in the post-British scenario was well known. His vehement opposition to partition of India on communal lines and his close association with the All India Congress Party was neither forgotten nor forgiven. The party against whom he had campaigned in the Frontier and elsewhere, the Muslim League, had successfully led the movement for the creation of Pakistan and it came to power in Pakistan in 1947. Worse still, his closeness and fondness for Gandhi was also well known and Muhammad Ali Jinnah, the founding father of Pakistan, had devoted his life, especially since the early 1930s, to fighting political battles against Gandhi and against the Congress and did not allow their political agenda for a post-British India to succeed.

Again, the Khan and his *Khudai Khidmatgars* had all along campaigned against the retrogressive Muslim forces and feudal lords who had collaborated with the British during the colonial days. Many of the *Mullahs* and feudal lords had jumped onto the bandwagon of the Muslim League and they were now running amok in the corridors of power in Pakistan. Finally, Jinnah, who was the father of the nation and who was a constitutionalist and a secularist, did not live long enough to put the country on constitutional, democratic tracks. He died in 1948 and the state was hijacked by the retrogressive religious forces, self-seeking bureaucrats, feudal and tribal lords, unscrupulous politicians and powerful military.

In fact, the going got tougher soon after the new state of Pakistan was created and even when Jinnah was alive and very much in power. The Congress government then in power in the Frontier was summarily dissolved soon after Pakistan's independence by the order of the central government. It was done without referring the matter to the Provincial Assembly where the Congress enjoyed majority support. In addition, the *Khudai Khidmatgars* organization was banned and not a single issue of the *Pashtun*, a journal that Ghaffar Khan had launched during colonial times and which was very popular among the Pakhtuns everywhere, was allowed to be published in Pakistan. The Khan was put behind bars for three years in 1948. The court proceedings against him were indicative of the way the Pakistani state was going to treat him.

Ghaffar Khan was arrested on June 25, 1948 on a charge of anti-state activity and the very next day he was given three years' rigorous imprisonment – the maximum punishment under section 40 of the Frontier Crimes Regulation. The Deputy Commissioner of Kohat tried him and awarded the sentence – all in one day. However, Ghaffar Khan was kept in jail even after the expiry of the term and was released after about five years on January 5, 1954 as a measure of amnesty to all political prisoners. Even afterwards, the Khan was frequently arrested, put under house arrest or imprisoned. As a matter of fact, he spent more years of his life in Pakistani jails than during the British period. Being totally disenchanted with politics in Pakistan, he also opted for self-exile and stayed in Afghanistan and India during part of the 1970s and 1980s.

While the going was tough for him in Pakistan, he also gave a tough time to the power elites of Pakistan. Repeatedly and fearlessly he demanded equal rights for the citizens living in the four provinces of Pakistan, called for equitable power and resource sharing among the provinces, condemned state terrorism and military rule, and criticized the retrogressive religious forces for their collaboration with the repressive forces in the country and for justifying violence in the name of Islam. He championed the cause of democracy, the rule of law and human rights for everyone. The state retaliated by projecting him as a separatist, and his love for the Pakhtuns, his demand to name the Frontier Pakhtunistan and his numerous statements advocating the redrawing of the boundaries in the territories where the Pakhtuns were living were seen as steps toward the creation of an independent Pakhtun state out of Pakistan. The government was also facilitated in its propaganda against the Khan as much of his struggle for political and social change through nonviolent action was focused on the region and on the future of the Pakhtuns. Furthermore, it was only the Pakhtuns who could join his *Khudai Khitmatgars* organization. Again, his longing for the freedom of the Pakhtuns and Pakhtun lands, his love for the Pakhtun language, heritage, culture and past and future and his advocacy in favor of peaceful and harmonious ties between and among Afghanistan, Pakistan and India earned him many enemies in the corridors of power in Pakistan.

Worse still, while successive Pakistani governments had all the power and resources to vilify, villanize, malign and project him as an enemy of Pakistan, Ghaffar Khan had very little opportunity to present his viewpoint on different issues. He was often immobilized due to imprisonment, banishment from one province to another and house arrest and both the print and electronic media were reluctant to present his case before the masses, as the media were under firm government control. Such a state of affairs saddened him greatly as his universalist and humanist ideas were not allowed to reach the people and he was presented as a local leader, as a leader of the Pakhtuns only.

However, it was the Afghan tragedy that saddened him most and the last decade of his life was a decade that broke his heart. This was the period when his dreamland – the Pakhtun belt comprising Afghan and Pakistani areas – was trampled under military boots. It was converted into a battlefield for the Soviet troops and Soviet-backed Afghan troops, as well as the American-, Pakistani- and Saudi Arabian-backed troops, which were euphemistically called *Mujahideen* and holy warriors. The Afghan crisis caused colossal destruction, war and war-related deaths, whole-scale displacements, and the major victims were the Pakhtuns living on both sides of Pak–Afghan borders. A major portion of the last ten years of his life was spent in Afghanistan during which he worked for peace in Afghanistan, but he was forced to witness the Pakhtuns taking up arms against one another and against the Soviets and the occupation of the Pakhtun lands by military forces and intelligence agencies and by the mercenaries coming from different countries. Before his eyes, his castle of nonviolence was being blown into pieces and his people whom he loved most, the Pakhtuns, were being sucked into war, conflict and violence.

For more than sixty years of his life, Ghaffar Khan had worked relentlessly for the liberation, progress and unity of these very Pakhtuns. For them he had bravely challenged the might of the British and successive Pakistani governments since 1947, suffered imprisonment and banishment and confronted the religious extremists and ruthless rulers. These were the Pakhtuns to whom he had taught lessons of nonviolence, to whom he had succeeded in disarming and unarming and to whom he wished to unite in the bonds of love, sharing and caring. It was for them that he had envisioned the eventual emergence of a just, progressive, modern, democratic, peaceful and nonviolent Pakhtun society, a society where the faith of Islam would not be used to fuel and justify violence. All his dreams were shattered as he neared the last days of his life.

Standing at the Khyber Pass and listening to the whisperings of unheard past, a past which was always there and which is nowhere, I think about the Siddhartha of Kapilvastu and the Gautama Buddha of Hashtnagar. Both were born with golden spoons in their mouths. Both belonged to the privileged and powerful families and both felt the seeds of discontent within themselves. Both were restless because of restless thoughts flooding in from all direction. Both were able to convince their reluctant fathers to let them wander in the wilderness and search for truth, harmony and peace. Both had wandered around near and far and preached peace and nonviolence. Both endured sufferings of all kinds at the hands of the powerful and faced ruthless Brahmins of their times with dignity and fearlessness. Both struggled for the common good and remained undaunted and unwavering in their resolve to serve the common people. Both fought heroically and nonviolently for the powerless. Both were adorned by the suffering, disempowered multitude. And both are needed by the past, the present and the future today.

Listening to the unheard past and unheard future, I see a gigantic stupa emerging from behind the Khyber Pass and see the two Gautama Buddhas together at its colorful balcony. I also hear them addressing the peoples of the world and saying: 'A day will come when the voice of the unheard past and unheard future will be listened to and when the banished gods of nonviolence and peace will return to confirm that the forces of nonviolence can never be defeated. On that very day, the powerful and the ruthless would realize that the Gautama Buddhas never die. They live forever and continue spreading the message of peace everywhere.'

Notes

1. The Khyber Pass, in western Asia, is one of the most famous mountain passes in the world. The 53 kilometer (33 mile) long passage through the Hindukush mountains connects Afghanistan and Pakistan. It is, in fact, one of the most important passes between the two countries. Winding northwest through the Sefid Koh Range near Peshawar in Pakistan to Kabul in Afghanistan, the Pass is an important strategic gateway. For centuries, numerous invading armies have used the Khyber as their entry point for their invasion of the Indo-Pakistan subcontinent. While the military importance of the Pass is widely known, little known is the fact that it was a major trade route for

centuries. In addition, it has also served as a cultural route connecting the people living beyond the Pass on both sides (*Afghan Network*, 2007).

2. The Pathans or Paktuns or Pashtuns (also known as ethnic Afghans) are an ethno-linguistic group with population primarily concentrated in eastern and southern Afghanistan and in the North-West Frontier Province (NWFP), Federally Administered Tribal Areas and Baluchistan Province of Pakistan. Additional Pakhtun communities live in the Northern Areas, Kashmir and Karachi in Pakistan. There are smaller Pakhtun communities in Iran and India, and a large Pathan migrant worker community in the Gulf and Middle Eastern countries. They constitute 15.42 percent of Pakistan's population and 42 percent of Afghanistan's population. The Pakhtuns are typically characterized by their Pashtu language, adherence to Pakhtunwali (an indigenous code of honor and culture) and Islamic faith. They have survived a turbulent history over several centuries and their martial prowess has been renowned since Alexander the Great's invasion in the third century BC. They belong to one of the few groups that fought very bravely against the British and managed to impede British imperialism during the nineteenth century. Again, the Pakhtuns played a pivotal role in the Soviet war in Afghanistan during 1979–1989, as many joined the resistance forces. They gained worldwide attention with the rise and fall of the *Talibans*, since they were the main ethnic contingent in the movement.

3. The exact date of birth is not recorded. Ghaffar Khan guesses that the year was 1890 and says that he guesses so because his mother used to tell him that he was eleven years old when his elder brother Dr. Khan Saheb got married in 1901.

4. When Ghaffar Khan was five or six years old, he was admitted to a mosque to take lessons from a *Mullah*, who was hardly literate and who could read the Qur'an but could not understand its meaning. He was also cruel and harsh. When the young Khan finished reading the Holy Qur'an, his father organized a celebration. At the age of eight, Ghaffar Khan was admitted to the Municipal Board High School, Peshawar, in 1898. He gained admission to the Edward Mission School, Peshawar, in 1901. While studying there, he applied for a commission in the British army and when he appeared at the matriculation examination, he was informed that the commission was granted to him. He was also asked to present himself the following day at 10 am before the recruiting office. He then left his exam unfinished and went to the recruiting office. He was examined there and enrolled for direct commission. However, he could not stay in the army for long and left when he realized that the British officers' attitude toward the Indian army men was discriminatory and degrading. He then went to Aligarh in 1908 to study there. Later, arrangements were made for his study in England where his elder brother was studying medicine. While he was willing to proceed abroad for studies, he decided against it in 1909 as his mother opposed his going abroad. The year 1909 marks the end of his quest for formal education, but it also marks the beginning of his deeper interest and involvement in the spread of literacy in his village and elsewhere in NWFP in particular. He opened a school in his village Utmanzai in 1910 and subsequently a number of schools were opened in other areas of the province. Later, these schools became the launching pad for his movement for political and social change in the Pakhtun belt, in the present-day Pakistan.

5. See also Khan Abdul Ghaffar Khan (2004, p. 9).

6. *Khudai Khidmatgars* or Servants of God represents a nonviolent freedom struggle of the Pakhtuns of NWFP against the British in undivided India. It was founded by Ghaffar Khan, almost on the eve of the Qissa Khawani Bazaar massacre, in November 1929. Initially intended to be a movement for self-reform and introspection, it soon

blossomed into a gigantic grassroots movement for social and political change in NWFP and for challenging the British colonial power in India. It was an extremely popular movement in the Pakhtun belt in the province and at its peak it consisted of almost 100,000 members. The membership of the organization, one may point out here, was voluntary. In order to crush the movement, the British resorted to all sorts of violent means including torturing the members, throwing them into ponds in winter time, shaving their beards off, charging the protest marchers with cars and horses, arresting the leaders, members and sympathizers, looting and destroying their houses and bombing the troubled areas. Though very popular and very powerful in the 1930s, the decline of the movement began by the middle 1940s for a variety of reasons. It suffered critically after the creation of Pakistan in August 1947. In September 1948, only a year after independence, the organization was declared unlawful and banned, a large number of its members were arrested, the center of the organization at Sardaryab – built in 1942 – was destroyed and the Babra Sharif massacre occurred. Though the ban was formally and officially lifted in 1972, the movement could never take off again.

7. The *Taliban* came to prominence in the year 1994 when a group of *Talibs* (students) from Darul Uloom Haqqania Madrassah in Akora Khattak in NWFP, led by their teacher Mullah Mohammad Omar, successfully battled an Afghan Mujahideen Commander who had reportedly assaulted three women in Kandahar in Afghanistan. During the same year, they were reportedly appointed by Pakistan to protect a convoy attempting to open up a trade route between Pakistan and Central Asia. Comprising Pakhtun tribesmen and trained in various *Madrassahs* (religious seminaries) of Pakistan, the *Taliban* soon metamorphosed into a powerful military force and went on to capture the larger part of Afghanistan including Kabul in 1996. Claiming to be a reformist force from the Deobandi tradition of Islam, the *Taliban* government soon degenerated into a fascist regime and let loose an era of ethnic and sectarian violence, political persecution and cultural suffocation. It was exceptionally harsh to the Afghan female population. The *Taliban* fell from power after 9/11, when US military action began in Afghanistan (*SATP*, 2007).

Reference list

Afghan Network (2006) http://www.afghan-network.net/culture/Khyber.html, date accessed November 19, 2006.

Afghan Network (2007) http://www.afghan-network.net/Culture/khyber.html, date accessed March 22, 2007.

Audarya Fellowship (2009) http://www.indiadivine.org/audarya/, date accessed June 30, 2009.

Banuri, T. (1990) 'Bacha Khan: Book Review,' *Frontier Post*, January 20, 1990.

Bult, J.M. (1989) 'Soldier of Peace,' *Frontier Post*, January 13, 1989.

Easwaran, E. (2001) *Badshah Khan: A Man to Match His Mountains* (New Delhi: Penguin Books India) [First published as (1999) *Nonviolent Soldier of Islam*].

Gandhi, R. (2004) *Ghaffar Khan: Nonviolent Badshah of the Pakhtuns* (New Delhi: Penguin Books India).

Ishaq, M. (2006) 'Peshawar's Illustrious Past,' *Dawn*, November 5, 2006.

Khan, K.A.G. (2004) *Aapbiti* [Autobiography in Urdu] (Lahore: Fiction House).

Korejo, M.S. (1994) *The Frontier Gandhi: His Place in History* (Karachi: Oxford University Press).

Lynch, D. (2004) 'Prism and Prisons: Religion, Abdul Ghaffar Khan, and the Khuddai Khidmatgars' http://www.asianreflection.com, date accessed June 30, 2009.

Majeed, M.A. (1991) 'A Man to Match His Mountains,' *Frontier Post*, January 20, 1991.

Malik, A. (1990) 'Kissa Khawani Incident,' *Frontier Post*, January 20, 1990.

Muhammad, J. (1989) 'Bacha Khan's Struggle on Behalf of Women,' *Frontier Post*, January 26, 1989.

SATP (2007) http://www.satp.org/satporgtp/usa/Taliban.htm, date accessed March 23, 2007.

Tendulkar, D.G. (1967) *Abdul Ghaffar Khan: Faith is a Battle* (New Delhi: Gandhi Peace Foundation).

27
The Inward Revolution: Aurobindo Ghose and Jiddu Krishnamurti

Samrat Schmiem Kumar

> There is hope in men, not in society, not in systems, organized religious systems, but in you and me.
>
> Jiddu Krishnamurti

Introduction

The cultural history of India is a story of countless experiments with spiritual truth and of a continual endeavor through the ages to organize life and society in accordance with most noble spiritual values. It would be no exaggeration to say that spirituality is one main keynote of Indian society, as Indian life cannot be lived in the sole power of its externalities. The lives of our two philosophers and peace thinkers of Indian origin, Sri Aurobindo Ghose (1872–1950) and Jiddu Krishnamurti (1895–1986), offer prominent insights to Indian culture's mesmeric perception on life and peace, giving both value to direct spiritual experience and intellectual understanding.

In their teachings, Aurobindo and Krishnamurti seek a transformation of society through invoking human's spiritual consciousness. In looking to the teachings of both outstanding personalities, one arrives to the understanding that reality can be found within, and by turning inwards a profound transformation of the individual self and humanity takes place. The outer is experienced in accordance with the inner reality.

Though Aurobindo's and Krishnamurti's philosophies and approaches deviate from each other due to their personal experiences and practices, their teachings share a distinctive commonality.

Aurobindo stands for a philosophy of peace that cannot be measured solely on rational and/or empirical grounds. His philosophy aims towards a transgression of the human mind and a spiritual evolution of humanity. Aurobindo's elucidating teachings are the result of his meditative practices and 'supramental' inner visions. His comprehensive and integrative system of yoga is primarily concerned with the spiritualization of society.*

Jiddu Krishnamurti, on the other hand, translates his deep spiritual insights into a modern and accessible language, in the form of entering a fresh and dynamic dialogue with his audience. His teachings are concerned with our day-to-day struggles and with some of humankind's fundamental questions on existence and peace. In Krishnamurti's writings and discussions the reader finds a clear contemporary statement of fundamental human problems, together with an invitation to solve it in a unique and appealing way – for and by oneself. What is striking about Krishnamurti's approach is that while addressing social, political and economic issues of the period, his answers are rooted in a timeless and universal vision of life and truth.

Sri Aurobindo Ghose

Sri Aurobindo Ghose[1] (1872–1950) is today best known as a spiritual philosopher and yogi,[2] the author of numerous and voluminous works such as *Savitri* (1950), *The Synthesis of Yoga* (1932) or *The Life Divine* (1949), and the founder of an ashram in Pondicherry, South India, that bears his name. In a series of works written between 1915 and 1920, he presented a theory of social and human evolution that is part of his spiritual philosophy, personal experiences and empirical observations. These later works, together with some of the earlier pieces, constitute a significant contribution to political, social and cultural theory.

Before Aurobindo 'retired' from political activism and settled in Pondicherry to engage himself in practices of yoga and the spiritual elevation of humanity, he was famous throughout India as a political writer and activist. The editorials he published in the newspapers *Bande Matram* (1906–1908) and *Karmayogin* (1909–1910), and the speeches he delivered during the same period, are among the most remarkable expressions of anti-colonial nationalism to come out of the Indian freedom struggle. Many of these pieces are still worth reading, because they deal not only with transient political issues but also with some of the perennial problems of human society.[3]

Thus, scholars and seekers alike will find in Sri Aurobindo not only an original philosopher and unconventional yogi committed to humanity's spiritual and social evolution, but also they can find in him a visionary with a profound sense of historical, socio-political and cultural processes.

Sri Aurobindo's importance is not limited to his early revolutionary activity or to his later spiritual teachings, but embraces a wide range of human achievements

---

*   Ed. For more on the topic of yoga (in this case from a Buddhist view), see Chapter 12 by Karma Lekshe Tsomo.

and developments. In addition to his political activities and political thoughts, his legacy includes a systematic philosophy, literary works, yoga system and the spiritual force attributed to him by his followers and contemporary companions. It becomes a difficult task to find any other great modern Indian spiritual personality who has developed such a comprehensive, original and critical philosophical system as Sri Aurobindo.

His system is further unique in its autobiographical authenticity. In its philosophical comprehensiveness, his philosophy finds its contemporary Western analogue among the systematic thinkers A.N. Whitehead (1861–1947) and Martin Heidegger (1889–1976). In its spiritual and autobiographic quality, it more closely resembles Søren Kierkegaard (1813–1855) and Martin Buber (1878–1965), and perhaps even Ludwig Wittgenstein (1889–1951) (McDermott, 2005, p. 23). Still, in the end, it can be said that the primacy of Aurobindo's spiritual practices and realizations in his experiences renders his philosophical system almost unique. More than any figure in India, Aurobindo's life exemplified vividly the blending of socio-political activism and spiritual insight.

Biographical traits

Much of Aurobindo's work in the fields of politics and culture bridges the East and the West. This should come as no surprise, as he was born in India and formally educated in England. His early cultural formation was almost entirely British.[4] Although he eventually transcended the limits of any *one* culture, he was able to move beyond Indian and Western ideas because he had assimilated the creative elements of both traditions (McDermott, 2005, p. 16). The first 'ingredients' in his intellectual formation were Western, especially the classical British education he received in London and Cambridge from 1879 to 1893.[5]

Between 1897 and 1906, Aurobindo served as a professor and administrator in a small college in the princely state of Baroda. In 1906, he went to Calcutta and became involved in the national education movement, which was part of the larger anti-colonial *swadeshi*-boycott movement.[6] In 1906 – together with another great nationalist, Bipin Chandra Pal (1858–1932) – he launched the English daily, *Bande Matram*, which was to be the first newspaper to proclaim publicly the goal of complete independence, and a powerful instrument for India's awakening (Satprem, 2008, p. 154). He also formed a 'revolutionist' party and set out an agenda of national action: boycott of British goods, boycott of British courts, boycott of British schools and universities (Satprem, 2008, pp. 154–155). In the same year, he became the principal of the Bengal National College. A year later, he had to resign this post after he was arrested by the British colonial authorities.

During his imprisonment for conspiracy to overthrow the British government (1908–1909) yoga became the central focus of his life. In prison, while waiting for trial – including several months in solitary confinement – he experienced moments of deep and profound spiritual insights that would never leave him again (Satprem, 2008, p. 164):

> [...] within me a great, pure, detached Self was felt as immersed in a peaceful bliss. [...] I cannot describe what transcendental peace possessed my mind and heart at the development of this inner state. The hard crust of my heart burst open and a love for all creatures flowed forth in a steady stream. Along with love, sattwic feelings like kindness, compassion, non-injury (ahimsa) etc. overpowered my rajas-ridden (active and impassioned) nature and began to grow apace. And the more they developed, the more increased my inner joy and deeper became the sense of a pure tranquility. (Aurobindo in Rishabchand, 2001, p. 286)

Although the combination of outer and inner life, or historical and spiritual concerns, runs throughout his life, it was during this year in prison, at the conclusion of three years of intense revolutionary activities, that Aurobindo resolved to work for the renewed spiritualization of Indian and human culture (McDermott, 2005). He resumed his political activities after his release from prison, but soon retired to devote himself to the study and practice of meditation/yoga and its applicability on public and human social life. The roots of this synthesis ran deep in the Indian and Western traditions from which he was drawing.

During his years as a political activist, especially the years of his revolutionary leadership in Calcutta (1905–1910), Aurobindo sought to prove that as long as India remained politically oppressed it could not express its distinctive spiritual and cultural genius (McDermott, 2005). Like Gandhi, who took leadership of the national independence movement, some years after Aurobindo had withdrawn from political activism, he was more deeply committed to the liberation of Indian consciousness than to political independence.

His withdrawal from active political life into spiritual retreat in 1910 can be explained as a coherent expression of his developing spiritual awareness. What appears to have been a conflict between political and spiritual activity is better understood as 'a dramatic instance of Sri Aurobindo's conviction that the historical form will adapt to the prior spiritual realization' (McDermott, 2005, p. 14). His political work conformed to his belief that historical evolution expresses the demands of spiritual consciousness. He read the historical process of humanity in terms of possibilities and necessities first realized in human's inner life. For Aurobindo, the spiritual discipline of yoga and the practical concerns of history function as equally necessary ingredients in the evolutionary process. Aurobindo's life, thoughts and influence have so creatively related the spiritual and historical that they 'jointly serve as a model of spiritual evolution' (McDermott, 2005, p. 15).

Soon after his year in prison, and four decades before India would gain her independence, Aurobindo settled in Pondicherry to concentrate on the elevation of Indian consciousness through spiritual and yogic forces. His integral yoga system and his program for historical transformation gained a universal expression essential for contemporary religious and cultural thought (McDermott, 2005, p. 19).

Philosophy of integral yoga

The teaching of Aurobindo starts with that of the ancient sages of India; behind the appearances of the universe, there is the reality of divine being and consciousness, a self of all things, one and eternal. Human, so says Aurobindo, lives mostly in his/her surface mind, life, and body, but there is an inner being within him/her with greater possibilities to which s/he has to awake. The first process of Aurobindo's yoga is therefore to open the ranges of this inner being and to live from there outward, governing one's outward life by an inner light and inner peace. In doing so, one discovers in one's true soul/self, which is not this outer mixture of mental, vital and physical elements, but something of the reality behind them, a spark from the one divine source (McDermott, 2005, p. 40).

The system of yoga that Aurobindo developed, practiced and taught during his lifetime, differs clearly from traditional paths in that it does not exclude any aspect of life, nor does it suggest a renouncement from the world, but it promotes a profound transformation of humanity. Aurobindo's teaching and method of practice aims towards an inner self-development by which each one who follows it can in time discover the One Self in all and evolve a higher consciousness than the mental, a spiritual and 'supramental' consciousness that will transform and divinize human nature (Aurobindo, 2006, p. 6).[7] Aurobindo called the highest form of this truth and power the *supermind*, and his life after 1926 was dedicated to making the supermind effective on earth (Heehs, 2005, p. 36).

According to Aurobindo, the human's mind or intellect is the principle of dichotomous thinking. The result is that the mind can think of establishing unity only by crushing diversities, imposing peace only by ignoring justice, expressing love only by smothering freedom. The supermind is the principle of integral consciousness in which all opposites are harmonized. So, the supermind alone is capable of laying the foundation for a unified world order in which unity and diversity, peace and justice, love and freedom can coexist (Chaudhuri, 1972, p. 7).

Aurobindo's integral yoga system regards a human as a divine spiritual being involved in mind, life and body. According to the integral view of Aurobindo, there is no ultimate dichotomy or discontinuity between the divine Self and the body–mind structure. The different aspects of human personality, such as the physical, the instinctual, the rational, the supramental and the pure spiritual are various modes of expression of the same fundamental energy, which is the creative dynamism of the Self.* The dichotomy of nature and spirit, as well as the dualism of matter and mind, and that of nature and supernature, is resolved for Aurobindo in this creative dynamism of the Self. A person, even after the attainment of complete self-realization, inner peace and being awareness, need not feel alienated from his body–mind personality. Moreover, the body–mind is capable of being perfected and transformed into an effective instrumentation of the illumined Self. This is the task the spiritual discipline of integral yoga sets before itself.

Aurobindo's yoga system, though based on essential texts of Indian spiritual tradition,[8] is not limited to any particular religious orientation. Throughout his life and writings, Sri Aurobindo consistently distinguished his spiritual discipline from traditional religion. He repeatedly emphasized that his teaching was concerned with the spiritualization of society. He gave special value to Indian scriptures because from him they contained truths reached by inner experiences that were accessible, in principle, to all human beings.

Through these practices, systematized in India as yoga but found also in other cultures, sincere practitioners eventually would come in contact with the truth and power that was needed for the transformation of human society. A seeker could approach the truths of yoga not only through practices associated with Indic religions, but also with any other religion or no religion at all. What is of primary importance in Aurobindo's teachings on yoga is for each individual to attempt to overcome the limitations of the ego and to be guided by an inner awareness. A transformation of many individuals then makes it possible for society as a whole to be transformed (Heehs, 2005, pp. 19–20). A first step in this direction would be the gathering of individuals striving for change in spiritually orientated communities.[9]

Social harmony and the integration of East and West

In his writings on philosophy and yoga, Aurobindo emphasized that the right way for society to move towards a harmonious and peaceful state was for each individual in it to achieve the greatest possible self-realization and self-expression (Heehs, 2005, p. 261). Social harmony, according to Aurobindo, can only be reached when the inner self of man is awakened, free and generous, not enslaved to selfish thoughts and aims. Social harmony is not a result of social machinery but the freedom of the human intellect and the nobility of the human soul (Heehs, 2005, p. 145).

---

* Ed. For another perspective on this topic, see Chapter 11 by Swami Veda Bharati in this volume.

Aurobindo thus cautioned in his political and social writings that it would be in vain to imagine that a solution to the pressing problems of the world could come from arrangements that were – what he called – solely mechanical (Aurobindo, 1997). As a believer in a reality that would express itself in time through a spiritual revolution, he affirmed that 'a deeper, wider, greater, more spiritualised subjective understanding of the individual and communal self and its life and a growing reliance on the spiritual light and the spiritual means for the final solution of its problems are the only way to a true social perfection' (Aurobindo, 1997, p. 183). This would come through a deeper understanding of the spiritual truth of existence, supported by a persistent effort after knowledge and harmony in all domains of human activity.

Aurobindo thus was not primarily a social thinker, but a mystic and philosopher who was interested not only in spiritual matters but also in secular problems. His exalted ideas about human society depend to such a degree on the influence of a power superior to the human mind that they might easily seem to be of no practical use in dealing with contemporary human concerns. He certainly believed that a general change of consciousness had to precede the final solution of such problems, but he did not believe that the striving for harmony and peace had to be pursued on the spiritual level alone.

Like other famous Indian figures, such as the noble laureate Rabindranath Tagore (1861–1941), former Indian President Sarvepalli Radhakrishnan (1888–1975) and Mahatma Gandhi (1869–1948),* Sri Aurobindo combines impressively traditions of India and the West, and envisions a fuller and more subtle integration of Indian and Western cultures. Sri Aurobindo firmly believed that the two great components of the future evolution of man were Indian spirituality and Western intellectuality. Thus, Aurobindo did not view and categorize the world in terms of fixed dichotomies: East and West, spiritual and material, conservation and progress. When two cultural systems came into conflict, he would see it as an occasion for them to move towards a synthesis in which both would be harmonized and exceeded (Heehs, 2005, p. 237).

For Aurobindo, East and West have the same human nature, a common human destiny, the same aspiration after greater perfection, the same seeking after something higher than itself. East and West have always met and mixed more or less closely, they have powerfully influenced each other (Heehs, 2005, p. 287).

There is a common hope, a common destiny, both spiritual and material, for which both are needed as co-workers. It is no longer towards division and

---

*   Ed. For a further discussion on Mahatma Gandhi as peace thinker, see Chapter 25 by Arun Gandhi.

difference that we should turn our minds, but on unity, union, even oneness. (Aurobindo in Heehs, 2005, p. 287)

Sri Aurobindo's life and thought have so creatively related the spiritual East with the intellectual and historical West that they jointly serve as a new model for human spiritual and rational development. Similar to Aurobindo, Jiddu Krishnamurti's life and teaching combine in an unparalleled manner thoughts of India and the West. Born in South India and educated in Europe, Krishnamurti spoke a philosophical language that could be understood by people from diverse backgrounds. He explained with great precision the subtle workings of the human mind, and pointed to the need for bringing to one's daily life a deeply meditative and spiritual quality.

Jiddu Krishnamurti

Jiddu Krishnamurti is regarded as one the most revolutionist thinkers of the last century. In his writings and speeches, Krishnamurti challenges norms and values of modern individual human life as well as social life. His teachings stress universal spiritual values, personal insight and autonomous self-knowledge, synthesizing both Indian and Western philosophical and psychological thoughts. Krishnamurti's teaching and approach have deeply influenced many people, offering them insightful solutions to the plethora of human problems of living in modern society.

Krishnamurti did not expound any particular philosophy or religion, nor did he formulate or develop a comprehensive philosophical system as Aurobindo did, but rather he talked intensively of everyday matters that concern all human beings. In a charismatic and even mesmerizing style of lecturing, he attracted large audiences around the world. His teachings and discussions were fundamentally based – like Aurobindo's – on his own personal insights into the human mind and his relationship with the sacred (Sanat, 1999; Mehta, 2002).

Biographical traits

Krishnamurti was born in 1895 in Madanapalle, a small town in South India, north of Chennai (then known as Madras). He nearly died of malaria when he was two years old and the disease would continue to reappear and sicken him during his years of adolescence. Krishnamurti's father was a civil servant in the British colonial revenue department and a part time worker at the Theosophical Society.[10] After his wife died in 1905, Krishnamurti's father retired from his job and sought full-time employment with the Theosophical Society. The family moved to Adyar near Chennai, and it was there at the age of twelve that Krishnamurti attracted the attention of Annie Besant (1847–1933) and C.W. Leadbeater (1854–1934), heads of the Theosophical Society.[11] The leaders of the Society prophesized that Krishnamurti would play an influential role in modern society, and would be used as a vehicle of the so-called 'World Teacher' whose coming they had predicted (Mehta, 2002, pp. 27–29). They gained guardianship of Krishnamurti and his younger brother, Nityananda, and privately educated them in the Society.

To prepare the world for the coming of the World Teacher, Besant and her colleagues founded in 1911 a worldwide organization called the Order of the Star in the East (OSE), and the young Krishnamurti was made its spiritual head. Chosen to be the new World Teacher, he began a long period of training directed toward fulfillment of this role. Krishnamurti's father was worried by Besant's and the Society's influence on his sons, and he tried to regain custody of them, but eventually failed. Krishnamurti and his brother continued their studies in England and France far away from their father (Mehta, 2002, pp. 28–29).[12]

By the early 1920s, Krishnamurti had begun to take on more of a leadership role in the Order of the Star. Accompanied by his brother, he embarked on a series of lectures, meetings and discussions around the world relating to his duties as the head of the organization. However, as Krishnamurti was growing up, he showed signs of adolescent rebellion and emotional instability, having doubts about the future prescribed to him (Lutyens, 1997).

Then, in 1922, Krishnamurti went through an intense, life-changing experience.[13] It has been characterized as a deep spiritual awakening that brought him endless joy and profound peace (Sanat, 1999, p. 3; Jayakar, 1986, p. 46):

> [...] I was supremely happy, for I had seen. Nothing could ever be the same. I have drunk at the clear and pure waters and my thirst was appeased. [...] I have seen the Light. I have touched compassion which heals all sorrow and suffering; it is not for myself, but for the world. [...] Love in all its glory has intoxicated my heart; my heart can never be closed. I have drunk at the fountain of Joy and eternal Beauty. I am God-intoxicated. (Lutyens, 1997, pp. 159–160)

In the next few years Krishnamurti's new vision and consciousness continued to develop and reached a point where, amid increasing popularity, he began internally to struggle under the worldly institutional restraints imposed on him. Thus, in 1929 he broke openly with the Order of the Star and disbanded with the formal order of some 50,000 adherents, saying:

> I maintain that truth is a pathless land, and you cannot approach it by any path whatsoever, by any religion, by any sect. That is my point of view, and I adhere to that absolutely and unconditionally. Truth, being limitless, unconditioned, unapproachable by any path whatsoever, cannot be organized;

nor should any organization be formed to lead or coerce people along a particular path. (Krishnamurti, 1996, p. 257)

He officially resigned from the Theosophical Society in 1930, and returned all the money and property that had been donated for this work. From then, for nearly sixty years until his death in 1986, Krishnamurti travelled throughout the world talking to large audiences and to individuals about the need for a radical transformation in mankind and human consciousness.

Krishnamurti spoke to his audience not as the new World Teacher but, as many would call it, a kind-hearted friend. His talks and discussions were based not on traditional scriptural knowledge or modern epistemology but on his own insights into the human mind and his vision of the sacred. His teachings were thus free from conditioning influences of the different systems of philosophy, religious dogmatism, political ideology, intellectual speculation and cultural bias. Krishnamurti left a large body of literature in the form of public talks, writings, discussions with teachers and students, with scientists and religious figures, conversations with individuals, television and radio interviews, and letters. Many of these have been published as books, such as *The Awakening of Intelligence* (1973), *Commentaries on Living* (1967), *Education and the Significance of Life* (1953) and *The First and Last Freedom* (1954).

'Truth is a pathless land' and the need for an inward revolution

In Krishnamurti's speeches and talks, many Westerners heard a modernist language, speaking of humanitarianism, compassion for the other, individual integrity and revolution; yet many Indians heard the voice of classic Indian philosophy shining through his words.[14] Not surprising, as Krishnamurti's life – similar to Aurobindo's – was subject to an identity that went beyond a crossing of regional and cultural boundaries to a point where he believed it was unproductive for life to even acknowledge the existence of such borders.

For Krishnamurti, a radical transformation of consciousness/mind requires one to abandon one's identifications with a particular culture, system of ideas, religion and with the expectations built over a lifetime (Sanat, 1999, p. 69). Krishnamurti accentuated on many occasions his independence from any religious organization, sect or country, and nor did he subscribe to any school of political or ideological thought. On the contrary, he maintained that these are the very factors that divide human beings and bring about conflict and war. He reminded his listeners again and again that we are all human beings first and not Hindus, Muslims or Christians, that we are like the rest of humanity and are not different from one another (Krishnamurti, 1989, p. 52).

Humanity, so Krishnamurti told repeatedly, has built images as a fence of security – religious, political and personal. These manifest as symbols, ideas, beliefs. The burden of these images dominates human's thinking, his/her relationship, and daily life. These images are the causes of our problems for they divide human from human. One's perception of life is shaped by concepts established already in one's mind. The content of one's consciousness is one's entire existence. The individuality is the name, the form and superficial culture one acquires from tradition and environment.

The core of Krishnamurti's teaching is thus contained in the statement he made in 1929 when he said, 'Truth is a pathless land.' Man cannot come to it through any organization, through any creed, through any dogma, priest or ritual, or through any philosophical knowledge or psychological technique. S/he has to find it through the mirror of relationship, through the understanding of the contents of her/his own mind, through observation and not through intellectual analysis or introspective dissection (Jayakar, 1986, p. 142). Krishnamurti's teachings transcend man-made belief systems, nationalistic sentiments and sectarianism. At the same time, they give new meaning and direction to mankind's search for truth.

Krishnamurti's teachings are non-dogmatic, centered on his own spiritual experiences and oriented to the particular needs and capacities of his listeners. He regarded life as a journey of self-discovery in which self-doubt, uncertainty and self-criticism are inextricably related to inward spiritual transformation. Krishnamurti believed spiritual ripeness and transformation come only with the willingness of radical self-analysis and an investigation into deeper levels of human psychic resources, which, once explored, can lead to dissolving the debased superficiality of the ego state (Krishnamurti, 2000, pp. 59–63). It is not the result of simple moral striving but of critical self-reflection, doubt, final enlightenment and self-knowledge that leads to the integration of the human personality, freedom, peace and love in pure, selfless compassion (Krishnamurti, 2006, pp. 2–7).

He thus urged for an inward revolution, which alone could bring about a radical transformation of the outer – of society (Krishnamurti, 2008, p. 24). Krishnamurti brought out a simple but clear message: what we are, the society is. Man tends to bring a change in life through a change of system or a revolution in ideas or values, forgetting that it is him/her that creates society. Krishnamurti stresses the human to begin a change with him/herself, to concern him/herself with his/her daily existence, with his/her daily thoughts, feelings and actions (Krishnamurti, 2008, p. 25). The world is no different from us and our activities, because it is what we are which creates the problems and conflicts of the world. The majority of men seek a solution to the problems of the world not within themselves but in a myriad of external systems and methods. In order to transform the world about us, with its misery, wars, violence, unemployment, starvation, class divisions and utter confusion, there must be first and foremost a transformation in ourselves (Krishnamurti, 2008, pp. 34–36).

At age 90, Krishnamurti addressed the United Nations on the subject of peace and awareness, as he was awarded the 1984 UN Peace Medal. In his speech to the UN in New York Krishnamurti said: '[...] there can only be peace when mankind, when you and I, have no conflict in ourselves' (Krishnamurti, 1985). Krishnamurti always stressed that a radical individual human transformation is essential as a prerequisite for any approach to peace, love and compassion. In order to have love and compassion for others, one has to move beyond the mind, beyond societal organizations and ideologies, to the core of the self: 'Love is something that is new, fresh, alive. It has no yesterday and no tomorrow. It is beyond the turmoil of thought. It is only the innocent mind which knows what love is, and the innocent mind can live in the world which is not innocent' (Krishnamurti in Mehta, 2002, p. 393).

Krishnamurti believed that humanity would be set free from conflict through discovering love in the core of the self. He maintained that the individual is freed by becoming aware of their own psychological conditioning, and that this awakening will enable them to give love to another. In his eyes, love alone can transform the present madness and insanity in the world, not systems, not theories. 'It is only when there is love that all our problems can be solved and then we shall know its bliss and its happiness' (Krishnamurti, 2008, p. 214).

Finally, one can subsume that Jiddu Krishnamurti invites us to look at life from an inward perspective and transcend all mental and dogmatic barriers. The approach of life and peace Krishnamurti presents is intensively dynamic and supremely practical. 'It is so simple that very often its simplicity gives to one a feeling that it could not be real. This is because we are accustomed to complex and complicated approaches to life – the more difficult it is, the more acceptable it becomes' (Mehta, 2002, p. 116). Krishnamurti unveiled with his unique approach a new dimension of living.

Aurobindo's and Krishnamurti's contribution to a culture of peace

Sri Aurobindo Ghose and Jiddu Krishnamurti have emphasized more than any other thinkers of their times that what the world needs today is a radical change in human consciousness, an inward revolution which will ensure social harmony and a culture of peace by removing the motives for engaging in activities that bring about a conflict between man and man. Society talks of peace but forgets the essential condition for it. Both Aurobindo and Krishnamurti have affirmed that without a radical transformation of human consciousness, it is idle to hope for any lasting improvement in human relations. Aurobindo and Krishnamurti emphasize(d) that the right way for society to move towards a harmonious and peaceful state is for each individual in it to achieve the greatest possible self-realization and self-expression.

Compassion, freedom, nonviolence and love, as foundations of a culture of peace, can only come about in a pure sense through the self-awareness and transformation of consciousness. When one has once achieved a true consciousness and knowledge, there is no longer any difference and conflict between oneself and the other; for then one acts freely out of oneself and lives spontaneously in accordance with the truth of one's spirit and one's highest nature.

In Aurobindo's and Krishnamurti's view, the world in which we live is not a dichotomy of nature and spirit, but rather a nature–spirit continuum and an evolutionary movement endowed with the possibility of enormous growth beyond the present human level dominated by the divisive forces of the rational mind. The total being of human is not a dichotomy of matter and spirit, nor a dualism of body and soul, but a body–mind–soul continuum. The being in the world and his/her non-temporal dimension of oneness with the divine/sacred are inseparable aspects of his/her whole reality.

Aurobindo asks for the integration of spirituality into a more complete vision of humanity. He analyzes the nature of reality primarily through the spectrum of spiritual evolution. The life and teachings of Aurobindo appeal to a culture of peace that recognizes the spiritual dimension of life. Spirituality and human mind in Aurobindo's thinking are not opposed to each other, but harmoniously integrated.

Aurobindo's philosophy is attractive for a culture of peace since it values spiritual experiences as essential for human and societal harmony. The secret of Aurobindo's yoga lies in human's conscious cooperation with the creative energy of 'Being' toward the integral transformation of his/her entire being, including the social and global dimension. Such integral transformation heralds the advent of an integral human as an effective force for social harmony and a culture of peace.

Krishnamurti's practical and sublime teaching marks an important contribution to modern social thinking as well as to a culture of peace. At the core of his teaching is the realization that fundamental changes in society can be brought about only by transformation of individual consciousness. Krishnamurti's teaching stresses that a radical individual human transformation is essential as a prerequisite for any approach to peace, harmony and compassion. In order to transform the conflicts and wars in our world there must be – first and foremost – a transformation in ourselves, which will lead to a change in society.

Aurobindo's and Krishnamurti's thinking transgresses the modern images of humans through recognition of the spiritual nature of mankind. Their teachings contain a unique and timeless perception of humanity's transformation and a culture of peace, bearing brilliant testimony of the vibrant and dynamic spiritual realism that is native to Indian life.

Notes

1. The Sanskrit and Indian word *Sri*, with a primary meaning of radiance, loveliness or diffusing light, is often used as a title of veneration. It stands as a respectful affix to the names of revered and celebrated persons.
2. The words yogi and yoga derive from the Sanskrit verbal root *yuj*, meaning 'to yoke' or 'connect;' lit. 'to re-unite,' 'to meet,' 'to join.' Yoga denotes a variety of human practices, disciplines, teachings and different stages of awareness about the relationship between the individual self and the cosmic self. It is referred to meditative systems of harmonizing mind, body and soul; a yogi is someone who generously and deeply follows a practice of yoga.
3. For more on Aurobindo's political writings, see Heehs (2005).
4. Aurobindo Ghose was born on August 15, 1872 in Calcutta, India. His father, Dr. Krishnadhan Ghose, had studied medicine in England and had returned to India as a confirmed anglophile. As a child living in rural Bengal, Aurobindo and his siblings were not allowed by their father to learn their mother tongue. After passing two years at a Convent School in Darjeeling, North India, Aurobindo at the age of seven, together with his two brothers, was sent to England for further studies. Not until the age of twenty would he learn his mother tongue, Bengali. He was never to see his father again, who died just before Aurobindo's return to India, and hardly his mother, whose illness would prevent her from recognizing him. Here was thus a child who grew up outside any influence of family, country and tradition – a free spirit. The first lesson Sri Aurobindo perhaps gives us is that of freedom (Satprem, 2008, p. 21).
5. In his early intellectual development, Aurobindo was influenced by late Romantic poets and post-Romantic critiques, such as Mary Shelley, Thomas Carlyle and Matthew Arnold. Five themes developed by these and other writers were especially important in his intellectual development: the worship of nature and the condemnation of mechanism; the importance of high culture; the concept of the nation-soul; the necessity of revolution to bring about social change; and the inwardness of truth (Heehs, 2005, p. 2).
6. The *swadeshi* (lit. 'of one's own country') movement was part of the larger Indian independence struggle against British colonialism at the beginning of the twentieth century. It was a quite successful economic strategy to oppose British supremacy and to improve economic conditions in India through self-sufficiency. Strategies of the *swadeshi* movement involved boycotting British products and the revival of domestic-made products and production techniques. *Swadeshi* strategies were also adopted by Mahatma Gandhi who described it as prerequisite for self-rule.
7. A systematic overview on Aurobindo's philosophy teachings can be found in his illustrative and outstanding work *The Life Divine* (1949).
8. His spiritual teachings are based in part on Indic texts, notably the Vedas, Upanishads and the Bhagavad Gita. Other lines of Indic practices (i.e. yogic meditation, tantric sadhana and bhakti) also left their mark on his integral yoga and philosophy.
9. A community of sorts had taken form around Aurobindo during the early years of his stay in Pondicherry. This group assumed a more organized shape after the arrival of Mirra Alfassa (1878–1973) (also widely known as 'The Mother'), a spiritual seeker from France whom Aurobindo acknowledged as his spiritual equal and companion. In 1926, he handed control of the ashram to her. The Mother directed the inner and outer lives of the members, while Aurobindo oversaw things from behind. The life in the ashram is based on Sri Aurobindo's teachings, which he derived from his spiritual experiences and certain yogic practices. Aurobindo sought to guide others to same level

of experiences and make them discover the divine self and consciousness concealed within each one of them (Heehs, 2005).

10. The Theosophical Society was an organization formed in 1875 promoting the religious unity of all men chiefly within the framework of Indian values.

11. During his forays to the Theosophical estate's beach at the nearby Adyar river, Leadbeater had noticed Krishnamurti (who also frequented the beach with others), and was amazed by the 'most wonderful aura he had ever seen, without a particle of selfishness in it' (Lutyens, 1997, p. 21).

12. In this period, he apparently enjoyed reading parts of the Old Testament and was impressed by some of the Western classics, especially Mary Shelley, Fyodor Dostoyevsky and Friedrich Nietzsche.

13. As with Aurobindo, an understanding of Krishnamurti's inner life is essential to a clear understanding of the deeper aspects of his teachings and approaches (Sanat, 1999).

14. Perhaps the fact that hundreds of thousands of people who read Jiddu Krishnamurti's work found wisdom in what he said without knowing anything of Indian philosophy might argue for a universality of language and message in his 'teachings,' which were adaptable across the ground of cultural and nationalist prejudice, language barriers and religious bigotry.

Reference list

Aurobindo (1997) *The Human Cycle: The Ideal of Human Unity. War and Self-Determination* (Pondicherry: Sri Aurobindo Ashram).

Aurobindo (2006) *The Integral Yoga. Sri Aurobindo's Teaching and Method of Practice* (Pondicherry: Sri Aurobindo Ashram).

Chaudhuri, H. (1972) 'The Philosophy and Yoga of Sri Aurobindo,' *Philosophy East and West*, 22, 1, 5–14.

Heehs, P. (2005) (ed.) *Nationalism, Religion, and Beyond: Writings on Politics, Society, and Culture by Sri Aurobindo* (Delhi: Permanent Black).

Jayakar, P. (1986) *Krishnamurti: A Biography* (New York: Harper & Row).

Krishnamurti, J. (1985) Speech at the United Nations, http://www.k.thequest.org.np/themes/peace.html, date accessed January 2, 2009.

Krishnamurti, J. (1989) *The Flight of the Eagle* (New York: Harper & Row).

Krishnamurti, J. (1996) *Total Freedom: The Essential Krishnamurti* (New York: Harper Collins).

Krishnamurti, J. (2000) *Commentaries on Living. Second Series* (Chennai: Krishnamurti Foundation India).

Krishnamurti, J (2006) *On Self-Knowledge* (Chennai: Krishnamurti Foundation India).

Krishnamurti, J. (2008) *The First and Last Freedom* (Chennai: Krishnamurti Foundation India).

Lutyens, M. (1997) *Krishnamurti: The Years of Awakening* (London: Shambhala).

McDermott, R. (2005) *The Essential Aurobindo: Writings of Sri Aurobindo* (Mumbai: Jaico).

Mehta, R. (2002) *J. Krishnamurti and the Nameless Experience: A Comprehensive Discussion of J. Krishnamurti's Approach to Life* (Delhi: Motilal Banarsidass).

Rishabchand (2001) *Sri Aurobindo: His Life Unique* (Pondicherry: Shri Aurobindo Ashram).

Sanat, A. (1999) *The Inner Life of Krishnamurti: Private Passion and Perennial Wisdom* (Varanasi: Pilgrims).

Satprem (2008) *Sri Aurobindo or the Adventure of Consciousness* (Mysore: Institut de Recherches Evolutivés).

28
Peaces, a Gift of Grace, Turned into Modern Horror: Ivan Illich Visionary of the Twentieth Century

Martina Kaller-Dietrich

> Illich insists on the need to trace, comprehend and then dismantle the link between peace and development as the primary way of challenging the monopoly of the elite over peace, naming this act of defiance as the most urgent task of peace research.
>
> Josefina Echavarría and Norbert Koppensteiner

Under Roman imperial rule, hegemonic *pax* replaced the many peaces of common people. Since 1949, the conjuncture of this imperial kind of peace and *development* forced *pax economica* over people's peaces. Ivan Illich (*1926–†2002) witnessed this last global corruption of peace. Only two small texts out of his vast oeuvre focus directly on peace (Illich, 1973b, 2006), whereas his remaining books, talks and articles reflect the modern violent war on subsistence. Illich's aim was to discover and to describe what imperial unique peace in combination with development does to us.

In early 1968, Illich gave a talk titled 'Violence: a mirror for Americans' (Illich, 1973b). He spoke mainly to resisters engaged in organizing the march on the Pentagon. He wanted to share with them the fear that after ending war in Vietnam, their commitment with modern ideologies and idols for bettering the world 'would permit hawks and doves to unite in a destructive war on poverty in the Third World' (Illich, 1973b, p. 19). The other talk referring explicitly to peace was delivered in 1980 at the Asian Peace Research Association in Tokyo by the then famous key speaker in international conferences: 'Peace vs. Development' by Ivan Illich today is considered as one of the key texts of peace studies (Dietrich et al., 2006, pp. 173–182).

Ivan Illich was born in Vienna in 1926 of mixed ancestry – on his mother's side descendants of Sephardic Jews, on his father's side descendants of a noted

Catholic Dalmatian family. Ivan was raised in the old house of his Dalmatian grandfathers until he turned six. This house had stood on its island in the Adriatic off the coast since the Middle Ages. Remembering the first years of life, he described the place around the house as a world in which life was in the hands of the commons: 'People lived in houses they had built; moved on streets that had been trampled by the feet of their animals; were autonomous in the procurement and disposal of their water; could depend on their own voices' (Cayley, 1992, p. 2). Friends who knew about his origin and his deep bond to these commons understood what was on his mind when Illich referred to vernacular subsistence of the commons: 'He took this fading world within himself where it would nourish a stance so radically traditional that for a few years in the late 1960s and early 1970s excited North American audiences thought it avant-garde' (Cayley, 1992, p. 2).

Ivan Illich also was a child of war times. When he had to move to Vienna, he lived at his grandfather's house. This was a place where a wealthy Jewish environment allowed the family Regenstreif to host extraordinary thinkers of their days. Among so many others, the '*Büble*' (boy) Ivan knew Rudolf Steiner, the founder of anthroposophy. Ivan Illich was expelled from his Vienna school in 1941 and together with his mother and the younger twin brothers was forced to flee to Italy because of his Jewish ancestry. He had been twelve when Hitler's troops reached the capital of Austria and by Annexation to the Third Reich the First Republic of Austria disappeared from the map. This changed his life forever. Decades later, in a conversation among friends, he mentioned: 'Whether they kill me for being Croatian or for being Jew doesn't make any difference to me' (Kaller-Dietrich, 2008, p. 37). And he kept wondering how Austrians could have been trapped into such a stupidity as anti-Semitism (Kaller-Dietrich, 2008, p. 23).

'War tends to make cultures alike,' Ivan Illich stated in 'Peace vs. Development' (2006, p. 175). Instead, culture means that a peculiar (hi-)story was being given to everybody, and this story must be lived and can be told. In war, this does not count. Instead of being a common woman or common man who has a story to tell, war reduces everybody to soldier and civilian, to enemy and allies, to cannon fodder or perpetrators, to dead soldiers and victims, to a starving population, surviving in collaterally damaged regions. War makes women and men disappear through the necrophilic fetish of *survival*. The history of war silences the many stories women and men could have told. 'People who speak about survival – this is my experience, I have no studies to prove this –' Illich said, 'speak not out of finely developed senses of smell and taste or a feeling for atmosphere, they speak out of a terminology and as a result of a propaganda, which goes through the head and through the heart' (Illich cited in Cayley, 1992, p. 263).

Who was this Ivan Illich, a man carrying the same name as the protagonist of one of Leo Tolstoy's most well-known novels? After completing his university studies in theology and history at Florence, the Gregorian University in Rome and the University of Salzburg, he was ordained as a priest in 1951 when he was just twenty-six years old. Ivan was invited to enter the Vatican's diplomatic corps but refused and, instead, he served as parish priest in Washington Heights, New York – an older Irish working class neighborhood that was host to the arrival of new Puerto Rican immigrants. Ivan worked hard at making that parish more receptive to the new immigrants. He 'Latinized' the church and St. Patrick's Day was forced to take a back seat to San Juan's day. Illich despised the smugness, the chauvinism, the Byzantine bureaucracy of the 1950s anglicized Catholic Church and he referred to some of his fellow priests as 'ecclesiastical conquistadors.' He felt that the ethos of the American Catholic Church was indistinguishable from the anti-social market values of global industrial capitalism. He became vice-rector of the Catholic University at Ponce, Puerto Rico, in 1956. Five years later he founded the Center for Intercultural Documentation in Cuernavaca, Mexico, 'as an agency to prevent implementation of a papal order in 1960 for ten percent of United States and Canadian priests and nuns to be sent to Latin America in ten years' (Underwood, 1975, p. 405). There, he called on young priests and nuns to take a new vow, a vow of 'cultural poverty' and thus to free themselves from their loyalties to old ideas and institutional repression.

Despite of all the wondering he created around him, the question of who was Ivan Illich remained open: was he a priest educator, a realistic dreamer, a thinker? Was Illich a sociologist, a theologian or was he a historian? For some, Illich was an 'intellectual gadfly, a guru and a heretic' (Scheper-Hughes, 2001, p. 1). Some of his friends, like Harvey Cox at Harvard, insist on asking whether Illich was a 'maverick intellectual' (Cox, 2002, p. 16). Ivan Illich himself never cared about professional markers. He preferred to tell stories. And, as named medievalist Ludlof Kuchenbuch analyzed in detail, Illich's stories cannot be proved, but his big explanations on history are fascinating and correct (Kuchenbuch, 2009).

Violence

Ivan Illich argued that according to each time and each place the very different conditions of peace always gave different meanings to the many epochs and cultures. He started from the vernacular character of peace. The Latin term vernacular, described in Roman laws, traces back to *vernaculum*: 'whatever was homebred, homespun, homegrown [or] homemade' (Illich, 1981, pp. 57–58). This includes shelter, food, handicrafts, abilities, words and stories, blessing and greed, children and slaves.

But, where does violence come from? Illich lived for two decades in Latin America where, with support of US counter-insurgency policy, one military regime after the other had taken over control in the name of peace and progress.

He had observed this closely. In 1968, he spoke out. For Illich, the symptoms of war in Vietnam

> are too horrible to permit a lucid analysis of the causes that produce them. It is therefore more important to focus United States attention on the other two programs, the war on poverty and the Alliance for Progress: one, a war conducted by social workers; the other, an alliance that has maintained or swept into power military regimes in two-thirds of the Latin American countries. Both originated in the name of good will; both are now seen as pacification programs; both are pregnant with violence. (Illich, 1973b, p. 22)

And he concluded:

> Both programs failed. The poor refused to dream on command. The order to dream and the money they got only made them rambunctious. Huge funds were appropriated to start the United States minorities and the Latin American majorities on the way of integration into a United States-style middle-class: the world of college attendance, universal consumer credit, the world of household appliances, insurance, the world of church and movie attendance. An army of generous volunteers swarmed through New York ghettos, and Latin American jungle canyons pushing the persuasion that makes America tick. (Illich, 1973b, p. 23)

By the end of the Second World War, the US had become the most potent food supplier that ever existed in world history. What later would be called *Green Revolution* received full support of the government. In the Cold War period, food programs spread over the whole globe and became one of the United States' most important weapons in its foreign policy: at first, interventions were carried out by policies, with the US defending zones of influence without representing a threat to its territorial sovereignty of the nation in question. In a second step, the US shed its provinciality by defending the values of a civilization supposedly most advanced, which it believed to represent and therefore was chosen to defend. Finally, in a third phase, a US intervention was not a military coup only. Following the defeat of the adversary, reconstruction of the territory and the redefinition of living standards according to the *American way of life* seemed to be the very goal of an intervention. In this context, peace policy and food aid became interrelated features of the same policy (Kaller-Dietrich, 2010a).

Almost twenty years later, President John F. Kennedy successfully established the domestic New Frontier programs, which aimed to fight poverty, help cities and expand governmental benefits to needy Americans. On the international stage, the US President also was eager to revitalize moribund economic aid programs and to counter negative images of the 'Ugly American' and 'Yankee' imperialism. As a new army of 'agents of change,' the *Peace Corps* thus participated in an overall campaign to revitalize the image of the US in the world. In the 1960s, the Peace Corps was very popular with college graduates whose ideals reflected generational attitudes of the time, such as a commitment to peace and international goodwill.

According to the historian Elizabeth Cobbs Hoffman (1998), this spirit of the sixties was the product of a combination of several different phenomena. The first was the conviction, shared by an entire generation of young people, that America's victory in the battlefields of the Second World War was a justification for America taking worldwide moral leadership. In the Cold War diction, the United States above all stood for democracy and the dissemination of this socio-political system throughout the world. Second, global interventionism was seen as positive, due to the belief that young Americans would best represent – through their conduct and their way of life – the ideals of democracy, personal freedom and justice (Cobbs Hoffman, 1998). That these concepts did not clash with the rebellion against mass society and the many critical demands of the sixties generation was based on the fact that 'the Peace Corps emphasized emotions and personal commitment as keys to social change, as did the civil rights and peace movements.' Indeed its second director, Jack Vaughn (1966–1969) declared that 'The Peace Corps is about love' (Kaller-Dietrich, 2010b).

To help the young volunteers along their path, Ivan Illich established the famous Center for Intercultural Documentation (CIDOC) in Cuernavaca, Mexico. In the early 1960s, it served as a site for developing a new school for North American and European Catholic missionaries, Peace Corps types, humanitarian workers who were preparing for the villages and shanty towns of Central and South America.

> CIDOC tried to exorcise ethnocentrism and to replace it with a sense of wonder and humility in the face of difference – face-to-face with the *other*. ('Whenever you say "we" remember that it includes "them" as well,' he would say.) In Latin America, that 'other' had gone by many different names – from savage, to Indio, to Wildman, to native, and finally (by the time of CIDOC) the 'under-developed', a term that Illich hated and mocked. (Scheper-Hughes, 2001, p. 2)

Out of the multicultural circles and critical consciousness seminars at CIDOC came Illich's succession of great books: *The Seamy Side of Development, Energy and Equity* (1974), *DeSchooling Society* (1973a), *Celebration of Awareness* (1973b), *Tools for Conviviality* (1975) and *Medical Nemesis* (1976a). Later would come *The Disabling Professions* (Illich et al., 1977), *Toward a History of Needs* (1978), *Gender* (1982) and *In the Vineyard of the Text* (1993).

In 1968, in his talk about violence, Illich spoke to the new armies of volunteers in development aid:

Next to money and guns, the United States idealist turns up in every theatre of the war; the teacher, the volunteer, the missioner, the community organizer, the economic developer. Such men define their role as service. Actually they frequently wind up nimbing the damage done by money and weapons, or seducing the 'underdeveloped' to the benefits of the world of affluence and achievement. They especially are the ones for whom 'ingratitude' is the bitter reward. They are the personifications of Good Old Charlie Brown: 'How can you lose when you are so sincere?' [...] I submit that foreign gods (ideals, idols, ideologies, persuasions, values) are more offensive to the 'poor' than the military or economic power of the foreigner. It is more irritating to feel seduced to the consumption of overpriced sugar-water called Coca-Cola than to submit helplessly to doing the same job an American does, only at half the pay. It angers a person more to hear a priest preach cleanliness, thrift, resistance to socialism, or obedience to unite authority, than to accept military rule. If I read present trends correctly, and I am confident I do, during the next few years violence will break out mostly against symbols of foreign ideas and the attempt to sell these. (Illich, 1973b, pp. 25–26)

Ivan Illich had foreseen this in 1968.

To prove his statement, we will return to the legacy of the Peace Corps. As times changed, the Peace Corps program as well as its position within the US administration changed accordingly, matching the different profiles of successive administrations. The Vietnam War and Watergate crisis led to a cut in government funding. 'Richard Nixon predicted it would become a haven for draft dodgers. To avoid this possibility, service in the Peace Corps provided young men with draft deferment, but not exemption. To allay fears that the Peace Corps would harbor secret agendas or become a tool of the CIA, Peace Corps volunteers were sent only to countries that requested their services' (US National Archives and Records Administration, 2009). These criticisms had become stronger during the 1960s and 1970s. President Nixon incorporated the Peace Corps under the agency named ACTION. Then, in 1979, President Jimmy Carter declared it autonomous. During the Ronald Reagan administration, Congress made the Peace Corps an independent federal agency expanding also its fields: 'Reagan attempted to diversify the Peace Corps program by branching it out from its traditional tasks with education and agriculture to more current concerns like computer literacy and business-related education by initiating several new business related programs.' (John F. Kennedy Presidential Library and Museum, 1960).

The Peace Corps is still growing and President George W. Bush pledged to double its size. After the declaration of the 'War on Terror,' and in response to growing global anti-US sentiment after 9/11 and the invasion of Iraq, the Corps volunteers were supposed to once again improve the US image in the world. Throughout the almost fifty years of its existence, it can be observed that the

Peace Corps program always reflected the evolving and expanding ideology and global reach of the United States, as well as its opposition, represented to a high degree by the volunteers themselves (Kaller-Dietrich, 2010b).

Illich's learning center in Mexico, CIDOC, was closed in 1976. He himself died in 2002. Most recently 9/11 showed the meaning of his words. Coming back to his definition for the causes of violence in 1968, his words could be called prophetic: 'The recent violence in Detroit, Washington, and Cincinnati after the murder of Martin Luther King shows how the impatience of the ghetto dwellers in the United States can erupt into violence and vandalism at the slightest spark' (Illich, 1973b, p. 26). Violence

> covers a broad spectrum of experience: from the explosion of frustrated vitality to the fanatical rejection of alienating idols. It is important to stress this distinction. But as United States thinkers are horrified by the heartless slaughter in Vietnam, and fascinated by the inability of a white majority to suppress the life of people, it is not easy to keep the distinction clear. [...] Living violence always breaks out against the demand that a man submit to idols. Planned violence is then promoted as justified by the need to reduce a man or a people to the service of the idol they threaten to reject. (Illich, 1973b, pp. 26–27)

The author of these words recommended studying violence always as a response to the introduction of *pax economica* by taking into account the regime of scarcity produced by peace itself.

One of the books Illich frequently recommended was *The Great Transformation*, written by Carl Polanyi in 1944. From the history of Britain in the nineteenth century, it teaches that there exists a starting point when scarcity really affected everybody's daily life on a global scale. According to Polanyi, scarcity is fully fletched when land turns into private property and humans are reduced to working forces. The meaning of this kind of scarcity was amplified by Ivan Illich. He added to Polanyi's analysis that 'scarcity defines the field in which the laws of economy relate to: 1) subjects (possessive, genderless individuals – personal and corporate), 2) institutions and 3) commodities, within 4) an environment in which the commons have been transformed into resources private or public' (Illich, 1982, p. 19).

The end of common culture and the growing intensity and variety of scarcity are two sides of the same process and they always come along with so-called pacification programs. To say it in peace terms, this is the *pax economica*. It separates the world into few players and many backward people hardly surviving under miserable conditions of subsistence. The world was apparently divided into few winners and a sea of permanent losers. In the opinion of Illich, this occurred due to development, not for lack of it.

The war on subsistence in the twentieth century

In all of his radical de-constructionist writings, Ivan Illich challenged us to rethink late modern industrial society, and the perverse social relations that have grown up around it. He encourages us to free ourselves from the disabling discourses and practices of expert professionalism, to rid education of formal schools and schooling, medicine of doctors, cities of urban planners and the so-called Third World of development specialists, international bankers and their armies of practical technicians. Additionally, Illich warned us: if a peace builder came along, run away as fast as we can.

In each essay of his early years, Illich used the method of radical doubt – not in the Cartesian but rather in the Socratic sense. Challenging the nature of certainties that have been purveyed as truth, he particularly analyzed the deception embodied in institutions. Illich stated that the dogma behind powerful institutions is the so-called certainty of the ideological liberal who assumes that man makes his life by his institutions and that therefore the institutions of North American industrial civilization can and should be translated to the Third World for its own good: especially the institutions of schooling and technical assistance designed to help a given nation emulate the affluence of the United States.

Instead of universities, e.g., he asked, why not informal intellectual gatherings around tables – universities without walls, without lectures. Illich once said it was easier to teach a new idea to Mexican peasants than to academically trained professionals. Gustavo Esteva,* Mexican activist and de-professionalized storyteller, was a friend and follower of Ivan Illich since early 1982. Esteva underlings Illich's experience:

> My fascination with Ivan was born out of the fact that his ideas, his words, his writings, were a brilliant intellectual presentation of ordinary people's common discourse. He was describing ways of living and being I encountered all the time at the grassroots, in my grandmothers' world; the world of other indigenous peoples; the world of *campesinos* or *marginales*. 'Vernacular' and 'convivial', two words that are central to Ivan's work, were magnificent symbols for my people's worlds. I heard them there, for the first time, not in reading Ivan. All those pre-Illich years, I felt and sensed and smelled and touched and experienced those words and what they symbolized, in the villages, at the grassroots. Illich's work held up for me a brilliantly lit torch in the middle of all the intellectual darkness defining the experts' reality. Illich stood out from the majority of published voices, illuminating for me what I could not make clear sense of before at the grassroots. His was neither a new theory nor

---

*   Ed. This book contains several articles by Gustavo Esteva, see Chapter 31 on Raimon Panikkar and Chapter 19 coauthored with Arturo Guerrero, where he further refers to his biographical context within the frame of peaces as the following quote suggests.

ideology. In my conversation with peasants or marginals, each time I shared Ivan's ideas, they showed no surprise. Their comfortable familiarity with Illich's ideas, I began to call the 'aha effect'. 'Aha', they were saying, every time I was quoting Ivan. Yes, they knew, better yet, understood by the seat of the pants what he was publishing. No surprise there. But the experience of hearing their own experiences and ideas so well articulated in Ivan's words held up for them a magnificent mirror affirming what they already knew from common sense. Ivan once said that 'people can see what scientists and administrators can't'. And he said something more: that the people in our countries, rather than the dissident elite in the advanced ones, were implementing the political inversion he conceived in *Tools for Conviviality*. (Esteva, 2004, p. 5)

In the 1970s, Illich stood for many people on the side of the rebellions against the dominant system and its overwhelming effects on our minds. But his answers were often more radical, more irritating than the ones found by the classical 1960s activists in Berkeley, Paris and Berlin. Illich did not search for reforms. He stood for the idea of total transformation, especially of modern institutions, which did not serve the people for whom they once were planned. Not surprisingly, they turned against them. They are the real weapons of the war against subsistence in the name of peace:

> *Pax economica* protects a zero sum game, and ensures its undistributed progress. All are coerced to become players and to accept the rules of *homo economicus*. Those who refuse to fit the ruling model are either banished as enemies of the peace, or educated until they conform. By the rules of the zero sum game, both the environment and human work are scarce stakes; as one gains, the other loses. Peace is now reduced to two meanings: the myth that, at least in economics, two and two will one day make five, or a truce and deadlock. (Illich, 2006, p. 181)

And it was not only such arguments he introduced into conversations, talks and academic venues. David Cayley summarizes: 'Illich is an anomaly among modern scholars because he insists that the habits of the heart are as crucial to scholarship as the habits of the head' (Cayley, 1992, p. 4).

If we watch closely, the two texts *expresis verbis* related to peace written by Ivan Illich, one in 1968 and first published in 1969 (1973b) and the other first held as a talk in 1980 (2006), do differ according to the audience addressed. 'Violence: a mirror for Americans' speaks about common people and addresses the angry, young 1968-resisters against the US establishment. It is a text that tries to explain to them what they should really oppose (Illich, 1973b). The text of 1980 is more philosophical in its epistemology and etymology, and Illich does not speak about concrete commons and the stories told to him. 'Peace vs. Development' (Illich,

2006) addresses established experts in peace building, professional employees in the development-peace business. They might have preferred Illich advising them what to do, instead of terrifying them with insights into the kind of business they were engaged in.

Pax economica in progress

Ivan Illich wished modern people did not want what they wanted. He seriously questioned the arrogant caste of professionals and experts, who always and everywhere knew better what to do when. However, at the same time, they were convinced that there were no alternatives to what they suggest and support. Illich acted according to his conviction that there must be a possibility to think beyond the reachable and seemingly desired answers provided by *pax economica*, considered to be unique, omnipotent and omnipresent. Illich reminded us that, in fact, this very unique peace had almost successfully corrupted our minds and our free will. Are we ourselves already convinced that we cannot see anymore, that we are not able to escape and finally agree to the notoriously unjust implications of *pax economica*?

Illich found examples of the side effects of the *pax economica* and the overwhelming impotence in which it traps us in many different fields: church and school, transportation systems and health care, housing, justice and development aid. In his opinion, they all share the following four characteristics, which corrupted them and corrupt us and everything within their reach.

1. Institutions have powerful, unknown side effects. Illich called them *hidden curriculum*, because institutions implicitly teach us things that do not figure visibly in their agenda. Churches do not only liberate the soul, they also assume that such liberation cannot happen without religious caretaking. Schools do not only provide students with knowledge and skills, but they make us understand the importance of schools in order to obtain these indispensable faculties. Medicine does not only cure, but makes patients dependent from the medical care system. All these institutions hide their side effects behind impressing rituals; often they do not even recognize their own rituals, even though they themselves established them.
2. Hence, institutions became what Illich called a *radical monopoly*. This means that an institution does not serve a goal anymore, but invades and dominates all aspects of life – far beyond its original meaning and function. A good example of this argument was the usage of individual cars: originally, a car serves the transport of goods and people. But, as it can be easily recognized, cars define the way how our cities are built and conformed, how we make use of our time, how much money we think that we have to earn and how we organize our economy. For the sake of employment in the car industry,

more cars are produced: cars which run faster than we need to move; and because cars are made to be sold, they are made cheaper, more dangerous and of less durability.

3. Institutions sooner or later tend to *form part of the state*, find their legitimacy and outcome under the legal and financial protection of the state and so far are not exposed to the market laws anymore.

4. Most institutions act in a *therapeutic* or *missionary* way: instead of taking their users with their desires seriously as partners, therapists and missioners undertake treatments for their users. Finally, all these users of such treatments turn into patients. This effect can easily be studied with an attention to verbal expressions notoriously used: institutional caretakers inform, they coach, they allow, they hide, they detect symptoms, they recognize and follow cases and they solve problems. In schools, learning processes are organized (seemingly without involving people) until they fail. Then, a diagnosis will be provided. This diagnosis will not explain what a pupil did or did not, e.g. had been lazy, did not understand, did not pay attention, had other interests, does not want. Instead of recognizing what happens with the individual, therapeutic institutions will discover an abnormal behavior, a trauma, a deficit or apathy. This sounds like the description of a kind of clinical record of the learner, the constitution of the learner or the climate of learning. Under such a diagnosis, therapeutic measures are recommended: motivation, compensation, socialization and programming. For an individual these measures might seem accurate. But summing up such treatments for learners, the subject disappears, something quite irritating happens to the society as well as to the single learner.

In Illich's eyes, pastoral care, development aid, criminal justice, welfare, insurances or medicine were originally charitable facilities, but their inherent dynamics to convert arbitrary autonomous men and women into patients of the system destroy their originally charitable intentions and effects. So they weaken instead of strengthen what originally was their intention. And it is the users of institutions themselves who know best about these effects:

Many students, especially those who are poor, intuitively know what the schools do for them. They school them to confuse process and substance. Once these become blurred, a new logic is assumed: the more treatment there is, the better are the results; or, escalation leads to success. The pupil is thereby 'schooled' to confuse teaching with learning, grade advancement with education, a diploma with competence, and fluency with the ability to say something new. His imagination is 'schooled' to accept service in place of value. Medical treatment is mistaken for health care, social work for the improvement of community life, police protection for safety, military poise for national security, the rat race for productive work. Health, learning, dignity, independence, and creative endeavor are defined as little more than the performance of the institutions which claim to serve these ends, and their improvement is made to depend on allocating more resources to the management of hospitals, schools, and other agencies in question. (Illich, 1973a, p. 9)

Surprisingly, Illich did not blame only experts and institutions. He also denounced the victims who accept these side effects without contesting or at least trying to escape from them. Illich insisted that nobody remains responsible for his or her own health or faith. If there is any way out, it might be found in collective abstinence from all kinds of truth productions, to say in a radical and tenacious impotency. Erich Fromm, in his introduction to *Celebration of Awareness*, described Ivan Illich, who was his neighbor for fifteen years, as follows:

The author [Illich] is a man of rare courage, great aliveness, extraordinary erudition and brilliance, and fertile imaginativeness, whose whole thinking is based on his concern for man's unfolding – physically, spiritually and intel-lectually. The importance of his thoughts [...] lies in the fact that they have a liberating effect on the mind by showing new possibilities; they make the reader more alive because they open the door that leads out of the prison of routinized, sterile, preconceived notions. (Fromm in Illich, 1973b, p. 11)

Ivan Illich's critique of development and his call for the creation of a radically new relationship between human beings and their 'environment' has not played a significant part in the mainstream of policy and practice (Finger and Asún, 2001, p. 14). In recent years, one of the strongest arguments for peace building efforts also concerns ecology. Relating peace to ecology could mean something like the balance among each other and the many different culturally defined ways of relationship between micro and macro cosmos. Besides his prophetic book *Energy and Equity*, released in 1973, throughout his whole long life Ivan Illich did explore this in depth.

As ultimate conversations with David Cayley (2005) reveal, in his last years Illich allowed us to see in him a man who had not given up, and maybe this can help us open our eyes, hearts and thoughts. He himself had found balance in *philia*, friendship (Illich, 2001). If we want to share this, we can read his work, where incidentally one of the sayings he used to tell most often while still being with us can be found: 'Perhaps, I can tell you a story which will make clear...' (Illich in Cayley, 2005, p. 133).

Reference list

The list below, besides matching the references in the text, further includes suggested readings and some commentaries to the works of Illich that could be helpful for researchers interested in his peace thinking.

Cayley, D. (1992) *Ivan Illich in Conversation* (Concord: House of Anansi).

Cayley, D. (2005) *The Rivers North of the Future: The Testament of Ivan Illich* (Toronto: Anansi Press).

Cobbs Hoffman, E. (1998) *All You Need is Love: The Peace Corps and the Spirit of the 1960s* (Cambridge: Harvard University Press).

Cox, H. (2002) 'A Prophet, a Teacher, a Realistic Dreamer: Priest and Thinker Ivan Illich dies at 76; he Founded Influential Mexican Centre,' *National Catholic Reporter*, December 20, 2002, 16.

Dietrich, W., J. Echavarría and N. Koppensteiner (eds.) (2006) *Schlüsseltexte der Friedensforschung/Key Texts of Peace Studies/Textos claves de la Investigación para la paz* (Vienna: Lit).

Esteva, G. (2004) 'Notes for the Presentation in "Schooling and Education: A Symposium with Friends of Ivan Illich",' Homepage of Gustavo Esteva, http://gustavoesteva.com/english_site/back_from_the_future.htm, date accessed April 22, 2010.

Finger, M. and J.M. Asún (2001) *Adult Education at the Crossroads: Learning our Way Out* (London: Zed). Helpful review of the current state of adult education thinking and policy. Useful (but flawed) introductions to key thinkers. The writers take the contribution of Ivan Illich as their starting point and make some important points as a result.

Illich, I. (1973a) *Deschooling Society* (Harmondsworth: Penguin). [First published by Harper and Row 1971; republished by Marion Boyars.] Argues for the disestablishment of schooling. Chapters explore the phenomenology of schooling; the ritualization of progress; institutional spectrums; irrational consistencies; learning webs; and the rebirth of Epimethean man.

Illich, I. (1973b) *Celebration of Awareness: A Call for Institutional Revolution* (Harmondsworth: Penguin). [First published by Harper and Row 1971; republished by Marion Boyars.] Fascinating collection of essays exploring violence; the eloquence of silence; the seamy side of charity; the powerless church; the futility of schooling; sexual power and political potency; a constitution for cultural revolution.

Illich, I. (1974) *Energy and Equity* (London: Marion Boyars).

Illich, I. (1975) *Tools for Conviviality* (London: Fontana). [First published 1973 by Harper and Row, republished by Marion Boyars.] Argues for the building of societies in which modern technologies serve politically interrelated individuals rather than managers. Such societies are 'convivial,' they entail the use of responsibly limited tools.

Illich, I. (1976a) *Medical Nemesis: The Expropriation of Health* (New York: Pantheon).

Illich, I. (1976b) *After Deschooling, What?* (London: Writers and Readers). Includes a substantial opening essay 'Deschooling revisited' by Ian Lister.

Illich, I. (1978) *Toward a History of Needs* (New York: Random House).

Illich, I. (1981) *Shadow Work* (London: Marion Boyars).

Illich, I. (1982) *Gender* (New York: Pantheon Books).

Illich, I. (1993) *In the Vineyard of the Text: A Commentary to Hugh's Didascalicon* (Chicago: University of Chicago Press).

Illich, I. (2001) [1996] 'Philosophy...Artifacts...Friendship,' *The Aisling Magazine*, 28, http://www.aislingmagazine.com/aislingmagazine/articles/TAM28/Artifacts.html, date accessed December 22, 2009.

Illich, I. (2006) [1980] 'Peace vs. Development' in W. Dietrich, J. Echavarría and N. Koppensteiner (eds.) *Schlüsseltexte der Friedensforschung/Key Texts of Peace Studies/ Textos claves de la Investigación para la paz* (Vienna: Lit), 173–182.

Illich, I. et al (1977) *Disabling Professions* (Boston: Marion Boyars).

Ivan Illich Archives (2002) http://www.davidtinapple.com/illich/, Homepage of David Tinapple, date accessed April 23, 2010. Very useful page with links into key obituaries and to his writings. Includes e-texts of *Deschooling Society* and *Tools for Conviviality*.

Ivan Illich Writing on the Web (2010) http://www.preservenet.com/theory/Illich.html, Homepage of the Preservation Institute: Beyond Progressive and Conservative, date accessed April 23, 2010. Useful listing of links.

John F. Kennedy Presidential Library and Museum (1960) 'Peace Corps,' Historical Resources: JFK in History, http://www.jfklibrary.org/Historical+Resources/JFK+in+History/ Peace+Corps.htm, date accessed January 12, 2010.

Kaller-Dietrich, M. (2008): *Ivan Illich (1996–2002): Sein Leben, sein Denken* (Wietra: Bibliothek der Provinz).

Kaller-Dietrich, M. (2010a) 'Food and Peace' in N. Young (ed.) *The Oxford International Encyclopaedia of Peace* (New York: Oxford University Press).

Kaller-Dietrich, M. (2010b) 'Peace Corps' in N. Young (ed.) *The Oxford International Encyclopaedia of Peace* (New York: Oxford University Press).

Kuchenbuch, L. (2009) Interviewed by M. Kaller-Dietrich (Vienna, January 23, 2009).

Polanyi, C. [1944] *The Great Transformation: The Political and Economic Origins of Our Time* (Boston: Beacon Press).

Reimer, E. (1971) *School is Dead: An Essay on Alternatives in Education* (Harmondsworth: Penguin). Highly readable analysis and positing of alternatives.

Sachs, W. (1992) *The Development Dictionary: A Guide to Knowledge as Power* (London: Zed).

Scheper-Hughes, N. (2001) 'Introduction to Ivan Illich Speaking on "Reading Technologies" at Doe Library at UCB' (Manuscript), 1–3.

Smith, M.K. (1997, 2004, 2008) 'Ivan Illich: Deschooling, Conviviality and the Possibilities for Informal Education and Lifelong Learning,' *The Encyclopedia of Informal Education,* http://www.infed.org/thinkers/et-illic.htm, date accessed April 23, 2010.

Thinking after Illich (2007) http://www.pudel.uni-bremen.de/500en_Themen.html, Homepage of the Circle for Research on Proportionality (CROP), date accessed April 23, 2010. It collects some essays of Ivan Illich and those of some of his friends and collaborators.

US National Archives and Records Administration (2009) 'Educators and Students: Founding Documents of the Peace Corps,' http://www.archives.gov/education/lessons/peace-corps/ index.html, date accessed January 22, 2010.

Underwood, R.A. (1975) Review [untitled], Reviewed work 'Celebration of Awareness: A Call for Institutional Revolution by Ivan D. Illich,' *Journal of the American Academy of Religion*, 43, 2, Book Review Supplement, 405–406.

29
Pagans and Nomads: The Post-modern Peaces of Jean-François Lyotard and Gilles Deleuze

Norbert Koppensteiner

A biography? Lyotards and Deleuzes

> The two of us wrote *Anti-Oedipus* together. Since each of us was several, there was already quite a crowd. [...] We have assigned clever pseudonyms to avoid recognition. Why have we kept our own names? Out of habit, purely out of habit. To make ourselves unrecognizable in turn. To render imperceptible, not ourselves, but what makes us act, feel and think. [...] To reach, not the point where one no longer says I, but the point where it is no longer of any importance whether one says I. We are no longer ourselves. Each will know his own. We have been aided, inspired, multiplied. (Deleuze and Guattari, 2005, p. 3)

> [...] proper names have that property of attracting to themselves phrases belonging to different regimes and to heterogenous genres of discourse. (Lyotard, 1984a, p. 20)

This chapter is supposed to begin with some introductory words on the lives of the two authors discussed here, Jean-François Lyotard and Gilles Deleuze. However, reading the famous opening lines of *A Thousand Plateaus* next to Lyotard's comments on the properties of proper names shows the whole difficulty of writing about Deleuze's and Lyotard's biography. On the one hand, it is one of the virtues of post-modern philosophy, and theirs is no exception, to move beyond the disembodied voice of reason that appears to come out of nowhere, beyond the illusions of neutrality and objectivity. At its best, post-modern philosophy is about the concrete, embodied experience, about the joys, pains, pleasures of the flesh. Life, here and now, in all its forms, actual and potential. One even can make the argument that this is particularly the case for Deleuze, as his philosophy

525

specifically aims to combine living and thinking, which would make writing about Deleuze's life an almost natural and necessary choice for understanding his thinking. Yet, just like Lyotard, Gilles Deleuze remains suspicious about the unifying functions attached to proper names. They both resist the notion of narrating a story as one coherent whole, as if when taking the single moments together they would form the stability of subjects and their lives, as if there was some kind of causality and linear teleology inherent to those lives. It is then as if one would be saying 'their life was like this and could have been no other.' A life-story. Ascribing a single identity to Lyotard and Deleuze by narrating their life in that manner would violate the multiplicity of their becomings – the heterogeneity of the many actual and still possible Deleuzes and Lyotards – and run the danger of destroying that inspiring, intuitive plurality they aimed for, which can never be completely captured. Both their versions of post-modernity are about difference and plurality – and about respect for these.

So, in the few paragraphs available I do not want to give the impression of narrating each of their lives as one coherent story. That is impossible, no matter how exhaustive and detailed the biographical account. But neither do I want to just efface those lives, or give the impression that their living was inconsequential for their thinking. Each life is many and out of the unfathomable multiplicity of Deleuzes and Lyotards I have thus picked up some elements of living and thinking, made connections and worked on differences, thereby also transforming myselves in rhizomatic conjunction with and differentiation from them. Trying to respect the many other possibilities, I have therefore chosen what resonated at the moment. In doing so I have been guided by highlighting their specific contributions as thinkers of peace and focused on aspects – like the very notions of paganism and nomadism – that might have remained unduly underfocused in many of the studies on their works. While I therefore do not claim completeness, after all many other Deleuzes and Lyotards are possible, I do accept responsibility for my choices.

In the following, I will thus proceed to highlight some of the stories around Lyotard's biography and then engage with his thinking, followed subsequently by a similar section on the lives and works of Gilles Deleuze. I will then conclude by drawing the figures of the pagan and nomad together in the context of peace.

Jean-François Lyotard

Small stories

Jean-François Lyotard is born in Versailles, France, in 1924 to a middle-class family. After graduating in philosophy from the Sorbonne, he takes up a teaching position in Algeria in 1950, at a time when the conflict over the French colonial rule is just heating up. Lyotard's political stance is clear: in 1954 he joins the Marxist group *Socialisme ou Barbarie* and becomes involved in the struggles for Algerian independence (Malpas, 2009, pp. 4–5). Increasingly disillusioned with Marxism, he subsequently returns to Paris to take up a teaching position at the Parisian University VIII Vincennes, where he also meets Gilles Deleuze. What ensues is his 'evil book' (Lyotard, 1988, p. 13) the *Libidinal Economy* (2004). This book signifies Lyotard's break with Marxism and is a conceptual response to Deleuze and Guattari's *Anti-Oedipus* and what Lyotard sees as their continued enthrallment with Marx. Written in sometimes-polemic manner, it also is Lyotard's reaction to the demise of Structuralism and his move towards that tradition of thought that soon comes to be labeled Poststructuralist. The French originals of his following main works *The Postmodern Condition* (1984b), *Just Gaming* (Lyotard and Thébaud, 1999), *The Differend* (2002) and *The Inhuman* (1998) appear during the subsequent years in the decades of the 1970s and 1980s.[1] Most of his work following *The Postmodern Condition* deals with the question of how it might be possible to feel, act and think while being embedded in fragmented and discontinuous worlds that are not or no longer organized by a central story or coherent subject. While Lyotard's philosophy does not provide an answer, it strongly argues for the importance of the questioning itself and holds that the irrevocable plurality of small and often contradictory stories that emerges from the dissolution of metanarratives is cause for celebration rather than lament. Jean-François Lyotard dies of leukemia in 1998.

Lyotard's biographical introduction to the *Peregrinations* (1988) tells the story of his early ambitions of becoming a monk, historian, artist or novelist. It can be argued that besides the well-known Lyotard-the-philosopher also the other four Lyotards do not disappear over time. They resurface in various guises, as in a preoccupation with Christianity and paganism; with the remnants of history after Auschwitz and totalitarianism; in the question of art, artistic production and the sublime; and in the attempt at a zero degree style in the writing of *The Differend* (cf. Hamilton Grant, 2004, pp. xx–xxi).

Jean-François Lyotard does not specifically call himself a thinker of peace. Yet if the reflection on peace is supposed to be more than a stale one-size-fits-all, then no thinking on peace that takes itself seriously can avoid engaging with his works. Many of the main topics that the different Lyotards keep returning to – plurality and difference, dispute and conflict, justice – are crucial concerns for peace. The approach of the Lyotards is often highly unconventional and radical, challenging established wisdom and self-evident truth and calling upon its reader to unthink the previously thought, thus making space for something new to emerge. New Lyotards and new Deleuzes are still emerging and, indeed, it is not far fetched to think differently yet again and find also peace thinkers in both of them.

The Postmodern Condition – language games, the death of metanarratives, history

The Postmodern Condition, Lyotard's probably most often referenced work, is a book commissioned by the government of Quebec on the status of knowledge in the most highly developed Western societies. Indeed, the very choice of words in the commission is telling, for it is exactly this linear narrative that would allow one to speak of (human) development that Lyotard's report comes to doubt. Lyotard uses this commission as a springboard for an inquiry into the question how human life is formed within and through narrations and whether it is (still) possible at all to tell the story of human existence along the lines of one grand story. In order to do so, *The Postmodern Condition*, following Ludwig Wittgenstein, approaches human communities as being perpetually engaged in language games. To say that language is a game implies three things. First of all a game means that there are rules which do not carry their own legitimation, but are the result of a contract between the players, whether this contract is explicitly stated or not. This is to say that the rules of a game are not naturally pregiven but need to be formed. Second, 'if there are no rules, there is no game' and any change in the rules, alters the game as such. Third, any utterance is a move in the game (Lyotard, 1984b, p. 10).

Lyotard perceives societies as constantly engaged in a multiplicity of different language games. Science, politics, arts, in fact all areas of human life have their own games, which define the utterances that are admissible (that can meaningfully be made) and how they can be formulated. The rules for how a statement needs to be formed in order to be meaningful are different in science, than, for example, in the political realm, yet one can be engaged in both games. The different games one plays at any given time may be contradictory or overlapping and influence each other. In this universe of games, every human being is furthermore formed as player by virtue of being embedded in a multiplicity of different games. Players do not exist independently from the games, but only within them. Who we are, after Lyotard, is a function of the games we play, not the other way round. On the basis of this method of language games, Lyotard describes narratives – the stories about themselves and the world that communities of players tell through the games.

Metanarratives in turn organize narratives in terms of an overarching master-story that holds the single narratives together and combines them in a meaningful whole. Using a more poetic language, Lyotard says apropos of Hölderlin that through metanarratives past, present and future are narrated together in a manner that makes them rhyme (Lyotard, 1998, p. 25). Metanarratives dictate the rules for the individual language games and provide an overall meaning to the different narratives told through the games. Who 'we' are, how belonging is defined or what is the concrete significance of our time. Metanarratives hold the different smaller stories together and show how all of existence is part of the same grand design.

Metanarratives are not unique to modernity, yet the modern metanarratives all tell the human story as a coherent story unified under the notion of progress. Humanity emerges from a less advanced past, passes through the now and is heading toward the advanced future. Societal time is narrated in them as linearity pointing upwards. This is the case for both types of modern metanarratives that Lyotard defines.

Marxism, the Enlightenment, liberal democracy or Capitalism are some examples for the emancipatory metanarrative. This metanarrative tells the tale of the successive human emancipation towards freedom: Marxism in the revolutionary advance towards a just social order; liberal democracy and universal human rights tell the story of the successive global realization of human freedom through a specific order of institutional organization; the Enlightenment narrative is about the process of humanity stepping out of the immaturity of superstition; the invisible hand of capitalism successively leads to greater welfare for all, etc.

The second kind, speculative metanarratives, tell the story of the progress of knowledge that culminates in truth. The advance in knowledge cumulatively leads onto an ever higher path of understanding reaching its pinnacle – as, for example, in the philosophy of Georg Friedrich Wilhelm Hegel – in truth as absolute spirit. The true, after Hegel, is the whole.

Lyotard assumes that those metanarratives have become implausible and obsolete during the twentieth century. The uprisings against the communist regimes in Berlin 1953, Budapest 1956, Czechoslovakia 1968 and Poland 1980 refute the Marxist understanding of historical materialism; May 1968 refutes the story of parliamentary liberalism; the crises of 1911 and 1929 shatter the dreams of universal prosperity promised by economic liberalism (Lyotard, 1989b, p. 318). What is more, totalitarianism and the technologically organized mass killings of the Holocaust have cast a stain of doubt over the very ideal of such a universal history. After Auschwitz, Lyotard argues, the whole can no longer be regarded as the true and history no longer be told as one unified story. The post-modern condition marks the increasing doubt towards both the factual claims and the ethical validity of modernity's metanarratives:

Simplifying to the extreme, I define postmodern as incredulity towards metanarratives. [...] The narrative function is losing its functors, its great hero, its great dangers, its great voyages, its great goal. It is being dispersed in clouds of narrative language elements – narrative but also denotative, prescriptive, descriptive and so on. Conveyed within each cloud are pragmatic valencies specific to its kind. Each of us lives at the interstices of many of these. However, we do not necessarily establish stable language combinations, and the properties of the one we do establish are not necessarily communicable. (Lyotard, 1984b, p. xxiv)

This denotes the post-modern as a state of mind of doubt, of skepticism towards the great promises of the metanarratives. Post-modernity, as Lyotard subsequently makes clear, defines that moment or moments of a loss of certainty, when the great modern narrations of salvation – Marxism, liberal democracy, enlightenment, humanism, the subject, etc. – and their underlying ideas of progress and development are no longer credible and the very value that is attached to them becomes suspicious. Far from being one universal tale of progress, history has become scattered into signs of history, into events whose meaning is no longer readily apparent. The twentieth century for Lyotard is strewn with the ruins of the once glorious grand stories of progress. With the advent of post-modern doubt and the caducity of metanarratives, it cannot be denied any more that time no longer rhymes with time (Lyotard, 1988).

The question of how this finding is to be evaluated also marks the beginning of Lyotard's debate with Jürgen Habermas during the 1980s. While not disagreeing with all of Lyotard's analyses, the conclusion for Habermas (1994) is that modernity is still an unfinished project. He sees the urgent necessity to work for uniting the differing language games. For Habermas, their splintering is the very malaise of the current times and he proposes a theory of communicative action to unite them again, upholding the ideals of emancipation (Habermas, 2006). Consensus between the different language games, for Habermas, is still possible and in any case should be upheld as an ideal.

Lyotard takes the opposite approach. His philosophy is an inquiry into heterogeneity, into the potentials of the manifold. He remains suspicious of the propensity for exclusion, intolerance and violence inherent to any grand story that tries to explain it all. The twentieth century has drastically shown the dangers lurking beneath the seemingly universal tales of progress and truth. The obsolescence of the metanarratives, while often accompanied with a feeling of disillusionment and loss, to him also is a cause for celebration. The ruin of the one grand story is the condition of possibility for the many small stories. Lyotard here often appears to follow Immanuel Kant and his insistence on the dissimilarity between the different types of reason (Lyotard, 1989a, p. 133). Yet, if this is indeed the case then it is a Kant pervaded by Nietzsche, for while Kant draws out possibilities for bridging and connecting the different forms of reason and discourse, Lyotard radically emphasizes their uniqueness, the singularity and heterogeneity of all that is alive (Zima, 1997, p. 178).

Consensus to Lyotard is a suspect value (Lyotard, 1984b, p. 66). It is difference – dissent and dispute – that opens up as of yet unthought and unthinkable possibilities. The story of the One – one truth, one progress, one humanity, one way of political organization – to him always bears the danger of becoming total. To aim for the one, global peace after Lyotard would mean silencing the multiplicity of the many small peaces. The challenge he poses in many different fields – politics, arts, philosophy – is how to recognize this difference without thereby immediately destroying it. His account of history thus is one of a post-structuralist dissolution into (hi)stories:

> [...] history consists of a swarm of narratives, narratives that are passed on, made up, listened to and acted out; the people does not exist as a subject; it is a mass of thousands of little stories that are at once futile and serious, that are sometimes attracted together to form bigger stories, and which sometimes disintegrate into drifting elements, but which usually hold together well enough to form what we call the culture of a civil society. (Lyotard, 1989a, p. 134)

An inquiry that organizes history along one linear vector of progress, with the human being as central subject and hero of the tale, according to Lyotard, is no longer possible. Yet neither does he follow Jean Baudrillard's notion of a reversal and complete dissolution of history based on the media-fueled hollowing out and anemic disappearance of events (Baudrillard, 1994; Malpas, 2009, pp. 79–80). Lyotard holds that events do still take place, in small, often infinitely simple forms, yet instead of being immediately understandable, they posit potential points of irruption, enigmatic signs that happen as a question mark even before happening as a question. What is necessary in approaching them is a certain privation, that is, not a thinking in terms of the already-known, but an unthinking that disarms what is already known as thought (Lyotard, 1998, p. 90). This question mark of the event calls for a careful *is it possible?* before even the question of the meaning of an event can be raised. It is an approach that does not pretend to already know what an event might be and look like. This notion of the event as an as-of-yet unprecedented possibility resonates in Lyotard's main philosophical treatise on the differend.

The Differend

The points Lyotard looks for in history, just as well as in art and communication, are the as-of-yet unpresentable. The moment when language falters, when the sublime is encountered in art, when something might occur for which we do not yet have the words. Lyotard's philosophy is a philosophy of respect towards this radical heterogeneity that in this sense exists only as potentiality. This is what a differend would be, an instant when something needs to be expressed but within the genre of discourse available cannot (yet) find its proper idiom. One, quite simply, is lacking the words. In Lyotard's definition, in the differend something 'asks' to be put into phrases, yet suffers from not being able to be put into phrases right away (Lyotard 2002, p. 13). If that idiom is not found, then a differend results in a wrong, that is, a damage which goes together with the loss of the means to prove that damage (Lyotard 2002, p. 5).[2]

Lyotard's differend leads right into the heart of questions around peace and conflict. The heterogeneity of language games points to the impossibility of avoiding conflicts. The absence of a universal genre of discourse to regulate those conflicts (Lyotard, 2002, p. xii) implies that a wrong occurs whenever the rules of one genre of discourse are imposed over the other. Also twenty years after *The Differend* has been published this raises burning issues, as, for example, around questions about the universality of the Western liberal democratic model and the legitimacy of nation building in places where this model has no tradition, or about the universality of human rights and the very ideal of humanity it espouses. After Lyotard, any attempt to state a universal law, to put oneself in the position of 'enunciator of the universal prescriptions,' is absolute injustice, infatuation itself (Lyotard and Thébaud, 1999, p. 99). His philosophy dissolves the notion of any single standard of measurement in a multiplicity of small measures that correspond to the size of human communities and their different language games.

The differend points towards the limitations of any prescriptive system of thought and action. It challenges all notions of conflict solution and casts into doubt the very pretension that one could know in advance what a conflict is or predefine a set of tools for its resolution. The task of philosophy, according to Lyotard, is to bear witness to the indeterminacy of the differend:

> One's responsibility before thought consists, on the contrary, in detecting differends and in finding the (impossible) idiom for phrasing them. This is what a philosopher does. An intellectual is someone who helps to forget the differends, by advocating a given genre, whichever one it may be [...], for the sake of political hegemony. (Lyotard, 2002, p. 142)

This is a task the scope of which can never be fully known in advance. It demands a fine sensorium of intuition and willingness to engage with the new, to unthink the previously thought, much rather than expert knowledge. Art plays a crucial role in this respect, with its propensity for dislocating one's faculties and figuring even that which cannot be figured (Lyotard, 1998, p. 98).[3] Indeed, if there is such a thing as a commonality among the many post-modern philosophies and philosophers, then it might reside in this commitment to difference, in understanding, as Lyotard does, philosophy to be the task of finding new rules, new idioms of expression. As we shall see further on, this task is echoed in the philosophy of difference of Gilles Deleuze.

Paganism, justice

Paganism, one might say, is Lyotard's response to the monotheistic religions and the metanarratives in history and politics. Taking the case of Christianity, he points out that monotheism is characterized by the One God's mastery over the world and the fidelity of the believers to His word. Christianity narrates the world as one coherent story, originated in God's performative (world-creating) first utterance. The metanarrative constructed upon this word places the believer in the position of somebody who is always the addressee, the commentator and interpreter of something that s/he has heard, yet never heard entirely or completely understood. The believer so never passes over into the position of speaker, that is, s/he 'must never assume the authority that the one who addressed him is supposed to have with respect to the meaning at hand' (Lyotard and Thébaud, 1999, p. 39).

Against this pragmatics of fidelity, Lyotard posits paganism as what might be termed a pragmatics of infidelity. However, this term is not to be understood in a moral sense, but much rather denotes the putting into action of the notion that it is possible to play several language games at once, switch between them and that each game may be interesting in itself, without thereby bestowing truth or exclusivity. Paganism works from the assumption of an uncountable multiplicity of competing stories (a multiplicity of competing gods) and the notion that everybody, including the gods, is immanent to the stories in the making (Lyotard and Thébaud, 1999, p. 43). Since the gods are equally part of the stories, a pagan knows that truth does not arise from either their word or the story itself. On the contrary, one can argue with those gods, deal with them, and they themselves are competing, can be treacherous, vain and fallible. Within pagan stories the human being is always both addressor and addressee, speaker and spoken to. In this situation of continuous embedding it is impossible to locate a first utterer or origin of the story (Lyotard and Thébaud, 1999, pp. 39–40). While 'I' can so enter into different language games, 'I' do not exist independent of the games, am not a unitary vantage point onto the whole set of games. 'I' do not play the game, the game makes 'me' into its player. The different games played make 'me' at least a severality and this narrative function works the same for everybody, gods and humans.

Lyotard deploys paganism as an instructive figure for how to break away from the exclusivity of metanarratives and operationalize his notions of the multiplicity of language games. Paganism utilizes those games as a strategy to open up possibilities and choices. The very absence of a unified subject and the inescapability of stories turn into the pagan's advantage, which s/he seeks to safeguard, expand and upon which s/he plays. As political strategy, it implies a commitment to the multiplication of small narratives. Paganism is infidel to stories of origin, its root term *pagus* implies a border region or the frontiers of towns, but not the stability of *Heim* or home (Lyotard, 1989a, pp. 135–136). Being pagan then means the subversive dissolution of the center from the unsettled margins, cheerfully playing the many small gods against the universal, monotheistic One God.

534 Peace Thinkers

Within Lyotard's theory of language games, this corresponds to the more technical term of paralogy (Lyotard, 1984b, pp. 60–67). Paralogy describes the power to destabilize an existing language game by deploying a move, an utterance that goes against the established rules. Paralogy emphasizes the subversive side of the new, it attempts to bring into play the as-of-yet unpresentable, the event, sublime or differend, thereby unsettling the existing game's power of explanation (Malpas, 2009, p. 31).

Lyotard holds on to the notion of justice, but does not ground it in either truth or the autonomy of the subject. In line with the commitment to the multiplicity of small stories and language games, justice then implies two things: First of all a multiplicity of justices arising within the different games. Those justices may be incommensurable to each other, yet in themselves are not arbitrary, but defined in relation to the rules specific to each game. Second, a justice of multiplicity that holds on to the prescriptive idea of justice but places it under the rule of divergence (minorities) rather than convergence (majorities). Lyotard here reverses the standard political imperative of liberal democracies. Society, to him, is made up of a multiplicity of language games and in terms of those games each member always belongs to at least several minorities. A Lyotardean justice of multiplicity implies that justice is not when the majority rules, but what is just is the avoidance of the domination of any one language game. Unjust would then no longer be the opposite of just, but 'that which prohibits that the question of the just and the unjust be, and remain, raised' (Lyotard and Thébaud, 1999, p. 67). Within the pagan universe, human beings so are *Just Gaming* (Lyotard and Thébaud, 1999), as the English translation of Lyotard's corresponding book *Au Juste* is entitled. There are just language games, yet one way of playing is playing them justly, respecting the difference, mindful of the possibility of a differend.

Working through modernity – post-modern peaces

Post-modernity after Lyotard mounts an insurrection against the homogenizing tendencies of everything that smacks of metanarratives – truth, state, capitalism, Marxism, Christianity, the Enlightenment ideals of Humanism among them. This rejection and doubt, however, do not derive from claiming to possess an even higher truth in the light of which the previously thought could now be assessed as faulty, a knowledge that would be even more total than the modern metanarratives against which it sets out. It derives, on the contrary, from the realization of the impossibility and inhumanity of such a grand knowledge and can thus only arise from a small, unstable multiplicity of local stories and forms of knowledge.

Post-modernity, as Lyotard never tires to point out (1984b, 1998), is therefore also not a new epoch after modernity. The 'post' cannot be read in the sense of an 'after' but as something that constantly refers back to modernity. Doubt as a sentiment has always been inherent to modernity. In fact, Lyotard argues, modernity's project of progressive self-overcoming necessitates this very post-modern doubt. Rather than something that comes later in time, post-modernity is thus nothing else but the radicalization of certain trends always inherent to modernity, which thus is constitutionally and ceaselessly pregnant with its post-modernity (Lyotard, 1998, p. 25). Post-modernity in all its colors and facets is not the overcoming of modernity, but the constant, unfinished and interminable reworking and rewriting of some of its aspects.

As pointed out above, Lyotard did not explicitly consider himself a peace thinker, yet his philosophy is immediately applicable here. In the wake of his philosophy, the plurality of post-modern peaces might be said to derive from the sentiment of doubt inherent to modernity. They derive from the disillusionment with modernity's promises of salvation and are skeptical towards notions of perpetual peace, the end of history through the triumph of liberal democracy and capitalism, the promises of Global Governance, Universal Human Rights and Millennium Development Goals. After Lyotard, one could say that post-modern peaces dissolve those metanarratives and from their vestiges build a heterogeneous multiplicity. Communication is always a possibility to them, understanding no guarantee and dispute almost a certainty. Post-modern peaces celebrate this Babel and see the so arising conflicts as opportunities for transformation and change, rather than detriments to be avoided or overcome.

Before returning once more to Jean-François Lyotard at the end of this chapter, the chapter will now proceed with outlining the nomadic version of the post-modern peaces after Gilles Deleuze.

Gilles Deleuze

Perhaps one day...

Repetition 1
The philosopher of itinerant nomadism is reluctant to travel – least of all abroad. His close friend Michel Tournier later on will speculate that Deleuze's visit during Tournier's stay in Tübingen, Germany, might have been his only foray abroad (Tournier, 2001, p. 201). While the figure of the nomad turns into one of his key concepts, Deleuze insists that physical movement is only one way of remaining itinerant. Deleuze is much more interested in thought as category for the itinerant. Movement, hence, is not just physical.

Repetition 2
Much more than Lyotard, Gilles Deleuze today is widely read and received in international academia. During the late 1980s and 1990s, a whole generation

of post-modern authors comes to prominence focusing on different Deleuzes. From the works in Poststructuralist Feminism of the early Rosi Braidotti (1994), to Brian Massumi (1992), the Post-Marxist interpretations of Michael Hardt and Antonio Negri (Hardt, 1993, Hardt and Negri, 2000) until more recently Manuel DeLanda (1997, 2002). These highlight some of the better-known Deleuzes – activist, materialist, anti-religious, anti-state, critical of Marxism – while at the same time in many ways remain beholden to the Marxist critique of capitalism. Perhaps less known is the cinematic Deleuze of Cinema 1 and 2 (2005a, 2005b), or Deleuze-the-philosopher both with works on his own topics and his many treatises on a wide range of other thinkers, for example Spinoza (Deleuze, 1988b), Kant (Deleuze, 2008) to Nietzsche (Deleuze, 2005c), Bergson (Deleuze, 1991) and Foucault (Deleuze, 1988b), or the Deleuze of literary studies.

Repetition 3
Gilles Deleuze is born in Paris, France, in 1925 and spends most of his life in that city, until his death by suicide in 1995 after suffering from lung cancer. During the second half of the 1940s, this Deleuze studies at the Sorbonne and also begins his academic career there, before moving to Lyon for a short period between 1964 and 1968. When he begins working, Phenomenology and then Structuralism dominate the French intellectual climate. Later, in 1969, he returns to Paris to take up a teaching position at the infamous Parisian University VIII Vincennes, which after its foundation in the same year rapidly becomes a hotspot of student activities. Its staff soon contains many of the leading French intellectuals, among them Michel Foucault, Jean-François Lyotard, Deleuze himself and one Félix Guattari.

Repetition 4
One Félix Guattari (1930–1992) is a disciple of Jacques Lacan and radical political activist. Deleuze and Guattari write some of their most influential works together, chief among them *Anti-Oedipus* (2003a), *A Thousand Plateaus* (2005) and their last collaboration *What is Philosophy?* (2003b).[4] In this cooperation Guattari's background of clinical psychology and militant activism productively combines with Deleuze's philosophical training towards a mixture that in the intellectual climate of Paris past the events of May 1968 is as explosive as it is unconventional. The fact of their cooperation, the visible move beyond the single author-as-subject is important to them, as they famously make clear in the very first lines of *A Thousand Plateaus*. Quite a crowd indeed.

Repetition 5
'[P]erhaps one day, this century will be known as Deleuzian' (Foucault, 1998, p. 343).

The power of philosophy – living and thinking, immanence, becoming, difference

This section is dedicated to thinkers of peace. Including Gilles Deleuze in this category is certainly appropriate. For one, the question of thinking remained one of the key concerns throughout Deleuze's life. And while, like Lyotard, he never called himself a peace thinker, his message is highly relevant for all those peaces that do no longer entirely fit the modern mold, without having an equally powerfully counterproposal available. If the emergence of post-modern peaces has been highlighted in the past pages with Jean-François Lyotard, then it is now Gilles Deleuze whose philosophy goes a long way towards conceptualizing the actualities and virtualities of those peaces. In fact, without going so far as to underwrite the bold forecast of the above repetition 5, I think that Deleuze's relevance for post-modern peaces is only now starting to be understood. While the post-modern debate may be drawing to a close, Deleuze's relevance for thinking and living peace has never fully been explored.

Deleuze's philosophy is aimed at critically reworking and subverting the tradition of thinking that has been built upon the ancient Greek model. Deleuze heeds the Lyotardean notion of a working-through of modernity and takes to the task some of the most important European philosophers of the past, to show the critical potential that is also inherent to them. He is interested in finding the doubtful, skeptical alternative, in short the post-modern element in some of modernity's pillar saints like David Hume and Immanuel Kant. After Plato, Western philosophy had hitched itself to the notions of representation, to the stability of being and truth. Deleuze, on the contrary, unearths the outlines of a different tradition, and he does so very often not by rejecting or refuting the modern thinkers, but by brushing them against the grain of their established reading. Philosophy, for Deleuze, after all is not the aspiration towards truth or the attempt to fix the meaning of existence. Philosophy, much to the contrary, is a creative task. Not to describe what is, not to find out what ought to be, but to enable a creative transformation and difference. He therefore distinguishes between images of thought and concepts.

Images of thought work as prefabricated boxes that help us orient ourselves in daily life. As labels or habits, they fix our world in certain forms and for Deleuze thus are not thinking, but the avoidance of thinking. Images of thought presuppose that we already know what it means to think, that thought is known. Descartes was only able to arrive at his philosophy of the subject by presupposing thought as the already known. Under the sway of images of thought, experiences similarly are stripped of their creative power and subsumed under already established categories. Images of thought further reinforce the known. The task of philosophy, on the contrary, is the creation of concepts (Deleuze and Guattari, 2003b).

Concepts answer to a given problem in a novel way. Concepts are not descriptions or definitions; they do not fix meaning but move beyond the already-known to open up creative potentials. They are thus not determined by what they are, but by what they can do, which ways of becoming-different they enable. To give an example: love, after Deleuze, is the encounter with another person that opens up a possible world. Such a concept does not determine what love is – does not fix a stability, but points beyond the known towards a transformation (Colebrook, 2008, p. 17).

Philosophy for Deleuze, just as for Michel Foucault (1990, p. 9), is predicated upon thinking differently; it implies to free oneself from what is already known, from images of thought. What so occupies Deleuze throughout his life is that movement of thought that instigates new becomings. To think for him quite simply means to voyage (Deleuze and Guattari, 2005, p. 482), yet a voyage from which one would never return the same, but always emerge altered, become-differently. In allusion to Martin Heidegger, thinking for Deleuze implies being on the road, a road that is not pregiven but made in the walking (Marks, 2005, p. 279).

Thought therefore is a productive category, one that has the potential to enable a transformation of the self. Yet, by the very same token of thinking-as-creativity, thought for Deleuze does not pose an absolute arbiter or final ground of judgment. Thinking is productive, not normative or descriptive. Indeed, he sharply turns against the Western tradition since Plato that places thinking on the highest pedestal, as the only possible venue to truth, thereby mutilating life – the concretely lived experience of (everyday) existence. Whenever thinking is related to truth, for Deleuze this leads to passing judgment on life. In the Post-Platonic, Cartesian West only that can be affirmed which is rationally held to be true; everything that is perceived by the senses is under the suspicion of being mere appearance and thus false. Living and thinking, instead of posing a fruitful union, so begin to fall apart.

What Deleuze criticizes is the Western trend of perceiving the world dualistically, with binary or dialectic oppositions. Wolfgang Dietrich (2008) has characterized the corresponding images of peace as *moral* or *modern*.* This dualistic perception, Deleuze argues, is to the detriment of both living and thinking. Under the rule of thinking life is mutilated, becomes subdued, disciplined and normalized. A thusly disfigured life in turn fosters a propensity for mad derailment in thought:

> We now only have instances where thought bridles and mutilates life, making it sensible, and where life takes revenge and drives thought mad, losing itself along the way. Now we only have the choice between mediocre lives and mad

---

* Ed. On the five families of peace – energetic, moral, modern, post-modern and trans-rational – see also the conclusion to this volume.

thinkers. Lives that are too docile for thinkers and thoughts that are too mad
for the living: Immanuel Kant and Friedrich Hölderlin. (Deleuze, 2001, p. 67)

Deleuze's caustic observation here is equally philosophical as psychological.
In the guises of living and thinking, he thereby rediscovers Friedrich Nietzsche's
Apollo and *Dionysus* (Nietzsche, 1967; Deleuze, 2001, 2005c) and the latter's
claim that Apollo unchecked leads to neurosis – *white man's disease*. Just like
Nietzsche, Deleuze proposes a fruitful union between living and thinking, a
unification of contradictory principles that is neither Hegelian-dialectic nor
binary-exclusive: life that activates thought and thought that in turn affirms
life (Deleuze, 2001, p. 66).

This is an insight that is shared by the energetic notions of peace (Dietrich,
2008)* and that differentiates Deleuze's peaces from the modern one. Yet the
coincidence with the energetic and unmodern traditions is also not total, as the
example of Jiddu Krishnamurti in the current volume shows.† In their own way,
both Deleuze and Krishnamurti criticize the modern predominance of rational
thought. Yet while Deleuze aims for a creative balance of living and thinking and
therefore affirms the potential of thought for transformation, for Krishnamurti
thought and living remain antithetical. For the latter life is always here and
now, whereas thought is tied to memory and is thus of the past. Krishnamurti
champions living; thought for him is dead. Peace implies the immersion into
the present and is therefore freedom from thought (Krishnamurti, 1969, 1975,
pp. 104–114). Thought has its place as a tool in the narrow realm of technical
application, but the crucial point for Krishnamurti is that it cannot transform
life. Thought for Krishnamurti goes no further than what Deleuze calls the image
of thought.

While the modern tradition thus occupies one pole and judges living by
thinking, the unmodern ones – like Krishnamurti or also Osho – move to the
other pole and try to get rid of thinking in favor of living.

Deleuze's post-modern peaces opt for a third possibility and aim for a
Nietzschean dynamic balance of living and thinking, proceeding along a complex
unity: 'One step for living, one step for thinking. Modes of life inspire ways of
thinking; modes of thinking create ways of living' (Deleuze, 2001, p. 66). Living
so offers the possibility for becoming, for a creative transformation of oneself –
and so does thinking. Ultimately, the two cannot be separated and keeping open
the creative potential necessary for peaces needs both.

To live and think peace after Deleuze, furthermore, would imply to radically
think it immanently. Deleuzian philosophy rejects any founding grounds,

* Ed. A deeper understanding of energetic peaces is discussed in Chapter 11 by Swami
Veda Bharati.
† Ed. The author refers here to Chapter 27 by Samrat Schmiem Kumar.

first principles – God, Being, Truth and anything that could provide a stable position or lead to transcendence towards an outside. This pure immanence also implies doing away with the privileged position of an experiencing subject that would exist independently of the experience. Deleuze dissolves subjectivity in a multiplicity of experiences. Instead of a stable being, there only is the permanent flow of becoming. Like earlier Nietzsche, Deleuze recognizes the subject as an illusion and posits instead an oscillating play of forces (affects, desires), propelled by difference that is not be captured within stable boundaries of a cogito.

Similar to Lyotard, Deleuze so drops the Enlightenment ideal of 'Man' and even the very idea(l) of the human. His philosophy thus often is characterized as anti-human, yet this is correct only if this term is given an affirmative and productive connotation. Becoming, another one of his key concepts, is thereby freed from those pregiven forms and opened up to a much wider array of possibilities. Once more the question is what a concept can do, and in terms of becoming Deleuze and Guattari (2005, pp. 233ff.) suggest becoming-animal, becoming-woman and becoming-imperceptible as only some of the multiple potentials then opening up. The point about becoming is not to know what, say, an animal *is* and neither to imitate it or identify with it, but much rather to open oneself up to different experiential categories, to different perceptions, movements, feelings (Deleuze and Guattari, 2005, pp. 238–239; Colebrook, 2008, p. 136). Becoming-woman, Deleuze suggests, is something that everybody needs to undergo in order to free oneself from the stability of being. Again it has to be emphasized that also this becoming-woman has to be understood as a vector of transformation – a line of flight in Deleuzian terminology – and not in the sense of performing woman as identity category, which would lead back to the stability of being, exchanging one mold for another. That is why there also is no becoming-man for Deleuze, because man has been set as the very standard for being. Becoming is the movement by which a transformative potentiality is actualized, it is the process of becoming-other-than-oneself. Yet this change is always an inclusive one that moves beyond the either-or of stable identity categories to an unending series of the 'and...and...and...' that reproduces and expands multiplicities. The whole series of becomings is perhaps best exemplified by becoming-imperceptible, the point of blending into the cosmos, relinquishing all notions of stability and individuality. This becoming-imperceptible has a spiritual quality, yet one that is not transcendent but radically immanent and embodied (Braidotti, 2006, pp. 258–259).

For such an immanent understanding, the decisive ethical question is then no longer the one between good and evil, but between an active and a reactive life, as it had been opened up in Nietzsche's *Genealogy of Morals* (1989). The notion of a single morality, of resentment and bad conscience (guilt) falls on the side of the reactive life, which is an investment in negation. Instead of assuming pre-established values and judging according to them, the active life seeks to actualize potentials, liberate from images of thought and affirm the creative power of becoming. It is not so much knowing what we are that is crucial, nor striving for what we should be, but opening the passageways to what we might yet become. This sounds very appealing, yet as ethical stance also raises the problem of violence, to which Deleuze refuses to give an easy black-and-white answer.[5]

What propels the movements of becoming is difference. The Platonic West sees difference as a derivative of identity. First, there is identity, then something else can differ from it. In *Difference and Repetition* (2004), Deleuze's 'reversed Platonism' (Foucault, 1998, p. 344) undoes this relation. Deleuze calls for seeing each event of life as unique and particular, for experiencing it here and now, without immediately ordering it along the lines of pregiven categories. This lets a radical difference emerge within each event, within each moment and aspect of life. This difference is internal to the event; it is difference-in-itself. It is no longer beholden to some standard of identity or sameness and neither is it grounded in a representational model in which it refers to something else. Deleuze joins difference-in-itself with Nietzsche's (1982) doctrine of the eternal return, thereby dynamizing it and turning it into a process, while keeping each moment of life unique and irrecoverable: Nietzsche's eternal return postulates a perpetually ongoing movement of repetition, to which Deleuze adds that what repeats itself is difference. To repeat an act is not to simply copy it but to reactivate the transformative potentials – the difference – that enabled it in the first place. The movement of becoming then is the repetition of difference, in which each new event of life also transforms the whole of life, and does so over and over again (Colebrook, 2008, p. 128). Thereby the notion of difference-in-itself attains its full meaning.

If we can speak of post-modern peaces after Gilles Deleuze, then it is this perpetual play of differences that enables them. Peaces are plural because what repeats itself is the difference in them and no two understandings of peace can thus be the same.* What is more, each time a new peace is enacted, all of them change. Peace can therefore never be stabilized but becomes the site of an ongoing series of questionings and creative reinventions. Peace never is, peaces become. Working for peace thus is the most universal yet most intimate task, for it implies activating the creative potential for transformation, without having recourse to pregiven recipes and how-to manuals. The moment those peaces are perceived they are already gone again and want to be repeated differently. The repetition is eternal, no safe haven and final resting place beckons at the end of all times. Yet it is this very repetition that gives them their beauty and uniqueness. Deleuzian peaces hence are, as we shall shortly see, nomadic, that is they are made, unmade and made-again in movement.

---

* Ed. For more on this, see also the last chapter – Final Remarks.

Desires, plateaus and nomads

Desire is one of the key terms in Deleuze's vocabulary, yet it is a concept that is as crucial as it is easily misunderstood. The discussions between Deleuze and Foucault on the topic of desire and pleasure give testimony to this (Deleuze, 1997). Desire, for Deleuze, is not to be equated with the psychoanalytic notion of lack and can also not be understood in Buddhist terms as one of the defilements. The psychoanalytic notion of desire derives from what is absent and forbidden – the inaccessibility decreed by the Oedipal law that leaves human beings forever yearning. The desire that Buddhism deems a defilement is geared towards fulfillment or orgasmic release. Unlike in psychoanalysis, in Buddhism desire is a defilement not because it is morally bad, but because it builds up only to be dispersed again and thus subtracts energy. Desire as defilement is ultimately reactive, negative and diminishing. This desire blocks Nirvana understood as the 'non-leaking realm' (Glass, 2001), the realm in which energy is no longer diffused but maintained.

The Deleuzian desire, much to the contrary, is a positive desire. It is the desire to remain itinerant, to remain in becoming. It is therefore not driven by lack and not aimed at climactic release and satisfaction in the future, but only at maintaining the permanent circulation of energies. This desire does not lead to a vertical build-up, but to horizontal circulation – to a plateau. Borrowing from Gregory Bateson (2000, p. 113),* Deleuze and Guattari famously define a plateau as a 'continuous, self-vibrating region of intensities, whose development avoids any orientation toward a culmination point or external end' (Deleuze and Guattari, 2005, p. 22). This aligns the Deleuzian concepts of desire and plateau with certain Tantric sexual practices and meditative states that are not geared towards orgasm and avoid goal-oriented thinking (Lorraine, 2005, p. 206). Deleuzian desire is a productive, active category and not reactive.

The figure that operationalizes this desire is the nomad. Unlike the goal-oriented movement of the migrant or the exile, nomadic movement is characterized by the very act of going, without a teleological purpose (Braidotti, 1994, pp. 22–23). Nomadism is thus characterized by movement-as-becoming:

> The water point is reached only in order to be left behind; every point is a relay and exists only as a relay. A path is always between two points, but in-between has taken on all the consistency and enjoys an autonomy and direction of its own. The life of the nomad is the intermezzo. (Deleuze and Guattari, 2005, p. 380)

Nomadic movement desires nothing outside of itself, no ultimate goal to be reached. In the vast spaces of the steppes – plateaus in their own right –

---

*   Ed. Victoria Fontan delves into Bateson in Chapter 32.

movement becomes a trajectory which knows neither beginning nor end, but only intermediate points of location – oases and grazing grounds which are reached only to be left again for somewhere else. And nomadic space itself is no fixed constant, but variable, open and unbounded – transiently fluctuating with shifts of vegetations, seasons, rain, sun, snow and the paths that traverse its surface. While nomadism thus knows points of reference, it follows no overall fixed structure. Deleuze calls its space smooth and opposes it to the striated space of the state and capitalism, whose territory is structured, hierarchically organized and whose movements follow pre-established channels and pathways.

Nomadism traverses different plateaus without diminishment or increase, lack or gain. Its desire is that which is forever already realized in the very walking and is thus constantly present. In the terms of Deleuze, it is neither transcendent nor vertical, that is, it does not have a teleology or aim for another world, but is, in this sense, pure immanence – *hic et nunc*. In the realm of perception, it describes the shift from figures to flows and fields, from the fixed patterns of striated space to the variability of smooth space on which the trajectory of all becoming is but a flecting, temporary, trace.

Yet nomadism is no recipe for perfect nonviolence, far from it. The corresponding section 'Treatise on Nomadology' in the *Thousand Plateaus* is aptly subtitled 'The War Machine.' Deleuze insistently points out that real existing nomadic tribes often were organized as counter-armies. Roving war-bands without the steep layered hierarchy of a military structure, yet therefore often no less ferocious. The clash between empires/states and the nomadological war machine at the edges of the deserts and steppes at times certainly was highly unpeaceful and by no means were the nomads always the victims. By focusing on the productive element of nomadic becomings, Deleuze highlights the whole potential of going beyond the morality of good and evil. His argument is not that nomadism is inherently superior or more peaceful, but only that it opens vectors for transformation that enable new horizons and the possibilities to live and think differently. Under modern conditions, those possibilities can be perceived as liberating, they can be used for new peaces yet also to repeat violence. Realizing the one always implies also being aware of the potentialities for the other.

Nomadism is fiercely resistant to anything that spells blockages to the flow of energies – the flow of movement – like the institutions of state and churches, absolute norms, organized religions and theological canons. Its peaces offer no failsafe protection from violence. Nomadism is neither modern nor moral and at times also halfway leaves post-modernity to roam those twilight borderlands between a post-modern dissolution of reason and a trans-rational spirituality. The patterns of its peaces are rhizomatic, that is, they form a non-hierarchical multiplicity that never collapses into the identity of the One Peace. They are made, unmade and made-again in the movement, are small, contingent, relational and forever circulating.

Pagans and nomads: The post-modern peaces of Lyotard and Deleuze

What I have tried to show throughout this chapter is the relevance and actuality of Jean-François Lyotard and Gilles Deleuze as thinkers of peace, paying special attention to their ideas on the nomad and pagan as ways of operationalizing their understandings. They may also be chiffres for two further Deleuzes and Lyotards that emerge out of their writing.

Pagan and nomad furthermore stand for figures of resistance that safeguard an affirmation. What they resist is the idea of One Peace, global and universal. They are cheerfully infidel to any canonical story and subvert the hegemonic apparatus in all its guises – whether it may appear in form of state, church, party or the ubiquitous sign of the dollar or euro. Yet their rejection can never be total and their position never outside, but in post-modern manner always is already implicated and part of that modernity which can no longer be overcome but only worked-through or *verwunden*, as Gianni Vattimo (1997) following Martin Heidegger would probably call that.

With Lyotard and Deleuze one equally remains suspicious of the facile gesture that tries to see in peace the morally good, that perpetual global goal which all decent people know, want and work for. Much to the contrary, following pagan and nomadic trajectories entails the liberating admission that one does not know what form the peaces might yet take. What Lyotardean pagans and Deleuzian nomads try to safeguard and affirm are the always risky and insecure potentialities for an open-ended plurality of peaces. Post-modern peaces after Deleuze and Lyotard are the site of an ongoing questioning and permanent instigation for new becomings. Keeping the question of the peaces open allows focusing on the expressions of peace in the here and now, in the experienced actuality, while nevertheless not foreclosing the potential that elsewhere and tomorrow might be different. Post-modern peaces in the vein of those two thinkers never form a stability, they are fraught with conflict and dispute, yet enable communication beyond moral judgments and the pretensions to know it better.

In the discipline of the academic research on peace, this post-modern spirit carried fruit in Wolfgang Dietrich's (2006) proposal of the Many Peaces and it similarly finds its expression in the plurality of notions of peace assembled in the current volume. Indeed, what better way to put to use Deleuze and Lyotard's philosophies and how better to underpin their relevance as peace thinkers than to show, as this handbook does all throughout, the beautiful diversity and heterogeneity of concretely lived and thought peaces?

Notes

1. The dates of the first French publications are 1979 *La Condition postmoderne*, 1979 *Au Juste*, 1983 *Le Différend*, 1988 *L'Inhumain*.

2. Reading Lyotard, Simon Malpas (2009, pp. 55–56) highlights a concrete case for a differend, which is worth summarizing here to show what is at stake in the differend. A land dispute, Malpas recounts, is brought before a judge in an Australian court. On the one side, a construction company, claiming this land for development, on the other side a group of aboriginal women contesting that claim, pointing out that the land is a sacred site to them. According to law, the women prevail if they can prove their claim. Yet, instead of doing so they simply point out that the sacredness of the site rests on a secret, which can only be passed on from mother to daughter. Revealing the secret profanes the land. The ensuing silence of the women as regards the proof of their claim faces the judge with a differend. In the idiom of law, which rests on proving your damages, the concrete damage suffered cannot be expressed. The case of the women can find no expression in law and they suffer a wrong if the judge, according to law, finds in favor of the construction company. Yet, it is impossible for the judge not to react upon the differend: if he does respect the women's silence and finds in their favor, the construction company is wronged for the rules according to which the judge finds are no longer those established by law. The judge is thus faced with a legal dilemma, upon which he can either react with accepting the dilemma, ruling within the law and ignoring the differend, thus solving the case but wronging one of the two parties. Or he can take that difficult, insecure and conflictive path of an only potential third option, which is trying to find a new idiom in which the differend might find expression.
3. Much of what Lyotard proposes here in terms of philosophy will later reappear in a different guise in John Paul Lederach's approach to elicitive conflict transformation. In concepts like serendipity, understood as accidental sagacity, as 'the wisdom of recognizing and then moving with the energetic flow of the unexpected,' Lederach (2005, p. 115) will put into action many of the notions Lyotard proposed twenty years earlier. Even if one might consider it too far fetched to suggest a direct link, in a broader context the evolution of John Paul Lederach's elicitive conflict transformation or Wolfgang Dietrich's (2008) trans-rational understanding of peaces nevertheless can hardly be thought without the initial work of the post-modern philosophies of difference.
4. The dates of the first French publications are 1972 *L'Anti-Œdipe*, 1980 *Mille Plateaux*, 1991 *Qu'est-ce que la philosophie?*
5. Rosi Braidotti, one of Deleuze's most astute readers, has extensively dealt with this question on the example of nomadic ethics (Braidotti, 1994, 2006) and, following her lead, I will engage with that towards the end of this chapter, after drawing out the features of the Deleuzian nomad.

Reference list

Bateson, G. (2000) *Steps to an Ecology of Mind* (Chicago: University of Chicago Press).

Braidotti, R. (1994) *Nomadic Subjects: Embodiment and Sexual Difference in Contemporary Feminist Culture* (New York: Columbia University Press).

Braidotti, R. (2006) *Transpositions* (Cambridge: Polity Press).

Baudrillard, J. (1994) *The Illusion of the End* (Stanford: Stanford University Press).

Colebrook, C. (2008) *Gilles Deleuze* (New York: Routledge).

DeLanda, M. (1997) *A Thousand Years of Nonlinear History* (London: Zone Books).

DeLanda, M. (2002) *Intensive Science and Virtual Philosophy* (London: Continuum).

Deleuze, G. and F. Guattari (2003a) *Anti-Oedipus: Capitalism and Schizophrenia* (Minneapolis: University of Minnesota Press).

Deleuze, G. and F. Guattari (2003b) *What is Philosophy?* (London: Verso).

Deleuze, G. and F. Guattari (2005) *A Thousand Plateaus: Capitalism and Schizophrenia* (Minneapolis: University of Minnesota Press).

Deleuze, G. (1997) 'Desire and Pleasure' in A. Davidson (ed.) *Foucault and His Interlocutors* (Chicago: University of Chicago Press), 183–195.

Deleuze, G. (1988a) *Foucault* (Minneapolis: University of Minnesota Press).

Deleuze, G. (1988b) *Spinoza: Practical Philosophy* (San Francisco: City Light Books).

Deleuze, G. (1991) *Bergsonism* (New York: Zone Books).

Deleuze, G. (2001) *Pure Immanence: Essays on a Life* (New York: Zone Books).

Deleuze, G. (2004) *Difference and Repetition* (London: Continuum).

Deleuze, G. (2005a) *Cinema 1: The Movement Image* (London: Continuum).

Deleuze, G. (2005b) *Cinema 2: The Time-Image* (London: Continuum).

Deleuze, G. (2005c) *Nietzsche and Philosophy* (London: Continuum).

Deleuze, G. (2008) *Kant's Critical Philosophy: The Doctrine of the Faculties* (London: Continuum).

Dietrich, W. (2006) 'A Call for Many Peaces' in W. Dietrich, J. Echavarría and N. Koppensteiner (eds.) *Key Texts of Peace Studies* (Vienna: Lit Verlag), 282–301.

Dietrich, W. (2008) *Variationen über die vielen Frieden. Band 1 Deutungen* (Wiesbaden: VIS Verlag).

Foucault, M. (1990) *The Use of Pleasure*. The History of Sexuality Volume 2 (New York: Vintage Books).

Foucault, M. (1998) 'Theatrum Philosophicum' in J. Faubion (ed.) *Aesthetics, Method and Epistemology*. Essential Works of Michel Foucault 1954–1984 Volume 2 (New York: The New Press), 343–369.

Glass, R. (2001) 'The Tibetan Book of the Dead: Deleuze and the Positivity of the Second Light' in M. Bryden (ed.) *Deleuze and Religion* (New York: Routledge), 65–76.

Habermas, J. (1994) 'Die Moderne – ein unvollendetes Projekt' in W. Welsch (ed.) *Wege aus der Moderne: Schlüsseltexte der Postmoderne-Diskussion* (Berlin: Akademie Verlag), 177–193.

Habermas, J. (2006) *Theorie des kommunikativen Handelns*, 2 volumes (Frankfurt: Suhrkamp).

Hamilton Grant, I. (2004) 'Introduction' in J.F. Lyotard (ed.) *Libidinal Economy* (London: Continuum), xix–xxxii.

Hardt, M. and A. Negri (2000) *Empire* (Cambridge: Harvard University Press).

Hardt, M. (1993) *Gilles Deleuze: An Apprenticeship in Philosophy* (London: UCL Press).

Krishnamurti, J. (1969) *Freedom from the Known* (New York: Harper One).

Krishnamurti, J. (1975) *The First and Last Freedom* (New York: Harper One).

Lorraine, T. (2005) 'Plateau' in A. Parr (ed.) *The Deleuze Dictionary* (New York: Columbia University Press), 206–207.

Lyotard, J.-F. and J.-L. Thébaud (1999) *Just Gaming* (Minneapolis: University of Minnesota Press).

Lyotard, J.F. (1984a) 'Interview: Jean-François Lyotard' in *Diacritics*, 14, 3, Autumn 1984, 16–21.

Lyotard, J.F. (1984b) *The Postmodern Condition: A Report on Knowledge* (Minneapolis: University of Minnesota Press).

Lyotard, J.F. (1988) *Peregrinations: Law, Form, Event* (New York: Columbia University Press).

Lyotard, J.-F. (1989a) 'Lessons in Paganism' in A. Benjamin (ed.) *The Lyotard Reader* (Oxford: Basil Blackwell), 122–155.

Lyotard, J.-F. (1989b) 'Universal History and Cultural Differences' in A. Benjamin (ed.) *The Lyotard Reader* (Oxford: Basil Blackwell), 314–324.

Lyotard, J.-F. (1998) *The Inhuman* (Cambridge: Polity Press).

Lyotard, J.-F. (2002) *The Differend: Phrases in Dispute* (Minneapolis: University of Minnesota Press).

Lyotard, J.-F. (2004) *Libidinal Economy* (London: Continuum).

Malpas, S. (2009) *Jean-François Lyotard* (New York: Routledge).

Marks, J. (2005) 'Thought' in A. Parr (ed.) *The Deleuze Dictionary* (New York: Columbia University Press), 278–280.

Massumi, B. (1992) *A User's Guide to Capitalism and Schizophrenia* (Cambridge: MIT Press).

Nietzsche, F. (1967) *The Birth of Tragedy* (New York: Random House).

Nietzsche, F. (1982) 'Thus Spoke Zarathustra' in F. Nietzsche *The Portable Nietzsche*. Edited and translated by Walter Kaufmann (New York: Penguin), 103–440.

Nietzsche, F. (1989) *On the Genealogy of Morals* (New York: Random House).

Tournier, M. (2001) 'Gilles Deleuze' in M. Bryden (ed.) *Deleuze and Religion* (New York: Routledge), 201–205.

Vattimo, G. (1997) *Beyond Interpretation: The Meaning of Hermeneutics for Philosophy* (Stanford: Stanford University Press).

Zima, P.V. (1997) *Moderne/Postmoderne* (Tübingen: A. Francke Verlag).

30
Ngũgĩ wa Thiong'o: Listening for Peace and Resilience in Africa from Makerere 1962 to Asmara 2000

Astier M. Almedom

> We answered many questions on the problems we faced when we fled our homes, but nobody has asked how we managed to stay well so far. We don't want to talk about trauma. Why don't you ask us how we survived, against the odds?
>
> Group of internally displaced women in Adi Qeshi IDP Camp

These poignant words, spoken to me in Tigrinya in December 2001, were translated into a formal research question. An interdisciplinary scientific inquiry into resilience in Eritrea ensued. This is where I began, where we began: they listened to what I had to say; I listened to their responses summed up as above; and we agreed. It is implicit in the Tigrinya word for 'agreement' that the parties to the agreement have listened to one another. *Listening* is the essence. It is understood that there are different points of view, competing, even conflicting interests. Agreement does not imply absence of differences. Nor does peace imply absence of conflict. When competing interests, conflicting opinions and each party's understanding of the problem and potential solutions are not listened to, there remain division and discord. The parties involved have to listen to one another and understand their differences. This ultimately leads to compromises reflecting the shared visions and aspirations of the whole and not just the parts.

Listening to one another is the key word in Tigrinya that connotes agreement.[1]

nisamama' ንስማማዕ Tigrinya, lit.,
Let us listen to one another; Let us agree.

The literal meaning is real and not disconnected from the metaphorical. Like all living languages, Tigrinya is spoken, sang, felt, thought and lived by the people for whom it is the mother tongue. Indeed, 'language is not merely a transparent container for ideas but the ideas themselves.'[2] This was also the central thesis of Ngũgĩ wa Thiong'o, famous Kenyan writer and scholar whose long journey from Makerere 1962 to Asmara 2000 is charted in this chapter using resilience as my compass for navigating the ever more turbulent waters of African and international affairs.

It is noteworthy at the outset that this is a gendered field. Women and men may listen and subsequently act differently. Their motivation and means for peace and harmony may not be rooted and executed uniformly and in the same site. According to the constitution of the United Nation's Educational, Scientific and Cultural Organization – UNESCO – 'since wars begin in the minds of men, it is in the minds of men that the defenses of peace must be constructed.'[3] However, we know that women are also implicated. More importantly, the consequences of war are most evident in the lives of women and their families, for the most part in the absence of men due to the skirmishes of military combat. This is indeed the case in both the traditional kind of war that is fought by combatants, and the unconventional kind that targets civilians.[4] It is therefore as necessary as it may be natural for women to actively broker peace, to foster the culture of listening in their homes, communities and in the public sphere.[5] In the case of Eritrea, women's participation in the armed struggle for independence, constituting a third of the Eritrean People's Liberation Army – EPLA – is one of the most well-documented features of the Eritrean Revolution. Among their notable achievements in the latter half of the last century were the key social and economic reforms that secured Eritrean women the right to own land, to participate freely in public office and to exercise choice in marriage.[6]

The implications of listening to one another are profound. This chapter aims to explore the gendered context of language, culture and meaning of peace in Eritrea, the newest yet ancient country in Africa at the dawn of the second decade of the twenty-first century. Peace is broadly understood as a state of relative harmony in the coexistence of diverse views, beliefs and interests; and not merely the absence of war. A complex interplay of language, culture, geography, history, economics and politics of research as a system of knowledge production and attribution of meaning is also subjected to interrogation.[7] The concept of *listening to one another for peace* is examined within the general framework of resilience – a multidimensional and interdisciplinary field of inquiry that has rapidly gained currency in the twenty-first century. The language of resilience embraces multiple narratives with built-in plurality in expression. Of course any discussion of language, particularly African languages, would also have to acknowledge at the outset the limitations of using the English language – in my case a third 'second language.'

In his seminal essays collected in the classic book *Decolonising the Mind: The Politics of Language in African Literature*, Kenyan – Gĩkũyũ speaking – writer and scholar Ngũgĩ wa Thiong'o explained how 'The choice of language and the use to which language is put is central to a people's definition of themselves in relation to their natural and social environment, indeed in relation to the universe' (Ngũgĩ wa Thiong'o, 1986, p. 4).

Ngũgĩ was reflecting on the historic meeting of African writers held in 1962 at Makerere University College, Kampala, Uganda, then an East African wing of the old University of London. The meeting was called 'A Conference of African Writers of English Expression.' Reflecting on it more than twenty years later, Ngũgĩ lamented the lost cause that the meeting represented for prominent African writers like himself who had done their very best to excel in getting published in the English language, using African ideas to enrich English and other colonial languages. In the process, African writers had neglected their own and other African languages in which African lives are lived and the struggles and triumphs of African peoples expressed.

Looking back at the 100 years of the history of Africa* and its languages and cultures starting from the Berlin Conference of 1884/5 – when the various territorial demarcations of the continent were formalized, not only by political boundaries but also by the masters' languages as English-speaking, French-speaking or Portuguese-speaking. Ngũgĩ decried post-independence African leaders such as Léopold Sédhar Senghor[8] of Senegal and Hastings Kamuzu Banda of Malawi, whom he saw as neo-colonial rulers perpetuating the old colonial structures and mindsets. Neo-colonial Africa had continued to alienate its people by taking them closer and closer to their old colonial masters' ways and farther and farther away from their own languages and cultures.

It was therefore most remarkable and exhilarating for Ngũgĩ wa Thiong'o to find himself in the company of about 250 African and non-African writers, cultural activists, publishers, and artists, from all over the world including North America and Europe writing and publishing in or with African languages, in Asmara, Eritrea, for a world class international conference called for the sole purpose of deliberating in and on African languages in a way that had never been done before. How did this come about, and what has it got to do with listening for peace in Tigrinya and resilience in Eritrea? Was Ngũgĩ's journey from Makerere 1962 to Asmara 2000 not inevitable? Where was Eritrea in 1962? And how did Eritrea come to offer such a coherent new beginning for African languages and literatures at the turn of the millennium? These are profoundly intriguing questions for this chapter to tackle.

Ngũgĩ wa Thiong'o was born and brought up in Kenya under the 'British East Africa Company.'[9] His primary education was in Gĩküyü, his mother tongue, for

---

* Ed. For further information on African history, see in Section V Peace Concepts in Africa especially Chapters 23 by Belachew Gebrewold and Chapter 22 by Kofi Asare Opoku.

the first four years when there was harmony between the language of his formal education and the culture of his Limuru peasant community. This harmony was severely disrupted after the Mau Mau uprising and the declaration of a state of emergency in Kenya. In 1952, all schools run by patriotic nationalists were 'placed under District Education Boards chaired by Englishmen [...]. In Kenya, English became more than a language, it was *the* language, and all the others had to bow before it in deference' (Ngũgĩ wa Thiong'o, 1986, p. 11). Ngũgĩ's recollection of the level of violence endured by Gĩkũyũ-speaking schoolchildren is vividly documented with details of the physical punishment and psychological assault to the children's core identity as human beings.

> Thus, one of the most humiliating experiences was to be caught speaking Gĩkũyũ in the vicinity of the school. The culprit was given corporal punishment – three to five strokes of the cane on bare buttocks – or was made to carry a metal plate around the neck with inscriptions such as I AM STUPID or I AM A DONKEY. Sometimes the culprits were fined money they could hardly afford. And how did the teachers catch the culprits? A button was initially given to one pupil who was supposed to hand it over to whoever was caught speaking his mother tongue. Whoever had the button at the end of the day would sing who had given it to him and the ensuing process would bring out all the culprits of the day. Thus children were turned into witch-hunters and in the process were being taught the lucrative value of being a traitor to one's immediate community. (Ngũgĩ wa Thiong'o, 1986, p. 11)

The 1962 meeting at Makerere University was for – the perhaps resilient minority of – 'African writers of English Expression' who had survived the adversity of a violent system of education. They adapted well and transformed themselves from deeply damaged personalities – as modern-day psychoanalysts reading Ngũgĩ's account might be prone to label them – to successful, even glittering literary figures in the English language. Using my multidimensional lens of resilience, it is difficult to see those 'African writers of English Expression' who met at Makerere in 1962 – including Ngũgĩ wa Thiong'o – simply as vulnerable victims of the European colonial era,* but Ngũgĩ's point may be more about the resilience of the colonial system that sustained itself by training Africans to betray their own systems of communal and cultural life in the interest of furthering its own.

Certainly, Ngũgĩ did not use the vocabulary of resilience that I have learned to use in order to meet the challenge posed at the start of this chapter. It would be natural for him to express regret about the fact that the questions he was asking in 1986 had not been posed much earlier, specifically at the meeting

---

* Ed. For a European perspective on the same issue, see Chapter 4 by Nigel Young.

in Makerere in 1962. However, the global geo-political climate of the early 1960s was qualitatively different from that of the mid–late 1980s. The Makerere meeting took place at the cusp of a critical shift in power dynamics as the overtly dominant British 'Sphere of Interest' made its transition to a more subtle form of existence. As Ngũgĩ reflected, the British colonial rule was giving way to its neo-colonial successors who remained true to their schooling, by and large keeping the colonial system intact. By the 1980s, post-colonial East, West and Central Africa had matured as the neo-colonial sites of inhospitable, even dangerous places for Ngũgĩ wa Thiong'o and other scholars like him who wanted to return to their roots.[10]

In the case of Malawi whose president, Dr. Hastings Kamuzu Banda, had established a boarding school named the 'Kamuzu Academy' in the style of English grammar schools, the brightest Malawian children were being trained to master the English language in order to go to top British and American universities while the vast majority of ordinary schools were neglected. As Ngũgĩ's sharpest criticisms highlight, Hastings Banda could not trust Malawian teachers, however qualified, to teach English in his Academy. So he imported English teachers from overseas. Those teachers may have been more humane than their colonial predecessors, but their job was to sustain the British 'Sphere of Influence' albeit implicitly. The English language was destined to remain dominant for the foreseeable future, and if Banda himself did not care about Malawian children's mother tongues, his English employees were not likely to.[11]

Banda and other African leaders like him had clearly taken on the mantle of oppressive colonial rulers. The downward spiral of poverty and deprivation continued to perpetuate the cycles of violence that still plague many African countries today. By the mid-1980s when his book came to be published, Ngũgĩ had had enough of neo-colonial African literatures that created English-speaking or French-speaking or Portuguese-speaking African peasantry and working class in their novels and dramas, portraying them as mentally anguished and in a state of 'torn-between-two-worlds' existential human condition. As Ngũgĩ declared in exasperation, 'if it had been left entirely to this class, African languages would have ceased to exist – with independence!' (Ngũgĩ wa Thiong'o, 1986, p. 22).

In sharp contrast, and apparently unknown to Ngũgĩ wa Thiong'o, Eritrean children and adults in the 'Liberated Zone' were seriously being schooled in Tigrinya, Tigre, Arabic, as well as English not only in purpose-built schools, but also in make-shift improvised 'classrooms' sheltered under trees or in caves and other underground locations where the people had to be protected from Ethiopian military attacks involving tanks and supersonic jets with relentless bombing missions carried out during the 1970s and 1980s. According to the British government opposition Labour Party's delegation sent on a fact-finding mission to Eritrea in 1984:

In developing its own educational system, the EPLF started from the basic principle that the aim of education must be to reinforce and strengthen the Eritrean revolution. Education must serve the masses in the constant theme of posters and wall paintings in areas controlled by the EPLF. In line with this objective, the EPLF is attempting to link the school to the rest of society, by encouraging community contributions toward building and running schools, and by promoting participation by schoolchildren in the services and production of the village.

Nevertheless, the first educational priority the EPLF set itself was to make every fighter literate – a goal that was achieved by 1972. All new recruits with less than seven years of schooling complete their education within the EPLF, and during our visit we often saw fighters sitting in the shade of trees studying. In this respect the EPLA differs from almost every other Third World army. For the EPLF, high levels of literacy and education among the fighters ensure a more effective fighting force, because fighters are highly motivated combatants, not just passive recipients of orders. We were surprised by how well-informed and interested many fighters were about world affairs.

When the EPLF turned its attention to civilian education it was hampered by the unsuitable curriculum inherited from the colonial period and the lack of textbooks in Eritrean languages. The civil war with the ELF delayed the preparation of the EPLF's elementary school curriculum until 1976, when it was introduced experimentally in the newly established 'Revolution School' in the EPLF base area. By 1978 seven grades had been prepared in Tigrinya and Tigre, and the EPLF were teaching some 30,000 students in 150 schools, many in towns captured during the EPLF advance of 1977.

This extraordinary expansion was possible not only because of the efforts of the Education Department, but also because the People's Assemblies and mass organizations built new schools, supplied materials and volunteered teachers. The EPLF withdrew from many of these areas during the retreat of 1978 [...].

One of the tasks of EPLF cadres is to convince poorer peasants of the importance of education. They are often reluctant to send their children to school because they are needed for agricultural and domestic tasks. The EPLF is finding it most difficult to reach the children of nomads, but has set up schools by the main watering places where nomad families camp for several weeks at a time.

The education system is designed to encourage young people to participate in the economic and social life of the village. As members of the Red Flowers organization they help the local clinic or with cultivating the village communal land. At the time of our visit Revolution School[12] had not reconvened after its holiday break because of a severe shortage of water at the school. Instead, middle and secondary level students had been sent to learn new technical skills in the base area workshops and at the laboratories and wards of the

Central Hospital. We met some of them at She'eb and were impressed by their self-assurance and enthusiasm, and by the curiosity they showed towards us.

The EPLF is developing a new culture and art out of the traditions of the different nationalities. Performances by the Red Flowers cultural groups of the dances of Eritrea's nine nationalities stress Eritrean unity and their songs and poems express new revolutionary values. The Red Flowers also perform short plays, illustrating such themes as exploitation by landowners, oppression of women, and the brutality of the occupying regime. (Firebrace and Holland, 1984, pp. 119–120)

These visitors had certainly not anticipated what they found in Eritrea. James Firebrace was working as a program officer for 'War on Want,' a non-governmental organization (NGO), and Stuart Holland, Labour Member of Parliament (MP) for Lambeth Vauxhall/South London, was appointed Shadow Minister of Overseas Development Cooperation in 1983. These authors included a number of photographs to illustrate the key results of their fact-finding assignment. Most striking among them are the array of books printed by the Department of Political Consciousness, Education and Culture in five languages: Tigrinya, Tigre, Afar, Kunama and Arabic (Firebrace and Holland, 1984, p. 119). Most of the photographs were taken by the authors, but they also included historic illustrations of the economic and psychological damage inflicted on Eritrea during the British administration of the 1940s. A striking photograph originated from *Eritrea on the Eve* by E.S. Pankhurst (1952) captioned: 'British administrators supervise the dismantling and removal of an Eritrean cement works in 1947' (Firebrace and Holland, 1984, p. 19). At that time, it looked as though a future British Labour government would open a new chapter of reconciliation and cooperation with Eritrea in good faith.[13]

Firebrace and Holland's report was taken seriously by the then leader of the British government opposition Labour Party, Mr. Neil Kinnock – a Welshman – who wrote in the preface to Firebrace and Holland's book in 1984 that the next Labour government would: (i) provide financial and material assistance to the EPLF and the Eritrean Relief Association (ERA); and (ii) back the EPLF's proposal for an internationally supervised referendum on the future of Eritrea.[14]

However, as Firebrace and Holland established first hand, the Eritrean policy of democratic governance through popular participation, self-reliance and political non-alignment was heralding a new model of development in post-colonial Africa.

Had Ngũgĩ wa Thiong'o been aware of *Never Kneel Down* published two years before his own *Decolonising the Mind*, he might have taken a more optimistic view. His discussion of neo-colonial African leaders might have compared Hastings Banda and others like him with the alternative, liberated young Eritrean leaders whose commitment to the true liberation of African peoples and their languages and literatures might have offered him a ray of hope. Unfortunately, Ngũgĩ's encounter with Eritrea was not to be for another ten years or more, when he found himself planning to co-chair an international conference on African languages and literatures to be held in Asmara, Eritrea's capital city, in the first month of 2000. In the meantime, the Eritrean leaders visited and interviewed by Firebrace and Holland in 1984 had finally liberated Asmara and the Southern Red Sea Port of Assab in May 1991. They started out with a renewed determination to rebuild a nation that was rising from the ashes of Africa's longest war.

Their first challenge was to prepare for a UN-supervised referendum in order to formalize the country's official membership in the family of nations. Although the outcome of the Eritrean Referendum was unlikely to be a surprise, it was critical to ensure that it was conducted properly, paying attention to women's participation. Women were then and still remain in the majority, on account of the war that decimated the male complement of the adult population. Yet, in some of the conservative traditional cultures of the western lowlands bordering with the Sudan, women's emancipation and voting rights were being negotiated from scratch. This was done in earnest, using the historical precedent of Beni-Amer and other minority women's participation in the ranks of the EPLF, contributing to historic social, cultural and political reforms during the war for independence. Two years of EPLF-style mass education and participatory discussions involving the entire population proved necessary to simply determine clearly whether theirs was a 'Yes' or a 'No' for independence. The Referendum of 1993 resulted in a resounding affirmative in Eritrea and in all the countries of the Eritrean diaspora.[15]

However, the 'international community' did not appear to be interested in allowing the process of *listening to one another* to take its normal course of local participatory deliberations. The new country came under increased pressure to conduct Western-style 'multi-party elections' within time frames as short as twelve months in the early 1990s.[16] While the first five years of independence saw the country emerge from war with its social fabric intact, determined to build its economy from the ground up following its well-documented policy of self-reliance, external aid was being offered with prescriptive external timetables attached. Before long, echoes of the divisive and destructive geopolitical influences of the 1940s began to be heard within the first five years of the Referendum, unleashing the so-called 'border war' during 1998–2000.[17] However, the country's development of a comprehensive education policy including language emancipation for all children and adults across the nine nationalities – ethnic/language groups – remained on track, as part and parcel of the long-standing national policy of 'Unity in Diversity.'

The new millennium was ushered in with a spectacular, historic international conference titled 'Against All Odds: African Languages and Literatures into the 21st Century' during January 11–17, 2000. Over 250 academic scholars, practitioners, writers, publishers and cultural activists from all over Africa, Europe and North America deliberated, listening and responding to a diverse array of presentations including performances of poetry, music and drama. They included Ngũgĩ wa Thiong'o and Nawal al Saadawi who co-chaired the conference with Zemhret Yohannes, Charles Cantalupo, Mbulelo Mzamane, Kassahun Checole, Kofi Anyidoho, Akinwumi Isola, Alemseged Tesfai, Abena Busia, Abdulatif Abdalla, Senait Lijam, Papa Susso, Musa Aron, *Mamma* Zeinab and many others.

The Asmara conference seemed to be an antithesis of the 1962 Makerere meeting of African writers of English Expression. Deliberately employing as it did modern African languages such as Fulani, Hausa, Kiswahili, Tigrinya and Zulu in the proceedings, albeit with necessary translations into English in order to overcome existing barriers of communication, it gave African and other writers a forum to discuss African languages. Famous African scholars and writers lamented the very limited volume of published literature in African languages, recognizing the impact of their being schooled in European languages. Colonial institutional structures of linguistic dominance and protective post-colonial policies had rendered African languages and literatures virtually invisible on the world stage. Seven days of intensive listening and responding to multiple narratives of vulnerability as well as resilience of African languages and literatures, written and unwritten, staged in venues as diverse and wide ranging as the city's top cinemas, theaters, university buildings, cultural exhibition centers, as well as the rural amphitheater in the 'Valley of Sycamores', the parties crafted and ratified the 'Asmara Declaration on African Languages and Literatures.' This summed up the participants' aspirations and realities of linguistic independence for the continent.[18]

There was an obvious discongruity between the realities of the Asmara conference and the international development and humanitarian sector expectations. While donor countries in Europe and North America predicted a vulnerable and depressed state of low morale, disarray and destitution to prevail in Eritrea in the immediate aftermath of the war, the capital city had remained a disciplined, virtually corruption and crime free, safe and warmly hospitable place proceeding with life as normal. The implementation of social and cultural policies had remained on course. Focus on long-term development began in earnest in Asmara and other newly liberated parts of the country – in the same way as had been documented by Firebrace and Holland in 1984. The Asmara conference took political pundits and development practitioners by surprise, particularly those who expected Eritrea to turn into a 'Failed State.' Organizing and hosting an international conference of that scale and significance, while rebuilding lives and livelihoods affected by the war, was far from the expectations of the international community.[19]

Eritrea was defiantly showing the world that it is still on track for collective self-determination, and looking out to the entire continent for global engagement in the 'big conversation.' Senait Lijam, Senior Research Officer of the National Union of Eritrean Women, spoke eloquently on the concept of 'armed struggle,' which she interpreted liberally with reference to the war for independence.

I would like to interpret the concept of 'Armed struggle' in this way: armed with what? You can be armed with a gun. You can be armed with a pen. You can be armed with an idea, a notion of social justice. You can be armed with commitment and steadfastness [...]. Whatever helped achieve success, the goal of the national liberation movement. (Senait Lijam)

Closer attention to early childhood development and pedagogy resulted in the convening of the Second International Conference on Early Child Development (ECD) in Asmara in 2002, following the First International Conference on ECD that was held in Kampala, Uganda, in 1999. The government of Eritrea co-sponsored this conference with the World Bank, UNICEF and the Association for the Development of Education in Africa (ADEA), with an evaluative policy agenda focusing on effective community approaches to the mainstreaming of beneficial indigenous knowledge and practices of child rearing with particular reference to disadvantaged children. It endorsed the conduct of systems analyses on relationships between preschool and primary education to achieve the following objectives:

- prepare children for school and schools for children and parent involvement;
- reduce school attrition and repetition; and
- assess the learning outcomes of children who received preschool education; including continuous monitoring, evaluation and research at community, district, provincial and national levels to ensure quality. The conference concluded that 'Education begins at birth.'

Underlying these developments in multilingual education and multicultural ethos in Eritrea is also an ongoing struggle to eliminate the cognitive and perceptual basis for 'second class' citizenship. The idea is that children brought up to freely use their mother tongue in both private and public spheres will not develop a sense of status of inferiority or minority in relation to other ethnic and/or language groups. Much in line with the argument put forward by Ngũgĩ wa Thiong'o in *Decolonizing the Mind* (1986), Eritrea's multilingual education and multiscriptal literacy policy has been examined to find out how much progress has been made in making minority languages and their scripts publicly available, particularly in rural settings where the languages of concern – Afar, Bidhaawyeet/Hidareb, Bilen, Kunama, Nara and Saho – use the Latin alphabet

(Asfaha et al., 2008).[20] The picture is complex, however, when it comes to the associations between cultural, linguistic and economic factors that determine language and script preferences. The majority of those for whom literacy in the mother tongue was novel saw literacy as a gateway to better jobs and income; while those for whom literacy, and indeed education beyond basic literacy is not new, did not (Asfaha et al., 2008, p. 230). Although the intrinsic and economic values attributed to literacy and education explained less than fifty percent of the variance in Eritrean attitudes to multilingual and multiscriptal education, the sociolinguistic survey conducted by Asfaha and others in 2005 confirmed the assumption that self-confidence and a sense of identity and belonging as a valued citizen were ingrained by the evident realization that one's mother tongue is not inferior to the language of the majority. This appears to be a cognitive value that fosters and builds human resilience.

The research initiated by listening to my Eritrean study-participants involved qualitative and quantitative assessment/measurement of resilience using the 'Sense of Coherence' scale adapted from Aaron Antonovsky's original scale, short form.[21] Resilience is a multidimensional construct defined as the capacity of individuals, families, communities and institutions to anticipate, withstand and/or judiciously engage with catastrophic events and/or experiences; actively making meaning out of adversity, with the goal of maintaining 'normal' function without fundamental loss of identity.[22] Why did Eritrea present itself as a natural laboratory for the study of resilience? Resilience to what? Whose resilience? These were among the key questions addressed by my interdisciplinary inquiry involving multiple perspectives, methods and sources.

Historically, the Eritrean struggle for self-determination and nation building has involved continual resistance of domination and hegemony imposed by imperial and colonial conquerors over many centuries. Modern Eritrea was, however, carved out as an Italian colony in 1885 at the instigation of Great Britain. Italian colonial rule ended in 1941 upon the defeat of the Axis powers by the Allies. This marked a new chapter in the Eritrean struggle to remain united in resistance to British attempts to divide up the territory between the two powers: Highland portions to be absorbed by Ethiopia in exchange for the Ogaden region, which Great Britain wanted to take over and unite with Greater Somalia but failed when Ethiopia forged a new alliance with the US;[23] while the Western Lowlands were meant to be integrated with Anglo-Egyptian Sudan. The collective Eritrean will and stamina to persevere against the most powerful machinery of misinformation became the hallmark of human – psychological, emotional and moral – as well as institutional resilience spanning more than half a century.

As the people of Eritrea continue to *listen* for peace, the cacophony of misinformation and level of distrust of the international community have persisted

(Almedom, 2006). It is clear that the recent United Nations Security Council sanctions announced to limit Eritrea's access to military capabilities without equally limiting the other party (Ethiopia), which happens to be in favor of the United States regarding a common enemy (Somalia), diminishes the weight of moral and ethical principles of peace and justice espoused by the international community. Both Ethiopia and Eritrea have retained the same leadership that ushered in independence in 1991, using different means. In the case of Ethiopia, so-called multi-party elections have served to maintain the domination of a minority regime, overtly employing violent strategies to incapacitate opposition parties. The May 2005 election witnessed high levels of violence as documented by the British Broadcasting Corporation (BBC) whose print, audio and video coverage of the election time bloodshed did not result in UN sanctions or any other sort of reprimand. The Ethiopian leader appeared to remain actively engaged in African Union and G-20 deliberations while the Eritrean government continued to be seen as isolated from international meetings designed to broker agreements. This breakdown in listening has continued to prevail unchecked, seemingly with the tacit approval of the powerful countries represented in the UN Security Council, G-8 and G-20.

The old international political 'anxieties' outlined in the first chapter of *Never Kneel Down* (Almedom, 2006) have remained in place:

> There is a further anxiety that allowing Eritrea to exercise its right to self-determination would set a dangerous precedent and give encouragement to opposition fronts among constituent nations of the Ethiopian empire. Whatever the strength of the case of the national liberation fronts within Ethiopia, theirs is a different case from that of Eritrea with its distinct history of European colonization [...]. Peace and stability in the region will not be secured until the issue of democracy for the Ethiopian nationalities is resolved.
>
> Elsewhere in Africa, governments are afraid that concessions to Eritrea will set off 'secessionist' demands within their own states. This is the concern of the Organisation of African Unity which in its founding charter 'determined to safeguard and consolidate [...] the sovereignty and territorial integrity of our states' (OAU 1963) [...].
>
> The OAU resolution of 1964 which calls for respect for the borders 'existing on the achievement of national independence' should support the case for Eritrean independence. Ethiopia can be said to have achieved her national independence either at the turn of the century when she successfully avoided colonisation by a European power or later in 1941 when she emerged from her 6 year occupation by the Italians. At both times Eritrea was treated as territorially distinct [...]. (Firebrace and Holland, 1984)

This view of Ethiopia is at variance with the Eritrean people's experience and understanding of Ethiopian colonial rule. As explored in my earlier re-reading of the history of Eritrea, comparing and contrasting English language records with the vernacular, successive Ethiopian emperors – aided in part by the geo-physical terrain of impenetrably mountainous fortresses – had succeeded in warding off European domination by playing sophisticated diplomatic games with rival French and British neighbors in the region, while also building up their own military capacity to match those of the Europeans (Firebrace and Holland, 1984). However, as the cold war came to an end with significant reforms initiated in the USSR reverberating across Eastern Europe and Africa, the long Eritrean struggle for self-determination achieved its goal. Eritrean languages and cultures expressed and communicated it in universally intelligible terms – starting with Reesom Haile and Charles Cantalupo 'joining' in poetry originally written and performed in Tigrinya (Haile), and given a meaningful rendering in American English (Cantalupo) demonstrating cross-cultural listening in both 'vernaculars.' Three of Haile's most apt poems are presented and discussed as they pertain to listening for peace on three interconnected themes: Unity, Self-determination and Peace.

The armed struggle for independence (1961–1991) had forced Eritreans to be scattered around the world. Nevertheless, they continued to shine their light and by and large succeeded in listening to one another and remaining united. In the words of the late Dr. Reesom Haile, international humanitarian communications expert and Tigrinya poet, as translated into English by Charles Cantalupo (Haile and Cantalupo, 2000, pp. 46–47), the Eritrean people outshone the stars in the sky:

> *Stars in the Sky*
>
> A sky full of stars –
> They outnumber us by far,
> Yet we have more light.
>
> A night full of stars
> Fade in the sun.
> But one
>
> Called the shepherds
> And three kings to our Lord
> And they adored
>
> The light
> Like stars, despite
> The wintry darkness.

> Light can be borrowed,
> Light can be bred.
> We have more light
> Because we're united.

The international community's neglect of Eritrea was a *cause célèbre* for many a Western journalist and writer, as well as scholars of history and academics in political science. Many made their name as friends of Eritrea during the war years of the 1970s and 1980s. However, in the end, the Eritrean people's sacrifice was the only deliverer. In this poem, Reesom Haile conjures up a deep sense of pride in the collective Eritrean resistance of divisive influences. Characterized by defiantly positive and constructive engagement with everyday life, the Eritrean people are portrayed exhibiting high morale: shining the 'light' that is self-generated, coming from within, and enduring – unlike the stars in the sky whose light is 'borrowed from the sun' and short-lived as they fade away when the sun appears.

Eritrea's location as a gateway to the sea and into Africa had destined it to having to build resilience to foreign invasions over centuries. Examples of peace building among neighboring ethnic and language groups through listening to each party's *tarikh* – story or history – and *Himam* – 'dis-ease' or grievance – are plentiful in both the oral and written tradition in the vernacular. It could be argued that these are in fact earlier examples of 'trans-rational peace'* in the region whereby agreements were made to 'live and let live' albeit with seemingly contradicting and diversely plural interests. Multiple traditional institutions, formal and informal, maintained harmonious coexistence of hierarchically structured associations. These were often interconnected by hereditary and conjugal ties of kinship. It is deeply ingrained in the Eritrean mind and heart, body and soul that peace comes from within and not without. Again in the words of Reesom Haile translated into English by Charles Cantalupo (Haile and Cantalupo, 2002, pp. 174–175):

Peace Will Come

> Peace will come.
> From the USA?
> No way!
> But dream on.

> Peace will come.
> From the UN?
> Are you hallucinating?
> Dream on.

---

* Ed. For an examination of the concept of trans-rational peaces, see Chapter 1 by Wolfgang Dietrich.

Peace will come.
From the OAU?
If wishes were horses.
Dream on.

Peace will come.
From Ethiopia?
Go get 'em.[24]
But dream on.

Peace will come.
From Eritrea?
Where else?
God bless.

When peace came to Eritrea in 1991, it looked homemade. The people of Asmara, the capital, and other towns that had been under Ethiopian rule until the fall of the Menghistu regime, received the EPLF, otherwise referred to as *Deqina*, 'Our Children' with wide open arms. Over 65,000 documented and honored martyrs of the war for independence were mourned a year later upon the completion of the hand-written individual national certificates of honor which were delivered in each village, town and city, following the period of national mourning. It was highly remarkable that the EPLF had kept meticulous records of its membership with the relevant details of each martyr, including dates of joining the EPLF, individual history of engagement/s in battle – with date and location – and the date and location of his/her fall. The three-day period of national mourning allowed families to sit together in large communal tents purposely erected for every community and neighborhood to share meals and reminisce over the experiences of the war years.[25] This collective activity reflected the social cohesion and bonding social capital that had long nurtured – against the odds – the self-sufficient mind-set of Eritrea, the new country (Haile and Cantalupo, 2002, pp. 2–3).

A Country

She lays her cool head
And warm feet
By the sea.
Small, self-made
Independent,
With a belly full of fire
And a big heart of wisdom,
She is blessed

> With love and children.
> I hear what she says
> And rely on what she does,
> Fierce as a tiger
> With new cubs.

The Eritrean people's participation in multilingual and multiscriptal education for development at the grass-roots level is ongoing. As a tangible result of the process of community-organizing and problem-solving culture, the resilience research participants quoted at the start of my chapter are no longer 'internally displaced.' By the end of 2004, the lengthy and meaningful process of listening to one another had resulted in a binding agreement that the displaced communities of Adi Qeshi would be assisted to return to their home villages during the eleven days between January 31 and February 10, 2005, coinciding with school vacation time. It was possible for everyone involved to concentrate on the move.

It was in the middle of the cold/dry season when the risk of contracting malaria was nil, and just as importantly, the roads were expected to be good [...]. Communication networks were tested to make sure they were functioning properly, and radio communications and mobile telephones were used to exchange information all the way from Adi Qeshi IDP camp to Shilalo. There were about 200 trucks and about 40 buses deployed in transporting the IDP and their assets [...] the trucks made 1815 trips from Adi Qeshi to Shilalo. Every household was given its own truck to load its property. This minimized loss of property and confusion. The most surprising part of the repatriation process was that livestock were also taken by trucks. As one of our respondents put it laughingly: 'Every thing about the return journey was good. Not only for us but also for our livestock; they made history; they had their first opportunity to ride trucks' [...]. The community organized itself to prepare make-shift classrooms out of wood and leafy branches until they could build shelter for themselves [...]. UNICEF had assisted in the renovation of war damaged schools and built new ones in areas that lacked schools before the displacement. Thus there were no obstacles to children's continued schooling. When asked what kind of problems they had faced during their return, ninety-six percent of our study participants responded that there were none worth mentioning. They reported that they were surprised by the organizing capacity of the government bodies and their own capabilities. One returnee summed it up by saying, 'I didn't know that we were so able.' The way the repatriation/resettlement was organized also surprised UN agencies and other international humanitarian agencies, and members of the international Diplomatic Corps who came to observe the process. Why were no major problems encountered? Why was it so successful? This can be attributed to many factors, five of which are most important:

i.   Lessons learned from previous experience of displacement
ii.   Clear and consistent government policy
iii. Detailed and coherent levels of organization
iv.   Sustained commitment
v.   Involvement of defense forces in relief and development activities.

This is a major achievement for Eritrea and a model for other countries in Africa and indeed elsewhere. Minimizing the duration of displacement of disaster and war-affected communities reduces conflict. Governments interested in their own sustainability often using foreign aid as a base of their power are unlikely to show such levels of commitment to their own populations. The Eritrean system of adaptive governance with respect to language emancipation and education has endured for nearly forty years, over twenty years of which were spent under the severely adverse conditions of war, drought and subsequent threats of famine.

As UNESCO declared 2010 the International Year for the Rapprochement of Cultures (and February 23, 2010 'International Mother Language Day' including an 'International Symposium on Translation and Intercultural Mediation'), Eritrea's implementation of the UNESCO Literacy Initiative for Empowerment (LIFE) is noteworthy.

The social cohesion and deliberative democracy that has marked Eritrea's human and institutional resilience is not peculiar to Eritrea. The larger African culture of *ubuntu* is the foundation of African communal life based on a sense of inter-connectedness, common humanity and sense of responsibility for each other. Malawian scholars in political science Richard Tambulasi and Happy Kayuni (2005, pp. 147–161) listed several variations of the term in different African Bantu languages: *umunthu* in Chewa, *umundu* in Yawo, *bunhu* in Tsonga, *unhu* in Shona, *botho* in Sotho or Tswana, *umuntu* in Zulu, *vhutu* in Venda, *ubuntu* in Xhosa and Ndebele. They explained that the central doctrine of ubuntu is expressed in a Zulu proverb: '*umuntu ngamuntu ngabantu abanye*' translated as 'a person is a person through other persons' (Tambulasi and Kayuni, 2005, p. 148). These authors mention that Dr. Hasting Banda's Malawi Congress Party (MCP) had lacked ubuntu. The MCP's popular slogan was '*zones zimene nza Kamuzu Banda*,' 'everything belongs to Kamuzu Banda.'

The concepts of trans-rational peace and resilience are perhaps most poetically linked in the story of intercultural transfer of Ngũgĩ wa Thiong'o's play *I will Marry when I Want*,[26] whose title came from a popular Gĩkũyũ song of the Mau Mau uprisings of the early 1950s. The play was translated from Gĩkũyũ into English by the author, and then translated from English into Tigrinya by Alemseged Tesfai, one of Eritrea's celebrated playwrights and historians. *I will Marry when I Want* was performed at the Cinema Odeon in Asmara for the participants of the 'Against All Odds: African Languages and Literatures into the 21st Century' international conference on January 15, 2000. In what seemed in-keeping with the spirit of ubuntu, and in honor of Ngũgĩ wa Thiong'o, the Eritrean actors sang in unison, waving Kenyan flags at the end of the performance on the stage. To critical acclaim,[27] the play then toured the country as

Miste berhani emer'o ምስተብርሃኒ እምር'ዖ

The story of the play resonated with the Eritrean people's experience of adversity and resilience, and thus was meaningful and important in meaning-making of the current struggle to rebuild lives and livelihoods, in both rural and urban communities. At the local and national levels, human and institutional resilience in Eritrea are unfaltering. Again, much to the surprise of the international community whose message to Eritrea was negative, the new monument of Russian poet Alexander Pushkin – whose Eritrean heritage was publicly celebrated – was ceremonially unveiled in Asmara in November 2009, before the UN sanctions were announced. Similarly, the Copenhagen Conference on Climate Change – COP15 – witnessed the story from Eritrea by a South African female journalist win the Earth Journalism award. This positive news was not included in the international reportage of COP15. It would appear that UNESCO and other UN bodies including UNDP and UNICEF are yet to take notice of the Eritrean process of *listening to one another*, the underpinning of agreements.

Conclusion

In conclusion, while it is still important to revisit Ngũgĩ's *Decolonising the Mind* as we embark on the second decade of the twenty-first century, the Eritrean experience has clearly demonstrated that human and institutional resilience are embedded in the vernacular languages and literatures. These are more forgiving, accommodating and inclusive of diverse points of view, including those in the diaspora who were brought up with little or no trace of African languages. As the English language itself has become Africanized, for example by taking a different identity when spoken by African-Americans, Black British and other hybrid renditions, it has become more important for African and other 'global citizens' of the world to seek and hold on to African concepts like *ubuntu* in order to foster and nourish principles of harmonious coexistence that appear to resemble Eritrea's policy of Unity in Diversity.

Notes

1. The *English-Tigrinya-Arabic Dictionary* published by the Eritrean People's Liberation Front (EPLF), 1985 edition, translates 'agreement' as 1. *simimi'*, *sinit* and 2. *wi'il*. The first meaning connotes a state of *listening to one another*, harmony, while the second refers to a contract. A Tigrinya dictionary published in Asmara by Girmatsion Mebrahtu, *Lisane agaazi zeiim girma* አሳነ ዘአጋዚ ዝኢም ግርማ offers *sima'* (Lit., listen) meaning *teredaa'* (Lit., understand). Government Printing Press, Asmara, 1976.

2. Dr. Charles Cantalupo, Distinguished Professor of English, Comparative Literature and African Studies, Pennsylvania State University – commenting on an earlier draft of this chapter.

3. This may be reflective of the rational Eurocentric view of human action that prevailed at the end of the Second World War. UNESCO's vision has remained focused on 'Building Peace in the Minds of People' – as its website still announces (UNESCO, 2010) – a twenty-first century revision may be expected to acknowledge that emotions – often believed to be seated in the heart or in the guts – underlie human motivation for violence; including hearts and minds of men and women.

4. Modern wars have been waged as deliberate assaults on civilian women and their families; see, for example, Sharratt and Kaschak (1999).

5. It is also my aim in this chapter to present an inclusive and interdisciplinary understanding of *listening* as a holistic process of perception and cognition involving all the senses: sight, smell, touch and taste, besides hearing. See, for instance, the work of Dame Evelyn Glennie (2010) – internationally acclaimed percussionist who has mastered the art of listening – and Dr. Paul Whittaker (2007).

6. Amrit Wilson's (1991) *The Challenge Road* and Glenys Kinnock's eye-witness accounts of the EPLF women's social, political and cultural accomplishments were among the powerful independent testimonies that informed and inspired many supporters in Europe and North America during the 1980s.

7. It should also be noted that the study of resilience my team conducted in Eritrea had been approved by the Tufts University's Institutional Review Board (IRB), following standard ethical guidelines for the conduct of research involving human subjects. This is an important requirement that ensures that study participants are properly informed about the purpose of research conducted upon their consent.

8. Senghor was also an acclaimed African poet and writer in the French language in which he was widely credited for forming a bridge between colonial and mainland France – reflecting the French brand of territorial expansion in which the colonies were officially called 'Overseas Departments' of France. The British and the French were competing colonial powers in Africa and other parts of the world where they were prone to transmitting their rivalry to their respective subjects.

9. One of the most succinct and amazingly accurate summaries of the highly complex system of British colonial 'Spheres of Influence' in East Africa – particularly Kenya and Uganda – is former TV-personality Bamber Gascoigne's (2001) summary of the 'History of Kenya'. Gascoigne's summaries and timelines of Eritrean and Ethiopian histories appear to be less reliable.

10. Kenya has certainly remained bedeviled by ethnic (and gender-based) violence, as seen in the last national elections in 2007.

11. Although strictly speaking this is the sort of transition from colonial to neo-colonial culture that gave rise to human rights activism. Post-colonial generations of British and other European young adults immersed themselves in the largely non-governmental mission to deliver Africans from their oppressive systems. These were mostly one step

ahead and therefore likely to be condescending of their African counterparts whom they saw as competitors. The field of international development is now more inclusive of a diverse workforce.

12. The Eritrean Revolution School ቤት ትምህርቲ ሰውራ has produced some of the most confident and highly adaptable young minds, a number of whom have gone on to attend top European and American universities successfully.

13. Previously, Mr. Martin Plaut, another official representative of the Labour Party, had represented the Party at the Eritrean Congresses of Workers and Women's Unions in December 1982. He is a prominent senior writer and broadcaster/commentator on African affairs for the BBC and other British and international media outlets.

14. Neil Kinnock's Labour Party did not win an election until well after Eritrea's liberation and UN-supervised Referendum. By the time it won (in 1997), Eritrea had gained independence and was already embarked on a new economic trajectory, having announced its own currency. Under Tony Blair's leadership of the ruling Labour Party, relations between Eritrea and the UK began to take a different tone.

15. See, for example, George W. Shepherd's (1993) eye-witness account reported in his capacity as a member of the international group of observers on the conduct of the Referendum.

16. My own contribution to Oxfam-UK's retrospective assessment (in 1992) of the Agricultural Rehabilitation Programme (ARP) and Food Distribution Programme (FDP) implemented cross-border (via the Sudan) before independence, and my follow-up discussions with key stakeholders including the National Union of Eritrean Women and government departments of social affairs, revealed that their attention was focused on the psychosocial aftermath of the war. When asked how they saw Oxfam-UK best helping to meet their needs, the reply was firmly clear: they asked for funding support to document and publish the social history of the war – to have the stories of courage and survival against the odds told. This was not exactly what a hands-on project-oriented international humanitarian agency expected to hear and/or respond to at that time. I drafted the job description for Oxfam's first ever field officer in the new country (a position taken by the best fitting candidate, a British woman with previous familiarity with Eritrea and research experience of the 'Liberated zone'). Meanwhile, Eritrean publications began to flow from Hidri and other publishers, filling the bookstores with new books in Eritrean languages.

17. The mid-1990s saw the rapid rise of Western development aid and human rights culture and the power of consultants emerge as an invincible force that still remains unchecked. Clark Gibson's (2005) team conducted what stands out as the most rigorous and authoritative analysis of the political economy of development aid. Eritrea was victimized as the power struggle between individual and corporate consultants played political leaders against each other, using the language and strategies of calculated speculations and vicious misinformation. I have previously examined this problem by tracing its roots to an 'anonymous' newspaper editorial planted by a British military administrator posing as a 'native' Eritrean in 1942, and the sense of *déjà vu* conjured up by the more recent state of negative peace in Eritrea (Almedom, 2006, pp. 103–142).

18. Details of the 'Asmara Declaration' are available, including full text of the Preamble at the Conference Site *Against All Odds* (2000). In addition, there is a documentary film that sums up the key points of the Asmara conference and preamble of the Asmara Declaration in one hour, written and directed by Charles Cantalupo, edited by Saba Ghebremeskel, and published by Hidri in Asmara (Cantalupo, 2007). It has served as part of the educational tools I have used in resilience workshops and seminars across university campuses in Europe and North America, and international

scientific meetings including 'Resilience 2008' (Stockholm, Sweden) and European Forum Alpbach 2008 and 2009 (Alpbach, Austria) generating positive feedback from discussion participants.

19. Elsewhere, the 'Asmara Declaration on African Languages and Literatures' seems to have generated a vicious battle among non-participating academic scholars – for example, on the pages of the journals of *Sociolinguistics* and *Applied Linguistics*. The war of words took a nasty and gendered tone as a Belgian dominant male expert/ specialist (Blommaert) leveled attacks on a Swedish–Finnish female scholar with a holistic ecological approach to the study of language and human rights (Skutnabb-Kangas). Interested readers may find the details in the opinion piece of the *Journal of Sociolinguistics* (2001, pp. 131–142) and rejoinder (2001, pp. 143–155) responding to myriad points of apparently calculated misinformation. While the responder (Tove Skutnabb-Kangas) exercised her right to reply to a negative and dismissive review of her book by the same 'emotional' attacker in the *Journal of Applied Linguistics* (2001), neither party seems to have followed up on the positive developments and successes of the 'Against All Odds' movement, which continued to impact education policy and practice in Eritrea and South Africa among other African countries. See also UNESCO (1953) and UNESCO (1999), which included the prospects of restructuring to transform the Ministry of Education to be more effective at working in partnership with local and international agencies concerned with health and nutrition – key requirements for the cognitive development of primary school children whose enrolment had risen dramatically in the 1990s.

20. Y.M. Asfaha, J. Kuvers and S. Kroon (2008) found that up to 36 percent of the variance in people's attitudes to multilingual education and multiscriptal literacy could be explained by the 'intrinsic values' of literacy and education; while only 11 per cent of the variance were explained by the 'economic value.'

21. The Sense of Coherence scale was originally called the 'Orientation to Life' questionnaire and the short form (thirteen items) translated well into the nine Eritrean languages with the exception of one item, which had to be altered to convey the appropriate and relevant concept of hope in Eritrean languages. My research team discovered that hope and loss of hope were closer to the Eritrean sense of agency and pathways to achieving individual and collective goals than the concept of 'loser or *sad sack*' as presented in Antonovsky's original (Almedom, 2005).

22. This definition was first proposed at the International Resilience Workshop held in Talloires, France, in July 2007, and published in the special issue of the journal *African Health Sciences on Resilience* (2008) following review by the panel of scientists who selected me to serve as one of the key speakers in the inaugural conference organized by the Resilience Alliance – Resilience 2008.

23. As documented by John Spencer in *Ethiopia at Bay*, the Ethiopian Emperor's meeting with US President Roosevelt had weakened the power of British influence, and Ethiopia had secured American support to keep the Ogaden – a region still contested with Somalia.

24. The literal translation of this line is 'with hardship,' implying that peace 'from' or 'with' Ethiopia had been tried and failed to bring comfort to Eritrea. Another poem by Haile entitled 'Believe it or Not' dwells more on that hardship.

25. Upon reviewing an earlier draft of this chapter, Zemhret Yohannes also pointed out the uniqueness of this practice of issuing individual 'Certificates of Honor' with hand-written names of each martyr to the families of those who died in service to the country. In Ethiopia, the families of soldiers were told that if their family member(s) did not return home, they should be assumed to be dead. No further information or acknowledgment of their services was offered.

26. This play emerged from his work with Ngũgĩ wa Mirii of the Kamĩrĩĩthũ Community Education and Cultural Centre, Nairobi University, which was later destroyed by *Askaris* (in 1982).
27. Alemseged Tesfai, 1999. The 'Songs' in the play are attributed to Mesgun Zerai, with 'Against All Odds' copyright.

Reference list

Against All Odds (2000) 'The Asmara Declaration on African Languages and Literatures,' http://www.outreach.psu.edu/programs/allodds/declaration.html, date accessed April 19, 2010.

Almedom, A. et al. (2005) '"Hope" makes Sense in Eritrean Sense of Coherence, but "Loser" does Not,' *Journal of Loss and Trauma*, 10, 5, 433–451.

Almedom, A. (2006) 'Re-reading the Short and Long-Rigged History of Eritrea, 1941–1952: Back to the Future?' *Nordic Journal of African Studies*, 15, 2, 103–142.

Asfaha, Y.M., J. Kuvers and S. Kroon (2008) 'Literacy and Script Attitudes in Multilingual Eritrea,' *Journal of Sociolinguistics*, 12, 223–240.

Cantalupo, C. (dir.) (2007) *Against All Odds: African Languages and Literatures into the 21st Century* (Eritrea: Hidri, DVD).

Firebrace, J. and S. Holland (1984) *Never Kneel Down: Drought, Development and Liberation in Eritrea* (Nottingham: Spokesman for War on Want), 119–120.

Gascoigne, B. (2001) 'History of Kenya', History World, http://www.historyworld.net/wrldhis/PlainTextHistories.asp?historyid=ad21, date accessed March 6, 2010.

Glennie, E. (2010) 'Evelyn Glennie Shows How to Listen,' http://www.ted.com/talks/evelyn_glennie_shows_how_to_listen.html, date accessed April 19, 2010.

Gibson, C. (2005) *The Samaritan's Dilemma: The Political Economy of Development Aid* (Oxford: Oxford University Press).

Haile, R. and Ch. Cantalupo (2000) *We have Our Voice: Selected Poems of Reesom Haile* (Lawrenceville and Asmara: The Red Sea Press), 46–47.

Haile, R. and Ch. Cantalupo (2002) *We Invented the Wheel: Poems by Reesom Haile* (Lawrenceville and Asmara: The Red Sea Press), 174–175.

Journal of Sociolinguistics (2001) 1, 5.

Ngũgĩ wa Thiong'o (1986) *Decolonising the Mind: The Politics of Language in African Literature* (London: James Currey & Nairobi: East African Educational Publishers).

Sharratt, S. and E. Kaschak (eds.) (1999) *Assaults on the Soul: Women in the Former Yugoslavia* (Oxfordshire: Haworth Press).

Shepherd, G.W. (1993) 'Free Eritrea: Linchpin for Stability and Peace on the Horn,' *Africa Today*, 40, 2, 94–96.

Tambulasi, R. and H. Kayuni (2005) 'Can African Feet Divorce Western Shoes? The Case of "Ubuntu" and Democratic Good Governance in Malawi,' *Nordic Journal of African Studies*, 147–161.

UNESCO (1953) 'The Use of Vernacular Languages in Education,' *Monographs on Fundamental Education*, 8.

UNESCO (1999) 'Education for All in Eritrea: Policies, Strategies, and Prospects,' *EFA 2000 Assessment Country Report* (Asmara).

UNESCO (2010) http://www.unesco.org/new/en/unesco/, Homepage, date accessed April 21, 2010.

Whittaker, P. (2007) 'Music and the Deaf, Dr. Paul Wittaker OBE – Clips from See Hear 2007,' http://www.youtube.com/watch?v=YOUP0Eh6FxQ, date accessed April 19, 2010.

Wilson, A. (1991) *The Challenge Road: Women and the Eritrean Revolution* (London: Earthscan).

31
Intercultural Inspiration:
The Life and Work of Raimon Panikkar*

Gustavo Esteva

> Peace has a different meaning for each epoch and for each culture area...
> Culture has always given meaning to peace. Each people, community,
> culture, has been mirrored, symbolically expressed and reinforced by
> its myth, law, goddess, ideal of peace. Peace is as vernacular as speech...
> Peace remains unreal, merely an abstraction, unless it stands for an
> ethno-anthropological reality.
>
> Ivan Illich

I would not have dared write on Raimon Panikkar. The theme – the man and
his work alike – is beyond my capacities. It is overwhelming even for him. In
his reaction to the papers presented in a symposium about his intercultural
philosophy in 2004 he confessed: 'Sincerely, I had imagined that it would be easy
[to comment on them], because I thought I knew the topic, since it concerned
ideas that I had published. I thought that after a quick reading I would be able to
write something. But I was wrong. I have learned a lot' (Panikkar, 2004a, p. 153).

And so when, perhaps with some irresponsible lightness, I did accept the
invitation to write this chapter celebrating Panikkar's contributions to peace, I
was well aware of my limitations. I accepted, however, because I thought it was
important to reflect on Panikkar's ideas in the context of this book. And because
he inspired this specific adventure.

As Wolfgang Dietrich mentions in the Preface, the book was originally
conceived as the first volume of an intercultural encyclopedia. It was not to
be an encyclopedia in the etymological sense: the course of general education
or a pedagogical encyclical (*encyclos paideia*), the circle of sciences and arts for
liberal education among the Greeks; it was not an encyclopedia in the modern
conventional sense either: a work, book or treatise, or a group of works, books

---

* Ed. On August 26, 2010, during the final stages of editing this book, we received the
  sad news of the passing away of Raimon Panikkar.

or treatises about one or many themes or sciences; nor was it an encyclopedia in the tradition of the French encyclopedists, who attempted in the eighteenth century to compile all the knowledge of their time; nor was it a dictionary, a word-book, a vocabulary list, a lexicon or a book of information or reference work on any subject or branch of knowledge.

Our dream, instead, was to generate a collection of books, produced after extensive research on homeomorphic equivalents[1] for certain fundamental social functions in different cultures, in order to explore their possible commonalities or points of overlap. By means of a dialogical dialogue, we wanted to search for an intercultural expression for those social functions. This was explicitly our interpretation of Panikkar's approach. We assumed that peace would be one of the easiest themes with which to begin the adventure. But it was not easy at all, as Wolfgang describes in the Preface. We are satisfied, though, with having attempted it.

The word *peace* rarely appears in a title of the innumerable essays and books of Panikkar. Peace, as a theme, does not seem to occupy a central position in his thinking. He is not an expert in the field or a prominent peace activist. But a book published in 1992 in honor of his life and work found it appropriate to call his position a philosophy of peace (Siguan, 1992). And he has a clear and important place in our own book because he deals seriously and rigorously with the preconditions for peace, no matter which notion of peace we adopt. Panikkar's *dictum*, 'Without interculturality, peace is only utopia,' was selected by Wolfgang as the epigraph for his introduction. What Panikkar has been doing in his long, productive life, in a thousand different ways, is to explore the conditions under which peace ceases to be a utopia.*

Being intercultural?

A philosopher; a theologian; a scientist; a prodigiously erudite scholar; a polyglot who writes comfortably in several languages; a dedicated and celebrated professor ('libero docente' at the University la Sapienza, in Rome; visiting professor at Harvard University; emeritus professor at the University of California in Santa Barbara); a committed international lecturer (as for the *Warner Lectures Series* or the *Gifford Lectures*); the founder of institutions like the *Center for Cross-Cultural Religious Studies* (Santa Barbara, California), *Vivarium, Centre d'Estudis Intercultural* (Tavertet, Catalogna) and *Pax Romana* (an NGO with consultative status at the United Nations); the president of organizations like the *Pipal Tree* (Bangalore) and the *Sociedad Española de Ciencias de las Religiones* (Madrid); the participant in numerous international consultations and the special envoy for the Indian

---

* Ed. In the last part of Chapter 16, Peter Horsley explores Panikkar's guiding thoughts on peace against the backdrop of Maori and European settlers' relationships in New Zealand.

government on cultural missions, Panikkar resists any conventional classification. He innovates constantly and constantly alludes to old traditions and wisdom. 'The more we have the courage to walk new paths – he once said – the more we must remain rooted in our own tradition, open to others who let us know that we are not alone and permit us to acquire a wider vision of reality' (Terricabras, 2008).

He was born in Barcelona in 1918, of a Hindu father and a Catholic mother. His father came to Spain as a representative of a German chemical company, when he thus escaped from Britain, where he had studied but whose colonial rule he had been fighting. Raimon studied with the Jesuits, in Barcelona, where he graduated in Chemistry in 1941, after some years at the University of Bonn. In 1942, he graduated in Philosophy in the University of Madrid. In 1946, he got a doctorate in Philosophy in that university, with a thesis on the concept of nature. That same year he was ordained as Catholic priest. In 1954, he graduated in theology at the Pontifical Lateran University in Rome and traveled for the first time to India, already 37 years old. In 1958, he completed a doctorate in Sciences, at the University of Madrid, with a thesis on the ontonomy of science. Back in Rome, he finished a doctorate in Theology (1961). His doctoral thesis, *The Unknown Christ of Hinduism* (Panikkar, 1981), was published in London in 1964 and immediately translated to four languages.* From 1964 to 1971, he divided his time between Varanasi (to whose diocese he was ascribed, while he continued his research in the University of Mysore), Rome and Boston (where he taught at Harvard University). From 1971 to 1987, he held the chair of Comparative Religious Philosophy at the University of California, in Santa Barbara, where he became Emeritus Professor, while continuing his research in India. He later retired to Tavertet, in Spain, where he directs *Vivarium*, an institute of cross-cultural religious research, but continues to lecture around the world.

'*Salí cristiano, me he descubierto hindú y regreso buddhista, sin dejar por ello de ser lo primero,*' says Panikkar (I started as a Christian, I discovered I was a Hindu and returned as a Buddhist, without having ceased to be a Christian). How is this possible? How can one combine a heritage that is both Christian and Hindu? Panikkar himself explains the apparent contradiction in the following terms:

> I was brought up in the Catholic religion by my Spanish mother, but I never stopped trying to be united with the tolerant and generous religion of my father and of my Hindu ancestors. This does not make me a cultural or religious 'half-caste,' however. Christ was not half man and half God, but fully man and fully God. In the same way, I consider myself 100 percent Hindu and Indian,

---

* Ed. The author refers to the translations of *The Unknown Christ of Hinduism* to German in 1965 as *Christus der Unbekannte im Hinduismus*, to Spanish in 1970 under the title *El Cristo desconocido del hinduismo*, in 1972 under the French title *Le Christ et l'Hindouisme* and 1975 in its Italian version as *Il Cristo sconosciuto dell'induismo*.

and 100 percent Catholic and Spanish. How is that possible? By living religion as an experience rather than as an ideology. (Panikkar, 2000b, p. 834)

'The dialogue route that I propose is existential, intimate and concrete,' says Panikkar. Any study of his intercultural philosophy should take into consideration how 'existential, intimate and concrete' it really is: it expresses a life experience and transforms that human – very human – experience into a philosophical attitude. His purpose is not 'to establish some universal religion, to end up with a kind of United Nations of religions' but 'to facilitate communication among men and women, for them to live in small huts on a human scale, with windows and streets, rather than on information superhighways' (Panikkar, 2000b, p. 834). His argument is explicitly constructed on experience.

As long as I do not open my heart and do not see that the other is not an other but a part of myself who enlarges and completes me, I will not arrive at dialogue. If I embrace you, then I understand you. All this is a way of saying that real intrareligious dialogue begins in myself, and that it is more an exchange of religious experiences than of doctrines. If one does not start out from this foundation, no religious dialogue is possible; it is just idle chatter. (Panikkar, 2000b, p. 834)

The dialogue Panikkar has been exploring during his entire life is always personal, not abstract: 'between you and me, between you and your neighbor; it should be like a rainbow where we are never sure where one color begins and another ends.' But this is not cultural relativism. It rejects any absolutization of the truth, but does not pretend to abandon truth, your truth. 'Truth is always relational, and the Absolute (*absolutes*, untied) is that which has no relation.'

I am not such a relativist as to believe that the truth is cut up in slices like a cake. But I am convinced that each of us participates in the truth. Inevitably, my truth is the truth that I perceive from my window. And the value of dialogue between the various religions is precisely to help me perceive that there are other windows, other perspectives. Therefore I need the other in order to know and verify my own perspective of the truth. Truth is a genuine and authentic participation in the dynamism of reality [...] I hold to my truth. I am even ready to commit my life to it and to die for it. I am simply saying that I do not have a monopoly on truth, and that what is most important is the manner in which you and I enter into that truth, how we perceive it and hear it. Thomas Aquinas said, 'You do not possess the truth; it is truth that possesses you.' Yes, we are possessed by truth. That is what makes me live; but the other lives, too, by virtue of her truth. I do not engage myself first of all to defend my truth, but to live it. And the dialogue between religions is not a strategy for making one truth triumphant, but a process of looking for it and deepening it along with others. (Panikkar, 2000b, p. 835)

Dialogue starts in yourself, with your self – which can only exist with the other: it is a knot in a net of relationships. Panikkar is not trying 'to be right' but rather to offer paths to deal with our predicaments. He does not aspire to defend this truth but to live it out. He invites us to think and to engage in dialogue, and dialogue, insists Panikkar, particularly dialogical dialogue, is a path towards peace. 'In the dialogical dialogue theory and praxis cannot be separated – although they should certainly be distinguished. Dialogical dialogue is more realistic: it deals with human problems, not only theoretical problems' (Panikkar, 2004b, p. 161); it looks for both our differences and what we have in common, to generate mutual fecundation.

Culture and intercultural dialogue

Interculturality, for Panikkar, does not allow for any reductionism, theoretical or practical. 'Culture is as physical as meta-physical and meta-empirical' (Panikkar, 2004b, p. 163). Perhaps the best way to introduce Panikkar's complex ideas about culture and intercultural dialogue is to use his own words, in the way he synthesized them for a virtual dialogue in preparation for the International Dialogue between Cultures, organized by UNESCO in Barcelona in 2004.[2]

1. We understand by culture the encompassing myth of a society in a given space and time. Myth is the horizon of intelligibility where all of our perceptions of reality make sense. Myth gives us the frame for our worldview, it is what makes possible and shapes any interpretation of reality. Therefore we are not fully conscious of our own myth, of those beliefs on which a given worldview is constructed. We become conscious of our own myth when somebody else shows it to us, or once we have abandoned it, at least in part.

2. Culture is not objectifyable. We can only approach the knowledge of a culture by somehow participating in its myth. Each culture is a galaxy, containing the experience and perception of the world out of which emerge the self-understanding of that culture and its particular questions, which will specify what is significant for that society: criteria for truth, goodness and beauty, as well as the limits of the world and our place in it.

3. We can distinguish between nature and culture, but in human beings they cannot be severed. Culture is the way in which human nature is expressed. We are cultural beings. Culture is the field on which we consciously walk towards our destination, towards full experience of life. Every person exists and is actualized in a given culture.

4. Cultures are mutually incommensurable. As all of us are part of a culture – at least –, there cannot be any outside 'neutral' standpoint from which to value or judge another culture; we are always dependent of the language and the criteria for truth of our culture. Therefore, there is no way to establish a hierarchy of cultures, or to pretend that the values of a culture can be always applied to others, that is, there is no way to absolutize or universalize our own values. We can only speak of *human invariants*, that is, those invariants common to all humanity like thinking, speaking, believing, loving…, which nevertheless are interpreted by each culture in different and specific ways.

5. Cultures are not folklore, they cannot be reduced to accidental ways to see life and to live it. They are not species of a purported genre 'universal culture' that would include all peoples and epochs. But there are some *transcultural* values at some given moments in history, for instance, some ethical norms for peace, justice and human welfare.

6. Each culture has its own values, but these cannot be absolutized. All values are relative. But this does not imply relativism. Relativism destroys the possibility of believing in anything. *Relativity*, on the other hand, means that every worldview and every assertion are relative to their contexts. Nobody has a complete and absolute view of reality, a reality that, far from being valueless, is constituted by indivisible network of the cosmic, divine and human dimensions. Every human being, as well as every culture, is a knot in this net, it is a centre in the reality and so it has intrinsic value, it is truly unique. Cultural relativity gives us the message of the crucial importance of every culture and every being. At the same time, it makes obvious the impossibility to absolutize them.

7. The belief in the universality of one's own cultural contents is the essence of monoculturalism and results in colonialism. Cultures are incommensurable but not incommunicable between them; this would be solipsism. Interculturality is half way between the absolutization of a culture and the absolute incommunication between cultures.

8. Interculturality describes the dynamic situation of the person who lives consciously and, being conscious of the existence of other people, values and cultures, knows that isolation is not possible. Intercultural dialogue is an imperative for our world today. Interculturality springs from the consciousness of the limitations of every culture, from the relativization of all that is human; it manifests itself as an intrinsically human, and therefore cultural feature.

9. All cultures are the result of an ongoing mutual fecundation. Cultures, like reality, are not static: they are in a process of ongoing transformation. Dialogue between cultures, as well as the philosophical task of trying to be conscious of one's myth, to question and to transform it, and to find equivalents among diverse cultural discourses, are a process through which every human person and every culture contribute to the destiny of humanity and of the universe, which, to a great extent, is in our hands. This is the human dignity and responsibility.

10. A forum of cultures could be an ideal way to open them to an intercultural dialogue that may bring forth the recognition of values that make possible a free and worthy human life.

We can establish a certain distinction among different dimensions or aspects of culture (*Interculture*, 1995, p. 53):

- **The morphological dimension:** entirely visible, like the foliage of a tree, is made up of the traits that constitute the external manifestations of cultures: language, dress, food, customs, arts, habitation, etc., what you see in entering the physical cultural of a specific culture. There are today some global standards. If you wake up in a Sheraton, you will not know, at first sight, if you are in Bangkok, Cairo or New York; at most you will get some 'local color' in the decoration. But beyond this homogenized fully westernized world, you will be able to find the local manifestations of cultures.
- **The structural dimension:** partly visible and partly invisible, like the trunk of a tree, is composed of the forms for organizing behaviors according to shared norms: medical or religious practices, governmental requirements, legal and social norms, etc. If you come to a village the day of an assembly or to a modern city the day of elections, you will be able to see a specific behavior, people gathered to discuss their affairs or in line for voting, but you will not be able to see the rules for such behavior, which can be analytically explored and described but are not evident.
- **The mythical dimension:** entirely invisible, like the roots of a tree, is the source of meaning. Its substance is the cosmovision, the notion of being, the perception of time and space, spirituality, etc.
  The morphological and structural dimensions or aspects usually manifest great dynamism: they change continually in response to external and internal influences. But the mythical–symbolic dimension of culture can maintain itself – at times for millennia. With the deeply traditional analogy of the tree, indigenous peoples in Mexico and Central America have been saying recently: 'They wrenched off our fruits, they ripped off our branches, they burned our trunk, but they could not kill our roots.'

Culture, says Raimón Panikkar (1975, p. 76), is 'the encompassing myth of a society in a given time and space'. And myth, in this context, is 'the horizon of intelligibility where all of our perceptions of reality make sense' (Panikkar, 1975, p. 76). The myth offers the frame within which the worldview is inscribed; it is that which permits and conditions any interpretation of reality. It is not seeing something or believing something, but rather believing that one sees, as the poet Machado said. 'Myth is what we believe, without believing that we believe in it.' It is 'what makes the meaning meaningful without being meant in the meaning' (Panikkar, 1975, p. 46). 'Myth is what makes one see but cannot be seen, like light itself' (Panikkar, 1987b, p. 76).

'Myth is outside the logical truth' (Panikkar, 1970, p. 199), but mythos and logos 'are two human modes of awareness, irreducible one to the other, but equally inseparable' (Panikkar, 1979, p. 100).

> *Mythos* and *logos* go together, because they designate two aspects of the word, the first being the word which expresses thoughts (as *realities*), the second being the act of intelligence and the operation run by the thing expressed in the word. *Logos* designates the word in reference to the subject who thinks or speaks: what is thought and calculated. What *mythos* designates primarily is not the word in reference to *what is thought*, but in reference to *what is real*. (Panikkar, 1970, pp. 181–182)

Another crucial distinction, for Panikkar, is the one between human invariants and cultural universals.

> There are human invariants: we all have a body, we all eat, we all walk, we all speak, we all like some things, etc. There are human invariants, but not cultural universals. The dominant culture has attempted to make us believe that there are cultural universals. Food, for some is to ingest proteins, for others is to keep yourself in shape, for some others is something communal and very beautiful, for some others is to communicate with the divine, for some others...is something entirely different. There are no cultural universals. (Panikkar, 1993b, pp. 16–17)

Conditions for peace

Panikkar (1995a) expressed in nine *sutras* the conditions for peace, what constitutes peace – the *sutras* being like the threads of a necklace, in which one leads to another, all depending on each other and only when interwoven constituting the necklace.

1. **Peace is participation in the harmony of the rhythm of being** (Panikkar, 1995a, p. 15). Peace implies participating in the rhythm of reality and at the same time contributing harmoniously to that rhythm. This requires participating, actively and passively, in the adventure of Being [...] going from the *status quo* to a *fluxus quo* towards a cosmic harmony constantly new.

2. **It is difficult to live without external Peace; it is impossible to live without internal Peace. The relationship is non-dualistic (advaitic)** (Panikkar, 1995a, p. 17). Peace is not only the absence of an armed conflict. Only with internal peace we can have external peace [...] but you cannot have genuine internal peace if you do not have external peace. There is a reciprocal, *sui generis*, causality between the two.

3. **Peace is neither conquered for oneself nor imposed on others. It is both received, discovered and created. It is a gift (of the Spirit)** (Panikkar, 1995a, p. 18). Peace is a gift, a revelation, a discovery, a grace, a responsibility. Peace should be continually nourished and recreated.

4. **Victory never leads to Peace** (Panikkar, 1995a, p. 18). None of the 8000 peace treaties that we know brought true peace. Peace is much more than a mere agreement for domination.

5. **Military disarmament requires cultural disarmament** (Panikkar, 1995a, p. 19). Cultural disarmament is a requisite for peace. This is fundamental for Panikkar; it is the title of his book on peace: *Cultural Disarmament: The Way to Peace* (1995a). Cultural disarmament does not imply a return to primitivism. It means instead adopting a critical attitude towards culture, particularly the dominant culture, in order to get a truly intercultural approach.

6. **In isolation, no culture, religion or tradition can resolve the problems of the world** (Panikkar, 1995a, p. 20). Only radical pluralism, with respect to cultures, religions and traditions, may bring peace.

7. **Peace pertains essentially to the order of *mythos*, not to that of logos** (Panikkar, 1995a, p. 21). Peace is polysemic; it has many senses. And it is pluralist: there can be many incompatible interpretations. The imposition of our *concept* of peace cannot bring peace.

8. **Religion is a way to peace.** For Panikkar, religion is the ultimate way, an expression that can be translated into a specific content like 'way to salvation' – a word used in diverse religious traditions. When he affirms that religion is the way to peace, peace represents the homeomorphic equivalent of earlier interpretations of 'salvation.' Panikkar does not allude only to political peace or internal concord, but to 'a complex and polysemic symbol standing for the cosmic and personal harmony of (and within) reality.' (Panikkar, 1987a, p. xxv)

Peace is the blend of harmony, freedom and justice. Some cultures stress freedom, and often only individual freedom. They are sensitive to the constraints that hamper human blossoming from without. Human life is seen as development. Some other cultures stress justice, often viewed collectively. They are sensitive to the structural obstacles to the constructions of a just social order. Human life is seen as well-being – and this well-being is usually framed only in terms of the material needs of the people. Some other cultures stress harmony, viewed most often in connection with nature. They are sensitive to the kind of human happiness that comes from playing one's part in the unfolding drama of the universe. Life is the main category, and human integration into that Life, the main value.

Freedom points to truth. Justice points to goodness. Harmony points to beauty.

A genuine peace would have to blend these three values, visions, experiences, both in a time-less/time-full (sempiternal) way and in a personal/cosmic manner. The traditional word for this blend is Love. And all of these, I submit, are religious categories... (Panikkar, 1987a, pp. xxiv–xxv)

For Panikkar,

the object of religion is not God, it is the destiny of Man – and of Man not just as individual, but also as society, as species and genus, as microcosm, as one constitutive element of reality which both mirrors and shapes that reality... God, a traditional name for the object of religion, may indeed represent the true destiny of the human being, but surely is not the only such symbol. The study of religion properly deals not with any one symbol alone, but with any symbol standing for the ultimate meaning of life and the means to reach it. In a word, the concern of religion is human destiny, and it is this human destiny which is at stake today. (Panikkar, 1987a, p. xxvi)

One aspect of the encounter of religions that has critical importance for a reflection on peace in Panikkar is the following:

The meeting of two differing realities produces the shock of the encounter, but the *place* where the encounter happens is one. This one place is the heart of the person. It is within the heart that I can embrace both religions in a personal synthesis, which intellectually may be more or less perfect. And it is also within my heart that I may absorb one of the two religions into the other. In actuality religions cannot sincerely coexist or even continue as living religions if they do not 'co-insist', i.e. penetrate into the heart of each other. (Panikkar, 1981, p. 12)

The real theology task...begins when the two views meet head-on inside oneself, when dialogue prompts genuine religious pondering, and even a religious crisis, at the bottom of a Man's heart; when interpersonal dialogue turns into intrapersonal soliloquy. (Panikkar, 1978, p. 10)

But such kind of dialogue is always in connection with the other: it is only possible through the other.

> Dialogue is, fundamentally, opening myself to another so that he might speak and reveal my myth that I cannot know by myself because it is transparent to me, self-evident. Dialogue is a way of knowing myself and of disentangling my own point of view from other viewpoints and from me, because it is grounded so deeply in my own roots as to be utterly hidden from me. It is the other who through our encounter awakens this human depth latent in me in an endeavor that surpasses both of us. In authentic dialogue this process is reciprocal. Dialogue sees the other not as an extrinsic, accidental aid, but as the indispensable, personal element in our search for truth, because I am not self-sufficient, autonomous individual. In this sense, dialogue is a religious act par excellence because it recognizes my *religatio* to another, my individual poverty, the need to go out of myself, transcend myself, in order to save myself. (Panikkar, 1979, pp. 242–243)

9. **Only forgiveness, reconciliation, and ongoing dialogue lead to peace and shatter the law of *karma*** (Panikkar, 1995a, p. 23).

These nine *sutras* can be seen as the introduction to Panikkar's thesis on peace, which consists of two parts and a corollary: '(1) Peace is an eminently religious affair. (2) The journey to peace requires interculturality, not as an academic luxury, but as an exigency of *lèse-humanité* (it requires what I have called cultural disarmament). (3) Post-modernity stands in need of a *metanoia*' (Panikkar, 1995a, p. 33).

For Panikkar, peace is one of the very few positive symbols for the whole of humankind: it is perhaps the most universal unifying symbol. To sum up, he says,

> Peace is not a simple state of mind, but is rather a state of be-ing (the gerund), a state of Being (as a noun denoting all reality). Peace is that state of Being corresponding to the being in question. That is, peace is a welfare in Being. When a being is in its place, it is at peace. When a bone, an individual, or a society is not in its place, it is not at peace. The bone hurts, the individual is disturbed, the society is unstable. And so with every being. But the spatial metaphor must be understood dynamically and freely. The 'place' of which we speak is not a predetermined space, or static locality, in which each being occupies its spot in a rank and file as in a regiment on parade, nor is each part localized after a manner of a part functioning in a machine. Instead of 'place', we could have said 'duty.' Peace emerges when a being complies with its duty. But here again the metaphor could be misunderstood. The duty in question

is not an extrinsic one. Each being's ought-to-be is its being-where-it-belongs. 'When each being fulfills its "function"' might be a third formulation of the same notion. (Panikkar, 1995a, p. 77)

[...] in the first place, that peace is not a static state, and that, accordingly, it is found to be constantly *in fieri*. In the second place, it shows us that peace is neither purely subjective not exclusively objective. It is relational. In the third place, it shows that peace is never perfect – that is, that it is never finished and complete. In the fourth place, it shows us that peace is not available to precise definitions, because of its character of ultimacy. In the fifth place, it shows us that peace has no biunivocal relation with the rest of reality. I can be at peace with others without others being at peace with me. In the sixth place, it shows us that peace is not a monolithic block. It is polyfaceted, and even pluralistic. It has facets, degrees, nuances. It is not subject to quantification, since these very facets are not homogeneous. And finally, it shows us that peace is the relation that joins us, equitable and with freedom, to a harmonious whole. (Panikkar, 1995a, p. 78)

A sense of urgency

For a long time, Panikkar has been living, thinking and writing with a sense of urgency.

I am convinced that we live in a state of human emergency that does not allow us to entertain ourselves with bagatelles of no relevance whatsoever. But [...] mere short-term solutions and technical stopgaps will not do [...]. We need an insight into the deeper strata of reality that might permit us to go to the roots of the problems. (Panikkar, 1979, p. 2)

The political and economic situation of the world today compels to radical changes in our conception of humanity and the place of humanity in the cosmos. The present system seems to be running toward major catastrophes of all kinds. This situation brings near the thought that if the change has to be radical and lasting, it also has to transform our ways of thinking and experiencing reality. (Panikkar, 1990b, p. 69)

There are in the world today a hundred social conflicts that can be called civil wars and we now live in a culture of war. Violence erupts daily everywhere in the world in the interaction among people of different cultures. No intercultural dialogue is truly attempted to cope with these conflicts; they are usually dealt with instead in the terms of the stronger party.

Given the current conditions of the world and stimulated by unacceptable reactions of intolerance, many sensible calls for tolerance are emerging everywhere. Despite the olive branch, however, this call for tolerance also has the thorny prick of intolerance. It stings, wounds. Tolerance can never embrace.

Tolerance means to suffer with patience. The person who tolerates perceives the other as someone who has the wrong color of skin, the wrong God, the wrong behavior. He enjoys the generosity of tolerating the other, of suffering him with patience. At times, though, the one who tolerates loses his patience, no longer able to tolerate the other. Though more gentle and discreet, tolerance is merely a different form of intolerance. 'Toleration,' Goethe observed, 'ought in reality to be merely a transitory mood. It must lead to recognition. To tolerate is to insult.'

Hospitality, on the other hand, is a recognition, an association, a coming together of an entirely different sort. In being hospitable, you recognize the pluralism of reality. You host the other even when you disagree with his arguments, his versions of the multiverse of the real world. To be hospitable does not mean to follow the other, to adopt his views, to affirm or negate him. Hosting the other simply means to open your arms and doors for him and to accept his existence in his own place.

As never before, we are now compelled to take a stance in the presence of the other. The reality of our daily lives makes it impossible to avoid mutual intertwining, intermeddling. Conflicts emerge.

What we now feel and suffer, the impasse implicated in every kind of violence, is the incompatibility of different worldviews. The question of pluralism is thus urgently posed to every one of us: the current situation throws us into the arms of one another. Are we going to open our arms hospitably, or arm ourselves?

It is true that democratic procedures, when different opinions, views and attitudes interact, offer consolation prizes to the minority and the possibility of improved power positions in the forthcoming contest. Not bad. It is better than fighting, and oftentimes the best or the only feasible solution for many conflicts. But democratic procedures cannot resolve the confrontation between incompatible worldviews. A plural world requires pluralist accords, not democratic, provisional agreements.

What is needed is to create a mutual opening to the concern of the other. We do not share ideas, concepts, beliefs, even words with the other. But we can find and share an element, something that can offer to both of us some guidance, inspiration, light, ideal, whatever both parties acknowledge and neither party controls. We can thus re-enact a dialogue, transcending the logos of both parties, our conceptual systems.

For this kind of opening, the life and work of Raimon Panikkar is a privileged path. 'What we need today,' he wrote thirty years ago, 'is not so much intellectuals saying what has to be done, or scholars writing what is the case, or, for that matter, preachers proclaiming the truth, but people living it, people writing with their blood and speaking with their lives' (Panikkar, 1979, p. 16). And he added, in closing the introduction to the book that he still considers the most complete expression of his thinking (Panikkar, 2004b, p. 190), 'after the excruciating experience of trying to put these studies together by revising them, I shall revert to where I began: to being coauthor of my life' (Panikkar, 1979, p. 16). When asked recently if his books are autobiographic, he answered:

> I don't speak about me, it is my I who speaks and everything he says is a confession and is, if you want, biographic, but my books are not merely an autobiography. In fact, all are autobiographies in the measure in which they emerge from the experience of my life (my bios). But it will seem as objectifying myself to present myself to others in that way. I am not an object, but a subject. (Panikkar, 2004b, p. 190)

Notes

1. Homeomorphic equivalents is a central concept in the intercultural philosophy of Panikkar. They 'are not mere literal translations, any more than they merely translate the role that the original word claims to play, but they play a function which is equivalent (analogous) or comparable to that supposedly played by (the original word). It is therefore not a conceptual but a functional equivalent, i.e. an analogy of the third degree. One does not seek the same function...but the function that is equivalent to that exercised by the original notion in the corresponding cosmovision. Let us consider a few examples that may help us. "Brahman" is not a translation for "God", since the concepts do not correspond (their attributes not being the same), and since the functions are not identical (brahman not having to be creator, providence, personal, as God is). Each one of these two words expresses a functional equivalence within the corresponding two cosmovisions. There is more. In that example, the correlation is almost biunivocal (one word homeomorphically corresponding to the other); but it could not be. We can for example translate "religion" by dharma without necessarily translating dharma by "religion". Dharma equally means duty, ethics, element, observance, energy, order, virtue, law, justice, and has been even translated by reality. But the word "religion" can also mean sampradâya, karma, jati, bhakti, marga, pûja, daivakarma, nimayaparam, punyasila [...]. Each culture is a world...We must seek a middle way between the colonial mentality which believes that we can express the totality of the human experience through the notions of a single culture, and the opposite extreme which thinks that there is no communication possible between diverse cultures, and which should then condemn themselves to a cultural apartheid in order to preserve their identity.'(Panikkar, 1998c, pp. 101–102)
2. http://www.barcelona2004.or/dialegs/dialeg4/s/panikkar/html was the page in which this text and the exchange among a group of participants – including the author of this chapter – took place. The page is no longer available.

Reference list

This list comprises the sources to the references made in this chapter and further includes the most relevant texts on peace by Raimon Panikkar.

Interculture (1995) 'Intercultural foundations of Peace between Mohawk Nation and North American States: Towards a Common Language,' 127.

Panikkar, R. (1970) *Le mystère du culte dans l'hindouisme et le christianism* (París: Cerf).

Panikkar, R. (1973) *The Trinity and the Religious Experience of Man* (New York and London: Orbis/Darton, Longman and Todd).

Panikkar, R. (1975) 'Percées dans la problématique interculturelle,' *Monchanin*, 50, 3–74.

Panikkar, R. (1978) *The Intrareligious Dialogue* (New York, Ramsey and Toronto: Paulist Press).

Panikkar, R. (1979) *Myth, Faith and Hermeneutics* (New York, Ramsey and Toronto: Paulist Press).

Panikkar, R. (1981) *The Unknown Christ of Hinduism. Towards an Ecumenical Christophany*, revised edition (London: DLT).

Panikkar, R. (1987a) 'The Challenge of Religious Studies to the Issues of Our Times. Foreword' in S. Eastham (ed.) *Nucleus: Reconnecting Science and Religion in the Nuclear Age* (Santa Fe: Bear & Company).

Panikkar, R. (1987b) 'Logotimia e pensiero occidentale,' *Rosmini e l'Iluminismo*, Atti de XXI Corso della Catedra Rosmini (Stresa: Centro Internazionale di studi rosminiani).

Panikkar, R. (1990a) 'The Religion of the Future,' Vol. I, *Interculture*, 107.

Panikkar, R. (1990b) 'The Religion of the Future,' Vol. II, *Interculture*, 108.

Panikkar, R. (1990c) *Sobre el diálogo intercultural* (Salamanca: Editorial San Esteban).

Panikkar, R. (1992) 'A Nonary of Priorities' in J. Ogilvy (ed.) *Revisioning Philosophy* (Albany: State University of New York Press).

Panikkar, R. (1993a) *A Dwelling Place for Wisdom* (Louisville: Westminster/John Knox Press).

Panikkar, R. (1993b) 'La diversidad como presupuesto de la armonía entre los pueblos,' *Wiñay Marka*, 20, 15–20.

Panikkar, R. (1995a) *Cultural Disarmament: The Way to Peace* (Louisville: Westminster/John Knox Press).

Panikkar, R. (1995b) *Invisible Harmony: Essays on Contemplation & Responsibility* (Minneapolis: Fortress Press).

Panikkar, R. (1996) 'The Defiance of Pluralism,' *Soundings*, 79.1–2, 170–191.

Panikkar, R. (1998a) *La plenitud del hombre* (Madrid: Ediciones Siruela).

Panikkar, R. (1998b) *Iconos del misterio* (Barcelona: Ediciones Península).

Panikkar, R. (1998c) 'Religion, Philosophy and Culture,' *Interculture*, 135, 99–120.

Panikkar, R. (1999a) 'The Foundations of Democracy: Strength, Weakness, Limit,' *Interculture*, 136, 4–23.

Panikkar, R. (1999b) 'The Discovery of the Metapolitical,' *Interculture*, 136, 24–60.

Panikkar, R. (1999c) *The Intrareligious Dialogue*, revised edition (New York, Ramsey & Toronto: Paulist Press).

Panikkar, R. (1999d) 'Religious Identity and Pluralism' in A. Sharma and K.M. Dugan (eds.) *A Dome of Many Colors. Studies in Religions Pluralism, Identity and Unity* (Harrisburg: Trinity Press International).

Panikkar, R. (2000a) *El silencio del Buddha: Una introducción al ateísmo religioso* (Madrid: Ediciones Siruela).

Panikkar, R. (2000b) 'Eruption of Truth: An Interview with Raimon Panikkar,' *The Christian Century*, August, 16–23, 834–836.

Panikkar, R. (2001) 'Politics, Religion and Interculturality' in K.L. Nandan (ed.) *The Earth Has No Corner* (Delhi: Shipra).

Panikkar, R. (2004a) 'Epileg. Diàleg a diverses veus' in I. Boada (ed.) *La filosofia intercultural de Raimon Panikkar* (Barcelona: Pòrtic).

Panikkar, R. (2004b) 'Entrevista amb Raimon Panikkar' in I. Boada (ed.) *La filosofia intercultural de Raimon Panikkar* (Barcelona: Pòrtic).

Siguan, M. (ed.) (1992) *Philosophia pacis. Homenaje a Raimon Panikkar* (Madrid: Símbolo).

Terricabras, J.M. (2008) 'Laudatio of Raimon Panikkar Alemany during the Solemn Academic Ceremony of his Investiture as Doctor Honoris Causa of the University of Girona,' http://raimon-panikkar.org/english/laudatio.html, date accessed February 18, 2010.

32
Gregory Bateson:
A Practitioner's Perspective

Victoria Fontan

I turn my eyes to the schools & universities of Europe
And there behold the Loom of Locke whose Woof rages dire,
Wash'd by the Water-wheels of Newton: black the cloth
In heavy wreathes folds over every Nation: cruel works
Of many Wheels I view, wheel without wheel, with cogs tyrannic
Moving by compulsion each other, not as those in Eden, which,
Wheel within wheel, in freedom revolve in harmony & peace.

William Blake

A colleague recently told me that Afghanistan has become a cemetery for peace projects. Over the past ten years, billions of dollars have been spent to alleviate people's suffering, to ensure that the country would embark on a sustainable recovery; this to no avail, Taliban or no Taliban. To the average observer, throwing money and goods at a country's economy can only serve the overall goal of its recovery; this for the general good. To the local farmer, the free supply of grounded wheat from benevolent nations to post-war Afghanistan means that he has no choice but to abandon the culture of wheat to the benefit of poppies, hence contribute to the exponential increment in opium trafficking towards Western nations.

After spending the last ten years visiting conflict areas and teaching Peace and Conflict Studies, I was left with the distinct feeling that I would not be able to spend the next ten years of my life doing more of the same. Mission after mission, course after course, I came to the realization that our field is more part of the problem than it is part of the solution. When peace has become more of an industry for the general good than a way of life, how can we, well-intentioned human beings, fit in? How can we reconcile our ethics with our activities?

Gregory Bateson wrote that a message about peace is not part of the peace and that the more we feel that we can wage 'war' on a problem, eradicate it, the more we contribute to it (Bateson, 1972a). What would he have said? Had he been alive to witness the 'Yes We Can' campaign of US President Barack Obama? Crowned not by his election but by his immediate showcase decision to close the Guantanamo Detention Centre, a decision yet to be applied? What would he have said to our growing concerns about climate change, he who more than forty years ago documented environmental changes on the coastal region of California? The discovery of Gregory Bateson's work has inspired me to spend the next ten years of my career focusing on how Peace and Conflict Studies can become part of the peace that is so often taken for granted. This chapter will review Gregory Bateson's work in light of the challenges faced by our discipline; this alongside his life.

Transdisciplinarity in the making

Gregory Bateson was born in England in 1904 and died in San Francisco in 1980. He owes his first name to biologist Gregor Mendel, rediscovered by his father William, a pioneer of modern genetics (Harries-Jones, 1995). Bateson's youth was dominated by the death of his two brothers, John, during the First World War, and Martin, who committed suicide by shooting himself in Piccadilly Circus, after a failed attempt at becoming an artist (Harries-Jones, 1995). While being promised to a career in zoology by his father and rebelling against the rigid system of science, Martin Bateson left a deep concern in the heart of his younger brother: how to reconcile science with arts. How to ensure that one becomes as sacred as the other. Gregory Bateson's fascination for the work of William Blake, centered on the sacred unity of mind and spirit, contributed to this search (Nachmanovitch, 1981). It is at the origins of his transdisciplinary epistemology.

While modern society can only function ascribing as many precise names as possible to people, Gregory Bateson still confuses most academics. This is because he never chose to pertain to one academic discipline *per se*, but instead, to adopt a transdisciplinary approach to the creation of knowledge and communication as early as possible in his career. Bateson never focused on content, but the relationships and patterns linking contents. To some, he remains an intellectual scattered between disciplines as varied as anthropology, oceanography, psychiatry, communication and ecology. To many, he is one of the fathers of cybernetics, through what he refers to as the ecology of the mind.

Being destined to a career in zoology after the death of his brother Martin, Bateson conducted a first field research in the Galapagos Islands in the mid-1920s, where he affirmed his desire to embark on a career of anthropology (Lipset, 1982). His first field research was conducted in Indonesia, followed by New Guinea and in the early 1930s Bali, where he met his first wife, the famous anthropologist Margaret Mead. He then embarked on a career mostly in the US, where he remained until his death in 1980 (Lipset, 1982). He first taught at Harvard University as a visiting professor, before joining the Veterans Administration Hospital of Palo Alto to head a study of abstraction within communication. His most famous finding from those years was to be the theory of 'double bind,' or dilemma in communication. Later, he led the Oceanographic Institute at the University of Hawaii, where he researched communication in porpoises. His last professional years were spent as part-time lecturer at the University of California, Santa Cruz.

Bateson's bibliography is as eclectic as his scholarship, most of his thinking being expressed in the recursiveness of his communication with his readers. Reading Bateson is a complex undertaking, since he engages the reader to mentally stretch in a feedback loop both during and in between the discovery of his articles, speeches and metalogues. Without active intellectual involvement, Bateson's words do not stick; his ideas fail to blossom. Bateson does not deliver content; he plants seeds of interconnectedness, he invites the reader to come back to his works over and over, to discover new ideas and, more importantly, make more connections between ideas, every single time. Reading Gregory Bateson is like journeying through the infinite complexity of a fractal.

Cybernetics of self

There are many entry points into Bateson's ecology of the mind, the most relevant to peace studies being that of cybernetics, where he proposes to rediscover the territory hidden by the map so commonly discussed in mainstream peace studies. The map, interventions for peace, often hides the territory, the patterns of communication that lead to conflict in the fragmentations of peacekeeping, peacemaking and peace building.

The essay he wrote on the cybernetics of the self, a reflection on the symmetric aspects of alcoholism, becomes resounding when one studies the many failures of peace operations worldwide (Bateson, 1972b). In his essay, Bateson explains how alcoholic pride, deriving from a Cartesian symmetric epistemology, invariably maintains the alcoholic in a state of addiction. This pride alludes to the addict and the understanding of the situation of his or her *entourage* as one to be conquered, won over and dominated. According to this common assumption, the addict must vanquish his or her desire to drink. He or she is thought to be in total control of his situation and locked onto a duel with the substance, a duel that is inexorably to be won by the substance as often as the situation repeats itself, with increasingly damaging consequences for the vanquished.

At the root of this situation lies the epistemological error of understanding the situation as one of symmetry between the addict and the substance, as well as the division between mind, matter and spirit. By believing that one has complete power over the situation, one is also left alone to confront it, hence unable to address the complimentary-related roots of the addiction. Conversely, the first of the famous 'Twelve Steps' of the Alcoholics Anonymous 'message to the alcoholic' is to make him or her 'cut through all this mythology of conflict' in making them admit that they 'are powerless over alcohol – that [their] lives ha[ve] become unmanageable' (Bateson, 1972b, pp. 312–313).

The myth of 'war over' is therefore diffused towards a reconnection between body and mind, mind and matter, matter and society, society and spirit. Combined to this is also the shock effect of having hit the bottom, which can be the loss of a job, the failure of a marriage, a blackout of a few hours. The shock generated by this awakening to one's situation is understood as a key to the recovery process. In sum: no hitting bottom = no recovery.[1] Yet, many actors in the life of the addict will ensure, knowingly or not, that the bottom is never reached. They can be understood as enablers. This can be the addict him or herself, the entourage, in their plight to hide the addiction to themselves, their families, society. This prevention of hitting rock bottom is a form of negative feedback. It regulates the addiction so that the amplifying effect of the shock never materializes. This is peace and conflict studies' own entry point into the ecology of the mind: conflict is to addiction what peace is to negative feedback. Both complement one another in, among other disorders, leading our world to its destruction.

From the point of view of a peace practitioner, this has been a rather grim, sobering, realization. We, from the vantage point of prescriptive peace as a discipline, can be seen as enablers to the conflict meme that animates us on a daily basis. How?

Conflict is to addiction what peace is to negative feedback

'War on Terror,' 'War on Drugs,' even 'War on Poverty,' these are the daily aberrations presented to us by political systems, relayed by the infotainment media industry (Nacos, 2002). In our certainty over our power to defeat terrorism, we have forgotten that not only are we powerless over this symptom, but also that we are addicted to the social, political and ideological conflicts that drive us. Terrorism is symptomatic of a greater conflict meme that animates our lives (Wilber, 2001). Our dualistic view of the world in 'us' and 'them' has made us unable to realize that we all have conflict within us and that our illusion of power over the other, terrorism, drugs, makes us part of the problem.

Bateson (1972b) asserts that we are the mirrors of our own demons. For as long as we are to engage in a symmetrical relationship with our addiction, we will be unable to transform it. The decision by President Obama to close Guantanamo Detention Centre was a message of peace, yet his administration's collateral killing of civilians in Northern Pakistan renders his message void in the eyes of the populations towards whom this message was aimed in the first place (Almeida, 2010). Worse, this message failing to materialize into concrete actions deepens political polarization, rendering moderate discourse obsolete.[2]

By declaring war on terrorism, or by attempting to hide skeletons in our human rights violations closet, we hereby declare war on ourselves, in the same way that the addict declares war over himself when he or she confronts the substance in a conflict that he or she is bound to lose every time. We instead have to examine the patterns of our involvement in conflict, in order to transform our symmetrical dualistic relationship into a complementary one. Bateson's ecology of the mind asks: can we imagine 'Twelve Steps' to our addiction to conflict? Can the sacred unity between mind, body and spirit help? Let us examine first if we have hit bottom.

Double bind

Bateson once asserted that 'language is a remarkable servant and a lousy master' (Bateson in Nachmanovitch, 1981, p. 11). In his research on communication, he wrote that digital, linear, communication was often symptomatic of a double bind that could only be transcended through an analogical approach to communication (Harries-Jones, 1995). Put simply, if digital communication can be the expression of robots, analogical communication is speaking with one's heart, mind, body and soul.

Double bind is the effect of a contradictory message given by someone to someone else, often within a power-dynamic. It results in pathological relationships. An illustration of double bind can be a parent telling a child that he or she is loved, but never with the gestures and actions that are the expressions of that love (Harries-Jones, 1995). It can be a post-Bush administration address to the Muslim world, alongside daily killings of civilians. Words but no hugs, no closeness, no connection: this contradiction creates different reactions, one of which being schizophrenia. Words but no human dignity or justice, this can result in disillusionment, or acts of terrorism (Fontan, 2007). In this, the digital communication of the parent or authority figure creates a pathological reaction (Bateson, 1972c). Under this light, language can certainly become a lousy master.

A sacred unity

Can aesthetics save us from ourselves? Can it bring meaning to our actions as peace practitioners? Bateson's deep connection to British painter and poet William Blake seems to foster this realization. Aesthetics in the work of both Blake and Bateson takes on the role of reconnecting the spirit to the mind and body, as well as nature, humans and the spiritual. It takes the spirituality out of organized religion and back to the cognitive domain of the individual and collective self. Aesthetics brings the territory back to the map in the same way that it connects both spheres of our brains. It connects nature, humans and their spirituality through the acknowledgment of what Bateson referred to as ECO, or the 'gods' of ecosystem (Harries-Jones, 1995). It redirects the message of peace into peace itself. Aesthetics is the missing link between our wishful thinking for the general good and our actions. It derives in our emotions, our ethics, our values and principles. It alludes to making peace with peace, to teaching peace with peace. It tells us that a 'Yes We Can' attitude is devoid of any connection to the reality of us creating more of the same by seeking to negate the connection patterns between our actions. Emotions, values and principles become visible in our actions.

Changing the bias of the system

We want to know that we are hitting the bottom, yet we refuse to acknowledge it in our belief that we can quit conflict, pain, hunger and death whenever we want to. We refuse to admit that we are addicted to conflict, yet it permeates every aspect of our lives, as deep as our entertainment patterns or our compartmentalization of peace building. We say 'never again' each time we speak of Auschwitz, yet refused to call events in Rwanda genocide (Albright, 2006). We believe that we are better than them, whoever they are, the Nazis, the Muslims, the terrorists, the freedom haters: the Others. Yet how would 'they' have sprung to life if it were not for us?

Bateson's essay on the Treaty of Versailles (Bateson, 1972a) is another revealing connection, another kick in the stomach of the peace practitioner. Evelin Lindner (2006) started her work on human dignity with an analysis of the Treaty of Versailles, on the humiliation that established the systemic bases for the Second World War to occur. Bateson made the same proposition, naming our 'peace' as a catalyst to the state of today's world, via the Second World War.

Bateson, in his essay 'From Versailles to Cybernetics' (1972a), contended that the treaty of Versailles changed the bias of the international system, a bias that inherently led to a century of international conflict. Bateson explains this with the metaphor of a house heating system's thermostat. If the temperature outside a house falls, the thermostat regulates the temperature in the house, this according to the temperature range within which the system operates; the bias. If the bias changes, the parameters for the room temperature change also.

His argument is that the Treaty of Versailles, with its short-term good intentions, for the general good, changed the bias of the international system away from one of justice for all, including 'losers,' which in turn increased the world's propensity for conflict. Many observers of the international politics have since also made the connection (Fisk, 2005). For as long as the bias of the system will be placed according to a dualistic understanding of the world, into 'us' and 'them' and a fragmented symptomatic solution to conflicts, peace initiatives will contribute to the overall sustaining of long-term conflicts (Anderson, 1999). It is the bias of the system that needs to be changed into a holistic and sacred one, not our response to its symptoms.

Peace and negative feedback

When I reflect on how Afghanistan has been mishandled since 2001, this by all actors involved in its reconstruction, I cannot help but wonder how the bias of the system can be changed, since we were conditioned into believing that this was a fight between good and evil, that there was absolutely no way to negotiate with the 'stone-age' Taliban rulers. Hence, I was very surprised during a recent meeting with the *hakim* (or 'witch doctor') of Mollah Omar, the former Head of the Afghani Taliban, who gave me a contextualized account of their rule. He mentioned the founding of a university for women, something new to me, the reasons behind the 'banning' of electricity, which actually was not banned but unavailable after thirty years of conflict, and the several logical reasons behind, for instance, the 'banning' of kite 'flying,' which, more accurately called kite-fighting, has also been banned in Pakistan since 2005.[3] He also mentioned how opposed the Afghani Taliban are to the Pakistani Taliban, deemed too radical for them.[4] I left his house wondering if Western politics in the area had not created the 'evil' that it was denouncing while justifying its 'invasion' of Afghanistan in 2001, albeit in Northern Pakistan. To this day, I am wondering what was our collective role in worsening the situation in Afghanistan and now its neighboring Pakistan.

In his resigning letter to the Board of Regents of the University of California, dated 1979, Bateson laments the preoccupation of national egos with the possibility of their own death, hence their need to develop nuclear weaponry, the reason for his resignation from this particular board (Harries-Jones, 1995). In his logic, the impossibility to find a valuable interlocutor and communicate with the 'other' is symptomatic of the Cartesian bias of the system, hence contributing to the negative loop of conflict.

We as peace practitioners are led to believe that we can initiate *ad hoc* interventions to suppress symptoms of conflict, to restore good conscience to the collective, in the same way that environmental agencies address degradation in a symptomatic manner (Bateson, 1972d). We linearly divide peace and conflict studies into conflict management, resolution and transformation, combining it with peacekeeping, peacemaking and peace building and we address the world's woes in as good a manner as we can. We intervene, mostly reactively, as a fire brigade, according to the decisions of an organization created by and for states, not with individuals in mind. We intervene within the conflict bias, instead of holistically addressing the patterns of interconnections that set the conflict bias. I have seen the eviction of illegal settlers in Bosnia, but yet have to see it occurring in Palestine. We say that we care, that we work for human rights, justice, democracy, but we only act politically, economically and selfishly (Easterly, 2006). Sending in rogue peacekeepers that abuse local populations, as occurred in many UN-sponsored missions across the world in relation to sexual slavery, only recently made it to the headlines in connection with the UN mission in the Congo; this after years of systematic malpractice on behalf of UN personnel (Firmo-Fontan, 2003; Lynch, 2004).

We talk of bringing peace to Afghanistan, but through what means? As Bateson's double bind creates schizophrenia, our collective double bind creates anger at best, terrorism at worst, depending on the person or group of people it is touching. In this sense, the peace practitioner that does not bring meaning to his or her words can be seen as an agent of negative feedback and not of social transformation. The digital communication of peace does not contribute to peace. It often spoils it. The digital communication of peace acts as a pesticide. It renders the soil sterile for years to come. Returning to the addiction entry point, the digital peace practitioner buys us a collective good conscience, hence prevents us from ever realizing that we have hit rock bottom.

A negentropy of peace?

Bateson might not have wished to paint peace practice black, or to throw the peacekeeper out with the bathwater, but he would have strongly objected the notion of general good that is often invoked in most missions. While most peace practitioners are dedicated individuals, this is not the question at stake when reflecting on Bateson's epistemology. It is fair to assert that *ad hoc* practices that do not help to sustain the peace we are all after, that acting in urgency without sustainability in sight can contribute to a worsening of a given situation, that all talk and no walk can alienate people and render them violent at worst. From our hubris to bring peace at all costs, to enforce it, stems the negative feedback that alienates the addict to the substance.

Gregory Bateson wrote of negentropy in terms of cybernetics and analogical communication. The concept of entropy stems from the Second Law of Thermodynamics, concerning the irreversibility of nature and energy. While negentropy does not completely point out towards a reversal of the Second Law, it is defined as a '*temporal reversal of disorder, when order is considered as a statistical rate of events in some closed system or channel*. In other words, our knowledge of probable events moves in a direction opposite to the time path of entropic systems' (Harries-Jones, 1995, p. 107).

In terms of cybernetics and the study of closed systems, negentropic conditions occur out of analogical communication, that is to say, a communication that lives, expresses, means, embodies. While too many peace efforts can damage peace on the long term, as, again, the Afghan example illustrates, an analogical communication/expression of peace can reverse the entropy created by its digital expression. In sum, peace can be brought back from the dead through communication.

This communication has to be systemic, transformative through the positive feedback that it can prompt, connecting the two hemispheres of our brain. It also has to be transcendent of our human condition towards ECO, the greater life system, as characterized by Bateson, of which we are only a small part (Harries-Jones, 1995, p. 107). All in all, analogical communication generates a wealth of ideas that live and die, according to their fitting with one another within their interdependent, interacting contribution to life of ECO (Bateson, 1991). Since Bateson's ecology of the mind is a constant appraisal of life, ideas that do not contribute to the life of ECO will die out naturally. An ecological understanding of peace would embody the same parameters, hence not repeat the same mistakes mission after mission.

Aesthetics, consciousness, the sacred and ecology

Bateson's work highlighted the importance of aesthetics as a shortcut to consciousness (Harries-Jones, 1995). The connection that he felt with William Blake's vision of the world led him to formalize his understanding of aesthetics as a means to express what cannot be expressed with words, a means to allow us to enter our consciousness through our unconscious. Photojournalism can be an embodiment of Bateson's aesthetics, as a means to enter our collective consciousness.[5]

However, the road to consciousness via aesthetics could not have sufficed to conceptualize what Bateson understood as the 'patterns which connect' between beauty and destruction, life and death. The sacred had to come to the rescue in order for his argument not to fall within a Cartesian dualistic pattern (Harries-Jones, 1995). Towards the end of his life, Bateson allowed the sacred to take a connecting space; it provided a vision of unity necessary to the ecology of the mind (Bateson, 1991).

According to Harries-Jones (1995, p. 213), the author of an intellectual biography of Bateson, 'the sacred indicates a form in which life cannot be opposed to itself, in which even death is part of the rhythms of life.' This trinity represents the ecology of the mind, whose sacred expression Bateson saw in the Hindi deity of Shiva the Destroyer. Harries-Jones (1995, p. 210) explains: 'of the qualities of beauty and ugliness that pervade the biosphere, these primary rhythms of life and death are those to which we must pay particular attention, for these are the "patterns which connect".'

One can negate death if one does not accept the greater implicate order of ECO.[6] Our modern rejection of it can account for the current state of resources depletion. Can we seek to live through the ecology of the mind if we do not understand, accept and live through our own mortality? Will ECO remind us of our own mortality, as it does through photojournalism when we allow it to permeate through our public sphere? Are we ready to surrender to it?

Bateson's epistemology of peace

A questioning of the epistemology of modern peace must be initiated before unethical, fragmented and dualistic actions spoil the soil where it is being applied. Recently, more and more NGOs have to resort to private security to continue their operations in increasingly difficult environments. Should that not be a sign given by ECO of our falling into disunity? Does this point towards the destruction of a dysfunctional industry? Does it have to be replaced by any alternative? I do not claim to give answers to the peace industry, but only to frame it within an ecological meme. More questions will undoubtedly come before any kind of resolution, if any ever occurs. If we are not meant to ever live in peace, then let ECO remain the guardian of the patterns that connect.

Notes

1. While psychiatric discourse has since disputed this notion of 'hitting bottom,' I remain attached to Bateson's desire to keep this as prominent as possible in the understanding of addiction. My own understanding of this stems from the fact that no one who does not want to be helped (hence has reached a certain bottom – and it is understood that bottom can be reached several times in a lifetime) can initiate a cure without ever falling into relapse at any given time.
2. Author interviews with various Pakistani political and intellectual leaders, Karachi, April 2010.
3. For an account on the debate over kite flying, see *The News* (2009).
4. Their opposition to the Pakistani Taliban stems from the incident of the flogging of a girl that shocked the Pakistani nation in 2009 (The DAWN Media Group, 2009).
5. See Photography by James Nachtwey (2010). I believe that all his shots are interconnected as Bateson highlighted it in his essay 'From Versailles to Cybernetics' (1972a).
6. I use here 'implicate order' in reference to David Bohm's writings (1980).

Reference list

Albright, M. (2006) *The Mighty and the Almighty* (New York: Harper Collins).
Almeida, C. (2010) 'Civilian Deaths in Drone Attacks: Debate Heats Up,' *Dawn Newspaper*, May 9, 2010.
Anderson, M.B. (1999) *Do No Harm: How Aid can Support Peace – Or War* (Boulder: Lynne Rienner).
Bateson, G. (1972a) 'From Versailles to Cybernetics' in *Steps to an Ecology of the Mind* (Chicago: University of Chicago Press).
Bateson, G. (1972b) 'The Cybernetics of "Self": A Theory of Alcoholism' in *Steps to an Ecology of the Mind* (Chicago: University of Chicago Press).

Bateson, G. (1972c) 'Culture Contact and Schismogenesis' in *Steps to an Ecology of the Mind* (Chicago: University of Chicago Press).

Bateson, G. (ed.) (1972d) *The Roots of Ecological Crisis* (Chicago: University of Chicago Press).

Bateson, G. (1991) 'Ecology of the Mind: The Sacred' in R.E. Donaldson (ed.) *A Sacred Unity: Further Steps to an Ecology of the Mind* (San Francisco: Cornelia & Michael Bessie).

Bohm, D. (1980) *Wholeness and the Implicate Order* (London: Routledge).

The DAWN Media Group (2009) 'Flogging in Swat Outrages Nation,' April 4, 2009, http://www.dawn.com/wps/wcm/connect/dawn-content-library/dawn/news/pakistan/govt-condemns-sc-acts-on-swat-girl-flogging--zj, date accessed May 18, 2010.

Easterly, W. (2006) *The White Man's Burden: Why the West's Efforts to Aid the Rest have Done So Much Ill and So Little Good* (London: Penguin).

Firmo-Fontan, V. (2003) 'Responses to Human Trafficking: From the Balkans to Afghanistan' in C. Van den Anker (ed.) *The Political Economy of New Slavery* (London: Palgrave).

Fisk, R. (2005) *The Great War for Civilization: The Conquest of the Middle East* (London: Fourth Estate).

Fontan, V. (2007) 'Understanding Islamic Terrorism: Humiliation Awareness and the Role for Nonviolence' in R. Summy and R. Senthil (eds.) *Nonviolence: An Alternative for Defeating Global Terror(ism)* (Hauppauge: Nova Science).

Harries-Jones, P. (1995) *A Recursive Vision: Ecological Understanding and Gregory Bateson* (Toronto: University of Toronto Press).

Lindner, E. (2006) *Making Enemies: Humiliation and International Conflict* (London: Praeger).

Lipset, D. (1982) *Gregory Bateson: The Legacy of a Scientist* (Boston: Beacon Press).

Lynch, C. (2004) 'U.N. Sexual Abuse Alleged in Congo,' *The Washington Post*, December 16, 2004.

Nachmanovitch, S. (1981) 'Gregory Bateson: Old Men Ought to be Explorers' *Free Play Productions*, http://www.freeplay.com/Writings/GregoryBateson.pdf, date accessed May 9, 2010.

Nacos, B. (2002) *Mass-Mediated Terrorism: The Central Role of the Media in Terrorism and Counterterrorism* (Oxford: Rowman & Littlefield).

The News (2009) 'Kite flying can't be Allowed at Expense of Lives: LHC,' March 14, 2009, http://www.thenews.com.pk/daily_detail.asp?id=167136, date accessed May 18, 2010.

Photography by James Nachtwey (2010) http://www.jamesnachtwey.com/, Homepage of James Nachtwey, date accessed August 4, 2009.

Wilber, K. (2001) *A Theory of Everything: An Integral Vision for Business, Politics, Science, and Spirituality* (Boston: Shambhala).

Conclusion

Josefina Echavarría, Daniela Ingruber and Norbert Koppensteiner

Peace is plural. In this manner, one of the outstanding results of the current volume could be summarized in the briefest fashion. From the Peruvian Andes of Grimaldo Rengifo's essay all the way to the Indogenic traditions rendered by Swami Veda Bharati, the contributions in this book give testimony to a multiplicity of cultural, linguistic, legal, spiritual and religious ways of defining, living and thinking peace. Recounted by voices emerging from within the respective communities, they so stand for an irreducible plurality of peaces, affirming a difference that neither easily or without violence can be reduced to the homogeneous One of a worldwide peace of whichever shade or color. Hence, each article presents one voice out of many and one perspective in an entire universe of perspectives on peace.

This *post-modern* state of affairs confirms a finding that was announced more than a decade ago by Wolfgang Dietrich in his essay 'A Call for Many Peaces' (2006). Since then, it has led to what might be termed an emerging cultural turn within the discipline of Peace Studies, a turn which is enthusiastically embraced by some authors in the field and is severely fought by others. This difference in perspective, just as the difference between the peaces themselves, may well give rise to arguments and conflicts, but from where we stand this is a fact that is to be accepted and welcomed rather than lamented or even overcome.

The fascinating aspect about the contributions collected here is that they can serve to open up new and strange perspectives to the careful reader; they might function as vectors of transformation towards new horizons and understandings. From our point of view, they do not need to be believed in or swallowed wholesale. The pertinent question does not concern right or wrong, but what those essays can do for the reader's perspective and to which forms of living and thinking differently they hint at. The current volume is grounds for neither fear nor hope, but calls for new frames of interpretation.

To orient ourselves within this multiplicity, we chose to employ a system following the five families of concepts of peace developed at the Innsbruck School of Peace Studies (Dietrich, 2008). To speak about families of peaces – *energetic, moral, modern, post-modern* and *trans-rational* – is to speak about groups, it is to speak of relations. Families are not monolithic blocks, but shades of differences and degrees of affiliations. In a similar manner, neither one of those five traditions of peace is pure, essential or unadulterated. They all have formed syncretistic variations, inspired and contradicted each other. For brevity's sake, we will proceed to shortly outline a distilled version, a concise framework to help orientation within the multiplicity of voices in this volume.

Our commitment to pluralist approaches, however, also demands refraining from the temptation to integrate those families into an overall standard of evaluation or render a final judgment. It is common practice within the Idealist tradition of Peace Studies to follow an evolutionist approach, in which the chronologically more recent is perceived as the more evolved, as if humanity as a whole would be striving upwards towards some kind of culmination point. From our perspective, to the contrary, each of those five types of peaces has the potential to provide a comprehensive understanding of the world. While some emerged historically earlier and some later, this placement in time does not imply a 'better' or 'worse,' a more or less 'developed.' It is their very differences that make it possible to distinguish them from one another, yet to align them according to a single yardstick of progress would violate and colonize this difference; an attempt that furthermore bespoke of intellectual arrogance. In this sense it remains true, as Ivan Illich (2006, p. 175) said, that 'peace is the condition under which each culture flowers in its own incomparable way.'

Energetic peaces are holistic. They perceive all existence as an inextricable fabric interrelating nature, society and divinities (cosmos). The individual is thus never separate, but always part and parcel of the larger relationality that, in turn, ultimately is a temporary manifestation of the primal *energetic* Oneness of all being. Being-in-the-world, therefore, calls for awareness of this relationality from which no part of existence is exempt. As Elida Jacobsen's chapter on the Scandinavian *friðr* shows, energetic understandings of peace are represented in notions of fertility and harmony, which concern such a multitude of events and relations as the growth of crops, the fertility of the soil, the reproduction of animals and the good health of human beings. Consequently, peace arises from the harmony or disharmony as it is perceived by the experiencing subject within this relationality.

Harmony is one of the most discussed topics in this volume. The lost harmony that Zapotec, Andean and Enlhet communities have experienced through centuries of colonization and post-colonial relationships is a subject that constantly reappears. Yet, such lost harmony is coupled with practices of balance. Harmony is not lost forever, yet neither can it be achieved once and for all. Many chapters in this volume testify that harmony is a constant doing and being. Harmony is dynamic and, in manifold languages, speaks to what peace could be. Multiple practices of sharing, reciprocity, determination, joint action and dialogue, as Hannes Kalisch shares with us on the Enlhet in the Paraguayan Chaco, make *nengelaasekhammalhkoo* a contextual social practice, a movement striving for equilibrium. Such movement, as Gustavo Esteva and Arturo Escobar tell us about *tu chh'ia*, also takes the form of attempts to recover harmony in the Zapotec communities of Mexico. They are accompanied by rituals of balance for the community as a whole, including compensation for those who could have suffered under a moment of disequilibrium. The cultivation of harmony, hence, goes beyond forgiveness and reparation. It speaks to the reestablishment of equilibrium among peoples, supranatural forces and nature.

As Grimaldo Rengifo recounts about indigenous peoples in the Amazonian region, in order to reestablish harmony, disharmony has to be acknowledged. Furthermore, the ability to open and deepen our perception of the signs of nature and the deities that signal disharmony, necessarily entails acting in accordance with the moment. In other words, to be able to perceive (listen, see, hear, smell and touch) the signs of disharmony, we need to focus our attention on the present moment. It is the present moment, which signals the disturbances in the relationships.

Echoing Rengifo, we could so characterize energetic peaces as small, context-bound and often tied to concrete practices. Karma Lekshe Tsomo describes such a peace from within the Vajrayana Buddhist tradition. In the tantric practice, peace is not just a matter for the outside societal conditions, but much rather begins on the inside, with the person's work on herself. Awareness of self implies the increasing realization of the impermanence of all things and the non-dual nature of the universe that knows neither separations nor divisions. Violence is created via egoic-attachments and identifications, as well as mental defilements like anger or desire. In the tantric practice those defilements, however, are not suppressed or rejected, but on the contrary acknowledged and actively used in the process of awareness.

In contrast, the Confucian perspective on harmony, portrayed by Kam-Por Yu, is classified in an unexpressed duality: a so-called 'higher' concept of peace is thinkable but regarded as unrealistic, the other concept is part of a path that needs to be chosen well. Conflicts here become resolvable. His contribution allows us to enter *moral* interpretations of peace.

Moral understandings of peace are organic. The material world and everything in it is still perceived as an interconnected whole, yet the realm of the divinities is separated. Instead of an all-connecting primal energy, *moral* peaces often proceed from a single, personified (male) creator God, who brings the universe into existence, yet Himself stands apart from it. He is an acting agent and peace shall be the reward for the ones following His rules. Those are set down in form of an absolute code of norms, which in turn calls for institutions and experts to authoritatively interpret and explain His law to the people. Thereof derives the absolute dualism between true and false, good and evil in *moral* understandings of peace, which is foreign to the *energetic*. While true peace remains a transcendent matter to be realized only at the end of all days, this-worldly, apparent peace is achieved via doing good and overcoming evil.

Within this framework, Marc H. Ellis reminds us that *shalom* is also related to *shelemut* (wholeness), meaning that there is a sense of harmony understood as the right living and relationships. This would point into an energetic direction. Yet, whereas the opposite of *shalom* is *mahloket* or divisiveness, Ellis argues that peace can only be thematically linked to justice. In other words, for Ellis *shalom* necessarily implies that the world has to be repaired (*tikkun olam*) beyond the privileged relations of empire. Likewise, from the viewpoint of Islamic values as Aurangzeb Haneef recounts, in order to restore *Salaam*, the Qur'an urges Muslims to stand up firmly for justice. And although patience and forgiveness are also preferred in order to resist oppression, demanding action against wrongdoing is permitted. This so describes the attainment of peace as a struggle between what 'is' and what 'should be.' Exactly at this point Amadou Lamine Sarr connects African Islam and African politics, believing that the desire for peace is a desire for tolerance, too.

This transcendental character of peace, as Uzma Rehman elaborates on Sufi practices, can so translate the concepts of *Wahdat al-Wujud* ('unity of being'), unity in diversity and inner *jihad*/peace into love for the humanity and love for the divine as essentially one. In this line of thinking, we find that the nonviolent character of *jihad* and the unity of being were exemplary lived by the figure of Ghaffar Khan, as Sikander Mehdi narrates in this volume. While making clear that his concept of nonviolence was directly derived from Islam, Ghaffar Khan created a movement where its members swore never to use violence, retaliate or take revenge, and forgive anyone who indulges in oppression and excesses.

Thus, the thematic of peace and justice takes innumerable and often contradictory shapes in this volume. Such richness does not only emanate from alternative interpretations of the same scriptures or differentiated cultural practices, it also derives from the constant crisscrossing between the above-mentioned concepts. For instance, this notion of trans-cultural hybridity is developed in this volume by Francisco Muñoz and Beatriz Molina. They argue that *Eirene, Shalom, Pax* and *Salam* – along with other terms and concepts from Greek, Jewish, Roman, Islamic and Christian, as well as other ancient and medieval Mediterranean, cultures – shared an ample worldview to compose a Mediterranean universality of peace. This universality, however, does not entail homogeneity, since peace is portrayed in various forms as a desire, an ethical horizon, a goddess, the establishment of diplomatic relations, the signing of a treaty, the end of a war, a political slogan or a social project.

And once more the subject of justice reappears, as the insights lead Muñoz and Molina to formulate that 'there is no Peace without Justice,' a dictum that also takes a unique form in Pat Lauderdale's contribution. Departing from the distinct perspective of North American Indians, Lauderdale claims that the recognition that humans are part of nature (not separate from it) and harmony are essential to peace and justice. Thus, it demands a communal approach to preventive and restorative mechanisms for there to be healing. Here it becomes evident that notions of peace as harmony, restoration and balance, overlap in some particular instances with moral understandings of peace as justice. This combination, although not exempt from inherent contradictions, seems to produce a tense relationship that is finally broken by the institutionalization and formalization based on sovereign subjects, like nation-states or, what we could also term, by the cooption of peace by modernity's inventions.

At the edge between a moral and a modern view lies Johan Galtung's contribution to this volume. Here the different doctrines in Buddhism emphasize a holistic approach to peace, clearly asking for certain ways of behavior that can lead to a peace, while peace is regarded as the goal – or a promise – of the future.

Modern peaces are mechanic. The spiritual realm is neglected or rejected altogether in favor of a purely this-worldly perception of the universe. God is replaced by a dogmatic reason as founding principle. In a modern, secular understanding, the universe functions like a machine according to eternal laws of cause and effect that, via the natural sciences, at least in principle can be deciphered. Knowing how the clockwork world ticks then opens the possibility for improving upon it, managing, repairing and perfecting it. The same notion also applies to the human realm, where knowledge about the functioning of individual and society paves the road towards the possibility to actively perfect the human condition and produce peace. Peace so turns into the promise of a final stage of human evolution that will become possible if the corresponding analyses are detailed enough and the tools and methods of science are applied correctly. The eschatological promise of *moral* peaces here appears in a secularized version as peace on earth at the end of all days. This is underpinned by a linear understanding of history guided by the belief in progress, enlightenment, development or civilization.

One can so observe that while energetic *peaces* are small, both *moral* and *modern* ones also know large variations. Dis-embedding peaces from their concrete contexts allows for abstractions of potentially universal character. In philosophy, Immanuel Kant's *Perpetual Peace* is an expression of such a *modern*, absolute and idealist understanding of peace, just as the Declaration of Human Rights is an example from the legal sphere. In the current volume, this approach is represented, for example, in Karlheinz Koppe's essay. His recount of Central European history follows a linear narrative that can be interpreted as a story of progress, even if it is interrupted by what the author perceives as the Dark Middle Ages. The progress of peace here is measured and expressed as the task of increasingly civilizing war via legal regulations. This peace can be actively brought about by the strength of the (post)national institutions.

Nigel Young chooses a similar chronological approach, talking about the lack of theoretical innovation for Peace (Studies) in the Anglo-Saxon world. Anglo-Saxon peaces are peaces of the action, and more creative in concrete peace work. The English-speaking countries and societies, Young argues, were always good in collecting ideas from different cultures and intermingling them – e.g. in Mohandas Gandhi's ideas of peace.

Certainly, Gandhian peace-concepts are mentioned frequently in this *International Handbook of Peace Studies*. His grandson, Arun Gandhi, contributed an essay with a very personal perspective of his grandfather's *satyagraha*. Peace here becomes an attitude of life, nonviolence a role model, morality an important tool and love the core of every human action.

The name of Ivan Illich stands for small variations of *modern* peace. Martina Kaller-Dietrich highlights Illich's understanding of common peace as convivial and vernacular, as something that is quite literally homemade in the sense of tied to a concrete context. He challenges the violence of the capitalist *pax oeconomica* and its promise of development. As a radically doubting mind Illich is a precursor for many of the critical *(post)modern* authors on peace during the last decades and rightly deserves a place among the original peace thinkers of the twentieth century.

Like multiple other encounters narrated in this volume, often concepts of peace collide, sometimes they embrace each other, yet at other instances they clash in violent forms. Robert Vachon shares with us such an example of the encounter of competing understandings in the specific case of *Tehona- tenentshawā:kon* (kinship alliance) as they were practiced between Native Nations and how Europeans framed them. Whereas the Great Law of Peace referred to an alliance of communitarian or extended family reciprocity, in which the Confederacy and other Native Nations committed each other to share hunting grounds, counsel, foods, furs, flint, wampum, etc., such an alliance was never one of subordination, subjection or sovereignty over subjects. Therefore, whereas for the Iroquois it meant the kinship alliance of brothers for protection and peace, for Europeans it was a kingship and friendship-based alliance with 'subjects and allies' for their own self-protection and to facilitate further conquest.

Both the *post-modern* and the *trans-rational* understanding of peace have already been described in Wolfgang Dietrich's contribution to this volume. We will not repeat his detailed argumentation, but only summarize and expand some points.

Post-modern peaces co-emerge with the *modern* ones, as their critical and doubting counterpart. The *post-modern* state of mind occurs whenever, under conditions of *modernity*, the latter's promises are no longer believed in. *Post-modern* peaces very often emerge as concrete counterproposals to the homogenizing tendencies in *moral* and *modern* peaces, or are instigated as practices of resistance. As Munir Fasheh points out, the disillusionment, disbelief and fear of a singled undifferentiated path to progress for achieving peace, looms large especially in post-colonial settings, such as Palestine.

Post-modern understandings of peace celebrate the exuberant multiplicity and contradictoriness of lived existence, without attempting to resolve the corresponding tension deriving thereof. The notion of resolution is replaced by an open-ended series of transformations, without final resting point or teleology. *Post-modern* peaces attempt to *twist* the dogmatism of *modernity's* reason, to turn its analytical tools on itself, thereby crowning and dissolving it by its own means. Abstaining from a *modern* foundation in reason, *post-modern* understandings of peace remain small, local and contextual, but here unfounded. Unlike the *energetic* peaces, *post-modernity* promises no hope for reconciliation in non-dual Oneness. As such, *post-modern* peaces do not provide certainties or the prospect of a stable and lasting state of being. Life to them is a permanent process of transformation and becoming. *Post-modern* peaces therefore constantly need to be reinvented and struggled for anew, as they perpetually remain transitory and unstable.

Jean-François Lyotard and Gilles Deleuze are considered two of the most important names within *post-modern* philosophy and Norbert Koppensteiner aims to highlight their specific contributions as *post-modern* thinkers of peace. Pagans and nomads here stand as emblematic figures of resistance against the homogenizing tendencies of the one, global peace. In Deleuze and Lyotard's thinking, they safeguard and affirm the irreducible plurality of the many peaces.

Astier M. Almedom aligns Ngũgĩ wa Thiong'o's arguments on the continued influence of the colonial languages in Africa with Eritrean efforts to put in place a multilingual and multiscriptal language policy. The key concept of *nisamama'* – listening to one another – in the language of Tigrinya ties together Ngũgĩ's concerns about language as crucial for self-understanding with the potential for peace that opens up through actively fostering the multiplicity of vernacular languages within societies.

Ikuro Anzai gives a beautiful example of the variety and contradictions of *post-modern* religious approaches to harmony: In Japan, the members of religious groups exceed the number of inhabitants of Japan. People choose the suitable religion for each occasion, and this also forms part of the search for peaces. Finally, it is Buddhism that presents an idea of harmony and balance.

Empathically intercultural is Raimon Panikkar's understanding of peace, as rendered in Gustavo Esteva's chapter on this prominent peace thinker. Relative without being relativistic, peace after Panikkar is never perfect but in the making, it is as pluralistic as it is unavailable for precise definitions. Relational without being biunivocal and joining us human beings to a harmonious whole, peace thus is a task for that particular brand of dialogical dialogue that Panikkar has strongly advocated.

Harmony in various ways, wrapped in mystic stories about peace, can be found in Swami Veda Bharati's text for this *International Handbook of Peace Studies*, when he opens up a huge universe of Indogenic perspectives on peace. Finally, it is the combination of the individual and the collective consciousness that forms the definition of peace – which is *shanti*.

Trans-rational concepts of peace share the *post-modern* commitment to plurality, yet additionally reintegrate the spiritual component. *Trans*-rational implies having passed through the rational, yet without clinging to its purely this-worldly perspective. Reason is acknowledged as one possible mode of perception among others. *Trans-rational* peaces do not found themselves in ultimate reason, but accept the impossibility of final statements about truth. As Alev Çakır puts it in relation to the Alevi concept of peace, the claim to truth is *unconditional* as it is always embedded in relations and, hence, contextual. Existence is perceived as an interrelated network of events, in which no part or element is fundamental. As such, for example, science appears for Alevis as a way of combining rationality with mystical experience by realizing the connection between human beings, nature and the universe.

Philosophical and scientific approaches based on *trans-rationality* deal with this lack of founding by way of what Fritjof Capra (1988), following the work of Geoffrey Chew, has termed a *bootstrap* approach. Bootstrapping implies accepting a multiplicity of overlapping yet not completely coinciding viewpoints, a shifting of perspectives between overlaying lenses that never completely merge. The corresponding descriptions of reality thus differ according to perspective. The spiritual might as well be expressed in terms of a systemic approach, in terms of deep-ecology, as the transpersonal or yet again the holistic. In the realm of Peace and Conflict Studies, *trans-rational* inquiries are thus not so much guided by questions of *why?* (diagnoses, based on first principles and following a linear model of cause–effect) but by questions of *how?* (observations of patterns and processes as vectors of transformation). This corresponds to a shift from the analytic to the descriptive. The trans-rational perspective is exemplified in both the work and biography of Gregory Bateson. Victoria Fontan's chapter captures the shifting interests of this trans-disciplinary academic polyglot and his main contributions to the current practice of peace work. The systemic perspective of ECO advocated after Bateson seeks to overcome the dualistic divisions of modern peaces. Through the ECO the human being, nature and spirituality are once more linked and the sacred reenters the discussion around the peaces, a thread that is also prominent in Samrat Schmiem Kumar's rendering of Sri Aurobindo and Jiddu Krishnamurti. Rather than dichotomous divisions, the latter two propagate a view of the human being as a body–mind–soul continuum and connect the social peace of communities to the individual transformation of human consciousness.

Peter Horsley puts dialogue into the center of his chapter; it is the dialogue between the different ethnical groups in New Zealand. Wisdom is connected to the heart and at the same time, the political search for peace needs talks and listening to each other. Partnership and plurality are two of the magic words and all of them are connected to ancient beliefs of peace.

Also connected to ancient traditions and beliefs but at the same time looked at from a modern perspective, religious life in western Africa seems to be full of contradictions and still gives us an example of a trans-rational form of thinking and living, as Kofi Opoku shows in his contribution. The similarities between the notions of peace in the West and the East of Africa become visible in the comparison with Belachew Gebrewold's article on the Kambaata. In both cases, ancient beliefs form part of everyday life and influence the concepts of peaces. Social life forms peaces and dissolves them again in the Kambaata community: it is the community that creates and preserves peace.

When read together, the distinct and complementary chapters in this handbook show how peace always seems to spill over from one category to the next. Better said, we might not be able to neatly and tightly categorize our experiences, thoughts, ideals, practices and findings on peace. Peace can be an idea(l), it can be a state of mind, a state of being, it might point to loving relationships as well as to achievement of institutional legal reforms and it might also mean the presence of equality. Consequently, peace can pose challenges to who we thought we were and who we might become. These paradoxes and indecisiveness, hand in hand with experiential knowledge that defies language, reach beyond a pure rational definition. As Munir Fasheh argues, mind and language can be quite useful for organizing and planning, yet are quite limited in their ability to comprehend life – and so peace – in its fullness, richness, depth, beauty and diversity.

Within the framework of this handbook, the inability to codify peace or offer a definite and final statement about what peace is, entails or might mean is a wonderful insight. Henceforth, although the above interrelated contributions speak to different predominant views on peace and, individually, each of the chapters in this volume stands alone for itself as exemplars of the Many Peaces, when taken together they are intended as an inspiration to peace and conflict scholars to reflect on their own peaces as particular readings of being-in-the-world. When seen through the chapters in this volume as prisms, this world is an open invitation to perceive the intercultural realities of peace.

Reference list

Capra, F. (1988) [1982] *The Turning Point: Science, Society, and the Rising Culture* (New York: Bantam Books).

Dietrich, W. (2006) [1997] 'A Call for Many Peaces' in W. Dietrich, J. Echavarría and N. Koppensteiner (eds.) *Schüsseltexte der Friedensforschung/Key Texts of Peace Studies/Textos Claves de la Investigación para la Paz* (Vienna/Münster: Lit), 282–305.

Dietrich, W. (2008) *Variationen über die vielen Frieden. Band 1: Deutungen* (Wiesbaden: VS Verlag für Sozialwissenschaften).

Illich, I. (2006) [1981] 'Peace vs. Development' in W. Dietrich, J. Echavarría and N. Koppensteiner (eds.) *Schüsseltexte der Friedensforschung/Key Texts of Peace Studies/Textos Claves de la Investigación para la Paz* (Vienna/Münster: Lit), 173–182.

Index

Compiled by Sue Carlton

Page numbers followed by 'n' refer to end of chapter notes

as normal state 34
as referent for peace 192–3, 198
relationships during 201–2
resistance to 60–1
  see also conscientious objection
role of Christianity 27
  see also Crusades
War on Drugs 589
War Jaabi, King 445
War on Poverty 589
War Resisters' International (1921) 63
war on terror 516, 589–90
War on Want 554
Waris Shah, Syed Pir 159
Watergate crisis 516
Watzlawick, P. 5
weak thought 8–9, 13
Wei Xiang 248
West
  perceptions of Palestine 100–1
  and post-modern condition 7
West Africa 417–27, 605
  community/commonality 418–19
  education 419–21
  indigenous judicial system 426
  and Islam 442–62, 600
  peace symbols 421–3
  proverbs 418, 420, 421, 423–4
  traditional religion 424–5
Whitehead, A.N. 498
Wiesel, Elie 94
Wilber, Ken 19, 313
Wilhelm I, King of Prussia 36
Wittgenstein, Ludwig 498, 528
women
  in Eritrea 555
  peace and war 549

Women's International League for Peace
  and Freedom 63
women's movement, and nuclear bases
  63–4
Woolf, Virginia 64
World Bank 100, 113, 116, 557
worthiness 111–12, 118
Wright, Quincy 64
Wu, Emperor 248–9

Xiong Nu (the Huns) 248, 249

yamas 213–14
Yasukuni Shrine 263–4, 265, 271–2
yoga 191, 194–6, 202, 210, 213, 497–9
  deity 237, 238
  integral 500–1
  sexual 238
Yoruba 422, 423–4
Yusuf Ali, Abdullah 132

Zapatistas ix, 107, 112
Zapotecs 352–68, 598
  assembly 362–3
  communal experience of social
    relationships 360–7
  conflict resolution 358–9
  justice
    and atonement 359
    consolation and compensation
     357–8
    and differential treatment 357
    and oral tradition 356–7
  languages 354–5
  and notion of peace 353–4, 356
  oral tradition 360
Zevallos, B. 376